# nxlevel™ guide *for entrepreneurs*

## Editor

David P. Wold

## Primary Authors

David P. Wold

Dennis Sargent

Martha Sargent

entrepreneur

On behalf of those involved in developing this program, we at the NxLeveL™ Training Network
dedicate this guide to entrepreneurs everywhere striving to reach the next level of success...

## Third Edition

Reprint February 2002

**Published in the United States of America by:**
NxLeveL™ Education Foundation
E-mail: info@nxlevel.org
Website: http://www.nxlevel.org

Designer: Michele Renée Ledoux, www.mledoux.com

ISBN: 1-931852-04-9

*"Helping Entrepreneurs Reach the Next Level of Success..."*

# NxLeveL™ guide
## *table of contents*

## To NxLeveL™ Participants, Instructors and Interested Readers:

Thank you for choosing NxLeveL™. We know there are wide variety "off the shelf" entrepreneurial training programs from which to choose and we appreciate you selecting NxLeveL™. Our goal is to help people reach their next level of success. We also understand that a strong small business sector builds a strong community, which furthers our primary goal of developing better, more viable communities.

This is the third edition of the *NxLeveL™ Guide for Entrepreneurs*. It incorporates feedback received from NxLeveL™ participants and Instructors over the past two years. Over 18,000 people have now enrolled in NxLeveL™ courses in communities located in over 30 states. The text is designed to capture an understanding of the process of starting and/or growing a business by thinking and acting as an entrepreneurial business. While no single text is designed to answer every question, it is hoped that you will find the *Guide* a useful tool for the continued improvement of your existing operations.

As with any program, one must acknowledge significant contributors to the total project. NxLeveL™ is no exception. NxLeveL™ is thankful for the continued support of the US WEST Foundation and its Executive Director Jane Prancan. Her insight into the needs of western communities made NxLeveL™ possible. The original 14 western state network (states comprising U S WEST Communications' corporate territory) of organizations and their staff were extremely helpful in providing feedback, identifying writers and providing the sites to test the training materials. Their willingness to share information has been invaluable. Without the support of the Foundation and the agencies implementing NxLeveL™ on a statewide basis, NxLeveL™ would not be the quality program that it is today.

Lastly, we want to know what works for you and where we can improve. NxLeveL™ is a program designed for people like you: Entrepreneurs. Please let us know what you think about NxLeveL™ and that together we will continue to improve to the next level in entrepreneurial training programs—NxLeveL™.

To contact us, visit our Website: http://www.nxlevel.org

*"Helping Entrepreneurs Reach the Next Level of Success..."*

# Letter From the Editor

My fellow contributors and I believe that entrepreneurship thrives in the United States primarily because of our legal and social structure and the diversity of its people. Therefore, we conceived, researched, and wrote this course of study for students of all professional and educational backgrounds, and of every gender, age, and race. The only prerequisites for taking this course are curiosity, and passion for starting or growing a business.

This text presents the theories and practice of entrepreneurship through real-life stories about small businesses, because we believe that nothing is as inspiring to entrepreneurs as the experiences of successful business owners.

All of the contributors to this book have either started a business or helped others to do so. The result is a composite of our experiences, which gives you an opportunity to learn from our mistakes as well as our successes.

In preparing this third edition of the *NxLeveL™ Guide for Entrepreneurs*, we have tried to be responsive to the comments and suggestions of our students and instructors. Their contributions are reflected in this edition; many changes were made to the text and format as a result of their feedback. We are a market-oriented publisher, so this feedback is not merely welcome—it is essential! We would very much appreciate your suggestions or comments about improving future editions.

One of the most important features of this edition is the inclusion of information on the Internet, which is not only an invaluable research tool and communications medium, but can also form the basis for a successful entrepreneurial venture. We have added information on the Internet and other technical resources to each chapter, and there are two new chapters dealing with the business potential of the Internet.

You may be certain that no matter who you are or what you know, entrepreneurship will indeed present many challenges. In the businesses I started, I had a love/hate relationship with the challenges I faced. I can't say that I always enjoyed them, but I knew that the day they ended, I would be out of business. Challenges were proof that my business was covering new ground and growing. Surprises and obstacles are part and parcel of managing a dynamic business. Our goal is to help you avoid the predictable obstacles, and inspire you to overcome the unpredictable ones.

Entrepreneurship is about freedom. Few things in life are as satisfying as being able to decide what work you will do, and to choose when, where, how, and with whom you will do it. With this freedom, inevitably, comes responsibility. Entrepreneurs do not answer to bosses, but we do have responsibilities to lenders, investors, and family; and we are bound by the laws of profitability. Above all, we have responsibilities to ourselves. We must be true to our vision, and design our businesses to reflect the best of what we have to offer.

I believe I speak for all of the contributors to this text when I say that entrepreneurship has enriched our lives by allowing us to share remarkable experiences with wonderfully unique and talented people. When confronting obstacles, it was very often the dedication and humor of the people we worked with that kept us moving onward and upward.

It is this sense of the pioneering spirit and joy of entrepreneurship that we want to pass along to you. We wish you the best of luck and many good times as you set out on your own entrepreneurial adventures.

*David Wold*
*Mill Valley, California*

## About the Authors

Preparing the NxLeveL™ text books was a challenge, and to meet that challenge in the best possible way, we asked several individuals to help us. The authors have a combined 250 years in business, making the sharing of their experiences just that much more beneficial. The authors include professional educators and entrepreneurs who have both educational and practical experience. We'd like to recognize them here.

## Primary Authors

**David P. Wold** is an international entrepreneurship consultant, advising start-up and growing businesses on strategy, management and marketing. He has over 20 years' experience growing businesses in the U.S., Latin America, the Middle East, Russia and Eastern Europe. A graduate of the University of Wisconsin, he has an M.I.M. from the American Graduate School of International Management.

**Dennis Sargent** is Director of the Small Business Development Center at Linn-Benton Community College. He is a C.P.A. and holds an M.B.A. from Oregon State University. Dennis has more than 25 years experience in business consulting, systems design, teaching and management.

**Martha Sargent** is an Assistant Professor of Accounting and Director of the Small Business Development Center at Western Oregon State College. She holds an M.B.A. from Oregon Sate University and is a C.P.A. Martha has more than 18 years experience in accounting and teaching.

## Contributing Authors

**Helen LeBoeuf-Binninger** holds B.B.A., M.B.A. and C.P.A. certificates. She has been involved with small businesses as an entrepreneur and consultant. She currently provides business consulting and training services to small businesses near her home in Idaho.

**Virginia Campbell** is the Assistant State Director for the Washington Small Business Development Center. Ms. Campbell has 10 years of Human Resource experience in the private sector working for an electronic manufacturer and has nine years experience as the owner of a small business in the construction industry.

**James Deffenbaugh** is the Executive Director of a nonprofit community planning and loan organization. He is a past administrator of the California Regional Parks System, and has been an administrative partner for a C.P.A. firm. He has many years counseling and consulting experience with both small and large businesses.

**Dawn Gardner** is currently Director of the Colorado Rural Development Program (CRTP) which is part of the Colorado Commission on Higher Education. CRTP continues to explore new ways to increase economic activity in rural areas in the telecommunications environment. Previously, Dawn served as Small Office/Home Office Studies as the Center for the New West and Vice President of the Rocky Mountain Home-Based Business Association based in Denver, Colorado. She served on the board of the Colorado Rural Telecommunications Project. Dawn owned and operated a small business from 1976 to 1985, served as Press/Public Relations Officer to Governor Lamm from 1985 to 1987 and developed the first entrepreneurial training program in Colorado which she delivered throughout the state from 1989 to 1996; Recently, Dawn has been providing entrepreneurial training workshops and curriculum development for USDA employees, the artistic community, *Energizing Your Community,* Internet Masters Program and various workshops for the home-based business.

**Kris Jon Gorsuch** is a graduate of the University of Iowa College of Law. Kris is an attorney specializing in helping entrepreneurs establish successful businesses. He has written and spoken extensively on business development and teaches continuing education classes. He holds Martindale Hubble's highest achievement rating.

**Joseph B. Harris** is a Business Development Specialist for the Washington Small Business Development Center in Pullman, Washington. He is a former owner of a scientific instrument manufacturing company and recently started a new business venture. He teaches entrepreneurship and business planning at Washington State University.

**Robert Horn** is the Director of the Colorado Center for Community Development at the University of Colorado at Denver and founder of the NxLeveL™ Training Network. He is an educator and professional planner by training. He holds a masters of Urban and Regional Planning, and has been involved in community economic development for the past twenty years.

**Randy Johnson** is Director of the Small Business Development Center for the Community College of Aurora, Colorado. Randy has developed several entrepreneurial training classes and has spoken on such topics as financing, economic development, home-based business and marketing. He is currently President of the Rocky Mountain Home-Based Business Association.

**Paul Karofsky** started working in his family's business in 1967 and has been involved with small businesses since. He is Director of the Northeastern University Center for Family Business and a lecturer at the University's College of Business Administration, and writes a family business column for several publications.

**Brandan Kearney** is a freelance writer and editor who has written extensively on environmental regulations, pollution control, and the chemistry of hazardous materials. He has written several manuals on the qualitative analysis of unknown chemicals for HazTech Systems, Inc., a San Francisco-based industrial hygiene company, and has conducted training on safe shipping and handling of chemicals.

**Yolanda Collazos Kizer** is the president of Builder's Book Depot and Casa Feniz Merchandizing, Inc. She has an M.B.A., and serves on several civic organizations throughout Arizona, including the Governor's Strategic Partnership for Economic Development and the City of Phoenix Commission on the Economy.

**Johanna Leestma** is a graduate of Vassar College. She has worked in Hong Kong and Thailand. Johanna owned a successful backpack design and manufacturing business before earning her M.I.M. degree from the American Graduate School of International Management. She is a freelance writer and entrepreneurial consultant.

**Lorre McKeone** of North Platte, Nebraska, has managed three small businesses and spent 7 years as a loan officer before starting her own business, The Executive Extra. She teaches classes, workshops and provides consulting services for small businesses. Ms. McKeone graduated with honors from Hastings College.

**William Mullane** is a consultant at the Center for New West. He is working on Ebits, an Internet business technology project in Idaho. He is a former newspaper publisher and was the communications manager for Schweitzer

Mountain Resort. Bill helped create the Royal Saudi Air Force Survival Training Center and curriculum. He has an M.I.M. from the American Graduate School of International Management.

**Cameron Wold** is a Community Development Specialist of the NxLeveL™ Training Network. A former commercial banker, his expertise includes entrepreneurial training, welfare transition, shared-use commercial kitchens and the specialty food trade. A graduate of Amherst College, he holds an MBA from the University of Southern California.

**R. L. Wolverton** is a freelance writer and photographer who teaches small business planning. He has owned and published newspapers and magazines, and his writing has appeared in several national magazines. He makes his home in Wyoming.

## Editor

**David P. Wold** is an international management and marketing consultant. He has won awards in advertising in Europe and the U.S. Mr. Wold lives in Mill Valley, California.

## Production Staff

NxLeveL™ Training Network
University of Colorado at Denver

*Project Management*

Robert Horn

Cameron Wold

*Layout & Design*

Michele Renée Ledoux

Amy Elizabeth Norton

J Fay Design

# PART I
# UNDERSTANDING ENTREPRENEURSHIP

## Chapter 1
## UNDERSTANDING ENTREPRENEURSHIP

*About This Chapter:*
- *The importance of small businesses*
- *What makes a good entrepreneur?*
- *Risks and drawbacks of entrepreneurship*

## Introduction

You can be a successful small business owner without being an entrepreneur, but you can't be an entrepreneur without starting out as a small business. What is the difference? Small businesses, such as a "Mom and Pop" dry cleaner or grocery store, tend to remain relatively small and local. Their owners maintain a small group of loyal customers and a steady level of income, but do not seek opportunities for growth. In contrast, the entrepreneur is a builder—one who sees an opportunity to create a new business venture, sizes up its value, and finds the resources to make the most of it. Entrepreneurs are never content with the status quo; they're always looking for new markets, new ideas, and new challenges. They are innovative, visionary people with a strong desire to create something new. It may be a new product or a new process, but it's always a "better idea." The entrepreneur has a vision of how the business will grow, and the drive to make it happen!

Most small businesses have the ability to become entrepreneurial, but their owners choose to keep them small to avoid the risks and complications that come with growth. For instance, the owner may not want to hire, train, and manage the new employees a larger business would require.

This chapter identifies a few of the most valuable qualities an entrepreneur can possess, and encourages you to find and develop these qualities in yourself.

> Our greatest weakness lies in giving up. The most certain way to succeed is to always try just one more time.
>
> —Thomas Edison

## The Importance of Small Businesses

Small business operators are the backbone of this country. Anywhere you go, you'll find examples of small businesses that contribute to the local economy, provide jobs, pay taxes, and earn a comfortable living for the owners. The Small Business Administration (SBA) reports that America's small businesses (those with less than 500 employees):

- Employ 54 percent of the private work force
- Generate 52 percent of all sales volume
- Are responsible for 50 percent of private production

Small businesses also provide the majority of new jobs, and these jobs are more likely to be filled by younger workers, older workers, and women.

Studies show that small firms produce twice as many innovations per employee as large firms. Some attribute this to the adventurous spirit of the small business, others to the ability of a small firm to move and change more rapidly than a large, bureaucratic company.

Small businesses also help to lead the country out of economic downturns. The SBA reports that between 1980 and 1990, all of the net new jobs in the economy were created by small firms. During this period, the nation's smallest firms (those with fewer than 20 employees) created almost 4.1 million new jobs, while large firms lost more than 500,000 jobs, and firms with 20-499 employees lost 850,000 jobs.

## What Makes a Good Entrepreneur?

Every day, millions of people dream of starting a business. Every day, hundreds of entrepreneurs turn their dreams of starting a business into reality. What is the difference between those who dream about it, and those who do it?

Well, entrepreneurs are usually young, old, or somewhere in between. They're either male or female. They're often college-educated, or not. In other words, they come from every imaginable background; no gender, age, education level, or ethnicity bestows a particular advantage in entrepreneurship.

But certain personality types *do* have an advantage. Most observers agree that successful entrepreneurs have certain characteristics in common. These include:

### Passion

Loving what you do is essential to doing it well. Successful entrepreneurs are passionate about their businesses, and it shows. Effort means little when we are passionate about our work, and often leaves us feeling exhilarated rather than exhausted! None work harder, more happily, or more productively than those who work for themselves.

### Persistence

Entrepreneurs are determined. They're willing to work longer and harder than others, which is often crucial in overcoming the daily challenges they face. They may have to do things that they don't enjoy, but they don't allow themselves to get discouraged. Although routine chores such as accounting are seldom enjoyable, they are vital to business success, and the true entrepreneur has the discipline and commitment to complete such tasks properly and on schedule.

### Good Health and High Energy

Starting a business requires a tremendous amount of effort and time. Without good health and high energy, it's very hard to maintain a successful business. (In fact, when the owner's health fails, the business is usually not far behind.) If you wish to be an entrepreneur, take care of your health...you're going to need it!

Passion is the cornerstone of the entrepreneurial spirit

## Creativity

It takes creativity to come up with innovative products and services. It also takes creativity to solve problems like losing an important supplier or a prime business location. An entrepreneur must always be willing to experiment with new ideas and strategies, which also means being open to creative suggestions from others.

## Independence and Self-Reliance

Entrepreneurs like to make things happen. They enjoy making their own decisions and carrying them out; this is what draws them to self-employment. They're also willing to take on the responsibilities that come with this freedom.

## Intuition

Intuition is the ability to see beyond the obvious. The intuitive entrepreneur has an uncanny ability to predict how a given situation will affect his or her business, and to make the right decisions in advance.

———————◆———————

*Dale Brundage is a good example of an intuitive businessman. One day, an inventor walked into Dale's office with something that can only be described as a chainsaw on a stick. This "extension saw" could cut branches up to 15 feet off the ground! Dale believed this invention could be marketed to parks, transportation departments, and others who maintain trees and shrubs in public areas. By using this new tool, these agencies would avoid the danger of climbing trees, and the expense—and inconvenience—of bringing in large machinery. Dale followed his instincts, and they paid off!*

———————◆———————

## Self-Confidence

Entrepreneurs are confident in their ability to make their businesses prosper, even when the people around them aren't. They're optimistic and have faith in their own ideas. This self-confidence also allows them to be realistic and open to change; they're not afraid to recognize that they must sometimes ask questions or seek advice.

## Willingness to Work Hard

Entrepreneurs are invariably hard-working. There is a common misconception that entrepreneurs have the freedom to set their own hours. In reality, starting a small business demands much more time than people realize. As one entrepreneur said, "I work only half the time—twelve hours a day!"

Creating and successfully running a new business takes hard work

## NxLEVEL™ TECH TIP

**There are hundreds of Web sites devoted to entrepreneurship. Here are a few of the best:**

**EntrepreneurMag.com** (http://www.entrepreneurmag.com). This remarkable Web site comprises thousands of pages, with chat rooms, a bookstore, over 300 free downloadable business forms, free membership and e-mail accounts, several years' worth of back issues of *Entrepreneur* and *Small Business Startups* magazines, and many links to related sites.

**Startup** (http://www.startup.wsj.com) is an offshoot of the *Wall Street Journal*, and features lots of news, advice, anecdotes, and ideas for the entrepreneur. **Entrepreneurial Edge** (http://edge.lowe.org) is a well-designed, incredibly detailed site with interactive business tutorials, a large library of pertinent documents, links to related Internet sites, an e-mail subscription newsletter, and much more.

Don't forget the **NxLeveL™ Training Network** at http://www.nxlevel.org.

## Risks and Drawbacks of Entrepreneurship

There are always risks in going into business for oneself, but they can be minimized with careful planning, information gathering, and analysis. Successful entrepreneurs may take calculated risks, but they are not gamblers; they seldom act until they have assessed the situation and done everything in their power to minimize risk.

Let's look at some of the risks and drawbacks that entrepreneurs face.

- **Failure.** Entrepreneurs must assume the emotional burden of failure.
- **Loss of money.** Most start-up entrepreneurs have their own money at risk.
- **Long hours.** Most entrepreneurs report 60-70 hours per week as normal.
- **Family problems.** Because of the strain of operating a business, the entrepreneur's family relationships may suffer.
- **Bad timing.** While people in all stages of life have started successful businesses, it seems that certain times are more conducive to taking on a new business venture. Sometimes, it is just not the right time to start a new business. In these situations, it's much better to put off one's venture temporarily than to let overwhelming distractions and difficulties harm one's prospects for success.

### Potential Weaknesses

Entrepreneurs, like all human beings, have weaknesses that can get in the way of their goals. Here are a few to watch out for:

- **Personnel problems.** Often, entrepreneurs are not very good at perceiving the "people problems" occurring around them. They don't like dealing with personnel issues, and have little tolerance for those who aren't equally focused on business goals. Because they are a confident lot and believe that they can do everything single-handedly, they often have a difficult time working as part of a team, or fostering teamwork among employees.

- **Controlling too much.** If you believe that no one can make decisions as well as you can, you may be unable to delegate authority. The result? A customer or client who walks into your business and finds that no one but you can make what appears to be a routine operating decision may go away frustrated. This is a common problem in businesses run by individuals who try to do everything themselves.

- **Workaholism.** Some people consider their work the only important activity in life; nothing else is quite as fun or exciting as business, so family and outside pursuits don't receive enough attention. This can make for unhappy families...and ultimately, unhappy entrepreneurs. A balanced life—one with plenty of time for family, friends, and relaxation—will serve the entrepreneur infinitely better than the tunnel vision of a workaholic.

*New venture owners believe in their ability to make the business prosper*

## Rewards

Different individuals have different motivations and different ideas of success, but some of the most attractive rewards for entrepreneurs include:

- **Independence.** The freedom to act independently, to "be your own boss," is a very powerful incentive for entrepreneurs.

- **Money.** The financial rewards of running a successful business can go far beyond what one can expect from a normal job, and provide much greater personal satisfaction!

- **Fun.** Most entrepreneurs really enjoy what they do. The entrepreneurial lifestyle presents opportunities for fun, excitement, and creativity that most businesses cannot offer their employees.

*Don't forget to have fun—that's what it is all about!*

# Conclusion

Entrepreneurship requires an ability to spot opportunities and act wisely on them. And just like other occupations, providing a product or service at an attractive price is the basis for getting paid.

Because of the widespread outsourcing, downsizing, and re-engineering at large corporations, entrepreneurial skills may be the key not only to economic independence, but even to survival in the 21st century. Naturally, there are many risks in entrepreneurship. But for most entrepreneurs, the joy of running a business outweighs the drawbacks!

# Chapter 2
# THINKING ENTREPRENEURIALLY

*About This Chapter:*
- *Why do businesses succeed?*
- *The nature of profit*
- *Bootstrapping*
- *The power of outsourcing*
- *Effective time management*

## Introduction

How does one think and act like an entrepreneur? Many entrepreneurs would answer that question with, "By understanding and adhering to the demands of profitability, managing time effectively, behaving ethically, leveraging scarce resources, and planning a fulfilling, balanced personal life."

The goal of this chapter is to inspire you to learn and practice these skills. You'll find that doing so will dramatically improve the efficiency of your business and the quality of your personal life.

## Why Do Businesses Succeed?

Businesses can fail for many reasons: They ignore their customers, they disregard market conditions, they miscalculate prices, they don't stick to plans and budgets, or they lack managerial control.

As helpful as it is to learn what not to do by analyzing the reasons a business fails, it's even more helpful to understand what makes a business successful. Business success can be defined in all sorts of ways—including business size, market share, profitability, efficiency, and ability to innovate—but there are certain qualities that every successful business shares.

*Businesses succeed because they:*
- Have a clear sense of purpose
- Base their goals on realistic expectations
- Understand their strengths and weaknesses relative to those of their competitors
- Target the right group of customers
- Specialize in solving customer problems, and experiment with new approaches
- Are organized for maximum flexibility
- Create customer loyalty and repeat business by offering a unique value
- Build enduring relationships based on quality, honesty, and responsiveness
- Develop a new product or service that captures a large market share
- Keep a close eye on costs, pricing, and profit

## The Nature of Profit

Businesses exist to make money. **Profit** is the positive difference between what a business earns for selling its products or services, and what it pays to produce those products or services. Profit is a return for time and money invested, and a reward to the entrepreneur for assuming risks.

However, using profit as the sole measure of your business's success can be deceptive. No matter what your profit margin, you must have sufficient **cash flow** to run your operations. Remember: a sale cannot be considered "cash" until you receive the money! It's not uncommon for profitable ventures to fail because of cash flow problems. In addition, a business may have customers lining up to buy its products, but if its costs are too high or its prices too low, it will not make a profit. It's essential for businesses to make regular calculations of profitability; this keeps them focused on revenues and expenses, and forms the basis for budgets, forecasts, and controls. Understanding profitability makes it possible to manage your resources more effectively.

*When Barbara Gillies first opened Cook's Kitchen, a gourmet kitchenware store in an upscale neighborhood, sales were brisk and profit margins high. Before Barbara patted herself on the back, she did some thinking about who her customers were and how she could maintain their loyalty. Because she wanted to ensure a constant cash flow, Barbara held a series of cooking classes at the store, for which she charged a fee. The classes were so successful that Barbara decided to offer a curriculum of classes throughout the year. In this way, she created a steady demand for her products, and satisfied her customers' desire to expand their culinary horizons.*

The lesson? Understand where your profits come from, and create strategies to maximize them. When planning your business's growth, consider short-term strategies that will ensure the long-term goal of customer loyalty.

## Bootstrapping

Often, entrepreneurs must use all their creativity to beg, borrow, or find the resources they need to support a new venture. This is called **bootstrapping**; it's the practice of getting by with as few resources as possible, and getting the most out of those you have. This might include holding down three different jobs, borrowing money from family and friends, selling assets, mortgaging a house, or even resorting to credit card financing. Entrepreneurs who use all of their wiles to make their business viable are bootstrapping. But bootstrapping is not just a way to finance a new business; it's also a way to keep a successful business lean and flexible. Successful entrepreneurs are always looking for aggressive, unconventional ways to generate revenue, minimize costs, and maximize profits.

*Top Drawer Publishing is a four-person team that designs newsletters, company reports, brochures, and other publications. Last year, they signed a large contract with Medis Corporation. By mid-year, they needed to buy computer equipment and move to a larger office space, but did not have sufficient cash. What to do? Top Drawer had sizable 60-day accounts receivable from Medis, so they searched out a factoring company that was interested in buying accounts receivable. The factoring company knew that Medis was a reliable firm with a solid reputation for paying its bills, and agreed to buy their accounts receivable at face value (minus a 10% commission). The result? Top Drawer received its cash immediately, and was able to buy the equipment and sign a new office lease.*

*Here are some hints for the bootstrapping entrepreneur:*
- Share office space with a larger business
- Cut down on the need for full-time employees by using independent contractors, temp workers, or services from other businesses
- Use barter arrangements to procure supplies
- Sell wholesale rather than direct to retailers—wholesalers are experts at setting up and managing distribution channels
- Collect accounts receivable as soon as possible
- Build strong relationships with suppliers, and arrange for longer payment terms
- Use computers to create promotional material, manage sales efforts, and keep track of your budgets and bookkeeping
- Most important: always be honest, creative, and reliable—never unethical

## NxLEVEL™ TECH TIP

**Here are a couple of ways to cut your costs and save time by going online:**

You can save on paper and phone bills by using e-fax services such as **Efax.com** (http://www.efax.com) or **Comfax** (http://www.comfax.com). Both companies offer a free service that allows you to send and receive faxes through your e-mail account. They can also provide a bulk e-faxing service that enables you to reach hundreds of customers at a fraction of the cost of a traditional direct mailing.

If you're tired of making trips to the post office and waiting in line (or getting there just as it closes!), new Internet postage systems like **Stamps.com** (http://www.stamps.com) allow you to buy postage over the Internet and print digital stamps using a computer and a standard laser or ink-jet printer. To prevent fraud, each stamp is unique and can't be photocopied, and postage can be printed only with a valid mailing address. Other systems, such as Neopost's Simply Postage or Pitney-Bowes Personal Post Office, require the purchase of hardware, and a monthly subscription fee.

## The Power of Outsourcing

**Outsourcing** is the practice of hiring **independent contractors,** consulting firms or temporary employment agencies, rather than hiring additional employees to help with business operations. Independent contractors own their own businesses and hire themselves out to perform specific jobs for their clients; these jobs may include accounting and bookkeeping, sales, product design, promotions, or logistics. Independent contractors are usually specialists in their particular field, and can be hired on a short-term or as-needed basis. Since they don't need to have social security tax or income tax withheld, or to be paid health insurance in their compensation package, they cost considerably less than full-time employees. The clever use of independent contractors can allow a small business to imitate the professionalism, expertise, and high-quality performance of a much larger firm. This strategy offers many benefits. You have limited resources and time, and you must carefully choose the battles you will wage. If others can do something better than you, why not benefit from their expertise? This is not just a technique for new entrepreneurs; many established businesses regularly use outsourcing to reduce their overhead, lower costs, and focus resources on their core strengths.

Additionally, entrepreneurs are turning to consulting firms or temporary employment agencies to provide the (non-employee) human resources necessary for short-term job positions, special projects, and other personnel needs that can be better served by these groups than by hiring new employees.

*Many businesses use independent contractors during their start-up phase. Frank Lang began his kitchen remodeling business by hiring independent contractors to help him with cabinetmaking as sales dictated. As his business grew, Frank eventually hired a cabinetmaker as a full-time employee. In this way, he was able to grow his business without having to worry about funding a regular payroll regardless of sales, or complying with federal payroll requirements (taxes, insurance, etc.).*

*When outsourcing, it is important to:*
- Select contractors with whom you can work and communicate easily
- Establish the contractor's level of expertise
- Discuss deadlines and performance standards thoroughly
- Have appropriate operating licenses
- Make sure contractors are covered by their own workers' compensation insurance
- Use a clear and professionally written legal contract
- Clearly state in the contract that for tax purposes the contractor will not be treated as a full-time employee

Use outsourcing to imitate the expertise of big business

# Effective Time Management

Smaller staffs and budgets, combined with the challenges of getting a young business up and running, make time one of an entrepreneur's scarcest resources. Many start-up business owners work between 60 and 80 hours a week, and still cannot get all of their tasks completed. Why? Because they are not effectively organizing their time.

Entrepreneurs who fail to manage their time often fall into a cycle of inefficiency and poor performance. They're too busy to teach employees how to work effectively, so they end up trying to do too many tasks themselves. They do not have enough time to weed out mistakes and improve practices. They cannot build strong relationships with customers and suppliers, nor can they fully enjoy their leisure time.

Effective time management leads to effective business management. No matter how small your business, you usually cannot single-handedly do all of the tasks it requires. You must delegate duties, and give people the authority to perform the tasks in the most effective ways. After all, you should focus your efforts on the tasks that only you can do: guiding the business by setting goals, and devising strategies that will achieve those goals.

*How to practice good time management:*
- List all business activities, and record how much time is spent on each over a one-week period
- Identify wasted time and "gaps" that can be used more efficiently
- Create an agenda of prioritized tasks, and cross them off as they are completed
- Finish tasks in one session
- Create agendas for meeting goals and deadlines
- Keep work areas clear of clutter, and file papers immediately
- Schedule the most important work for first thing in the morning
- "Batch" tasks that can be done together

Good time management takes discipline and organization, but it makes you more efficient and improves the quality of your performance!

## Personal Planning

Because entrepreneurs have so much flexibility in creating their work environment and schedule, they need to address personal priorities very early in their ventures. Where will the boundaries be drawn between work, family, and leisure time?

For many, the traditional boundaries between private and professional time are blurred. It's easy for entrepreneurs to focus too intently on the rewards they reap from their efforts. Unfortunately, this preoccupation with the business sometimes alienates them from family and friends, and leaves them with no time for community, athletic, or creative pursuits.

From the outset, smart entrepreneurs take the time to evaluate their personal priorities, and plan a schedule that allows them to fulfill these priorities.

Delegating responsibility and authority is one of the toughest but most important things an entrepreneur must do

*Baked Alaska, a start-up handbag manufacturing firm, demanded at least 80 hours a week from entrepreneur Antonia Bolt. She designed and sewed samples, did the books, and sold the finished product. She also spent time meeting with sewing shops, checking on orders, and negotiating bulk supplier contracts. She was very, very busy!*

*After four months in business, she realized she hadn't been out on a date in three months. And because she had no time to jog or go to the gym, she had gained ten pounds. At that point, she realized that she needed to create firm boundaries between work and play.*

The following is an example of an entrepreneur's weekly plan:

|  | February |
|---|---|
| S M T W T F S | |
| | 1 |
| 2  3  4  5  6  7  8 | |
| 9  10  11  12  13  14  15 | |
| 16  17  18  19  20  21  22 | |
| 23  24  25  26  27  28 | |

# Weekly Planner
# February 10-16, 2000

**Monday 10**
10:30 AM - 12:30 PM Meet with Richard Hersey/Textiles Unlimited - discuss supply agreement and schedule
2:00 PM - 3:00 PM Interview Frances Klein for asst. position
4:00 PM - 5:00 PM Aerobics class

**Tuesday 11**
9:00 AM - 10:30 PM Women in Business breakfast
11:00 AM - 1:00 PM Review March - June orders
3:00 PM - 4:00 PM Appointment with Flair Boutique

**Wednesday 12**
8:30 AM - 12:30 PM SBDC Conference - "Financing Sources"
1:00 PM - 3:00 PM Lunch with Robin Grant re: design concepts

**Thursday 13**
9:00 AM - 10:00 AM Finalize lease with MMC Management Co.
11:00 AM - 12:00 PM Contact Hilton gift shop re: July - Dec. orders
7:30 PM - Class - Marketing/Internet

**Friday 14**
9:00 AM - 10:30 AM Meet with accountant - review tax returns
1:00 PM - 2:00 PM Present designs to Shelly's Shop
4:00 PM - 5:00 PM Yoga class

**Saturday 15**
11:30 AM - Golf with Ann
8:00 PM - Movie with Bill

**Sunday 16**
12:00 PM - Lunch with Mom and Dad

*Antonia bought a day planner and created a weekly schedule—not just for business tasks and appointments, but also for social and athletic activities. Every day at 4 P.M., she would stop working and go for a run, or visit the health club. If she didn't feel like working out, she would take a walk, go shopping, or drop in at her favorite bookstore and read. She also decided that to keep her creativity and enthusiasm up, she needed to go out with her friends at least three nights a week, even if it was only to have a cup of tea at a local café. Her final rule? All work ended at 9 P.M.*

The best way to approach personal planning is to identify your family and community responsibilities. You should also:

- Prioritize activities
- Set working hours and family time
- Allow time for athletic and creative activities
- Take vacations
- Create work time cut-offs
- Reward yourself for completing major projects

## Conclusion

What is true entrepreneurial thinking? It is keeping one eye on profit and the other on "quality of life" issues. It is finding clever ways to maximize one's resources. It is using time wisely, and being guided by one's values and commitments. It is evaluating one's priorities, strengths, interests, and goals, and creating a business that fulfills them. Entrepreneurs are truly successful when they find a comfortable balance between business responsibilities and personal needs.

*"Work needs to fit your personality just as shoes need to fit your feet."*
—Marsha Sinetar, organizational psychologist and business consultant

# Chapter 3
# SELF-ASSESSMENT AND YOUR BUSINESS CHECK-UP

*About This Chapter:*
- *Your personal assessment*
- *Your business skills assessment*
- *Your lifestyle assessment*
- *Personal mission statement*
- *Your business check-up*

## Introduction

This chapter contains a series of questionnaires designed to help you assess your business skills and lifestyle preferences. You may find it helpful to solicit feedback from family, co-workers, and friends; ask them to answer these questions with you in mind, then review their answers with them.

After completing the questionnaires, and doing some soul-searching, you can draw upon these insights to create a personal mission statement that will guide your efforts to grow your business.

The point of this exercise is not to identify "true" entrepreneurs and screen out the rest. It is simply a tool to gauge your personal and business skills, to help you make the best decisions about whether to go into business, and to identify the skills that you need to improve. Your scores do not guarantee success or failure—entrepreneurs are made, not born! The purpose of this chapter is simply to clarify your priorities, and inspire you to develop your portfolio of skills. If you routinely go through these exercises, you can develop effective entrepreneurial skills that will grow as your business grows. Remember: Successful entrepreneurs never stop trying to identify areas for self-improvement.

And now, find a quiet place to work, sharpen your pencil, and start getting to know a new entrepreneur!

## Your Personal Assessment

People are defined by their actions: how they interact with people, how they make decisions, what their natural talents are, and how they get things done. In general, our personalities are revealed by a unique composite of daily habits that reflect our skills, motivation, and past learning. Habits are learned and modified every day; they contribute to our view of ourselves, and to the impression we make on others. The following personal assessment will help you see your own habits more clearly, so that you can compare them to the habits of successful entrepreneurs. This allows you to identify skills you might need to improve as you begin your venture.

Knowing what you know…the starting point for real learning

Read each statement carefully, and enter a score in the right-hand column based on how well the statement agrees with your own feelings. Use a scale of 1 to 4:

1 = strongly disagree
2 = disagree
3 = agree
4 = strongly agree

When you have finished the test, calculate your total by adding all points in the score column. A score of 25 to 62 points in this exercise may mean that starting a business is not the right choice for you. Becoming an entrepreneur is stressful and challenging, and if the ability to focus your energy wholeheartedly on a goal is not among your strengths, you may want to consider an alternate profession!

That said, a low- to mid-range score may simply mean that you have not yet had a chance to develop these skills. With a little training and experience—such as you'd get from partnering with more experienced people, or going to work in a small, entrepreneurial business—you can easily overcome this handicap.

Perhaps your self-confidence is lower than you'd like. You may feel that you're not as creative as you need to be, or that you lack "natural" leadership abilities. Chances are, if you look closely at your achievements, you'll find that you possess more good qualities than you think! This book will help you to develop many of the personal qualities entrepreneurs need, including leadership skills, creativity, and a capacity for innovative problem-solving.

If you scored between 63 and 100 points, you are well on your way to having the skills you'll need to tackle the challenges of entrepreneurship; you enjoy setting goals and achieving them, and are comfortable with taking some risks. However, since the success of your venture depends on discovering and improving upon your weak areas, we recommend that you consider ways to develop those skills for which your score was below 3.

## Personal Assessment

| Statement | Score |
|---|---|
| I enjoy competition in both work and play. | 2 |
| I often set goals for myself. | 3 |
| I often meet the goals I set for myself. | 4 |
| I set limits for myself and follow them (with money, time, projects). | 2 |
| I am happiest when I am responsible for myself and my own decisions. | 4 |
| If given a choice, I prefer to work with other people on a project. | 2 |
| In group situations, I usually take a leadership role (setting the agenda, organizing duties, recording decisions, establishing criteria, etc.). | 3 |
| I do things on my own. Nobody has to get me going. | 4 |
| I work best when there are no precedents for what I am doing. | 3 |
| I enjoy putting myself "on the line." | 4 |
| When I start something, I am able to generate enthusiasm and commitment among other people. | 3 |
| I believe that "luck favors the prepared mind." | 4 |
| I do not perform well when other people set goals and define tasks I am to do. | 1 |
| I am an on-time kind of person. | 3 |
| I enjoy seeking out new challenges. | 3 |
| I thrive on inventing new ideas, products, concepts. | 3 |
| I find it exciting and exhilarating when circumstances change and I must adapt or expand my abilities. | 4 |
| I enjoy speaking in front of groups of people. | 2 |
| I have strong intuition, and I listen to it. | 3 |
| I have many natural talents. | 4 |
| I often identify new skills I need and work at acquiring them. | 3 |
| I prefer to be very busy. | 4 |
| I enjoy the task of juggling several tasks at once. | 4 |
| I can make up my mind in a hurry if I have to. These decisions usually turn out to be good ones. | 2 |
| I get excited about new opportunities, ideas or projects just about every day. | 3 |
| **Personal Total Points** | 78 |

## Your Business Skills Assessment

Entrepreneurs have limited time and resources, so they must focus on what they do best. It's important to know early on which skills you have, and which you'll have to learn, or find in co-workers.

Many of the skills discussed in this exercise are not difficult to acquire. In fact, it's very possible that you use them often without knowing it! To rate yourself fairly, consider past and present participation in community, church, and family activities; hobbies; and professional organizations. You are likely to find that you possess far more business skills than you realize, and can learn those skills you *don't* have much more easily than you might think.

Read the following statements, scoring yourself on a scale of 1 to 4.

1 = strongly disagree
2 = disagree
3 = agree
4 = strongly agree

If you score between 25 and 62 points, there are many steps you can take to improve your business skills. For instance, you may wish to find a community college or continuing education program that offers basic accounting, financial management, and marketing classes. Talking with experienced business people is another great way to get real-life knowledge about business skills; seek out people who work in your targeted field and ask them about the skills they feel have been crucial to their success. Learning new business skills is a continual process in today's marketplace.

If you score above 63 points, you may already possess basic business knowledge. However, the advice above applies to you, too: Identify the business skills you need to learn and focus on them!

## Business Assessment

| Statement | Score |
|---|---|
| I keep track of my personal finances and balance my checkbook every week. | 2 |
| I create monthly and yearly budgets for myself and follow them. | 2 |
| For any given period of time, I know what I spend on medical costs and living expenses. | 3 |
| I know within $100 how much it cost me to operate my car last year. | 2 |
| I prepare my tax return myself. | 1 |
| I have borrowed money from a bank. | 4 |
| I have an excellent credit rating. | 2 |
| I enjoy getting "out there" and selling an idea or product to people I have never met. | 2 |
| Give me five minutes, an audience, a great product, and I can make a sale. | 2 |
| I understand how to calculate profitability and perform break-even analysis. | 4 |
| I understand the difference between fixed and variable costs. | 4 |
| I believe that "luck favors the prepared mind." | 4 |
| I am able to utilize a computer to efficiently manage my work and personal finances. | 3 |
| I have an e-mail address and use it. | 4 |
| I regularly read *Inc.* and other weekly business magazines. | 2 |
| I would press customers for full payment up front, or if they refused, negotiate with them for a 50% deposit. | 4 |
| I have work experience in the industry or field in which I am interested in starting a business. | 1 |
| I have successfully managed people by setting goals, delegating responsibility and addressing performance. | 3 |
| When negotiating a decision with a friend, co-worker or salesperson, I am confident in identifying and communicating my interests and succeed at maximizing my outcome. | 3 |
| I understand the basics of how different products and services are distributed and why. | 4 |
| I have hired and fired people. | 4 |
| I know how to effectively interview and assess potential employees. | 3 |
| I understand how the concept of "cash flow" impacts business decisions. | 4 |
| I am comfortable giving talks and know how to create professional, effective presentations. | 3 |
| I know how to use computer software to create effective presentations. | 4 |
| I know how to prepare an invoice. | 4 |
| **Business Total Points** | 84 |

## Your Lifestyle Assessment

Assessing lifestyle preferences means measuring what you value as a human being. Carefully studying your motivations, and the priorities that guide your decisions, will ensure that the demands of your work and your personal life are compatible.

Read the following statements, and score yourself as you did in the previous assessments.

1 = strongly disagree
2 = disagree
3 = agree
4 = strongly agree

Are you flexible enough to take on the challenges and uncertainties of a new business? If you score below 62 points, financial, family, community, or other personal responsibilities may be a considerable source of conflict to you!  By looking at the statements for which you scored a 1 or 2, you may be able to draw some conclusions about how time, money, family, health, and other issues will affect your ideal lifestyle.  This does not disqualify you from pursuing your venture; it simply reveals some of the realities of your life, and presents the parameters within which you must make business decisions.  The same holds true if you score between 63 and 100 points: this is your starting point for understanding what type of business opportunity is best for you to pursue, and how you can make it fit your lifestyle.

## Lifestyle Assessment

| Statement | Score |
|---|---|
| My friends would describe me as a high-energy person. | 3 |
| My health is good. | 3 |
| I can support myself without taking money out of my business for 1 year. | 1 |
| If I needed to, I could keep my full-time job and run my new business on the side. | 1 |
| I have no problem working 10-12 hours a day, 6 days a week, including holidays. | 4 |
| I am willing to work 60 hours or more a week. | 4 |
| My family will tolerate me working 60 hours or more a week. | 4 |
| I consider myself a high performer. | 4 |
| I know I can work productively for long hours and meet deadlines, no matter what it takes. | 4 |
| I have very good physical stamina. | 3 |
| My family obligations rank number one on my list of priorities. | 2 |
| At the expense of professional stability and perhaps higher income, it is important to me to be able to determine when and where I work. | 3 |
| Foremost among my personal goals is the freedom to pursue my own ideas. | 4 |
| I am prepared to lose my savings. | 4 |
| Beginning my own business is all about making money. | 1 |
| I am prepared to sacrifice the amount of money and/or time that I am able to commit to community, church, or charity obligations during the first five years of my business. | 4 |
| I can go a year without a vacation. | 4 |
| I have the enthusiastic support of my family to pursue an entrepreneurial venture. | 4 |
| I am comfortable setting, evaluating and achieving my own 1, 3 and 5 year plan. | 3 |
| I understand that part of my job description in my new business would include sweeping the floor, typing letters and taking out the trash. | 4 |
| When I think about the future, I envision positive, new growth opportunities. | 4 |
| It is important to me to create my own space in which to work. | 4 |
| I am comfortable working in a "gray area" where the boundaries between my work and personal life are sometimes hidden. | 4 |
| I don't get sick often. | 3 |
| **Lifestyle Total Points** | 79 |

## Personal Mission Statement

With these insights in mind, now is a great time to write your mission statement. The statement represents the values and principles on which you base your life. Many of us seldom take the time to examine how or why we do things; however, this is precisely what you should do if you wish to make your business thrive! Your personal mission statement is unique to you, and can look and sound any way you want it to. Let the following sample serve as an outline for the creation of your mission statement. Be creative, be true to yourself, and let inspiration guide you!

### Sample Personal Mission Statement:
- My family comes first
- I strive to be honest in everything
- I will finish everything I start
- I want to set standards among my peers for commitment and dedication
- I will take time to daydream
- I will laugh at myself when appropriate
- I will ask others' opinions and learn from them
- I want to listen more than I speak
- I will always make time for others

After making a list for your personal mission statement, fit these goals into your business's mission statement.

### Sample Business Mission Statement:
- I believe the future of the U.S. economy lies in the ability of Americans to increase their rate of savings
- My business will help people accomplish this through low-cost investment advice
- I will limit my client base to those people who have between $1,000 and $10,000 to invest; these people are in need of financial advice, but are never solicited by financial advisors because they aren't considered worth the effort
- I will call my business "Net Worth"

## Your Business Check-up

Before you can plan for growth, you need to assess your operations and measure efficiency. This is a chance for you to look into the nooks and crannies of your business, and address any problems you may have been putting off. This check-up will help set your course for the future. As you perform the assessment, look at your business as a potential buyer would. Some of the issues to consider are:

- What are your business's strengths and weaknesses?
- What could you be doing better?
- Which areas of the business have given you the biggest challenges?

- Which areas of the business have you been ignoring?
- Has your business realized its potential?
- Has it demonstrated profitability?
- Does it consistently deliver quality goods and services?
- Does it have a rich skill base and distinct expertise?
- Do you have a realistic vision for the future—and the strategies and tactics to realize that future?

These are the concerns you must address before you take your business to the next level of growth.

## Status of Your Customers and Your Market

Successful businesses begin every self-assessment by evaluating how well they are serving their customers. Why? Because customers are the reason businesses exist. The needs and tastes of customers constantly change; what is ideal for one group of customers may not satisfy another. Therefore, one of the biggest challenges for a growing business is to have a thorough understanding of its customers and market. How well does your business serve its customers? Consider the following questions:

- What percentage of your business is repeat business?
- How large is your overall market?
- How large is your customer base?
- Have you defined your target customers? Where are they located? What is important to them? What makes them unique? How much are they willing to pay?
- How has your market changed since you've been in business?
- Do you periodically gather new information about your market?
- Who are your competitors? How do you differentiate your business from theirs'?
- What legal or government regulations affect your business?
- Has your market continued to grow, or is it leveling off or shrinking?

## Your Profitability and Prices

Even the most talented entrepreneur cannot grow an unprofitable business. Before you go any further, you need to assess whether or not you are generating a profit.

- What are your **variable costs**?
- What are your **fixed costs**?
- What is your target profit margin?
- How are you currently pricing your products or services?
- Do your sale prices allow you to earn your target profit margin?
- How do your prices compare to those of your competitors?
- How do your prices position you in your customers' eyes?

Is your business efficient?

Profitable?

# NxLEVEL™ TECH TIP

The right technology can tremendously improve productivity, customer service, sales, and employee morale. Every serious entrepreneur needs a computer (with Internet capabilities), a phone, a fax machine, and perhaps a copier. Here are a few less obvious items that every business should have:

**Computer backup system** Your files should be backed up at least once a week. (Note: It's a good idea to practice recovering lost information before you have a problem!) Many data protection systems are available, including tape, CD-RW, and optical drives. As an alternative to these in-house backup systems, some companies now offer Net-based backup for a subscription fee, allowing you to transfer important files (and in some cases, entire systems) onto the Internet for safekeeping. With a conventional modem, this can be quite time-consuming; luckily, most services allow you to schedule your backups for nights or weekends. Online backup systems include **Connected Online Backup** (www.connected.com), and **Internet FileZone Plus** (www.atrieva.com).

**Router** A router is basically an office-wide modem that allows you to connect additional computers to the Internet without paying for multiple modems or overloading your phone lines. Routers are inexpensive, and can save you a good deal of money!

**Ergonomic computer stations** Almost everyone is aware of carpal tunnel syndrome and other repetitive motion disorders, but surprisingly few businesses take steps to correct the conditions that cause these serious injuries. To help prevent these problems, it's essential to have keyboards at the proper height. A low-cost solution is to purchase adjustable keyboard platforms that attach to the underside of existing desks and tables.

**Uninterruptible Power Supply (UPS)** Chances are, you already have surge protection for your electronic equipment, but surge protectors do not protect you from blackouts, which can not only damage your equipment but cause valuable, unsaved work-in-progress to be lost. A UPS is a battery-powered outlet that acts as a buffer between the incoming power and your computer, regulating voltage spikes and surges. In the event of a blackout, the UPS provides enough electricity to let you close your applications and shut down the computer normally. For a single computer, the cost is under $100. Many UPS systems are expandable to accommodate growth. Look for a good warranty; many manufacturers offer up to $25,000 in the event of damage to or loss of equipment protected by their UPS.

It's a good idea to ask your employees what equipment they feel they need. Let them explain how a color printer, a faster connection to the Internet, or networking capabilities will help them do their jobs better. Obviously, you don't want to spend your money on frivolous equipment just to entertain a bored employee, but you also don't want to hamper the efforts or enthusiasm of a dedicated employee who wants to see your business grow. Also, ask your customers what technical improvements they'd like to see. Would they order more if they could place orders online? Would they appreciate fax-back service, or the ability to subscribe to an e-mail newsletter? If the answer is "yes," you need to ask yourself if you have the time and money to provide these services.

## Your Time Management

Growing businesses place unique demands on your time. Multiple tasks, short deadlines, and new challenges can easily cause quality performance to slip. Are you managing time effectively? Ask yourself the following questions:

- Do you routinely schedule your time?
- Do you set deadlines for completing projects? Do you meet them?
- Do you regularly take time to evaluate your efforts?
- Are you able to solve problems and move on to new challenges?
- Are you delegating responsibility and authority?
- Are you satisfied with the amount of time it takes you and your team to complete routine tasks?
- Do you take time off?

## Your Team

Growing businesses must assess how well employees and outside contractors have performed in the past, and identify areas for improvement.

- What tasks are performed? Who performs them?
- How satisfied are you with your team's performance?
- Do your people have the skills they need?
- Are you compensating your team appropriately?
- Is your team happy and having fun?
- Do you set performance goals for your team?
- How do you reward your team?
- What is your rate of employee turnover?

Are your employees happy and productive?

## Your Operations

How well a business manages its operations determines its ability to tackle new challenges and grow. How does your business measure up?

- How are you managing your raw materials? How are inputs ordered, counted, inspected, and stored?
- How good are your relationships with your suppliers?
- Do you negotiate favorable terms? Extended payment plans?
- Is your equipment up-to-date and well maintained?
- Is your work space conducive to productivity and efficiency?
- How much inventory do you keep on hand?
- Are you able to fill orders reliably?
- Are you satisfied with the overall quality of your operations?
- Do you keep organized, accurate records?
- Are you in a location where customers can easily find you?
- Is your product being distributed in the most cost- and time-effective way?
- How does the Internet affect your business?

### Your Financing

The growth of your business depends on how well capitalized it is, and how well it manages its resources. Consider the following:

Do you need more

financing to grow?

- What are your sources of financing?
- How much does your financing cost?
- Are you adequately capitalized?
- What is the value of your business's assets?
- What is the value of your business's debts?

## Conclusion

What motivates you? Independence? Money? Fun? Creativity? Recognition? Security? Understanding your personal issues, skills, and talents is essential to developing your ideal business. The assessments you have just completed should clarify your goals, prepare you to acquire the skills you need, and inspire you to create the business you want...so regardless of what you scored, give yourself an A+!

For businesses, good health means profitability, and happy, emotionally involved personnel. The business assessments above are valuable instruments for testing any business's health. How did your business fare? You should now have a clearer picture of what your business is doing well, as well as the areas most in need of improvement. Take time to fine-tune your operations and, by learning from your mistakes, your business stands a better chance of success in the future.

# Chapter 4
# A CUSTOMER-DRIVEN PHILOSOPHY

*About This Chapter:*
- *Pitfalls of product-oriented and inward-looking companies*
- *Understanding your customers*
- *A customer service plan*
- *Managing customer service*
- *Customer service and your employees*
- *Customer service practices*

## Introduction

Businesses cannot thrive without satisfied, loyal customers, and they cannot grow unless they continually attract new customers. This is why successful organizations commit themselves to delivering exceptional customer service. For many larger corporations, this often entails trying to simulate the more intimate relationship that a small business has with its customers; Coca-Cola, General Motors, 3M, and even the United States government are creating smaller operating units known as project teams, profit centers, or work groups in order to be more accessible to and communicative with their customers.

As a small business owner, you are already in an excellent position to listen to and learn from your customers, which means that you can adapt to customer needs more quickly and creatively than your larger competitors. Why is this essential to running a successful business? Because it is increasingly difficult to differentiate a business simply on the basis of such "tangibles" as quality, technology, and price. Nor does a business want to limit itself to these factors! Competing on the basis of price alone offers the customer no other way to compare businesses. Besides, even if nobody is offering a lower price than you today, someone may tomorrow!

On what other basis can your company compete? Friendly, unique, responsive, and flexible customer service! This is one of the small business's greatest advantages; those who aren't taking advantage of it are throwing away one of their most powerful competitive tools.

> "There is no product devoid of an accompanying relationship between buyer and provider."
> —Karl Albrecht

## Pitfalls of Product-Oriented and Inward-Looking Companies

Companies that focus on a particular product or technology instead of on the market are limiting their sales today and their growth (or survival) tomorrow. The same is true for companies whose internal bureaucracies and politics overshadow focusing on the customer. This is not to say that internal issues are not important; they are critical, but they should never take precedence over customer issues.

Customers' needs change, and a business must watch and listen so it can change, too. Yesterday's product may not serve tomorrow's needs.

The task of an outward-focused business is not simply to "make the customer happy"; it must also understand customers' lives, anticipate changes in their needs, and identify new opportunities to serve them. This includes seeing customers' complaints as opportunities to learn and improve.

Customer complaints are opportunities to learn and improve

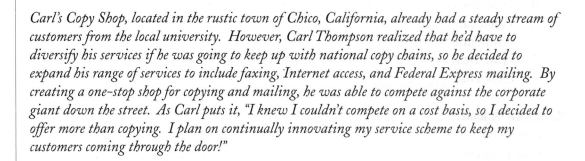

*Carl's Copy Shop, located in the rustic town of Chico, California, already had a steady stream of customers from the local university. However, Carl Thompson realized that he'd have to diversify his services if he was going to keep up with national copy chains, so he decided to expand his range of services to include faxing, Internet access, and Federal Express mailing. By creating a one-stop shop for copying and mailing, he was able to compete against the corporate giant down the street. As Carl puts it, "I knew I couldn't compete on a cost basis, so I decided to offer more than copying. I plan on continually innovating my service scheme to keep my customers coming through the door!"*

## Understanding Your Customers

Understanding your customers means knowing how they use your product or service, and why they choose you over your competitors. It means knowing about the customer's life—at work or at home, wherever the product or service is used.

Successful businesspeople can provide a highly accurate profile of their customers, and they know when that profile changes. As noted elsewhere in this book, this knowledge is reflected in the business plan, and in the firm's marketing and operating plans.

### Create a Customer "Value Profile"

How does your customer define value, and what does your customer value most? Does your customer see your products or services as low, average, or excellent in quality? Your job is to find answers to these questions, and use them to deliver better customer satisfaction than any of your present and future competitors. The way you achieve this will invariably be different from the way your competitors do; this is what gives you a competitive edge. By understanding the goods and services your customers value, you can add value to your products and services. For instance, Carl added value to his basic copying service by providing his customers other services (e.g. Internet access, packaging, shipping, etc.).

To begin, ask yourself, "What do I offer? What is my product or service?" Think in terms of intangible qualities you offer, such as convenience, creativity, reliability, time, or comfort. An example of this is a pizzeria that delivers children's birthday pizzas to their customers' homes. This restaurant is in the business of doing much more than delivering tasty pizzas; they are selling convenience, spare time, and fun to their targeted customers.

*Six basic questions can identify your customer's idea of value:*
1. What does our customer want?
2. How does our product/service help our customer solve his or her problem?
3. What aspects of our customers' dealings with us are most important to them?
4. How does our customer view doing business with us or our rivals?
5. What can we do to improve our customer's experience and distinguish ourselves from our competitors?
6. How are our customer's needs likely to change, and how are we preparing for these changes?

## Create an Organization that Helps People Serve People

Your first task in creating value for your customer is to be sure your business has the tools it needs to deliver innovative, reliable service. Remember: Creating customer orientation is not a one-time event; it is an ongoing process!

*People*

The way a business treats its employees mirrors the way it treats its customers. Whether you have three employees or three hundred, your business must become a place where quality people want to work, and where quality service is delivered. This requires openness, trust, and participation at all levels. To achieve this, you should:

- **Lay out the goals** of the organization clearly and often.
- **Establish employee training as an ongoing process** by offering opportunities for people to learn about other functions in the business. Create mixed teams to tackle specific problems and brainstorm solutions. Encourage employees to visit customers, keep tabs on the competition, and set aside special times to take a fresh look at your business and customers.
- **Ask employees how they contribute to customer value—and how they could do more** by holding regular meetings, establishing an anonymous suggestion box, etc.
- **Create a system of measurement, recognition, and rewards** for excellent customer service.

———————————◆———————————

*As a small VCR component subcontractor, Randy Regner knows that his business depends on delivering quality components on-time to his client. In an effort to enthuse assembly line workers, he made it a policy to reward employees with additional vacation days for meeting or exceeding daily production quotas and deadlines, rooting out problems on the line, and coming*

Manage customer service well and you will have more customers

Customer Service—a unique and powerful competitive tool

Walk a mile in their shoes

Sample Customer

Service Goals

- Answer all written

  queries within

  2 days

- Answer the phone

  within 3 rings

- Reduce the number

  of returned or

  incorrect orders

  by 50%

- Increase rate of

  customer referrals to

  2 per customer

- Reduce customer

  order turnaround

  time by 50%

*up with innovations in production. Because their work is often monotonous, Regner brings in a masseuse every Tuesday and Thursday to give his employees stress-reducing neck massages. By engendering employee loyalty, he is consistently able to deliver the components his client needs.*

---

*Strategy*

Having a clear strategy to guide your efforts is essential to providing good customer service. It can also stimulate ideas for improving service. Effective strategies include:

- **Keep the customers you get.** Depending upon the type of business, experts estimate that it costs three to five times more to find a new customer than to keep an old one. Repeat customers represent an ongoing revenue stream that is essential to your business. Suppose a woman buys a bagel that earns the deli $1. If she buys her bagel and does not return, her business is worth exactly $1 to the deli. However, if she returns three times a week, every week, for a year, that $1 grows to an impressive $156.

- **Earn customers' loyalty by being loyal to them.** The secret to having long-term relationships with customers lies in demonstrating your ability to predict their needs, and to meet them in creative ways.

- **Continually challenge assumptions.** When the customer's priorities shift, the best businesses see it coming. They also help customers identify new opportunities.

- **Communicate with your customer.** Critical feedback from customers can direct your attention to things that need improvement. Nobody likes bad news, but gathering bad news is often more valuable than collecting pats on the back. Use every contact with your customers to learn to serve them better.

- **Embrace the concept of Total Quality Service (TQS).** This popular management tool can be as important for small businesses as it is to the larger corporations that pioneered it. Much has been written about TQS and **Total Quality Management (TQM)**; your local bookstore will have several publications on these topics.

*Systems*

Systems and processes are the tools employees use to implement your strategies. You should focus on specific operational tasks that speed up or enhance service, both internally and externally. To make customer service goals more real, write them down (see "Sample Customer Service Goals") and post them in a high-visibility spot.

You should also create a flow chart, focusing on where, when, and by whom customers are served. At each step, write a description of the tasks and goals involved and who is responsible. As the business grows, you can revise the chart.

## A Customer Service Plan

Every business should have a **customer service plan** within its marketing plan. This outlines who your customer is and how you deliver service to them. The CSP should include:

- Your customer service goals—presenting them clearly to your employees
- Your after-sales service practices
- Your return, exchange, and customer complaint policies
- Your special order or custom service policies
- How different areas of your business deliver service
- Your system of training and rewards for customer service excellence
- Your customer service benchmarks
- The effects of the Internet on customer service
- Your system for periodically reviewing and updating the customer service plan
- Appointing a "customer expert" who deals with customer needs, trends, and complaints; and regularly compiles internal **customer service history** reports
- Creating a formal system by which customers report their feedback.

Creating a customer service plan early on will ensure that customer service is central to your business.

*Everything that happens within an organization affects customer service*

---◆---

*When Linda Rogers and Gayle Corson decided to open La Femme, a fine lingerie shop in Grosse Pointe, Michigan, they knew they would be in competition with national lingerie chain stores. However, after doing some research, they realized that there was an untapped market for lingerie. Rogers and Corson decided to innovate by reaching out to larger women, petites, and pregnant women—a niche market not served by the larger stores. Their business supplies fine lingerie to women who have difficulty finding attractive lingerie elsewhere. By offering special touches like a complimentary glass of wine for shoppers, personal shopping services, and a frequent shopper card, the proprietors of La Femme developed a loyal following. They are now launching their mail-order catalog and will soon be opening up a branch in Ann Arbor, Michigan.*

---◆---

## Customer Service and Your Employees

Your staff is the first line of direct contact your business has with its customers, so every employee should embody your customer service policy. Let them know what you expect of them, and give them the freedom to invent new ways to deliver customer service. Let them contribute to and improve your customer service plan. Here are some additional suggestions for getting the best service out of your employees:

"Our goal as a company is to create customer service that is not just the best, but legendary."
—Paul Hawken

**Employees are the most important link to your customers**

- Hire inspired, curious, and committed people
- Incorporate customer service elements in every job description
- Post your customer service goals prominently in your office
- Help employees develop product expertise and encourage them to share this expertise with customers
- Teach your employees to find answers to customer questions: It's OK not to know all the answers as long as they know where to get the answers
- Let your employees know how much you value their extra efforts to serve customers; thank them often and publicly for good service
- Create a system of rewards and incentives for customer service. Tie rewards to things like minimizing customer complaints, product returns, and customer wait times; or devising new customer service ideas
- Identify and reward employees who share knowledge with customers and cooperate with other employees. Peer reviews and customer surveys are a great way to identify your service "stars"
- Educate all of your employees in customer service. Even back office and logistics people should know the important role they play in delivering quality service. Encourage them to view front-line people as their customers

---

*Saturn Motor Company was able to enter the already crowded world of car sales by offering something different—the no-pressure car sale. Saturn decided to create a welcoming atmosphere for customers tired of high-pressure, fast-talking salespeople. Saturn has built its softer image around the needs of car buyers who are unhappy with wheeling and dealing. Salespeople wear non-intimidating khakis and polo shirts. They do not work on commission. They have developed a reputation for customer service, even offering to fly a prospective customer to a showroom 200 miles away from her home. The purchase of a Saturn car is a celebration, where the new car owner is photographed as a memento of his or her pleasant car-buying experience. The value of these customer-focused business practices is evident in the number of Saturns you see on the highway today!*

---

If you hire people carefully, train them, and allow them to be creative, your business will develop a unique and unbeatable service "personality."

## Customer Service Practices

The sections above have described what a customer service business looks like from the inside. But what is it like from the outside? These **customer service practices** should be a starting point for your own strategies:

- When customers enter your place of business, greet them immediately and pleasantly
- When a mistake occurs, quickly and professionally accept responsibility and fix it

- Always make an extra effort to help customers find what they need
- Follow up on all customer contacts: always record the customer's name, phone number, and order type. After customers call for product information or service assistance, follow up within two days to check on satisfaction
- Make sure employees look professional and tidy when they deal with customers
- Thank your customers every chance you get
- Thank your employees for excellent service every chance you get
- Always answer the phone within three rings
- Call your own business and pretend to be a customer to gauge service quality
- Don't "dump" customers on hold. If you must, ask if you can put them on hold or call them back within five minutes
- Periodically survey customer satisfaction with brief questionnaires

## Conclusion

Your customers are a valuable source of information for your business. If you listen, they will tell you what they want. If you plan your strategy carefully, you can deliver what your customers want faster and better than any of your competitors. This will enable you to create long-term business relationships, generate enthusiastic referrals, and create new product and service opportunities. Remaining open to new ways of looking at your customers will keep you focused and fresh in your efforts. Businesses that succeed at this have fun watching their profits grow!

Customer Service Tips

- Solving your customer's problems requires persistence
- Great service is contagious
- Listen to the bad and act on it
- All employees are service employees
- Great service is marked by good manners and politeness
- Those who focus on customers grow, those who don't—won't!

## NxLEVEL™ TECH TIP

**A common customer service complaint is slow or no response to e-mail inquiries. Sudden growth or periods of intense customer interest can swamp you with e-mail, and slow your response time to a crawl. Here are some solutions:**

Auto-responders (also known as mailbots, autobots, and email-on-demand) are e-mail addresses that automatically send a form letter reply to inquiries. Free auto-responders are available at **MyReply.com** (http://www.myreply.com). You can set up auto-responders for job applicants, specific customer questions, or more general inquiries. Simply write the appropriate responses for each question, and put the e-mail addresses on your Web site.

Outsourcing e-mail systems is an increasingly popular option for small businesses whose rapid growth makes keeping up with e-mail difficult. The cost is often lower per user than administering your own in-house e-mail, and there's no need to add servers, disk space, or new lines!

# Chapter 5
# OVERVIEW OF MANUFACTURING, SERVICE, AND RETAIL

*About This Chapter:*
- *The world of manufacturing*
- *Operational & managerial challenges*
- *Product-focused organization*
- *Service businesses*
- *The service provider's business strategy*
- *Operational & managerial challenges*
- *Service quality essentials*
- *Retail businesses*
- *Operational & managerial challenges*

## Introduction

The three major types of business are manufacturing, retail, and service. This chapter presents basic information about the particulars of each. It is not designed to be a comprehensive guide on beginning a manufacturing, service, or retail business; there are many books dedicated to these subjects, which you can and should consult. What this chapter *does* offer is an understanding of trends, competition, organizational challenges, and the skills needed to excel in these businesses.

As we explore the differences between these businesses, keep in mind that they often overlap. For example, into which business category does McDonald's fall? Is it a manufacturer because it buys ground beef and turns it into hamburgers? Is it a service provider because it offers its customers time savings, convenience, and a pleasant meeting place? Or is it a retailer because it sells directly to the public? The answer is that McDonald's is all three; this is precisely why it has been so successful! McDonald's identified where several types of business overlapped and created a truly original concept.

## The World of Manufacturing

Huge conveyor belts chugging along, heavy machinery stamping out parts, sparks flying—this is what probably springs to mind when most people think of manufacturing. But manufacturing isn't limited to such large-scale operations. Small bakeries, specialty textile mills, microbreweries and piece assembly shops also manufacture goods for market, and compete fiercely to do so.

Manufacturing has traditionally been defined as the mass production of components and finished products. Mass production is based on the concept of **economies of scale**: the more goods are produced with the same machinery and overhead, the lower the per unit costs and the higher the profitability.

## Trends in Manufacturing

Manufacturing today is very different than it was 20 years ago. Increased international competition, technological innovations, and the rising cost of labor have revolutionized the way the world builds things, and have spurred the development of new managerial approaches like **employee work teams, Total Quality Management,** and **Just In Time Inventory**.

Today, manufacturing businesses of nearly every shape and size are influenced by the following trends:

- Increased speed and flexibility of operations
- Teaming of cross-functional employees
- Hiring and training multiskilled employees
- Giving more responsibility and authority to employees
- Flattening out traditional organizational hierarchies
- Creating flexible production systems to do smaller production runs
- Environmental issues and regulations
- Use of the Internet as a business tool

## The Time Element

Time is the most important element of client satisfaction. In the last five to seven years, **cycle times** have become compressed by over 50%. To retain their market share, manufacturers must redesign products and create entirely new models more frequently. They do this because their customers demand it. Increased competition has added to this trend, as has the introduction of innovative technology that speeds transactions.

The emphasis is on speed—customers demand it

More often than not, manufacturers sell to businesses, who in turn assemble a product and compete with other businesses to meet the demands of customers. With more businesses selling overseas, manufacturers must factor enough time into their production schedules to allow for shipping, customs processing, and multiple quality checks. All of these things take time—time that can be minimized by speeding **front end** processes like sourcing, product development, and manufacturing.

As a result of this emphasis on high-speed production, the definition of manufacturing is being reinvented. Today, what used to be considered central to manufacturing (product development, design, assembly, and logistics) is often performed by other businesses through outsourcing agreements, strategic alliances, and partnerships. In fact, some "manufacturers" do not manufacture any part of their product; they simply assemble it out of components bought from partners who may not operate in the same state, or even the same country! These businesses manufacture their products only in the sense that they control the trademark, patent, design, channels of distribution, and after-sales service to the customer.

This represents a shift in manufacturing towards "virtual" organization, as opposed to the traditional "vertical" organization. **Virtual businesses** are defined by the number of tasks that they pay other businesses or individuals to perform. The creation of value occurs outside the business. **Vertical businesses** are defined by the number of functions (sourcing inputs, shipping and warehousing goods, and distribution) they perform themselves. A **vertical integration** strategy implies that a business controls the supply of all or many of its own inputs, and performs its own value-generating activities. Perhaps the most famous example of this comes from the early days at Ford Motor Company, which owned and operated its own iron ore mines, steel plants, metal stamping and finishing shops, assembly lines, and showrooms. In many ways, Ford set the standard for vertical integration.

The virtual model of business spells major opportunity for even the smallest and newest of manufacturers. These businesses can step in to perform specific functions for larger manufacturing companies at competitive prices.

*The virtual model of business spells major opportunity for even the smallest and newest of manufacturers*

## Benefits of Vertical vs. Virtual Manufacturing Organization

*Vertical Benefits*

- Cost savings and economies of scale
- Employment security
- Control over strategic information or proprietary technology
- Lower risk: ensured supplies of inputs
- Ability to sell excess capacity for additional revenue
- Faster, shared learning among value-creating functions

*Virtual Benefits*

- Components are bought at lowest total cost, considering service, quality and impact on lead times
- Lower overhead, quicker break-even point
- Business is able to do more tasks with fewer people
- Supplier consolidation reduces administrative costs and variation in quality, increases control and cooperation

### Competitive Challenges

For large manufacturers, competition is tougher now than it has ever been. Lower trade barriers, the availability of cheaper overseas labor, innovations in information technology and communications, strategic alliances, and shifting consumer demand continually alter the landscape of manufacturing.

### The Manufacturer's Business Strategy

Like all business people, manufacturers must decide where, when, and how to produce their goods. Their foremost strategic planning issues are:

- The degree to which they will be virtual vs. vertical
- Competitive positioning: Will they lead on price? Quality? Customer service?
- How to use innovative technology in their products or manufacturing process
- Which geographic markets they will serve

- Identifying their target customer segments
- What channels of distribution they will use
- How they will provide after-sales service and technical support

## The Customer

In manufacturing, supplier and customer relationships more closely resemble partnerships than those in service and retail businesses. Defining characteristics of customer relationships in manufacturing include:

- Anticipating and responding quickly to customer needs
- Varied customer bases, sometimes in other countries
- Designing and producing products tailored to a specific customer
- Quick delivery time
- Close communication via computer and phone lines
- Extensive technical support and follow-up service
- Cooperative sharing of information and production needs
- Service, service, service!

Since they often purchase inputs from a variety of competitors, business customers require that manufacturers conform to international standards for quality, performance, and size.

## The Suppliers

In manufacturing, solid relationships with suppliers can mean the difference between being in business, and being out of business! The most common aspects of supplier relationships include:

- Shared turnaround time
- Shared standards of quality
- Close proximity by geography and/or communication
- Flexible, collaborative problem-solving
- Joint production scheduling
- Use of backup suppliers
- Tough price competition among suppliers

A solid relationship with your suppliers is critical

# Operational & Managerial Challenges

A good starting point when analyzing any sort of business is to ask where and how value is created. Manufacturers (more so than retailers or service businesses) rely on equipment to produce their goods, and on employees with the expertise to operate the equipment. Let's look at how manufacturers approach their major business functions.

## People Management

Successful manufacturers consider their employees to be assets of greater value than their equipment. The more skilled employees are, the better they are at performing multiple functions, and troubleshooting manufacturing problems. Manufacturers tend to invest considerable time and money in training and updating the technical skills of their employees, and place a great deal of emphasis on reducing employee turnover.

Traditionally, a factory worker's hourly pay was based on seniority. Today, many compensation strategies focus on the total output of the business. In businesses with work teams, employee compensation may also be pegged to team performance.

## The Role of Technology

All manufacturers rely on new technologies to:

- Communicate with customers and suppliers
- Control product quality
- Standardize production processes
- Analyze product specifications
- Design products
- Simulate production runs
- Track products from sub-suppliers to delivery

## What Does a Manufacturer Look Like?

In a manufacturing business, organizational structures and processes tend to focus on reducing lead times, lowering inventories, speeding machine set-up, lowering costs, improving quality, and accelerating product delivery times. This adds up to competitive advantages in the marketplace. Many manufacturers have shifted away from the traditional organizational structure focused on functions (marketing, finance, engineering, etc.) towards product-oriented structures. There is also a trend among today's manufacturers to use the creative energies of all employees to solve problems innovatively.

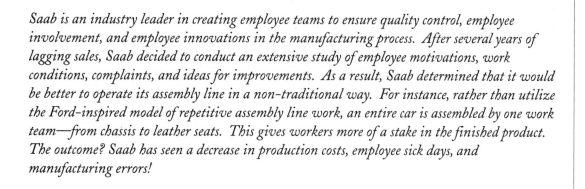

*Saab is an industry leader in creating employee teams to ensure quality control, employee involvement, and employee innovations in the manufacturing process. After several years of lagging sales, Saab decided to conduct an extensive study of employee motivations, work conditions, complaints, and ideas for improvements. As a result, Saab determined that it would be better to operate its assembly line in a non-traditional way. For instance, rather than utilize the Ford-inspired model of repetitive assembly line work, an entire car is assembled by one work team—from chassis to leather seats. This gives workers more of a stake in the finished product. The outcome? Saab has seen a decrease in production costs, employee sick days, and manufacturing errors!*

# Product-Focused Organization

## Quality and Manufacturing

Manufacturers must ensure that their processes consistently reproduce high-quality products, which means inspecting the product as it moves through the production process. Ideally, the manufacturer must maximize the number and accuracy of quality inspections while minimizing the time and cost required to do so. This is why they need high-performance, multiskilled employees who are adept at detecting and correcting manufacturing defects.

## Financial Issues

Unless you intend to build a retail store with gold fixtures and marble floors, starting a manufacturing business requires more financial investment than a retailing or service business. Plant, machinery, and equipment call for a heavy up-front investment. Once the business is set up, the manufacturer's major financial issues are controlling costs for inputs and materials, and counting and valuing inventory. The major elements of manufacturers' product and operational cost structure are:

- Worker hours
- Inputs and materials
- Machine time
- Capital overhead
- Product marketing and selling
- Research and development

## Are You a Manufacturer at Heart?

Most successful manufacturers have educational and professional backgrounds in production or engineering. People who perform well in manufacturing generally:

- Are gifted at identifying and managing new production processes
- Can talk and think like an engineer
- Enjoy working with assembly lines, production schedules, and machines
- Have found or invented a unique product or process
- Have long-range conceptualization and planning skills

## How is Manufacturing Different?

As noted above, manufacturing can require more technical expertise and financial resources than either retailing or service businesses. Manufacturers are also vulnerable to supplier problems, labor costs, and union pressures, and are often forced to create plans projecting well into the future. The timeframe for completing business transactions tends to be longer in manufacturing than in service or retail businesses. Furthermore, manufacturing businesses tend to be linked to long-term consumer patterns and cycles in the economy.

To compete, manufacturers of all sizes must:

- Be quick!
- Be quality!
- Be flexible!

## Start-up Opportunities

There are more opportunities now for the aspiring start-up manufacturer than ever before. Given the increase in virtual businesses, many opportunities exist for small, highly specialized manufacturers to provide inputs to larger manufacturers. Comparatively speaking, these limited production operations require less capital investment to begin; for instance, the small manufacturer may need to invest in only one or two high-quality pieces of equipment.

# Service Businesses

**Service businesses** provide expertise and convenience to customers when, where, and how they need it. Many service providers don't work even out of an office. Consider management consultants or computer support experts: during the length of their consulting engagements, they may take up residence within the company to which they are offering the service. Hospitals, telecommunications providers, shipping companies, house painters, even babysitters all fall under the heading of service businesses. The service sector comprises more small businesses and one-person providers than retailing or manufacturing. It is also the fastest-growing sector in the U.S. economy today.

### Trends in service businesses

The most important trends affecting this fast-growing business category are:

- **Downsizing of companies.** Large corporations have reduced their number of full-time employees and begun relying on a growing number of independent contractors to perform non-core functions.
- **Repairing and reusing existing products.** Consumers are buying more expensive, higher quality durables, which they repair and upgrade rather than replace.
- **The crunch for time.** As more members of households go to work, there are fewer people left at home to do basic household chores. Time is at a premium.
- **Obtaining and processing information.** Because of advances in information technology, there is more information that needs to be organized and processed.
- **Bringing order to chaos.** Specialized businesses provide order and create time savings for other businesses and individuals.
- **Targeting niche markets.** Businesses of all types have benefitted from dividing larger customers into niche markets. The smaller the market, the more focused a business's marketing efforts can be.
- **Higher expectations for service.** Individuals and businesses expect better service, increasing opportunities for new competitors.

## Competitive Challenges

Service providers must provide reliable and consistent service, at a competitive yet profitable price. Service businesses are just beginning to feel the international competitive pressures with which manufacturers have been contending for over 15 years. Providing services to international customers may require a business to perform in a variety of cultural, regulatory, legal, geographic, and linguistic environments. Even small service businesses are springing to life to serve international customers.

# The Service Provider's Business Strategy

### The Customer

More so than other businesses, the service business's strategy revolves around the customer. Service businesses sell to other businesses as well as to individuals. In each case, customer expectations are as different as the relationship between the buyer and the seller.

Service businesses need to make sure that their customers understand the intangible benefits of their service. Tax preparation consultants might point out the tax savings they offer, while employee trainers might focus on the higher worker productivity and long-term savings their seminars provide.

Customers of service businesses tend to be interested in the latest trends. When an idea or process gets old, opportunity arises for innovation. To keep the customer's interest and loyalty, service businesses must constantly update their expertise and improve their service.

Unlike manufacturing and retailing businesses, service businesses have a great deal of flexibility as to how, where, and when to deliver their service. They can serve customers face-to-face—as gardeners or doctors do—or indirectly via mail, telephone, or the Internet. Travel agents often deliver their services entirely through indirect customer contact; they may offer fare quotes over the phone and mail brochures about destinations to customers.

Another unique feature of many service businesses is that they can involve their customers in the design and delivery of their services. Doing so allows customers to make valuable contributions to the organization's structure, policies, and performance as well. Why is this? Because in service businesses—more so than in manufacturing and retail businesses—customers have an ongoing relationship with their service provider. This offers opportunities for feedback, rapport, and repeated assessment of customer needs.

Truly competitive service businesses maximize this opportunity to increase customer loyalty. Some service providers ask their customers to take part in teams responsible for hiring customer service agents. A more widespread practice is the use of customer satisfaction surveys; hotels, car rental companies, and even mail-order companies use these to gauge their performance and better understand customer preferences.

## Operational & Managerial Challenges

Major operational challenges for service businesses include:

- Identifying their core service
- Deciding to what degree they will customize or standardize their services
- Ensuring the professionalism of their employees
- Creating print, video, and voice media that communicate the nature of the service

---

*More so than other businesses, the service business's entire strategy should revolve around the customer*

- Accurately measuring costs and pricing services
- Ensuring consistency and quality in service delivery

## Organizational Structure

Some service organizations operate under the traditional **hierarchical management structure**, in which employees are organized in "layers" according to their rank or authority. Examples of hierarchical structures are the U.S. Army, traditional accounting firms, and some management consulting firms. Other service businesses have entirely flat management structures; examples include restaurants, photo processors, roofers, and landscapers.

## Employee Management

Service businesses train and manage their employees differently depending upon the industry in which they operate and the level of service they provide. As more expertise is required of employees, compensation demands rise, as does the need for other types of rewards.

Service business owners know that the employees who interact with customers make or break their businesses. Employees often have to assess customer needs, tailor the service accordingly, and control the quality of the service. This is a lot to ask! For this reason, service businesses tend to hire people capable of performing multiple tasks, train them to work in teams, and give them greater flexibility in how they perform their specific tasks.

---◆---

*The Walt Disney Company is famous for its intensive training of those employees who have personal contact with customers at Disney theme parks. Employees are called "cast members" to reinforce the idea that they are providing entertainment for the park visitors, who are called "guests." A cast members dressed up as a Disney figure is forbidden to talk to guests, because Disney does not want to shatter the illusion by using a voice that doesn't seem to fit the character. Employees enter and leave the parks through special tunnels so that guests do not see them outside of their outfits. Even corporate employees are called "cast members" and must work in a theme park for at least one day, in order to understand the importance of the entire Disney product. Disney's goal is to create a consistent and reliable image for the company through its cast members: they are courteous, competent, attentive, and fun!*

---◆---

## Quality in the Service Business

Characteristics of excellence in service business include:

- A quantitative approach to measuring customer needs
- Continual measurement of performance against that of competitors
- Focusing on service improvements to increase customer satisfaction
- Aggressive efforts to minimize the time taken to meet customer needs

Alternative Service Delivery Systems:

- Mail contact
- Internet
- Telephone contact
- Face-to-face standard delivery
- Face-to-face moderate customization
- Face-to-face total customization

- Focusing on core services that affect cost and customer satisfaction
- Use of technology to enhance contact with customers
- Consistency of performance by delivering the service at the promised time

**Service Quality Essentials**
- Politeness and respect
- Trustworthiness and honesty
- Responsiveness
- Expertise
- Easy access
- Good communication
- Security and confidentiality
- Knowing the customer's needs

## Financial Issues

Fixed costs generally make up the majority of service providers' costs. For example, a tree trimmer can trim an additional tree using his existing set of tools; therefore, his cost for pruning one additional tree is minimal. On the other hand, if he wants to trim trees for an entire neighborhood, he will have to hire an assistant and get more equipment. Having done so, he is able to trim an increased number of trees, until he hits his new maximum capacity. This is the concept of **incremental capacity gains**: service providers have relatively low marginal costs for serving small numbers of additional customers, but must increase capacity if they want to meet greater demands.

## Are You a Service Provider at Heart?

Service businesses are successful because they know their customers well, and often customize the services they provide to each customer. Communication and follow-up with customers are especially important. For these reasons, people who excel in service businesses tend to be:

- Good at interpersonal communication
- Confident
- Creative thinkers
- Self-disciplined and independent
- Flexible
- Able to adapt their knowledge to many different situations
- Expert in a specific field
- Interested in popular culture, and able to identify and act on major trends

## How Are Service Businesses Different?

The business of delivering services is comparatively flexible and inexpensive to enter. Service businesses tend to have:

The service business...

focus or disappear!

- Closer relationships with customers
- Lower overhead
- Easier entry and exit into business
- Less emphasis on geographic location of the business
- A smaller management team (often just one person)

### Opportunities

Given the explosive demand for services, there are many opportunities for start-up businesses in the service sector. Corporate downsizing, outsourcing, and the globalization of business have combined to create many new niche markets, and small businesses are stepping in to provide services to businesses and individuals of all types.

## Retail Businesses

Crowds are streaming in, registers are ringing, and a voice on a loudspeaker is saying, "Attention K-Mart shoppers!" This is the sound of retailing in action. Perhaps no other type of business is so familiar to Americans. Wal-Mart, Safeway, Nordstrom's, True Value, and Burger King have become part of our national consciousness; they offer us the latest in fashions, food, and fun, at the competitive prices we want. Today, nearly 30% of all new businesses are retail stores that buy merchandise from wholesalers or manufacturers and resell these goods directly to consumers. Other types of retail strategies include mail order, automatic merchandising, and direct door-to-door selling.

### Trends in Retailing

Retailing has gone through a profound shift in the past 15 years. More large-scale retailers have emerged, and shopping malls are cropping up to house scores of national chains. In many towns, malls have replaced downtown areas by offering a safe, clean, convenient, and stylish environment in which people can buy everything from sleeping bags to sushi. Internet retail business is also booming.

The trend toward large "chain" retailers notwithstanding, many retail businesses are still run by a single owner with expertise in a particular type of product. These retailers often lack sophisticated purchasing, planning, cost control, and merchandising expertise; they are in the business simply because they love their products and the customers they serve.

These small retailers have been remarkably resilient in the face of heavy competition from the retailing giants. Why? Because they offer consumers personal service, low-stress buying, and a down-home atmosphere. If you've ever tried to get technical information about a CD player from a salesperson at a huge department store, you know that many mass retailers do not attempt to provide this type of service. Instead, they focus on offering a wide selection of products at competitive prices.

### The Retailer's Business Strategy

Like other businesses, successful retailers segment their customer base and focus on meeting their needs.

*Best Buy sells electronic goods to middle-income families. Their customers want to browse and buy in one visit; they don't need extensive information or technical support. Best Buy has focused on delivering a wide selection of products, creating an open and light environment, and offering low prices. At the other end of the spectrum is Patagonia, a sports clothing store that offers luxury products and knowledgeable service. Some of their high-performance, all-weather coats retail for over $400, and are nearly indestructible. And what if your dog finds a way to chew a hole in your new Patagonia sailing jacket? The company will replace it immediately, no questions asked! Salespeople at Patagonia match the profile of their target customer: they are educated, serious outdoor types. They are experts on the clothing and the conditions in which they can be used. Unlike Best Buy, Patagonia spends money on hiring and training employees who will inspire customers to buy their gear. Both businesses are successful because they create their business strategies around their target customers.*

### Location, Location, Location!

Perhaps the single most important element that determines success in retailing is location. Identifying the right location for a retail store is a very tricky task. Large national retailers like Home Depot and Wal-Mart pay market research experts millions of dollars to identify the spot where their business will have the best chances of succeeding.

How do retailers choose a location? First, they need to know where their target customers live, work, and shop. Second, retailers consider the type of merchandise they sell. Retailers who carry convenience goods (coffee, fast food, photocopying services) locate themselves in convenient spots, while retailers who offer specialty products might not be as choosy about a central location, since customers will be willing to travel further to find their product.

When choosing a location, retailers must also consider:

- Corners of blocks (they have higher visibility and more traffic)
- Who their retailing neighbors are
- The cost of renting space
- The image or feel of the block or neighborhood
- The image of the building and retail space
- Parking availability for customers
- The location and number of competitors
- Zoning regulations
- Traffic flow
- Nearby landmarks, industries, and tourist attractions
- Opportunity for expansion
- Demographic characteristics of the area

Great locations:

where the customer lives,

works, and shops

## A Word on Shopping Centers

The popularity of suburban shopping centers shows no signs of subsiding. However, locating in a mall has some downsides: Tenants are required to join tenant's associations, and to pay dues and maintenance costs. They are also required to abide by rules and regulations regarding store hours, holidays, and window displays.

Many retailers feel that shopping malls, which have a proven record of success, are the surest long-term bet. Malls do have obvious advantages—such as security, high traffic, organized promotional events, lots of parking, and long business hours—and most consumers find that shopping malls are safer, cleaner, and more attractive than other shopping locations. Of course, the decision to locate a business within a mall depends on the customer a retailer is hoping to attract. The rule of thumb: If your customer is there, you should be too.

## Creating and Managing an Image

In retailing, image is everything. The newer, cleaner, more unique, and more exciting products look, the better they sell. The look of the retail space itself is also of critical importance. If retailing is like a theatrical performance, then the retail space is the stage, and the salespeople are the actors. This comparison is not as silly as it sounds. When customers buy a product they are "buying into" the store and the person who sells to them. Successful retailers know that every element of their retail package must consistently and effectively communicate the message of the business.

*Retail is like a theatrical performance*

## The Customer

Who are retail customers? Well...everyone! The relationship between customer and retail businesses tends to be informal, habitual, and convenience-based. Selling occurs at specific points in time, rather than as part of an ongoing sales and service relationship. Among franchises and mass retailers, very little customization of products occurs for the customer. For the most part, standard products at standard prices are offered, and there is usually no negotiation.

## Supplier Relationships

Most small retailers buy their merchandise from local wholesalers. However, a trend in supplier arrangements is for major retailers to bypass wholesalers (and their markups) entirely and push for direct purchase from manufacturers; this allows them to buy in large volumes and charge lower prices. Retailers who order large quantities can do what is called **specification buying**. This means asking the manufacturer to change the packaging or characteristics of the product to fit merchandising needs.

*To be successful— know your customer!*

Among the smaller, boutique segment of retailing, the number of specialized sales representatives is growing. These people act as liaisons between retailer and manufacturer, and tend to carry a whole line of varied but complementary products. One example of this is clothing and jewelry representatives.

In general, retailers enjoy a very different sort of relationship with their suppliers than do manufacturers. Rather than a close, collaborative partnership, retailers and suppliers tend to have more limited, traditionally structured relationships. (One exception is the relationship of franchisees with their parent organization, the franchisor. This is discussed thoroughly in Chapter 8 *Franchising*.)

## Operational & Managerial Challenges

Since retailers are fundamentally service providers, the managerial issues they must address are very similar to those of service businesses.

### Organizational Structure

Regardless of whether a retail business is run by a single owner or a team of employees, the same core functions must be performed: buying and selling merchandise, providing customer service, and managing finances. Unlike manufacturing businesses, only the largest retail businesses organize themselves into product departments; most smaller retailers simply have a salesperson or two who assist customers and sell merchandise. An employee or the owner may also perform the essential functions of ordering and pricing merchandise.

This chart depicts typical managerial and organizational functions:

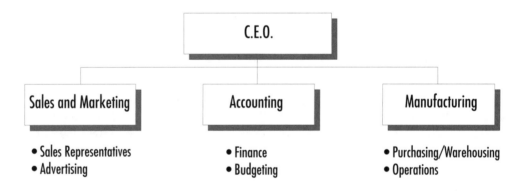

### Employee Management

Employees are powerful contributors to a retailer's profitability; they can project the image of the business and communicate the features and benefits of products. Unfortunately, retailers often focus their energies on merchandising, display layouts, and pricing rather than on their employees.

Like manufacturers, successful retailers know that trained employees are one of their best assets. Training strategies commonly used in retail businesses include:

- Assigned readings
- College courses
- Job rotation
- Management training

Train and reward your employees

- Customer profile training
- Successful selling practices
- Product specification and performance training

Many successful retailers typically compensate their employees with hourly wages and enhance their earnings with discounts on store merchandise, bonuses during peak sales periods, and commissions on sales. By encouraging employees to purchase store merchandise at discounted rates, retailers can create enthusiastic, real-life advertisers for their products. The Gap has been very successful at doing this; their employees embody the image of the retailing giant, and provide a handsome source of annual revenue for the business.

## Quality and Retailing

Quality for retailers is defined by two major elements: the quality of the merchandise and the quality of the service. Careful selection of suppliers and manufacturers is the first step in ensuring quality in a retail venture. The next step is ensuring that service is of the highest quality. What are the hallmarks of excellent retail service?

- Knowledge about the product
- After-sale service and assistance
- A fair return policy
- Willingness to special-order products
- Home delivery
- Customized products or services
- Availability of restrooms
- Gift certificates, credit, and check policies

## Financial Issues

Retailing start-up costs vary widely depending on your target market. Other factors include:

- Whether you rent, buy, or build your retail space
- The type of merchandise you will be selling
- The decor and image you want
- The size of the space you want

Is your business's image hip and trendy? Young and sporty? Seasoned and subtle? Natural and healthy?

PROJECT IT!

One of the major cost elements of retailing is **inventory management**, which includes all planning and stocking activities. Effective managers project their sales figures to plan for their inventory needs; this ensures the fastest possible **turnover** of merchandise. Limiting the amount of inventory held can also reduce storage, stocking, and maintenance costs.

Good inventory management means knowing which items are hot sellers and which are slow movers, and pricing them accordingly. Too many small retailers simply buy what they like without considering customer desires. The science of ordering appropriate merchandise, and pricing and displaying it to sell, is called **merchandising**.

## Use of Technology

There are hundreds of affordable, specialty software programs created specifically to help small businesses keep accounting records, create budgets and reports, process supplier invoices, manage payroll and inventory, and perform pricing calculations.

## NxLEVEL™ TECH TIP

**One area in which the lines between service, manufacturing, and retail businesses have blurred is the software rental market.** Some companies now offer their software applications as a service to subscribers or renters, at a fraction of the cost of buying the programs. Currently available programs run the gamut from single functions such as payroll, e-mail, and direct marketing; to multifunctional programs such as Enterprise Resource Planning (ERP), which include personnel, accounting, order processing, manufacturing management, and inventory; and Customer Relationship Management (CRM), which administer sales force automation, marketing, and customer service. These programs provide entrepreneurs with the computer capabilities of much larger companies at an affordable price, while allowing them to focus on their core competencies. To see an example of a rentable program that allows you to design and send a direct mailing, check out **Responsys.com** (http://www.responsys.com). For more information, check Sage Networks' **Interliant AppsOnline**, a catalog of software for hire on the Internet (http://www.appsonline.com).

## Are You a Retailer at Heart?

Are you people-oriented? Service-oriented? These are the two most important traits for retailers. Successful retailers have the ability to create a unique and seamless image for their store, in which all elements complement each other: the store sign, display windows, layout and design, and the appearance and service of employees. Successful retailers have an eye for detail, a flare for color and design, and an understanding of human temperament.

## Retail Opportunities for Entrepreneurs

There's always room in the market for a unique and well-conceived retail concept. If you feel you have the ability to seize upon or start the next big trend, retailing might be for you.

Fashions, changing lifestyles, innovative technology, and increasing discretionary income present opportunities for new variations on old themes. The key to successful retailing for the small entrepreneur is targeting a particular customer segment and going after it.

## Conclusion

Manufacturing, service, and retail operations all present unique challenges and rewards. Manufacturing tends to attract individuals who are intrigued by engineering processes, and are not intimidated by production schedules, machinery, and large capital investments. Businesspeople who start service ventures are usually good at interpersonal communication, have expertise in a particular field, and adapt to trends quickly and easily. Retailers generally love to help people and are very service-oriented. Your interests and passions will determine what type of business is best for you, but whichever you choose, start-up costs, the competitive environment, relationships with suppliers and customers, timeliness, and innovation all play vital roles in determining your success.

# PART II
# ENTRY AND GROWTH STRATEGIES

## Chapter 6
## ENTRY STRATEGIES

*About This Chapter:*
- *Common entry strategies*
- *Alternative entry strategies*
- *Buying into an existing operation*

## Introduction

Part two of this book is primarily concerned with business entry and growth strategies. It is included in this course for existing entrepreneurs because many people who have established businesses are looking at starting new divisions or businesses that compliment their operations. Also, this material will help existing businesses with buying and selling a business, franchising, running home-based and family-owned businesses, and exporting and importing.

There are many reasons why people go into business for themselves, and there are many options for entering into business. Not all opportunities are based on starting a business from the ground up. Countless alternatives are waiting to be developed or discovered by an inspired, creative mind. This chapter presents common and alternative entry strategies to help you get started on your quest.

## Common Entry Strategies

### Starting a Business
Starting a new business can be the most exciting method of getting into business, as it permits you the most freedom. You get to develop the strategies, marketing approaches, employment requirements—everything. You won't be constrained by someone else's way of doing business. If you're successful, you will have the satisfaction of knowing you did it all yourself.

### A new invention
One popular belief is that a new invention is the best way to guarantee success. In reality, this road to success may be long and arduous. Although an invention is exciting to the inventor, the device may prove to have little commercial value. Perhaps no one wants the product or the market is too small to be viable. Careful market research is the key to determining potential demand for the product.

Also, an inventor may be a genius at developing a new device, but may not have the aptitude for running a business. Most inventors do not realize how much time and money it takes to bring a new product to market.

If you intend to start a business based on an invention, it is best to face the reality of the marketplace. You must see if there is a viable market, determine how you will finance your endeavor, understand the limitations on a business built on one product, and be prepared to spend a lot of time and energy getting your product in front of your potential customers.

### Spin-off of an existing product or service

Suppose you are working for a landscaping contractor as a buyer. In the course of your work, you realize that no one has a good stock of seedless cherry or plum trees. With a little research, you locate a supply of seedlings, find an area where you can grow them, and discover a source for the capital you need. This is an example of a simple spin-off business grounded in your personal knowledge and experience. There are many opportunities to develop spin-off options, and they are often successful!

### Turning a hobby into a business

If you're going to start a business, why not do something you love? You may have a much better chance of success if you develop a business from a hobby you enjoy.

Two things stand out when developing a business out of a hobby. First, you must recognize that the product or service has an economic value, and that you need to make a profit. Second, remember that you are running a business, not pursuing a hobby. As the business develops, you may not have time to enjoy your hobby the way you did in the past. Let's say you love fly-fishing and have scoped out some of the best spots for fly fishing in your state. If you decide to start a business acting as a fly-fishing guide, be prepared to give up those leisurely fishing trips.

### Awareness of a given customer

Entering into business for yourself is a risk. The greatest risk is that there will be no customers to buy your product or service. Therefore, there is great advantage in starting a company if you have customers who are ready to purchase your product. In fact, there are cases where customers are so eager to purchase your product that they may be willing to provide financing or place an order large enough to give you the financial resources to establish your business.

However, there are some potential problems to consider. First, you need to ensure that your customers are financially capable of meeting their commitments. Second, even though they claim they need your product, it doesn't mean they are capable of marketing it. Third, if you rely on only one customer, you are subject to his or her economic cycles, which can dictate your price, production runs, and potential profitability.

*John Vail's River*

*John Vail lived in Mississippi, near the Tallahatchie River. He had always loved the river—for years he had spent every Sunday afternoon in his boat, fishing in the peaceful backwaters. One day, his line became tangled in the dense brush growing along the bank. While trying to get the line free, he saw the end of an old plank in the thicket. He pulled it loose; it was muddy and damp, but John knew good hardwood when he saw it. The next day, he and a friend returned with some pruning shears and went digging in the brush. They found over two dozen 12-foot planks, and began to wonder if any more were lying hidden along the river.*

*As it happened, these were just a few of the millions of planks cut over a hundred years ago by a long-defunct lumber company, which had floated the rough planks down the river to a finishing mill 20 miles away. Thousands of these planks had been caught by eddying currents, and had disappeared into the foliage. In the intervening years, the level of the river had dropped, leaving the planks hidden and relatively dry in the tangled brush at the water's edge.*

*John had an idea. He contacted a local mill that provided lumber to a furniture manufacturer in North Carolina. The furniture company prided itself on using recycled wood, so the mill owner was very interested in these historic planks. He and John came to an agreement: John would reclaim the wood and sell it to the mill; the mill would dry, treat, and finish the wood, and sell it to the furniture maker. There was one catch, though. John needed a larger boat, a motorized winch, and some brush-clearing tools before he could get started. Since the mill owner was eager to obtain wood of such high quality, he agreed to help finance the project. Everything went as planned, and John now runs a thriving business on the river he loves!*

## NXLEVEL™ TECH TIP

**If you're considering entering the market as an Internet business, a great place to get help online is eMarketer (http://www.emarketer.com/).**

This comprehensive site provides statistics and information about every e-commerce topic imaginable, from Internet advertising and marketing, to current and upcoming market trends, to the secrets of Web page design. The "eStats" section is especially helpful for the initial planning stages of your business; it has online statistics for ad revenues, Internet usage patterns, market size/growth, and demographics. Complete reports on Internet usage are available for a fee. Other features at this site: "eDirections," which offers step-by-step information on setting yourself up for e-commerce; an eGlossary; and the "eCommunity" section, which comprises discussion areas where you can exchange ideas and make business connections.

The number of major companies needing new products, services, or parts is almost unlimited. If you can find a fully qualified buyer, you may be able to establish your company with limited risk. Consider this customer only the starting point for your enterprise.

### Unfulfilled market need

Many successful businesses have been launched by entrepreneurs who recognized an unfulfilled need, and worked hard to deliver a product or service that would fill it. That being the case, you might think that all you have to do is find an unfulfilled need and leap into production before anyone else!

Unfortunately, it's not that simple. People sometimes deceive themselves into thinking that they've found such a need where it doesn't really exist. Friends may tell you that your idea is great and that your product is sure to sell like hotcakes, but their opinions may be clouded by friendship. Even if you do have an exciting, unique specialty product, the market niche may be too small to sustain your business for any meaningful length of time. This is why you must carefully determine how large your market is, and what percentage of that market will provide you with sufficient sales to grow your business.

### Expansion of a part-time activity

One way to develop a full-time business is to expand on a part-time activity. By keeping your full-time income and starting slowly, you can reduce the risks inherent in business start-ups.

*Grow part-time work to a full-time business*

---

### Specialty Pottery

*Jane Dillard had always made art in one form or another. She studied painting and on the side she dabbled in pottery. While exhibiting her paintings at various art shows, she began to bring along some of her pottery, and found that it sold more consistently than her paintings. Soon Jane began to concentrate on making pottery full time, and now she produces a specialty line that she sells to wholesalers. Because it was expensive to get started, Jane set up her production facility gradually and brought on skilled labor as her business expanded. Today she has customers throughout the western United States and Canada.*

---

There are other definite advantages to starting a business in this manner: you have the opportunity to observe market demand; to grow with your interests and capabilities; and to develop your client base to the point where it can sustain a full-time business.

### Chance

Many entrepreneurs are in business for themselves by chance. Opportunities come to all of us at some point in our lives; the real skill is recognizing the opportunity and having the energy to pursue it.

*Chance and Initiative*

*John Sullivan and Tim Tucker were hired to install new equipment for a large cable TV company. The equipment they replaced was in good working order, but it had been designed for a smaller operation; as the cable company grew, it was constantly forced to replace outmoded equipment. When John and Tim returned to the office and asked their boss what to do with the old equipment, he told them to throw it away.*

*John knew that there were many small cable companies nationwide, and thought that there must be a market for the used cable equipment. He and Tim decided to offer the equipment for sale by taking out a classified ad in an industry magazine. They were amazed by the number of calls they received; within a week, they had sold all their used equipment! They immediately made a deal with their boss to buy all the used equipment at a set price.*

*Next, they called a few other large cable companies and found that they were also disposing of equipment. After six months, their business was going so well that they decided to quit their jobs and start selling full-time. John and Tim had come upon the initial opportunity by chance, and they took the initiative to capitalize on a market they already knew existed!*

## Professional or technical expertise

Many people have a specific technical education or have acquired various skills through prior business experience. These skills can be used in building a business. The time and energy spent acquiring a specific skill will aid greatly in developing your business. If you are a nurse and want to move from hospital-based work to consulting for an HMO on healthcare costs, your schooling and work experience will obviously be major factors in your business's success.

While it is true that some technical skills are required for all businesses, it's also important to remember that your skills may need to be augmented by the expertise of others. Seek advice from professionals who have the skills you lack.

## Desperation

Although desperation is not the ideal way to discover your entrepreneurial creativity, it does provide an impetus for some people. You may be the victim of downsizing, right-sizing, reduction in force, merge and purge, or any of the other methods corporate America has found to reduce its work force. Once you lose your job, you may find that no one in your area needs your skills. Or the death of a spouse may make it necessary for you to find a way to earn a living. Any number of reasons can cause you to decide that your best option for earning a living is to work for yourself.

## Buying an Existing Business

Start up by purchasing

a going concern

Many businesses will buy an existing business to round out the services they can offer. For instance, a local marketing firm might be interested in purchasing a direct-mail fulfillment house in order to expand its business. Likewise, if you've always wanted to own your own gift shop and your favorite local store is for sale, you might consider buying the store in order to jump-start your dream.

By buying an existing business, you can:

- Avoid lead time required to launch the business
- Understand expected income, expenses
- Acquire an existing customer base
- Take hold of an established image

Although buying a business may not offer the same opportunity for creativity as starting a business, there will be many ways to express your ideas by improving the image, expanding the customer base, and streamlining operations. On the other hand, if the business is thriving, you can avoid much of the uncertainty of a start-up operation.

Most successful acquisitions are accomplished by knowledgeable, adequately financed business people. When acquiring a company, it's important to understand the numerous tax and financial maneuverings available for acquiring and financially restructuring an existing company.

## Purchasing a Franchise Business

**Franchises** are independently owned businesses that provide the business owner with much of the entrepreneur's independence, while often presenting less risk than other types of entry strategies.

**Franchising** is a method of business expansion whereby a business owner or manager allows others to market products or services under his or her name and trademark, in strict adherence to a prescribed system. In return, the franchisee pays a fee and, usually, an ongoing royalty. Moreover, the franchisee pays all of the costs of getting into the franchise.

In effect, a franchisee is able to launch a new business with fewer growing pains. Someone else has already developed an operating system that works. It is like a cook using a recipe created and tested by a master chef; he or she can be pretty sure of getting good results on the first attempt.

However, not every franchise is viable. Many small, less expensive franchises are under-funded, lack a good training program, and fail to provide necessary support. Many of the large, well-known franchises are too costly for beginning entrepreneurs. Still, the support and proven business successes of some franchises make them an attractive starting point for the entrepreneur. For more information, see Chapter 8, *Franchising*.

## Alternative Entry Strategies

In this section, we will explore some of the non-traditional methods that people have used to enter the world of self-employment.

### Technology Transfer

**Technology transfer** is a less common yet viable business entry method in which certain procedures and products developed by state and federal agencies are made available for commercial use.

*Separating Potatoes*

*The specific gravity separator developed at the National Energy Laboratory in Idaho is a good example of technology transfer. The process was a means to separate nuclear waste by its specific gravity, regardless of the size of the sample.*

*In southern Idaho, where many of the nation's finest potatoes are grown, a common problem in digging up the potatoes is separating them from rocks. A farmer in Twin Falls, Idaho, became aware of the process used to separate nuclear waste and wondered if the same process could be adapted to separate potatoes from dirt and rock.*

*After just a year of development, the farmer was able to adapt the separator to farm use. He felt that he could manufacture the machine and sell enough of them to establish the product name before the major farm equipment companies started developing and manufacturing their own separating equipment. Today, his machine is considered the premier potato separator.*

There are many other technology transfer options. In several universities and colleges, products are developed and offered for commercial development. NASA and other governmental scientific agencies are also good sources for technology transfer ideas.

### Purchasing a Business in a Different Locale

Most people who consider purchasing a business limit their search to businesses in the immediate area, and thus miss many excellent opportunities. Consider looking at communities where small manufacturing, publishing, catalog, or food processing companies might be available. The key elements to consider are:

Turning technology into

a business

Is the business:

- Simple to learn?
- In line with your goals?
- Transferable to your community?

If you buy a business in another town, you get all the advantages of buying an existing business, but are not dependent on your local market for support.

## Licensing Your Idea

**Licensing** is an option you might consider if you have developed a product or idea that you want marketed. Under a **licensing agreement,** you give another party the right to produce and/or market the product. In exchange for granting this right, you receive a percentage of income from the sale of the licensed product.

Licensing is also beneficial if you want to manufacture and/or distribute a product that is trademarked or copyrighted by someone else. You might manufacture toys based on a popular children's film through a license with the film company, or produce software for a small, independent software development company. In both instances, you are using your manufacturing expertise and creating a highly recognizable product.

Licensing arrangements are common in industries such as electronics, apparel, and software. Obviously, some products are more suitable for licensing than others. Licensing is not risk-free, as many people are in the business of producing "knock-off" products. If you license another party to produce and distribute your product, you should first take every precaution to protect the intellectual property rights associated with your product (such as trademarks, copyright, or a patent), and make sure that your licensee takes steps to protect your trademark as well.

Another risk you may face is selecting a party that is unsuccessful in marketing or manufacturing your product. Try to avoid getting stuck with a poor performer by making sure your license agreement contains measurable performance standards, or the right to license others to produce and market your product or idea.

———————————◢———————————

*Colonial License*

*Colonial Williamsburg, Virginia, is a lovely restored 17th century village where the life of early colonists is recreated for thousands of visitors yearly. However, the price of admittance to Williamsburg covers only a portion of the operating expenses of the village. The trustees of Williamsburg needed additional funds to help cover maintenance of the historic property. They entered into a licensing agreement with a large home furnishings company to allow the company to produce linens based on historic designs found at Williamsburg. Not only is Williamsburg bringing in income from its licensing deal, but it is getting publicity from tags included in the linen's packaging that explains the design period represented by the style of linens the consumer has purchased.*

Buy a good idea!

### Buying a Good Idea

It can be just as creative to find someone with a good idea, product, or business that you can purchase. Sometimes people are willing to sell an idea because they don't have the desire, time, or money to start a business of their own. As with any start-up or expanding business, you must research the market to determine if there is enough demand to support the business.

### Copy an Idea from Somewhere Else

The basic concept of fast-food hamburger restaurants is not exclusively a McDonald's idea. Long before there was McDonald's, there were Tasty Freeze and Dairy Queen restaurants. Many fast-food restaurants have patterned their operations on the successful chain operations that went before them. If you are going to pattern an operation on a successful business, use the essence of the approach to operations. Don't copy names, duplicate products, or infringe on the protected rights of businesses. If you choose to copy someone, do it within the framework of the law. In fact, you may find that the owner of the business you wish to emulate may be willing to be a mentor to you if you don't plan to infringe on his or her market.

### Joint Venture

If you have an idea you believe in, but lack the capital or knowledge to manufacture it, consider finding a partner who possesses the skills or resources you lack. It is best to set out in a joint venture agreement the rights and responsibilities of each partner. Often, large companies will consider a joint venture with you if you can add value to the venture. The corporation may be able to provide funding and guidance to make your idea a success!

## Buy Into an Existing Operation

Buying into an existing business can sometimes be less troublesome than starting a company from scratch. The major opportunities are found with:

- Companies in the developmental stage
- Small manufacturing companies
- Specialty companies

In pursuing this option, you should make sure the company is financially sound and that you can work with the current owners. Ask for a copy of their business plan and study it. Make sure all of your questions have been answered to your full satisfaction. Buying into an existing business is a lot like getting married. Make sure you invest enough time and effort to be completely comfortable with the arrangement.

## Conclusion

Use your creativity as you study various entry strategies. Common methods of entrepreneurship include starting a business from the ground up, buying an existing business, or purchasing a franchise. Don't forget to explore less common entry strategies such as technology transfer, licensing, and joint ventures.

Deciding whether to start or acquire a business is rarely easy. However, the process can be simplified by establishing criteria for evaluating your options. Exploring many options simultaneously is a time-consuming process, but it is well worth your effort!

# Chapter 7
# VALUING AND BUYING A BUSINESS

*About This Chapter:*
- *Pros and cons of buying an existing business*
- *Finding a business to buy*
- *Analyzing a business before you buy*
- *Valuing a business*
- *Valuation methods*
- *Consider buying a business as you would any other investment*
- *Generating cash*
- *How to value a company*
- *Let's make a deal—negotiations*

## Introduction

Entrepreneurs are often described as people who start businesses from scratch. However, entrepreneurs just as often purchase an existing business.

This chapter is designed to help you:

- Understand the advantages of buying a business rather than starting from scratch
- Establish criteria for buying a business
- Find businesses to buy
- Analyze a business to determine whether or not you should buy it
- Submit an offer
- Negotiate the deal and finalize the purchase

## Pros and Cons of Buying an Existing Business

It's difficult to say whether one method of getting into business is better than another. Each person has his or her own personality, criteria, and set of circumstances. However, exploring the advantages and disadvantages of purchasing a business may make it easier to decide whether this method is best for you.

### Advantages to Purchasing an Existing Business
- **The hardest work is already done.** The biggest advantage of buying an existing business is that someone else has already gotten things started.
- **Quick entry.** If you are eager to get into business fast, buying a business is the quickest way.

Buying a business is the quickest way to be your own boss

- **Lower cost.** It's often less expensive to buy a business than to start one. However, be careful about price; if the price looks too good to be true, it probably is!
- **Expanded market share.** Purchasing a going concern means that you already have an established market share, and won't have to create a presence in the market.
- **Initial capital.** Although the cost of buying a business may or may not be less than starting from scratch, at least you know the dollar amount. You will get fewer surprises than you would if you tried to estimate start-up costs.
- **Location.** Buying a business in an ideal location can be a real advantage, especially if all the other good locations are taken.
- **Personnel.** You won't have to search for employees with the right skills and training. (Of course, once you become boss, you will have to determine if you have the best people in the right spots.)
- **Inventory.** The seller should already have inventory on hand and be aware of what customers want. This reduces the risk of ordering unnecessary types and quantities of inventory.
- **Customers.** An existing business has an established customer base, so you don't have to go through the process of creating product awareness. The customer list can be a particularly valuable asset.
- **Contracts and licenses.** An established business should have all the licenses that it needs to operate in its city and state. It may also have contracts with vendors, landlords, etc.
- **Control systems.** An established business should already have accounting, inventory, personnel, and other control systems in place.
- **Image.** One of the biggest jobs a business has is to create the right image in the minds of its customers. If the business has already done this successfully, it can be a huge advantage to the purchaser.
- **Credit.** Going concerns already have relationships with vendors and suppliers. Also, it may be advantageous to establish your banking relationship with a banker that already knows this business.

## Disadvantages to Purchasing an Existing Business

Each of the above advantages can also be a disadvantage. For example, customers may have a negative image of the business, contracts may be restrictive, or the business may have bad relations with creditors. Other possible disadvantages:

- **Misrepresentation.** Although you don't want to assume that a person is dishonest, sellers of businesses are notorious for misrepresenting the condition of their businesses. Sometimes these problems are difficult to spot until after the purchase.

- **Unexpected changes.** Has a major change occurred that will affect the business? Has a new competitor moved into the area? Is the market shifting away from these types of products? Has a new government regulation been enacted? If you are unfamiliar with the industry in general, you may not find out about these problems until it's too late.

# Finding a Business to Buy

This section assumes that you have decided to purchase an existing business and are now beginning your search for the perfect candidate.

## Analyze Your Personal Criteria, Skills, and Abilities

The first step is to decide what kind of business you want to be in. Asking yourself the following questions makes it easier to look only at companies you would be happy owning:

- What do you want to get out of the business?
- How much capital can you put into the business?
- Do you have the right skills and experience?
- What skills do you lack?
- Do you enjoy this type of business?
- How much risk are you willing to take?
- Is this the size of company you want to buy?

*Armed with a personal criteria list, you can start the search for an acceptable business to purchase*

## Where to Find Businesses for Sale

Sources of information about businesses for sale generally fall into the following categories:

*Public Sources:*
- Small Business Administration
- Newspaper advertisements
- Landlords
- Trade journals
- Chamber of Commerce
- Real estate brokers
- Business brokers
- Business counselors
- Shopping centers

*Private Sources:*
- Personal referrals
- Acquaintances
- Attorneys
- Accountants
- Bankers
- Suppliers
- Stockholders
- Former employers
- Venture capitalists

The best strategy is to network among the private sources listed above. Let your banker, attorney, and accountant know that you are interested in purchasing a business, and ask them to keep their eyes open for likely prospects. Don't expect instant results—be patient and wait for the right opportunity.

## Analyzing a Business Before You Buy

Prepare a checklist prior

to purchasing a business

Once you have found a few businesses that fit your criteria, do a complete analysis of each to decide which of them are worthy of further consideration. This can be a daunting task; having a team of experts to help you will make a tremendous difference.

### Checklist for Analyzing a Business

Below are questions that you should ask when assessing the health of the company. (Of course, not every question will apply to your situation, but most questions are pertinent to most businesses.)

- ❑ Why does the owner want to sell?
- ❑ What is the physical condition of the business?
  - ❑ Equipment
  - ❑ Inventory
  - ❑ Building
- ❑ Does the company own or lease its facilities?
- ❑ What is the financial condition of the business?
- ❑ Who are the existing and potential customers?
- ❑ What is the competitive environment?
- ❑ What legal aspects should be considered?
- ❑ What is the overall history of the business?
- ❑ Who owns the company, and is it publicly or privately held?
- ❑ How is the company structurally organized?
- ❑ How many employees does the company have? How long have they worked there?
- ❑ How are personnel managed?
- ❑ What kind of accounting system is in place?
- ❑ What budgeting and expense controls are in place?
- ❑ What do the company's balance sheets, income statements, and cash flow statements reveal over a period of five years?
- ❑ How does the company manage its short-term and long-term cash and investments?
- ❑ How much debt does the company have?
- ❑ Does the company have any unpaid taxes and/or lawsuits pending?
- ❑ What type of insurance coverage does the company have, and how much?
- ❑ How solid are the company's supplier and vendor relationships?
- ❑ What kind of marketing and promotional activities is the company currently engaged in? What are the plans for future innovations/promotions?
- ❑ How tight is the market for the company's products, and how much market share does the company control?
- ❑ How does the company's current pricing structure match that of its competitors?

- ❑ Does the company offer deep discounts to large-scale customers?
- ❑ What is the company's sales history during the past five years?
- ❑ Does the company have an established distribution network and sales force?
- ❑ Where is the business located? Near transportation and shipping lines (if manufacturing)? In a busy suburban mall (if retail)?
- ❑ How strong is the company's manufacturing base? How old is its manufacturing equipment? Does the company own or lease its equipment?

## Narrowing Your Choices

Answering the questions above should give you a clear picture of the business you are considering. Now, use that information to define your best prospect. The following questionnaire will make the process easier.

Circle the number that best corresponds to your understanding of the prospective business. Be honest with yourself in answering these questions!

|  | Strongly Agree |  |  | Strongly Disagree |  |
|---|---|---|---|---|---|
| 1. I could never start a company this good from scratch. | 5 | 4 | 3 | 2 | 1 |
| 2. This business gives me exactly the kind of lifestyle I want. | 5 | 4 | 3 | 2 | 1 |
| 3. Success in this business requires skills and strengths I currently possess. | 5 | 4 | 3 | 2 | 1 |
| 4. This is the right part of the world, country, state, or city for me to live in. I will be happy living here. | 5 | 4 | 3 | 2 | 1 |
| 5. I have a good relationship with a banker or other lender who would be willing to help finance this business. | 5 | 4 | 3 | 2 | 1 |
| 6. The present owner thinks I will fit in well with the business. | 5 | 4 | 3 | 2 | 1 |
| 7. I have been very thorough in gathering information about the business. I have answered all the questions in the previous section. | 5 | 4 | 3 | 2 | 1 |
| 8. The current owner has been completely honest and has answered all my questions. | 5 | 4 | 3 | 2 | 1 |
| 9. I have done a thorough job of gathering the information I need to make an accurate cash flow projection. | 5 | 4 | 3 | 2 | 1 |
| 10. I have calculated an accurate price ceiling and applied my required rate of return (see next section). | 5 | 4 | 3 | 2 | 1 |
| 11. I have been objective in my evaluation, and have looked for reasons not to buy the business. | 5 | 4 | 3 | 2 | 1 |
| 12. I have done a good job of assessing the strengths and weaknesses of the company's present employees. | 5 | 4 | 3 | 2 | 1 |

Add up your score for each business; the highest score indicates the business to which you should give the most consideration.

## Valuing a Business

### How Much is the Business Worth?

Once you have decided to buy a business, the next question is, "How much is this business worth?" The answer is always the same: "The business is worth whatever the buyer and seller agree it is worth."

The buyer and seller have different incentives for placing a price on a business. The seller probably started the business from scratch, or watched it grow from his or her efforts; this is why sellers often have an inflated estimate of their business's worth. The buyer probably has limited resources, which will be used not only for the purchase price, but also to make any necessary changes. Therefore, the buyer wants to pay the lowest possible price.

There is always a middle ground between these two positions.

## Valuation Methods

There are numerous methods for valuing a company, and to make things even more complicated, different terms are often used to describe the same method. (Note: For a fee, a valuation firm will take on this task for you.) The box on this page lists some of these methods and terms.

Familiarity with the pros and cons of the following three methods will make you a stronger negotiator when the time comes to discuss price.

Once you have made the decision to purchase a business, the most important, and most difficult question to be answered is, "How much is this business worth?"

**Valuation Methods**
- Projected Discounted Future Earnings
- Market-Based
- Percentage of Gross Annual Revenues
- Multiple of Earnings
- Asset
- Stream of Earnings
- Estimates

## Asset Valuation

This method places a value on the assets of the company (building, property, machinery, inventory, etc.) and uses this value to price the business. Since this method tends to give lower values, it is commonly used by buyers. Common methods are as follows:

- Book value (known as the balance sheet method)
  - Tangible book value
  - Adjusted tangible book value
- Replacement value
- Liquidation value
- Excess earnings

## Stream of Earnings

This method derives the company's value from its profits, earnings, or cash flow (or their multiples or present values). It usually gives a higher value, and so is typically used by the seller. Common methods include:

- Multiple of earnings
- Price/earnings ratio (P/E) (If the company has listed stock)
- Discounted future earnings (discounted cash flow)
- Return on investment (ROI)

## Estimates

Estimates are based on what the business owner thinks the price should be, according to the selling price of other businesses or a hunch. Common methods include fixed price and market value; they are usually arbitrary and should be avoided if possible.

You're probably asking yourself, "Which of these methods should I use to establish a beginning price for negotiations? What do I really need to know to make an informed decision? How do I establish what the company should be worth to me?" This next section offers some practical answers to these questions.

# Consider Buying a Business As You Would Any Other Investment

As you search for a business to buy, you should also be looking at other things to do with your money, such as investing in the stock market, a money market fund, T-bills, a savings account, or other investment instruments. By regarding the purchase of a business as an investment, you can evaluate all investment possibilities on the same terms, and ascertain which investment will give the best return on your money.

Investment choices can be passive or active. A **passive investment** is one in which you are not actively involved in generating money (e.g., a savings account or the stock market). An **active investment** is one in which you are actively involved in generating money (e.g., owning and working in your own business).

Many times, business owners will estimate what they think the price should be based on such things as selling price of other businesses, or a hunch.

If you can make a 10% return on a passive investment (with little or no time required on your part), does it make sense to buy a business that gives you less than a 10% return, and requires your full-time attention? You must determine if the business you want to buy is a better investment than the other investing options open to you.

## Generating Cash

Many who value businesses place importance on a company's cash position and its ability to generate cash. A company's assets, both tangible and intangible, are good for only two things: 1) they can be sold for cash; or 2) they can be used by the business to generate cash.

### Sold for Cash

A company's **tangible assets**—such as equipment, inventory, buildings, etc.—can be sold for cash (liquidated). Even though they are more difficult to value, **intangible assets**—such as **goodwill**, customer lists, or the value of a patent—can also be sold.

### Used to Generate Cash

The most important function of a company's assets is to generate cash. To illustrate this point, let's look at Better Plastics, Inc., a manufacturer of auto parts. Their assets, including special machinery, were valued at $100,000. The company is currently up for sale.

> *Scenario 1:* Their records show that they had a negative cash flow of $1,000 for each of the past three years. How much would you pay for the company?
> *Scenario 2:* Their records show that they had a positive cash flow of $50,000 for each of the past three years. How much would you pay for the company?

The most important function of the company's assets is to generate cash

In Scenario 1, you probably asked yourself, "Why should I pay $100,000 for the privilege of losing $1,000 a year?" Perhaps you could sell the equipment for $100,000, but then you haven't really gained anything. However, if this equipment could generate $50,000 in positive cash flow each year, as it does in Scenario 2, it would be better to keep the equipment and use it as a cash generator. The emphasis of the valuation, then, should not be solely on how much the assets themselves are worth, but on how much cash they can generate.

Cash flow is simply the movement of money through the business

## How to Value a Company

As we have seen, **cash flow** is the best way to evaluate a business as an investment, and to place a dollar value on it. Cash flow is simply the movement of money through the business; cash comes in through sales, and goes out to pay the bills. **Net cash flow** is the difference between what comes in and what goes out. A **positive cash flow** means that at the end of a given time period, more cash has come in than has gone out of the business.

How can you use cash flow to evaluate the business as an investment, and to place a value on it? To answer this question, it is necessary to examine the company's past cash flows, and estimate its potential future cash flows. The results determine the price you should pay for the new business.

### Step 1: Historical Cash Flows

Obtain **historical cash flows** for as many previous years as possible; it is obligatory to get records for at least the past three years. (If the company is less than three years old, get as much of the company's financial information as possible.)

The majority of small businesses will not have a cash flow statement available for inspection. However, most businesses do prepare a **balance sheet**, which shows the company's assets and liabilities; and an **income statement**, which shows the company's profit (or loss) after expenses are subtracted from revenue.

If no cash flow statement is available, one can be created from the income statement and the last two ending-period balance sheets. To take accrual-based financial statements and create a financial picture based on "cash" accounting requires accounting expertise. An accountant's help in this area is vital.

To get a true picture of cash flow, you must further consider the income statement given to you by the seller. Most business owners try to make the income statement show as little profit as possible; the smaller the profit, the fewer taxes the business has to pay. Conversely, when selling a business, many business owners try to make the company look more profitable by not recording expenses, or by understating them.

An important area in which owners juggle profits and losses is **cost of goods sold**; overstating or understating inventory significantly changes the apparent profit or loss. Therefore, you should insist on an independent inventory count to verify the owner's estimate.

As the prospective owner, you need to know how profitable the company really is. Many accountants use a technique called "recasting" or "reconstructing" to get a true picture of profitability; they modify the cash flow to reflect the business's probable profits had it been run by the prospective buyer. They recast the statements as if the business were operated by the new owner under those guidelines, practices, and assumptions. For instance, in the case of an owner who tries to minimize profits, deductions for such items as company cars used personally by the owner and first-class travel are backed out, or the cost of professional management is substituted for the owner's sometimes inflated salary. In the case of an owner who tries to inflate profits, the accountant makes sure that the amounts listed for wages, taxes, legal and accounting fees, supplies, insurance, and all other operating expenses are reasonable. If there is little or no amount in these areas, adjustments must be made.

### Step 2: Projecting Future Cash Flows

Projecting or forecasting future cash flows simply means making an educated guess, with a strong emphasis on the word "educated." This is where doing your homework pays off in terms of finding a business that is selling for a bargain price, or that has great potential for future profits.

The information in Table 1 is an example of how to prepare a cash flow forecast. You can use a blank form to enter information about the future cash flows of the business you are evaluating.

### Step 3: Use Historical and Projected Cash Flows to Place a Value on the Business

The problem with projecting cash flows is that due to the loss of purchasing power, dollars earned in the future are worth less than dollars earned today. However, future cash flows can be "discounted" to today's dollar value. By using a **discount rate** (interest rate adjusted for risk), you can calculate a **net present value** that determines the dollar value of the business today, even though you are looking at annual cash flows for as many as five years ahead.

**There are four steps to calculating net present value:**

*1. Estimate cash flows for the future.*
We've already discussed the process of estimating cash flow, but part of our negotiating technique requires us to calculate two different sets of cash flow:

a. **Historical cash flow**. Use the historical cash flow to calculate the business's present growth rate, then use this growth rate to project a conservative future cash flow. If past cash flow has grown at 10% per year, your estimate is that future cash flow will grow 10% or less per year. If the company has not grown in the past three years, or growth has been erratic, this becomes a negotiating tool for lowering the price. This estimate gives you the minimum you will be willing to pay.

b. **Your confidential cash flow**. Next, calculate a "best case" cash flow, but for your information only. This gives you an idea of the upside potential for the business, and the maximum you will be willing to pay.

### Step 2. Determine an appropriate discount rate.

The discount rate is a risk-adjusted interest rate you would expect from a comparable investment. The risk adjustment is to compensate you for taking the risk of buying this business, since it's impossible to buy a "sure thing."

For example, if you could invest in a government-guaranteed security, such as T-bills, and earn 7% interest, and a relatively low-risk business opportunity seems to justify a small 2% premium, then the discount rate for valuing that business would be 9%. If the business seems risky, a risk premium of 10% could be assigned, resulting in a 17% discount rate. Most small businesses are assigned risk premiums between 5% and 10%. As a result, discount rates for most small business valuations range between 12% and 22%, but it's not uncommon to find discount rates as high as 35%.

In the negotiation process, it's important to understand the procedure of setting the discount rate. If you feel the business is high-risk, you should assign a higher discount rate; if you and the present business owner disagree on the risk involved, you can use this as a negotiating point to lower the price of the business.

### Step 3. Determine a reasonable life expectancy for the business.

Most experts agree that future cash flows should be estimated for no more than five years; estimates beyond five years are not reliable.

### Step 4. Determine the net present value of the cash flows.

The value of the business is determined by calculating the net present value of the projected cash flows, using the discount rate you have chosen. Using the data from the example in Table 1, a value can be calculated for the ABC Company. A growth rate of 10% per year is assumed for the data in the table.

Example: Using the information in Table 1, calculate the value of the ABC Company.

### Table 1: ABC Company Cash Flow Projections

| | 1997 | 1998 | 1999 | 2000 | 2001 |
|---|---|---|---|---|---|
| **Revenue** | | | | | |
| Product 1 | 100,000 | 110,000 | 121,000 | 133,100 | 146,410 |
| Product 2 | 100,000 | 110,000 | 121,000 | 133,100 | 146,410 |
| Total Revenue | 200,000 | 220,000 | 242,000 | 266,200 | 292,820 |
| **Expenses** | | | | | |
| Cost of Product 1 | 50,000 | 55,000 | 60,500 | 66,550 | 73,205 |
| Cost of Product 2 | 50,000 | 55,000 | 60,500 | 66,550 | 73,205 |
| Wages | 25,000 | 27,500 | 30,250 | 33,275 | 36,603 |
| Outside Services | 250 | 275 | 303 | 333 | 366 |
| Supplies—office & operating | 500 | 550 | 605 | 666 | 732 |
| Repairs & Maintenance | 500 | 550 | 605 | 666 | 732 |
| Advertising | 5,000 | 5,500 | 6,050 | 6,655 | 7,321 |
| Car, Delivery, and Travel | 500 | 550 | 605 | 666 | 732 |
| Accounting and Legal | 1,000 | 1,100 | 1,210 | 1,331 | 1,464 |
| Rent | 6,000 | 6,000 | 6,000 | 6,000 | 6,000 |
| Telephone | 2,000 | 2,000 | 2,000 | 2,000 | 2,000 |
| Utilities | 1,200 | 1,200 | 1,200 | 1,200 | 1,200 |
| Insurance | 1,000 | 1,000 | 1,000 | 1,000 | 1,000 |
| Taxes | 1,000 | 1,100 | 1,210 | 1,331 | 1,464 |
| Loan Repayment | 12,000 | 12,000 | 12,000 | 12,000 | 12,000 |
| Miscellaneous Expenses | 1,000 | 1,000 | 1,000 | 1,000 | 1,000 |
| Owner's Withdrawal | 35,000 | 40,000 | 45,000 | 50,000 | 55,000 |
| Total Expenses | 191,150 | 210,325 | 230,038 | 251,221 | 274,023 |
| **Net Cash Flow** | **8,050** | **9,675** | **11,962** | **14,979** | **18,797** |

ABC's value is found by applying the four steps:

*Step 1. Estimate cash flows for the future.* You have determined that the revenues and expenses for the next five years will be those in Table 1. Your evaluation of ABC Company's historical cash flows shows that they have been growing by 10% per year. The cash flows in Table 1 show an increase in revenues of 10% per year. These are the cash flows to be used:

Year 1 - $ 8,050    Year 4 - $14,979
Year 2 - $ 9,675    Year 5 - $18,797
Year 3 - $11,963

*Step 2. Determine an appropriate discount rate.* Let's assume you could invest in the stock market and make a return of 10%, and that this is your best alternate investment. We'll also assume that you believe the ABC Company is not very risky, so you assign a risk premium of 5%. This means the total discount rate is the sum of the best alternate investment rate and the risk premium, or 15%. Therefore, you want a 15% return on your investment.

*Step 3. Determine a reasonable life expectancy for the business.* In this case, we will use five years of projected cash flows.

*Step 4. Determine the net present value of the cash flows.* Using present value tables from a financial handbook, a financial calculator, or a computer spreadsheet, use the present value factors for 15% (the discount rate). Multiply the present value factor by the cash flows for each year. The total of the discounted cash flows is the value of the business.

|   | A | B | C | D |
|---|---|---|---|---|
| 1 | Year | Net Cash Flow | Present Value Factor | Today's Value |
| 2 | 1 | $8,050 | 0.8695 | $6,999 |
| 3 | 2 | $9,675 | 0.7561 | $7,315 |
| 4 | 3 | $11,963 | 0.6575 | $7,866 |
| 5 | 4 | $14,979 | 0.5717 | $8,563 |
| 6 | 5 | $18,797 | 0.4972 | $9,346 |
| 7 | Totals | $63,464 | | $40,089 |

The following example shows how to calculate net present value using Excel, a popular spreadsheet offered by Microsoft.

|   | A | B |
|---|---|---|
| 1 | Year | Cash Flow |
| 2 | 1 | $8,050 |
| 3 | 2 | $9,675 |
| 4 | 3 | $11,963 |
| 5 | 4 | $14,979 |
| 6 | 5 | $18,797 |
| 7 | NPV | $40,089 |

*In Excel:*

Enter the cash flows for years 1-5 in cells B2 through B6.

Type the following formula in cell B7: =NPV(15,B2:B6)

The discount rate of 15% is already entered in this formula. Change the discount rate and cash flows to fit your situation.

The calculated value of ABC Company is $40,089. This means that if you buy the ABC Company today for $40,089, and the projected cash flow is accurate, you would realize a 15% percent annual rate of return on your investment over the next five years.

You must remember one principle in price negotiations: The higher the price paid, the lower your rate of return. For example, if the price for ABC Company was $46,204, the rate of return would only be 10%. In order to set a **price ceiling** for negotiations, choose your lowest acceptable rate of return and recalculate the net present values at that rate. The resulting number represents your highest acceptable price. You should be prepared to walk away from negotiations if the seller will not accept it.

The higher the price paid, the lower your rate of return

As stated earlier, you should also prepare a confidential cash flow that reflects revenue-increasing improvements you will be able to make to the company. Using the net present value of the higher cash flows, recalculate the value of the company. This gives the company a higher value, meaning you may be willing to pay more than the historical cash flows justify. This can be risky, so weigh the evidence carefully before using this method.

Earlier in this chapter, we said that this method of calculating a business's value would allow you to answer two questions. Let's look at the answers to those questions.

1. **How does this investment compare with other investments available to me?** The answer: At a price of $40,089, given all the assumptions made, your investment in this business will give you a 15% return. You can now compare that return with alternate investments.
2. **How can I tell how much a business is worth?** You have calculated that the business is worth $40,089. You now have a starting place in price negotiations.

## Professional Appraisers

Should you hire a professional appraiser to establish the value of the business you want to buy? The advantage of hiring an appraiser is that they know how to gather the necessary information to value a company. They could be used to document, for tax purposes, the process of arriving at the agreed-upon price. The disadvantage of using an appraiser is that, as you have seen, there are countless ways to arrive at a price.

The advantage of hiring an appraiser is that they know how to gather the necessary information to value a company

The best approach is to work with an accountant or CPA whom you trust—someone who can help you gather the information, and cast accurate cash flow projections as if you were the owner. Proper discounting of these future cash flows can then be used to calculate your acceptable purchase price range and the return on your investment.

## Let's Make a Deal—Negotiations

Before you make an offer, it is essential that you establish your price ceiling—the top price you are willing to pay. This gives you considerable power in the negotiations.

### Negotiations

The objective of the negotiation process should be for both sides to walk away feeling reasonably satisfied. A win/win situation creates goodwill on both sides. Without that goodwill, situations may develop that could be detrimental to your business's success (such as the previous owner telling all his or her old customers that you are unreasonable). If it's not possible to make both sides happy during the negotiations, perhaps you should look for another business to buy. Be sure to look at Chapter 41 *Negotiating and Managing the Deal.* The entire chapter is devoted to the important subject of negotiations.

### Price

It seems to be a rule that when the first asking price is accepted, sellers wonder if they could have gotten more out of the deal. Likewise, if the first counteroffer is accepted, buyers always wonder if they could have gotten the business for an even lower price. To help avoid "buyer/seller remorse," you should generally not offer the full asking price.

What if the asking price is significantly below your price ceiling? You should still make a counteroffer, but by a smaller amount.

How much below the asking price should your offer be? Any counteroffer you make should be justifiable. If your assessment of the company shows that the cash flows will not support a certain price, this is ample justification for a lower price. In addition, your investigation of the company should have made you aware of other factors that justify a lower price, such as old inventory, an unproductive family member on the payroll, or repairs that must be made to the building or equipment. Be on the lookout for these bargaining chips.

If the asking price is significantly above your price ceiling, what should you do? The first step is to counter with a price that can be supported by the cash flow, which is your price ceiling or lower. If that does not leave you with negotiating room, you must decide whether to walk away or accept a higher price with more favorable terms.

### Terms

You must assess which is most important to your particular deal: the price or terms of the agreement. If the seller's price is firm, you should dictate the terms to your advantage. If terms are most important to the seller, you should dictate price.

Should you pay a higher price if you can dictate the terms? Always evaluate the deal in terms of the rate of return on your investment. Suppose your ceiling price for the plastics company is $100,000, which will give you the 15% return you require. The seller refuses to go lower than $150,000, but is willing to carry the contract for 25 years, with payments of $6,000 per year. Your original offer assumed you would need a $100,000 loan for 5 years at 10% interest, with payments of $25,488 per year. These new terms mean an increase in cash flows of more than $19,000 per year, which more than provides your 15% return. Should you pay more than your ceiling price? In this case, the answer is emphatically yes!

## Conclusion

There are no hard and fast rules about placing a value on a business; a business is worth what the buyer and seller mutually decide it's worth. The methods presented here merely serve as a starting place for negotiations. However, it is important that you know what rate of return you require; this knowledge allows you to set a price ceiling. The involvement of your team of professionals will ensure that you make an objective evaluation, so always include your accountant, attorney, and business advisors in the valuation process.

# Chapter 8
# FRANCHISING

*About This Chapter:*
- *Common franchise formats*
- *Regulation*
- *A turnkey operation*
- *The downside*
- *The preliminaries*

## Introduction

In a franchise, the **franchisor** allows the **franchisee** the right to sell or distribute a service or product under the franchisor's system. In return, the franchisee pays a fee called a **royalty** to the franchisor. A tremendous growth in the number of franchises has occurred during the last 40 years. Today there are over 600,000 franchises in operation in the United States. Worldwide, there are many thousands more. The economic impact of franchising is staggering. A few years ago it was estimated that one-third of all retail sales occurred in franchises, and this number is increasing annually.

Franchising is a growing method of doing business

The growth of franchising can be traced to three primary trends. Consumers have become much more mobile and subject to national advertising than in the past, and they find comfort in knowing that a franchise's goods and services are of uniform quality whether they're bought in North Dakota or New Mexico. Second, the small businessperson can begin a franchise without many of the problems of starting from scratch. Finally, the franchisor saves on capital and personnel by having franchisees start its stores throughout its service area. In this chapter, we discuss what franchises are, how they work, and whether one is right for you.

## Common Franchise Formats

Franchises can be structured in any number of ways, but generally they are categorized as:

- Business-format franchises
- Brand-name franchises
- Product-distribution franchises
- Affiliate franchises

The **brand-name franchise** allows the franchisee to market products or services under a brand name in order to take advantage of the franchisor's name recognition and goodwill. **Affiliate franchises** are groups of similar businesses that join for the purpose of marketing their services in a general way. **Product-distribution franchises** usually operate under a license from the franchisor, which allows marketing of the franchisor's products and services in specific areas. The **business-format franchise** is the most common and the fastest-growing type of franchise; therefore, we will use it as the model for our discussion, but the issues we address apply equally to the other types of franchises.

## Regulation

State and federal

franchise regulation

In a franchise, a person is usually given the exclusive right to sell a company's product within a defined region. These agreements are not considered restraint of free trade because they do not monopolize an entire market.

To illustrate the incredible growth in franchising over the past 20 years: It wasn't until 1978 that the Federal Trade Commission (FTC) adopted regulations covering franchises. California was the first state to regulate the sale of franchises, and it still requires that you register a franchise operation with the Department of Commerce. About 25 states have adopted some type of franchise regulations. These rules usually require registration by the franchisor prior to sale. They also address the parties' relationship under the franchise agreement, particularly regarding renewal and extension of the term. Most regulations also require that certain disclosures be made by the franchisor to the franchisee, but these disclosure laws rarely focus on the specific details of the deal. Therefore, you should review the franchise agreement carefully, and retain experienced legal counsel to assist you from the start.

Other laws affecting franchises include state securities laws and unlawful trade practices acts. In addition, the brokers who sell new franchises are often regulated under business transaction statutes that require disclosure of certain information to the franchise purchaser, establishment of escrow accounts, and other financial protection. If you are considering franchising your operation for sale to others or serving as a broker yourself, consult your attorney beforehand; the penalties for violating federal or state law in the sale of franchises can be severe!

## A Turnkey Operation

The primary advantage of franchising is that the franchisee is immediately able to compete with larger companies by utilizing the goodwill, quality standards, and experience of the franchisor. These assets would take years to acquire if the owner operated an independent shop. Other advantages include:

- Access to expert help
- Increased purchasing power
- Aid in lender negotiations
- Sample business and operating plans

*Jeff Martin wanted a change of pace. He had spent 15 years working as a salesperson for a computer company, and now he wanted to strike out on his own. He investigated various business opportunities and decided to buy an ice-cream store franchise. He received two months of training as part of his purchase, because the franchisor wanted to ensure that the quality of its franchises was consistent. Jeff found it exhilarating to own his own business while receiving support from the franchisor.*

## The Downside

Operating a franchise is not for everyone. Some franchisors are control-oriented, and will monitor and regulate virtually every aspect of your business. It is in the franchisor's best interest to see your franchise succeed, because the more you sell, the more money it makes. Other disadvantages are:

- Royalty payment problems
- Inflexibility on the part of the franchisor
- Insensitivity to local markets

### Scams

You should be aware that numerous corrupt franchising opportunities lure the uninformed entrepreneur into an investment scheme in which the franchisor literally takes the franchisee's money and runs. Let the buyer beware!

There are some problems
in operating a franchise

*Ada Briscoll signed a franchise agreement with AV Computing to open a local branch and to sell its newly created anti-virus software program. The franchise agreement required Ada to buy a large inventory of software from the franchisor. Because she wanted to get her franchise up and running, she agreed to this provision, although she questioned it while negotiating the franchise agreement. Ada felt that the extra inventory would sell quickly due to the huge demand she had read about in business trade journals.*

*Ada quickly sold the software to several local government agencies, who started frantically calling her when they found that the software did nothing to protect their data from the viruses that were plaguing them. After careful inspection of the software, Ada determined that it was seriously flawed. When she called AV Computing for assistance, she got a message saying that the number had been disconnected.*

One way to avoid a scam is to investigate the franchise meticulously before you invest in it. Face-to-face contact with the franchisor can provide a strong sense of the success of the organization. It's also a good idea to contact franchisees directly to identify any problems they've had with the franchisor.

# The Preliminaries

### How to Find Out About Franchise Opportunities

How do you get started? Go to the library and read what you can find. The Internet will have some useful information as well. Talk with people who currently own franchises and see what they say. Check the business section of financial and business newspapers and periodicals; many franchisors and owners of franchises advertise for buyers in these publications.

Franchise trade shows are a quick way to gather a lot of information

Franchise trade shows are now held in several large cities. There will be booths explaining how to select and operate franchises. You may even have the opportunity to obtain information on franchise fees, royalties, and related issues from a large number of possible franchisors. This allows you to see if a particular franchisor's terms are in line with the market. A word of warning: Many of the franchisors at these trade shows are small, disorganized operations. Caution is the byword!

### Investigating the Franchise Opportunity

Before making an application for a franchise, do your homework! Are the products and the systems proven? Is the franchise new to your area, or to the region as a whole? Is this product on the upswing of a new idea, or the downside of consumer desires? Have you seen an operation in place? Can you visualize one in your area? Would the demographics and economy of your area support this type of business? For example, a low-income retirement community may not be the best place for a trendy, expensive necktie franchise! Could you realistically learn this business, and would you like it? Do you respect the franchise's product or service?

### The Application

At this stage, the franchisor will want to know some things about you as well, including your financial status, experience, and ability to perform. These applications are often very detailed, and you may not like giving a stranger all this personal information. However, if the franchisor doesn't ask for much information about you, it may indicate that it is not careful enough about its business. You may not want to complete your franchise application with such a company!

### Deposit Agreement

After your application has been accepted, you are typically requested to make a "good faith" deposit of between $2,000 and $10,000. This is usually required before the franchisor will disclose to you many details of the operation. Before you make a deposit, review the deposit agreement and make sure that the deposit is refundable if you cannot strike a deal. Also, see to it that the deposit is in escrow and not commingled with the franchisor's operating funds. You will also want your deposit to serve as a reservation of your franchise.

---◆---

*Laura Phipps was not careful enough in her drive to own an interior design franchise. She deposited $7,000 with Designs on Wheels, a regional window treatment franchise that provides in-home design consulting and development. Unfortunately, she did not look very closely at the franchise deposit agreement. When she was rejected by the franchise, she lost 50% of her deposit to franchisor "investigation fees."*

---◆---

## Examining the Franchisor

By now you have made your application to the franchisor and have qualified. At this point, the franchisor should be willing to disclose to you its financial and operational details (you can expect to sign a nondisclosure agreement), and you must make a very detailed examination of this information before signing the franchise agreement. (Remember: If you negotiated your deposit agreement properly, you will be entitled to a refund if you don't like what you see!) If the franchisor appears reluctant to provide you with information, or is in a big hurry to sign you up, you should take these as warning signs and refrain from going forward with the deal. Here are some questions to ask before you get to the details of the franchise agreement:

- Can the franchisor deliver all that it has promised?
- Is the assistance to your business operations worth the franchisor's interference?
- Does the franchisor have a good track record?
- Have you checked a credit rating service like Dun & Bradstreet, called the Better Business Bureau in the franchisor's home town, the state's attorney general's office, and the FTC?
- Is most of the franchisor's income from franchise fees (immature business), or from royalty payments (ongoing successful franchises)?
- Do you understand what you will be getting and what you will be expected to do?
- Are you permitted to interview any franchisees you choose, or are you given an exclusive list?
- Is there any market research in your area for this type of product at this price?
- Has the location of your shop been carefully evaluated?
- How are you going to construct the type of store the franchisor requires?
- How does the franchisor administer the franchise, and what kind of help is it willing to supply to a new or struggling franchise?
- Are the training commitments more or less than you reasonably need?

- Do you have sufficient funds to make the purchase payments without severely affecting your capital needs in the short term?
- Does the franchisor have valid trademarks or patents on the products you'll be selling?
- How many franchises have been sold this year, and over the last five years? How many have failed?
- Do franchisees collectively have a voice in management or a seat on the board?

## Buying an Ongoing Franchised Business

There are additional questions to ask if you are considering the purchase of an ongoing franchise. First, you must make sure that the franchisee has the right to sell it to you; most likely, you will need the consent of the franchisor. Is your seller considering this a sub-franchise, where he or she will take royalty payments in addition to the purchase price and those royalties that you are obligated to pay directly to the franchisor? Does your seller operate competing franchises within your area? If so, are they successful, and would you want to become part of a team, or be a competitor, with your seller?

Because you will be buying into a complex business relationship, you should investigate the business as if you were buying the franchise directly from the franchisor, and study the terms of the franchise agreement accordingly. We recommend that you have a feasibility study prepared by an expert to determine whether you are buying into a booming or declining enterprise. (In retailing, this is often referred to as **product life cycle** analysis.) One thing that makes investigation difficult is that the franchisor often has restrictions against distribution of the information in its operations manual to third parties. But it is essential that you review these documents carefully before buying an ongoing franchise.

Is the location a good pick for your kind of business?

## Understanding the Franchise Agreement

You are now at the last step before you begin business as a franchisee. Every franchise agreement is different, but most of them address the following issues in one form or another. Remember, all your careful analysis is wasted if you agree to a contract that is unfair to you or that you cannot perform. Don't be afraid to ask the franchisor to explain why a particular term is fair or necessary; the agreement is negotiable even though it comes on a "standard form." Every franchise presents different issues and opportunities, and these must be included in your particular agreement. You can seek experienced legal counsel to help you negotiate a fair deal, and you can always walk away if you cannot reach a fair agreement with the franchisor.

## Contract Term and Extensions

Is the initial term long enough, and can the franchisor restrict renewal in some way? You may want a short initial term in case things don't work out, but you may want the automatic right to renew without additional fees. Many states regulate how franchisors grant extensions, so that they cannot be cut off early to the detriment of the franchisee. Also, the type and length of notice required prior to renewal is very important because if you miss that date you could find yourself unable to renew.

### Franchise Fee and Royalties

Usually, the initial franchise fee does not include the inventory, fixtures, or supplies you will be required to purchase. The royalty you pay can be based on net or gross sales. Issues to consider are: When is the royalty due? Is there a cap or a declining percentage in your favor as your sales go up? How often—and at whose expense—will an audit of your books take place? If your books are in error, the agreement will typically provide that you pay the expense of audit, which can be substantial. You should understand the extent and nature of your reporting requirements, and the required accounting methods.

### Supplies

Are you required to buy all your supplies from the franchisor? Do you get a discount based on economy of scale, or do you pay a premium for name familiarity? Are the initial stock-up requirements merely a disguise for a clever pyramid scheme?

### Territory

One of the critical elements in a franchise agreement is the extent of the territory over which you have been granted the franchise. You must determine whether it is exclusive or nonexclusive (i.e., whether other franchises can be granted in the area by the same franchisor). A franchise is not always an exclusive right. On the other hand, will you have the obligation to open additional stores in the area, or else lose your exclusivity or even your franchise? Is the exclusive market area so large that it will overextend your resources, or so small so that you will find yourself competing with another franchisee in your area?

*Territory can be the key to your success in franchising*

### Physical Plant

Identify the extent to which the franchisor controls or assists you in locating a site, making improvements, and furnishing the interior. Many retail franchises are promoted not only by the product they sell, but by the physical appearance of the store. Will the franchisor own the building and lease it to you, or will you be expected to construct the improvements? Determine what rights the franchisor has to inspect your premises and operations, so you can be prepared for franchisor visits.

*A franchise often requires a special building and fixtures*

### Training

Many franchisors will give you the equivalent of a master's degree in small business administration, while others throw you a manual and tell you to get to work. Your agreement should clearly state what training is offered, when and where, and at whose expense. Will your employees receive training from the franchisor, or is that your obligation?

## Management Assistance

One of the common elements of a franchise is that the business practices throughout the franchise system are uniform. This can be a great benefit to the small business owner who does not have the experience, education, or desire to work up management procedures for the business and maintain them. Your contract should spell out what ongoing management assistance the franchisor will provide.

———————————◆———————————

*Marvin Johnson of New Orleans was surprised and happy to learn of the extent of franchisor support behind his newly purchased Italian Café franchise. Not only was he trained for three months onsite at another Italian Café, but his training was ongoing. The franchisor provided seasonal promotional materials such as table tents and shirts for wait staff, as well as advertising in local papers for his franchise. Johnson knew he couldn't provide this type of marketing so early in his business's start-up phase, so he appreciated the franchisor's guidance and involvement!*

———————————◆———————————

## Marketing

One of the major advantages to a franchisee is the value of the existing marketing program of the franchisor. Name and product recognition are crucial to most retail franchises. Will you be required to spend a certain percentage of your gross sales on additional advertising? What percentage of your royalty payment will go to area, regional, and national marketing by the franchisor? Do you have the right to audit the franchisor's books to see that it is performing its obligations?

## Quality Control

It is important for both the franchisor and the franchisee to see that uniform standards of quality are maintained throughout all franchises. A bad product or sleazy business practice in one location will hurt all franchisees, because your trade name is theirs, too. The franchisor should insist that you and all other franchisees maintain an established standard of quality. You should insist that the franchisor keep the other franchisees on the same path and give you remedies if they fail to do so.

## Trade Secrets

Most franchises are largely based upon the franchisor's "trade secrets," which include the product, the operations manual, and the management system. The franchise agreement will often provide that every aspect of the business is a trade secret, and you may be required to keep that information confidential. You may also be prohibited from competing against the franchisor when the franchise terminates, and from opening non-franchised outlets while the agreement is in place. Without these protections, the

Your shop is judged by what other franchises do

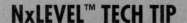

## NxLEVEL™ TECH TIP

**Many franchisors have elaborate Web sites that allow the prospective franchisee to take a virtual walk through the business. Here are a couple of Web sites with links to dozens of franchise home pages:**

**EntrepreneurMag.com**'s Franchise and Business Opportunities site (http://www.entrepreneurmag.com/oppguide) has information on franchises in every field imaginable, including candles, tanning, custard, vitamins, and autopsies!

**Bison Franchises and Franchising Online** bills itself as "the most comprehensive site devoted to franchising and franchises." The site showcases hot companies, provides contacts and basic information for 1500 franchises, allows you to download application forms, and discusses personal screening and loans.

franchisor is subject to unfair competition. However, you should review these provisions carefully to avoid undue restrictions on your right to operate other businesses or to earn a living once the franchise is terminated.

## Transferability

The franchise may be the most substantial asset in your estate. At some time, you may wish to sell the business or pass it on to your children. For this reason you must review the transferability provisions of the agreement carefully. The franchisor, on the other hand, has sold you the right to use its name, product, and operational methods on the basis of your financial position, experience, and reputation. Therefore, the franchisor will want to review your buyer's qualifications, just as it reviewed yours when it sold you the franchise. In addition, the franchisor may want to reacquire the franchise, and it is quite common to see options or rights of first refusal granted back to the franchisor.

*Can you sell the franchise to someone else?*

*Jim Timmons had owned a successful convenience store franchise for 15 years and planned to retire to Key West, Florida. Because he always dreamed of fishing off the Keys, when Timmons signed his initial agreement with the franchisor, he checked to make sure that the transferability provisions provided for the eventual sale of his business. Due to his long-range planning, Timmons enjoyed 15 years of business ownership and was able to sail off into the Florida sunset!*

## Termination

Careful consideration must be given to the termination provisions in any contract, but this is especially critical in a franchise agreement. The franchisor will want to be able to terminate the agreement if the franchisee fails to follow the program, is unsuccessful or goes into bankruptcy, takes the process to another location or provides it to a third party, or is delinquent and fails to make timely royalty payments. For these reasons, the termination provisions in a franchise agreement are often very strongly in favor of the franchisor.

On the other hand, you need to protect your investment in the franchise, and you also want the ability to terminate or get damages if the franchisor is not delivering all that it has promised. You may also want to include a buyout provision, just in case you wish to terminate the franchise voluntarily. Buyouts often have complex formulas because the franchisor may want the continuing royalty payment, but cannot quickly get a new franchisee in place. In a buyout, the franchisor wants you to pay damages based upon the expected return for the remainder of the contract term, less the franchisor's costs of performance of its duties to you.

If the franchisor defaults and the agreement is terminated, does the contract provide for your recovering some portion of your initial franchise fee? Does the contract provide for liquidated damages? What items must be returned to the franchisor? You will want a clear delineation of these matters so you are not subjected to claims after termination.

## Conclusion

Franchises are a popular way of doing business. They offer the franchisee incredible advantages in purchasing power, name and product recognition, tested physical plant layout, operations manuals, training, and business management assistance. However, they can also be burdensome in terms of paperwork and expense. Use caution when considering a franchise. If successful, the franchise arrangement will benefit both parties!

# Chapter 9
# HOME-BASED BUSINESS

*About This Chapter:*
* *Home-based business today*
* *Types of home-based businesses*
* *Legal, tax and insurance issues*
* *Managing a home-based business*

## Introduction

Home-based business is one of the fastest-growing forms of entrepreneurship in the United States. Corporate restructuring, and the rapid growth of telecommunications and information technologies, have resulted in an explosion of full- and part-time home-based businesses. According to statistics, a new home business starts every 11 seconds, creating 8,219 jobs each day. These businesses generate over $401 billion per year.

What is the economic impact of home-based businesses?

## Home-Based Business Today

### Trends

Dramatic changes in our society have forced many people to rethink traditional ways of earning a living. Although successful home businesses include everything from desktop publishing to dog-walking, an increasing number of home workers are professionals who serve new markets and provide needed services and products to fast-growing firms and corporations. As a result, home-based entrepreneurs are becoming a major force in the business world. This phenomenon is fueled by several factors, including:

* Corporate layoffs
* Military downsizing
* Advanced technology
* Growing family responsibilities
* Company outsourcing
* E-commerce growth

LINK Resources, Inc., a New York marketing research firm, shares basic facts about home-based business owners:

* 80.1% are married
* 51.9% have children under 18
* 24.4% have children under 6
* 55.4% have a college degree

- $49,000 is the average income
- 38.5 years is the average age

Rural areas tend to have a large percentage of home-based businesses for several reasons: 1) many small farms, ranches, and other agricultural operations are in fact home-based businesses; 2) in areas where jobs are often scarce and/or low-paying, many rural residents create their own jobs by running a part- or full-time business from home;  3) rural areas generally do not have the zoning and other restrictions that discourage home businesses in metropolitan areas; 4) corporate restructuring and changing lifestyle preferences are sending increasing numbers of former city dwellers to rural areas of the country because advances in technology have made it possible to "telecommute" or run small home businesses.

### Work-at-Home Opportunity Scams

Home-based business frauds and scams have been springing up all across the country.  If you suspect fraud in a home-based business opportunity, investigate the company through the Better Business Bureau, your state Attorney General's office, a consumer affairs agency, or the U.S. Government's Postal Inspection Service (if fraud is conducted through the mail).

Some business opportunities to avoid include:

- Chain letters
- Multilevel marketing
- Free seminar scams
- "Get paid for reading books"
- Vacation and free gift scams
- Envelope stuffing
- "Make money at home" ads
- Distributorship fraud
- Developing mailing lists
- Home assembly programs

### Advantages and Disadvantages

Is your home the best place to locate your business? As usual, there are advantages and disadvantages.

*Potential advantages*
- Flexibility in scheduling personal and work obligations
- Independence
- Lower start-up costs, less overhead, money saved on parking and lunches
- Tax breaks
- Home-based businesses can have a positive effect on the community

*Potential disadvantages*
- Feelings of isolation are common for home-based business owners
- Operating a home-based business can cause loss of privacy for family members
- The home-based business may have an uphill battle in gaining credibility
- Zoning restrictions may be a problem in some communities
- Work may be interrupted by family, friends, and neighbors
- Space may be limited when setting up a home office

## Types of Home-Based Businesses

According to recent information, there are over 200 different types of home-based business. *Entrepreneur Magazine* notes that the following 10 businesses are currently the fastest-growing:

- Bill auditing services
- Computer tutor and trainer
- Real estate appraiser
- Management consultant
- Public relations specialist
- Business plan writer
- Desktop publishing
- Export agent
- Janitorial and cleaning services
- Bookkeeping service

Here are some areas in which there may be future growth:

- Cleaning services
- Computer/E-commerce
- Executive search
- Management consultant
- Medical transcription service
- Paralegal
- Public relations specialist
- Temporary help service

### Setting Up a Functional Office

Understandably, home business working environments differ in relation to the type of business you run. Depending on your needs, you might furnish a home office with a simple folding table and chair, or with impressive office furniture and personal computers. However, it is important to set aside a specific work area. Consider the following questions:

- Where in the home will the office be located?
- What adjustments to living arrangement will be required?
- What are the start-up costs?
- How will your family react?
- Will customers ever come to your home office?
- Will household noise or activity pose problems?
- How convenient is the space for delivery of materials, or for a customer to enter and leave?

### Home-based office equipment

Here are some of the most common types of home-based office equipment:

- A separate business telephone line
- Answering machine or voice mail service

- Fax machine
- Personal computer and printer
- Computer modem
- Applicable computer software packages
- Photocopier or access to one
- Filing cabinets
- Miscellaneous supplies

A professional image is important

### Projecting a Professional Business Image

Developing a professional image is an important part of building credibility with your customers. What business image do you project? Factors to consider include:

- Your address—you may want a post office box instead of a rural address
- Business graphics—logo design, business card, letterhead, signs, etc.
- Telephone answering service, e-mail, fax
- Separate place of work and business entry
- Establish regular hours of work
- Prompt response to mail, phone, and e-mail messages
- Businesslike communications

## Legal, Tax and Insurance Issues

### Zoning

When considering a home business, you need to be familiar with the zoning laws in your neighborhood. Zoning laws vary from community to community, so contact your city hall and request the zoning ordinances for your area. The most common restrictions are:

- No onsite sales
- Space limitations/parking
- No deliveries
- No storage of inventory
- Restrictions on noise, hazardous waste, and odors
- No business signs
- Potential fire hazard
- No employees other than family members

In addition to local zoning, you must be aware of state and federal legislation on labor laws.

### Employee vs. Independent Contractor

People who offer their services to the general public are usually considered **independent contractors**. The most important characteristic of independent contractors is freedom from control and financial risks. If you plan to use independent contractors rather than employees, be sure to take the IRS test.

The IRS uses a list of 20 factors to determine whether a worker is a common law employee or an independent contractor. The state's Unemployment Insurance Liability Unit and the Division of Worker's Compensation use similar guidelines.

The general rule is that an individual is an independent contractor if the employer has the right to control or direct the result of the work, but not the means and methods of accomplishing that result. Independent contractors are hired to accomplish a particular job, and the relationship between the hiring party and the independent contractor is contractual.

## Taxes and Home-Based Business

The IRS is very exacting in its requirements for home businesses. Records must be meticulously kept.

What tax advantages are associated with a home business? In order to qualify for home business tax deductions, you must meet requirements outlined by the IRS. The part of your home for which you are claiming deductions must be used both exclusively and regularly as one or more of the following: 1) the principal place of business for any trade or business in which you engage; 2) a place to deal with your clients or customers in the normal course of your trade or business; and/or 3) a structure that is not attached to your house or residence and that is used in connection with your trade or business.

In any given year, deductions indirectly related to your business cannot exceed the gross earnings of the business. Indirect expenses include real estate taxes, mortgage interest, rent, utilities and services, insurance, repairs, and depreciation. The business portions of these expenses are deductible. You can only deduct a percentage of the home expenses equivalent to the square foot percentage of your home that your business occupies. Direct expenses that benefit only the business part of your home, such as painting or repairing your work area, are fully deductible.

The IRS publishes special guidelines and tax packages to assist the home-based business person in figuring his or her tax deductions. You may wish to hire an accountant to help you with your taxes.

## Home-Based Business Insurance Needs

Every type of business, in-home or not, requires insurance protection, yet many people starting home businesses fail to consider their insurance needs. A carefully planned insurance program is vital to the protection of your business and personal assets.

There are several types of insurance coverage that you should consider. Your business may not require all of the following forms of insurance, but it will probably require a few: Product Liability and Worker's Compensation; Burglary, Theft, and Robbery; Fire; Business Life; Credit; Fidelity Bonds and Security Bonds; and business use of home computers.

Check with the IRS on the 20-factor test

See IRS publication 587 on business use of your home

Home-based businesses need to check with an insurance agent or broker for pricing; shop around for services and price

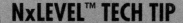

## NxLEVEL™ TECH TIP

**New Internet connections through ISDN (Integrated Services Digital Network), DSL (Digital Subscription Line), cable, and satellite offer speeds hundreds of times faster than even the fastest modem connections.**

ISDN and DSL use existing phone lines, and some residential areas are not zoned for connections of this type. To check the availability of ISDN and DSL in your area, call your local phone company and ask to speak to a representative who specializes in home business services. If you are not eligible for ISDN or DSL, don't despair; you may still be able to get a high-speed connection through your local cable or satellite companies. When dealing with these companies, bear in mind that unlike standard Internet service providers they usually have no competitors and therefore have no need to price their connection fees competitively. Also, since many people probably have cable service in your area, the connection speed offered by a cable company may be lower in practice than the advertised rate. As the demand for high-speed connections increases, new options are likely to become available in your area, so you may want to avoid getting into a long-term contract with cable or satellite providers.

When organizing your business insurance program, make sure you:

- Define the different perils your business may face, and rank them according to the greatest risk of loss
- Cover your largest risk first
- Shop around for the best, most cost-effective coverage
- Avoid duplicate coverage
- Periodically review your insurance program; coverage needs may change

Since insurance coverage is an important and complex matter, you should work closely with an insurance broker. See Chapter 26 *Managing Risk* for more information.

## Managing a Home-Based Business

To run a successful business you need to manage time, money, and people. The more efficiently you run your business, the greater its chances for success.

Here are some ways to create a professional home-based business:

- Establish and follow regular work hours
- Make business calls during normal work hours
- Treat interruptions as if you were working at a job outside the home
- Educate family, friends, and neighbors about your business

- Get out of the house at least once a day
- Keep up your contacts with trade and professional associations

Does starting a home-based business mean leading a life of loneliness and isolation? Not necessarily, if you follow a few basic tips:

- Have lots of work; loneliness is rarely a problem when you're busy with clients
- Don't procrastinate; force yourself to begin whatever task you're avoiding
- Become active in your related professional organization; stay abreast of changes in your profession; become better known among your peers
- Join a formal networking group; your local Chamber of Commerce or similar networking groups offer regular networking sessions and business seminars
- Start an informal support group; meet with other home-based business owners to discuss common business issues
- Take a course; learn a computer program or become certified in your industry
- Find a telephone buddy; connect with somebody who cares about you and who will welcome your calls to chat, complain, or brag
- Use the Internet to connect electronically with people
- Schedule regular social activities; plan a weekly breakfast with a friend or an exercise class at the gym
- Get to know your service providers by chatting with your suppliers, delivery person, or bank teller
- Give back to your community by volunteering

Creating contacts outside your home office will increase your business associates, and the networking opportunities may increase your bottom line! **Networking** business-to-business is one of the most important ways of marketing your home business. A network is a system of supportive people who are interested in one another and willing to help each other succeed. Your involvement in even one established home-based business network could mean the difference between success and failure.

## Conclusion

Home-based businesses have led many entrepreneurs to new freedom and prosperity. As a home-based business person, you can overcome feelings of isolation—and give and receive valuable information—by joining networks and being active in professional and trade associations. This will also build a marketing network for your service or product. You should continually evaluate which organizations and resources best serve your business information and networking needs.

Use the Internet and a telephone buddy to stay in touch

# Chapter 10
# FAMILY-OWNED BUSINESS

*About This Chapter:*
- *Family business today*
- *Family and business systems*
- *Managing by communicating*
- *Preparing for succession*

## Introduction

Family-owned businesses face unique problems that arise from overlapping family roles and work relationships. For this reason, many family business owners have professionalized their management practices by adopting policies that maintain clear boundaries between family and business systems. These policies include formal plans for training the younger generation; rules of entry, advancement, and exit that apply to all family members equally; and a willingness on the senior member's part to discuss company policies and succession plans candidly. In addition, business owners often consult outside advisors to get an independent, objective assessment of strategies and succession plans.

To build the strongest possible foundation for this new professionalism in family-owned businesses, owners and employees must learn the basic principles of MBC—managing by communicating.

## Family Business Today

A **family business** is one in which two or more family members have a substantial ownership interest and, in most cases, also participate in senior management. In most family enterprises, ownership is closely held and concentrated within the family.

Family businesses now employ more than half of the nation's work force. They account for 80% to 90% of all commercial enterprises in the United States, and are growing at a time when many large, publicly held corporations have been downsizing and restructuring. They account for more than 50% of U.S. gross domestic product (GDP), and constitute a third of all companies listed on the New York Stock Exchange. Some family-owned enterprises are not only quite large, but are well known to the public (e.g., Coors, Anheuser-Busch, and Bechtel).

### Professionalization: The Key to Family Business Survival

In today's increasingly competitive climate, success and survival require a professional management culture. Statistically, less than one-third of family businesses survive through the second generation, and fewer than one in ten last through the third

Family businesses account for more than 50% of U.S. gross domestic product (GDP), and constitute a third of all companies listed on the New York Stock Exchange

generation. The average life span of a family business is just 24 years. Bad economic conditions and poor business judgment explain some of these failures, but the major cause is an inability to develop a competent business succession plan. There appear to be four reasons for this:

- It's tough for senior family members to address their own aging and mortality
- Many seniors worry that the younger generation's way of running things won't be as good as their way
- Many seniors are concerned about their own long-term financial security, which sometimes causes them to postpone transferring control until it is too late
- Many are too personally tied to the business and lack other interests that would satisfy their need for fulfillment after retirement

Less than one-third of family businesses survive through a second generation

## Family and Business Systems

Family businesses are unique in that they represent the merger of two distinct and sometimes incompatible systems. As the story below demonstrates, the business system can easily become entangled with, and confused by, the family system.

———————◆———————

*Two brothers worked in a retail clothing business with their mother. Their sibling rivalry, which began in childhood, soon spilled over into the business. Although Mom held the position of president, she often found herself saddled with the added role of "chief emotional officer" when called upon to referee fights between the two brothers. The brothers' continuing childhood rivalry and their mother's need to intervene was inappropriate for the business. The solution? Mom placed the brothers in jobs where neither reports to the other. This helped to insulate the business from conflicts that developed much earlier in the family setting.*

———————◆———————

In a family-owned business, decisions can be guided not only by the goals of the business but by the expectations of the family. Sometimes this makes very good sense: a parent may naturally want his or her child to manage the business, even though a more qualified non-family member is available. Unfortunately, integrating the demands of both systems in ways that lead to satisfactory outcomes for both can be stressful.

The owner's offspring also have to grapple with the ambiguity of overlapping roles, as the following example shows.

One-tenth of family businesses survive through a third generation

———————◆———————

*Dad feels that his newly married daughter has done a good job on a research assignment for the business and decides to reward her with a bonus. He tells his daughter not just that she did a good job, but that she could probably use some extra cash, having just started a family of her own. The daughter may wonder whether she got a gift from Dad or a bonus from her boss.*

———————◆———————

Why do overlapping roles pose a problem?  In the family, fairness may require equal treatment of children without regard for performance; in business, reward is traditionally based on performance alone.  The family is characterized by strong emotional feelings having a long and complex history; rationality and objective judgment are applauded in business.  The family is based on love, while business relations are based on respect, which in turn depends on performance.

Integrating the expectations of the two systems is one of the most difficult tasks the family business leader must perform.  It requires competence in managing relationships, and then properly communicating expectations about those relationships to family members, especially where family and business roles overlap.  Although all family members share responsibility in this task, it is up to the leader to define the boundaries between the two systems.

### Establishing the Boundaries

Members of a family business are likely to disagree on the extent to which family interests should be allowed to intrude into the business.

*Mom feels that all her children should have equal ownership of the family business whether they have worked actively in the business or not, but Dad feels very differently.  A way must be found to reconcile the two contrasting views of fairness.  Perhaps the children who are active in the business can be given more ownership, while the other children receive help with education, or the capital needed to launch businesses of their own.  Or the active children might receive voting stock, while the inactive children get non-voting stock.  There are many ways to solve such problems, if communication between family members is frank.*

Family members must also work to prevent entrenched family expectations from entering the workplace.  For example, if the family has a history of dismissing Junior's ideas around the kitchen table—because age and experience are all that count when debating ideas at home—his good business ideas may be dismissed just as arbitrarily around the conference table.  When this happens, he is apt to question his value to the business and may decide to leave.

### Expectations for Performance

In well-functioning family businesses, family members are held to higher standards than non-family workers because of the **stewardship obligation** that comes with ownership.  Although this is usually an unspoken principle, it is intuitively understood by family and non-family employees alike, and is one of the unique strengths of a family-owned business.

Employee morale can suffer if family members are hired and promoted without meeting or exceeding the skill and education required of non-family employees applying for similar positions. A child who receives favored treatment may find that non-family employees are less likely to take him or her seriously. Many family businesses deal with this problem by encouraging younger family members to work elsewhere before entering the family business. (Sometimes this becomes a formal policy called a **rule of entry**.) After building a solid track record working for somebody else, they are able to enter the family business with more credibility.

It's a good idea to create and communicate rules of entry and exit as early as possible, so family members know that the rules are are fair and exist to ensure the well-being of the business. For example, if family members who leave the business know that they must sell back their stock, or that a college degree is a prerequisite for entering management, everyone knows the score in advance, reducing the likelihood of conflict.

## Managing by Communicating

Successful management of a family business depends on how well the younger and older members manage their communications within the family, within the business, and with non-family employees. Precisely because the leader of the business exercises ultimate authority, he or she must be a good listener so that all perspectives get a hearing when important issues arise. It all boils down to "MBC"—Managing By Communicating.

### Conflict Must Be Dealt With, Not Avoided

The expression of conflict is healthy. Avoidance of conflict can harm both the family and the business. Good MBC requires candid discussion of disagreements. If Dad fails to deliver an objectively negative assessment of his son's lackluster work performance because he doesn't want to hurt his child's feelings, the son won't be able to grow in the business.

## Planning for Succession

When the time comes to work out a formal **succession plan**, it will go smoothly only if family relationships have been managed properly during the early years, long before the attorneys and financial planners are called in to hammer out the details. If you are a senior family member and have ownership, you have a duty to initiate this planning. Make sure that family members participate, and that the next generation has been adequately prepared for senior management positions. All family members and non-family employees should be told the rationale for the choice of the successor.

The founder and other members of the senior generation need to understand that they have to pass the baton of leadership at some point, even though they may be reluctant to retire and let go of their "baby." Because so many owners have spent most of their lives building their businesses, letting go isn't always easy—especially if they really enjoy their work! Also, most of them know that their kids won't run the business the same way they did. And for many, "not the same" means "not as well."

It may not be pleasant to address one's own aging and mortality, but to transfer a family business from one generation to the next, thorough planning is essential.

## Planning for Financial Security

Seniors who depend on the success of the business for their post-retirement livelihood need a plan that provides the necessary safeguards for themselves, while giving the younger generation sufficient operational control over the business. Some retiring owners do this by maintaining control at the board level, transferring their voting shares to children in the business over a period of years. In other cases, the seniors may receive preferred stock with fixed dividends, or retain company real estate with a long-term lease to the company.

## Planning for Life Outside the Business

Planning for the post-management years should be just as important to retiring seniors as their financial planning. The succession is more apt to go smoothly when seniors have something useful to occupy themselves with after leaving the business. Before retirement, they should cultivate outside interests, and experiment with different hobbies and activities. Those who do not wish to exit the company completely may choose to stay on as an advisor or consultant, while others may launch a new career altogether. If the family has created a charitable foundation, involvement in philanthropy is an option.

*Senior family members must prepare for a new chapter in their lives*

## Whose Job Is It to Plan the Management Succession?

A succession plan is not something that owners can simply turn over to their attorneys, accountants, and financial planners. Although these specialists are certainly needed, the plan deserves the owner's serious attention. Family members and key non-family employees should be involved as well.

The children especially should be consulted about the plan. When the owner neglects to include members of the younger generation in this planning, he or she risks having the business controlled "from the grave." Successors then have very little choice but to accept the business as it was left to them. Indeed, the parents may find that they left the business in the hands of a child who—even in his or her own eyes—was neither the most motivated nor the most capable candidate for leadership.

By incorporating the younger generation's ideas into the final plan, the owner can rest more easily, knowing that the responsibility for the future of the business has been shared.

**NxLEVEL™ TECH TIP**

Here are a couple of Internet resources geared specifically to family businesses:

Check **http://www.fambiz.com** for over 300 articles on family business issues, many of which are also pertinent to more general entrepreneurial concerns. This site also has many links to other family business Web sites, and extensive news archives.

**Family Business** magazine is online at http://www.fambuspub.com. This site includes a bookstore and family business planning tips, as well as articles from the magazine's current issue.

Outside advisors can lend an objective view

### How Outside Advisors Can Help

Outside advisors and consultants can provide an objective judgment regarding the skills and experience successors will need, given the company's future direction. Because outside advisors and experts stand apart from both the business and family systems, they are not entangled in the emotional tugging and pulling that often goes on within the family. They are less apt to play favorites, and for that reason can help ensure adequate representation of divergent interests. In contrast, family members usually have vested interests to protect, which may conflict when it comes to determining the successor.

Another advantage of involving outside advisors is that parents are spared the painful dilemma of having to choose the successor from among several children. An objective judgment from non-family advisors may lessen the disappointment of those who are passed over for succession, which means that family relationships are less likely to suffer damage.

If you decide to establish a board of advisors made up of experienced individuals who provide occasional advice—but lack the authority and legal responsibilities they would have as directors—you must be certain you receive unbiased, objective opinions. As regards succession planning, advisors should have no stake in the outcome. Vendors, customers, professional service providers, consultants, employees, members of the board of directors, and relatives (unless they are principals) should not be included on a board of advisors.

Above all, your advisory group should focus on the long-term interests of the company. If you decide that compelling family needs come first—which could mean having to make sacrifices in the business—you will at least have had the independent views of unbiased outsiders to aid in this decision.

## Prepare the Younger Generation

For most members of the younger generation, preparation for a new leadership role requires the acquisition of more knowledge, skills, and experience. They need to be given the opportunity to learn, which also means learning from mistakes; allowing them to make mistakes is good for the business because it's the only way they can gain business judgment. Owners can give their children increasing amounts of authority over a period of time. With each accomplishment, more authority should be granted.

Younger members of the family need not stand idly by, waiting for new responsibilities to be thrust upon them; instead, they should actively seek new responsibilities whenever possible. This does not mean getting involved in a power struggle or an internal revolt. Rather, younger members should make their case for taking charge by bringing forth a careful plan for change, backed up by innovative ideas and compelling arguments.

There is an important difference between giving members of the younger generation more authority and responsibility because they insist on it, and giving it based on demonstrable achievement. Still, when in doubt, it's better to err in the direction of giving too much control rather than too little. This means that the senior generation must feel comfortable with relinquishing a reasonable amount of control before the succession occurs.

## Develop New Designs for Succession

Owners are coming to understand the advantages of innovative new designs for succession. For example, passing the business to the eldest child, which had been the prevailing succession pattern, is no longer an automatic decision. One solution that has worked for a number of companies is to hire an interim CEO—an experienced non-family outsider—to run the company and mentor younger family members until they are ready to take control.

The "president for life" pattern of tenure that characterized most family businesses in the past is also changing. Some owners decide that they are ready for a change well before the normal retirement age. In most organizations today, the average tenure in a managerial job is four to seven years. While this is not true of every family business owner, it is becoming an increasingly popular option. Of course, this means that the senior generation should be working on a succession plan and preparing the next generation sooner rather than later.

*The younger generation must acquire knowledge, skills, and experience*

What happens if the evaluation of two or more children who are active in management turns out to be a toss-up—just too close to call? Both may be equally eager to run the business, and both may be equally qualified. Although the rule against having a divided leadership is standard wisdom in mainline organizational practice, co-successor strategies—often called "co-presidencies"— sometimes work out well. One of the successors gets the title and responsibilities of chief executive officer (CEO), while the other assumes the duties of president. In other cases, several family members constitute the "office of the president," all sharing equally in the exercise of control.

How well this works out depends on how well the individuals get along; sibling rivalries, for instance, may preclude this type of arrangement. Yet there are also many cases in which sisters, brothers, and cousins with a good work relationship based on love, trust, and mutual respect can easily work together as co-successors.

## 7 Steps to Success

### For members of the younger generation:

1) Learn about the business; spend time with your parents and other senior relatives to demonstrate your knowledge of and interest in the business.
2) Don't short-change your education. Focus on training for leadership; interact with challenging minds; use your imagination to compete for excellence.
3) Broaden your experience by working full-time for another company before joining the family business.
4) Get paid fairly. Resist the "golden handcuffs" that would tie you to your parent's business too early; take no more nor less than you are truly worth to the business. Develop good financial judgment in both business and personal finances.
5) Try to avoid reporting to your parents in their business until you've worked at lower levels, reporting to non-family managers who will evaluate you objectively. Your parents may not be able to provide objective appraisals of your work.

### For members of the older generation:

6) Set a strategic direction for the future of the business and match future leadership to it. Plan for the transfer of management and ownership. Accept that you have to pass the baton. Secure your own financial future. Think about a new role and the challenge that new pursuits can provide.
7) Run with your children while passing the baton, then let the next generation move ahead. It's time to watch the race, and root for the new team!

## Communicate the Succession Plan

Passing the baton from the older to the younger generation involves more than just the drafting of a formal succession plan. It begins much earlier, and involves both generations in a process of communication and learning as preparation for the eventual transfer of control. When the time for passing the baton finally arrives, you need to communicate the succession decision in the right way to your children, other relatives, and non-family managers. No matter how rational the plan, no matter how objective the

*Even the best plan will fail if it is communicated poorly*

candidate assessment process, some relatives and employees are apt to be disappointed. Here, too, MBC can make the difference between success and failure. Even though you have put the company in the right hands and have used the right estate planning tools, you must still communicate the decision in a way that will preserve goodwill among family members and non-family employees.

As hard as it seems, the successful perpetuation of a family business may well be the closest you come to immortality!

## Conclusion

All family members in the business, both the senior and the younger generation, share responsibility for creating a professional business environment. This requires balancing the expectations appropriate for family relationships and the criteria appropriate for business decisions. Success in this collaboration between seniors and the next generation will determine whether the current owners will be able to pass the baton to the next generation, and whether the younger members will be prepared to accept the baton and run with it. Above all, it is important that family members candidly discuss their concerns and decide how to set the boundaries between the two systems. If the family neglects to do this at an early stage, it risks real trouble later when a succession plan is under consideration. Communication is the key!

# Chapter 11
# EXPORT AND IMPORT

*About This Chapter:*
- *A word about international trade*
- *Evaluating potential export markets*
- *Becoming an exporter: logical steps*
- *Evaluating products and services for import*
- *Becoming an importer: logical steps*

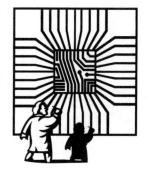

## Introduction

We are now living in the age of the global village. What does this mean for you? Opportunities! It means that in other countries, people just like you are looking for opportunities to import and export goods and services. Today, money and materials move at a faster rate than ever before. Many Americans have traveled overseas and seen products and services they think would sell quite well in the United States. Likewise, they have seen opportunities for the sale of U.S. products and services in other countries. Is the time right for you to explore opportunities around the globe? This chapter will help you decide whether you are ready to take on the challenges involved in international trade.

## A Word About International Trade

**International trade** is commerce between businesses from different nations. **Importing** is the purchase of goods or services from a party outside your political borders. **Exporting** is selling goods or services outside your political borders.

Why would you want to seek out international business when you have easier opportunities right here at home? Certainly, international business is more difficult, but many people involved in it enjoy overcoming the challenges of operating in an unfamiliar environment. By doing business in a foreign country, you will become an expert at foreign trade in your industry. Other companies who want to sell overseas may seek you out for advice, or to promote their goods along with your own.

The U.S. market has become a fertile ground for international commerce. In addition, English has become the accepted language of international business. Does this mean you will not have any problems doing business overseas? Well, not exactly. There are many obstacles to overcome when dealing with people of other cultural backgrounds. This means that you must do extensive research on the country, the industry, and the companies with which you plan to trade. You might consider another necessary tool of the trade: patience! Because of cultural barriers and varying levels of language proficiency, it takes more time to execute a deal. By being patient with international business partners, you will be more likely to develop lasting personal relationships, thus facilitating better business relationships.

### Cross-Border Payment

You might be thinking, "How do I know I'll get paid once the deal is done?" International finance has progressed right along with the movement of goods across borders. Investors seek out the most promising investment opportunities, based on a country's political and economic stability. As an example, European and Asian companies own interests in high-tech companies here in the United States. Part of the reason they invest here is that we have a politically and economically stable environment. How does their money get here? Huge amounts of capital move into and out of the United States with the push of a button. Cross-border payment—while complex—can be safely done through a competent financial institution. A banking partner can assist you with the financial aspects of import and export.

*Millions move from Miami to Milan in a millisecond*

### What About Tariffs?

One of the first issues you will encounter when you investigate worldwide markets is **tariffs** (taxes on imported or exported goods). The General Agreement on Tariffs and Trade (GATT), which is an international agreement to lower tariffs and trade barriers, has made international commerce easier. Although the majority of the world's countries subscribe to GATT, it has been difficult to get everyone involved in the treaty to agree. Each GATT conference has been a hotbed of complaints about unfair trading practices. This has led to an outcropping of trading blocs; these are regional agreements that allow for unrestricted trade between groups of countries, which are usually contiguous with one another (or at least geographically close).

Examples of trading blocs include the North American Free Trade Agreement (NAFTA), the European Community (EC), the Association of South East Asian Nations (ASEAN), and the Asia-Pacific Economic Conference (APEC), the last of which is planned for the year 2010. Within these trading blocs, tariffs—and sometimes border checks—have been reduced or eliminated, resulting in easier trading between member nations. With the tearing down of trade barriers and the formation of trading blocs, you can market your product to a group of countries by using one country as a hub. The World Trade Organization (WTO) carries on this work today.

### Challenges

In addition to tariffs, every country has non-tariff barriers (NTBs). NTBs can come in many forms, including language differences, excessive regulations, and quotas. Your ability to deal with these issues depends on how much you know about the foreign market in which you plan to operate. An inexperienced company might take one look at language and regulatory differences and decide that it's not worth the effort to sell to a foreign country, while more experienced companies can look at the same set of circumstances and see nothing but opportunities. The point is to have patience and persevere. If you go one step further than the next person, you may find that the extra step is all it takes for your product to gain acceptance in the market.

Foreign businesses differ in the way they value time, practice business, and treat their employees. For example, in many South American countries, businesses close during the hottest hours of the day. In other countries, such as Japan, formal rules of etiquette are an essential part of business dealings. You must pay close attention to the way in which business is conducted in other countries. The best way to do this is to visit the countries and companies with which you are considering doing business.

Another factor in doing business with a different country—especially those located across the Atlantic or Pacific—is the difference in time zones. A common problem experienced by employees working overseas for, or with, American firms is the lack of concern for a good night's rest. For example, if you get out of a meeting in your Denver office at 10 A.M., it's after midnight in Singapore. What do you do if you need to solve a problem right away? Sometimes, a situation just can't wait. However, in most cases a few extra hours will not do any harm on your side, and will mean much appreciated sleep for your employee or business partner in Singapore.

I'm sorry. Did I wake you?

Although English has become the language of choice in international communication, this does not necessarily mean that you can rely on it to carry you through an international business deal from beginning to end. Current thinking on this issue encourages those doing business abroad to obtain at least a basic understanding of common phrases in a given language. In addition, you might consider familiarizing yourself with the meaning of gestures and body language in the country with which you trade. You will more quickly pick up the nuances of gestures that your business partners make when they speak, and your conversation will go more smoothly. Your counterpart in the foreign business will appreciate your efforts to understand the basics of his or her language, culture, and history. Professional translators are available when you require in-depth negotiations.

---

*Annie Reilly has been running a specialty foods catalog company since 1977. In 1999, after a number of customers requested Thai food ingredients, she decided to offer these products. Before embarking on her venture, she asked several Thai restaurant owners who their suppliers were in the United States and Thailand. She investigated the etiquette of doing business with Thailand by attending a weekend seminar sponsored by her local university's MBA executive education department. Once Annie felt confident in her knowledge of both the business and culture of Thailand, she embarked on her mission. The addition of Thai spices and foods to her catalog was such a success that she is now looking to add other Asian foodstuffs in 2000!*

---

# Evaluating Potential Export Markets

One of the first steps when you form an export organization is to evaluate your market opportunities. If you plan to conduct your business on your own, you will have to think about the following factors:

- Which markets are large enough to justify a marketing effort?
- In which markets will your product most likely be accepted?
- Who is your competition, both foreign and domestic?
- What political and cultural factors could affect the success of your product?
- Are there any tariffs or non-tariff barriers to take into account?
- How will you price your product?
- What will your expected sales volume be?
- What additional costs will you incur?
- What would you expect your profit to be?

Answering these questions usually requires conducting extensive research on your targeted foreign markets.

Other methods include seeking the assistance of an export management company, or going through an export company (which we will describe in more detail later). No matter which avenue you take, you should know as much about the country and its markets as possible. This means researching the countries through such information resources as the National Trade Data Bank (NTDB), local and state international trade agencies, and international banks. Your local International Trade Administration (ITA) can offer valuable assistance, frequently at little or no cost.

## Measuring Competitiveness of Products and Services

How can you find out whether there is a demand for your product in a particular country, and how it measures up to the competition? Again, the ITA can provide you with valuable information. They have access to statistics by product and service category, and lists of manufacturers with whom you will be competing, or to whom you might sell your product.

In conducting your research, you should consider the following methods:

- **Historical information.** You should determine trends and seasonality.
- **Current environment.** By observing what has happened, or is expected to happen in the near future—such as tariff reductions or regulatory changes—you can ferret out niche opportunities for your products.
- **Market testing.** There are services available that evaluate your product against similar products in a given country's market. Many firms use this method to find out exactly where and when to initiate their marketing efforts.
- **Personal visits.** Before trading, it is imperative to visit your trading partners more than once. The personal insights you'll gain are invaluable.

Since you will be operating in an unfamiliar environment, market evaluation is a critical step in preparing to sell abroad. It will validate or alter your ideas, and may even steer you in a direction you had not anticipated.

## Product Modifications for Export

One of the major differences of doing business in foreign markets is the need to modify products for individual markets. Factors to consider include:

- Language changes to labeling and packaging
- Adjustments to product size
- Compliance with regulations
- Replacing the U.S. system of measurement with the metric system
- Different electrical standards
- Special transport requirements
- Local preferences such as color, texture, and graphics

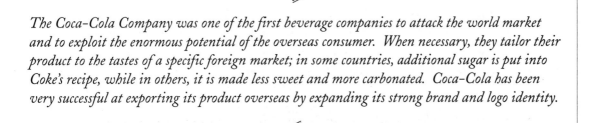

*The Coca-Cola Company was one of the first beverage companies to attack the world market and to exploit the enormous potential of the overseas consumer. When necessary, they tailor their product to the tastes of a specific foreign market; in some countries, additional sugar is put into Coke's recipe, while in others, it is made less sweet and more carbonated. Coca-Cola has been very successful at exporting its product overseas by expanding its strong brand and logo identity.*

Will you need to change or add to the language that appears on your product? You bet! Regulations in many countries require that you describe the contents of your product in the local language—frequently in excruciating detail! Some products sell well abroad primarily because of their trendy American lettering, but in most cases it's much easier to market a product with labeling and packaging printed in the local language.

Regarding transportation, most countries do not possess the capabilities you are used to in the United States. Loads will have to be broken down into smaller quantities and distributed by light rail, pickup truck, or hand cart. You might want to check on the capabilities of the freight carriers in the country to which you plan to ship and plan your shipment size accordingly.

## Are Other Countries Ready for Your Product?

There are a number of factors to consider regarding your product's viability in a given country's market, including:

- **Familiarity.** Are you entering an existing market, or will you have to promote a novel item or service?

- **Capacity.** Does the country to which you are selling have the infrastructure to support your product in terms of transportation, industrial need, or average home size?
- **Alternative uses.** How will the people of the country to which you are selling use your product? (For example, bicycles and satellite dishes are used in other countries in different ways; the former may be the primary means of transportation, and the latter may be used mainly for telephone communications rather than TV reception.)
- **Specifications.** Does your product meet safety codes?

By researching these factors and adjusting to them, you can maximize the foreign market's receptiveness to your product.

## Becoming an Exporter: Logical Steps

All U.S. companies interested in export should follow these basic steps when selling to other countries:

- Do market research
- Prepare a marketing plan
- Explore sales and distribution options
- Make sales
- Prepare your product for shipping
- Comply with documentation requirements
- Ship your product
- Manage risk
- Obtain payment

### The International Marketing Plan

Although many of the steps in preparing a domestic marketing plan apply to the international plan, there are significant differences. The international marketing plan steps are listed here:

- **Evaluate your export market alternatives.** In which country are you most likely to succeed? What are the population demographics of that country?
- **Distribution options.** How will you ship the product? Who will market and distribute your product once it gets there? What are the advantages and disadvantages of direct marketing, or of going through an importer?
- **Competitors.** Who are they? How will they react to your efforts? Might you be able to work with them to sell your product? Is there room for you in the market?

An international marketing plan Is essential!

- **Pricing.** How will you price your product? How will duties and non-tariff trade barriers (such as regulations affecting customs clearance) affect the price? Will your product still be priced competitively once it gets through all of the layers of distribution?
- **Promotion.** How will you promote your product? Is the channel that you are using the most efficient? What about advertising? How can you assist your sales representatives, through incentives, to promote your product most effectively?

Your international marketing plan will serve as your road map to success. The components of your plan are not fixed in stone, however. If you work with your representative to explore your options in each area, and weigh the benefits against the costs involved, you can achieve the flexibility necessary to adapt to the unique challenges of exporting.

## International Sales and Distribution Options

How do you get your product to your foreign customers? There are several possibilities:

### Direct marketing

Direct marketing can range from selling directly to the consumer through a foreign office, Web site, or a catalogue; to establishing a relationship with an import company in a given country. The advantages of direct marketing include retaining control of the product, and a higher share of the profits. However, this is the most expensive option, since you must support a full-time direct marketing staff and assume all of the marketing costs.

### Distributors and agents

Distributors and agents differ in one important way: a distributor takes title to your goods, but an agent does not. Using a **distributor** means that you will lose control of the product and gain the least in terms of profits. The advantage of this method is that the distributor is building business you would not be able to create yourself.

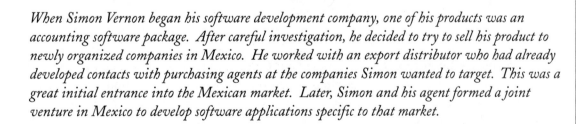

*When Simon Vernon began his software development company, one of his products was an accounting software package. After careful investigation, he decided to try to sell his product to newly organized companies in Mexico. He worked with an export distributor who had already developed contacts with purchasing agents at the companies Simon wanted to target. This was a great initial entrance into the Mexican market. Later, Simon and his agent formed a joint venture in Mexico to develop software applications specific to that market.*

**Export agents** promote your goods or services and receive a fee for their work, usually on a commission basis. This allows you to retain control over your goods and avoid paying an in-house export staff. However, the commission does cut into your profits.

### Partners and strategic alliances

Many overseas companies are looking for quality product lines and services to complement their current offerings. This is particularly important for service businesses. Two examples of strategic alliances are high-tech foreign companies investing in high-tech firms in Silicon Valley, and American consulting companies forging relationships with firms abroad. You can also approach other companies in your industry, either in the United States or in other countries, to explore export alternatives.

### Other export organizations

Two other types of export company deserve mention: **export management companies** (EMCs), and **repackagers**. An export management company is a hybrid between an agent and an in-house export staff. They work on a salary or commission basis to promote your product through their office. EMCs are useful when you desire maximum control over your product, but do not want to support an in-house staff. They can be very expensive in the long run, but may be worthwhile as a market entry strategy. Repackagers find markets for and sell domestically produced goods in other countries. They buy your products (which are usually not ready for export) and repackage them to meet the requirements of the target country. EMCs and repackagers are usually listed in the yellow pages, or in local trade directories in port cities.

## A Word About Making It Legal

When you develop an agreement with an individual or a company to export your goods, make sure the agreement is in writing! This protects you from infringement on intellectual property rights and other problems that can occur during cross-border trading. It is also wise to patent your goods in the countries to which you plan to sell. This will give you the most security possible against somebody else stealing your idea!

## Shipping and Documentation

The first time you export your goods, you might be amazed at the documentation required. Do not be alarmed! These procedures apply to all parties involved in export. Rest assured that this process does get easier as time goes by.

Better yet, have a **freight forwarder** handle your export shipping and documentation. Freight forwarders are experts in handling export documentation and shipping needs; using them will allow you to focus on what you do best, instead of tending to bales of incomprehensible paperwork. These companies can be found in the yellow pages of most major cities.

Protect your intellectual property rights with foreign patents

## Bill of Lading

A **bill of lading** is a shipping contract outlining the terms of the shipping agreement and the means by which the goods are shipped. When you receive a copy of the bill of lading depends on whether the freight is paid in advance or not. In the latter case, you receive a copy after delivery of the goods.

## Customs and Duties

The customs process and the duties you might have to pay are two very important factors in the export of goods. **Duties** are import taxes based on a preset tariff rate. These issues are interrelated (duties depend on the declared value of your goods and, in some cases, the freight and insurance costs), so an explanation of the customs process will offer insight on what to expect in terms of duties.

Be very careful not to make any mistakes in the documentation that accompanies your goods. A mistake in the date, port of origin, port of entry, or any other part of the forms can mean delays in shipment and unnecessary expenses. Make sure that your customer has access to the following documentation—free of errors—upon the arrival of your goods:

- Entry documents
- Letter of credit
- Commercial or pro forma invoices
- Bill of lading
- Packing lists
- Evidence of the (insurance) bond

---

*An entrepreneur in California mistakenly dated his shipment to arrive one year after the actual date. He was dismayed to find out that customs in Japan wouldn't clear his container load of chicory for an entire year! He had to fly to Tokyo to take care of the customs problem personally, which cost him all the profit he expected to make on the transaction!*

---

In addition, duties may be assessed on a number of different charges incurred through the trade. Be sure to provide information on any fees that have accrued between you, the seller, and your buyer. Some examples include:

- Packing costs
- Sales commissions
- Licensing or related fees
- Amount of sale

Providing your buyer with all documents and information related to the trade greatly reduces the chance that customs will hold up the transaction.

## Managing Risk

When you conduct business outside the United States, there are additional risks involved. The first issue to consider is whether your trading partner will follow through on the deal. You can alleviate some of this risk by going to see your customers, and by inviting them to visit you. This is very helpful in establishing a lasting relationship.

*Risk management is a critical component of international trade*

Also, you might take into account transportation and insurance. There are many transportation alternatives available. A competent insurance company can offer comprehensive coverage on your goods so that you can eliminate the risk if the goods are damaged, stolen, or lost.

A consideration unique to international trade is **currency fluctuation**. If you have the financial resources, you can hedge this problem through investment in currencies equal to the amount of your order; this is an effective way to balance out the risks of investing in goods headed to a foreign port. Another way to eliminate risk is to demand payment in U.S. dollars; this is a common practice of companies that do not wish to or cannot afford to hedge.

Political risk is yet another concern. Some countries have an unfavorable business environment due to political instability or unfriendliness toward American interests. "War risk" can be insured against through a blanket insurance policy with your freight forwarder. The U.S. Department of State can provide invaluable information on the status of the country with which you plan to do business.

---

*One unlucky entrepreneur who exported hand tools to Nigeria got caught in the middle of a civil uprising! His shipments were stolen by thieves posing as custom officials. He was unable to trace the disappearing shipments due to the breakdown in governmental control over the country. If he had read the U.S. Department of State's report prior to entering the Nigerian market, he would have been warned that civil strife was imminent!*

---

## Getting Paid

Financial organizations around the world have established ways to facilitate payment for goods or services traded between countries. The safest way to conduct business with a foreign buyer is to build a relationship with a bank in the foreign country. They provide a valuable link in the trading process by dealing with your customer's bank and arranging for payment upon receipt of the goods or services. The following list introduces the terms with which you must be familiar when arranging for international payment:

*Build a relationship with a foreign bank*

- **Irrevocable Letter of Credit (L/C).** This is a contract for payment arranged by your bank and your foreign customer's bank. Always make sure that your letter of credit is irrevocable!

- **Bill of Exchange.** This is a financial instrument that is used to pay you through your bank from a foreign bank.
- **Bill of Exchange—Bankers Acceptance.** This is a demand for payment from your bank to your foreign client's bank based on the L/C.
- **Documents Against Payment.** These documents are required in order to obtain payment on an international trade.
- **Cash Against Documents.** The payment, based on the letter of credit, that your customer makes through his or her bank to your bank.
- **Documents Against Acceptance.** The process of checking the original letter of credit against the documentation that your client provides after receiving the goods.

Your bank and freight forwarder will know a great deal about these documents. You should work with them to ensure that you do not miss a step in setting up a letter of credit or obtaining any other form of payment.

## Methods of Payment

Methods of payment are described below, along with their advantages and disadvantages for you and your customers.

- **Cash in advance.** This is the most favorable means of payment for you. Payment is made in advance of shipment, and there is no risk to you. This is not a standard method of payment in international trade, and is usually used only when circumstances make any other form of payment impossible or very risky (such as for a foreign client with an open account who has neglected to pay previous bills). Your customer is completely dependent upon you to ship the goods in the manner to which you agreed.
- **Sight Letter of Credit (L/C).** This type of payment is made when the goods are shipped. The only risk you face with this type of payment is the possibility of the order's cancellation. Your customer is assured of receiving the shipment, but is still dependent upon you to ship the goods in the manner to which you agreed.
- **Time Letter of Credit (L/C).** Under this mode, payment is made after the goods are received, regardless of the condition of the goods. There is little risk involved for you when you use this mode of payment. Your customer does not have the security that damage to the goods can be reconciled with you.
- **Sight Draft for Collection.** In this case, your customer does not pay for the goods until they are seen, and can refuse to pay if the goods are not satisfactory.
- **Time Draft for Collection.** This type of payment is made after your customer has received the goods. Your risk comes from the fact that your customer has possession of the goods before making payment.

- **Open Account.** This is similar to the method used for domestic payment. There is no risk to your client. This method might be used when your customer has a long-standing, stable relationship with you.

## Evaluating Products and Services for Import

Many of the topics discussed in the export section of this chapter can be applied to the context of import, simply by thinking of export in reverse.

In finding products or services for import, you need to examine your alternatives based on the following criteria:

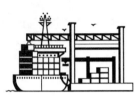

- **Quality.** Does the product or service meet your minimum requirements?
- **Price.** Is it low enough to justify sourcing a foreign firm?
- **Quantity.** Does your vendor have the manufacturing or labor capacity to fill your order on a continuous basis?
- **Familiarity.** Do you know about your vendor's culture, and do you feel comfortable operating in that environment?
- **Language.** If you are not fluent in their language, do they have a competent English-speaking staff?
- **Terms.** Will they agree to your shipping and payment terms?
- **U.S. tariffs.** Are there U.S. tariffs on the products you are importing? If so, do they apply only to imports from certain countries?
- **Political stability.** Will changes in the foreign government affect your business?
- **Distribution.** How many hands will the goods pass through before they leave the country? Can your price be lowered by importing more directly?
- **Dependability.** How dependable are your trading partners? Will they fulfill their commitments?

If you consider these issues in your search for a foreign supplier, you will be better able to choose the right vendor. It is no coincidence that quality is listed first; the most common problem with foreign products or services—and the most difficult to solve—is poor quality. Visit your potential overseas vendors several times to check on their capabilities and background!

## Becoming an Importer: Logical Steps

Take the following steps before you choose a foreign supplier:

- Perform a vendor search
- Evaluate quality and delivery
- Do market research on potential domestic buyers, or benefits associated with materials substitution
- Prepare a marketing plan
- Make sales

- Manage risk
- Anticipate payment requirements to your foreign vendor

These issues are discussed in the following paragraphs.

## The International Marketing Plan

You must consider your opportunities within the United States when you are establishing your import marketing plan. These considerations include:

- **Market demand.** Is there a demand for the product or service that you plan to import? Will importing give you an advantage over your competitors?
- **Market location.** Where is your market? What distribution channels will you use? Is the U.S. port of entry strategically located so that in-country transport is minimized? Will you be able to ship the goods directly from the port of entry?
- **Price.** How does the price of your imported good or service compare to its domestic counterparts? Is the price savings large enough to justify sourcing a foreign vendor over a domestic supplier?
- **Promotional considerations.** How will you market your imported goods or services? What particular markets will you target? Does the product or service deserve broad-based advertising or specific promotion?

Your plan should take into account the challenges you will meet while promoting your imported product or service, and should be flexible enough to allow you to adapt to unexpected obstacles—such as competitors' price-cutting.

## International Sales and Distribution Options

What form will your import business take? There are many possibilities:

### Direct

Direct marketing means that you are the first source to whom a foreign supplier sells, and that you will resell directly to the end user. The advantage of this method is that you retain the highest share of the profits from your domestic marketing efforts. The disadvantage is that your marketing costs can be much higher, since you are responsible for marketing the imported product or service to the end user.

### Being a distributor and agent

Perhaps you are debating whether you should become an import agent or an import distributor for an overseas company. For example, you might consider importing hot chili peppers from Mexico as an import agent. In this case, your role is to seek out customers for the peppers here in the United States. What will you do to research the U.S. market, make sales, and arrange the deal? How will you get paid? In most cases, agents receive a commission on the sales they produce.

As a distributor, your responsibilities extend beyond marketing. If you were importing sardines from Norway as a distributor, you would arrange for the purchase of the sardines—including all customs, insurance, and freight requirements. You actually take title to the goods, so the business risk transfers to you sometime after the goods have left your foreign vendor's facility (the exact time depends on the terms of sale). Acting as an import distributor involves more risk than acting as an agent, but the rewards can be greater. Once you take title to the goods, you set the sale price.

*Partnering and strategic alliances*
Many foreign companies hope to expand their business to the U.S. market through an American company.

## NxLEVEL™ TECH TIP

If you're not ready to invest in a connected organizer like the PalmPilot and you're sick of bulky paper organizers, you can keep track of contacts and appointments with free Web-based calendar services like those offered by **When.com** (http://www.when.com) or **MagicalDesk.com** (http://www.magicaldesk.com). These sites allow you to access files, consult your address book, and schedule appointments from any computer with Web access.

IBM's International PC Card Modem with GSM allows you to access your network and e-mail from 70 countries via a cellular connection or a standard phone line.

A new breed of digital, handheld translators with swappable language cards is now available, and may be useful to those who do business in foreign countries. Thanks to their "virtual keyboard," these translating devices even let you type in different alphabets! There are also free computerized translation services on the Internet that may help you to decipher messages written in a foreign language. However, bear in mind that no computer can be programmed to deal with the infinite number of sentences that can be spoken or written; they cannot understand what words mean, so they often transform straightforward sentences into gibberish, making grammatical mistakes that would be impossible for a two-year-old child! That's why it's essential to seek out the services of a human translator for important documents such as instruction booklets or business proposals. There are many such translation services online, specializing in just about every language under the sun; it's a good idea to test their accuracy by having a sample of their work carefully compared to your original by someone competent in both languages. Incidentally, the prevalence of jargon in the business world may cause additional problems for the international entrepreneur. When writing documents for translation, bear in mind that certain "buzzwords" and phrases—however common in our country—may translate unintelligibly! (If you're not careful, your mission statement may be interpreted as a "church invoice"!)

---

*An Australian training firm recently developed a program that teaches accountants how to market their services to individual clients. Their market research led them to the United States. The Australians partnered with a series of American professional training organizations, which had American CPA firms as their clients. The advantage for the Australians was the ability to establish their U.S. training program quickly. The advantage for the American professional training organizations was the commission received from the Australian training firm.*

---

### Other import considerations

The issues of shipping, documentation, customs, duties, and managing risk are all very similar to those addressed in the section on exporting. A **customs broker** can assist you with these concerns to ensure that your business deal goes smoothly. Your primary concern as an importer is to develop your market at home; provided you achieve sales targets, your overseas partner will likely be satisfied with your performance.

### Getting Paid

Paying your vendor through proper international banking channels requires keeping track of all necessary documentation. If you become an import agent, or work on any other kind of commission basis, you must keep tabs on all of the transactions taking place between the overseas company you represent and the domestic companies that purchase the goods.

## Conclusion

To succeed in an import or export business, you need an effective marketing plan. If you are planning to export goods or services, pay attention to the special cultural needs of your foreign markets. If you are planning to import, closely examine your market in the United States to increase the chance that your product or service will be a success. International trade is an exciting and rewarding field, so get ready and go global!

# PART III
# PLANNING YOUR BUSINESS

## Chapter 12
## WHAT IS BUSINESS PLANNING?

*About This Chapter:*
- *Importance of planning*
- *Defining the business concept*
- *When to plan*
- *Who does the planning?*
- *Feasibility studies*

## Introduction

Planning is the process of preparing your business for the future. The planning process is the subject of this chapter; subsequent chapters will focus on the results of this process. Although planning may sound like an academic exercise best suited to large corporations, the classroom, or consultants, small businesses are inevitably more affected than their larger competitors by changes in the economy. It is this fragility that makes planning so important for your business.

## Importance of Planning

Let's take a look at the benefits associated with the planning process.

Planning is a dynamic process

### A Look at the Whole Business

The planning processes described in this chapter require you to evaluate your entire business. Daily decision-making often focuses on solving a series of individual problems that may not seem to be connected. Planning helps you to discover the underlying causes of these recurring problems. It also helps you to identify overlooked business opportunities.

### A Guide for Daily Decision-Making

Small business owners are often frustrated that their employees don't make the right decisions when solving problems. A business plan guides each employee's daily actions. (This assumes that your employees are involved in the planning process or, at the very least, receive training about the parts of the plan that affect them.)

### Useful Communication Tools

The business plan puts useful information in writing, which can then be communicated to employees, investors, creditors, and other interested parties. The major problem with keeping your business plan in your head is the difficulty of communicating your plan to others.

### Increased Chance of Success

The business world is becoming increasingly competitive, so small businesses must find a well-defined market niche. Furthermore, they must service their market in a customer-oriented and cost-effective manner. The planning process forces you to address these issues, which means your business has a better chance of being successful.

### Future Business Opportunities

The products, services, and delivery systems offered by small businesses change constantly. Change always presents opportunities to the prepared business owner, and planning is a systematic way to identify these opportunities.

### Feedback Results in Improvement

The written plan is not the end of the planning process; in fact, the process is continuous. The ongoing comparison of planned to actual results provides a terrific opportunity to improve business operations.

### Action, Not Reaction

Small business owners often talk about suffering from "burnout," or feeling like a firefighter responding to the latest emergency. A business plan is analogous to a good fire prevention plan. Fires still occur, but not as often, and the best method of response has been pre-determined.

### Key Questions

The process helps you sort through hundreds of concerns about your business and focus on the handful that cause the majority of your problems. This is called the 80/20 rule: "In any organization, 80% of the problems can be solved by focusing on 20% of the underlying causes (customers/suppliers/employees/policies). Similarly, 80% of the opportunities result from 20% of your customers/suppliers/employees/policies."

## Defining the Business Concept

Every business is unique. For example, your business faces challenges different from those of your competitors or other types of businesses in your community. Planning helps you to define the factors that make your business unique.

Although you may be eager to start planning for a successful future, there are some questions to answer first. As you work on the questions in this section, make a list of any difficulties you come across; it will be helpful in the next section.

- What business am I in?
- What products or services do I offer to my customer?
- Who are my target customers?
- Why would the customer want to buy from my business?
- When will my customers buy?
- How will customers find my business?
- How much will my customers pay?

Major management

functions

- Planning
- Organizing
- Staffing
- Directing
- Controlling

Review your answers to the previous questions and write a one-page definition of your business. Here's how one business might go about doing this:

---◆---

*Simply Shoes: Business Concept*

*Simply Shoes—a partnership of Sara and Bob Abbott and Dave and Maria Brookes—is a retail shoe store located at the corner of Fifth and Main. Simply Shoes sells medium- to high-quality dress and casual shoes to adult and young adult customers. The owners purchased the business this year and plan to increase style and size selection, double sales, develop a loyal customer base, and emphasize good customer service.*

*Simply Shoes fills a void in the local retail shoe industry by offering quality shoes at discounted prices. This is made possible by careful attention to purchasing through direct contact with brokers and manufacturers. The marketing strategy calls for targeted marketing to identified customer groups, and projected sales of $350,000 for the coming year. To accommodate a wider selection, the partners propose to remodel existing space, providing more visibility of merchandise and room for displaying more styles.*

---◆---

## When to Plan

Planning is often simply a reaction to a crucial event, such as seeking financing or buying a business. However, this is not sufficient to start or grow a successful business. Planning requires constant attention—just like marketing and bookkeeping—so it needs to be integrated into the day-to-day management of your business. It makes sense to concentrate your planning activities during an annual process, but you should be working the plan constantly.

## The Planning Cycle

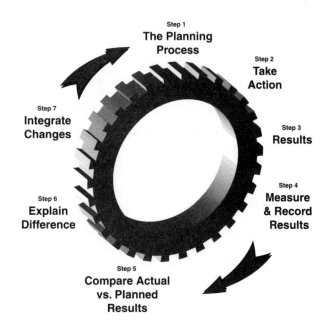

Step 1
**The Planning Process**

Step 2
**Take Action**

Step 3
**Results**

Step 4
**Measure & Record Results**

Step 5
**Compare Actual vs. Planned Results**

Step 6
**Explain Difference**

Step 7
**Integrate Changes**

A successful business completes all seven steps in the planning cycle!

### The Planning Cycle

Planning is a seven-step process. In a well-managed business, these steps take place every day.

Step 1:    **The Planning Process.** By making a commitment to the planning process, you can prepare your business for the future.

Step 2:    **Take Action.** Take action by making decisions that implement the plan.

Step 3:    **Results.** These result from the action taken in Step 2. (Something happens as a result of every decision, whether there's a plan or not.)

Step 4:    **Measure and Record Results.** Measure and document the results seen in Step 3.

Step 5:    **Compare Actual vs. Planned Results.** Compare the actual results to the results planned in Step 1.

Step 6:    **Explain Difference.** Explain why the actual results vary from the planned results. This is done whether the variance is positive or negative. This step will tell you a great deal about how your business really functions.

Step 7:    **Integrate Changes.** Make changes to the plan as a result of what you learned in Step 6.

## Who Does the Planning?

### Owners Must Take the Lead

It's important that you avoid the temptation of delegating all the responsibility for planning to an employee, a team, or a consultant. It's great to have others organize and participate in the planning process, but the owner must be seen as a strong and active advocate of the process.

### Assemble a Planning Team

Now that you are committed to being actively involved, you must identify the other members of your planning team.

Do you really need to form a team? Couldn't you just write the plan and then tell your employees what to do? No, not successfully! Giving key employees a sense of ownership in the plan greatly improves its chance of success. You may also want to involve professional advisors; businesses often hire an outside facilitator to keep the planning process running smoothly. (His or her role is to facilitate the process, not control or participate in it.)

The business owner must be actively involved

At the initial meeting, set a timeline for future meetings and for completing the planning process. Make sure that each person on the team understands his or her responsibilities, both at the meetings and in the work done between meetings.

## Types of Plans

- **Business Plan.** The document resulting from a planning process is usually referred to as a business plan. A complete business plan contains three major components: strategies, actions, and projected financial statements. (A fourth area, policies and procedures, is also important to the planning process but is not included in the business plan.)
- **Marketing Plan.** A plan that focuses solely on the marketing function of your business. Portions of the marketing plan appear in the business plan.
- **Strategic Plan.** Strategic planning is the systematic process of evaluating the impact of your business environment and the major decisions you face. The goal is to ensure long-term success. Focus your attention five years into the future when considering strategic planning. Strategic plans are the result of the strategic planning process. The strategic plan is contained, often in its entirety, in the business plan.
- **Operational Planning.** This process focuses on the actions that must be taken in the short term (usually one year). When operational planning is not based on a strategic plan, your business runs the risk of making decisions that seem good today but could have a negative long-term impact. Ideally, operational planning should occur after strategic planning is complete. However, small businesses are usually short-term oriented, and thus emphasize operational planning.
- **Annual Work Plan.** Annual work plans are the result of operational planning. An annual work plan is very detailed; only the highlights appear in the business plan.
- **Financial Planning.** Financial planning includes the process of preparing budgets and projected financial statements. These numbers must be updated whenever any planning activity is undertaken. The numbers are merely a numerical representation of the strategic and operational planning processes.
- **Financing Proposal.** A financing proposal is not really a planning document. Financing proposals are developed for the purpose of securing financing, not for the purpose of managing the business. The majority of the financing proposal is usually taken from the business plan, although it is really a by-product of the planning process.
- **Feasibility Study.** An entrepreneur investigating starting a new business may engage in an abbreviated planning process to determine whether to proceed with the new venture. The result is called a feasibility study. This is an important tool for anyone contemplating a start-up business, or adding a new component to an existing business.

Financial planning: the process of preparing budgets and projected financial statements

*Software Solutions, Inc.*

*Joe Murrow, owner of Southern Software Solutions Inc., wanted to promote his software products at the annual Comdex show in Las Vegas. He had read about the show in various industry publications but knew very little of the details, so he decided to do some research.*

*Joe gathered information about the number and types of people who usually attend Comdex, and estimated the cost to his company of exhibiting. Joe and his Marketing Manager Barbara Fabric then made a list of the advantages and disadvantages of attending. As part of their research, they looked into alternative ways of spending their marketing dollars. Finally, after three months of research, they decided to budget marketing dollars for the next Comdex show.*

*Joe and Barbara's research identified three primary benefits of attending the show:*

- *Their potential customers based their buying decisions upon contacts and information obtained at the show*
- *They would be able to demonstrate their products to potential customers in person*
- *Attending the show would generate greater sales*

*Joe and Barbara decided to develop a written plan for themselves and their employees. Since attending a major trade show requires a serious investment in terms of time and money, the plan would keep them focused and organized.*

## NxLEVEL™ TECH TIP

**Ameriwest Business Consultants, Inc.** offers a financial analysis template that allows you to put together financial projections for up to five years. Its capabilities include break-even analysis, month-by-month annual budgets for the first five years, and summary income statements. You can input data for an existing business or a start-up; the data can be historical, projected, or a combination of both. If your business is unique, the template can even be customized to meet your specific needs. For more information on this product, go to **http://www.abchelp.com/Ameriwest_Complete_Financial_Analysis.htm#Ameriwest**.

The method used by Joe and Barbara is an example of planning. They began by doing research, an important part of any planning process. They had a goal in mind, did some research to decide whether the goal was worthwhile, and then worked on how best to accomplish the goal. Note that the written plan is the last phase of the process.

# Feasibility Studies

John Gregson owns a successful sporting goods store. He has the opportunity to expand into an adjacent space that just became vacant. Is this expansion a good idea? If so, should he increase his inventory of existing products, or offer new product lines? How much can John afford to spend on remodeling? Will he need to increase his prices to pay for the expansion? An acquaintance recently expanded his auto parts business by getting into Internet sales, and John has been considering this option. What is his best course of action? How can he make a decision?

Small business owners are continually confronted with opportunities—and questions—like these. No business has the time to investigate each new product, target market, advertising strategy, pricing policy, or packaging alternative. You must respond quickly to the needs of your existing customers, or your competitors will. Expanding into new target markets is always an option for the small business owner, but how do you decide which opportunities to pursue? A feasibility study is the best planning tool you can use.

## What is a Feasibility Study?

The purpose of a feasibility study is to determine if a business opportunity is possible, practical, and viable. A business opportunity that is worth pursuing satisfies the following feasibility tests:

### Test #1: SWOT analysis

After you've considered the *strengths, weaknesses, opportunities,* and *threats* of the business concept, does it still seem like a good idea? To be feasible, strengths and opportunities should outweigh weaknesses and threats.

### Test #2: financial feasibility

Feasibility studies should quickly focus on determining financial feasibility. We assume that your business was formed to make a profit; therefore, if a business idea is not financially feasible, it is senseless to investigate it further.

### Test #3: Feasibility of sales volume

Almost any idea appears to be financially feasible if one assumes a high enough sales volume. Ask yourself if you are really able to achieve the sales volume you need to make your idea work.

### Test #4: Marketing feasibility

If your business opportunity passes the sales volume test, then you must develop a marketing plan that will outline how the business will reach the projected sales volume.

### Test #5: Feasibility of personnel

If your opportunity passed the previous tests, it is time to consider the issue of personnel. The best idea in the world won't succeed if you don't have—or can't hire—the staff to make it succeed.

Ideas that are not profitable are not feasible!

Look at both the positive

and negative aspects of

an opportunity

*Test #6: Other aspects of feasibility*

Other factors in determining feasibility vary by the type of business. Common considerations are: ability to find suppliers, ability to manufacture the product, and ability to provide customer support. In-depth analysis and planning beyond this would be part of your business plan.

## Why Do a Feasibility Study?

Entrepreneurs are optimists by nature. When faced with a business opportunity, they tend to focus on its positive aspects. A feasibility study enables them to take a realistic look at both the positive and negative aspects of the opportunity.

---

*Reality Check*

*Susan Connors is the owner of Sue's Accounting Service, a business she started three years ago. She provides accounting services to local small business owners and helps them computerize their accounting systems. She has earned a reputation for excellent customer service. Susan has dreams for the future, but never has enough time to develop a business plan.*

*She was contacted by a representative of In-Balance Software and offered the opportunity to be the exclusive state representative for their accounting software packages. Susan is so excited by the possibility that she has had a difficult time working. Plans for expansion of her business keep running through her mind and she has almost decided to pay the $10,000 fee for the two-year exclusive arrangement. The deadline is five days away, and she just knows that this is the opportunity she has been waiting for...or is it?*

---

In many cases, a comprehensive business plan cannot be completed in time for a decision. Preparing a feasibility study is quicker and can greatly reduce the risk for the entrepreneur. The feasibility study can be done before preparing a business plan or modifying an existing plan.

## When to Do a Feasibility Study

### Before starting a new business

The process of defining a new business is critical. A feasibility study is an important tool for making the right decisions. A wrong decision at this point often leads to business failure. Only 50% of start-ups are still in business after 18 months, and only 20% are in business after 5 years.

*Before acquiring an existing business*

---

*Health Food*

*Tom King is interested in purchasing the local health food store. He knows the present owner— she has a nice house and buys a new car every year! Tom's wife just inherited $50,000; Tom plans to use this for the down payment and to pay off the remaining $125,000 over seven years. Tom's wife is hesitant, but Tom is sure that this is a good decision. Besides, he is tired of working for the county as a building inspector.*

*Since the health food store is feasible for the present owner, Tom assumes that he'll do just fine. But business ownership is often not so simple. Tom would benefit from taking the time to do a feasibility study!*

---

### Before expanding an existing business

Owners of existing businesses continually face decisions about expansion (e.g., the addition of new product lines, hiring a new employee, or increasing the square footage of the business location). The owner who knows how to perform a quick feasibility study is more likely to select the right opportunities. Techniques covered in this chapter can also be used to look at changing prices, purchasing additional advertising, giving pay raises to employees, and almost any other decision that changes the "numbers" for your business.

## Outline of an Initial Feasibility Study

If you follow the process described in the next section, you will easily be able to prepare an initial feasibility study by assembling the following:

- Definition of the business concept
- Results of SWOT analysis
- Financial feasibility
- Sales volume assessment
- Conclusion

The five major parts should be prepared in the order listed above. The details will vary according to the details of your initial feasibility study.

### Starting a new business

**Step 1:** This step gives you the chance to describe accurately the business opportunity in which you're interested. The key questions to consider were outlined in the "Defining the Business Concept" section of this chapter.

**Step 2:** SWOT analysis provides a first glance at your idea's viability. **Strengths** and **weaknesses** relate to internal analysis of the business. Look at traditional functional areas such as marketing; engineering and product development; operations; personnel; management; and finance. **Opportunities** and **threats** relate to analysis of factors external to the business, including competition, technology, economic conditions, political conditions, and social factors. Note that external threats often result from internal weakness, and external opportunities from internal strengths.

**Step 3:** Determining financial feasibility is a three-step process.

a) Determine the start-up costs associated with your new business opportunity, and decide how much of these costs you need to finance. Start-up costs include professional fees, deposits, remodeling, licenses and permits, inventory, equipment, vehicles, and other fixed assets.

b) Budget your annual operating costs, and determine which are fixed and which are variable. Annual operating costs should be calculated on a cash basis, and should include servicing the debt you will need.

c) Determine financial feasibility by performing a break-even analysis (also called cost-volume-profit analysis). This calculation tells you the annual sales volume you will require to cover fixed and variable operating costs.

Initial feasibility study: a quick look at the possibilities

**Step 4:** The market assessment answers the question: "Is the break-even sales volume realistic?" Prior to this step, it is important to define your business concept concisely (this includes defining your target market). During the SWOT analysis, you examined the industry and the competition; these are also important considerations when answering questions about sales volume.

**Step 5:** The conclusion calls for a simple yes or no. At this stage, you may elect to return to Step 1 and revise your responses to the first four steps. This process is encouraged as it provides an opportunity to fine-tune your idea.

### Acquiring a business

In this case, the five steps are the same as in the previous section, but you will perform them a little differently. Include the present owner in the process and obtain copies of his or her business records whenever possible. The first time you go through the five steps, you should analyze current business operations. You are purchasing the business as it is, not as it could be.

For future iterations, you can modify the business concept, SWOT analysis, financial data, and so forth to reflect the potential of the business. Be very careful when making these modifications. If your first attempt suggested that you should not buy the business, but you still want to buy it, it is easy to make changes in order to prove to yourself that the business is feasible.

### Expanding an existing business

### Step 1: Impact on business concept

Does this opportunity for expansion require you to modify your current business concept? If so, how substantial is the modification? This is an initial feasibility check. Ideally, the opportunity will fit your business concept, or require that it be modified only slightly.

*A New Opportunity*

*Team Sports is a mail-order business that specializes in selling athletic equipment to adult players of recreational team sports. Its owners, Tom and Jim, started a mail-order business because they didn't want to keep regular business hours. (They both like to travel, especially to locations that offer outdoor adventures.) Their chosen market niche was the result of extensive market research performed during their last year of college.*

*A sales representative from WEBFOOT, makers of an innovative all-weather sports sandal, recently contacted Team Sports about selling their sandals. Tom was interested; he had worn these sandals during a rainy, four-day hike on the Milford Track in New Zealand. He was very satisfied with the sandals and even called WEBFOOT to say so upon returning home.*

*Adding the sandals seemed like a good idea. Their quality was impeccable, and they could easily be sold via mail-order. But WEBFOOT sandals had a different target market than Team Sports' products. Tom and Jim wondered whether the sandals would fit into their current product mix.*

*They decided to perform further analysis.*

## Step 2: SWOT analysis

Review the results of your previous SWOT analysis and determine whether any changes are required. Do the changes indicate an improved or worsened competitive position? A good business opportunity should result in an improved position.

*Team Sports SWOT Analysis*

*Strengths:*
- *Well-defined market niche*
- *Very productive mailing list*
- *Good reputation, as measured by many new customers from referrals*

*Weaknesses:*
- *Team Sports is poorly capitalized*
- *New product doesn't fit market niche*
- *New product requires substantial time from owners*

*Opportunities:*
- *Expand products offered to existing customers*
- *Market existing products to youth teams*

*Threats:*
- *Large mail-order companies might enter market*

*When Tom and Jim reviewed their SWOT analysis, they were very concerned that adding the sandals to their product line would weaken their competitive position. However, they decided to complete the Initial Feasibility Study before making a final decision.*

---

### Step 3: Cost analysis

Here, you have the same three steps regarding financial feasibility as those described for starting a new business. The difference is that you start with your present annual operating costs and make adjustments from this baseline.

Different steps are required to do a feasibility study when expanding an existing business

  a) **Start-up costs.** No opportunity is so simple that you won't have start-up costs!
  b) **Annual operating costs.** Analyze your annual operating costs. In most cases, you'll find that these costs will increase. They may not change, but take a good look just to be sure.
  c) **Break-even analysis.** This is done only for start-up costs and annual operating costs for the new business opportunity.

### Step 4: Sales volume

A sales volume assessment answers the question: "Is the incremental sales volume realistic?" Be sure to review your industry and competitive analyses.

### Step 5: Conclusion

The "yes or no" conclusion is a little more complicated for an existing business. A business owner may decide to pursue an opportunity that is not feasible in the short term because he or she has a strong belief that it is the right move in the long run. The existing business must be profitable enough to support this decision.

---

*Team Sports Reviews WEBFOOT*

*The sales representative from WEBFOOT told Tom and Jim that their minimum initial order would be 200 pairs of sandals. The sandals cost an average of $50 per pair plus freight, so their initial inventory would cost $10,000, plus $250 in freight charges. They estimated a cost of $350 to modify the layout of their catalog to make room for the sandals; a professional photographer would cost another $300. Based on their previous experiences, they budgeted another $500 for unknown costs. Therefore, the total start-up cost for adding the sandals was $11,400.*

*Tom and Jim estimated that the sandals required 4% of their total catalog space, and decided that the sandals must cover 4% of the printing, mailing, and mailing list maintenance. Using this formula, they estimated annual operating costs at $3,690.*

*Their research indicated that the sandals could be sold for an average of $80 per pair, plus shipping. Their cost of $50 per pair left Team Sports with a gross profit of $30 per pair. Thus, if they sold 123 pairs of sandals they would cover their additional annual operating costs of $3,690.*

*Tom and Jim believed they could sell this number and felt optimistic about the opportunity, but they were still concerned about having to order 200 pairs as initial inventory. Jim contacted WEBFOOT and negotiated an option to return any unsold sandals within six months for a restocking charge of $10 per pair. This arrangement greatly reduced Team Sports' financial risk.*

*With the ability to return unsold sandals, Tom and Jim felt that the sales volume question was less important. They viewed this as a chance to test-market the sandals, and decided to proceed.*

## Outline of a Complete Feasibility Study

Follow the process described in the next section, and you will assemble a complete feasibility study, comprising:

- Cover page
- Executive summary
- Definition of the business concept*
- Results of SWOT analysis*
- Financial feasibility*
- Sales volume assessment*
- Marketing
- Personnel
- Other
- Conclusion

*Indicates sections already completed as part of your initial feasibility study.*

## How to Prepare a Complete Feasibility Study

If the results of the initial feasibility study are positive, then it is time to do more research before implementing the business opportunity. You completed Steps 1-5 during your Initial Feasibility Study; now, proceed with steps 6-11.

### Step 6: Marketing
Having looked at the industry and the competition, you believe you can achieve the sales volume required to support your idea. Next, you must decide how to achieve it. Consider product, price, promotion, placement, and so forth.

### Step 7: Personnel
Now it's time to assess the ability of your personnel to take advantage of the business opportunity. First, look at the capabilities of your employees, owners, managers, and outside advisors. List the key tasks at your business, and determine who will perform

Complete feasibility study: a more thorough analysis

## Keys to Success

- The ability to do a quick feasibility study is invaluable to you as a business manager. Remember not to commit to an opportunity until you take a realistic look. There will always be new opportunities for the watchful entrepreneur!

- Design your business so that you have a market niche that makes your business unique in the eyes of your customers. Copying another business will not give you such a niche!

- Do a thorough analysis of each major competitor. Establish your market niche so that you have at least one major competitive advantage when compared with each competitor. This requires some work, but it's worth the effort.

- Investigate every start-up cost. Entrepreneurs always underestimate start-up and operating costs. Unfortunately, they also overestimate revenues. Spend some time identifying every start-up cost, and obtain two or more cost estimates for each item.

- Research the financial averages for your industry. These averages represent the performance of existing companies in your industry. If some of your financial figures differ greatly, you would be wise to determine why. Annual Statement Studies, published by Robert Morris & Associates, is an excellent source. Or, check with your trade association and your accountant.

- Are you smarter than the established competition? An established competitor (i.e., any business with at least five years of experience) is doing some things right. You may be focusing on their mistakes; look into their strengths as well. This is especially important for a start-up, or if you are buying an existing business.

- Research growth trends. How fast is the industry growing? What is the impact of international trade? Is it increasing or decreasing? What technological changes can be expected?

- Research the role of small businesses in the industry. What is the role of franchising? Is it increasing or decreasing? Is the industry dominated by large or small businesses?

them. (In your copy of the NxLeveL™ Business Plan Workbook, you will find a worksheet to help you do this.) Having no capable personnel to perform the key tasks you've identified is a warning sign that you should heed!

### Step 8: Other factors

What about other factors that might affect your ability to implement the idea? Remember, this is a reality check; if you have a doubt in the back of your mind, now is the time to investigate.

### Step 9: Conclusion

Last, take a thorough look at your feasibility study. Besides an overall answer, review the business opportunity in terms of personnel, finances, markets, and other factors. This is your final chance to refine your idea before implementation.

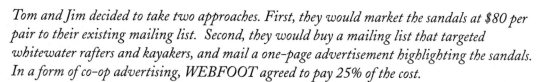

*Tom and Jim decided to take two approaches. First, they would market the sandals at $80 per pair to their existing mailing list. Second, they would buy a mailing list that targeted whitewater rafters and kayakers, and mail a one-page advertisement highlighting the sandals. In a form of co-op advertising, WEBFOOT agreed to pay 25% of the cost.*

*Tom and Jim felt that they'd identified all their concerns. They were still worried by the fact that the sandals didn't really fit in with their other products. But they also felt that they needed to expand their business, and the WEBFOOT opportunity gave them a good chance to do so. Accordingly, they decided to finalize their sales agreement with WEBFOOT.*

### Step 10: Executive summary

Write a one-page executive summary of your feasibility study that can be given to an outsider. A well written executive summary should be easily read and understood by those without any special knowledge of your business or industry.

### Step 11: Cover page

Prepare a cover page that includes your business's name, address, phone, and fax numbers; the date the study was prepared; and the names of the owners.

*The Perils of Operating Without a Plan*

*In 1994, Sandra Workman started a catering business called Affairs of the Heart. In two years, the business was successful beyond her wildest dreams. She moved twice to larger quarters, hired 10 additional full-time and 15 part-time employees, and had a well-deserved reputation as caterer to the "movers and shakers" of Omaha, Nebraska. The future for Sandra and her business looked bright!*

*In 1998, things started to go awry. Sandra was facing yet another move to accommodate increased business, she had increased her staff to 15 full-time and 30 part-time employees, and cash flow was an ongoing crisis. She couldn't figure it out: she was generating more revenue than ever, she still enjoyed her stellar reputation, and her business was growing—why couldn't she pay her bills? How would she ever find the time to locate and renovate another space?*

*Sandra was determined to make Affairs of the Heart a long-term, successful business, so she hired a business consultant. After several months of studying every facet of the business (and running up a significant bill), the consultant gave Sandra her analysis. Every problem Sandra was trying to deal with was a result of the lack of planning. Sandra had never developed a business plan; she hadn't thought she needed one! The consultant helped Sandra develop and write a business plan, including critical sections on future growth, marketing, and budgets.*

*At the end of 1999, Affairs of the Heart closed out its books with a profit, and was still the premier caterer in Omaha!*

As Sandra's story shows, a well-executed planning process can have a tremendously positive impact on your business. Conversely, inadequate or disorganized planning can be devastating. Here are some basics you should bear in mind to keep your planning process on track:

- Owner assumes the lead role
- Plans must involve everyone in the business
- Plan in definable steps
- Plans should be flexible, and reflect reality
- Have a contingency plan for the worst case
- Identify how to achieve specific objectives
- Build the plan on the skills of those who will implement it
- Document assumptions
- Revise the plan as needed

## Conclusion

Planning is the key to success for guiding your business through difficult times and terrific times. The various planning processes described in this chapter will help your business prepare for a competitive business environment.

Is the planning process really the same for all types of businesses? The steps in the process are the same, but the results are different. You wouldn't expect a manufacturing company that specializes in high-quality custom orders to have a plan identical to that of a fast-food restaurant. Nor would you expect a wholesaler of farm implements to have a plan identical to that of a consulting company that specializes in customer service training.

You must customize your plan for your business. If you do, you will be ready to compete today, and—even more important—you will be positioned to be successful in the long run.

# Chapter 13
# THE NXLEVEL™ BUSINESS PLAN

*About This Chapter:*
- *Who uses the NxLeveL™ Business Plan?*
- *What do readers look for in a business plan?*
- *Getting started*
- *A polished presentation*

## Introduction

The **NxLeveL™ Business Plan** outlines the basics of a business concept: the business's mission, objectives, products or services, management, marketing, and financial plan. Many businesses use the business plan as an exercise to test ideas and stimulate thinking.

When you prepare your business plan, you will learn whether your business idea is truly viable. You will also fine-tune your business concept, making it all the more likely that your venture will succeed and grow.

Why are we presenting the business plan here, before we have introduced basic marketing and financial concepts? Because this chapter shows you where you are headed, and highlights the concepts you must understand to get a business idea up and running. Each chapter in this book contains elements that are related to the business plan.

The NxLeveL™ Business Plan is the first step in growing your business

*The Birth of Bag-It Gourmet*

*Catherine Baggott began Bag-It Gourmet on the simple premise that most people want good food, but simply do not have the time to prepare it.*

*This was her own situation from 1996 to 1999, when she sold advertising space for a gourmet magazine. During the week, Catherine would work long hours, go to her health club, and get home late, tired, and hungry. Most of her favorite restaurants didn't deliver, so she often ended up ordering pizza or Chinese food. She soon found herself wishing there was more varied, higher quality food available for home delivery.*

*Catherine spent a year casually researching the feasibility of a gourmet food delivery business. By the end of the year, she had created a business concept: Bag-It Gourmet would take phone orders and deliver food from ten different restaurants to customers within a five-mile radius of her home.*

*Catherine was well versed in financial analysis. She created a business plan for Bag-It Gourmet, clearly outlining its costs (including the purchase of a new mini-van for deliveries), sales forecasts, and break-even point.*

*She decided the business was feasible, so she prepared a brief description of the business, bundled it with her financial plan, and prepared to leave her job.*

---

## Who Uses the NxLeveL™ Business Plan?

Business plans are written for three major audiences:

- The internal management team
- Potential lenders and investors
- Potential partners, advisors, and employees

Whether you're starting a new business, expanding an old one, or just wondering how to improve your current business, the NxLeveL™ Business Plan is an indispensable tool. It explains who you are, the direction in which you are headed, and your approach for achieving your goals.

The NxLeveL™ Business

Plan informs and inspires

A business plan presents essential information for anyone who is seriously considering involvement in your venture, such as prospective employees, mentors, and partners. Banks, investors, small business development centers, and other institutions review business plans before making loans, so that they can judge the abilities of the business owner and the potential profitability of the business.

Therefore, your business plan must be clear and concise, and should ignite in others the same enthusiasm that you feel about your business idea!

## What Do Readers Look For in a Business Plan?

Lenders, employees, and partners all look for the same information in a business plan:

- Is the business idea viable?
- Are its products or services new, unique, or better than current offerings?
- Does the business create or cater to a new market?
- Is it a growth market?
- Are the cash flow and sales projections realistic?
- Can the business be profitable and service its debt?
- Does the business understand and place priority on customer needs?
- Is the business concept clear, focused, and intelligently presented?
- Is the business concept based on sound research and analysis?
- Are key people experienced in this business?

## Major Components of The NxLeveL™ Business Plan

The major components of the plan are:

- Cover Page
- Table of Contents
- Executive Summary
- Mission, Goals, and Objectives
- Background Information
- Organizational Matters
- Marketing Plan
- Financial Plan
- Appendix Section

## Getting Started

Before you start drafting your plan, revisit your original business concept and review your assumptions. You should be perfectly clear and confident about the direction in which you want to take your business.

Next, list and prioritize the things you'll need in order to pursue your business idea. Imagine you want to open a combination cafe/laundromat. Although there are two other laundromats in your town, they are poorly lit and maintained, and completely lacking in appeal. Your vision is to create a place where people will want to wash their clothes. While they wait for their laundry, they can have a good cup of coffee and a fresh sandwich. They can socialize, or sit at a table and read.

Make a list of the skills you are going to need, such as maintaining laundry machines, and managing a cafe. You may eventually seek outside investors or lenders, so start to think like one. Ask yourself, "What is so great about my laundromat? What makes it unique? What resources are available to me? How long before I make a profit? What is my competition like? What are my long- and medium-term plans for growth?"

Once you've done this, it's time to start drafting your plan.

### The Executive Summary

The executive summary is the opening argument of the business plan. It's your chance to take the floor and convince your audience that your business is viable. Because it is the first thing readers see, it must capture and hold their attention. Potential investors will scan it to determine whether or not the rest of the business plan is worth reading.

The executive summary comprises condensed versions of the major sections of the business plan. Therefore, you must understand the preceding sections, and how they relate to one another, before you can write an effective summary.

Keep in mind the three Cs: Be clear, concise, and convincing!

The NxLeveL™ Business Plan presents the elements that will affect the success of your business

Be clear, concise, and convincing!

---◆---

*Bag-It Gourmet Grows*

*One year later, Bag-It Gourmet was making over 200 deliveries a week, charging a 15% commission on each delivery. Catherine had four enthusiastic young drivers who were as committed to customer service as she was.*

*But she could see that the landscape in which her business operated was changing. More and more customers were calling from outside her delivery zone, and customers were requesting deliveries from a wider selection of restaurants.*

*Clearly there were opportunities for growth. Catherine decided to jump in and trust her instincts. She was excited about the new housing developments north of town, and decided to expand her area of operation to serve them. She calculated that she would need another mini-van and three more drivers.*

*She heard about a successful businesswoman named Lissa Herman, who made loans to fledgling businesses. Catherine decided to give her a call.*

---◆---

## Mission, Goals, and Objectives

Your **mission statement** states, in the broadest terms possible, what your business hopes to be and do. Some examples: "To help people work more efficiently and comfortably," or "To provide healthy, energizing juices," or "To take the anxiety out of tax preparation."

Here is your opportunity to demonstrate the focus and scope of your business. You should spend a fair amount of time developing a mission statement for your company, and direct all subsequent strategies and tactics towards implementing this mission.

A good example of a simple, straightforward mission statement was developed by the publishers of a monthly outdoor magazine called TRiPS, which was based in Santa Cruz, California: "The purpose of TRiPS is to promote outdoor adventure and travel so people see, feel and know how good it is to be outside."

Finally, you should explore growth and product expansion potential. For example, if your business is a graphic design service, this could eventually lead to providing Web site design and editing services to small businesses in your community. Demonstrating foresight in the early stages of planning carries weight with those interested in participating. Use this section of the plan to state specific objectives for growth.

## Background Information

This section presents the industry in which your business operates. What past and present industry trends affect the business? Where is the industry headed in coming years? What economic, social, or political trends affect your industry? How attractive is the industry for your business? How does your business "fit" into the industry?

The business plan: a road map highlighting routes, road blocks, and detours

## Organizational Matters

This section usually begins by describing the legal form of ownership of the business. Will it be a limited partnership? A sole proprietorship? A corporation?

This section also introduces the people and structures that will make the business run smoothly and successfully. At what point do you estimate you will need additional personnel? What are the responsibilities and qualifications of your team? Businesses often attach resumes to this section to highlight the strengths of the team.

A good plan tests ideas and focuses goals

Describe how different parts of the business work together. Who will report to whom? Which areas of the business will be responsible for which functions? Businesses often illustrate this with an **organizational chart**, which is a blueprint of the management hierarchy. It details relationships and where different parts of the business exist in relation to one another.

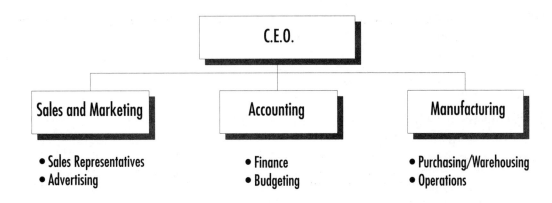

Which tasks will the business be responsible for in-house, and which will be outsourced—provided by outside services, temporary employment agencies, consultants, and mentors? Will you do accounting and payroll in-house, or hire an accountant? Will you use outside sales representatives, distributors, or agents?

The management section of the business plan is a good place to present potential problems, along with contingency plans for troubleshooting and solving these problems.

The organization section of the business plan should also explain how records will be kept and budgets and controls managed. It explains what strategies your business will use to manage risk.

## The Marketing Plan

The **marketing plan** identifies the markets your business intends to serve. It outlines your business's strengths, and describes how it will be positioned in its market. The marketing plan contains the following sections:

## Products/services description

What products or services will your business offer? What benefits do they provide to your customers? You might also include information about the seasonality of your product, and where it is in its **life cycle**. Is it in the introduction, growth, maturity, or decline phase? What growth do you anticipate? What new products or services will you offer in the future?

## Market analysis

Market analysis is the result of market research findings. It presents your business's **target market**, which is the segment of the overall market on which you will focus your marketing efforts. What is your business's market potential? How large is the target market? How fast is it growing, and what sales volume can it generate? What is the target customer profile?

**Demographic** and **psychographic data** are used to help describe the target market. Demographic data comprise quantitative information like people's addresses, age, income level, spending patterns, and family composition. Psychographic data are qualitative information about people's lifestyles, hobbies, beliefs, and attitudes. Together, these data determine all marketing strategies, including those regarding **product, price, promotion, and placement**.

The **competitive analysis** describes your competitors. Is the market already saturated with other companies? What does your business offer that's better than the competition? What are its strengths and weaknesses?

A major component of the market analysis is a list of possible barriers to entry. What are the initial start-up costs? What skills or expertise do you need? How long will it take to set up operations? Which government regulations apply? This section explains how you will overcome obstacles to achieve your objectives.

## Market strategy

This section outlines your business's product, pricing, placement, and promotion strategies. What sort of customer service will you provide? How will you package your products or services? Will the products be widely or selectively distributed? What marketing strategies will you choose? How much will promotional tactics cost, and how long will each tactic be used? Where will your supplies come from? How will you maintain production levels to meet customer orders?

General pricing information is also included in the plan. What will you charge for your product or service? How have you calculated your costs and your profitability? How will your price position you in the market? Will you offer any special discounts to entice new business?

---

*Bag-It Gourmet Meets An "Angel"*

*Lissa Herman was an entrepreneur whose success allowed her to take the time to mentor new women-owned businesses. When she spoke to Catherine Baggott on the phone, she was impressed by her enthusiasm and obvious head for business. In fact, Lissa had ordered from Bag-It Gourmet more than once, and thought the business had a huge potential.*

*But when Lissa read the business plan that Catherine had submitted to her, she found that it didn't present a clear picture of Bag-It Gourmet's target market and overall marketing strategy. How did Catherine intend to guide her business as it grew? Catherine had completely failed to address this issue in her business plan, and Lissa wondered if Catherine had overlooked other key elements. She wondered, in fact, what rationale Catherine had for wanting to grow her business in the first place.*

*Lissa knew that Bag-It Gourmet needed a clear picture of its customers and markets. Without this information, it was just a matter of time before the business got off course.*

---

## The Financial Plan

The financial plan is the longest and most important section of the business plan. This is where you list the financial requirements for launching or growing your business. The financial plan comprises four sections: financial worksheets, cash flow projections, financial statements, and additional financial information.

### Financial Worksheets

The financial worksheets present many important details on the management of the business:

- **Salaries, wages, and benefits.** How much will your business pay each month to compensate your team? What benefits will it provide, and how much will they cost?
- **Outside services.** What outside contractors or service providers will your business rely on? What duties will they perform? How will services be contracted and managed?
- **Insurance.** Which types of insurance will you use to minimize risk? How probable are losses? What are premium costs?
- **Advertising budget.** What is the overall budget for advertising and promotion? How much will be spent on advertising campaigns?
- **Occupancy expense.** What is the monthly cost of renting or leasing work space? What related expenses does your business have?
- **Sales forecasts.** How much do you anticipate selling in your target markets over the next one, six, and twelve months? Consider presenting separate sales forecasts for different product types, geographic regions, and markets.

- **Cost of goods sold (COGS).** What does your business pay for supplies and other inputs? This includes all costs related to buying, storing, counting, assembling, or enhancing inputs to create the finished product. This category is also known as **cost of product units**.
- **Fixed assets.** What land, plant, and equipment does your business own or lease? What is the market or book value of these assets?
- **Growth expenses.** What expenses do you require for growth? Consider additional equipment, space, personnel, inventory, promotions, distribution, and production.
- **Miscellaneous expenses.** What other business expenses do you anticipate? Are these one-time or recurring expenses?

### Cash Flow Analysis

Cash flow analysis calculates how much cash is coming in and out of your business. It is perhaps your most important financial tool; it is particularly useful for determining when and how much you will need to borrow during an annual cycle, and how much cash you will require to pay monthly bills.

This section is especially important for businesses that have a large number of **accounts receivable**. This is the unpaid balance of money owed to the business by customers. Suppose that a t-shirt business manufactures and ships out 500 shirts, along with an invoice due to be collected in 30 days. If the business has an outstanding bill due in two weeks, it won't be able to count on the income generated by this sale to pay current expenses. Thus, it runs the risk that it will not collect its accounts receivable in time to meet its obligations for the cost of materials and labor.

Entrepreneurs have a tendency to be too optimistic when developing cash flow projections. The truth is, business ventures often fail because of faulty predictions in the financial planning section.

To calculate your cash flow, start by calculating how much cash you have on hand, then add **cash receipts** (cash generated from sales and collection of accounts receivable, including any loans received from banks or other lenders).

Next, calculate **cash disbursements**. This is calculated by adding together all the uses or payments of cash, including selling, general and administrative expenses, payments of interest and taxes, and any expenses associated with the cost of your product. This would include all payments that decreased your **accounts payable,** which is the unpaid balance of money owed by your business for inventory and supplies. Add to this total the cash you have withdrawn under owner's withdrawls, and the sum of these figures equals **total cash disbursements**.

Subtracting total cash disbursements from cash receipts results in your business's **cash flow**. When there is more cash coming in than being paid out, businesses have a **positive cash flow**. If more cash goes out than comes in, then the business has a **negative cash flow**. When this occurs, businesses are unable to pay their bills. While it is possible for businesses to operate profitably with a negative cash flow, this is not an advisable course of action for a growing business! Maintaining a positive cash flow at all times ensures that your business can meet its obligations.

The **ending cash balance** for a given time period is calculated by adjusting the beginning cash balance by the current period cash flow you have just calculated. Subtract a negative cash flow and add a positive one.

You must also include a **break-even analysis** in the financial plan. The **break-even point** is the amount of units sold or sales dollars earned that the business must achieve to recover all the expenses associated with generating these sales.

To calculate your break-even point, you must total your fixed and variable costs. **Fixed costs** are costs that remain the same regardless of how many units you produce or customers you serve (e.g., costs for tools, equipment, and marketing efforts). **Variable costs** vary with the quantity of goods sold; these include costs of labor, supplies, and materials. Below is the equation for calculating your break-even point:

$$\textit{Break-even quantity} \quad = \quad \frac{\textit{Total fixed costs}}{\textit{Price – average variable costs}}$$

**Cash flow projections** detail the revenues and expenses anticipated for a given period of time. They entail the same type of calculations used to determine cash flow, but are based on assumptions about the business and its markets. For this reason, you must attach a statement describing the assumptions on which you have based your projections (e.g., assumptions about customers, the economy, competitors, available technology, or legal restrictions).

Most business plans contain **monthly cash flow projections** for the first year, and **annual cash flow projections** for years two and three.

*Financial Statements*
The financial statements section is composed of several items that give a quantitative profile of your business. The **income statement** is a financial report showing actual revenues earned, expenses incurred, and the resulting **net income** or **net loss**. A **projected income statement** presents the income you expect to generate in the future. Typically, this is done for the first year of business, and then quarterly for the two years that follow.

Once you have settled on the prices you will charge, estimate how much income, or **gross profit**, you expect to generate from sales each month. Then, subtract **cost of goods sold** to determine your **gross profit margin**.

Next, calculate how much you must pay each month for salaries, wages, rent, utilities, insurance, and so forth. The sum of these expenses equals **total operating costs**, and includes the **depreciation** of any equipment. (Depreciation is the decrease in value of buildings or equipment over time. For example, if your brand new computer is worth

$6,000 today, in a year it may be only worth $3,500. The depreciation of $2,500 must be added to your total operating costs.) Subtract operating costs from gross profit margin to determine your predicted **net profit before taxes**.

The **balance sheet** lists your business's **assets, liabilities,** and **net worth**. Assets are any items of value owned by the business, including equipment, accounts receivable, inventory on hand, cash, and any prepaid expenses. Liabilities are all debts, including rent, lease payments, accounts payable, bank mortgages, other bank debts, and equipment depreciation. To calculate your net worth, subtract total liabilities from total assets.

Net worth is sometimes shown as the **statement of owner's equity,** which presents the money that owners have invested in the business. This is known as **external equity**. **Internal equity** is profits that you have earned and reinvested in the business. Hence, the amount of equity in a business is determined by:

- The amount of the owner's initial investment
- Any additional investments in the business
- The income retained or reinvested within the business from earlier periods, minus any withdrawal by the owners

### Additional Financial Information

This section of the business plan summarizes the financial requirements of the business, its existing debt, and the financial position of the owner(s).

The **summary of financial needs** presents what your business requires to fuel its growth. The business's **existing debt** is a summary of all outstanding loans the business has received to date. The **personal financial statement** lists any assets that you are able to invest in the business, and any other sources of income you have.

*"What Do You Mean by a Marketing Plan?"*

*That was Catherine Baggott's response when Lissa asked her where her marketing plan was for her business plan.*

*Lissa explained that Bag-It Gourmet was at a critical point in its growth. If Catherine didn't know what type of customer she served and what needs the business filled, she wouldn't know how to guide and control her growth.*

*"Before you consider growing to serve that new housing development," Lissa said, "you have to know if the people who live there fit your target customer profile. Maybe they don't need the services you currently offer!"*

*Before making any decisions, Lissa asked Catherine to write down the answers to the following questions:*

- *Where do most of your customers live?*
- *What restaurants do they most want to order from?*

- *How long are they willing to wait for delivery?*
- *How much are they willing to pay?*
- *How frequently do they order?*

*Catherine was humbled. Although Bag-It Gourmet was profitable and she had made a success of her entrepreneurial vision, she worried that maybe it had all been just good luck. How could she have launched her business without knowing the answers to these basic questions?*

---◆---

## Appendix Section

This final section of the business plan presents a timetable for action (action plan), as well as any supporting documents that will enhance your business plan.

Use the appendix for timetables and action plans

Given your research, calculations, and projections, can your business continue to be a viable venture? Can you profitably operate your business? This is the time for you to make a judgment call about what you expect to achieve and when you expect to achieve it. What is your long-term vision for the business? This section prioritizes and schedules your tasks and tactics. What will you achieve in the next one, three, and five years?

Supporting documents might include resumes of the owner and other employees, market research findings, product specifications, brochures, and customer testimonials.

---◆---

*Was It All Luck?*

*Because she had provided all of her own seed money to launch Bag-It Gourmet, Catherine had never been required to research and write a complete business plan. She had simply launched the business on the basis of her financial projections and confidence in her idea.*

*She wanted answers to Lissa's questions, and more. Was it just dumb luck that Bag-It Gourmet had done well? She needed to know before she took another step.*

*She began work by gathering information from the local library, a real estate association, a food industry association, and the local Chamber of Commerce.*

*Three weeks later she scheduled another meeting with Lissa Herman. This time she was prepared.*

---◆---

## Is Your Business Venture Feasible?

You've drafted your plan, and completed the NxLeveL™ Business Plan checklist. Look at the information you've accumulated and ask yourself these questions:

- Does your business plan make sense?
- Is there a real demand for your product or service?
- Is there a potential for continued growth?
- Will you seek additional investors? If so, who they will be?
- Do you need to revise your business concept?

## The NxLeveL™ Business Plan Checklist

*Prepare Objectives and Mission*
- ❏ Growth plan description
- ❏ Stage of development
- ❏ Mission statement
- ❏ Objectives

*Prepare Background Information*
- ❏ Industry analysis and trends
- ❏ The business "fit" in the industry

*Design the Organization*
- ❏ Business structure
- ❏ Management
- ❏ Personnel
- ❏ Outside services/advisors
- ❏ Risk management
- ❏ Operating controls

*Prepare the Marketing Plan*
- ❏ Description of products or services
- ❏ Market analysis
- ❏ Competitor analysis
- ❏ Market size and trends
- ❏ Sales volume potential
- ❏ Marketing mix strategy
- ❏ Explain market strategy
  - ❏ Price
  - ❏ Placement
  - ❏ Product
  - ❏ Promotion

*Compile the Financial Plan*
- ❏ Financial worksheets
- ❏ Cash flow projections
- ❏ Financial statements
- ❏ Additional financial information

*Assemble Appendices*
- ❏ Timetable
- ❏ Supporting documents

*Write Executive Summary*
- ❏ Analyze target readers (investors/lenders) and write accordingly
- ❏ Consolidate and summarize all accumulated data
- ❏ Adjust original business concept as needed

*Finishing Touches*
- ❏ Proofread and edit document
- ❏ Create/collect graphs, charts, and photographs
- ❏ Reread entire business plan
- ❏ Determine overall feasibility of plan
- ❏ Give plan to friends, advisors, or family for review
- ❏ Make changes as necessary

- Are you targeting the right market?
- Are your financial projections correct?
- Are you operating as efficiently and profitably as possible?
- What additional education or skills do you need?

Be sure you have resolved these questions before seeking financial assistance from family, friends, other investors, or banks. When you are satisfied with your results, you can start putting together your executive summary.

A weak plan can be fatal, not only because it may turn away potential lenders and investors, but because it won't properly direct you toward success. Do yourself a favor and be honest when you are creating your plan. It is easy to paint a glorified picture of your idea, so do a reality check: Are your assumptions accurate? Have you addressed all the questions lenders or investors will ask? Do you have the right skills and resources? Get the input of friends, family, employees, and advisors before you commit to a plan.

A realistic business plan helps to identify your weaknesses and strengths so that you can budget the time, energy, and money to improve those areas that need it. Don't beat yourself over the head if you find major problems with your plan; Rome wasn't built in a day, and neither are successful businesses. You can always revise and improve your plan.

Finally, don't be a slave to your plan. If new opportunities arise, don't avoid them simply because they weren't anticipated in your plan. There's more than one way to get to your destination.

Above all, the NxLeveL™ Business Plan is a working document. It should evolve over time as you learn more about your market, your business, and yourself.

A weak plan is fatal.
You should:
- Strive for success
- Seek out the truth
- Continually revise and improve your plan

------------------------------◆------------------------------

*The Bag-It Gourmet Plan Takes Shape*

*Because she was still busy with the day-to-day operations of her business, Catherine hired a local business school student to help her write the marketing plan. Once they began to work, Catherine realized the power of a good marketing plan, and wondered how she could have missed it before.*

*She also made some startling discoveries. By reviewing her sales records, she found that her average customer ordered food three times a month. The average size of the order was $45.00. The most valuable information she gathered came from a questionnaire that her M.B.A. student suggested: Why not attach a simple ten-question flier to each delivery for the next two weeks?*

*This way she found out that most of her customers:*

- *Were professional, married people in mid-life*
- *Had no children at home*
- *Had a household income of more than $80,000 a year*
- *Enjoyed and paid more for high-end, gourmet food and wines*

*Catherine quickly realized that the new subdivision outside town did not fall within her target market. Her research showed that these were multi-family units, designed for budget-conscious, first-time home buyers with young children. She doubted that these people would pay premium prices to have gourmet meals delivered!*

*Obviously, she needed to reevaluate her growth options. She asked herself, "Do I want to grow my business after all?"*

*Catherine knew the answer already: a resounding yes! She loved the challenges and rewards of being in business, and felt that she had just begun to realize its potential. She even had ideas of franchising her business to her cousin in Colorado, but that was far off in the future. What would her first step be?*

*In the course of gathering market information, her business school intern discovered that construction for a large office complex was due to begin in the next month. In fact, the east side of town was rapidly expanding into one large commercial zone. If her goal was to expand business, why not look there?*

*Catherine's drivers began work at 6 P.M., and her mini-van sat in the driveway most of the day. What if she expanded her business into daylight hours? Bag-It Gourmet could deliver gourmet continental breakfasts, bagels, muffins, and fresh fruit for early business meetings. And why not also deliver gourmet food for lunch-time office meetings and seminars?*

*Catherine incorporated the idea into her revised business plan (she called it her "growth plan"). She was very enthusiastic when she shared it with Lissa Herman!*

---

## A Polished Presentation

Remember that the NxLeveL™ Business Plan is a tool for you to attract investors, advisors, and employees. For this reason, you should think about how you will present the plan, both in writing and in person.

A polished presentation is instant information delivered with impact

Painstaking research, planning, and documentation mean nothing if you cannot present your ideas clearly and convincingly in a few minutes. That's all the time most lenders or investors will take to look at your plan, so you must pique their interest with an organized plan that utilizes visual cues.

The NxLeveL™ Business Plan should be:

- Typed and printed on quality paper
- Absolutely free of spelling and grammatical errors
- Presented in a hard folder or binder
- Augmented by charts and graphs that are consistent in style
- Clear, to the point, and easy to read
- Free of industry-specific terms (unless they are briefly defined)

Once you've proofread your document and cleaned up its formatting, you should pass it along to a trusted friend, relative, or mentor for review. Keep an open mind as to their input.

## NxLEVEL™ TECH TIP

Need to do some research on trends, demographics, laws, or statistics before you embark on your business plan? The following U.S. government Web sites can help:

- **Library of Commerce Business Reference Services** (http://lcweb.loc.gov/rr/business/) is a good starting point for conducting research on business and economics. Supported by a reference collection of over 20,000 volumes, a network of CD-ROM services, and the Adams Building Computer Catalog Center, reference specialists in specific subject areas of business can help you gain access to the wealth of business information in the Library's collections.

- The **U.S. Chamber of Commerce Small Business Center** (http://www.uschamber.org/smallbiz/index.html) provides information on pertinent Chamber of Commerce resources; economic policies affecting small businesses; educational and training programs; employment opportunities and internships; expos and trade shows; Chamber of Commerce publications; retirement plans for small businesses, and more.

When you present your NxLeveL™ Business Plan in person, you should:

- Dress cleanly and professionally
- Speak slowly and clearly
- Look directly and confidently at your audience
- Prepare and budget your time in advance
- Present a compelling executive summary in the first 30 seconds, and use the next two or three minutes to provide details and supporting information
- Finish with a clear conclusion and detail what you want from the listener
- Use simple charts or tables to clarify ideas and focus attention

*Catherine Gets her Dough...and Bag-It Gourmet Grows!*

*Lissa was impressed with Catherine's research. She felt that Catherine's estimate of costs for implementing Bag-It Gourmet's creative new strategy was on target, and decided that the business was worth financing.*

*Catherine came away from the meeting with a commitment for funding and a new vision for her business. She felt more confident than ever! Growth no longer seemed like a hit-or-miss proposition. She knew who her customers were and what they wanted, and she knew how to get the information she'd need to keep her strategies up-to-date. It looked like Bag-It Gourmet was in the bag!*

---

## Conclusion

The NxLeveL™ Business Plan is an operating plan for the entrepreneur, a financing proposal for lenders, and a source of inspirational information for potential partners and employees. It is also the capstone of your participation in the NxLeveL™ training program for entrepreneurs. When you have completed the soul-searching and the hard work that go into the plan, you should be proud. You have taken a big step in making your entrepreneurial dream a reality!

We all have hopes and fears when we begin or grow a business. The NxLeveL™ Business Plan will help you confirm your hopes, confront your fears, and make your business a success!

# Chapter 14
# CONTINGENCY PLANNING

*About This Chapter:*
- *Setting your limits*
- *The nitty gritty of selling your business*
- *Selling your stock to the public*
- *Being shown the door*
- *The business failure*
- *It's really happening! What do I do now?*
- *You've sold your business...what now?*

## Introduction

It may sound odd, but the same day you begin your business you should start preparing your **exit strategy**, which means defining the circumstances under which you will consider leaving the business. Why do this? Because setting limits for your involvement in your business gives you a benchmark against which you can judge your business's progress or lack thereof.

This chapter discusses situations in which you may choose or be forced to end your business, including boredom, the pursuit of a better opportunity, a terrific buy-out offer, or bankruptcy.

## Setting Your Limits

### Why Would You Want Out?

It's sad but true: many young businesses go belly up and have no choice but to call it quits. But there are also happier reasons for exiting one's business—for example, if someone wants to buy it for a sizable amount of money! Here are some other reasons for calling it quits:

- You've identified a better opportunity elsewhere
- You're bored and want a new challenge
- You think that your business has achieved all the growth it can
- You lack the skills or desire to take your business to the next level
- You are no longer willing to work 70 hours a week
- You want to diversify your assets
- Your interests and/or those of your founding team have changed
- You are ready for retirement

Welcome aboard!

Got your return ticket?

## Knowing When To Say When: Your Business Limits

Preset exit limits are a safety net against personal and professional loss. Your exit limits, expressed in quantitative terms, might look something like this:

*"If my business experiences the following, I will seriously consider calling it quits":*
- The business has overdue bills exceeding $25,000
- The business has fallen below $500,000 in sales
- The business has accumulated over $100,000 in long-term debt
- Profit margins have fallen below 12% over two consecutive quarters

*"If my business experiences the following, I will call it quits":*
- The business has overdue bills exceeding $35,000
- The business has fallen below $200,000 in sales
- The business has accumulated over $150,000 in long-term debt
- The business has experienced three consecutive quarters of declining profits
- Profit margins have fallen below 10% over three consecutive quarters

You might also create limits to your involvement in the business once it becomes too large or too successful, as indicated by a certain level of sales, customers, or employees. Once your business reaches these limits, it will be your signal either to hire a full-time manager to take over, or to remove yourself in order to start your next business.

Remember, you don't have to carve these limits in stone, but you should define them carefully and write them down. Revisit them often as your business grows.

## Knowing When to Say When: Your Personal Limits

Having set the financial limits for your involvement in the business, your next step is to identify your personal limits. Knowing when to say "when" is a lot easier if you distinguish your goals from the goals of your business.

Every so often (maybe twice a year), you should update your one-, five-, and ten-year personal plan. Consider your personal ambitions, as well as your commitments to family and friends. Set goals for yourself just as you do for your business. Here are some examples:

- By age ___, I want to have a personal net worth of $___
- By age ___, I want to be earning $___ a year
- I want to retire at age ___
- I want to own a house by age ___
- I want to spend at least ___ hours a day with my children/family
- I want to take a ___ month trip to South America by age ___

Your goals should be concrete, measurable, time-bound, and attainable; otherwise, they are not goals but wishes. These goals might include:

- Personal investment targets
- Acquisition of personal assets

- Developing new skills
- Switching careers
- Travel and adventure
- Additional education or degrees
- Financially supporting your parents
- Moving to a different city, region, or country
- Community service or volunteer work

## Setting Your Exit Goals

Even in the most difficult financial times, you still have some power to decide if your business will continue, in what form, and what you will get out of it. Your choice of an exit strategy depends on how fast you want out, how much ongoing participation you want in the business, and how much of your ownership you want to liquidate.

*The Couch Potato*
*Consider for a moment the experiences of an inspired entrepreneur in Santa Cruz, California. Having grown a successful investment consulting business, she found that she was spending more time with her computer and telephone than with her young children. Working with a good attorney and banker, she sold off her interest in the business and used the profits to start a new venture in couch retailing. In structuring this business, she was guided by insights she gained in her investment business. Her priorities? Spending time with her family, and working in a relaxed environment with people who were part of her community. Her new business, Couch Potato Couches, was open for business four days a week. In those four days, she was able to do the administrative work for the business and sell enough couches to sustain the lifestyle she valued. This left her with plenty of time to spend at home being a mom!*

## How Do I Get Out?

You have several avenues by which to exit your business, each of which depends on how successful the business has been, and what your goals are. Common exit scenarios include:

- Selling out to an individual
- Selling out to another company
- Selling your stock within the company
- Selling your stock in a public offering

Also, consider these less pleasant exit scenarios:

- Business failure and bankruptcy
- Being shown the door by your investors or directors

## The Nitty Gritty of Selling Your Business

For one reason or another, you've decided to sell your business. This may seem like a confusing process, but at each step of the deal there is a whole cast of experts who specialize in buying and selling businesses. Attorneys, accountants, brokers, investors, bankers, and consultants come in all shapes and sizes, and can help even the smallest of firms. (For further information, see Chapter 7 *Valuing and Buying a Business*.)

There are two approaches small business owners generally use when selling their businesses. The most common, inexpensive, and informal approach is word of mouth; if you talk to your partners, your investors, your friends, members of your community, and your professional network, you might be surprised how quickly you will find a buyer!

If you want to approach the sale of your business more methodically, the other course of action is to seek the help of a professional business broker.

### Small Business Brokers

Business brokers are used primarily when one individual is selling his or her business to another. Business brokers evaluate the business; post listings in various journals, newsletters and newspapers; and advertise the businesses they broker in much the same way realtors do. They operate locally, regionally, or nationally, and often specialize by industry or geographic location. Check your local newspaper or the yellow pages for listings of brokers in your area.

### Valuing Your Business

No matter how unique your product or how knowledgeable your employees, your business is valued by buyers simply on the basis of cash flow and asset evaluation. This can be a simple listing of the valuables of a business, such as assets and real estate. (There can be exceptions to this rule, as in the case of a business possessing a key piece of real estate; if your shoe store is located on a busy corner in your neighborhood, and Starbuck's Coffee wants to come to town, you might find that your business is worth a lot more than the revenues it generates by selling shoes! However, most businesses rely on their cash flow and/or significant tangible assets as measures of their market value.) Other indicators of your business's worth are:

- sales growth
- historical profitability
- industry market conditions

### Evaluating Buyers

Should you choose not to work with a business broker, you will have to evaluate potential buyers. (Consider hiring a good accountant to assist you in this process.) You should set criteria for selecting a buyer, and rank them according to their importance. These criteria should include:

Spread the word... and suitors will come calling!

- Financial strength
- Type of industry
- Size of the company
- Reputation
- Their experience in acquisitions
- Knowledge of your industry and market
- Geographic location
- Ownership of the company (privately or publicly held)
- Degree of synergy between both business's core competencies

Entrepreneurs often strike a deal whereby buyers will pay them a small portion of the sale price of their business in cash, and then pay the remaining amounts in installments over time. Usually, these are paid out of earnings taken from the business itself. For this reason, you must assess the buyer's ability to manage your business profitably. Buyers often ask the seller to stay on and teach them the business. This allows the buyer to benefit from the seller's years of experience, and lets the seller guard the value of the business, which is especially important when the purchase is being financed out of the business's cash flow.

### Legal and Tax Implications

Taxes resulting from the sale of your business can seriously affect the structure of the transaction. Likewise, there are many legal guidelines (which vary from state to state) that govern the transfer of ownership in a business. Therefore, before you sell all or part of your share in a business, you should seek the assistance of an experienced tax attorney and/or securities lawyer.

*Maximize your gains by minimizing your taxes*

## Selling Your Stock to the Public

In the past decade, many companies, such as software or other technology-oriented companies, made headlines by going public at very early stages of their growth and with very minimal levels of sales. In the process, they have made millions for their founders, many without ever posting a profit. How did they do it? High-tech companies often possess unique technical knowledge or intellectual property that makes them particularly attractive to larger companies wanting to acquire that know-how. This explains the rush by large companies like Microsoft, Novell, and IBM to snap up small companies with small or no earnings, and pay handsomely to do it.

This is much less common in other industries, in which the value of a company is judged on the basis of its earnings and cash flow. This means that unless you have developed a unique and innovative technological process or product, you will probably not be participating in a public offering of your venture. However, if you grow your business to a significantly profitable level (between $5 to 20 million in sales), you might consider offering your stock to the public. Owners of high-growth businesses in select industries do this to raise additional capital or liquidate their ownership in the business.

If you decide to sell stock to the public, the first step is to select a quality investment banker. If you've never participated in an **initial public offering (IPO)** before, there are many experts out there to help you. Your investors, lawyer, accountant, consultants, and banker will all be essential to the process, and can help you select a good investment banker.

When structuring an IPO, you should identify the following:

- The percent of ownership to be sold
- The pricing of the shares of stock
- The timing of the offering
- The compensation to the investment banker

There are many legal and regulatory guidelines for public offerings of stock. Most of these involve having the business audited by outside accountants (to verify the accuracy of its financial data), and the release of timely, accurate information to potential investors. Your lawyer will be indispensable as you work to meet disclosure deadlines, file documents, and prepare contracts governing the transfer of stock.

Dreaming of

millions? Think:

- high tech

- high growth

- high profits

## NxLEVEL™ TECH TIP

**Here are some good Web sites for information on IPOs and related topics:**

- **Vistaweb** (http://www.vistaweb.com). Visit this site to get information and advice that will help you decide whether your company should consider an IPO of stock over the Internet.

- **Growth Company Guide** (http://www.once.com/gcg/). This detailed and comprehensive guide covers all the basics on structuring an IPO, legal and SEC rules, and various dealmaking strategies. Also features an extensive glossary of venture capital terminology.

- **Direct IPOs** (http://directipo.com/about/faq.html). See this site for information and advice about online IPOs of stock (or other securities) in your company.

## Being Shown the Door

This scenario usually occurs when the business has outgrown the ability of the entrepreneur to manage the enterprise. It can also occur when the entrepreneur's interest in operating the particular business is exhausted. In these cases, a group of major investors or the directors of the company might ask the founder to relinquish day-to-day control over management.

# The Business Failure

Unfortunately, for many entrepreneurs the exit path leads directly to **bankruptcy**. What is bankruptcy? It is simply the inability of a business to pay its debts. Sometimes this is the result of a major occurrence, such as the failure of a large customer to pay off its account, a major lawsuit, a loss of inventory or equipment due to fire, or the call of a large debt by a lender. It can also be caused by undercapitalization, poor cash management, or overexpansion.

Bankruptcy in the United States is regulated under the Bankruptcy Reform Act of 1978. Presented below are the major subchapters that cover different types of bankruptcies:

## Chapter 11—Voluntary

When an entrepreneur is unable to pay debts in a timely manner, he or she may voluntarily petition for the protection of the U.S. District Court. If approved, this protection allows the business to continue operations under a set of legal guidelines designed to protect the interests of the business's creditors. In this case, the business seeking protection is given 120 days in which to submit a reorganization plan that will guide the business for the duration of the bankruptcy. This plan includes provisions for paying off different classifications of creditors, the preference order and timetable for payments, and so forth. In some cases, the court may appoint a trustee to take possession of the company's assets and oversee operations. The bankrupt entrepreneur may also raise new funds by selling shares in the business, borrowing money, or selling assets.

## Chapter 10—Involuntary

Under this chapter, the creditors of a business have the right to petition the court to demand a company's reorganization. This petition may be submitted when a creditor's (or group of creditors') claims exceed $5,000. The debtor may contest this petition, and if successful, may seek reimbursement for all legal costs from his or her creditors. If contesting is unsuccessful, the procedure is similar to Chapter 11 Bankruptcy proceedings.

## Chapter 7—Liquidation

This chapter covers the most extreme cases of business bankruptcy—those in which the business must liquidate or sell off all nonexempt assets to cover its debts. If the entrepreneur submits a voluntary bankruptcy petition under Chapter 7, it is a voluntary recognition that the business is bankrupt. Along with this statement, a businessperson must usually submit an up-to-date statement of income and expenses. An involuntary bankruptcy under this act is very similar to those under Chapters 10 and 11, with the exception that the business's assets are liquidated to pay off its creditors.

## Learning from Bankruptcy

What about the effect bankruptcy might have on you personally and professionally? You may feel worn-out, dispirited, and embarrassed, but keep in mind that bankruptcy doesn't necessarily mean the end for your career as an entrepreneur. It is historically proven that most successful entrepreneurs have endured—and learned from—multiple failures before achieving success. This is why it is critical for you to ask yourself hard questions about what caused your failure:

Experienced entrepreneurs agree: learn all the lessons you can and move on

- Was it bad luck, or was it a weakness you have in one area or another?
- What skill should you acquire to improve the chances of your next venture?
- Did you create an exit strategy, and review it often?
- Did you stray from your core competencies?
- Did you undertake expansion too quickly?
- Were you undercapitalized?
- Did your business invest too much time in seeking additional customers, and too little time serving the ones it had?
- Did you file for bankruptcy protection too late?

Having failed once, you are likely to have a better grasp of market dynamics, and the correct mix needed to run a successful business: market research, capitalization, cash management, and personnel management. Your negotiating skills will almost certainly have improved!

## It's Really Happening! What Do I Do Now?

A great actor always knows when to exit

How do you know when you're going bankrupt? If you know the warning signs, you might be able to avoid trouble, or at least minimize it when it hits. These signs often are linked—once one happens, the others may not be far behind. At the outset, you should have a general understanding of the protections available under U.S. bankruptcy law, and a good relationship with a capable, trustworthy attorney.

### Bankruptcy's Red Flags

- Lack of management control and accountability over finances and spending
- Lack of inventory or supply to meet orders
- Lack of planning and paper documentation of major transactions
- Key people leave the company
- Business offers large discounts to customers who pay cash
- Bank requires subordination of its loans
- Payroll taxes are not paid
- Employee benefits are not funded
- Suppliers require cash payments
- Increase in customer complaints

Here's the scenario: Your creditors are calling on the phone in a panic, your two largest customers just failed for the fourth time to pay off their accounts, and your banker is getting antsy. What should you do? Contact your lawyer immediately, and if he or she recommends filing for bankruptcy, do it fast! Your best strategy is to file *before* your creditors join together and force you into bankruptcy. Why? Because a voluntary bankruptcy declaration will buy you a 120-day holding period in which to submit a plan of reorganization, and another 60 days while the court and your creditors evaluate it. During this period, your business is not required to pay off any of its debts. Afterwards, you have two courses of action: ensure that your plan to make your business profitable again works, or begin planning the liquidation of your business.

During this process, stay in contact with customers to inspire their confidence and continued loyalty to your business. Keep creditors and stockholders informed about all developments. Your investors are probably more concerned than anyone about your business and their investment in it, so keep them apprised of details through a newsletter, or for larger investors, a personal phone call. Last, but not least, you must communicate with your employees, who more than anyone else feel the uncertainty of the business on daily basis. Share with them the details of the business's reorganization, and keep them focused on the tasks at hand. After all, the very future of your business depends on them!

## You've Sold Your Business...Now What?

You were working 70 hours a week, and now you're sitting in your garden reading travel magazines. The thrills of the day-to-day operations of your business are behind you, and a lot of uncertainty lies ahead. What is your next step? As mentioned at the start of this chapter, looking at your personal and professional life before exiting your business will help you immeasurably.

Take some time to think about the business you've left and the lessons you've learned, and your transition into the next phase of your life will be a lot easier. Then, celebrate your victories and do some of the things you've always dreamed of doing!

---

*Exiting Doesn't Mean Having To Say You're Sorry*

*Anderson and Associates, a public relations firm located in a suburb of Washington, D.C., started up in 1990. Its owner, Dylan Anderson, had always planned to sell the business at some point, because she and her husband, who would retire in 1999, planned to relocate to the Maryland coast and build their dream house on the beach.*

*By late 1995, Anderson and Associates had become a very successful company. Clients included several national associations located in the Washington area, as well as some major corporations. Dylan had worked hard to establish her business, and all the key elements were there: attention to financial details, an energetic and creative staff, great customer service, and high profits. By mid-1996, Dylan had three serious bidders for her business.*

*Dylan and her husband ushered in the new year of 2000 in their new house overlooking the Atlantic Ocean. The new owner of Anderson and Associates celebrated the new year and his new venture in the company's office.*

---

Is the glass half empty or half full?

Half of all businesses fail in their first four years

—OR—

Half of all businesses succeed beyond four years.

## Conclusion

You have gotten a priceless education by starting your own business. You've learned about a particular industry, customer service, hiring and managing people, and keeping track of finances. You might even have learned a few things about yourself! With these insights in mind, you are uniquely equipped to set new goals and create the personal and professional life you desire.

Remember: The things that made you an entrepreneur—drive, fearlessness, and charm—will not disappear the day you cash out of your business. You might take some well-deserved time off, but before long, no doubt, the wheels of your imagination will be churning out new ideas and opportunities for professional growth.

## Chapter 15
# LEGAL STRUCTURE OF THE BUSINESS

*About This Chapter:*
- *Selection of the business entity*
- *Operating within a corporate structure*
- *Mechanisms for generating capital*

## Introduction

What type of business entity do you want to own? Selecting the one that is right for you involves considering taxes, estate planning, and financial issues. This chapter discusses the advantages and disadvantages of the most common types of business ownership. A note of clarification: The term **closely held business** refers to a business that is owned by a few people and whose stock isn't publicly traded. Normally, closely held businesses have 25 or fewer owners, and the majority are owned by one or two individuals.

Sole proprietorship is the most common form of business ownership in the Unites States

## Selection of the Business Entity

### Sole Proprietorship

The most common closely held business is the sole proprietorship, which is run by an individual, often under a trade name, and with no outside owners/investors. Although it is the simplest business entity and avoids the potential for double taxation assessed on corporations, sole proprietorship exposes you to personal liability for every act and debt of the business, and there is no room to expand through new owners and their capital. Also, many of the tax deductions available to other forms of business organizations, such as expenses for health benefits and defined benefit pension plans, are unavailable or the expenses for them are only partially deductible on your tax return. Sole proprietorships terminate at the proprietor's death, so they are difficult to work into an estate plan.

*When Mary Ligori opened her travel agency in 1996, she decided to do so as a sole proprietor. She wanted to avoid corporate taxation and felt her risk of exposure for personal liability would be minimal. Her successful agency now has three offices and continues to grow. Sole proprietorship has worked well for Mary Ligori!*

### General Partnership

A **general partnership** is formed when two or more persons enter an agreement (either written or oral) to operate a business together. The partnership files an "informational" tax return, and the partners must report their share of the partnership's profit or loss on their individual tax returns with what accountants call a **K-1 statement**. The Uniform Partnership Act, which has been adopted by most states, sets forth the rights and duties of the partners to each other and to third parties. It also provides uniform procedures for dissolution and wind-up of the business. You can customize your partnership agreement's terms to deal with management issues, distribution of profits, and the authority to conduct business on behalf of the partnership. You will also need to file an assumed business name form to protect your partnership's trade name.

Partners are jointly and severally liable for all the obligations of the partnership. This means that you can be held liable to a third party for all debts and torts of the partnership, even though you may only have a partial interest! This is the primary disadvantage of doing business as a partnership. Another disadvantage is that many partnerships terminate upon one partner's death, so it is hard to use them in estate planning. The third major disadvantage is that fringe benefits packages for owner/employees are only partially deductible on the partner's tax return.

---

*Joining an ongoing partnership to invest in oil well exploration in the South China Sea was an opportunity that Jim Carruthers did not want to pass up. The China Sea partnership needed more cash to expand its operations, so it was opening up to new partners. Jim's total investment of $200,000 bought him a 1/16th interest in the exploration company. Unfortunately, several months after Jim joined, a China Sea partnership tanker carrying tons of oil was overturned. The cost of environmental clean-up was too expensive for the partnership to bear, and because he was jointly liable, Jim's personal assets were used as collateral for a portion of the clean-up. Jim vowed he would never form a partnership again unless he read the partnership agreement with his lawyer.*

---

### Limited Partnership

In a **limited partnership**, individuals or corporations operate as general partners, and are in charge of managing the day-to-day activities of the business. **Limited partners** are **silent investors**, and do not participate in day-to-day management; they may, however, vote to dissolve and wind up the partnership's affairs. Limited partners are only liable for partnership debts to the extent of their investment, so if you invest $15,000 as a limited partner, you are exposed to no more than $15,000 of losses, regardless of the activities of that partnership or the extent of its obligations.

Limited partners must observe strict formalities to avoid the joint liability of general partnerships. In most states, the Uniform Limited Partnership Act addresses the partners' duties, liabilities, and rights in wind-up and dissolution. You must file a certificate of limited partnership with your department of commerce, and you'll also need to file to protect your trade name. Some states also require the use of "Ltd." to accompany the trade name of a limited partnership.

## Corporations

A corporation is a legal entity wholly separate from the shareholders who own it. All states have laws describing how corporations may operate within that state. How a corporation works will be discussed in greater detail later. For now, the different types of corporations that will be discussed are:

### C-corporation

Most large businesses in the United States operate as "C-corporations." (The letter "C" refers to a subchapter of the Internal Revenue Code for corporate tax purposes.) These are usually large, publicly held companies, but they also include small and even single-owner companies. A C-corporation may have a single shareholder who comprises the entire board of directors, holds all the corporate offices, and is the only employee! The distinguishing characteristics of a C-corporation are that it may have more than one class of stock (such as common stock and preferred stock) and an unlimited number of shareholders, and that the taxes on its profits are paid by the corporation. This may result in the double taxation previously discussed. However, this can often be avoided by careful year-end planning, since reasonable salaries and fringe benefits (medical and dental plans, insurance, and retirement plans) are deductible by the corporation. A word of caution. It is very rarely to your advantage to own real estate in a C corporation. It will almost always generate two levels of tax without any corresponding benefit to you.

Most large businesses are C-corporations

### S-corporation

These corporations are different from C-corporations in that their profits and losses are not reported at the corporate level. Instead, they are reported on the owner's personal tax returns in much the same way as partnerships. S-corporations are limited to one class of stock and must file their tax returns on a calendar year. They are restricted to 75 shareholders. In order for your company to become an S-corporation, you must file a special election with the Internal Revenue Service (within certain deadlines that depend on when you file your **articles of incorporation** with your state's Department of Commerce). The S-corporation provides a substantial tax benefit in that it may allow you to pass the losses of your business through to your personal tax return. This often has a significant benefit in the early years of a business, because the business may generate "paper losses," but still make enough money to pay a salary.

You can switch from being an S-corporation to a C-corporation (or vice versa) only once during the existence of your company, so consider the change carefully!

### Export corporations

If your business is organized for import/export, you may want to form either a Foreign Sales Corporation, or an Interest Charge Domestic International Sales Corporation. These highly specialized corporations provide significant tax advantages. You may even want to set up a subsidiary export corporation that will run under your regular manufacturing company. You should talk to your accountant and lawyer about this.

### Professional corporations

Most entrepreneurs cannot operate as a professional corporation, because most states permit such corporations to be used only by doctors, lawyers, accountants, and other persons who are licensed by the state as professionals. Limitations on liability will be discussed later in this chapter, but for now you should be aware that in most states, professional corporations do not offer shareholders any freedom from personal liability.

### Nonprofit corporations

In most states, this form of business entity is restricted to charitable, religious, or educational enterprises, which do not have the purpose of making a profit. Any profits earned by the business cannot be passed through to the individuals. Nonprofit corporations do not have shareholders, because the assets of the corporation do not belong to any individuals; most states require that when a nonprofit corporation is dissolved, its assets must be delivered to another nonprofit corporation operating with the same general purpose. A nonprofit corporation is run by a board of trustees, and generally hires an executive director to manage its activities (that person, and the other employees, can be paid salaries). Typically, nonprofit corporations include animal shelters, churches, youth organizations, senior citizen services, and similar types of public service enterprises. The state often monitors the activities of nonprofit corporations to ensure their compliance with applicable laws.

### Cooperatives

The employee-owned cooperative was a common method of doing business in the early 20th century. They do not offer the tax benefits of a corporation, but they do have the unique feature of passing all profits through to the owners (who are usually its employees). Members of a "community" may feel especially comfortable with the structure of a cooperative; communally run natural food stores often choose this form of operating entity. If you elect to do business as a cooperative, you will need a written contract establishing the cooperative enterprise and describing how it will be managed on a day-to-day basis.

### Business trusts

Business trusts were popular late in the 19th century, before many states recognized the existence of the corporation. Two or more persons can operate as a business trust by combining their resources and adopting a **Declaration of Trust**. The business is then managed by trustees for the benefit of holders of "certificates of beneficial interest." **Bylaws** are often adopted; these are official guidelines by which the business is governed. Unlike ordinary trusts, which exist to conserve and protect an estate, the purpose of business trusts is to make money. Business trusts are used infrequently today, because some courts have ruled that they are not distinct legal entities, and because corporate laws are so much more flexible than they were in the past. The primary disadvantage of the business trust is that the certificate holders may be personally liable, as partners, for the debts of the trust if they retain any control over the trustees. The IRS taxes the business trust as it would an association, so there is again the danger of double taxation.

*Limited liability companies*

The **limited liability company (LLC)** is a new form of ownership established by an operating agreement that is similar to the bylaws of a corporation. They are now permitted in almost every state and have been recognized as valid entities by the IRS. LLCs combine the best attributes of partnerships and S-corporations; they're taxed like a partnership, but liability is limited like a corporation. One of the distinguishing features of an LLC is that the parties may allocate in their operating agreement their shares of gain or loss, which do not have to be equal to the percentage of their investment. Therefore, if one party can utilize tax losses better than another due to his or her personal tax situation, operation as an LLC allows beneficial allocation of that tax benefit. In addition, you may have two or more members of an LLC, and you may establish classifications of owners through the operating agreement, unlike the restrictions on an S-corporation.

Transferability of ownership is addressed in the buy/sell provisions of the operating agreement. LLCs can also be used effectively in estate planning. Tax advantages and freedom from personal liability make the LLC an ideal business entity for joint ownership and operation of real estate. They are being used by many other closely held businesses as well. Note: Most states require that you file limited liability articles and annual reports with the Department of Commerce. Your lawyer can assist you in this process.

Since an LLC has many attributes of a corporation, many lawyers recommend that the members hold an annual meeting, keep minutes and maintain books and records like a corporation, as discussed in the next section.

# Operating Within the Corporate Structure

## How a Closely Held Corporation Works

The closely held corporation is the form of entity most familiar to accountants and lawyers; the rules and tax code provisions that apply to them are well established. Shares in corporations are also easy to transfer for business and estate planning purposes. The following discusses in greater detail how corporations work, and what you must do if you desire to operate your business as a corporation.

## Corporate Formation

You can form a corporation by filing **articles of incorporation** with your state's Department of Commerce (or your local equivalent). This document states why the corporation is being formed, and what type of business it will conduct; and specifies its incorporators, its principal place of business, and the duration of its existence. Corporations may have an unlimited life, extending far beyond the death of the initial shareholders. The articles also serve to register the corporate name. **Bylaws** are the operating guidelines for the company. They explain how the corporation is to function; the rights and duties of the board of directors, shareholders, and officers; and how the corporation is to wind up its business. Once the articles have been filed, the corporation must have an organizational meeting at which the bylaws are approved, stock is issued, the first board of directors is elected, and the corporation officially begins conducting business. A corporation is not completely formed until all of these steps have been taken. In addition, the organizational meeting is a good time to adopt a formal **buy/sell agreement** and an **employment agreement**.

## Board of Directors

The corporation's activities are managed by its board of directors, which generally consists of five or fewer people. In the case of a closely held corporation with a single owner, the board often consists of the shareholder, one or two family members, and one or two other trusted advisors. When there are several owners, each usually has a seat on the board, at least initially. A chairperson is elected at the corporation's annual meeting, and runs the board meetings until replaced or voted against at the next annual meeting. The board sets the policies of the company, and elects certain officers to be in charge of specific aspects of the business.

## Officers

Typically, a corporation's officers include a president, treasurer, and secretary. The officers actually run the company; they hire and fire the employees and work to grow the business. Most states allow for a closely held corporation to elect one person to one or more offices, so one person can be chairman of the board, president, treasurer, and CEO all at once!

## Shareholders

The shareholders of the company are those persons who own its stock; their rights and duties are set forth in the bylaws. Ultimately, all power in the corporation rests with a majority of the shareholders, for they elect the board of directors. If the shareholders are dissatisfied with the management of the company, they may hold a special meeting and either elect a new board of directors, or require that the board replace the officers or other employees. Individual shareholders are liable for the debts of the company only to the extent of their investment in the shares. (This will be discussed in more detail later.)

Shareholders own part of a company by owning "stock"

Keep good records!

## Annual Meeting

The board of directors and the shareholders must each have an annual meeting. However, most states allow for these meetings to be held jointly. The bylaws of the corporation state when the meetings are to be held, what type of notice must be given, and what activities may take place at the meetings. The bylaws should also address the number of persons to be elected to the board of directors each year.

## Books and Records

To ensure that your business remains classified as a corporation, you must observe certain formalities. As stated above, one of these is to hold an annual meeting. Another is to document the major activities of the corporation in the corporation's annual meeting minutes. Most states require that corporations keep certain records. The shareholders of the corporation have the legal right to review its books and records, such as annual minutes and financial statements. Your corporation should maintain a minute book containing the registry of shareholders, a copy of the articles of incorporation, the bylaws, the organizational minutes, and the minutes from each of your company's annual meetings. The annual minutes should describe salaries paid to the principals; loans to and from the corporation; major purchases or sales of equipment; real estate and leases; and major policy decisions. The minutes should also describe employment agreements; pension or medical plans; reimbursement for vehicle expenses; authorizations for major travel or educational expenditures, and similar actions. The annual minutes will assist your accountant in the preparation of the annual tax return, and serve as evidence to support that tax return if you are audited.

## Annual Reporting

Most states require that your corporation file an annual report with the Department of Commerce. This report may be a simple pre-printed form indicating that your corporation is still in business, and stating the location of your corporate office and the name of the principal person in charge. Other states have a more complicated form for annual reporting. In any event, it is important that you file the annual report to prevent the Department of Commerce from classifying your corporation as delinquent in filing and terminating its corporate charter. While all these formalities may sound complicated, your lawyer and accountant are there to help you and they should handle much of the paperwork.

Limited liability: the corporate shield against personal liability

## Liability—The Corporate Shield

One of the main reasons to do business as a corporation is the "corporate shield" doctrine, which limits personal liability. As mentioned previously, the liability of shareholders of a corporation generally extends only to the amount of their investment.

*If you invest $50,000 in ABC, Inc., your liability is unlikely to exceed that amount. For example, if ABC owed $1 million to its landlord and trade creditors, but you did not personally guarantee any of that debt, in most cases you would not personally owe any portion of it, even if you were the only shareholder.*

Corporations must strictly adhere to the laws that govern them; otherwise, the corporate shield can be "pierced" by the corporation's creditors. The most common reason for piercing is that the corporation did not have annual meeting minutes, or did not file its annual report. This can have extreme consequences to the investors! Courts also allow the shield to be pierced when the corporation is a sham, and the owners have depleted its assets for their own benefit and to the injury of its creditors.

The major exception to the rule of limited liability is the Doctrine of Primary Actor Responsibility. This applies to all grants of limited liability to limited partners, LLC members, and corporate shareholders. A person is always responsible for his or her own actions, regardless of whether they occur in the context of a corporation or sole proprietorship.

*Let's say you are a $20,000 investor in a corporation, but are also an employee. You will be personally liable for any damages that you cause to other persons, even though you are employed by the company. For example, if you are a shareholder of Welders, Inc. and are also its only welder, you may be personally liable for any personal injuries or damages caused by your faulty welding. In addition, your investment of $20,000 may be at risk if the company is found liable for your negligence!*

The principles of using insurance to allocate risk will be discussed in a later chapter. For now, you should remember that operating as a limited partner, LLC member, or shareholder in a corporation may not, under all circumstances, shield you from personal liability. The best way to allocate that risk may be through insurance against losses.

A final thought on this topic: Operating in a limited liability corporate form does not absolve you from personal liability for unpaid taxes if you are in a position of authority in your business; the government will hold you personally liable to make the payment!

## Mechanisms for Generating Capital

The following topics are covered in more detail in Chapter 40 *Money Sources*.

## Equity Financing

All states require that your business have some amount of **equity capital**. In other words, the owners must give some value to the company to give it life, and to support their possession of limited partnership shares, LLC memberships, or corporate stock. Corporations, limited partnerships, and LLCs allow the organizers to finance the business through their own investments, as well as by seeking capital from outside investors. (Note that financing your business through the investment of third parties results in loss of control. This will be discussed in greater detail in a later chapter.)

Some corporations use a device called "preferred stock" to raise capital from outside investors. This type of stock is often non-voting, and usually has a set dividend payable to preferred shareholders before any dividends are payable to "common" shareholders. Remember that taxes must be paid on dividends received by preferred shareholders.

---

*Bob's Wise Web Page started out by offering preferred stock to its initial investors at $5 per share. Once Bob's business took off, he decided to offer common stock to later investors at $3 per share. When his company profits rose by more than 150% in his third year of operation, he was able to offer a dividend to those first fearless investors who purchased his preferred stock.*

---

You should also be aware that the federal government and all 50 states have adopted regulations that restrict the ways in which you can sell the investment opportunities known as **securities**. These laws apply to shares of stock in a corporation, interests in a LTD and memberships in an LLC, among others. Federal regulations apply if you publicly offer a security for sale across state lines, if more than $5 million is involved, or if more than 35 investors are solicited. In these cases, your security sales will be regulated not only by federal law, but also by the Securities and Exchange Commission (SEC), with whom you will have to register your securities.

Many states have similar **blue sky** provisions, but their regulatory thresholds are lower to cover smaller businesses. Typically, states require registration if the solicitation is made to 25 or more persons, and over $1 million is sought. Even if state registration is not required, your sale of securities is subject to disclosure laws aimed at preventing fraud. Disclosure laws require that the company offering its securities for sale disclose detailed information about the company to ensure that the public has sufficient knowledge on which to base an investment decision. Be sure to consult with your lawyer before making a public or private offering of a security, to make sure you comply with registration and disclosure requirements. Be aware that if you are considering a public offering that requires registration, you can expect a complicated, time-consuming, and expensive process! Financing your business is discussed in much greater detail in a later chapter.

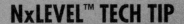

## NxLEVEL™ TECH TIP

A wide range of state business and tax information is accessible via the Internet. You can get most states' laws online, download tax forms, and find information on a wide range of business, tax, and regulatory subjects. Here are a number of reliable online business and tax information sources for each of the fifty states:

• **Yahoo State Information** (http://www.yahoo.com/regional/U S States/). This is a good starting point for a search of state Web sites. It lists all of the states; simply click on the state whose governmental information you wish to peruse.

• **50-State Map of State Web Sites** (http://www.state.ne.us/states.html). This site displays a map of the 50 states. Simply click on your state to go to your state's official or unofficial home page.

• **Corporate Agents, Inc.** (http://www.corporate.com). For a small fee, this private service will incorporate your business in any state, generally within a day or two. It contains everything you need to form a new corporation or limited liability company in any state for as little as $11, plus state filing fees. A helpful FAQ addresses many questions about incorporating, and there is also a collection of links to Web sites for entrepreneurs.

### Debt Financing

Another method of financing the business is through debt. This often takes place through the traditional relationship of a business and its bank. The bank typically requires shareholders to make a **personal guaranty** of the corporation's obligations, and will most likely want **collateral** to secure the debt. Thus, in order to get a loan of $50,000 for new equipment, you will probably have to sign the loan personally, and grant the bank a lien on the title to that equipment. You may even have to put up your personal assets as collateral. (As a side note, you may want to insist on the personal guaranty of the principal of a corporation to which you sell goods on credit. This gives you a guarantee on the debt in the event that the corporation proves to be an empty shell with no real assets.)

A second method of debt financing for closely held businesses is for the principal shareholder to loan additional funds to the company for its operation. You should document these loan transactions in your annual minutes, and prepare a promissory note payable to the principal by the business. The principal may also want to consider taking some collateral for the loan so if the business becomes insolvent, there is something of value remaining. This is important because if the business fails, creditors can attach the business's interest in that asset unless it has been previously pledged as collateral to the principals.

## Bonds

A **bond** is a cross between a stock and a loan; this instrument is a security too. The corporation sells the bond to a third party for a fixed price, and agrees to pay interest on that amount. The face amount of the bond is to be repaid from future profits on a certain date. The bond holder is given no collateral.

## Venture Capital

When a business is unable to acquire capital by borrowing money from the local bank, a common solution is to look to venture capitalists. These lenders often finance new businesses, but sometimes under onerous terms. They usually require the personal guaranty of the principals, together with a lien on all the assets of the business. And since they often demand a majority interest in the company through shares of its stock, you may find that your lender is also your majority shareholder! Many owners get squeezed out of their businesses this way, so you should very thoroughly discuss this issue with your lawyer and accountant before agreeing to such terms.

## Government Financing Programs

Many states have adopted grants, loan programs, and other financing devices to assist small businesses. These programs constantly change in response to the political and economic climate. The most well-known program is the Small Business Administration, which cooperates with local lending institutions to make loans that might exceed the risk tolerance of the bank. The bank loans the funds, and the SBA guarantees up to 80% of the loan. There are many other programs unique to each state; consult with your local economic development organization to determine which resources are available to your business.

| Forms of Ownership | Advantages | Disadvantages |
|---|---|---|
| Sole Proprietorship | Low start-up costs<br>Owner in direct control<br>Minimal working capital requirements | Unlimited personal liability<br>Lack of continuity<br>Difficulty in raising capital<br>Ownership limited to one person |
| General Partnership | Ease of formation<br>Low start-up costs<br>Broader management base<br>Direct sharing of profits | Unlimited personal liability<br>Lack of continuity<br>Difficulty in raising additional capital<br>Bound by acts of partner |
| C-Corporation | Limited liability<br>Separate legal entity<br>Transferable ownership<br>Ease of raising capital | Activities limited by the charter and regulations<br>Most expensive form to organize<br>Possible double taxation |
| S-Corporation | Limited liability<br>Taxed as a partnership to shareholders<br>Transferable ownership<br>Ease of raising capital | Must have calendar year<br>Limited to 75 shareholders<br>Expensive form to organize<br>Only one class of stock is permitted |
| Limited Liability Company | Freedom to choose options<br>Tax attributes of a partnership<br>Flexible management<br>Transferable ownership | Expensive form to organize<br>Relatively new legal entity<br>Limited transfer of interest |

# Conclusion

There are a number of different forms of business entities, but the most common form is still the closely held corporation. This may change in the future as most states have adopted laws allowing the formation of LLCs. The type of business entity you choose determines how easily the business can be transferred to your family, employees, or a third party purchaser; the amount of liability you assume personally; and how you and your business are taxed. Therefore, you must consult with your lawyer and accountant before you select an entity, so that you can devise the best possible strategy. Remember to follow all the rules governing your type of entity; this will ensure that the business is able to continue in that form, and that you retain all your rights and benefits as the business owner. Once again, always seek advice from your lawyer and accountant when considering the legal structure of your business!

# Chapter 16
# GOVERNMENT REGULATIONS AND TAXES

*About This Chapter:*
- *The American legal system*
- *International regulations*
- *Areas of governmental regulations affecting business*
- *Bankruptcy*

## Introduction

How does the legal system affect your business? How can you use it to protect your business interests and plan for your retirement? We will answer these and other questions by discussing the legal system, and some of the major areas of business regulation.

## The American Legal System

The American legal system consists of statutory laws, judicial interpretations, and administrative rules originating from the executive, legislative, and judicial branches of government. All of these can affect your business.

### Statutory Law

The U.S. Congress consists of the Senate and the House of Representatives. In order for a bill to become law, it must be enacted by both chambers. Once enacted, it becomes part of the U.S. Code. A similar procedure takes place in each of the 50 states. The **federal code** is subject only to the U.S. Constitution; **state statutes** are subject to their own state constitutional limitations, and must also conform to federal law and the U.S. Constitution. States can regulate activities that take place within their borders (for instance, how businesses may incorporate, or the requirements for obtaining a driver's license).

Since different statutes govern different aspects of business practice, it's a good idea to insist that your contracts with other parties include a statement by the other party that they are in compliance with all federal, state, and local laws. For example, if you are working with a toy manufacturer, you should ask the manufacturer to represent to you that they are in compliance with federal laws regarding child safety standards.

## Judicial Interpretation and Common Law

The federal court system consists of:

- United States Supreme Court
- Eleven appellate circuit courts
- Federal district courts
- Federal magistrates

In addition, there are federal courts established for:

- Bankruptcy
- Claims
- Taxes
- Customs
- Patent appeals

Federal courts hear cases of federal law, and those which involve the crossing of state lines or waterways. Each of the states has a supreme court, and most have an intermediate level court of appeal. All the states also use local (appellate) trial courts, which are usually based upon county lines.

The courts hold trials, hear appeals from lower courts, and probate estates. They also review the decisions of administrative agencies, and the actions of state and federal legislatures, for conformity with federal law and constitutional requirements. In reviewing the actions of the other two branches of government, the courts establish law through their interpretations. This is called **common law**. The courts use decisions from previous, similar cases as a basis for their judgments.

*Common law is made by the courts applying prior decisions*

## Administrative Rulemaking

The executive branches of the federal and state governments have established various administrative agencies to implement federal codes and state statutes. These agencies create laws by way of **administrative regulations**; in many states, they have established a hearing process that enforces these regulations within the state. Many laws affecting business originate from administrative rulemaking. One example is the worker safety regulations of the Occupational Safety and Health Administration (OSHA).

*Agencies make law through rules*

## Civil and Criminal Systems

There are two further divisions of the law: civil and criminal. A **tort** is a civil law action in which a **plaintiff** sues a **defendant** in order to be "made whole" after being injured by the defendant. Remedies are generally either **money damages**, or **injunctions** by which the court orders one party to cease doing something damaging to another party. In cases of outrageous wrongdoing, **punitive damages** may be awarded by the court or jury to make an example of the wrongdoer; punitive damages levied against a company for an accident caused by its drunken truck driver puts other trucking lines on notice that they cannot allow such behavior in their own companies.

A common example of a tort is a suit against a person who caused an automobile accident through negligence. The court can make the defendant pay money damages to the plaintiff; this may include compensation for any "pain and suffering" endured by the plaintiff. **Criminal law**, on the other hand, concerns the rights of society as a whole versus the actions of individuals; its purpose is to maintain public peace and safety. Criminal justice is enforced by the state or federal government, and penalties range from fines to jail terms.

The following story shows how one event can trigger various responses from the legal system.

———————◆———————

*Al's Asbestos, your next door neighbor, knowingly allowed toxic materials to leak onto your property, and one of your employees was killed as a result. You have a statutory civil law remedy for the injury to your property, and you may be able to get an injunction against Al's to prohibit further dumping. Your employee's family could bring a common law tort action for personal injury or wrongful death; punitive damages would probably be in order since Al had prior knowledge of his dumping. The state may also have a criminal complaint for homicide, and the state environmental regulating agency would bring an administrative action against Al's for violating environmental regulations.*

———————◆———————

### Local Government

In addition to the state and federal legal systems described above, you should also be aware of local regulations, which are often called **ordinances**. These cover zoning and building codes, requirements for business licenses, signage regulation, and so forth.

## International Regulations

If your company has offices in or does business with another country, it is wise to comply with that country's laws and regulations. An attorney whose focus is international business can advise you on this matter. The country's laws may seem strange to you, but it's important to remember that diplomacy, and respect for the law, will always help your reputation abroad.

### Arbitration and Mediation

Some states have recognized that the traditional method of resolving legal disputes (the civil lawsuit) is too expensive and time-consuming. One response has been arbitration administered under the court system. A person called an arbitrator is vested with the authority of the court to settle the conflict, and the informal proceedings take place under a fast-track time schedule. Many contracts now provide for this procedure in lieu of litigation. You may want to spell out in your contracts that the arbitration is binding and cannot be appealed, since in some states those issues are left to the disputing parties.

You must comply with local laws when doing business overseas

*Mike Laughton, an organic farmer in Gilroy, California, was having problems getting his distributor, Sun Products, to comply with their contractual obligation to distribute Mike's fruits and vegetables to chain stores throughout California. Over the course of one year, Mike saw his customer base slide from ten chain stores to three! He asked around and discovered that Sun Products was marketing other growers' produce in the same area. Mike was furious, and immediately telephoned Sun Products to complain. Sun Products claimed that their agreement with Mike was not exclusive. Because there was an arbitration clause in the contract, Mike called in an arbitrator to settle the dispute. The arbitrator ruled that Sun should pay Mike $100,000 for lost business and agreed that the two firms could terminate their working relationship. Mike was happy because he was compensated for his losses and he was free to find another exclusive distributor. The cost of taking Sun Products to court would have been prohibitive, so arbitration was a great solution for Mike.*

A similar, but wholly voluntary and even less formal process is **mediation**. The primary difference between arbitration and mediation is that the mediation process isn't binding. The mediator is usually selected to facilitate communication, to deliver an unbiased point of view, and to help the parties reach a settlement. Again, the savings to both parties in time and cost are often significant. Mediation often preserves business relationships, because the process is far less adversarial than a lawsuit or arbitration. Of course, the participants must have a desire to resolve the dispute amicably or the process is ineffective.

## Areas of Governmental Regulation Affecting Businesses

No one could hope to list or explain all the laws and regulations that may affect your business. Each state and city has its unique set of rules. Following are a few of the regulations you may encounter.

### Taxation
#### *Federal and state income tax*
Federal, state, and local governments all have the power to collect taxes. In most states, taxation of personal and corporate income parallels the federal system. One of the primary problems with doing business as a corporation is the potential for double taxation, in which your company's profits are taxed, and any income paid to the company's individual owners is also taxed. The legal structure of a business was discussed in the preceding chapter.

#### *Sales tax*
All but three states have enacted sales taxes, which affect businesses by taxing transactions. Some states tax nearly all transactions—including those for medical and legal services—while others exempt "necessity" items, like food and clothing. States often attempt taxation of transient visitors through motel and occupancy taxes, gas taxes,

and the like. States that use sales taxes usually require that you register your business with the state taxing authority; some even require a bond before they will issue you a tax reporting identification number. In a few states, counties and even some cities have local taxing authority. Check with your accountant or state Department of Commerce to find out how your business will be taxed.

Sales tax laws may require registration of your business

---

*The Brewmeister*

*Tom Davenport, the maker of a specialty microbrew called Brew-You Brew, was astonished to discover how much he'd have to pay in taxes once his business was operational. Not only was he responsible for federal and state income taxes on his profits, but he also had to pay sales and use taxes to each of the states for which he needed a business permit; bi-monthly sales taxes to the Bureau of Alcohol, Tobacco, and Firearms (BATF) for all his shipments of beer to wholesale distributors; and state alcohol beverage control agency taxes in forty states. The fines for missed or late payments to the BATF were enormous! After four years of dutifully paying all of his required taxes, Tom got so frustrated that he decided to name his latest flavored ale Tax-You Brew, and to introduce the beer to the public on April 15!*

---

### Property tax

Most states assess taxes against real estate as a means of funding state government. The property tax structure can have interesting twists, such as your equipment being taxed as real estate or personal property. Depending on its location, your business may have unique tax benefits or burdens; many states have adopted enterprise zones or similar devices whereby businesses are given tax breaks for locating in certain areas. Urban renewal districts can also result in favorable real property taxation assessments. Discuss your state's tax structure with your accountant and lawyer before starting a business, or making any major changes to an existing business.

### Business license fees

Many local jurisdictions can tax your business under a system of business license fees. Before you choose a business location, you should consult the city finance department to determine what, if any, local business fees they assess. Some states also assess special fees for regulated professions and industries (such as beer, wine, and spirit manufacturers), so check with your state Department of Commerce.

## Employees

### Payroll/withholding

The federal government has a standard system for requiring employers to deduct and pay various payroll taxes on their employees. These include the Federal Insurance Contributions Act (FICA), which is the social security tax, and the Federal Unemployment Tax Act (FUTA). The employer is also required to withhold sums from employees for state unemployment compensation, injured worker compensation, and consumer protection escrow. In large metropolitan areas, city taxes are often withheld. As an employer, you must make quarterly (sometimes monthly) payments of income tax withholdings to the government; incorrect or late payments can result in severe penalties! Anyone who has observed an IRS lock-out has seen the devastating effect of the failure to pay withholdings.

Some employers avoid federal withholding requirements by calling their workers independent contractors; before attempting this, you should carefully review IRS regulations and state laws regarding independent contractors. In most states, persons or businesses performing labor or services for others (called the owner in this example) are considered independent contractors only if they:

- Are free from the direction and control of the owner, except that the owner specifies the desired results
- Are responsible for obtaining their own licenses and business regulations
- Provide their own tools or equipment
- Have the authority to hire employees to assist them
- Are paid upon completion of specific portions of the project
- File tax returns as a business, rather than as a W-2 wage earner from the owner's business
- Advertise to the public as an independent business through business cards, advertisements, telephone listings, and the like
- Perform work for more than two owners in a year
- Have a place of business outside that of the owner

### Responsibility for the acts of employees
Under civil law, the employer is generally held responsible for any injurious act of its employees that occurs within the scope of employment. Thus, if your delivery person hits a child in a crosswalk while running a business errand, your business is probably liable. This is why many businesses buy liability insurance, and incorporate to avoid personal liability.

### Wage and hour regulation
The federal government has established a minimum wage under the Fair Labor Standards Act. Most states have also adopted such requirements. There are additional state and federal laws regulating child labor, overtime, provision for periodic breaks, consecutive hours worked, and related employment practices. You should familiarize yourself with these laws and keep updated on the most recent increases to the minimum wage.

### OSHA
The Occupational Safety and Health Administration (OSHA) sets guidelines for worker safety. Governing the guidelines are a complex series of regulations by both federal and state agencies. There are severe financial penalties for failure to comply with these regulations, but what is more important. It makes good business sense to provide a safe and healthy workplace for your employees!

### The hiring process

Under Title VII of the Civil Rights Act of 1964, your business is prohibited from discriminating against someone on the basis of race, color, sex, national origin, or age. Consequently, there are a number of federal and state codes and regulations that affect your hiring process; for instance, you may not inquire about a person's age, religion, or sexual preference. It is a good rule of thumb not to ask any interview questions that are not job-related. (It is also strongly recommended that you establish a standard set of questions for your interviews. These matters will be discussed again in more detail in Chapter 24 *Managing Human Resources.*)

### Harassment

The government has also enacted antidiscrimination laws to discourage harassment in the workplace. Harassment can take many forms, from unfair job placement and promotion to permitting sexual harassment to occur in the office. Your best guide for avoiding those problems is to adopt and enforce an employee policy manual specifying conduct that your company does not tolerate.

Your business cannot tolerate harassment

### Americans with Disabilities Act

Employers cannot discriminate against the disabled, whether in the work force or in facilities that are open to the public. These extremely broad regulations include the size of restroom doors, the height of keyboards, the type of door handles used, and so forth. Be aware of these regulations, and familiarize yourself with the sections that apply to your business.

### Organized labor laws

The National Labor Relations Board has adopted a number of statutes and administrative regulations relating to unfair labor practices and collective bargaining with labor organizations. Some states require union employment or its equivalent in public projects. If you are going to have a manual labor force or bid on public projects, you may want to consult with the state Department of Labor for the applicable regulations.

### Family and medical leave

The Family and Medical Leave Act, applies to employers of 50 or more people. It entitles workers to a maximum of 12 weeks of unpaid leave in cases of pregnancy, family illness, and elder care. Employers who do not comply with the requirements of this law may be subject to serious penalties! Also, state or local laws that provide greater family and medical leave rights than the federal act does are *not* superseded by it, which means that your employees may have a choice of whether to request such leave under federal or state law. Your state Department of Labor will be able to help you understand how these laws affect your business.

## Consumer Protection

There are a number of federal and state consumer protection regulations affecting everything from consumer credit to warranties. Your local chamber of commerce can assist you in learning and complying with consumer protection regulations. These regulations include:

*Unlawful trade practices*

Most states have established statutes defining minimum standards of fair dealing in consumer transactions.

*Warranties*

The federal government has established an "anti-lemon" law providing minimal requirements for written warranties in consumer transactions. This is in the nature of a disclosure requirement; it is not a requirement that you provide a warranty. Using the sale of a used car as an example, the seller is required to disclose any defects in the car to a potential buyer, but doesn't have to provide any type of warranty that the car will work next month.

Consumers are protected in most states from unethical business practices

## NxLEVEL™ TECH TIP

There are hundreds of tax software applications on the market, to say nothing of programs designed to aid you with government compliance. Some of these programs are quite expensive, others can be difficult to use, and still others may squander most of their functionality on capabilities that are unnecessary for your business. You can save time and money—and spare yourself a lot of frustration—by using the following checklist every time you consider a software purchase:

• Seek out software that is designed to serve the needs of small-business users. Many of the popular business applications on the market today are designed for use by enormous companies with in-house support teams; if you lack these resources, you should choose software that avoids technical language, operates intuitively, and is scaled to the size of your enterprise.

• Make sure the program is relatively easy to learn and use. Look for on-screen tutorials, complete printed and on-screen documentation, CD-ROM training courses, and the like. Along the same lines, many companies offer free technical phone support (for a limited time), advanced documentation by fax or Internet, and/or a money-back guarantee.

• Choose software with ready-to-use templates that allow you to create professionally formatted documents right away.

• Select a software program that can serve your needs today and in years to come. Perhaps a simple program is sufficient for your current needs, but it may become inadequate as your customer base and business expand.

### Uniform Consumer Credit Code

A number of states have adopted the Uniform Consumer Credit Code. This code establishes a uniform system of regulations for consumer credit contracts and **usury**, which is the legal rate of interest.

### Department of Commerce

Most states have a Department of Commerce or similar state agency that regulates specific businesses. For example, the state's real estate division regulates licenses for sales, property management, and escrow; while the insurance division regulates the types of policies that can be sold and who can sell them. A number of other divisions regulate persons engaged in specific business activities. A call to the Department of Commerce or its equivalent can often save you a great deal of frustration later.

### Business registry

A state's Department of Commerce often maintains the state's business registry. Its duties include the registration of assumed business names and trademarks, annual corporate and partnership filings, and administration of state securities laws.

### Banking and finance

Most states have a Department of Banking and Finance, which regulates mortgage lending, money brokers, consumer credit, formation and merger of banks, and bank holding companies.

### Telephone solicitation

Many states have enacted restrictions on telephone solicitations. The regulations are quite varied in their approach among the states. Some states require telephonic sellers to register with the Public Utility Commission or other similar agency. Other states prohibit calling at certain hours or placing calls to persons who have registered for non-solicitation. Some states have disclosure requirements or prohibit solicitations for certain types of products or services. Every state prohibits dishonesty or fraud in telephonic sales. Before you conduct telephonic sales or hire an agent to do so, you should check with the attorney general's office in your state for applicable regulations.

### Privacy of consumer information

Under recent federal legislation, firms which provide financial services are required to provide written notices to certain clients regarding disclosure of non-public personal information. Every such firm is now required to provide their clients a disclosure as to how and when non-public information may be disclosed and whether the firm maintains safeguards complying with federal regulations to guard their client's non-public personal information. A sample privacy disclosure statement is included at the end of this chapter. This is a sample only and will need to be tailored to your business if you provide financial services. You should consult with your attorney on this. If you are required to provide this notice, you must do so when the customer relationship is first begun and again annually thereafter. Failure to provide this disclosure could result in significant fines against you.

The UCC affects almost everything your business does

*Privacy Disclosure Statement*

Pursuant to the Gramm-Leach-Bliley Act, Public Law Number 106-012, and the rule issued by the Federal Trade Commission regarding the Privacy of Consumer Financial Information, 16 Code of Federal Regulations Part 313, firms which provide financial services are required to provide written notices to certain clients regarding disclosure of non-public personal information.

We may collect non-public information about you from you, and with your authorization, from third parties such as accountants, attorneys, financial advisors, insurance agents, banking institutions, and other advisors. We do not disclose any non-public personal information about our clients or former clients to anyone except as permitted by law, or as authorized by that client. If we are authorized by you, we may disclose non-public personal information to unrelated third parties. Such unrelated third parties would include accountants, attorneys, financial advisors, insurance agents, or government authorities in connection with work we are doing for you. We restrict access to non-public personal information about you to those employees of our firm who need to know the information in order to provide services to you. We maintain physical, electronic, and procedural safeguards that comply with the Federal Regulations to guard your non-public personal information.

## Uniform Commercial Code

The **Uniform Commercial Code (UCC)** was drafted in response to the need for uniform regulations covering such business contracts as bills of lading, warehouse receipts, and letters of credit. The UCC also regulates bank interactions, such as checks passing through interstate streams of commerce. The UCC was intended to remain uniform throughout the states (except Louisiana, which did not adopt it). The scope of the UCC is staggering; there are literally thousands of pages of written commentary on the UCC and each of its nine articles! Because of its breadth, most businesses directly or indirectly encounter the UCC every day.

The UCC is broken down into chapters dealing with checks and promissory notes, contracts between businesses, security interests and liens on personal property, and maintenance of security investment accounts. The UCC also requires manufacturers to protect the users of their products through product liability standards. A few states' commercial codes also regulate **bulk sales**, which is the sale of substantially all of a business's assets.

Article 9 of the UCC is very important in establishing rights to collateral. It provides for liens (comparable to mortgages on real estate) on personal property—such as inventory, equipment, or accounts receivable—and establishes a uniform system for filing these liens. In 2001, major changes to Article 9 were adopted throughout the country. These changes are far too detailed to discuss here. The major impact of the new legislation was on lien interests that cross state lines. So, if your business assets move between state lines, or if you take collateral on assets which move between state lines, you should consult with your lawyer regarding these new laws.

Make sure your business complies with environmental laws

Be cautious of any property which has had fuel tanks

This new law is important when you borrow money and the bank wants your assets as collateral. You can also use the provisions of Article 9 when you place goods with another business on consignment, or accept a note in lieu of a cash payment. Your lawyer can help you to understand these laws.

## Environmental Laws

### Hazardous materials

In the 1960s, a number of environmental laws were passed, such as the Clean Air Act and the Clean Water Act. Later, the Comprehensive Environmental Response Compensation and Liability Act (CERCLA or "Superfund") and the Resource Conservation and Recovery Act (RCRA) were adopted; together, these acts affect virtually every business and real estate transaction. Most states have laws and regulations parallel to RCRA and CERCLA. Under RCRA, the handling of hazardous materials is regulated from creation to disposal; any business that deals with potentially hazardous compounds is strictly regulated.

CERCLA and its equivalent state laws create a method for cleaning up hazardous substances that were previously released into the environment. Under CERCLA, responsible parties are identified in any cleanup activity, and are responsible for cleanup costs. You've probably heard of the "Love Canal" cleanup, but you may not realize that Superfund legislation also applies to your own dry cleaning or welding shop. Under CERCLA, a new owner of land or even a long-term tenant can be held liable to clean up an environmental dump caused by a prior owner or tenant! The one exception is if you tried to investigate the land's condition before you leased or bought the property, so it is very important that you review the history of a property before you buy or lease it. These issues are discussed at greater length in Chapter 17 *Business Ethics*.

*When Roger Zwicki bought the Morris Paint Company through a bankruptcy sale, he thought he was getting a bargain. Roger wanted to open his own specialty paint factory after having worked at a major paint company for over 20 years. However, in his eagerness to buy, he neglected to investigate the history of the property on which the factory was located. Three months into production of his specialty paint line, Roger was visited by federal officials who informed him that he was standing on a Superfund-targeted site. Four years later, he had to declare bankruptcy himself, due to the high cost of cleanup.*

Chapters 11, 12, and 13 involve a restructuring of the business and its debts

### Petroleum storage tanks

Many businesses use petroleum products in the operation of vehicles and machinery, or as heating oil for furnaces and boilers. Most states regulate storage tanks for these products, as well as the cleanup of any petroleum products that may have leaked from tanks in the past. These cleanups, for which the small business owner is held financially responsible, often cost several hundred thousand dollars.

### Wetlands, Endangered Species Act

Under the authority of the Clean Water Act, the Army Corps of Engineers and various state environmental agencies have adopted regulations that identify and protect wetlands. Primarily, these rules prohibit filling or other disruption of wetlands, and mandate mitigation of any injury to wetland areas. The regulations go far beyond riparian areas that lay along streams and lakes; they also extend to areas that are seasonally inundated with groundwater. Before you start a cut or fill project, you should check local regulations. The Endangered Species Act prohibits "taking" of an endangered species. List of salmon and the spotted owl as endangered species has had a major impact on business in the western United States. There are many other examples.

### Zoning

Zoning divides the community into districts or zones, and zoning laws regulate the use of land and the structures thereon in order to protect public health, safety, and general welfare. For more information, check with your local building or zoning department.

## Bankruptcy

### General

The Constitution establishes a bankruptcy court, and requires the federal government to offer relief from excessive debt through the Bankruptcy Code. Bankruptcy laws affect many businesses, and add considerably to the paperwork required when you request a loan. The best strategy for dealing with bankruptcy is to know the reputation and financial status of the parties with whom you enter into contracts. Do not let accounts become too stale, and consider retaining a lien on property under Article 9 of the UCC. The worst strategy is to wait until you receive a notice of the filing from the bankruptcy court, at which point you must stop your collection efforts. The best thing to do is gather your paperwork and go see your lawyer. There are four types of bankruptcies with which you should be familiar:

### Chapter 11—Business reorganization

The Bankruptcy Code under Chapter 11 provides an opportunity for viable businesses that find themselves unable to meet current cash flow needs to reorganize and pay off a percentage of their debts. The debtor remains in possession of its property and proposes a plan to the bankruptcy court for restructuring its debts. Until a plan is approved by the court or the case is dismissed, creditors are prohibited from foreclosing against the insolvent party. A creditors' committee consisting of the ten largest unsecured creditors is established to assist the court in formalizing the plan of reorganization. Even though the court supervises the plan, it's up to you to see that your rights as a creditor are protected. Creditors without liens usually get nothing.

### Chapter 12—Farm bankruptcies

Land-rich, cash-poor farming enterprises sometimes cannot make current loan payments because of cash flow problems that arise either from a seasonal crop that had a bad yield, or falling market prices. Under Chapter 12 of the Bankruptcy Code, farm enterprises may reorganize in much the same way that businesses do under Chapter 11.

*Chapter 13—Reorganization for individuals with regular income*
Individuals with regular income can adjust their debts under Chapter 13, which is also available for restructuring the debts of a sole proprietorship. The debtor continues in possession of his or her assets, and proposes a plan for payment of debts and reducing arrears on long-term debt. A trustee collects the payments and distributes the funds to the creditors. When the plan is fully performed, the debtor receives a discharge from all debts except for long-term secured debts, such as home mortgages, with maturity dates that extend beyond the term of the plan.

*Chapter 7—Liquidation*
This is often referred to as "straight bankruptcy." All states have adopted "exemption" laws allowing debtors to keep an interest in certain assets, such as a $25,000 home equity, a motor vehicle, tools of the trade, and clothing; these exemptions help the debtor to make a fresh start after the bankruptcy. At the beginning of the case, the debtor's nonexempt assets are collected by the trustee, creditors' claims are scheduled, and priorities are established. The nonexempt assets are liquidated and the claims are paid *pro rata*, according to their priority. (Obviously, creditors with property liens under Article 9 of the UCC will fare better than "unsecured" creditors.) The debtor then receives a discharge of financial obligations. Many Chapter 11, 12, and 13 cases ultimately end up in liquidation because the plans are not properly performed.

Note: when we went to press in late 2001 Congress was debating amendments to the U.S. Bankruptcy code. These debates have lasted over a year and appear to be no where near conclusion. The amendments seem to be of a technical nature and do not appear to change the basic principles described above.

## Conclusion

Virtually every aspect of business faces regulation to some extent, so it is a good idea to educate yourself about the regulations that apply to your business. Although laws and regulations may seem to be a maze, compliance will help you prosper. In the chapters that follow, some of these ideas and strategies will be discussed in greater detail.

# Chapter 17
# BUSINESS ETHICS

*About This Chapter:*
- *Defining values*
- *Ethics training for employees*
- *Treating employees ethically*
- *Worker safety and health*
- *Ethics and government*
- *Environmental ethics*

## Introduction

Entrepreneurs face many ethical tests as they struggle to get their businesses off the ground. They may be tempted to lower their taxes by understating revenues, to pay employees less than the fair market rate, to issue misleading advertisements, or to engage in manipulative selling practices.

Although many of these actions are illegal, business ethics go beyond what is legal or illegal. When we feel tempted to compromise our principles for the sake of business or personal advantage, adherence to ethics is a measure of our integrity and sense of responsibility. It is easy to have strong ethical beliefs; it is more difficult to behave ethically when times are tough and the survival of your business is on the line. But ultimately, a business has the same responsibility to be honest, fair, and socially responsible that an individual does.

Strong business and personal values help you make ethical business decisions

## Defining Values

Throughout history, all societies have defined the following traits as the best and most fundamental human virtues:

- fairness
- fidelity
- honesty
- integrity
- respect for others
- responsible citizenship

You undoubtedly look for these qualities in yourself and others, so it's only natural that you should strive to build a business that displays the same values! That being the case, there will almost invariably be an ethical dimension to your business decisions. You should regularly ask yourself these questions when making decisions:

- Is this decision consistent with my personal and organizational values and ethics?
- Will anyone be hurt or angered by this decision?
- Would I want to be treated the way I am treating someone else?
- Will this decision result in increased employee and customer trust?

## Ethical Dilemmas

Being ethical means choosing the right over the wrong, the fair over the unfair. In many cases, the proper course of action is perfectly clear. In others, it seems that we will compromise one or more of our values no matter which alternative we select. When this happens, we find ourselves in an ethical dilemma.

People compromise their ethics for many reasons, including financial worries, peer pressure, and deadlines. When you are operating under stresses like these, such compromises may seem justifiable. That's why it's important to ask yourself the following "mirror test" questions:

- Does the decision make you feel guilty, disappointed in yourself, or anxious about what someone else might think?
- If a child, spouse, or friend were in a similar situation and came to you for advice, would you recommend the same course of action you're choosing?
- Would you feel comfortable if your decision were subject to public scrutiny or media attention?
- If someone injured you through a conscious action and invoked one of your justifications in defense, would you accept it as a legitimate excuse?

These questions can help you to pinpoint the ethical dilemma, confront it without illusions, and resolve it. One of the hardest tasks in ethical decision-making is to be able to see a problem from someone else's point of view; always ask yourself how you would want to be treated if you were in the other person's shoes.

## Treating Customers Ethically

Customer loyalty is the result of trust, and trust is the result of fair dealing. A customer considers a transaction to be fair when it satisfies his or her expectations (i.e., an excellent product or service, delivered on-time, and at a reasonable price).

However, it takes more than meeting expectations to build customer loyalty. The customer must consistently receive service above and beyond his or her expectations, resulting in a cycle of ever-increased and ever-exceeded expectations.

Therefore, your employees must work towards establishing an ongoing relationship with each customer. You must empower them to do this by giving them the freedom and skill to add a value to the transaction that will exceed your customers' expectations. Above all, when conflicts or disagreements arise, your employees must try to see things from the customer's point of view, and bend over backwards to reach an equitable agreement.

Your commitment to treating customers ethically will distinguish you from your competitors, and give you the competitive advantage.

# Ethics Training for Employees

As the leader of your business, you represent the values by which your employees will operate. For this reason, you must handle ethical dilemmas precisely as you want your employees to handle them. If they feel that there is a double standard at work, they will not take your ethics program seriously.

There must be perfect congruence between what you ask of your employees, the values that guide your own behavior, and the type of behavior you reward. The consequence of ethical congruence is employees who consistently act in accordance with the organization's guiding principles, even in the absence of specific policy or direction.

You can best communicate your ethical expectations through daily interaction. Let your employees know what is important to you: if safety, quality, and customer service come first in your business, make sure your employees know what you expect them to do when conflicts arise between any of these values. They must understand that you will reward those who uphold your ethical code, and remove those who don't.

## Your Statement of Ethics

Once you have quantified the ethical ideals that will guide your employees' interactions with customers, management, and one another, it is time to draft a statement of ethics. Post the statement prominently, and explain that all your employees must adhere to the values it expresses. Another option is to include a brief statement of ethics in your mission statement. But remember, the most eloquent statement of ethics is worthless unless the code of conduct it dictates is an obvious, measurable force in your day-to-day business. If your employees see that compromises are often made and rules often broken, for the sake either of convenience or personal gain, they will form their own opinions about what your business really values.

## Codes of Conduct

Effective codes of conduct must instill your employees with the desire to make ethical business decisions. They should also address practical issues, so that your employees can easily act on that desire during their daily routines. It's impossible to have a specific policy for every situation that might occur, so you must clearly define what steps your employees should take when confronted with a dilemma. Encourage your employees to discuss ethical situations or decision-making dilemmas as they arise, and create an ethics "chain of command," so that your employees can always get the answers they need. This might comprise written guidelines, or a standard procedure.

# Treating Employees Ethically

Mutual trust and respect are prerequisites for running an ethical organization. In too many businesses, employees feel pressured, unappreciated, and mistrusted. Often, unethical behavior is caused by a perception that the employer's behavior is itself unfair or unethical. The anger and disillusionment that results can lead to poor performance, low morale, and indifference to the well-being of the business.

What earns employees' trust and loyalty? In a word, "fairness." Being fair requires first that you be honest with yourself, and second that you be honest with employees and customers. Without honesty, there can be no ethical management.

Your employees want an opportunity to succeed, and a reputable product to sell. They want your business to fulfill the promises they make to your customers. If they work hard and do what is required, they should have a reasonable expectation of reward.

Note that what gets rewarded gets repeated. The distribution of rewards communicates what is most highly valued by an organization. For example, if you reward people for great customer service, then great customer service becomes a priority, rather than mere organizational rhetoric.

### The Law and Your Employees

The main law affecting worker's pay is the **Fair Labor Standards Act (FLSA)**, which was passed in 1938. The FLSA mandates a minimum wage, premium pay for overtime work, and equal pay for men and women performing equal work. The FLSA applies to almost all small businesses, excepting those of which the owner is the sole employee. (Even if your business is covered by the FLSA, some administrative and professional employees may be exempt, provided they meet certain criteria. Check with the Wages and Hours Division of the U.S. Department of Labor, or with your state Department of Labor, for more information.) Here are a few points to remember:

- **Minimum wage.** Some states have a higher minimum wage than the federal rate; check with your state Department of Labor for the most current information.
- **Overtime.** It's illegal to change the start of the work week to avoid paying overtime!
- **Equal work.** Jobs do not have to be identical to be considered "equal work." They meet the definition of the Equal Pay Act when they require identical levels of skill, effort, and responsibility.
- **Pay interval.** Pay periods must be one month or less. Certain states require a shorter interval. Call your state Department of Labor for more information.
- **Time Off.** Although the FLSA doesn't require you to grant paid vacation days, holidays, or sick days, be aware that if you promise such days off in an employee handbook or other written form, or have paid these days in the past, you may be legally required to give these benefits to all employees. Some states mandate paid time off for voting, military service, and school conferences.
- **Breaks.** Nearly half the states have regulations on frequency of breaks and the minimum length of these breaks.

### Bending the Rules

Some employers try to avoid minimum wage and overtime requirements by labeling all entry-level employees "assistant managers," and then forcing them to work over 40 hours per week with no further compensation. The Department of Labor works to uncover such abuses, and the employers they catch face severe penalties. Most investigations occur after a disgruntled employee complains (note that it is illegal to fire or harass an employee for complaints of this type). If you are found to have violated the FLSA, you will most likely have to pay the employee all unpaid wages (including overtime), and you may also be fined or penalized. Especially willful abuses may result in fines of up to ten thousand dollars; a second offense may lead to jail time. Also, the animosity these proceedings generate can result in considerable loss of morale amongst your other employees, who are likely to side with the unhappy employee.

# Worker Safety and Health

There are many good reasons to create a safe and healthy workplace for your employees. First, and most important, is your humane concern for their well-being. Next, there are pragmatic reasons: healthy workers are happier, more productive, and less prone to absenteeism; also, health insurance and workers' compensation costs may be lower. Last, there are legal obligations. In the wake of well-publicized lawsuits, the average worker is quite knowledgeable about workplace health and safety issues, and will not hesitate to make legal claims against employers who fail to rectify unsafe conditions.

The best way to meet your legal responsibilities for keeping your workplace safe is to involve your workers. Schedule regular safety meetings at which you ask your employees to identify problems and suggest solutions. If workers can voice their safety concerns to you, they're less likely to complain to the authorities. (Organizing a worker's safety committee can also earn you a break on workers' compensation premiums!) Safety codes are another good way to let employees know that you take safety seriously.

## Occupational Health and Safety Act

In 1970, Congress passed the Occupational Health and Safety Act. This legislation states that as an employer, you must provide a workplace "free from recognized hazards that are causing or are likely to cause death or serious physical harm to employees." As you can see, this very broad definition covers almost every conceivable physical hazard an employee might encounter in your business.

To administer these regulations—and others that are added continually—Congress created the **Occupational Safety and Health Administration (OSHA)**. OSHA oversees exposure to hazardous chemicals; first aid and medical treatment; noise levels; protective gear; fire protection; worker safety training; workplace temperatures, and ventilation. One of your obligations is to post a notice called "Job Safety and Health Protection," which is available from OSHA. Workers have two basic rights under OSHA. First, they can complain to OSHA about safety or health violations without being penalized for doing so. Second, they can refuse to work if they have a reasonable belief that by working they face an immediate risk of serious injury or death.

*Jack Cannon owns St. Charles Flora and Gifts in New Orleans, a specialty florist shop offering 24-hour delivery of flowers, chocolates, balloon arrangements, and gourmet food baskets. One day, driver George Wilson was loading one of St. Charles's delivery vans when another driver told him that the van's brakes weren't working properly. George went to Jack and asked to be given a different van. Jack said that all other vans were currently in use or in the shop. George refused to drive the van unless a mechanic checked the brakes to make sure they were safe. Since getting a mechanic would take time and George's delivery was an important one, Jack ordered George to use the van. When he refused, Jack became frustrated and fired him. George complained to OSHA, and in the ensuing trial the court determined that because a fellow driver had warned him about the van's brakes, George had a reasonable and good faith belief that he'd be exposed to immediate risk of death or serious injury if he made the delivery—even though Jack proved to the court that the brakes were in good working order! Jack was ordered to rehire George and pay him for the weeks of work he had missed.*

OSHA inspectors can enter your workplace at any time—with no warning—and can issue citations or impose penalties if unsafe or unhealthy conditions exist. If you have ten employees or fewer, and are in a business with a low injury rate—a shoe store, for instance—you are exempt from inspections by federal OSHA officials. State inspectors may inspect smaller businesses, but unless you are in a high-risk field—such as construction, welding, or metal plating—you are unlikely to be inspected unless one of your employees makes a complaint to OSHA.

OSHA recordkeeping requirements apply only to businesses with ten or more employees. However, state OSHA regulations may apply recordkeeping laws to smaller businesses. In addition, certain businesses are exempt from recordkeeping, including most retailers; real estate, insurance, and financial businesses; and most service businesses. To see if your business is exempt, contact your state OSHA office.

Penalties imposed by OSHA depend on the seriousness of the violation. For willful or repeated violations, your business may be fined thousands of dollars. If a worker dies because you ignored OSHA standards, you could even be sent to prison. For less serious offenses, the maximum penalty is generally $1,000. In assessing penalties, OSHA looks at several factors, including the size of your business; the seriousness of the hazard; and whether you've made a good-faith effort at compliance.

### Safety Training

Under OSHA, you're responsible for safety training. Make sure that all employees know about the materials and equipment with which they'll be working. Don't let an employee begin a job until he or she has been instructed in how to do it safely. You must maintain records of your safety training procedures; it's a good idea to have employees sign a form each time they receive training. Be prepared to show these records to OSHA inspectors. Remember: even if no accidents ever occur, a noncompliant workplace provides disgruntled workers with a means of causing you considerable trouble!

If your state has a health and safety law that meets or exceeds federal OSHA standards, the state OSHA can take over enforcement of these standards from its federal counterpart. State standards and enforcement actions may be more strict than federal standards, and the requirements for posting notices and recordkeeping may be different. If your business operates in a state that has an OSHA law, contact the appropriate agency for the standards that are applicable to your business.

### Help with Compliance

In each state, an agency funded by the federal OSHA office offers free consultation. You and the consultant will tour your workplace together; the consultant will point out health and safety risks, and work with you to control or eliminate the hazard within a timeframe that you jointly determine. The consultant will not issue citations or impose penalties, nor will he or she provide information about your business to OSHA unless extremely hazardous conditions exist, or you fail to make the agreed-upon improvements within the stated time. For more details, contact your state OSHA office.

## Ethics and Government

Your relationship with federal, state, and city government is another area in which you must be ethical. This means abiding by hiring regulations, zoning laws, tax requirements, environmental standards, safety codes, fire codes, and all other areas in which your business falls under government regulations. This is an especially important area for a conscientious ethical policy, as the failure to live up to your obligations can result in fines or jail time. The federal government has issued a new set of sentencing guidelines for ethics violations, and fines can run in the millions of dollars.

Since the government wishes to encourage effective ethics programs, it will lower these fines by as much as 80% if the business provides proof of a good-faith ethics management program and cooperates with authorities. In fact, the *only* proactive step an organization can take to lower its vulnerability to these fines is to institute an ethics management program!

## Environmental Ethics

Looking back on the course of the twentieth century, we can say with some accuracy that it was an era of unbridled exploitation of natural resources, and pollution of the environment. Today, things are changing. For many businesses, it is no longer socially, legally, or economically acceptable to pollute the environment. In fact, the money one can make by cleaning up the environment almost rivals the money one can make by polluting it, and many entrepreneurs are finding highly profitable niches in fields related to environmental clean-up!

Federal and state laws mandating environmental protection are proliferating; very few businesses remain unaffected by them. For this reason, most of this section focuses on legal issues.

## A Maze of Regulations

The U.S. Department of Transportation (DOT), the Occupational Safety and Health Administration (OSHA), the Environmental Protection Agency (EPA), and the National Fire Protection Association (or National Fire Code) all have regulations pertaining to hazardous materials. Each agency has its own definition of which materials qualify for regulation, and its own specific handling requirements.

To further complicate matters, while each agency concentrates on its own specific area, the regulations and areas of concern overlap. For example, both DOT and OSHA have communication and training standards that you must meet.

The EPA's list of hazardous substances is based primarily on environmental impact and persistence. OSHA, meanwhile, simply defines a hazardous chemical as something that "may be considered explosive, flammable, poisonous, corrosive, oxidizing, irritating or otherwise harmful, and is likely to cause death or injury."

It may seem impossible to keep track of all these regulations, but you can do it by focusing on one area at a time. For instance, many organizations offer hazardous materials (or hazmat) shipping seminars to help you comply with DOT regulations. It is a legal requirement that all hazmat shippers undergo this training or its equivalent, so you may wish to sign one of your employees up and make him or her the company hazmat expert. Storage and handling within your workplace are regulated mainly by

OSHA, which has plenty of compliance information available. Emissions, spills, contamination, disposal, and the like are the primary concern of EPA; check their Web site for help with compliance.

## How the Laws are Enforced

Because environmental problems often require special understanding of local issues, responsibility for implementing federal environmental laws rests largely with state and local governments. In fact, many states have enacted local laws that are more stringent than federal laws. For example, more than half the states require environmental impact statements before they will permit industrial growth, and many have developed their own provisions for monitoring air quality.

To find out who is obeying the law, the EPA generally relies on the following:

- **Self-monitoring.** Most U.S. environmental laws require regulated facilities to keep track of their own compliance status and report all or part of the resulting data to the responsible agency. This not only gives the agency data it needs, but also helps the company's senior management to obey the law. Fraudulent reporting is a serious offense.
- **Inspections.** This is the EPA's primary means of officially assessing compliance.
- **Area monitoring.** Area monitoring looks at environmental conditions in the vicinity of a facility, or over a larger area. Methods used for area monitoring include ambient monitoring, remote sensing, and overflights.

## Penalties

It is impossible to predict how the EPA will deal with a particular violation of environmental law; its response usually depends on your willingness to cooperate, the severity of the situation, and any unusual or mitigating factors. Possibilities include:

- **Civil actions.** Most environmental laws authorize the EPA to obtain civil penalties and/or injunctions against violators. Your permit can be suspended or revoked, you will be required to take steps to correct the violation, and you will be subject to penalties that are at least equal to the costs your company saved by not complying with applicable requirements; penalties may also be imposed as a per-day charge (up to $50,000 under some acts), or per violation.
- **Criminal action.** Criminal prosecution is usually reserved for flagrant violations, such as illegal dumping of hazardous waste, or deliberate falsification of records. Criminal violations may be either misdemeanors or felonies, punishable by substantial fines (a maximum of $250,000 for an individual, or $500,000 for a corporation, on a per-day or per-violation basis, or both). Jail terms for corporate executives are less common, but not unheard of.

The EPA is responsible for most environmental protection in the United States

- **Administrative enforcement action.** This involves only the administrative agency, not the courts, and can range from informal advisory notices or warning letters—advising the manager of a facility what violation was found, what should be done to correct it, and by what date—to a more formal legal order compelling the recipient to take corrective action within a certain time.

Note that state and local governments may assess additional civil penalties.

## Environmental Laws That May Affect Small Businesses

### Clean Air Act

The Clean Air Act protects public health and the environment by setting and achieving National Ambient Air Quality Standards (NAAQS) in every state. Later amendments to the CAA focused on such problems as acid rain, stratospheric ozone depletion, and air toxics.

### Clean Water Act

The Clean Water Act gives the EPA authority to set water pollution standards on an industry basis, and makes it unlawful for any person to discharge any pollutant into navigable waters without a permit. The CWA allows for the delegation by the EPA of many aspects of the law to state governments; in such cases, the EPA still retains oversight responsibilities.

### Comprehensive Environmental Response, Compensation and Liability Act

CERCLA, commonly known as Superfund, was enacted by Congress in 1980. This law:

- provides broad federal authority to respond directly to releases of hazardous substances
- establishes prohibitions and requirements for closed or abandoned hazardous waste sites
- establishes liability of persons responsible for releases of hazardous waste at these sites
- establishes a trust fund to provide for cleanup if the responsible party cannot be identified

CERCLA was amended by the Superfund Amendments and Reauthorization Act (SARA) in 1986.

### Emergency Planning and Community Right-to-Know Act

EPCRA (also known as Title III of SARA) was enacted to help local communities protect public health and the environment from chemical hazards. To implement EPCRA, Congress required every state to appoint a State Emergency Response Commission, each of which was required to divide its state into Emergency Planning Districts and to name a Local Emergency Planning Committee (LEPC) for each district.

### Federal Insecticide, Fungicide, and Rodenticide Act

FIFRA provides federal control of pesticide distribution, sale, and use. It mandates that all pesticides used in the United States be licensed by the EPA, and that all users take exams for certification as applicators of pesticides.

### Resource Conservation and Recovery Act

RCRA gave the EPA the authority to control hazardous waste from "cradle-to-grave," and set forth guidelines for the management of nonhazardous wastes. RCRA focuses only on active and future facilities; it does not address abandoned or historical sites (see CERCLA). The Federal Hazardous and Solid Waste Amendments (HSWA) are 1984 amendments to RCRA that require phasing out land disposal of hazardous waste. Other mandates of this strict law include increased enforcement authority for the EPA and more stringent hazardous waste management standards.

### Safe Drinking Water Act

This act was established to protect the quality of drinking water in the United States. This law focuses on all waters actually or potentially designed for drinking use, whether from aboveground or underground sources.

### Superfund Amendments and Reauthorization Act

This act, which amended CERCLA in 1986, stresses the importance of permanent remedies and innovative technologies in cleaning up hazardous waste sites. It also provided new enforcement authorities and settlement tools.

### Toxic Substances Control Act

TSCA gives the EPA the ability to track and screen industrial chemicals currently produced or imported into the United States, and to ban the manufacture and import of those chemicals that pose an unreasonable environmental or human health risk.

## It Pays to Cooperate!

The EPA's **Policy on Compliance Incentives for Small Businesses** offers a waiver of penalties for environmental violations to encourage small businesses to participate in onsite compliance assistance programs and to conduct environmental audits. The policy applies to small businesses that employ 100 or fewer individuals.

The EPA will waive civil penalties if your business:

- Received onsite compliance assistance from a government or government-supported program (during which the violations were detected); or conducted an audit and disclosed the violation(s) to the appropriate regulatory agency in writing and within ten days.

- Was not subject to an enforcement action for the current violation in the past three years, and has not been subject to two or more enforcement actions for environmental violations in the past five years.
- Fixes the violation and any harm associated with it within six months of discovery. (Businesses that use pollution prevention technologies to fix the violation receive an additional six months to comply.)
- Did not cause serious harm or present a significant threat to public health, safety, or the environment; and is not guilty of criminal conduct.

If your small business meets these criteria, the EPA will waive up to 100% of the gravity component of the penalty. However, in the unusual event that your small business obtained a significant economic benefit from the violation, such that you put your competitors at a serious marketplace disadvantage, the EPA may fine you the full amount of this economic benefit.

For more information on the EPA's Small Business Policy, go to http://es.epa.gov.oeca/ smbusi.html.

*Chris Hendrickson is the owner of Bull's Eye Graphics, a small but successful graphic design and printing shop in the Hunter's Point area of San Francisco. One day, she noticed that her head printer, Ed Apperson, was pouring fixer and developer waste into the sink. Ed is an expert at offset printing; in fact, Chris feels that she couldn't run her business without him.*

*Unfortunately, Ed learned the trade when he was considerably younger, and has become a bit set in his ways. When Chris asked him to stop pouring the waste into the sink, Ed replied that he'd been pouring wastes down the drain since his high school print shop class, and saw no reason to stop now. When Chris insisted, however, he agreed to dispose of the waste properly, and she thought no more about the matter.*

*As it happened, Ed disposed of the waste properly only when Chris was on the shop floor. Most of the time, he felt he was too busy to do anything more than dump the waste in the sink. He figured what she didn't know wouldn't hurt her; besides, he was saving time and money!*

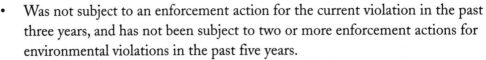

**P2 Program=**

**"Don't pollute in**

**the first place!"**

## Pollution Prevention

A great new strategy for dealing with toxic waste is **pollution prevention** (or P2), which the EPA defines as "elimination of or reduction in waste quantities or toxicities at the point of generation." In plain English, this means not making pollution in the first place! Even the smallest businesses can benefit from a P2 program. How? By cutting wastes, you cut disposal costs, energy fees, and water fees; and you increase the efficiency of your business.

If you wish to begin a P2 program, here are some hints:

- **Write a policy on pollution prevention for employees and customers.** A sample follows:
  *"At Melmoth Economy Shoe Heel Corporation, we believe that a clean, healthy environment is very important. We are committed to preventing pollution by eliminating or reducing our use of toxic materials, conserving energy, and reducing wastes."*
- **Educate and involve all employees.** A safer working environment increases employee morale and productivity. Once employees understand the P2 goal, they will generate valuable new ideas.
- **Set defined and obtainable goals.** For example, you may want to decrease your solid waste output by 25% in one year, or reduce your hazardous waste by 10% every year for five years.
- **Collect data.** Determining the types and amount of waste your company generates helps you evaluate your options, and establishes a baseline for measuring progress.
- **Publicize your efforts.** Tell your community that you are implementing a P2 program; this demonstrates your concern for the environment and your neighbors.

The following P2 methods cost little or nothing to implement, but can result in considerable long-term savings.

## Good Housekeeping

- Install spigots and nozzles to dispense fluids from bulk containers, and use drip pans and splash guards to avoid spills.
- Check for leaks at least once a week. Even the smallest leaks can lead to waste problems and exposures if not remedied. Also, check closures to prevent spills and evaporation of liquids.
- Keeping track of where spills have occurred may help you prevent future spills.
- Use absorbents to clean up minor fluid leaks and spills. (Note: Used absorbent may be hazardous waste, either because it contains hazardous materials or it exhibits a hazardous characteristic.)
- Reuse partially saturated floor absorbent to cut down on waste. If you use absorbent pads instead of floor absorbent, wring out the pad and recycle the liquid. The pad can be reused.

## Purchase and Inventory

- Be sure to factor in waste management costs when buying materials. Remember: Materials that generate hazardous waste cost more than the purchase price!
- A large inventory ties up money that might be needed elsewhere, and increases the potential for spills. Order materials in smaller unit sizes to reduce inventory.

- Broken packaging or expired materials may increase your waste load. Do not accept deliveries of materials that are damaged, have an odor, or show signs of leakage. Also, make sure all materials have legible labels.
- Follow proper storage methods for perishable materials. Using stock on a FIFO (first in/first out) basis reduces the chance that materials will deteriorate in storage. If possible, arrange to return expired materials to your suppliers.

### Material and Waste Storage
- Make certain that spills or leaks will not contaminate sewer or storm drains.
- Keep different wastes separated; mixing wastes can be dangerous, and may make reusing or recycling impossible. Also, mixing hazardous and nonhazardous wastes increases the volume of hazardous waste, thus increasing disposal costs.
- Store hazardous waste indoors or in a covered area to prevent moisture from seeping in. Moisture may increase the volume of your hazardous waste, increasing disposal costs.
- Store hazardous waste in a safe location out of major traffic areas, and have emergency equipment ready for immediate use in case of spills and leaks. Make sure employees are trained to use emergency equipment.

### Equipment Changes
- Consider the cost of waste management when purchasing new equipment, and try to find the best nonpolluting equipment within your price range.

### Material Substitution
- Substitute nonhazardous or less hazardous materials for those you presently use. This can reduce or even eliminate hazardous waste generation from your business. Look into substitutes carefully; some will solve one problem but cause another. Try to contact other users to learn how the substitute materials worked for them. Also, when considering a substitute, remember to look at the Material Safety Data Sheet (MSDS). Less toxic substitutes may still have a low flash point, or be regulated for their volatile organic compound (VOC) content.

### Who Pays the Costs of Clean-Up?
Clean-up of environmental contamination is supposed to be paid for by all those who are responsible for the contamination. If many parties are responsible, they bear a proportionate share of the costs. If negotiations fail or responsibility is disputed, the EPA can either require potentially responsible parties to clean up the contamination, or conduct the clean-up itself and then sue those responsible to recover its costs (up to three times the amount). The state also can sue those responsible by filing a separate action.

If the responsible parties cannot be found, will not pay, or cannot pay, federal clean-up activities are covered by Superfund and the Oil Spill Liability Trust Fund (both are financed by taxes).

If you unwittingly buy contaminated property, it is essential that you consult with an attorney immediately. You can be held liable even if you had no knowledge of the contamination at the time of your purchase, and thus may be required to pay all or some of the clean-up costs!

If you're considering the purchase of an abandoned site for a new business, your state can provide you with previous use information, such as whether the site was formerly used as a gasoline station or plating shop. You can also check with your EPA region to see if they have any record of contamination for the site. (There are environmental consultants who will conduct this "Phase 1" research for you.)

---

*Business was booming at Bull's Eye Graphics. Chris needed to hire a few more employees, so she interviewed an applicant named Peggy Murray. She asked Peggy if she'd worked in a busy print shop before; Peggy said she had, but not for some time. Chris really wanted a worker with years of experience in high-volume, fast-turnaround printing, but none of the applicants fit the bill perfectly. Peggy seemed enthusiastic and confident, so Chris decided to hire her on the understanding that she would undergo a three-month trial period, during which she could be dismissed for any reason.*

*The weeks went by, and Peggy didn't seem to be working out. When her second inking mistake in two months caused Bull's Eye to miss an important deadline, Chris suspected that Peggy had exaggerated her qualifications and fired her.*

*Peggy was angry and disappointed. She felt that she hadn't been given a fair chance to prove herself. On a couple of occasions, she'd seen Ed pouring developer down the sink; thinking back on this, she became convinced that Bull's Eye was an unethical company. She considered it her duty to notify the Department of Environmental Protection.*

*The DEP looked into the matter, and found grounds for a criminal complaint. Bull's Eye was fined $4000 and placed on two years' probation after pleading no contest to two violations of the state's Solid Waste Management Act. Chris wasn't happy about paying the fine, but she was well aware that it could have been worse. She signed Ed up for a DEP-sponsored waste training program, and used P2 processes to cut down on her wastes. After that, no more wastes went down the drain, and neither did Bull's Eye Graphics!*

---

# Conclusion

Entrepreneurs are members of their communities. As such, they have a responsibility to make positive contributions to their communities, and to adhere to local, state, and federal laws. By acting ethically, you establish a valuable reputation for fair dealing. Not only is this good for your conscience, its good for your business! Whether we are talking about customers, employees, stockholders, suppliers, or regulatory agencies, the benefits of ethical business practices are obvious. From referrals by loyal customers to the favorable credit terms offered by vendors, the rewards for doing business ethically are real and measurable.

# Chapter 18
# MANAGING RISK

*About This Chapter:*
- *Seek the help of qualified advisors*
- *Important business protection techniques*
- *Squeeze-outs*
- *Dissolution*
- *Insurance*
- *Your insurance checklist*

## Introduction

You've worked hard to establish your business, so you want to protect it against risks. This chapter explains precautions you can take to protect your business from internal risks, such as your fellow investors forcing you out of your position because you no longer agree on the company's direction; and external risks, such as a customer suing you for damages.

## Seek the Help of Qualified Advisors

It is essential that you find qualified advisors to help you with the legal aspects of protecting your business. You should interview your potential advisors to find a fit in personality, objectives, and business philosophy. Look for someone who is experienced and efficient, and who will remain in his or her career during your business's future. The hourly rate your advisor charges is another consideration. Lastly, trust your gut feelings; you have not become successful in your business by ignoring your intuition!

Find advisors you can really rely on

### Accountant

A qualified accountant is probably the most important advisor you can have. Apart from organizing your books, an accountant can help you with business management, tax reporting, and strategic planning. A business that starts without the help of an accountant may later find that the accounting system is not set up properly, that tax reporting has not been done accurately or on time, or that there's no room for expansion within the system as it stands. Performing daily bookkeeping chores in-house or through a bookkeeping service will save money, and your accountant can then be used for more complex planning and organizational issues.

### Insurance Agent

We strongly recommended that you establish a good relationship with a qualified **business insurance agent**. Throughout this text, we refer to the need to insure various risks as a means of avoiding disastrous consequences. We will discuss this topic further later in this chapter.

### Banker

It is almost inevitable that you will need outside capital during the course of your business, either for major improvements, such as buying a new computer system or a new building; or for cash flow management and operating funds. It's difficult for a banker to respond quickly to a loan request without having had the opportunity to review your business plan and tax returns, and to visit your facilities, so it's a good idea to establish a relationship with a banker well in advance. A periodic lunch meeting with your banker and accountant is a great way of protecting your business!

### Lawyer

The world of **business law** is infinitely complex, so you'll want to find a lawyer or legal firm specializing in business issues. The most practical way of selecting a business lawyer is through a referral from your accountant, who will be familiar with the business law firms in your area. Another person to ask is your banker. You might also place a call to the president of the local county bar association, or the director of your Chamber of Commerce. A lawyer who is not familiar with the issues discussed in the previous chapters may not have the necessary experience to protect your business.

## Important Business Protection Techniques

Now that you have your professional advisors on board, you should plan for some of the difficult situations you may have to confront in the future, and devise strategies to protect your business from internal and external attacks. (Note: The rest of this chapter assumes that you will be in business with someone else.)

### Participate Prior to Purchase

If you are buying an ongoing business, you can learn more from the former owner than you could ever learn from a textbook, or from talking to dozens of professional advisors. Keep your eyes and ears open, and you'll see firsthand what works and what doesn't.

### Retain the Prior Owner in an Advisory Capacity

If you have not had an opportunity to work directly with the former owner prior to purchase, you should consider retaining that person as a consultant. The business contacts and practical experience of the former owner are invaluable assets to almost any business acquisition.

### Participate in Management

If you are one of several owners in a business, you should not overlook your role in management. You may be in charge of only one department, but that does not mean you should ignore the big picture. Take the time to review management reports, and talk with other executive staff members to make sure that all business functions are flowing smoothly.

## Maintain a Majority Position

When you are doing business with other co-owners, it's easy to forget that the majority owners ultimately control the business. If you must take a minority position, try to have all other owners have equal minority interests (i.e., all of you hold one-third interest).

## Importance of Bylaws/Operating Agreement

One of the first things you can do to protect your business from internal threats is to draft the **corporate bylaws** or **operating agreement**. (Remember that bylaws are adopted by a corporation, and an operating agreement refers to the contract between partners or limited liability company members.) Some things you should consider in your bylaws are:

- Location and timing of meetings
- What percentage of ownership is required to call a meeting?
- What business can be conducted by what percentage of the ownership interests?
- How are the officers and members of the board of directors elected?
- Who has the authority to enter into contracts, sign checks, and bind the business to other obligations?
- How is employment handled?
- What method is in place for terminating the employment of personnel who have ownership interest?

*Carefully consider your bylaws or operating agreement*

## Buy/Sell Agreements

A properly drafted **buy/sell agreement** is one of the most important business protection devices you can have; it's crucial to the success of your business, no matter what type of entity you operate, and regardless of whether there are two or twenty owners. The issues it should address are:

- How can an owner be expelled from employment or ownership?
- How do you voluntarily terminate the business relationship and get your money out?
- What happens upon divorce or death?
- Do you fund the buy-out upon death or disability with an insurance policy?
- How do you feel about future generations inheriting the interest of a deceased or retiring owner?

You should consult with your business advisors to help you resolve these questions.

## How to Deal with the Vocal Minority

Some owners attempt to dominate all of your business's operations, regardless of their percentage of interest. It's important to recognize these individuals early on. You may have to rely on the terms of your buy/sell agreement to buy out the disruptive minority owner. It is better to just avoid getting into business with these types of individuals from beginning.

### Avoiding Problems with Inactive Shareholders

Certain owners always remain inactive. Others are content to be a "silent investor" until things go bad, at which point they take the opportunity to question everything you've ever done. The best way of handling such individuals is to keep them advised of the business operations by providing regular reports and inviting their participation at annual meetings.

A totally different approach applies to an inactive owner who is expected to be an active participant. For example, if three partners agree to contribute equally to the duties of the business, and one is not pulling his or her weight, appropriate action must be taken. If there is a personal problem, counseling may be effective. If the problem persists, it may be necessary to terminate the inactive owner's interest. Your professional advisors can be of great assistance in dealing with problems relating to inactive owners.

# Squeeze-Outs

Business **squeeze-outs** typically take place for one of three reasons: the company is merged into or taken over by another business; the owners have a divergence of business interests; or one of the owners has wrongfully taken business opportunities for private benefit.

A **merger** is a blending of two businesses. Mergers most often happen because two businesses have compatible opportunities. The result can be very positive. Negative consequences include loss of opportunity for former owners, and the dilution of their percentage of ownership interest.

---

*Sally's Sodas, a new-age beverage company, merged with Just Juice Company, a subsidiary of a major food and beverage manufacturer. At first, Sally's shareholders were excited by the increase in their share price due to the merger. After some months, they were dismayed to find that instead of having a 10% share of the small start-up, they now owned less than one-tenth of one percent of a major corporation! This severely limited their ability to exercise control over corporate decision-making.*

---

Divergence of business interest takes place when some of the owners see the business going in one direction, and one or more of the other owners see it going elsewhere.

Of the three most common reasons for squeeze-out, misappropriation of the business's opportunities is the most difficult. Sometimes individuals will take advantage of the business's opportunities because they do not feel the company is qualified to handle them. For instance, a partner in a construction company might refer a project to his cousin's construction company for a commission if he believes that his own company can't handle the assignment. Most often it is the result of one owner attempting to better his

Squeeze-out warning

signs include:

- deteriorating

  relationships

- removal from the

  board or termination

  as an employee

- stock dilution

- disappearing assets

- withholding

  dividends

or her position at the expense of the others. Your buy/sell agreement should address whether potential opportunities belong to the business, or each owner can seek out and retain these opportunities for personal gain.

### How to Protect Yourself

An owner who actively participates in management will usually be able to detect the warning signs of a squeeze-out well in advance. The best way to protect yourself against squeeze-out is to have provided for a fair way of treating each other in your bylaws or operating agreement. If the rules for termination are well defined in your buy/sell agreement, and the method of valuing the business interests is clearly set forth, the disputes may not go away, but they certainly will be less adversarial.

## Dissolution

There are three phases to the dissolution of a business:

### Windup

Windup occurs when the owners decide that the business should stop functioning rather than have one owner's interest bought out by the other owners, or by a third party.

### Liquidation

After the affairs of the business have been wound up, the outstanding contracts performed, the obligations paid, and the various entanglements separated, you must liquidate the assets of the company and distribute the funds (or the assets themselves) to the owners based on their percentage of interest.

### Reorganization

Once the old company has been dissolved, many owners take the opportunity to reorganize.

## Insurance

When business owners get together for coffee, one of the things they often talk about is insurance. They complain that they feel overwhelmed and overcharged, and tell horror stories of local businesses that were wiped out because they thought they had adequate coverage, but discovered after a disaster that they were underinsured.

This feeling of frustration often stems from not understanding insurance and, in some cases, relying on insurance agents who are not qualified to serve the small business owner's needs.

Insurance is a complicated issue. Lawsuits abound in our society and virtually all businesses are at risk. Remember, you may be legally liable for damages even in cases where you exercised reasonable care! Similarly, you may be liable for acts of employees or persons under contract with you, and for any property of others placed in your care. All of these risks are insurable with the right policy. "Better safe than sorry" is an old adage that applies to insurance coverage for your business.

Merger/take-over can result in loss of position

## Choosing an Agent

People buy insurance in two ways: through an agent or through a broker. **Agents** work for one or more insurance companies and receive a commission for each policy they sell. They tend to offer standardized coverage. **Brokers** are hired by their customers for a fee; they generally do business with large companies that want customized insurance packages.

There are two types of insurance agents: **direct writers** and **independent agents**. Direct writers represent one insurance company, so they tend to be quite familiar with the policies they offer. Independent agents represent multiple insurance companies, which often means that they offer more competitive prices.

Personal referrals are the best means of choosing an agent. Ask your banker, accountant, or other businesses for a recommendation. You may need several agents for the various types of insurance your business requires. Consider the following when selecting an insurance agent:

- Personal referral about reputation
- Services offered
- Agent's communication skills
- Cost

Getting three bids and checking references is recommended. You should understand exactly how your premium is calculated and make sure the agent's estimate is correct. A good insurance agent will ask enough questions about your business to determine all potential areas of loss and liability. For your part, you need to be honest with your insurance agent, who can only give good advice on complete information.

The agent you choose should pick the policy that is in your best interest, and sell it at a competitive price. Since your agent is your contact with the insurance company, you will need to have confidence in him or her should a claim arise.

## What Kind of Coverage Do I Need?

There is no specific answer to this question, because not all businesses are alike. The standard advice is to insure what you can't afford to lose. In other words, if you can't afford to pay 100% of a given business loss, you need insurance.

Many business owners naively believe that their businesses don't need insurance. But even if you're operating a business from home, your household insurance will probably not cover your business venture. You are not likely to be covered if your office equipment is stolen, or if a client slips on your sidewalk and is injured. Buying a separate policy, or upgrading the existing insurance, is a necessary cost of doing business.

In most cases, insurance is required as a condition for a bank loan. In a sole proprietorship, adequate insurance is critical because you are personally liable for all debts.

Do not assume one business policy covers all your insurance needs!

Insurance contributes to your success by reducing the risks under which your business operates. As a business owner, it is your responsibility to find out what coverage you need before you are faced with a claim. Trying to save money by keeping coverage to a minimum is false economy, and can have disastrous results!

The basic steps to developing your insurance program are:

1. Obtain professional advice
2. Go over the coverage you already have
3. Determine what further insurance is needed, and how to buy it economically

Your agent should look at your present coverage to identify uninsured areas of risk, and recommend the amount of additional insurance you require. Most businesses should have fire, automobile, liability, and workers' compensation insurance.

## Types of Insurance

The insurance industry divides coverage into two categories: **property and liability** and **life and health**. Life and health coverage is usually part of employee benefit packages, but it may also insure the owner and/or partners. Property and liability are the most important types of insurance for business. A property policy provides insurance on your building and other physical assets; liability protects you against claims of injury or property loss resulting from negligence on your part.

Property and liability coverage is often offered to businesses as a package policy covering a number of risks at once. You should be careful with these plans; don't assume that a package policy covers all of your insurance needs!

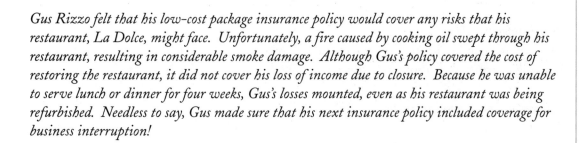

*Gus Rizzo felt that his low-cost package insurance policy would cover any risks that his restaurant, La Dolce, might face. Unfortunately, a fire caused by cooking oil swept through his restaurant, resulting in considerable smoke damage. Although Gus's policy covered the cost of restoring the restaurant, it did not cover his loss of income due to closure. Because he was unable to serve lunch or dinner for four weeks, Gus's losses mounted, even as his restaurant was being refurbished. Needless to say, Gus made sure that his next insurance policy included coverage for business interruption!*

Property losses must be reported within 60 days, unless an extension is granted. Liability policies generally require immediate notification. There must be proof of loss. Insurance companies compensate your losses in four ways:

1. By paying cash for the actual cash value of the loss
2. By repairing the insured item
3. By replacing the insured item

4. In liability cases, by paying court costs, legal fees, and interest on judgments in addition to the liability judgments themselves

There are other specialized types of property and liability insurance your firm may need. Insurance companies have developed coverage for almost everything. In most cases, all are written as separate policies. Examples include:

- Credit insurance
- Title insurance
- Aviation insurance
- Crop insurance
- Errors and omissions insurance

If you need specialized insurance, your agent can tell you about coverage available. The plans most businesses should consider are as follows:

### Liability Insurance

Liability insurance protects your business if, for example, someone suffers a bodily injury while on your site and sues you for damages. Your insurance policy should cover your costs for these damages. Many policies also cover injuries like libel and slander (if you are in the publishing business, for instance). The cost of liability insurance is generally related to the risk of your industry. Thus, if your company deals with toxic waste disposal, the cost of your liability insurance will be much greater than it would be for a florist shop.

### Product Liability

Product liability insurance protects you against claims of injury or property loss due to your product's defects or design flaws.

### Professional Liability

Professional liability insurance protects people who are self-employed in fields such as law, engineering, and accounting from being sued for malpractice by their clients.

### Completed Operations Insurance

CPAs and other licensed professionals need this type of insurance to protect themselves against errors or omissions in the services they provide to their clients. For example, suppose you asked an accounting firm to value a company that you're thinking of investing in, and after investing, you learned that the valuation was highly inflated. If you chose to sue the accounting firm, their completed operations insurance would help cover any damages they had to pay you.

### Business Property Insurance

Most businesses need business property insurance to protect company equipment or assets that are stolen or damaged by fire, flood, vandalism, or other unfortunate incidents.

Other hazards, such as windstorms, hail, smoke, and explosion can also be covered. The coverage is written for a specific value, such as the cost of replacing a building or its market value. Premiums are based on the insurable value.

## Business Interruption Insurance

This type of insurance protects against the loss of business due to disasters such as fire or weather damage. It is particularly important for businesses with a high risk of fire damage, like restaurants.

## Commercial Auto Insurance

Commercial auto insurance is not much different from the automobile insurance on our personal cars. Most commercial auto policies include property coverage for the vehicle itself, liability coverage for damage to other vehicles and persons, and the cost of injuries to the driver and passengers of the insured vehicle. If your company has more than five vehicles, **fleet insurance** will cover them all on one policy. If you are transporting people for a fee, you need a special type of endorsement or policy.

## Surety or Fidelity Bonds

Bonds are similar to insurance. You can buy a bond to guarantee that you will perform some specific action for a customer. Bonding is very important in the construction industry, where the bond guarantees that you have the financial capacity to perform. If you fail to perform as agreed, the client can get a settlement to cover their losses. You can also buy fidelity bonds for employees to protect the business against employee dishonesty and theft. Fidelity bonds should be used to cover both cash and merchandise losses.

## Key-Person Insurance

One of the problems faced by many small firms is the loss of a key employee or partner. **Key-person insurance** protects the company against financial loss caused by the death or disability of such individuals. The key person is covered by life and disability insurance, and the business is usually the policy owner and beneficiary.

## Life and Health

Employee benefits—such as group life, health coverage, and pension plans—are commonly offered as additional compensation in lieu of salaries or wages. Not surprisingly, health care is the fastest-growing component of employee benefits, but the high costs make it a major investment for small businesses.

The reasons most companies provide employee benefits include:

- Attracting and retaining good employees
- Improving morale and worker satisfaction
- Helping employees stay healthy and productive

In some instances, benefits are required by state or federal statutes.

### Workers' Compensation Insurance

Workers' compensation is required by law in every state

Workers' compensation covers employees who are injured on the job. It is required by law, but specific requirements vary by state. Most states require that worker's compensation benefits cover medical and rehabilitation costs, and lost wages for employees hurt on the job. Worker's compensation consists of two components: the first covers medical bills and lost wages for the injured employee; and the second encompasses employers' liability, which covers the business owner against lawsuits by the spouse or children of a worker who was permanently disabled or killed. In some states, a third optional element has been added to protect the business against employment practices liability, such as claims from sexual harassment, discrimination, and the like.

### Life Insurance

Life insurance often comes as part of a health insurance package. Otherwise, term life insurance can be purchased for your employees at a reasonable cost.

### Group Health/Medical Insurance

Health care coverage— the riskier the occupation, the higher the cost

Choosing the most economical and effective health insurance plan can be difficult. There are many providers and policies, including HMOs, private providers, and Managed Care Programs. Your agent can be invaluable in finding the best coverage. Health care is designed to cover the cost of care associated with a serious illness or accident. Many plans now include "wellness" programs, which include screenings for breast or colon cancer, and high blood pressure. Most plans are either comprehensive or scheduled. Comprehensive plans provide universal coverage to an employee after a deductible amount has been paid by the employee; in other words, they pay health care expenses up to a certain amount. Scheduled plans specify the amount they will pay for each health care item. The cost of any health care plan is determined by the work done by the employees; the riskier the occupation, the higher the cost of coverage.

### Pension Plans

A retirement savings plan is one of the most effective incentives a business can offer to recruit and retain good employees. However, because of the costs involved, only 20% of companies with less than 20 employees have an employee-based pension plan. Generally, there are two types of plans. A defined plan—the best example of which is the public employee retirement plan—pays a set amount, and guarantees a certain level of income at retirement, based on length of service and wage level. A contribution plan promises, but does not guarantee, a set amount. Profit sharing, in which a company makes an undefined contribution based on a profitability formula that changes from year to year, is a good example of this type of plan.

### Self-Insurance

Many small firms are looking at self-insurance as a way to cover the medical needs of their employees. Self-insurance is the practice of choosing not to purchase health coverage, but paying claims of a specific type and cost as they occur. The business only purchases what is called "stop-loss" insurance, which protects the business against major catastrophic illness/accidents and expenses. Consider the advantages and disadvantages carefully before choosing self-insurance!

# Your Insurance Checklist

This checklist is an excellent way to evaluate your insurance needs:

| Types of Insurance | Required | Type/Coverage | Annual Cost |
|---|---|---|---|
| **Protecting Your Business** | | | |
| General Liability | | | |
| Product Liability | | | |
| Completed Operations | | | |
| (Errors/Omissions) | | | |
| Professional Liability | | | |
| Automobile Liability | | | |
| Fire and Theft | | | |
| Business Interruption | | | |
| Fidelity Bonds | | | |
| Surety Bonds | | | |
| **Protecting Yourself** | | | |
| Personal Disability | | | |
| Key-Person | | | |
| Life Insurance | | | |
| Medical | | | |
| **Protecting Your Employees** | | | |
| Group Health | | | |
| Life | | | |
| Pension Plan | | | |
| Workers' Compensation | | | |

## Protect one of your most important assets—your computer.

The business information stored on your computer system is one of your most important—and most vulnerable—assets, but if you're like many companies, your insurance doesn't cover its loss. (For example, a theft policy may cover some or all of the replacement cost of a computer, but does not address the loss of the data stored on the computer, which are often infinitely more valuable than the hardware itself.) Loss of important computer data—such as accounting information, employee records, crucial work-in-progress, or a customer database—can deal just as crippling a blow to your business as a fire or flood, yet this risk is seldom adequately addressed by conventional policies. That's why you should consult your insurance agent about Electronic Data Processing (EDP) insurance, which covers theft, loss, and costs incurred when computers break down. If you're considering EDP coverage, look for coverage of losses due to virus attacks; utility-based damage (e.g., voltage spikes and blackouts); lightning strikes; and fire or water damage. It may also be possible to get coverage of damage to peripheral systems that are an integral part of your computer network. This is a relatively new (and often confusing!) form of insurance, but its popularity and importance are likely to grow as computers assume an even more central role in business.

A basic first step is to make sure that all your sensitive electronic equipment (e.g. computers, printers, fax and copy machine, etc.) have a proper surge protector (not a cheap "outlet strip") between the equipment and he wall outlet. Additionally, many firms also use a back-up power supply that provides enough power—and time— for you to save and back-up your computer files when the power goes off.

## Conclusion

You must work hard to establish your business, so it stands to reason that you'll want to protect your investment of time, money, and effort by taking precautions from the beginning. Seeking out the advice of professionals in accounting, insurance, banking, and law enables you to make informed decisions about protection techniques. Developing lasting relationships with your advisors will help you manage such business risks as partnership or shareholder problems, squeeze-outs, and insurance coverage. Take the time now to begin a program that will protect your business. You'll be glad you did!

# Chapter 19
# INTELLECTUAL PROPERTY RIGHTS

*About This Chapter:*
- *Why protect your ideas?*
- *How to protect your ideas*
- *Agreements to protect your secrets*
- *Getting outside help*

## Introduction

Your ideas and know-how—otherwise known as **intellectual property**—are among your business's greatest assets. Intellectual property law consists of regulations that help you protect your ideas from unlawful use or infringement by others. There are two reasons why you should legally protect your ideas: 1) to prevent other businesses or former employees from unlawfully using them in competition with you; and 2) to clarify who owns the right to intellectual property developed by your business and employees.

## Why Protect Your Ideas?

If you don't protect your intellectual property, you can lose it to your employer, dishonest employees, or your competitors. Under the doctrine of **work done for hire**, ideas you create while employed or commissioned by someone else are owned by your employer. For this reason, you should have a clause in your employment or engagement agreement addressing the ownership of your ideas. If you create ideas while employed by your own corporation, and you do not reserve them as an individual, the corporation may own those ideas. This means that if the corporation sells its assets to a third party, or its assets are seized by the court or creditors, you may find that your copyrights, patents, trade secrets, and other intellectual property belong to a third party! This is a further reason to identify the ownership of the intellectual property in your employment agreement, even if you are a single-shareholder corporation.

*Your ideas may belong to your employers unless you agree otherwise*

## How to Protect Your Ideas

### Business Names

Most businesses operate under an **assumed business name**, sometimes signified by the phrase, "Doing Business As" or "DBA" for short. Customer recognition of your business name—and the goodwill associated with it—is invaluable to your business, so you will want to protect it against misuse by other parties.

Most states provide for the registration of an assumed business name, which can usually be done either statewide or by county. This is most often accomplished by filing a simple form with the state Department of Commerce. Most states require that the assumed business name be filed at the time you begin using that name in order to offer full protection. If your car repair business is named "Action Automotive" and you reserved this name in one county, it may be available for use by a business in another county unless you reserve it statewide. And even if you register your name statewide, it is possible the court will allow another business to use it, provided the competing business operates in a different area and does not cause you any harm.

When selecting a name, be careful to avoid using any term that describes the product itself. Some of the best trademarks are names that have no dictionary meaning at all, such as Nerf, 7-Up, or Oreo.

## NxLEVEL™ TECH TIP

If you have an idea for a new product, but you're not sure that it's really marketable, you might wish to consult an independent product developer (IPD). For a fee (usually less than $500), IPDs will objectively evaluate your product's potential, so that you can decide whether to pursue further development. Here are three very reputable IPDs to consider:

The **Wisconsin Innovation Service Center** at the University of Wisconsin, Whitewater, will send you an evaluation of your product with regard to competition and technical feasibility in about 30 days. It will also conduct a preliminary patent search. Call (414) 472-1365 for more information.

The **Washington Innovation Assessment Center (WIAC)** will identify the positive and negative characteristics of your idea, and provide a quantitative measure of its potential for commercial success. For an additional fee, they'll also conduct a preliminary patent or trademark search. For more information, call (509) 335-1576.

The **Wal-Mart Innovation Network (WIN)** is another option. For $175, the students at Southwest Missouri State University in Springfield will evaluate and score your idea for market potential. If your score is high enough, Wal-Mart buyers may consider your product for placement in their stores; however, WIN should be looked at primarily as a source for product evaluation. To find out more, call (417) 836-5671.

Note: All three of these IPDs will sign confidentiality agreements, so you don't have to worry that sharing your idea with them will release it to the public domain!

In the event a third party uses your business name, or one that is deceptively similar, you may seek a court injunction to prevent them from using that name. Most often, courts rule that the first business to use or register the name has the right to continue using it, so it is important that you register your business name as soon as possible.

## Trademarks

A **trademark** is a word or symbol used to identify a company or its services and products. For example, the Nike® "swoosh" is a symbol of that company's products. A trademark is different from your business name in that your name identifies your business, while the trademark is your insignia or brand name.

How to register your trademark

Virtually every retail business trademarks its name. Think of Starbucks Coffee, The Gap, or the Pottery Barn. When these companies started, they might have been local or regional concerns, but they soon caught on and became national chains. Even if you are contemplating growing to a national enterprise, it pays to protect your trademark early on. When you first start using your trademark to identify your business or product, use the ™ symbol. This shows you are claiming your common-law rights in regards to the mark. If your business is a service business, use the ℠ symbol.

The federal trademark office provides nationwide registration of trademarks. Once you have created a trademark, you should conduct a trademark search at the federal trademark office to determine if your mark is unique enough to register nationwide. Federal registration takes about a year and is good for 20 years. The mark must be unique and cannot be recognized by the marketplace as belonging to another company.

------------------------◆------------------------

*If the Posh Pita Company has been baking pita bread for ten years and using a smiling pita as its symbol, you wouldn't be able to trademark a smiling pita bread as your new company's logo. Even if the Posh Pita Company never registered its smiling pita with the federal trademark office, the smiling pita is still instantly recognizable as the logo for the Posh Pita Company.*

------------------------◆------------------------

A state trade name search is no substitute for a federal trademark search. There are firms in Washington, D.C. that conduct searches for a fee, or you can retain a patent lawyer to help you. Some states also register trademarks; check with your state Department of Commerce. For most closely held businesses, state registration may be sufficient. Either way, registering your trademark is easy, inexpensive, and very valuable. Register your trademarks as soon as possible to avoid losing your rights to another party!

Before you use your trademark on a product sold through interstate commerce (i.e., shipping across state lines), it's wise to file an application to register it with the U.S. Trademark Office. Keep in mind, however, that registration will not be granted until the mark is actually in use. Important advantages of registration include a presumption of validity in the mark after seven years of continuous use, and the option of filing with U.S. Customs to prohibit imported knock-offs from entering the country. The trademark symbol ® is used to show you have registered your trademark.

How to stop infringement

on your copyright

You can stop **infringement** of your trademark by suing the infringer. Normally, you can get a court injunction to stop infringement of your trademark; most state statutes provide for triple damages to the winner. Note that merely registering your trademark will not protect you from infringement; if another company can show that it was using the mark before you registered it, has a valid defense. Also, if their use is not causing you injury or confusing your customers, then the court may not protect you; therefore, federal registration of the logo of your local coffee shop would probably have little practical value unless you plan to go nationwide. Companies that maintain nationwide surveillance of trademarks (for a fee) can assist you in protecting your mark.

A good starting point for your trademark search is the United States Patent and Trademark office website: **http://www/uspto.gov**. It has an online searchable database of registered trademarks, as well as a wealth of information on trademarks.

## Copyright

Another way of protecting your ideas is through a **copyright**. Any original work that can be printed can be copyrighted. Magazine and newspaper articles, songs, pictures, novels, computer software programs, and similar creative works are subject to **copyright protection**. You can protect your copyright by registering it with the Register of Copyrights in Washington, D.C., or by noting on the document itself that it is subject to copyright by using the term "copyrighted" or the symbol ©, giving your name, and showing the year of first publication. However, you can lose copyright protection if you allow publication of your work without the copyright notice. Copyright notices and registration are both very inexpensive and remain good for up to 50 years after your death.

Many recording artists and composers have been financially hurt over the years because they signed away copyrights on their recordings to large record companies. Every time a song plays on the radio or on a jukebox, the copyright holder of that song is due a royalty fee. If the songwriter did not copyright his or her song, he or she misses out on thousands of dollars in royalties.

Enforcement against copyright infringement is similar to the process used to protect trademarks. You can sue to prevent someone from using your copyrighted work, or for monetary damages, or both. If the work is federally registered, you may also get statutory damages and attorney fees. Many companies are having difficulty operating in the international marketplace because some foreign countries do not protect intellectual property to the extent that we do in the United States. This has been a recurring problem in China, where bootlegged computer software, CDs, and similar materials have cost American businesses millions of dollars. You should note, however, that many Asian countries are considering stronger intellectual property laws. And in Europe, the Community Trademark law will allow one-step international registration in the EC. In the United States, there is much discussion about ensuring that copyrighted material remains protected as it is transmitted over the Internet.

## Patents

Let's say you just invented a great new way to remove wine stains from fabrics, and you want to make sure your competitors won't copy your product's ingredients. How do you do this? By obtaining patent protection. A **patent** is the protection of a unique invention or process by registration with the United States Patent Office in Washington, D.C. In order to apply for a patent, you must conduct a patent search. Unless you are extremely familiar with the operations of the Patent Office, you should engage an attorney who specializes in intellectual property to apply for your patent. The cost depends on the complexity of the invention; it often costs more than a trademark search.

Once your search is complete and you've determined that your invention is unique enough to be eligible for patent protection, it's time to file a patent application. The application must describe the invention and include drawings. The process is complicated and most applications are examined very carefully by the patent office. Generally, patents are good for 17 years. A **utility patent** lasts for 20 years from the date of the application (or "date of grant"), and usually relates to mechanical or electronic devices, or a new process. A **design patent**, which may be obtained for the ornamental appearance of a manufactured product, is good for 14 years after the date of grant.

Once you obtain your patent, you have the right to exclude others from using, selling, or manufacturing your product. You must mark the product with the patent or you lose your protection. (A word about using the term **patent pending** on your product: First, if you are not intending to apply for a patent, then using this term may be illegal. Second, it gains you nothing—you either have a patent or you don't!)

With a patent, you can license your patent to someone else who will produce and market your product. Typically, you do this for a fee or a royalty based upon the frequency of use of the product. Even without a patent, you can allow others to use your product for a fee under a well-drafted **licensing agreement**.

Enforcement against patent infringement is much the same as enforcing copyrights and trademarks. As a practical matter, it is often difficult to protect a patent because of the complexity and the expense. You may want to consider carefully whether a patent application is really the best thing for your business. The application requires that you disclose a great deal about the steps taken in the process and the diagrams of your invention. You may simply be providing a means for your competitors to take advantage of your products without having to put all their money into the research and development of such a product. You may be better off keeping your invention or process to yourself and protecting it as a trade secret.

Hire a patent lawyer to search records at the U.S. Patent Office

A good starting point for your patent search is the United States Patent and Trademark Office website: **http//.uspto.gov**. It has an online searchable database, as well as a wealth of information on patents.

### Trade Secrets/Customer Lists

Trade secrets consist of the confidential business information, methods, and processes used in your business; they are not common knowledge, but have not been protected by patent registration. Trade secrets are the primary intellectual property of most small businesses.

*Your trade secrets are your most valuable intellectual property*

In many states, trade secrets and customer lists are given statutory protection against theft or misuse under the Uniform Trade Secrets Act, as long as you take reasonable steps to maintain their secrecy. Even if an invention or process is not eligible for patent registration, it may still be a protected trade secret under state law.

Typically, misuse of trade secrets occurs when an employee has left your employment and attempts to use your secrets to compete against you. The remedies against such acts are often injunctions; the court requires the offending party to stop using the information and to return it to the owner. Monetary damages may also be awarded against the offending party, since in many instances you cannot undo the harm done to your business. Finally, if trade secrets and customer lists are protected by statute, it may be a crime to steal those items.

You should also think about protecting your computer files. If you are on a network, make sure that you have password protection for files that should only be seen by you. Disgruntled employees have been known to erase crucial files before they leave; a tape backup system will help avoid this problem.

In addition, more and more companies are trying to maintain the confidentiality of e-mail correspondence. If you are thinking of establishing a Web site, it is a good idea to install controls that prevent hackers from changing or destroying the material on your site.

## Agreements to Protect Your Secrets

### Noncompetition Agreements

**Noncompetition agreements** are intended to restrain a person from competing with your business. They are typically used when an employer does not want employees to leave with unique knowledge developed by the company. Noncompetition agreements are also used when a business is acquired by a new owner who does not want the former owner to start another business in the area, contact all his or her old customers, and compete against the very business he or she just sold.

*You can use a contract to protect your trade secrets*

Most states regulate noncompetition agreements, and some also address the content of trade secret agreements. You should have your lawyer check into this, and help you draft these agreements so they will be enforceable. Generally, one of the requirements is that the agreement be entered into at the beginning of the employment, or at the time of a significant promotion. Another common requirement is that the noncompetition agreement be limited in time and distance. This is to avoid **antitrust** (monopoly) law violations, and to allow for future employment of former employees or owners.

Most noncompetition agreements are narrow in scope and duration

———————————◆———————————

*If Sally's Hair Salon were to employ Betty as a stylist, it would more than likely be a violation of these legal requirements if Sally insisted upon a noncompetition agreement that prohibited Betty's competition statewide for ten years. These prohibitions would not be reasonably limited in time or distance, because it is unlikely that Sally's customers come to her from all over the state. It is also unlikely that Sally's business would be hurt even if Betty competed in the same town more than a year after the termination of her employment.*

———————————◆———————————

## Nondisclosure Agreements

A **nondisclosure agreement (NDA)** typically requires that parties receiving information about your business cannot disclose it to any third party or use it for themselves. These agreements are useful when you must allow another company to acquire nonpublic information about your business, such as when a company reviews your operations, books, and records for purposes of a potential acquisition or merger; or when you retain a consultant to assist you in the management of your enterprise. We recommend that you have such an agreement in place before you allow an outsider or another company to have access to any of your books or records, trade secrets, customer lists, or even to inspect your physical plant. A well-drafted agreement will provide for injunctive remedies as well as damages in the event of a breach of that agreement.

NDAs are also a means of protecting your ideas while they are in the development stage. Since you may have to share an idea in development with potential partners, investors, consultants, or manufacturers, you should consider requesting that these individuals sign NDAs. Your lawyer will be able to advise you on this matter.

———————————◆———————————

*When Mike Johnson fired his assistant, Shirley Frasier, for nonperformance, he never imagined all the trouble she would cause after she left the company! Johnson's Marketing Works provided strategic marketing services to several beverage companies. When Shirley Frasier left, she took with her several crucial files on competitive industry analysis after deleting them from Johnson's computer. Because Johnson did not have the foresight to have Frasier sign a nondisclosure agreement when she started working at Marketing Works, Johnson had a difficult time trying to right the wrongs that Shirley did.*

———————————◆———————————

## Getting Outside Help

In many cases, it becomes necessary to consult an expert while perfecting a new invention or process. This can get expensive, so you should first do as much research as you can on your own, using your public library and the Web. (Make an effort to learn all the pertinent terminology; if you end up having to pay an expert for advice, it'll be a big help!)

Consider other sources of free or low-cost advice, including knowledgeable friends and associates. Many communities have nonprofit groups composed of retired business veterans who will share their expertise for free. You can call your Chamber of Commerce for similar services.

If you need to consult a professional, start by checking under "consultants" or "engineers" in your local business-to-business telephone directory. Also, most industry trade groups will provide you with a list of reputable experts on request.

Next, make an outline or flowchart that describes what you hope to accomplish, using as much detail as possible. If it's computer software or an electronic circuit of some sort, write down the algorithms or step-by-step instructions. If it's a mechanical device, explain exactly how it should look and work.

It's a very good idea to ask for references and check with the Better Business Bureau before disclosing your ideas to an outside expert. And, as always, you should consult your attorney to see if he or she recommends that you utilize a nondisclosure agreement.

There should be no charge for your first meeting with a consultant. Keep your presentation brief and to the point. The consultant will assess your needs, and get back to you with a written proposal indicating what services he or she will perform, and the fee. Avoid open-ended, per-hour charges, and make sure to set a ceiling limit on the final amount. Be aware that if your expert contributes any innovations, he or she may be considered a co-inventor, and will have to be included on the patent application. Your written agreement should specify both parties' rights and obligations.

## Conclusion

Even if you do not think your business has intellectual property, such property is probably your greatest asset. You do not have to be engaged in biotech or computer research to have methods or processes that are not commonly known. Who your customers are, and what and how often they order, is vital information that you should seek to protect. There are various methods of protecting your intellectual property under both state and federal registration and state safeguard statutes. Our best advice is to see your lawyer early and use these protections to your full advantage!

# Chapter 20
# CONTRACTS AND LEASES

*About This Chapter:*
* *Elements of a contract*
* *Common contract issues and terms*
* *Remedies*
* *Drawing up a contract*
* *Leases*

## Introduction

Contracts are central to business activity. Without them, there would be no agreement on the terms of purchase or sale, and businesses could not exist! In transactions involving the sale of goods, the **Uniform Commercial Code (UCC)** has a significant impact on the common law of contracts. Article 2 of the UCC applies primarily to the sale of goods; most of its provisions are limited to transactions between businesses. The following chapter focuses on some of the UCC's most important provisions, and discusses how they affect your business. It also explains the differences between the UCC and the common law of contracts.

## Elements of a Contract

Suppose you walk into the corner grocery store where you have been shopping for 15 years and pick up a bottle of milk. You take it to the counter and show it to the owner, who enters the price on your account. Although this is an informal transaction, all the elements of a contract are present: the owner offered the goods for sale, you agreed to buy them at a specific price, and value was exchanged when you got the milk and the owner recorded an account receivable.

Now let's discuss the more formal requirements of contracts and how they can affect your business transactions.

### Formation

In order to determine whether you have a deal, the first question is, have you both agreed to the same thing? Under the common law, there must be a valid offer for goods or services, and an acceptance of this offer at an agreed-upon price. If the buyer proposes any alternate terms, this becomes a **counteroffer** from the buyer to the seller. The counteroffer terminates the original offer, and is then subject to the seller's acceptance or rejection. At this point, the seller isn't required to agree to the counteroffer *or* the original offer.

This common law rule caused problems in the modern business world, because so much of our business dealings are done by a preprinted form. In other words, the fine print of a proposal may be different from the purchase order, which may be different from the shipment statement, and so on. In response to this exchange of paper with conflicting terms, the UCC has a "battle of the forms" provision. In most instances, this means that the identical terms of different forms are deemed the contract terms, and those which are different—so long as they are not material to the transaction—are thrown out and replaced by the standard "gap filler" terms of the UCC. However, if the terms in the differing forms are so much at variance that the parties in effect don't have an agreement, then the UCC states that no legal contract was formed. The UCC also recognizes contracts established by the conduct described in the milk-buying scenario above, even in the absence of a written document between the parties.

Under common law, an offer of contract is only open for a reasonable amount of time, or until the seller withdraws it. The UCC allows the parties to agree to leave the offer open for a stated period of time. This agreement is in itself a contract.

### Consideration

In order for a contract to be enforceable, there must be some value or **consideration** passing between the two parties. In the corner grocery store, for example, you received the milk as consideration and the grocer received your promise to pay at the end of the month. Consideration can consist of many different kinds of value. Forbearance, or the giving up of a right, can be consideration. For instance, if you had the right to buy shares of stock under an option (as we'll discuss in a later chapter), you could agree to give up that right as consideration for the company performing some other duty, such as agreeing to ship you two boxes of parts you wanted. Contracts can also be supported by mutual promises: if you promise to design computer software for a company with delivery six months from now, and they promise to ship you a new laptop two months thereafter, this constitutes a contract. The court does not usually concern itself with the fairness of the consideration unless one party has acted fraudulently or under undue influence (a threat of physical harm, for example).

### Capacity

Both parties must have the mental capability to enter into a contract. For that reason, most states rule that contracts with minors for unessential goods or services are unenforceable against the minor. Likewise, you cannot enter into a contract with a person who does not have the mental capacity to understand the nature of the transaction, regardless of his or her age (e.g., someone with Alzheimer's). Another example of lack of capacity is when the person with whom you are dealing is intoxicated or under the influence of drugs, prescribed or otherwise. In short, a contract made with a party who does not have the capacity to enter into that contract is legally voidable.

### Legality

For a contract to be **enforceable**, the terms of the transaction must be legal. In most states, for example, one could not enforce a contract based upon, prostitution, child labor, or other illegal transactions.

### The Statute of Frauds—Written Agreements

The Statute of Frauds, which has been adopted in most states provides that any contract that exceeds $500, or that cannot be performed within one year, must be in writing. Most states require that any type of transaction involving real estate be in writing, regardless of the value or duration. The writing does not have to be fancy—you just need to outline the essentials. (A contract written on the back of a cedar shingle was once enforced for the sale of a subdivision lot. The parties were identified by their initials, the price was "10K cash," and the property was described as "lot 16.")

Like every general rule of law, the Statute of Frauds is different in every state and there are many exceptions to it. The UCC allows the contract to be any type of written communication between the parties, such as a series of letters which collectively could be construed to represent the contract terms. The UCC specifically excludes specially manufactured goods from the Statute of Frauds, because the existence of goods made to the specifications of the buyer is evidence enough that the parties had an agreement.

## Common Contract Issues and Terms

When you receive a contract, you should make sure that you understand all the conditions of the deal. Most business contracts include many of the following terms:

### Performance

Performance means the actions you must complete under the contract. For instance, you might be required to deliver ten desks to an office by a particular date.

### Price

The UCC will fill a nonexistent price term in a contract if the parties' actions indicate there is a contract. However, you should understand the price term of your agreement before you start performance. Your contract should also establish how many units you are to deliver, at what price, and whether the price is in U.S., Canadian, or some other funds.

### Quality Control

Does your contract require an international standards (ISO) certification, or total quality management (TQM) reporting? Do you need to deliver a sample before the contract takes effect? Are you manufacturing the product to the buyer's specifications? Are any tolerances allowed? Does "class A goods" mean the same thing to the buyer and the seller? Have you done business with this party before, so that prior performance establishes these standards?

### Bailout

Does the agreement allow for an escape? Are you bound to deliver goods in the future, or is this a single-delivery agreement, so that once you have performed you can bail out?

## Time to Perform

If the parties do not identify the time for performance, the UCC implies that a "reasonable time" must be allowed. Of course, what is reasonable to you and what is reasonable to the other party may be different, so you should identify specifically when performance is due, both from the delivery and payment sides of the transaction.

## Nonconforming Goods

Under common law, the seller must deliver exactly what the contract specifies or the buyer does not have to accept the goods. However, if the seller ships goods reasonably believed to be acceptable to the buyer—even though they do not exactly match the terms of the agreement—and the buyer doesn't reject those goods within a reasonable amount of time, the UCC recognizes the deal as complete.

## Place of Delivery

Where are the goods or services to be delivered? Who pays for shipment? Who bears the risk of loss while the goods are in transit? Does training on how to use the item take place in your office or theirs? Are your travel time and expenses covered? Failure to review the delivery terms of the agreement carefully can result in your profits being used to pay for these costs! You should also consider when payment is due and what, if any, carrying charges apply.

## Warranty

A warranty is a promise or representation about the goods, which creates an expectation that the goods will conform to the promise. A warranty can be created by a description of the goods, a sample or model, or a verbal or written statement. It is not necessary to use formal terms, such as "warrant" or "guaranty", but a warranty must be more than an off-handed opinion that the quality is "good" or some other vague term. Obviously, it is best to deal with warranties in writing so that there is no confusion. Take note that you may have made a warranty by sending a sample unless you disclaim any implied warranties on the sample.

The UCC provides for implied warranties of "fitness for particular purpose" and **merchantability**, as does most state warranty legislation. The shorthand definition of merchantability is that the goods are fit for their normal use, and are equal in quality with similar items manufactured by others. "Fitness for particular purpose" means that the seller has reason to know of a particular purpose for which the goods are required, and that the buyer is relying on the seller's skill or judgment in furnishing suitable goods. You can avoid both of these implied warranties if you expressly disclaim them in bold print, by name, in your written contract. We recommended that you consult your lawyer before offering any warranty, or disclaiming the UCC-implied warranties.

*Friendly's Auto agreed to sell Dana Buckle a standard model American car and then failed to deliver. Dana had to buy a replacement at Honest John's, which cost $500 more than the car at Friendly's. More than likely the court would find that Dana could be "made whole" by having Friendly's pay damages, which it would calculate as the difference between the price at which Friendly's had agreed to sell the car and the price Dana had to pay Honest John's for the same car (namely, $500). However, if Friendly's had agreed to sell Mr. Buckle the one-of-a-kind customized motorcycle that Dennis Hopper rode in* **Easy Rider**, *then the court could find that the motorcycle is so unique that damages are not adequate compensation. Under those circumstances, specific performance might be required by the court, and Friendly's would have to locate the specific motorcycle Mr. Buckle requested.*

## Venue

Many contracts provide that they are to be judged under the laws of a certain state, and that any lawsuit or arbitration must be brought within that state. You must be extremely cautious when using these provisions. The laws of each state can be quite different; commonly accepted practice in your state may be unenforceable in another. In addition, your lawyer may not mind handling the arbitration in Hawaii, but you may not be able to afford that if you live in Colorado!

## Notice

Are you required to provide notice under the agreement when you have reached a certain production level, or even prior to beginning your performance? Whom do you notify, how often, and where? You should not ignore these provisions.

## Parties

With whom are you dealing? Is it the parent corporation, or a shell with no assets? You may wish to consider the requirement of a personal guaranty if the party turns out to be Blue's, Inc., rather than the financially secure Ms. Blue. A guarantee by Ms. Blue places her in the position of responsibility if her corporation breaches the deal. For more information, see our discussion of guarantees in an earlier chapter.

## Clarity

Is the agreement written so that a third person (such as a judge) who is not in your industry could understand its terms? If you have to submit this contract to arbitration or litigation, it is most helpful if the judge is able to understand it.

## Modifications

Does the contract require that any modifications be in writing, and does it exclude all other prior agreements? These terms can have very serious consequences to a party who relies on verbal change orders. There is a rule, both in the common law and the UCC, stating that if the parties intend the written contract to be their final agreement, it cannot be contradicted by oral terms. This is known as the "parol evidence rule." There are many exceptions to this rule and it is different in each state. However, the courts are much more likely to enforce the parol evidence rule where the contract contains a clause requiring all changes to be in writing.

### Estoppel

Generally, a party to a contract may not deny the existence of that contract, or a change to the performance under the contract, when the other party has begun performing under the agreement and the first party knowingly allows the other party to continue its performance. Therefore, even if the other party's performance is not identical to the terms of the original contract, the doctrine of **estoppel** can modify the written contract.

---

*Let's say your greeting card design business contracts with a large greeting card supplier, Sentimental Thoughts, Inc., to deliver 15 birthday card designs on a monthly basis. For the first three months, you deliver exactly 15 birthday card designs to Sentimental Thoughts per month. Suddenly, you get writer's block; for the next year you deliver only seven birthday card designs per month, and make up the shortfall with anniversary and "bon voyage" card designs. If*

## NxLEVEL™ TECH TIP
### Hiring a Lawyer

Hiring a lawyer can be quite expensive, running $200 per hour or more, yet much of what lawyers do is routine. Many legal documents are merely templates that can be filled in with basic information, so why not fill them in yourself and save some money? That's the premise behind legal software, which provides templates for a wide range of commonly used legal documents. Users fill in blanks with the appropriate information, aided by pop-up windows describing the type of information that should go in each blank. Some programs provide a proofing function to make sure you've filled in all the blanks in the template (although none of them check whether what you've filled is accurate). The templates included in legal software packages vary; typical documents include estate planning, finance, power of attorney, consumer credit, wills and gifts, buying and selling real estate, goods, or a business; borrowing and lending money; operating a corporation; and general contract clauses. (Some legal software packages even provide general legal information of interest to small-business owners, including articles discussing employment, corporate, intellectual property, financial, and legal issues.) Remember: Legal software programs simply help you produce legal documents more quickly. Like accounting or tax software, they can reduce the cost of legal services, and they also give you a better grasp of the legal documents your business deals with. However, you'll still need to have the documents reviewed by a lawyer specializing in that issue, or in your particular business.

*Sentimental Thoughts does not complain about this, the doctrine of estoppel states that you have effectively changed the terms of your agreement. However, in order to protect yourself, you should document any changes by way of letters or other written memoranda.*

---

### Good Faith

Many states have adopted the requirement of "good faith" and "fair dealing" in consumer contracts. The UCC specifically provides that every contract, including those between businesses, has an implied obligation of good faith in its performance or enforcement. Many courts are now enforcing these good faith requirements. (This does not mean, however, that the court will allow you to escape a bad deal just because you entered into it foolishly; the courts are reluctant to interfere much in transactions between businesses!) The UCC also provides that if the court finds any clause of a contract to have been "unconscionable," it may refuse to enforce the contract, or may enforce the contract minus the unconscionable clause. The Code does not define the term "unconscionable"; rather, it looks to the prevention of oppression and unfair surprise. It is not intended to disturb the allocation of risk because of superior bargaining power, so once again, don't think this rule will allow you to get out of a bad agreement!

## Remedies

### Liquidated Damages

Sometimes the parties to a contract provide for specific consequences if one party breaches the agreement. This is generally referred to as **liquidated damages**. The courts do not allow the recovery of liquidated damages if they are really a penalty rather than an accurate forecast of the reasonable cost of obtaining the goods or services elsewhere. Nevertheless, you should review these provisions very carefully; if enforceable, they can be quite severe.

Liquidated damages: the accurate forecast of cost to obtain goods or services elsewhere

### Arbitration

Many contracts provide for **mediation** or **arbitration** in place of a party's right to bring a lawsuit to enforce the agreement. You should consider whether this is beneficial to you before entering that term into the agreement. Many small businesses prefer to use arbitration or mediation because of the high cost of trying to pursue a lawsuit in court.

### Professional Fees and Expenses

Most well-drafted contracts provide for the winning party to recover attorney and other expert's fees (for appraisers, accountants, and the like), and all court costs from the losing party. You should make sure that this term also covers arbitration, defense of your position if the other party goes bankrupt, and other such fees and costs in any appeal.

When drawing up a
contract, always:

• consider your role

• seek legal advice

• read the fine print

## Specific Performance

Specific performance is a remedy that is rarely allowed by the courts outside of real estate transactions, or transactions involving unique and irreplaceable property. The "specific performance" decree requires the party to perform, instead of granting the injured party money damages.

# Drawing Up a Contract

## Your Role

As you see, contracts can be simple or quite complex. You should always determine whether the proposed agreement fits the way you do business. For instance, if the agreement requires "ISO certification" and you thought that term had something to do with the speed of the film in your 35mm camera, then you should research that term until you understand what it means. Prior to signing any agreement, you should always review the contract's provisions as if the contract was in default, and ask yourself if you're prepared for the consequences, positive or negative. It does you no good to enter into an agreement to manufacture 1,000 specially designed, highly technical parts when your company has never manufactured even one part to such exacting standards. Can you, and do you want to, perform this agreement under these terms and circumstances?

## Legal Counsel

Always review any complex contract with your lawyer. To save time and expense, you should be thoroughly organized before visiting your lawyer. Outline the elements of your understanding, and any terms that are different from the contract provided to you. Helping your lawyer to understand the common practices in your industry will make it easier for him or her to protect your interests.

If you ask your lawyer to draft a contract for you, outlining the basic terms ahead of time will save money. Look at other agreements that people in your industry have used in the past; your Chamber of Commerce may be able to put you in contact with someone in your business, or you might find relevant information at the library or on the web. You may want your lawyer to prepare a blank contract that you can use again and again. There are even contracts available on computer software. However, always remember that every contract is special to its circumstances, and your lawyer should review the agreement before you finalize it.

Understand the
boilerplate before you
sign the contract

## Boilerplate

It should be apparent by now that the **boilerplate** (also known as **fine print**, or **standard clauses**) found in most business agreements is important. In the event of a dispute, every term in that contract will be reviewed and utilized by one party or the other. You should never assume that a printed form is "standard" and cannot be modified. As we discussed in earlier chapters, you should always attempt to modify the form to fit the specific deal. If a contract contains boilerplate that is unacceptable, you can always cross out or change a term, initial the change, and have the other party initial it too. Remember that small print can have huge consequences!

# Leases

A lease is an agreement giving one party possession of another party's land or personal property (e.g., equipment) for a stated period of time. Leases are addressed in this chapter because they are one of the more important contracts your business may sign. They involve long-term, ongoing relationships, and often represent one of your largest fixed costs. Here are some things to think about when leasing your business premises:

## Area

What space are you actually renting? If you are in a shopping center or office complex, a suite map is helpful. This map should also indicate common areas (see below).

## Rent Escalators

How does the rent change over time? Is it based on a consumer price index adjustment, appraisal, or the landlord's caprice?

## Triple Net

This is a shorthand expression for requiring the tenant to pay the insurance, maintenance, and taxes on the property. These payments are in addition to your regular lease payments. There are many variants of these provisions, and you must review them very carefully to understand the full cost of the lease.

## Common Area

Are you sharing any space with other tenants, and if so, how are the costs for those spaces allocated between you? Who takes care of it? Who pays for insurance on those areas? Examples of common areas include lobbies, elevators, parking lots and lawns.

## Parking

Is there enough? Is it conveniently located? Are any spaces reserved for you or your customers? Can the landlord later develop an additional building in what was your parking area, leaving you with inadequate parking?

## Renewal

Is your right to renew the lease clearly stated, and is the mechanism for arriving at the rental for the renewal period clearly defined?

## Purchase Rights

Do you have an option to buy the property, and if so, under what terms? Do you have a first right of refusal to buy the property under the terms offered to a third party by your landlord?

## Exclusivity

Does your lease state that yours will be the only paint store in the complex, or can other paint stores come in and compete against you? Do you want the landlord to be able to lease the parking lot to a Christmas tree vendor, or a circus?

### Permitted Uses

Do you want your Christian bookstore to operate next to a body-piercing salon? Is your assembly facility sensitive to vibrations or noise from the warehousing operation next door? These are the kinds of issues you need to consider if the space you are leasing is in a business park, shopping center, or other multi-use complex.

## Conclusion

Contracts can be simple or complex, written or verbal, performed or breached, but no matter what, if you do a deal there will be a contract. Be sure you know what you intend to do and what the desires of the other party are. The best practice is to put everything in writing, and to avoid signing an agreement until you are completely comfortable with it.

# Chapter 21
# BUSINESS SUCCESSION AND ESTATE PLANNING

*About This Chapter:*
- *Executive compensation*
- *Estate planning*
- *Succession planning*
- *Exit strategies—children*
- *Death/disability among shareholders*
- *Retirement plans*

## Introduction

We have discussed the legal system and how it affects your business operations. You have made it through the rocky start-up stages of business and are starting to experience the fruits of hard work and careful planning. Now comes the fun part—handling success! It may be that your planning has just begun!

## Executive Compensation

### The Most Commonly Challenged Deduction

Since your business has become successful, you have just paid yourself a hefty salary. Your C-corporation has filed its tax return and along comes an audit! The IRS often tries to characterize compensation paid to the owner as a dividend, because dividends can be taxed once on the corporation and once on the owner's personal return, resulting in **double taxation**. (Remember, C-corporations are separate taxable entities.) For this reason, most closely held corporations try to "zero out" taxable income by paying out most of the profits at the end of the year to the owner as compensation. The corporation then takes a deduction for the compensation paid and the individual is taxed only once on his or her individual return.

The IRS may challenge the compensation amount as not being "reasonable," so if you pay yourself a very high salary to avoid double taxation, you should document the reasons for that high salary in the corporate minutes and in your employment contract. Be sure to include your qualifications and achievements, your duties and responsibilities, the complexity of your work, and the long hours you spent on the job. Your accountant may also want to review how your salary compares with owners of comparable companies. Unreasonable compensation disputes seldom arise in S-corporations, LLCs, or partnerships, because the income of those entities is "passed through" for purposes of taxation.

Be careful with non-cash compensation because it's taxable

## Non-Cash Compensation

Many owners of closely held business fall into the temptation of compensating themselves with **non-cash distributions**. For example, a business owner might have a number of his or her personal expenses paid by the corporation directly. Or a business owner who collects antiques might have the company buy antique office furniture and end up taking it home. In these cases, IRS auditors would probably characterize these non-cash transactions as income to the individual. A tax would then be levied, but the individual has no cash income with which to pay that tax obligation. In addition, the IRS may consider such practices as fraud, and civil or criminal penalties could be imposed. We suggest you talk with your CPA about non-cash compensation.

# Estate Planning

### Objectives

Careful business owners consider estate plans to be part of their business plans. **Estate planning** should provide for your future support; minimize your taxes, or provide for the payment of taxes due; and facilitate transfer of the business to the next generation, or to a third party.

The place to start is with your **will**. If you do not have a will when you die, the state writes one for you under the probate statutes. The state's will (or "intestate succession") usually provides that your surviving spouse receives half of your estate, and the remainder goes to any surviving children. Also, in most states, the estate—your business—is sold and the cash is distributed. Obviously, the state's will does not allow you to accomplish the three objectives described above! Therefore, our first recommendation is that you see your lawyer and discuss the preparation of an estate plan that will accomplish your goals.

### Planning for Taxes

Both spouses should use their estate tax credit to pass on twice as many assets tax-free

If your net estate exceeds $675,000 at your death in 2001, your estate may owe federal estate tax. In addition, many states have inheritance taxes. Most states follow the federal taxation structure. Congress recently passed a new tax act that made significant changes to the estate and gift tax laws. Between 2002 and 2010 the estate tax exclusion will increase to $3.5 million per person. Estate tax may be completely repealed in 2010 pending further action by congress. Under these new laws, many estates which were formerly taxable will avoid such taxes in the future due to the increased exemptions. A **net** estate is the value of your assets minus liabilities. Under federal law, you may leave any amount of assets to your surviving spouse without paying any estate tax. However, if your estate exceeds the federal exemption then this could lead to a bunching of assets in the survivor's estate, which may result in even higher taxes when your spouse dies. The time to plan is while both spouses are alive and able to utilize their estate tax exemption. Simply splitting the estate into two entities can save several hundred thousand dollars of unnecessary tax!

Since one purpose of estate planning is to pass your business on to future generations, you do not want it sold to pay estate taxes! It's often advisable for the owner of a closely held business to anticipate the payment of estate or inheritance taxes with an insurance policy, thus avoiding any liquidation of business assets to pay taxes. You must not own the life insurance policy yourself, however, or it will be included in your estate and be subject to estate tax; instead, either the business, or a third party—such as your children—should own the policy. Be aware that a provision under the federal code allows your estate to defer payment of portions of the estate tax attributable to the closely held business; these payments may be spread out over a period of up to 14 years. With careful planning, you can avoid this situation entirely. Undoubtedly, the new Tax Act will affect many of the tax oriented estate and succession planning techniques which were formerly recommended by lawyers and accountants. To what degree, however, is yet to be seen. Many of the strategies and techniques have multiple benefits – i.e., both estate tax benefits and family succession benefits. For this reason, we will still discuss most of the well-recognized planning strategies, because one or more of them may be useful for you.

### The Use of Trusts

By utilizing a trust, your heirs can most often avoid the substantial time and expense of a probate. Trusts are a very effective way of planning for someone to assist you in the event that you become physically or mentally disabled. You can provide for care and maintenance of minor children or a surviving spouse, and avoid the costs of court-administered probate. After the new Tax Act of 2001, these advantages of a trust are the best reason to continue to use trusts in estate planning. However, if your state is in the taxable range, then certainly trusts are also an effective way of lowering estate taxes by having each spouse utilize his or her $600,000 federal exemption to its maximum. The various types of trusts are too complex to detail here; you should see your accountant and a good estate planning lawyer.

### Probate of Estates

If you die without a will, or your will does not include a trust, your estate is subject to the procedures of the state probate court, and a personal representative will be appointed to administer its assets under the supervision of the court. Legal documents disclosing your assets will be filed at the courthouse as public records. Filing fees, administration expenses, attorney fees, and accountant's fees are included in this procedure. The probate is ultimately resolved by the distribution of assets to the heirs pursuant to the court's order; this can take anywhere from six months to several years, and is a process you will definitely want to avoid in your estate planning!

## Succession Planning

To begin the process of passing your business on to one or more of your children, you should allow them to assume gradually increasing responsibilities in running the business. Before taking this step, ask yourself these questions: Are your family members capable of running the business after you die or retire? Can they work together, and do they want

*Gifts are an effective estate planning tool*

to? It's surprising how few parents ask themselves and their children these questions! Sometimes it's a bad idea to leave the family business to siblings who could not get along as children; it may be better to leave the business to one child, and buy life insurance on yourself for the other to equalize their inheritance. A family meeting, along with your lawyer and accountant, is a very good idea before you develop a final succession plan. See Chapter 10 *Family-Owned Businesses* for other ideas on this subject.

### Gifts

The new Tax Act did not repeal the gift tax. However, it did raise the exemption to $1 million. So, you can make a gift of your business, or a portion of it, while you are alive and if the gift is valued at less than $1 million, there will be no gift tax due. You are also permitted to make a gift of up to $10,000 a year in cash or other assets to anyone. Your spouse is able to make the same gift, even though he or she may not actually own the asset given. Therefore, one very common method of succession and tax planning before the new tax act was to make gifts of up to $20,000 interest per year in your business (if you are married) to each of the family members who will carry on the business. If you start early enough, and live long enough, you can reduce your estate to the nontaxable level simply through the use of gifts. By making gifts of portions of a business that is appreciating, you can also reduce the growth of your estate. If your business is worth more than $1 million, this tax strategy may still be viable. Remember that your estate is also entitled to take the federal state tax exclusion at your death. In the future, "gifts" of part ownership in your business may be used more for succession planning than for estate tax planning.

One disadvantage of such gifts is that the income tax basis of property you give is your cost of the asset, minus the depreciation you took on tax returns. Often, the tax basis in a closely held business is quite low because it grew on sweat equity over time, and the owners took as much depreciation as possible. Conversely, the income tax basis for

*You must know to make a gift and retain control*

## NxLEVEL™ TECH TIP

There are many documents related to business succession and estate planning. A good source for these documents can be found at **http://www.legaldocs.com**, which allows you to prepare customized legal documents online. Choose any of the documents offered, complete the questions, click the "Submit" button, and the finished document is ready for you to download or print. Many documents are free; others are available for a fee ranging from $3.50 to $27.75. As with the legal software discussed earlier, remember that online documents are supposed to save time and avoid the preparation fees your lawyer would charge, not to replace your lawyer! All legal documents prepared through online or downloaded services must be reviewed by your lawyer.

property inherited after death is stepped up to the value of that asset at the date of death up to a maximum of 1.3 million dollars, under the new tax act. The second disadvantage of using gifts is that every gift of an interest in your business, reduces your percentage of control. (However, this can result in a positive tax effect known as a minority discount, which we will discuss later.) If you operate as a sole proprietorship, you cannot give away portions of your business during your lifetime unless you restructure your business.

You must relinquish control of the business interest given in order for it to qualify as a gift. If you retain the right to vote the shares of stock, or the interests in the LLC, the IRS will take the position that the gift was never made. Unlike an S-corporation, a C-corporation may have more than one class of stock with different voting rights. In some instances, a trust or other corporation can be made a shareholder under a different class of stock, and you may be able to retain control of the corporation even after giving away substantial amounts of stock.

A new technique in estate and succession planning is the **family limited partnership**. This is a standard limited partnership, but it is composed only of family members. After setting up a family limited partnership, you start a planned giving program of limited partner shares. You retain general partner interest so you have the ability to control the business.

You may not want an underaged child to control a substantial portion of your business or property if you die unexpectedly. Therefore, gifts to minors are usually made by way of a trust or the family limited partnership. Again, gifts in trust require special planning to qualify for the gift exclusion.

## Sale During Your Lifetime

Sale of your business is fully discussed elsewhere in this book, but it's worth mentioning here since it's another way of reducing your estate for tax purposes, transferring the business to your children during your lifetime, and providing lifetime income for you and your spouse. One consideration is that you must have confidence that your family members can run the business and make payments, or you risk losing control over your major income-producing asset. By using the installment sale method, you should be able to defer a portion of the tax on the gain through the term of the sale contract. You can often structure the transaction so that you retain a lien on the business assets, but provide family members with the flexibility to make payments from business profits. The main disadvantage to this method of succession planning is that family members do not receive a step-up in tax basis equal to the value of the business at the owner's death.

We previously discussed the use of **buy/sell agreements** in closely held businesses. They can have an estate planning benefit by ensuring that the business remains in the family's control, and by establishing the value of the business for estate tax purposes. There are also a number of hybrid agreements, which you should discuss more thoroughly with your lawyer. One is a **stock redemption agreement** that requires or allows the corporation to buy the interests of the deceased shareholder, thus permitting the use of

Minority discounts can

reduce estate taxes

corporate money to fund the purchase agreement. Another is a **cross-purchase agreement** requiring or allowing the other shareholders to buy the right of the deceased shareholder. The use of insurance to fund these agreements is often recommended.

### Options
**Stock options** are another method of freezing the value of the business in order to remove future appreciation from your estate. You may grant an option to your family to buy shares of the business at a set price, but you should be aware that under specific provisions of the Internal Revenue Code, this option agreement will be disregarded in valuing the property for estate tax unless it meets certain requirements that ensure it is a legitimate business transaction.

### Minority Discounts
Closely held businesses always present difficulty in valuation, because shares in such businesses—unlike shares of a corporation sold on a public exchange such as the New York Stock Exchange—have no established market value. Traditional appraisals have difficulty in valuing the **going concern and goodwill value** of a closely held business when that goodwill rests primarily with the former owner. Therefore, one of the most effective estate and succession planning techniques is the **minority discount**. If you reduce your interest in your company to a minority position prior to your death, you may be able to take advantage of the minority discount. The idea is that a minority owner's lack of control reduces his or her true value below the book value of that interest. For example, if your estate owned only 30% of a closely held corporation and the book value of the shares was $10 a piece, your 10,000 shares would in fact be worth less than $100,000, because a buyer would not pay that price to buy into a minority position. There is no set percentage for minority discounts, so you must work closely with your accountant and estate planning lawyer.

A company retirement plan may be better than an IRA

## Exit Strategies—Children
Let's assume that your parents established a business, and even though you took it to its present level of success, they are unwilling to hand over the reins. Most often, they just want something useful to do with their lives, so it's necessary to create an environment where they can take an "active" retirement. You need to convince them that they'll be ensured future income under a buy-out or salary continuation plan, that you are capable of handling the business, and that their other children will be provided for in their estate plan. Talk to your business lawyer and accountant about these ideas, since they will have an understanding of both the current management and the history of the business. Purchase agreements, coupled with parental consulting contracts, can often solve these problems. Of course, any successful strategy requires your parents' active involvement.

## Death/Disability Among Shareholders
Sudden death or disability of an owner of a closely held business can have devastating consequences. As discussed earlier, you should always prepare for the death or disability of one of the owners by devising a means of acquiring that person's interest. The use of

**life and disability insurance** is highly recommended. Certain disability policies cover business overhead when an owner is temporarily disabled, and convert to permanent disability policies in the event that the owner cannot return to work. If you plan for these emergencies before they occur, you will increase the chance of your business's survival.

# Retirement Plans

Many of us do not entirely trust the Social Security system to provide for us after retirement. Some of us have been saving for retirement under **Individual Retirement Accounts (IRAs),** and similar personal savings plans. Under the new Tax Act, allowable contributions to an IRA will triple between the years 2001 and 2008. Taxpayers over 50 years of age may also be able to make "catch-up" contributions to IRA's, 401(k), and SEP plans. However, many closely held businesses are capable of funding retirement plans with even greater benefits than the plans mentioned above. Your bang for the buck greatly increases if the contribution is through a qualified plan, and is made by the business rather than by you personally. The payment will be deductible by the business and will consequently be paid by the business with pre-tax dollars. The income the plan earns is not taxed until you begin to withdraw the funds; presumably, you will be in a lower tax bracket when you retire. There are a number of different qualified retirement plans available, depending upon the size and nature of your business. These are regulated under the federal Employee Retirement Income Security Act (ERISA). Generally, ERISA requires that the plans have formulas for allocating contribution and distribution to the parties. They may not discriminate in favor of highly compensated persons, i.e., the owners or highly paid employees (usually over $500,000 per year). There are disclosure requirements to the participants, and of course, there are reporting forms to the IRS. You may be able to roll over the amounts from one qualified plan or your IRA. The new tax act, effective in 2002 makes rollover much easier. Another very valuable feature of the new act is that a tax credit is given to lower income persons for pension plan contributions and qualifying IRS of up to $2000 per year. So, you can make a retirement investment with money you would otherwise be paying in taxes.

Even if you don't completely trust Social Security, this doesn't mean you should ignore it. You may lose benefits if you have excess earnings after starting Social Security, so you'll want to arrange your pension plan benefits and any income from your business to take advantage of the best opportunities. For example, stock dividends are not defined as earnings, and salary can be shifted to family members who provide services to the business. Also, many pension plans allow you to defer benefits until a later age.

### Simplified Employee Pension Plan (SEP)

The SEP is designed for the small business owner with a limited number of employees. It uses an IRA for each employee to receive and invest the funds. The contributions are based on a maximum of 15% compensation. Contributions may not exceed $10,000 per year, and this amount increases to $15,000 by 2006 under the new tax act. Employees typically end up with a bigger share of the annual contributions under a SEP, as compared to a profit-sharing or pension plan. The major benefit of a SEP is its

simplicity; IRS filings are not required, and no plan documents need be prepared and maintained (other than a one-page 5305-SEP form). The drawback is the amount of the employer's contribution.

## 401(k)

Your business may set up a plan whereby the employees make additional contributions—which may be matched by the employer—to the retirement plan trust. There are limitations on the amount of contributions that can be made by the owners or highly paid employees. However, 401(k) plans do have the distinct advantage of being paid with income before it is taxed.

## Pension and Profit-Sharing Plans

A number of qualified pension and profit-sharing plans are available to the closely held corporation. These include profit-sharing plans to which discretionary contributions are made from profits; defined benefit plans with a benefit formula based on each employee's years of service and final pay; and money purchase pension plans that fix a percentage of the employee's compensation as the employer contribution. These plans offer much greater benefits than a SEP or a 401(k) plan, but picking the right plan can be complicated. Discuss your alternatives with your accountant and a pension plan lawyer.

## Transfer of Stock/ESOPs

Transfers of stock to family or other employees provide an opportunity for the recipients' retirement planning, and for succession planning by the owner. They can be given as additional compensation and/or as a percentage of company ownership. Stock bonuses often create an incentive for long-term employment. Before you utilize this technique, however, you may want to have a stock sale restriction in your buy/sell agreement that either requires the corporation to repurchase the stock, or gives the other shareholders a first right of refusal to buy the stock. Thus, you will not have outsiders owning a piece of your business. One other caution regarding stock bonuses: Although they are a low-cost method of providing additional interest in the business to family employees, they have a negative consequence for your children, who will have taxable income equal to the fair market value of the bonus share, without generating any current cash with which to pay the tax.

**Employee Stock Ownership Plans (ESOPs)** may provide you with an opportunity to sell stock to the plan—thereby raising cash to provide for your support during your life—and to transfer a portion of your business to employees. One advantage of an ESOP is that it allows you to transfer stock of your company to the plan without any income tax if you reinvest the funds in qualified replacement property, which includes publicly traded stocks and bonds. Another advantage of an ESOP is that the purchase of the stock by the company through the ESOP is tax-deductible.

## Conclusion

When your business becomes successful, it becomes a major portion of your estate and it is time for you to take some of the actions suggested in this chapter. Due to recent changes in federal tax laws you should meet with your accountant and lawyer to formulate plans for estate taxes, income for you during retirement, and transfer of your business to your children or third parties. It is essential to involve your family in this planning.

## Chapter 22
## MANAGEMENT OVERVIEW

*About This Chapter:*
- *What is management?*
- *Other management issues*
- *Map out your business*
- *Get advice*
- *Don't forget to have fun!*

## Introduction

Just because you have sales, orders, expenses, and employees doesn't mean you are managing a business. Your goal as a manager is to set strategies that will make your employees productive and the business profitable. First, you must understand the environment in which you operate and identify your business goals. Second, you must create the structures and policies necessary to achieve these goals.

This chapter offers a broad introduction to the mindset of an effective manager. It is a realistic guide to the tasks that lie ahead. Whether yours is a small or large, local or national, service or manufacturing business, management fundamentals remain the same.

Remember, you're not a superhero! You needn't perform all management tasks yourself. In fact, your challenge is to manage your time by limiting yourself to those duties that only you can do effectively—such as assigning duties, setting goals, and assessing performance—and delegating responsibility for the rest. The key to being a successful entrepreneur is the ability to identify quality performers, and let them do their jobs.

---

*Smashed Bagels Come to Hoboken*

*Angela Minghella loved baking, and she really loved bagels...big, chewy bagels like her grandmother used to make every Saturday morning. She always knew that someday she would open her own bakery. In 1999, she made that dream a reality when she opened The Bagel Smash in her hometown of Hoboken, New Jersey.*

*The Bagel Smash offered 12 flavors of bagels that could be toasted and smeared with a variety of toppings. But the store's real specialty was "Bagel Smashes"—bagels topped with a choice of butter, peanut butter, fruit preserves, bananas, ham, eggs, or cheese (or any combination thereof), then put into a special hot plate, toasted until brown, and smashed to perfection. They were a big hit!*

*Angela opened The Bagel Smash with the help of Eloise Stein, the previous renter of the bakery space The Bagel Smash now leases. Their partnership was completely unexpected; they had met and hit it off as Eloise was preparing to close her business, and Angela was being interviewed to lease the space for her new business.*

*Eloise's small gourmet pastry shop was closing in part because the business was simply wrong for the location. She had operated her shop for two years, selling baked goods for special events. Few of the local professionals bought from her shop during the week as they waited for the bus in front of her shop, or made their way to the subway station one block away. Still, Eloise loved baking and when she and Angela hit it off, she found a way to stay in the business.*

---

## What is Management?

### Management Planning is Contingency Planning

Good management helps businesses grow and meet challenges. Regardless of the obstacles you encounter, your business will thrive if you build a management structure that fits your needs and contains the potential for learning and innovation.

As you grow, neither well-timed ideas nor innovative products and services are enough to sustain success. Don't wait until you have a crisis; make a deliberate effort now to create structures that support consistent performance.

Intelligently created structures allow your business to be uniquely responsive to its customers. As the manager of your new business, you should assume that your product or service will find uses in markets neither you nor your competitors had anticipated.

IBM originally marketed machines capable of complex mathematical calculations to scientific users. Blue jeans were created to be durable work clothing for ranchers and miners. These are examples of businesses that started in one market and migrated to another. They succeeded because they changed their business strategies and upgraded their management structures as circumstances demanded.

Remember that a good manager is very different from a boss. Managers build teams of people to meet business objectives; they give team members the responsibility and authority to perform, they measure and reward performance, and they create the structures and policies that support business objectives.

### Structure and Processes

**Structure** refers to the manner in which responsibility for various tasks is divided among the people in a business. **Processes** refers to the manner in which people within a business work together to get the job done.

Your task is to create durable structures and efficient processes, not to stifle creativity and fun. Contrary to some people's fears, structures allow businesses to succeed on more than the energy and drive of the entrepreneur.

Managers should know enough about all business tasks to direct and measure performance

*A Smashing Partnership*

*In the spring of 1994, Eloise and Angela started their new business. Their biggest challenge was earning the loyalty of the hundreds of commuters who passed within 100 yards of the shop twice a day, on the way into and out of Manhattan. The Bagel Smash had stiff competition from the Starbucks coffee down the street and a large bagel chain two blocks away. To succeed, it would have to be managed impeccably; they knew they wouldn't get a second chance to win their customers' loyalty.*

*Eloise and Angela evaluated the situation, then set the following managerial objectives:*
- *Absolutely clean and sanitary conditions*
- *Speedy, efficient, friendly customer service*
- *The best, freshest, most authentic bagels available*
- *The most delicious and creative toppings for bagel smashes*
- *Well-trained, motivated, happy counter staff*

## Creating the Right Management Style

Reflect on the feeling you want your business and office to have. What type of environment do you thrive in? What kind of people do you most enjoy working with? What sort of behavior do you want to encourage and reward?

Next, review your business goals as set forth in your **mission statement**. Discuss these with your friends, family, and advisors.

Good managers work to maximize their business's strengths. Today, corporate managers call these strengths **core competencies**. This is just a trendy way of describing the things your business does better than any competitor—the things your customers value the most. Your goal is to leverage these strengths for maximum competitive advantage.

Lastly, business management must fit the industry and the markets in which it operates. Get to know your customers and competitors, industry trends, and the strengths of competing products and services. These elements determine the design of your business's internal functions such as marketing, finance, accounting, and sales.

*Decide what you do best and delegate the rest*

*Neither Angela nor Eloise had a problem with working long hours; they knew it came with the territory, and looked forward to the challenge. But they wanted to build a business that would operate reliably even in their absence. Angela was the mother of a two-year-old, and Eloise still enjoyed preparing specialty cakes for custom orders. Neither wanted to run a business that caused undue stress!*

*Before hiring anyone, they decided to list the activities that needed to be performed at The Bagel Smash, and to describe how critical each one was to the business's success. This would help them decide where to put the most time, energy, and resources.*

| *Most Critical Activities* | *Critical Activities* | *Least Critical Activities* |
| --- | --- | --- |
| *1. Baking bagels* | *1. Managing supplies* | *1. General maintenance* |
| *2. Serving customers* | *2. Organizing the store* | *2. New product decisions* |
| *3. Training* | *3. Pricing and promotion* | *3. New locations* |
| *4. Managing cash* | *4. Coffee making* | *4. Community activities* |
| *5. Cleaning the store* | *5. Financial planning* | *5. New technology review* |
| *6. Employee management* | *6. Budgeting* | |
| *7. Payroll and accounting* | *7. Long-range planning* | |
| *8. Ordering supplies* | | |

*With this list in hand, Eloise and Angela began to form a picture of their successful business. Angela was responsible for all baking. She would bake from 4:00 A.M. until 8:00 A.M., then help to serve the morning rush of customers. She would bake all bagels for the first three to six months. Then, as business warranted, she would hire and train an experienced baker or two to help. She would also order and manage all supplies.*

*Eloise took responsibility for managing the store. She would ring up sales, price the bagels, prepare toasted bagels and smashes, train all non-baking employees, and maintain the store's impeccable organization and cleanliness. In short, she would create a welcoming and smooth-running environment where customers came first.*

Be prepared: your business will take on a life of its own!

---

## The First Step: Identify Activities

The first step in designing management structures is to identify the main activities of the business. Which steps must be done every day to ensure your survival and success? Which are less critical on a daily basis, but important for ongoing performance? Some of these activities may be specific to your business, and may not fit neatly into traditional functional categories. Listed below are the functions that most businesses must perform every day. Many of these topics are discussed in greater detail in other chapters of this book. For now, use this list as a starting point for your own brainstorming.

- Accounting
- Inventory
- Human resources
- Marketing & sales
- Logistics management
- Quality control

- Financial planning & budgeting
- Research & development
- Manufacturing
- Engineering
- Customer service
- Purchasing

Try the following exercise as you define these functions to fit your business.

## Identifying, Simplifying, and Allocating Tasks

| Task | Explanation |
|------|-------------|
| Identify | Look at your past and future performance. Review the different ways you get various tasks completed. Define a "good" or "successful" process. Pool insights of your team. |
| Set the boundaries of these tasks | Identify context in which you perform individual tasks. Separate one task from another. These are discrete service jobs that your business performs. |
| Identify ways to simplify your tasks | Pare down individual tasks to the most basic elements. How can you make them more efficient? This focus allows you to avoid redundancies. |
| Allocate the necessary resources | Identify what your business requires to perform the highest quality work. This is the starting point for creating a system of budgetary forecasts and controls. |

Now is a good time to consider the different types of tasks businesses perform. **Operational processes** directly create value for your customers, employees, owners, and stockholders. **Strategic planning** and **controlling processes** create the context and resources for operational processes. They provide short- and medium-term guidance of operations. Some of these processes include developing performance measures, setting policies for rewards and recognition, and allocating resources. Lastly, **navigational processes** create the purpose and character of a business; they guide decisions, personnel interaction, and overall organizational objectives.

### Step Two: Allocate Tasks

The next step is to allocate responsibility for various tasks. Begin by asking yourself which tasks you do particularly well, and which you're less comfortable with. Based on this, identify the activities you will perform and those you will delegate.

If you have a team assembled, which individuals are most suited to which tasks? You or your employees are, or will be, performing several tasks at once; do these tasks fit together logically? Would it be more efficient to separate tasks and reassign them?

When we use the word "team" we are not necessarily referring to a group of full-time employees hired by your business. It can be a **virtual team** composed of you and a collection of part-time or outside service providers. Virtual teams work together via phone, fax, and computer modem; they allow you to benefit from the skills of many different people without having them inside your business.

*You are in the midst of creating the kind of business that people will want to work for, buy from, and partner with*

*Outsourcing at the Bagel Smash*

*Once Eloise and Angela had sorted out the most critical duties, they took a look at less critical issues. Who would manage payroll? Clean up? Design the menu? The partners decided that they simply didn't have enough time or energy to do all of the duties themselves. They would have to allocate some tasks to full or part-time employees, or even to outside contractors. The financial management of the business concerned them. Neither knew very much about accounting, so they decided to use the accountant who'd helped Eloise manage her business. Art Donner was an accountant and financial manager, who worked part-time with many small business clients. They met with him and worked out a contract whereby he would keep all of their books, manage payroll, and pay bills. He would meet with Eloise and Angela every two weeks to review the business's financial health. If they needed additional financing for equipment or an upgrade of their store, he could help them with that, too.*

*The remaining duties—cleaning and organizing the store, making coffee, and ringing up sales during peak business hours—would be handled by three or four part-time counter employees whom Eloise would hire and train.*

### Step Three: Set Expectations
The next step in creating management systems is to set objectives for employees. What does the business expect of each person? Who will be held accountable for specific tasks? What is the deadline for task completion and assessment?

Building a great organizational structure takes time. It also takes a real commitment to thinking critically and creatively about your business. Give your team plenty of time to learn how to work together and share ideas. Most importantly, try to identify what each person needs to do to help others perform well.

## Other Management Issues

### Good Communication
One of the biggest obstacles for businesses is poor communication. Imagine an army in which privates set their own marching orders without ever hearing from the general. Obviously, things would not run well! For businesses, failure to communicate effectively can lead to marketers selling at the wrong price, financial planners creating wrong budgets, and operations producing the wrong products. Failure to communicate can also cause:

- Lack of cooperation
- Poor coordination between different functions
- Inefficient use of time and resources
- Missed opportunities for creative problem-solving

- Diminished morale
- Resistance to change
- Lack of discipline
- Failure to meet long-term goals

How can you ensure effective communication? Begin by establishing formal practices, such as daily or weekly staff meetings, in which employees can be updated on goals and performance, raise questions, and get feedback. Here are a few additional suggestions:

- Regularly compile and circulate a one-page operating report of problems and proposed solutions
- Schedule a "war room" meeting for all team members
- Schedule regular company sessions to address problems and opportunities
- Pursue suggestions for process, product, and structural improvements
- Manage by walking around; don't stay in your office
- Don't be afraid to open your books to employees

*Job Descriptions at The Bagel Smash*

*Together, Angela and Eloise described what their employees would have to do, how they would be evaluated, and how each job would fit within the business. They focused on the counter employees, who would represent the store for customers:*

*"Counter employees should think of working at The Bagel Smash as an opportunity to become friends with all the people who come in. Our customers are our neighbors, and you will be responsible for treating them as you would a very special guest in your home. When they come in, smile and greet them. While they're here, make them comfortable and provide them with whatever they want. When they leave, thank them for coming, and invite them to come back soon.*

*"Most customers are in a rush, particularly in the morning, so speed is of the essence. Counter employees must know how to operate and troubleshoot all equipment, including the cash register. The customer must be able to walk in, order, pay, and leave with a bagel in less than five minutes."*

*Angela saved the less enjoyable duties for last:*

*"At the end of each shift, employees will sweep the store (mopping only for closing shifts); thoroughly clean counters; wipe down smashing machine, cash register, all table tops, display counter, and coffee area; clean the bathroom; restock supplies; and list any inventory that needs to be reordered."*

# Map Out Your Business

Businesses often create an **organizational chart** to represent how different business functions fit together. Think of this as a strategic map or a visual record of the relationships among people.

The most common structure for businesses is **functional**. Functional organization allows businesses to group people who share responsibilities and skills. In its simplest form, the functional organization chart begins with the president or CEO and moves down to include sales and marketing, finance, and operations.

3 key processes:

• operations

• planning

• controlling

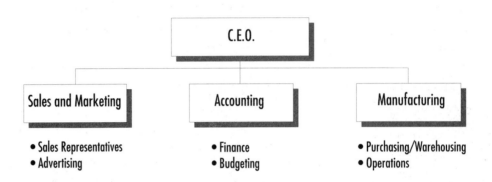

An example of a business structured along functional lines would be a metal foundry that supplies small parts to tractor manufacturers. It has a finance department to manage financial resources; an accounting department to allocate costs; a marketing and sales department responsible for pricing, promotional, and distribution strategies; and a manufacturing department that produces the goods. Each functional area works together to achieve the organizational goal of manufacturing and marketing tractor parts.

Functional organization is best for hiring, training, and managing people within the context of their individual functions. The downsides to functional structure include diminished attention to customer service, less employee flexibility, and a tendency to focus on narrow tasks rather than business goals.

## Testing Structural Integrity

Develop the habit of looking back on structures you've created and decisions you've made in the past. Using the following criteria, test the appropriateness of each of your business practices:

- Does it provide a means for getting into business more quickly?
- Does it lower the risk of market entry?
- Does it enhance flexibility?
- Does it build on your personal strengths?
- Does it maximize your business's resources?
- Does it allow you to evolve, and to redirect resources easily?
- Does it make your business attractive to investors and lenders?

The dedication, vision, and ethics of a manager determine whether a business is managed or mismanaged

- Is it appropriate for your kind of industry?
- Is it consistent with the kind of life you want to lead?
- Will it result in the kind of company you'd be proud to call your own?

## Get Advice

One of the most important things you can do for your business is to seek outside advice. Ask a mentor, a colleague, or a professor to evaluate the way you plan to structure your business. Or, if you can afford it, try a paid consultant. Today, there are more voices of experience for entrepreneurs to consult than ever before. You should also seek out advice from friends or business acquaintances who work in larger businesses. You can learn from their successes and mistakes, improve upon their ideas, and tailor their advice to fit your business.

### NxLEVEL™ TECH TIP

Ever wonder how other managers deal with the stress and responsibility of running their businesses? A good place to find answers to this question—and countless others—is the *Institute of Management and Administration's Business Management Supersite* (http://www.ioma.com/). This enormous site (nearly 1,000 pages) publishes a broad range of information for business professionals. According to IOMA, "The role of the site is to provide our subscribers, and the general business community, a place to learn, communicate, and explore the breadth of information provided in the form of sample articles from 40 business management newsletters. We want to foster a sense of community, a place where the busy business professional can seek out answers to questions by posting them to the bulletin boards, or asking our editors."

*The Bagel Smash's Management Processes*

*Angela and Eloise did not want The Bagel Smash to become a huge operation. They conceived of it as a neighborhood spot, where regulars could drop in, get a smash and a coffee, hang out if they had time, or be on their way if they didn't.*

*The owners imagined that they would have a team of 10 to 12 employees, including bakers and counter people. To keep the tight, family feel of the business they decided that every month all employees would meet for an afternoon tea at the store. This would be an opportunity to voice concerns, ask questions, suggest improvements, and chat.*

*The Bagel Smash would have no formal hierarchy or management structure. People would fulfill their specific job responsibilities and if they wanted to help out in other areas, they could. Eloise and Angela were quite happy to evaluate their employees' talents and interests, and match the job to fit them. They wanted happy, satisfied team members, who would be guided by the shared purpose of making their customers equally happy and satisfied.*

### How Will Your Business Look?

Don't underestimate the importance of the physical layout of your work space. Remember that summer job you had at the office with no windows? Or the flickering track lighting that made your head pound and sapped your energy? Or the messy warehouse where you couldn't find anything?

Take some time to consider the way your working space will look. Your work area should be inspiring, comfortable, and ideal for teamwork. The space you create can help make you and your employees happy, productive, and successful! Many extraordinarily successful businesses allow employees to stamp their own personalities on their work spaces. Possibilities include bringing pets to work (one software company even has dog food stations), creating larger kitchens for lunch time cook-ins, selecting music to work by, and rearranging the work space to fit employee preferences.

## Don't Forget to Have Fun!

One of the most valuable things you can do is ensure that you and your employees have fun and work creatively. The more people enjoy their work, the better they perform. The more creative businesses are, the more innovative they can be in solving problems and outperforming competitors. The happier your employees are, the better they will serve customers. You must create an environment where people will want to spend their time!

Is the business you've created one for which you'd want to work? If there's any doubt, you need to question how you've structured your business. Here are several ideas for making your business more fun.

Management tip: encourage creativity and innovation

**10 Ways to Have Fun & Be Creative**
- Hire curious and creative people
- Take vacations
- Bring in guest speakers and pursue interesting educational programs
- Make your work space wacky and colorful
- Give a party for your best clients
- Take your employees on a picnic
- Rearrange your schedule and insert random activities
- Send your employees to a ballgame

*Making the Team a Reality at The Bagel Smash*

*To encourage team spirit, Eloise decided that employees who stayed for the first six months of operations would get a percentage of the profits. All employees would be trained for three days (seven days for bakers) and evaluated by the owners after their first two weeks. After that, performance would be evaluated every six months. Angela suggested that the employees should also be able to evaluate the owners' performance, and Eloise loved the idea! They decided that at their afternoon teas they would collect and discuss "Eloise and Angela Scorecards."*

*At these meetings, The Bagel Smash employees would also get a health report for the business. Angela wanted employees to know all about daily sales, major costs, sources of revenue, and profitability. She believed that employees with a big picture of the business would perform better and have greater pride in the business. This "open book" policy has worked well for them. Today, Angela and Eloise's planning has paid off. The business is thriving! Not only is it a favorite of locals, but it has begun drawing weekend customers from Manhattan, Newark, and beyond. Angela and Eloise are even contemplating a change from their original plans: opening a second store!*

## Conclusion

In designing your company, you are doing nothing less than creating a model work environment: a business that performs its tasks in a competitive way while protecting its spirit of independence and creativity. At the same time, it must fit your management style, your personality, and your environment. Defining tasks, processes, organizations, and structures that will help you manage your business is essential. You should manage by design, not by default!

# Chapter 23
# TEAM BUILDING AND LEADERSHIP

*About This Chapter:*
- *What is a team?*
- *Why do you want a team?*
- *Being a leader vs. being a boss*
- *Developing leadership skills*
- *Empowering your team*
- *Building your team*
- *Team challenges: manage, learn, & overcome*

## Introduction

Creating an organization in which teams can perform is the cornerstone for growing a successful company. This chapter introduces the basics of creating, managing, and benefiting from teams within your business.

## What is a Team?

A **team** is a group of people who work together to achieve shared objectives and rewards, each contributing individual strengths. This may seem like a simple concept, but given the internal and external challenges a small business faces, operating a team can become very complicated.

It has been said that a team is the fundamental building block of an organization. Families, groups of friends, and civic organizations demonstrate that individuals naturally form groups with different allegiances. Teams, however, do not form naturally; they must be initiated and maintained. Ideally, a team is defined by participatory leadership, shared responsibility, open communication, joint purpose, and focus on the future. A team that is performing at its highest level responds rapidly and creatively to challenges. Do you think your business is oriented towards groups or teams?

Teams can perform many functions within a business. The categories of teams presented below are in hierarchical order from the most detailed to the most basic:

- **Strategic Planning Teams** determine strategy, mission, and policy
- **Issue Managing Teams** are responsible for specific technology or work issues
- **Directing Teams** are ongoing, part-time teams that coordinate complex organizational tasks
- **Project Specific Teams** are temporary teams composed of individuals with mixed skills and backgrounds, and are formed to address a specific issue

Groups versus teams

- **Brain Trust Teams** are catalysts and supporters of decision-making and change
- **Task Teams** are responsible for the basic tasks of the business

Depending on your needs, you may choose to create several teams to perform specific functions, or simply organize your personnel into a single team with a broad range of responsibilities. Either way, your goal is the same: to create a cooperative, interdependent unit, committed to open communication, creative thinking, and a single vision.

---

*The Business That Sells Fun*

*Red Speed, Inc. is a southern California start-up dedicated to fun. Started by Nate Miguel and his cousin Jamie, Red Speed rents out ATVs (All Terrain Vehicles), Harley Davidson motorcycles, Jet Skis, and Sea-Doos. They rent to weekend fun seekers who want to explore the desert, mountains, or beach on their own terms.*

*Most of Red Speed's customers are tourists visiting from Europe. Red Speed delivers rental vehicles to customers' hotels, complete with trailers, helmets, and other accessories. They will even deliver rental trucks to pull the trailers! Red Speed was conceived as a full-service business providing no-worry, no-hassle weekend escapes for true outdoors adventurers.*

*Aside from Nate and Jamie, Red Speed has nine other employees: two telephone order/sales people, six mechanics, and the office manager. Once reservations are taken and processed, most of the business's time is spent maintaining and upgrading equipment. Red Speed is dedicated to staying ahead of the latest adventure sports trends and making its rental equipment the easiest to use, most reliable, and highest quality available.*

*Today Red Speed has earnings of over $7 million a year, and one of the largest fleets of rental Jet Skis and Harley Davidsons in the country. Its rentals have an impressive 90% utilization rate; they are out of commission for repairs only one out of ten days. The business doesn't have to do much advertising, since it generates as much business as it can accommodate from word-of-mouth referrals and repeat customers. In the busiest months, Red Speed has a waiting list for every type of equipment it rents. Red Speed's customers are loyal, the equipment is reliable and impeccable, and the business profitable and growing.*

*How do they do it?*

---

## Why Do You Want a Team?

At times it must seem like an impossible task: being customer-focused, market-driven, forward-thinking, and detail-oriented. You might ask yourself, "On top of all that, why do I need to create a team-based organization? Isn't that for the McDonalds and Motorolas of the world to do?" Or perhaps you subscribe to the Groucho Marx school of thought: "I wouldn't want to join any club that would have me as a member!"

Large corporations are forming teams in order to infuse their organizations with the excitement and sense of empowerment that entrepreneurial ventures enjoy. Businesses of all types have realized that creating teams rejuvenates employees, making them more creative and responsive to customers.

Teams reduce communications logjams

A strong team demands performance, and encourages people to give their best. **Multidisciplinary** teams increase the range of problems your organization can solve. By leveraging a variety of skills and personalities, teams allow a few people to do the tasks of many; this can reduce management costs and communication logjams. Because they require clear goals, teams can aid in promoting your business vision.

Your employees also benefit from being part of a team. Team members enjoy a greater sense of identity, recognition, and fulfillment in their tasks. When expectations and rewards are clearly defined, people feel a greater sense of control.

### Evolving Away from the Lone Ranger Model

Creating a team requires moving away from the "Lone Ranger" mentality. Whether you have two people or 200 in your business, you must shift your focus from your individual capabilities as an entrepreneur to those of your entire staff. Your suppliers, customers, partners, and employees don't judge your business on the basis of what you are capable of as an individual, but by what it can accomplish as an organization.

Many start-ups fail because the entrepreneur tries to do everything single-handedly. The transition from being a one-person show to sharing responsibilities is difficult, but you can't grow if you can't change, and changing requires that you look at your business in a new way.

## Being a Leader vs. Being a Boss

A boss instructs and disciplines people, sets goals and expectations, and limits the ways in which people can achieve their tasks. Under this traditional model of management, the major source of motivation is avoiding penalties or earning the boss's favor; in the absence of the boss, motivation suffers, performance falls, and focus is lost.

In contrast, a leader generates an emotional connection with people, attracting and inspiring them towards a common cause. The traits of a true leader are trust, excellent interpersonal skills, inspiration, motivation, and direction. A successful leader has learned the art of managing through influence, and understands that people prefer to do things for their own reasons. When employees are given the opportunity to identify their own goals, and the freedom to select the best way to achieve them, their performance improves dramatically.

Do you have the necessary skills to lead? Perhaps you're good at one-on-one communication, but how are you at one-to-group communication? Some people are born with the skills needed to be outstanding leaders. The rest of us must learn these skills.

Take a moment to reflect on what you know about leadership. Ask yourself these questions:

- What are your reasons for wanting to be a leader?
- When in a leadership role, how did you perform? How did you feel?
- What was the outcome?
- What are your greatest misgivings about being a leader?
- What do you think are the most important attributes of a leader?
- Who are the leaders you've most admired or responded to, and why?
- Which leadership traits and skills do you think you have? Which do you lack?

Having reflected on your ability to lead, consider the skills necessary to empower teams. A team leader should be:

- Coherent, forward-thinking, and consistent
- Able to commit team members to their efforts
- Able to understand team roles, functions, and expectations
- Skilled at leading efficient, focused meetings
- Able to sustain a positive climate
- Able to diagnose weakness in the team and correct it

A leader inspires:

- trust
- motivation
- direction

---

*How Red Speed Works: Good Leadership*

*Nate and Jamie Miguel have built Red Speed's success on good leadership and teamwork. Though each member of the team has specific responsibilities and criteria for performance review, all have the same goal in mind: maximizing customer satisfaction. This means staying on top of ordering parts, upgrading equipment, and anticipating problems.*

*Nate spent six years in the Navy, as part of a jet fighter maintenance crew aboard the aircraft carrier U.S.S. Enterprise. There he learned that the keys to having a team that "thinks with one mind and works with one body" are division of duties, continuous and clear communication, common goals, and shared rewards. With the help of his cousin Jamie, he made these things pay off at Red Speed.*

---

## Developing Leadership Skills

Start by focusing on who you are. Be true to your vision and to yourself, and be consistent in your campaign to achieve your goals. Pay attention to the way you interact with people, and work to improve your "self-leadership" and self-confidence. Before you know it, you will be more comfortable with positions that require you to set and achieve goals, and to lead other people.

## Leaders Persuade

As a leader, you must provide your people with the focus and inspiration that will persuade them to share a goal and participate in deciding how to reach it. By providing structure, and a forum for people to contribute ideas, you can facilitate a process by which the team allocates its own tasks, arrives at a plan, and sets a reasonable deadline for completion.

## Leaders Have Charm and Wit

The best leaders—those who inspire loyalty, trust, and a desire to work hard—are always friendly and likable. Who wouldn't want to work for a charming and engaging person with a great sense of humor? By demonstrating that you don't take yourself too seriously and are able to keep a healthy perspective, you will inspire others to do the same.

## Leadership Hints

- Know what you stand for, and what you're willing to take a stand against
- Be nice
- Have a sense of purpose, and the courage to make tough decisions
- Ask for help, and accept it when it is given
- Make other people look good
- Create other leaders

## NxLEVEL™ TECH TIP

As team leader, your biggest challenges are coordinating your team's efforts and making sure that all team members have access to the information they need. Here are a number of software applications to make your job easier:

- **Teamsoft's TeamAgenda.** This cross-platform application can help you to coordinate projects and optimize time management. For a free demo, go to http://www.teamsoft.com:8888/downform.html.

- **Alexsys Team 98.** With this multi-user database, you can track work assignments for all team members and analyze the team's productivity. You can download a demo at PC World's FileWorld (http://www.pcworld.com/fileworld/file_description/0,1458,4534,00.html).

- **Microsoft Team Manager 97.** This program helps team members stay in sync by coordinating and tracking team activities. It automatically consolidates tasks, progress, and status reports entered by team members; and helps coordinate individual activities with the overall team plan. It also tracks and reports details, so the manager can focus on the big picture. More information about this program is available from Microsoft (http://shop.microsoft.com/store/products/).

- Be consistent
- Use other people's ideas, and give them the credit
- Be truthful and honest
- Practice what you preach
- Listen to what people say, as well as what they don't say

## Empowering Your Team

**Empowerment** is a term that has been used so widely by management consultants that it has become a management philosophy. This simple concept guides everything from stuffing sausages in Wisconsin to the development of supercomputers in Silicon Valley. But what does it mean exactly?

Empowerment means giving employees the authority to manage themselves. In many cases, this requires stripping away layers of management so that functions traditionally performed by managers—such as setting goals, assessing performance, and restructuring work processes—can be performed by line employees. Some organizations empower teams to hire and fire members, and to evaluate and contract with outside suppliers.

Regardless of your industry or the size of your business, an empowered team must set its own goals and be given the responsibility of selecting the best way to achieve those goals. Leadership of an empowered team comes from within, and decision-making is by consensus.

How can you implement this process in your business? The starting point for creating an empowered team is establishing a shared **vision**. A vision is more than a business goal—it provides a context for all decision-making, and is a yardstick to measure progress; it gives your employees a focus for collaboration, and a motivation for excellence.

Your second task is to create a climate of shared responsibility within your team. This means that in order to reap the rewards, every member of the team must perform; if any member does not, it is the responsibility of the entire group to assess the difficulty and remedy it.

## Building Your Team

The best way to create an empowered team is to break the process into these easy steps:

### Identify Needs
Businesses use teams to do everything from selecting suppliers to creating new marketing strategies. Let your knowledge of your business and your creativity determine which area of your business would benefit most from the strength of a team.

### Identify Key People
First, identify the skills your team must possess in order to accomplish its goals. By mixing people with different backgrounds (e.g., a sales person and a financial planner), your team will be able to explore a wider range of solutions.

*Empowerment equals authority plus responsibility*

## Gather, Inform, and Listen

Having assembled your team, explain why you have chosen to create the team, and what you hope to accomplish. Encourage and listen to your people's feedback. At this early stage, your active participation as a leader is crucial.

## Set Your Sights!

At this point you must clarify the purpose of the team. Clearly set forth specific, measurable, and time-bound team objectives. Without these parameters, teams tend to lose focus.

*You must play to win, not to avoid losing*

## Establish a Forum

Open communication and constructive confrontation are the essential attributes of an effective team. Your team members must:

- Identify common ground and points of disagreement
- Encourage full expression of all viewpoints
- Regularly share both positive and negative feedback
- Monitor the resolution of issues and conflicts
- Listen, listen, and listen some more!
- Support and trust one another

---

*Training: The Beginning of Teamwork at Red Speed*

*For Red Speed, teamwork begins with hiring good people who have excellent skills. Nate and Jamie hire and train their employees carefully. Red Speed focuses the bulk of its energy on the employees who are most critical to the business's success: the mechanics. All Red Speed mechanics have at least three years of experience working on motorcycles. Nate tries to hire former Navy or Army mechanics, because they understand better than others the kind of operation he strives to run. Mechanics are trained by spending two weeks repairing each type of equipment Red Speed rents out. New mechanics work as buddies with experienced employees; by the end of their eight-week training period, they develop considerable expertise and a solid working relationship with their new team-mates.*

---

## Set Ground Rules and Procedures

You've assembled your team and identified your mission...now you've got to make your first team decision. How do you ensure the participation of all members?

The team should decide how it will make decisions on a day-to-day basis. This is dictated by the size of the team and the challenges it faces. Will its decision-making be formal or informal? If you are a member of the team, will you remain the leader? Will leadership become a collective function, or migrate to another member? What are the time constraints?

Here are some additional issues you should address:

- Who holds authority in which situations?
- Is relevant information collected quickly enough?
- Are authority and responsibility matched when tasks are assigned?
- Are decisions effectively communicated?
- Is the team coordinating its resources?
- Does the team learn from experience?

Keeping your team focused yet open to new ideas requires dedicated attention to group dynamics. Your team must learn to identify issues, explore problems, gather information, seek new perspectives and alternatives, and select the best possible course of action. This process, which should become second nature, is the critical cycle through which your team will perpetually move.

As you continue to build your team, remember that progress occurs incrementally. Taking small steps can make the team-building process smoother and a lot more fun!

---

*Responsibility and Authority at Red Speed*

*It is the responsibility of every mechanic at Red Speed to help the company meet its goal of 90% equipment utilization. This means that on average, a broken motorcycle, Jet Ski, or Sea-Doo must be repaired and out the door within 24 hours. Routine maintenance checks between rentals must average no more than 30 minutes.*

*How does Red Speed ensure quality with such a short turnaround time? By clearly allocating responsibility, giving team members authority to make decisions, and encouraging initiative. All the mechanics at Red Speed have the authority to order new parts, and to allocate their time as they see fit. They work in pairs, with every member of the team qualified to repair any type of equipment.*

*Rentals are generally returned in the late afternoon, and rented out again in the morning. Therefore, the busiest time of day is between 3 and 7 P.M. During this "Jam Time," new parts must be easily accessible, the floor organized and uncluttered, and the team working at its best. When Jam Time ends, it is the responsibility of each pair of mechanics to organize and clean their workspace. They also quickly complete an equipment status report and update the supplies list. This takes only a few minutes on any one of three computer terminals in the repair area.*

---

## Evolving and Adapting

Continual improvement is essential to teamwork. Teams can improve only by assessing how successful their actions have been. Ask the following questions as a guide in post-project team review:

- Did you use the procedures set up by the team? What were the biggest challenges and successes? Solicit feedback from all members.
- Are members pleased with the team's performance? What would they most like to change for the next time?
- Which team members communicate freely? How can you encourage those who don't?
- What is the quality of the team's output compared to others?

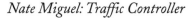

*Nate Miguel: Traffic Controller*

*The most important component of smooth operation at Red Speed is team coordination. This responsibility belongs to Nate. Every evening, after Jam Time, Nate reviews computer reports to determine what supplies are needed. Before the mechanics head home, Nate quickly debriefs them to uncover any problems they encountered or challenges they anticipate.*

*It is Nate's job to restock the repair area, estimate turnaround time for repairs, and allocate team responsibility for specific jobs based on rental demands. Several of the mechanics specialize in Harley Davidson repairs, so he makes sure that if bikes are being returned in the morning, those mechanics are ready to jump on the maintenance job.*

*Because most of its business comes from Europeans on vacation, Red Speed often has reservations six months in advance, and thus usually knows ahead of time what its equipment needs will be. Nate maps out the flow of equipment through the shop, and allocates extra time for the larger repair jobs that inevitably crop up.*

*Each day, the mechanics arrive knowing which pieces of equipment they must do quick maintenance on, and which larger repair jobs are pending. They plan their time with their work buddies accordingly, knowing that the supplies and support they need are waiting for them.*

Reward successful teams

## Reaping the Rewards and Having Fun!

Everyone who has ever played a team sport has experienced that brief moment of ecstasy when all team members do the right thing at the right time. This feeling that one is part of a collective mission is one of the most rewarding aspects of being part of a team. When your team has one of those euphoric moments, take time out to savor it! Do something to celebrate, like taking a team photo or having a team dinner.

Rewards propel and motivate your team, so remember to take notice of the special people who surround you! How do you reward your team for a job well done? Here are some suggestions:

- Peg performance to financial rewards
- Offer nonmonetary rewards such as time off or a better office
- Hand out props, trophies, or other small incentives
- Offer promotions and new responsibilities to effective team members

---

*Pie Time at Red Speed*

*During peak business months, Nate and Jamie meet with Red Speed's team of mechanics at the end of every week. During these 60-minute gatherings, the team reviews its performance for the past week. What was the average utilization rate for equipment? What special repair challenges came up? What team coordination or cooperation issues came up? This is the time for members to speak up, ask questions, and resolve conflict. Nate has found that it is during these informal meetings over coffee and pie (his mother makes a great strawberry rhubarb) that some of the shop's most successful improvements have come about. The best to date? The idea of installing an easy-to-use software system for managing inventory and tracking projects; that upgrade alone helped the business jump from 70% to 90% utilization!*

---

## Team Challenges: Manage, Learn, & Overcome

The biggest challenge in creating and maintaining a team is managing group dynamics. Personality conflicts, peer pressures, conflicting loyalties, and old habits can cause a team to work at cross purposes. Your daily task as team leader is to create an atmosphere in which people can freely express positive and negative views. In this way, they can vent frustrations and overcome negative feelings, which will allow them to focus their energy on the mission rather than on team dynamics.

Positive conflict can be a tremendous source of energy and spirited debate—use it to improve team performance. In the following contexts, constructive conflict can bring creativity and realism to a team:

- When there is flexible thinking among group members
- When dissenting thoughts are clearly and fully expressed
- When team members feel free to give their honest opinions
- When conflict resolution techniques are understood and used

Constructive conflict is a tremendous source of team energy

One of the most common problems encountered by teams is the tendency towards **groupthink**. A team afflicted by the groupthink mentality develops a distinct personality that limits its ability to investigate issues completely and to create a full range of robust alternatives. In the rush to make decisions and see progress, the minority view is often rejected in favor of a reactionary majority mindset.

Keeping clear lines of responsibility and accountability within the team is also a major challenge. However, this difficulty can be overcome by helping your team to return to the basics: talk, listen, encourage one another, and focus on the mission.

---

*Rewarding the Red Speed Team*

*The final ingredient of Red Speed's recipe for success is a unique team compensation strategy. For every month that the company achieves its equipment performance targets and other customer service goals (number of complaints, refunds, and referrals, to name a few), each employee earns a percentage of the profits. When the business falls short of its goals, the percentage of profit sharing drops. If the business earns no profits in a slow month (this has happened only twice in four years), no bonuses are paid out. Employee performance is reviewed by Nate and Jaime every three months, and employees anonymously review each other's performance every six months. Red Speed pays for regular employee training seminars, enabling its mechanics to hone their skills and upgrade their expertise.*

*Other employee benefits—such as the spring and fall adventure weekends, Christmas parties, 75% discounts for friends and family, and all the strawberry rhubarb pie you can eat—make Red Speed a fun place to work. Red Speed has a team that is trained, managed, and rewarded for success...and they truly do deliver—fun!*

---

# Conclusion

By virtue of being a small business, you already enjoy many of the qualities that corporate America covets: a collaborative atmosphere, fast communication, and the ability to respond rapidly to the market. Chances are, this has not occurred as a result of deliberate planning on your part, but because you only have a couple of people in your business. With just a little foresight, you can lay the foundation for an effective team or group of teams that will commit your company to a course of continual innovation and improvement, and open the door to steady growth. As many management consultants have pointed out, teamwork is not a destination, it is a journey.

# Chapter 24
# MANAGING HUMAN RESOURCES

*About This Chapter:*
- *Tool kit for managing people*
- *Interviewing and hiring people*
- *Compensating your people*
- *The personnel and company handbook*
- *Corporate culture*

## Introduction

The most important asset any business has is its people. For this reason, hiring, training, and motivating your employees is one of your most important jobs. If you do these things well, you have a good chance of building a stable, sustainable business.

If you want your business to grow and perform consistently—even in your absence—you must empower your people to perform. This means devising a system of rewards, policies, guidelines, and practices for all your employees; writing job descriptions and performance evaluations; setting salary levels; and creating a competitive mix of compensation.

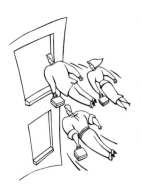

## Tool Kit for Managing People

The fact that you've seen certain human resource practices used elsewhere doesn't mean you should necessarily emulate them in your own business. Think how differently the employee handbook at a computer company with 20,000 employees would look compared to the handbook used at a bicycle repair company with 20 employees! Begin with the basics (policies for hiring, training, rewarding, and motivating), and fit them to your own needs. This is a good time to consult your business plan, because the industry in which you operate, the products you produce, your business goals, and your core competencies all govern how you manage your employees.

## Interviewing and Hiring People

### Job Descriptions
Before hiring even one employee, the first thing a good manager does is write clear, concise job descriptions, including:

- Tasks to be performed
- Performance criteria
- Necessary skills or qualifications

- Importance of each duty
- Supervision
- Future projects
- Training
- Growth and advancement

Consider this job description for a marketing manager:

———————————————◆———————————————

*Rosann's Rockin' Rollin' Tires*

**Job Title:** *Marketing Manager*

**Department:** *Sales and Marketing*

**Reports to:** *President*

*Responsible for: Creating market development strategies and processes for our line of environmentally friendly recycled tires; focusing on new product introductions; working closely with sales force to ensure that they have the tools necessary to launch product and meet schedule commitments; managing communications between the president and the sales staff; acting as an advocate for the different product and customer segments; tracking progress against plans and communicating any changes to plans. Must be willing to work on accelerated schedule and manage many tasks simultaneously. Must also be flexible, and an effective communicator.*

**Minimum Qualifications:** *BA/BS in Marketing/Communications or equivalent; three years of product management experience; creative ability; marketing skills; and independent judgment. PC Skills: word processing, spreadsheet, and presentation software.*

*The ideal candidate will flourish in a fast-paced, entrepreneurial setting, and know how to have fun. Knowledge of tire or automobile markets is essential.*

———————————————◆———————————————

**A sample job description** *(margin note)*

## Hiring Smart People

**Fix your weak spots by hiring people with different skills, experience, and personalities** *(margin note)*

Hiring smart people is the second step in creating strong, capable management. It's important to hire talented people to whom you can delegate responsibility and authority at the outset. No doubt you're under time pressures, but investing time in selecting good people now will pay off later.

Your first employees will perform the primary functional tasks of your business: marketing, accounting, selling, producing, financial management, and customer service. Your standards for these people should be high but realistic. Beware of expecting too much and rewarding too little; this creates resentment, resulting in poor performance and high employee turnover.

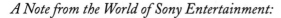

*A Note from the World of Sony Entertainment:*

*Consider this example of a hiring policy: The former president of Sony, the multinational electronics company, instituted a policy whereby managers were required to seek and hire employees who were smarter than they were! In the aggressive, fast-paced, and technically innovative industry of home electronics and entertainment, this policy was the key to Sony's survival; it ensured that the company cultivated the industry leaders for tomorrow.*

Two criteria guide the hiring process: the first is functional or technical qualifications; the second has to do with style, attitude, and personality. Here are some hiring basics:

### Have face-to-face interviews

You should like the people you work with, and they should be personable. It is important to get to specifics as soon as possible. What exactly has this person achieved in the past five years? Get the person to talk about his or her achievements, goals, and values. Try to pinpoint specific projects the candidate has started and finished. When finished, you should clearly understand his or her past performance record. Don't forget to take notes!

Learn good interview techniques

### Use "what if?" questioning

Presenting prospective employees with a selection of possible business and interpersonal scenarios offers insight into personality and work style. Ask the candidate how he or she would react to a specific crisis, an ambiguous or uncertain situation, or a given challenge.

### Check references

Use reference checks to verify the candidate's qualifications and get information on work habits. How does the candidate work under pressure? Is he or she disciplined, detail-oriented, and able to complete tasks without constant supervision? Use your interview notes and the resume as a guide as you dig for more information.

### Characters to avoid

Let's take a moment to examine a few composite sketches of employees your business should avoid. These people can be a drain on your resources and a thorn in your side, and they will almost certainly appear at some point in your business's life.

- **The Master of The Universe.** This person is eager to identify, quantify, and correct all ills of the organization, and continually demands attention and recognition of status from you and your staff.
- **The Ambitious Policeman.** This person is self-appointed to police standards and procedures within your business. This usually involves patronizing other employees, concentrating obsessively on their alleged faults, and wasting countless hours on small or useless projects.

- **The Sales Vulture.** This person may have come highly recommended as a "great seller," but mostly seems downright abrasive. These people earn the highest salary by virtue of commissions and incentives, and constantly remind you of their "fair market value" at competing firms.
- **The Troublesome Techie.** This theoretical genius seldom misses an opportunity to demonstrate technical superiority, and is notoriously bad at sharing knowledge and helping others to learn. These people can be stubborn, limited in their thinking, and unwilling to adapt to new design or product specifications.
- **The Business Stiff.** When the business is not doing well, this person—who has a lot of education but little actual experience in your industry—may be recruited by investors or your partners to inject some "good old-fashioned business sense" into the organization. The focus will be on trimming the "fat" from the organization (this usually means firing people) and setting strict guidelines for "turning things around."

## Compensating Your People

The rewards that businesses offer their people can be divided into two categories: regular compensation and benefits, and additional rewards and incentives. Basic benefits are the things that all employees receive, regardless of their level of performance. Rewards and incentives are given in order to motivate employees to exceed performance targets, and increase innovation.

It's hard to find capable people who are truly motivated. Those special people who can invest their spirit in your business are treasures. Challenge, compensate, and reward them well!

*Compensation packages are your employees' meat and potatoes; rewards and incentives, their dessert!*

### Salary
This is the annual or monthly dollar amount you offer your employees for the job they do. You should know what your people are worth, and create competitive compensation packages to pay them accordingly. Many small businesses lack the cash flow to pay out big salaries, but you can compensate and reward your people in other ways, such as stock options, flexible work hours, and vacation time. An employee who is concerned only with earning a large salary is not the kind of person who should be working for you anyway!

### Vacation time
Vacation leave practices are often dictated by the geographic region and industry in which a business operates. Your main decision is whether to have staggered vacation times, or plan for a two-week shutdown once a year.

### Holidays
Although some holidays—such as Christmas, Thanksgiving, New Year's Day, and President's Day—are considered standard paid time off, it is entirely at your discretion which holidays you choose.

### *Sick leave*

Sick leave practices are usually dictated by the region and industry in which a business operates. You can manage your policies any way you please. Decide how many sick days you will pay, and how many you will tolerate before taking disciplinary action.

### *Health and medical coverage*

This is one of the fundamental benefits that many employers offer their employees. However, providing this benefit simply may not be financially possible in the earliest stages of a business's life. As soon as possible, you should consider getting some form of group medical coverage for your company. It is better to have a modest plan with high deductibles and simple benefits than to have no insurance at all. You can begin by paying a small fraction of the cost of coverage, and increase the contribution as you grow. Many medical coverage packages also include some form of life insurance and dental care coverage. Shop around and ask a lot of questions in order to find the best deal!

## Motivating and Rewarding Your People

What does it mean to motivate people? It means to inspire and stimulate them to realize their potential, and help them to have fun in the process! Some people assume that salary is the most important motivation for employees, but this isn't always the case. Often, new challenges and opportunities for learning are what employees consider most important. This type of motivation is critically important for a growing business.

You should develop year-long motivational training strategies for your business. These may include a schedule of programs that your sales people can look forward to throughout the year: in February they will attend a tactical sales seminar, in August they will be trained in international selling techniques, and to ring in the New Year in January, they will participate in a class on fun and selling. You may also want to create an agenda for internal sales, productivity, or quality contests. Each month, gains can be measured, winners selected, and fun prizes awarded.

This schedule provides markers throughout the year that will keep your people motivated and forward-looking. You should also post your business's performance goals prominently around your work space. For example, if your t-shirt printing business is shooting to hit an all-time production high of 1,000 shirts per week, the number "1,000" might be posted at key spots on walls, or printed on shirts to be worn by your employees.

Employee Motivation:

- $'s
- Learning
- New challenges
- New opportunities

---

*In the notoriously low-profit world of travel, where travel agents earn little besides commissions, travel businesses have had to use creative tools to attract and compensate their employees. One particularly clever executive allows her agents to purchase mileage points for their own use at rock-bottom prices, take several vacations annually (for field research!), and work out of their homes on their own terminals. Her best achievement is the annual office party. These events are legendary: the turnout is huge, people have fun, and best of all, the expectation before the parties is a powerful employee motivator. The most popular part of these parties? Creatively devised and enthusiastically received contests with exceptional prizes for everyone: around-the-world airline tickets for agents and their spouses, hotel vouchers, and free rental cars! Now that's an incentive!*

---

Good people managers continually refresh their employees' awareness of the business's goals and rekindle their enthusiasm. One method is to build incentives for exceeding targeted levels of performance into your system; most businesses do this by rewarding employees who exceed sales quotas or complete projects ahead of schedule. How much employees are rewarded depends upon how much they have exceeded their targets. Your incentives can be as creative as you like! Consider creating incentives for:

- Meeting or exceeding quality standards
- Lowering customer complaints
- Exceeding standard order turnaround time
- Acquiring new skills or expertise outside of one's functional area
- Exceeding targeted inventory turnover
- Exceeding accounts receivable collection targets
- Exceeding sales quotas

Incentives allow the business to pay for performance once it has been delivered. The best example of this is an incentive-based compensation system for a salesperson. Two of the most common ways to reward employees are:

### Stock purchase plan
The stock purchase plan (which is the opportunity to buy shares in the business) is one of the most common systems of rewards in entrepreneurial ventures. Everyone wants a piece of the action! This is particularly true in high-growth, high-tech industries like those in California's Silicon Valley, where the issue of stock options invariably comes up during the first interview with prospective employees. The stock purchase plan gives employees an added incentive to help the business succeed, and allows the business to compensate its employees with earnings it has not yet produced. As your company grows, you should tailor the plan to fit your business. Always engage your attorney to help you review your choices, and the tax and business benefits of each.

### Profit sharing
In the early stages of your business, stay away from promises to share profits. It will be a while before your business generates profits, and it will be even longer before you've generated enough cash to pay out on a formal plan. If you choose to share profits, consult your attorney and bankers for guidance.

## Mentoring

An integral part of your job as leader is to help other people succeed in your business. As your business grows, your time should increasingly be spent mentoring or coaching. This means relinquishing your role as the "shining star" of the team and helping others to bask in the spotlight of success. This means delegating responsibility for functional tasks, and focusing your energy on the strategies that allow your business and its people to succeed.

*Help others to bask in the spotlight of success!*

## NxLEVEL™ TECH TIP

An increasing number of companies have taken outsourcing to a new level by contracting with a Professional Employer Organization (PEO), which enables the PEO to serve as the business's virtual human resources department. Unlike temp agencies, PEOs do not provide personnel. A PEO manages complicated and time-consuming human resources functions, including payroll and tax filings, unemployment and workers' compensation reports, 401(k) plan and health insurance administration, and compliance with regulations. Certain PEOs provide additional services, such as employee handbook and policy development, or employee counseling and training; some will even act as your personal workplace issues consultant, providing up-to-date advice on new or pending labor regulations that can protect you from costly noncompliance penalties.

For some business owners, PEOs offer a chance to increase efficiency while reducing stress. For example, by delegating personnel responsibilities to a PEO, you can spend more time developing new products or satisfying customers.

Before entering into a co-employer relationship, check to see whether the PEO is a member of the **National Association of Professional Employer Organizations (NAPEO)**, or better still, is accredited by the **Institute for the Accreditation of Professional Employer Organizations (IAPEO)**. You should also investigate how long the PEO has been in existence, and if it will furnish names of current and past clients for reference checks. For more information on how best to search for a PEO, contact NAPEO at (703) 836-0466, or visit the organization's home page (http://www.napeo.org/peo/).

## Firing People

You've selected your employee carefully, written a clear job description, and set attainable goals. But for some reason, the employee just isn't performing. One of the least pleasant duties a manager has is to ask someone to leave. There are several reasons you might arrive at this difficult decision:

- The employee has stolen from the company
- The employee has not performed as expected
- The employee has a personality conflict with other members of the team
- The company can no longer afford to pay the employee

When you do act, it should be quick and clean. There is a standard process used to terminate an employee:

- Have a private conference with the employee in a private area
- Describe the problem, the performance you expect, and the date by which it must be delivered
- Schedule a follow-up review
- Meet again to share your assessment of the employee's performance
- At each stage, document the issues in writing; thoroughly describe the problems your business has with the employee, and his or her improvement or failure to perform
- Make the decision to keep, terminate, or transfer the employee

When you terminate employees, it is important to explain why they are being fired, and if possible, suggest how they might improve in their areas of weakness.

## The Personnel and Company Handbook

Early in your business's life, you should develop an employee and company handbook. It should contain the following:

- A letter from you—the founder, team leader, and coach
- The company mission statement
- Your employee relations policy
- Your employee benefits package
- A "principles of doing business" statement, including its purpose and author; who should use it; an explanation of its terms, and the time frame it covers
- Your employee performance appraisal and problem resolution procedures
- Vacation and holidays policy
- Organizational reporting structure and functions

Consider the following examples of a company mission statement and statement of business principles:

The company handbook sells the company from the inside out

*Couch Potato, Inc. Mission Statement*

*Couch Potato, Inc. is a homegrown company founded on the principle that a comfortable couch makes for a comfortable home. We are committed to selling and servicing the most comfortable, long-lasting couches in California. We strive to maintain the highest standards of customer service and product quality. Our goal is to educate our customers about the benefits of buying durable, high-quality, ergonomically correct couches for their families. Lastly, we will always, and without exception, do things the Couch Potato Way!*

*Couch Potato, Inc. Principles of Doing Business*

- *We source, sell, and service the highest-quality couches*
- *We accept all returns, no questions asked*
- *Whatever is best for our customers is best for us*
- *We deliver our couches on time, intact, and with a smile*
- *We hire creative, committed, fun, and honest people*
- *We want to help our employees exceed their personal and professional expectations*
- *We laugh at ourselves when we need to*

The handbook provides information needed by managers and employees regarding all issues, practices, and procedures related to employee relations. The key elements are:

## Employee Relations Policy

This is a clear statement of your business's commitment to its employees. What qualities and skills does your business value in its people? Consistency? Humor and wit? Creativity? Speed? Accuracy? Loyalty? Pick and choose and write it down! This statement also broadly outlines the structures and policies by which your business manages its people. This can include a brief summary of health, educational, and training benefits; and promotional policy.

## Problem Resolution Policy

This is management's tool for resolving failures to perform, personal conflicts, and employee complaints. It provides employees with a clear indication of how and to whom they can present their issues and problems. Consider some of the situations you might want to address:

- Drug or alcohol abuse
- Excessive absenteeism
- Interpersonal conflict
- Poor performance
- Theft

The 'open-door' policy— easy access for problem resolution

Corrective action should include:

- Verbal warnings
- Written warnings
- Counseling
- Termination

### Employee Development and Performance Appraisal Policy

Outlining this policy is vital to the professional development of your employees. This statement should emphasize the ongoing responsibility of your business and its employees to develop and demand the highest standards of quality. Here again you will lay out in broad terms the core objectives of the business. This statement may offer an explanation of your business's policy regarding employee development and training. It can also outline how frequently and by which criteria employee performance is judged.

### Employee Benefits Policy

This clearly describes the benefits that your business offers its employees. It identifies who is eligible for which benefits, and when.

### Employee Compensation Policy

This explains how your business compensates its employees. It should address full-time, part-time, contractual, and temporary employees; and the various job classifications that exist within your business. It should also address:

- How and when salary is paid
- The hours of work
- Overtime compensation
- Holiday pay

As with all employee-related issues, you must make sure you are in compliance with federal, state, and local regulations. Be sure to have your legal advisor review your company handbook and any other policies and practices.

## Corporate Culture

A business's **culture** is usually a function of its values. These values may range from how employees dress, to the language they use, to how they deal with each other and their customers. Values govern both the spoken and unspoken rules of behavior in a business. These vary from company to company, and can be very difficult to change once they are in place. (For example, the corporate culture of a skateboard shop would be very different from that of an accounting firm.) For this reason, you should pay particular attention to the values you endorse and reward at the outset of your new business.

## Conclusion

In the rush of day-to-day pressures to make products, fill orders, and collect payments, the important task of creating company policies is often pushed aside. Skilled managers create organizational structures that motivate employees to invest themselves in growing the business. If you create a fulfilling and enjoyable place to work, hire smart people, motivate them, and compensate them fairly, you will have a better chance of success in your business. Employees are crucial to your success, so treat them well!

# PART VI
# MARKETING YOUR BUSINESS

## Chapter 25
## THE MARKETING PLAN

*About This Chapter:*
- *Why every small business needs a marketing plan*
- *What are objectives, strategies, and tactics?*
- *Contents of the marketing plan*
- *Creating a sales forecast*

## Introduction

Would you consider taking a long car trip without knowing where you wanted to go, which route you would take, or what stops you would make along the way? Of course not—you would plan your trip and develop an itinerary!

A plan is just as important for your business's marketing efforts. Your business's **marketing plan** tells what you want to accomplish, how you plan to go about doing it, and what tools you will use in the process. It's your chance to demonstrate your expertise, and your knowledge of your customers and market. It is an opportunity to spotlight the actions you will take to be competitive and successful. The time spent in researching and designing your marketing plan will more than pay off in the end!

## Why Every Small Business Needs a Marketing Plan

As a small business owner, you have limited time and resources with which to achieve your marketing goals. Your margin for error is smaller than that of large businesses. You may have loan payments due, another job to hold down, or a family to support. This is no time to spin your wheels! A good marketing plan organizes your thoughts, prevents you from duplicating your efforts, and keeps you from spending your business's precious capital on the wrong things.

Potential investors and lenders pay particular attention to a business's marketing plan. They look to the plan as an indicator of the business's potential. Who will the business sell to? How will it position itself in the market? How realistic are its objectives? What strategies and tactics will it use to achieve these objectives?

*A Marketing Case Study: The Boot Doctor*

*Mary and her brother Sam grew up on a ranch outside of Denver, wearing sturdy leather cowboy boots while they rode horses and worked the cattle. Over the years, Mary became an expert at resoling and stitching her favorite boots to extend their life and improve their appearance. She and Sam revived old cowboy boots as a hobby; they repaired their own, their parents', and eventually their friends' and neighbors' boots. They even created a unique mixture of glue and rubber cement that could be formed to fit onto the old sole and extend the life of the boot.*

*After working in a local bank for several years after college, Mary became interested in starting her own business. What could she do? What did she know well and what were her hobbies? Why, boots of course! She remembered how important well-maintained boots were to her, and how great it felt to revive a favorite pair. Inspired, she decided to look more closely at the market for boot repair.*

---

## What are Objectives, Strategies, and Tactics?

Marketing objectives, strategies, and tactics— the cornerstones of the marketing plan

**Objectives** describe what the business plans to achieve in chosen markets. This could mean controlling 20% of the market, increasing sales by 50% in the next six months, or having 100 new customers by the end of the year.

**Strategies** describe the business's plan for achieving its objectives. These may include targeting customers who are between 24 and 40 years old, or targeting a niche market for customized bridal gowns. In marketing, your strategies show how customers will be segmented into target groups, and how products will be positioned in the market to emphasize the business's competitive advantages.

Strategies are also used to guide each element of the **marketing mix**, which is composed of product, price, promotion, and placement. (Each element of the mix is presented in greater detail elsewhere in this book.) The goal of a marketing strategy is to align these four elements so that they complement each other in order to achieve the same marketing objectives.

**Tactics** are specific actions that support strategies and achieve objectives. Businesses use marketing tactics for each of the major elements of the marketing mix. Businesses work to achieve their marketing objectives by designing complementary strategies, and mixing and matching different tactics for each. Marketing tactics might include repackaging heavy products in smaller, easier-to-lift containers; offering a two-for-one promotion; creating a classified ad that emphasizes your customized service; or distributing your products only through specialty boutiques.

---

*The Boot Doctor Researches Her Market*

*Before Mary could prepare her marketing plan, she needed information. She began her market research by gathering census data from the Chamber of Commerce. She checked demographic patterns for her community and estimated how many cowboy boot wearers there were, based on the number of farms and ranches in her area. Next, she counted the number and types of cowboy boot sellers within 100 miles. She estimated how often people needed their boots repaired by interviewing friends, neighbors, and family. She also created a simple one-page survey, which she distributed at the local mall. Using open-ended questions, she asked where and how often existing needs were being met, what were the most common boot problems, and what people wanted most from a boot repairer. She also asked which businesses provided similar services, and how much people were willing to pay. At the end of her efforts, Mary had confirmed her hunch that there was a market for a custom boot repair business in her area.*

*She identified her market: loyal cowboy boot wearers of all ages—both ranchers and city professionals—located within 100 miles of her town, who spent $100–300 on their boots, and were willing to spend $60 annually on boot repairs. These people would have at least one pair of boots repaired in the fall and the spring, depending on how often and where they wore their boots.*

A good marketing plan will help you get and stay in business

## NxLEVEL™ TECH TIP

The Internet is a marketer's dream. Not only can you find plenty of essential raw data online, you can also find countless services and products that will help you make the most of those data! Here are some sites to visit for a look at the possibilitites:

• **American Marketing Association** (http://www.ama.org/). This useful site provides all sorts of information about the American Marketing Association and its services.

• **D & B MarketPlace** (http://www.dnb.com/products/mktghome.htm). Registration with this site gives you access to reports on any U.S. industry. D&B's Marketing Connection provides marketing tools to help you research your market, identify your best prospects, and locate marketing service providers. It also offers desktop access to D&B's information base of more than 10 million U.S. businesses.

• **MarketPlace Pro** is a versatile, easy-to-use software suite that integrates the Dun & Bradstreet marketing database with a "match engine" and analytical tools. For more information, go to Icon, Inc.'s Web site (http://www.iconinc.com/bzone/db.cfm).

• **Drayton Bird Partnership** (http://www.draytonbird.com/). Provided by a leading direct marketing firm, this site features answers to 277 common marketing and direct marketing questions, as well as articles, examples, and case histories.

• **United States Census Bureau** (http://www.census.gov/). Need demographic information? There's no shortage of it at this site, which provides access to complete U.S. census information.

• **EXPOguide** (http://www.expoguide.com/). This site allows you to search for trade shows, conferences, and seminars either alphabetically, by date, geographic location, or concept. Many of these events have a small business orientation.

# Contents of the Marketing Plan

The marketing plan summarizes all market research and analysis. The entrepreneurial marketing plan contains the following three sections:

## Product/Service Description

- Describe your product/service
- What are its features/benefits?
- Does your product/service have any cycles or seasonality?
- What are your growth plans (products/services)?

## Market Analysis

- Who is your target customer?
- What is the size of your target market?
- What are the major segments of your market?
- How will your product or service deliver unique benefits to customers?
- What major market trends will have an impact on your business?
- What external opportunities and threats does your business face?
- Competitor Analysis
    - Who are your major competitors?
    - What are their strengths and weaknesses?
    - What competitive advantage does your business have?

Think creatively as you write your marketing plan

*The Boot Doctor: Marketing Schedule and Budget*

| Marketing Tactic | Monthly Cost | Timeframe | Comments |
|---|---|---|---|
| Networking | $40 | 6 months | Attend trade shows, rodeos, community events |
| Classified ads | $50 | 3 months | 2 newspapers, once a week; evaluate after 3 months |
| Fliers | $70 | 3 months | Designed and printed by sister, distributed by self and teenage neighbor |

## Marketing Objectives, Strategies, and Tactics

- What does your business want to accomplish, expressed as specific objectives?
- How will you position your business in the market?
- What is your marketing niche?
- What is your business's marketing mix?
  - What **products** or services will you offer?
  - How will you **price** your products or services?
  - How will you **promote** your products or services?
  - What **channels of distribution** will you use?
- In which geographic areas will you sell?
- What product or service enhancements will you offer?
- What financial and human resources will you require to implement your strategies?
- What is your timeframe for achieving specific goals?
- What is your schedule and budget for specific marketing tactics?
- What level of sales do you forecast for the next 1, 6, and 12 months?

Your finished marketing plan might be several pages long, but first try containing it in a single paragraph. Give it careful thought—make it brief, to the point, and focused. Never lose sight of your purpose: to maximize profits. This requires meeting your customers' needs, setting clear goals, and accurately forecasting and budgeting.

A marketing budget and schedule might look like the sample on the previous page.

Eventually, you will need to create a more detailed marketing plan that includes long-, medium-, and short-term projections. You may even want to include in your expanded marketing plan several "what if" scenarios and contingency plans. Customers and markets are dynamic, so your marketing plan will invariably require fine-tuning. Prepare for this by building these elements directly into your plan.

The most important part of any marketing plan is committing yourself to it and using it. This should be a living document—one you consult and re-examine at least every three months.

---

### The Boot Doctor Identifies Her Mission

*Mary knew her product, knew her market (she'd been living there for 29 years!), and knew there was a need for her service. Initially, she would work out of a small room in her house; as the business grew, she could rent a more central location in town. She would promote her business in three ways: word of mouth and referrals; classified ads in her local newspapers; and a colorful display with fliers, which she would place in the major western supply stores in her area.*

*What was Mary's positioning strategy for her service? She would return worn-out boots to top form with the best tools, materials, and expertise around. Her competitive advantage? In-depth knowledge of cowboy boots and unique tricks for extending their life. She was a true professional—and a likable, neighborly one to boot! Mary had successfully begun her marketing efforts long before she invested a penny in her business: she had preliminary knowledge of her customers, her service, her price range, and where and how she would deliver her service. Now that's aggressive, smart marketing!*

## Creating Sales Forecasts

A **sales forecast** is a prediction of how much of a product or service will be sold during a specific period of time. Businesses create forecasts for target markets, geographic regions, and specific products or services. They're also used to plan production schedules, and to allocate responsibility, time, and resources.

Forecasts are a critical component of your marketing and business plan; they help to pinpoint exactly how and when your business will be profitable. By carefully researching and updating them, you increase the probability of success.

For entrepreneurs—who might be selling an innovative product or service for which there is little precedent or market information—forecasting can be particularly difficult. For this reason, small businesses often rely on industry publications, trade associations, or other business periodicals for information on market trends and sales predictions. There are also many professional forecasting companies that sell both general and highly specific forecasting information.

Some approaches to forecasting are presented below.

- **Breakdown forecasting** means looking at your largest population of prospective customers, then breaking that group down to define the level of sales you can expect from target customers. Begin by gathering data on the population of your state, city, or town, then quantify the number of target customers by using **qualifying criteria** such as age, income, buying needs, preferences, or buying patterns. Lastly, narrow your focus to the average number of times the specific customer is predicted to buy your product or service per year. Businesses use several different sources of data to perform breakdown forecasts, including U.S. census reports, surveys, articles in national marketing periodicals, state Department of Commerce data, and information gathered through their own surveys or focus groups.
- **Buildup forecasting** requires you to estimate the size of each market segment, then add them together to arrive at a forecast of sales. A business that sells children's bathing suits would first calculate how many children aged ten and under there are in the four surrounding counties, then add these numbers to estimate total market size.

*Forecasts are an important guide for on-going marketing activities*

- **Indirect forecasting** is a method that businesses use when they cannot obtain specific market information. To create forecasts, businesses gather related data to indicate the size of the market. For example, lacking specific information on bathing suit buying patterns for its markets, a children's bathing suit business might gather information on total spending on summer play clothing for children. It could also gather data on the number of swimming pools in the surrounding counties, and the number of children enrolled in swimming lessons. You often have to be creative to find data that provide relevant, reliable insights into your target markets!

---

*Mary Meets Her Goals*

*With her market research done and her positioning strategy in place, Mary created her marketing plan. The most important part of her plan? Her goals. She would average 60 pairs of boots a month during her first year. After introductory discounts, she would settle on her preliminary price of $60.00 per pair. After six months, she would investigate extending her services to include delivery service, custom decoration, and repairs by mail. Mary was excited to take on bigger challenges, but she knew she had to meet her preliminary goals first.*

*Eighteen months later, Mary had met her goals. Things had been slow at first; she'd needed to perfect her technique, find reliable, cost-effective sources of supplies, and develop her routine. Her biggest challenge? Scheduling her time and sticking to her budget. She beat these challenges by hiring a local accountant to keep her books for a small monthly fee. She also sought out owners of other service businesses and studied how they managed their time and money. She attended her first western wear trade show, and also shared a booth with two other entrepreneurs at several local rodeos. After eighteen months, Mary was the name of the game in boot repairs in her 100-mile area!*

---

## Conclusion

The entrepreneurial marketing plan identifies your customers, what you will sell, and how you will achieve your business objectives.

The marketing plan also steers management efforts. It summarizes your marketing objectives, strategies, and tactics. It presents the specifics of your business's marketing mix and the sales that you expect to generate. Research and write your marketing plan carefully, and revise it often. A good marketing plan can be the most compelling argument you have for the viability of your business; it gives potential investors, lenders, employees, and advisors a reason to believe you will be successful.

Continually review customer needs: your business depends on it

# Chapter 26
# MARKET RESEARCH AND ANALYSIS

*About This Chapter:*
- *What is market research?*
- *The market research process*
- *Using the Internet for market research*
- *Market analysis*
- *Competitive analysis*
- *SWOT analysis*
- *Look before you leap*

## Introduction

**Market research** is the process of gathering information to make informed, intelligent, strategic decisions. What product should you produce, and in what quantity? Which stores should you target? Where should you locate your retail shop? What should you charge for services?

**Market analysis** tells you how attractive the environment is for your chosen industry. Who are your competitors? How fierce are they? On what basis do they compete?

Your marketing strategy is a road map for your business, so you must make sure that the information on which it is based is sound. In order to be useful, market research and market analysis must be valid, reliable, and representative of target customers.

Think of the time you spend analyzing your markets as an investment in your business that will save you time and money in the future. Market research and market analysis are powerful tools for focusing your business's goals and increasing your odds of success.

## What is Market Research?

Market research allows you to identify opportunities, test alternate strategies, evaluate marketing performance, and predict changes in your market. It also gives you feedback so you can challenge your assumptions and fine-tune your marketing mix.

Effective market research means planning, collecting, and analyzing data about your customers, industry, and competitors. It is an ongoing process of understanding the changing environment in which your businesses operates.

### Demographic vs. Psychographic Data
**Demographic data** describe specific characteristics of an individual such as age, level of education, occupation, income, marital status, and address. Businesses gather demographic data to discover who and where their customers are.

Market research helps you find out if your hunches are correct

**Psychographic (or lifestyle) data** describe an individual's activities, interests, opinions, and beliefs, and give marketers insight into such things as how their potential customers live, make buying decisions, and plan for the future.

Good demographic and psychographic data are particularly useful for small businesses, whose success usually depends on offering more personal customer service than larger competitors.

Here are some demographic and psychographic trends that affected marketing in the 1990s.

*Three major demographic trends*

- **Shifts in the age make-up of the American market.** In the United States, 77 million baby boomers (people born between 1946 and 1964) make up one-third of the population, and represent more than one-fourth of the economy's purchasing power. In the last decade of this century, baby boomers' income is expected to double. The size of the youth market (people aged 12-19) is expected to continue decreasing, but their spending is increasing. The mature market (50 years old and up) commands half of the discretionary income in the United States and holds 77% of its assets. Within 30 years, one-third of all Americans will fit into this group.

- **Changes in family composition.** Increases in the divorce rate and the percentage of working women, and a decrease in the birthrate after 1960, have caused major changes in the make-up of the typical American family. (In fact, it seems no one can agree on whether there exists a typical American family anymore!) Single-parent homes, smaller families in married households, and a decline in the proportion of teenagers are related trends.

- **Increasing proportion of working women.** In 1990, 58% of women worked, as compared to 33% of women in 1950. Women are entering the work force at younger ages and changing the face of American business in nearly every industry. The resultant "time crunch" that many working women feel has fueled a boom in catalog and Internet shopping, and other time-saving services.

*Three major psychographic/lifestyle trends*

- **Shifting male/female purchasing roles.** Because more women are working, in addition to having a family, men are playing a larger role in child care and household duties. And because women are earning more money and achieving more independence, they are spending more money on travel, dining out, entertainment, and luxury products.

- **Increased interest in "healthy" lifestyles.** In 1990, half of all American grocery shoppers read the labels on the food they bought. Americans are giving up smoking, drinking less alcohol, and eating less meat. Fat-free, low-fat, low-salt, sugar-free, and "natural" products are increasingly popular. Americans are more interested in fitness, too; they are jogging, climbing, hiking, biking, and swimming more than ever before.

- **More conservative lifestyles.** In the 1980s, the youth market became more concerned with career, personal style, and lifestyle choices. Today, they are spending more on clothing, personal grooming products, and automobiles. Young adults and teenagers are also getting more involved in household and food purchases. The increase in the number of divorced households, and the frequency with which young adults are transplanting themselves to pursue jobs and education, means that more people are setting up their own households at younger ages.

## Trends Spell Opportunity for Small Business

Trends like these present a tremendous opportunity for new businesses, and not just for businesses in large cities. Even the smallest rural communities are affected by such trends and thus have business opportunities to match.

For example, you may think that the increase in working women has no importance for you. But when you look closer you might find that in the past two years, traffic on your local highway has increased by 20%, and that 30% of that traffic consists of women commuting to work. Seeing an opportunity, you might investigate opening an express dry cleaner/coffee shop catering to professional women. Where? Somewhere along the highway, of course!

Get the picture? Look around, ask questions, and use market research to put your business in the right place at the right time!

# The Market Research Process

While large corporations have the budgets to create entire market research departments or hire research consultants to test their ideas, smaller businesses have to be more creative. Limited budgets mean most entrepreneurs depend on salespeople, distributors, and themselves to conduct and gather market research. Quality market research can indeed be gathered for little or no money, but it does take effort!

## How Do Small Businesses Gather Market Research?

Market research can be expensive or low-cost, depending on your sources and the scope of your research. All research should be guided by an initial set of objectives, which will help to keep the project within budgetary constraints. It's also a good idea to break the research process into small parts. This organizes your efforts, and makes the task a lot less intimidating.

## Understanding Your Customers' Buying Behavior

To create a profitable business, you must identify and satisfy your customers' needs. One of their most important needs is the ability to buy in the manner, time, and place they choose. Market research helps identify customers' needs, and uncovers **buyer behavior**—the attitudes that influence what and how they buy.

Before you begin your market research process, it is important to understand how and why different types of customers make purchases.

Surf the tide of changing trends

*How do individual consumers make purchase decisions?*

Consumers who buy products through retail outlets make their decisions in different ways depending on the products they buy. Just think how differently you go about buying a car, a candy bar, or aspirin. In general, consumers' buying behavior involves identifying a need, gathering information, evaluating alternatives, making the purchase, and evaluating their degree of satisfaction.

Consumer purchases vary according to the following:

- **Level of involvement in the purchase.** How important is the product to customers? What percentage of their income does its price represent? How often do they buy? How complex or unique is the product? How risky is the product?
- **Degree of brand loyalty.** How important is a particular brand to customers? Do they associate the brand with particular events, memories, related products, or people? Or do they fail to distinguish between different brands altogether?
- **Habits and learning.** How complex is the decision process? How much must customers know to make an informed purchase? Is the product purchased habitually? Or must customers learn something new or change old behavior before buying?
- **Consumer motivation.** Why is the customer making the purchase? Is it satisfying physiological (food, shelter), safety (protection, security), social (acceptance, friendship), ego (prestige, success), or self-actualization needs?
- **Consumer perceptions.** How do consumers perceive different brands and product offerings? By what criteria do they evaluate different products? Do consumers have a positive or negative image of a product?

*How do organizations make purchase decisions?*

For the most part, organizations buy very differently than consumers do . The products they buy tend to be essential to their operations, and thus require more planning and involvement. Their purchases are riskier, because if the components they buy fail, so will their finished product. Because there is generally more negotiation and ongoing business between buyers and sellers, personal selling tends to be more important in organizational markets than in consumer markets; buyers and sellers tend to form more stable and intimate business relationships.

For important or expensive purchases, businesses often rely on teams to make **product specifications**, which are requirements that dictate product performance and type. Within the buying team, individuals tend to fall into the following roles:

- The **gatekeeper** regulates the flow of information to the team, and finds alternate products and vendors.
- The **influencer** has some leverage from experience, position, or technical expertise to influence the other members of the team.
- The **buyer** decides which product or service to purchase, and may help to evaluate different choices (although he or she often defers to others on the team who have more technical expertise).

"You have to see the future to deal with the present."

—Pop-culture tracker, corporate consultant, Faith Popcorn

- The **user** helps set product specifications, and evaluates the product after it is purchased.

Note that these roles may all be filled by the same or different people. What is the importance of all this for the small-business owner? By knowing how your customers make decisions and who fills these roles, you can focus your sales efforts and maximize your resources. For more information, see Chapter 44 *Dealing with Large Organizations*.

Now, let's move on to the process of gathering your market research.

## Define Your Research Objectives

In market research, starting at the beginning means quantifying what you do and don't know about your market. If you are considering a foray into an industry that is new to you, there will probably be a great deal of information you don't have. Your research objectives might be to identify events, trends, or cause-and-effect relationships in your marketplace; or to define specific problems for additional research.

This initial phase of your market research process should include writing down, as precisely as you are able, the information you need to fill the gaps in your knowledge about your market. Are customers spending less on your type of product? Is there a viable distribution channel for your product? Are production costs prohibitively high?

As you define your research objectives, try the following:

- Rephrase questions about your market to get a new perspective
- Prioritize your questions
- Test your objectives by creating sample data about your market. Do they help answer questions and set strategy?

———————————◆———————————

*Twila's Wedding Dresses*

*Twila Robinson was in seven weddings in one year, and ended up with seven bridesmaids' dresses that she felt were ugly, ill-fitting, and of poor quality. She was fed up! While she was helping a girlfriend plan yet another wedding, her friend suggested that they work together to design and sew her wedding dress and bridesmaids' dresses. Twila was enthusiastic about the idea; she loved to sew and make clothing for her friends (she'd even helped design and sew wedding dresses for two very tough customers, her sisters-in-law). The project went so well that Twila became intrigued by the idea of starting a new business—one that would generate a little extra income and allow her to use her creativity. She decided to investigate opportunities for designers and seamstresses of wedding and bridesmaids' dresses in her community. She wanted the following information:*

- *The geographic area of her market*
- *The market for wedding gowns and bridesmaids' dresses in her region, as determined by tracking marriage rates, population size with age breakdowns, and income levels*

Market research is basic exploration that tells you the who, what, where, why, and how of your business

- *Potential sales volume for the first year*
- *How much brides were willing to pay for dresses*

*Twila's major marketing problem: Could she count on the current wave of weddings to continue and support her in a full-time business? Or would she have to operate part-time and continue her sales job? How could she compete with the high- and medium-end bridal sections in local department stores?*

---

## Conduct a Situation Analysis

A **situation analysis** is a preliminary look at the market information that is already available to you; it tells you whether you must spend time and money gathering your own, original market research. A good situation analysis takes little time and delivers a lot of information.

**Primary data** are collected for the purpose of answering questions about your customers or markets. This may involve observing customer behavior, or designing questionnaires and surveys to learn more about a representative customer population.

**Secondary data** comprise information that has already been gathered and published. This information might come from academic research studies; articles in magazines, trade journals, or newsletters; census reports; or contact with distributors, middlemen, customers, competitors, or other knowledgeable people in the industry. Many research questions can be answered through readily available (and free) secondary data.

## Identify and Plan Primary Research

If you complete a situation analysis and find that there are insufficient secondary data available about your market, you'll need to gather your own primary data.

When businesses gather primary data they are generally gathering **qualitative data**, which are data that cannot be quantified or counted. They reveal the quality of a subject's experience or beliefs, and are gathered by allowing customers to answer questions in an unstructured manner. A person's political beliefs, interest in backpacking, or preference for chocolate over vanilla are examples of qualitative data.

**Quantitative data** describe quantities that can be measured and analyzed with statistical analysis. What do your customers earn each month? How old are they? How much do they spend each month on groceries? Rent? Gas? How many kids do they have?

Businesses use two major methods to gather this data:

*Surveys*
Surveys are the most important and widely used means of collecting primary data. They provide both qualitative and quantitative information from respondents, including facts, opinions, and attitudes. The first step in creating a survey is to decide to whom it will be

*Remember: As you research your market, you are not seeking to confirm your opinions...you are seeking the truth*

given. This group, chosen from the **target population** (i.e., the people whose opinions, behavior, preferences, and attitudes influence your marketing strategy), is known as a **sample**. Sample selection can be random or non-random.

**Random sampling** ensures that each member of the target population has an equal chance of being included. These samples have a greater statistical validity, but can be time-consuming, expensive, and more complex to design and execute.

**Non-random sampling** is usually done to save time, money, or simply because it is more convenient. On the other hand, it is harder for a researcher to calculate the degree to which the non-random sample represents the larger population.

Businesses that use non-random samples try to choose respondents who are representative of their target customer base. Respondents might be selected because they live in a specific geographic region or fall into an age, income, or lifestyle bracket.

*Twila's Research Plan*

*Twila decided to give herself one month to gather her market research data. She began by buying every magazine she could find on brides and wedding planning. What sort of dresses were women buying? What styles were popular? Who were the major manufacturers, fabric suppliers, boutiques, and designers? Where were women buying dresses?*

*Next, she went to the library and gathered the census data for her city and county, and scouted out the yellow pages for bridal gown shops and tailors. She telephoned and visited each one to find out what products and services they offered, what they charged for dress design and sewing, how many fittings they required, and how long it took them to deliver the finished product. She even asked for the names of past clients with whom she could speak.*

*This information was helpful, but Twila needed more specific information about the needs and tastes of her prospective clients. She decided to organize several focus groups. She used non-random sampling to select her participants. She chose two girlfriends and eight other women who had been referred to her, and divided them into two separate focus groups. Twila was careful to use open-ended questions, and to encourage all of the women to participate. She also made sure that the discussion stayed roughly on track and covered the following topics:*

- *How satisfied were they with their wedding and bridesmaid dresses (price, service, style, quality, selection)?*
- *What were the most important criteria to them in selecting a bridal boutique and wedding dress?*
- *What would they change about their dress buying and alteration experiences?*
- *What was the ideal environment for trying on, buying, and being fitted for a dress?*
- *How important were friends' recommendations in selecting boutiques and dresses?*
- *How far they would be willing to travel for a good seamstress and designer?*

- *How much they would be willing to pay for a good seamstress and designer?*
- *What would be the ideal wedding dress buying experience?*

*Twila rounded out her research by going to her Chamber of Commerce, which offered free Internet access. Using the search engines Yahoo! and AltaVista, she punched in several of her subject words: bridal, fashion, and weddings. She was pleasantly surprised to find a number of Web sites that gave her information on the latest wedding trends, buying patterns, and colors for dresses.*

*At last, Twila felt she had a solid level of knowledge on which to base a marketing strategy.*

---

Which sampling method you choose depends on the type of research you are conducting, and the amount of time and money you budget. Because your new business is small, you will probably opt for the convenience of non-random sampling. This may include a list of current customers, people whom you believe fit your customer profile, members of your church, or people who shop at your grocery store. However, as you gather your list of respondents, make sure they represent a reasonable mix of your customer base; too many of any type of respondent will skew your findings.

Below is a brief summary of random and non-random sampling techniques:

Keep your research objectives simple, specific, and clear

| Random Sampling Techniques | Non-Random Sampling Techniques |
|---|---|
| Computer programs can select random samples from electronic lists of names (telephone books or customer lists) | Select targets to question on the basis of convenience |
| Using a list of people (i.e., telephone list), assign a number to each name, select numbers from a table of random numbers, and choose the numbered entries on the list that correspond to those random numbers | Use your judgment to determine who is best to include in the sample on the basis of how well the person represents your targeted population |
| Decide on a "skip interval" and select names that are every *n*th on the list | Use a quota system that designates how many respondents of each gender, income bracket, geographic location, educational level or other criteria that you will sample |
|  | Gather respondents on the basis of referrals from other respondents |

The most common types of survey research include:

- **Personal interviews.** These can either be focus groups or individual interviews. Focus group interviews are the most widely used questioning technique for gathering market research because they can yield very in-depth information. Interviews are used to gather qualitative data about a target group. They can be conducted door-to-door, by intercepting people as they shop in a mall, or at a booth or trailer set up by the business conducting the research.

- **Telephone interviews.** These are best for shorter interviews (five to ten minutes). They can be more economical and time-effective than personal interviews. However, it is getting harder and harder to find people who are willing to interrupt their at-home time to speak with a stranger over the phone. For this reason, your telephone questionnaire must be short and concise.
- **Mail surveys.** These can be inexpensive for the researcher and convenient for respondents to complete, but the response rates for mail surveys are lower than for other types of surveys, and they can take a lot longer to compile. Offering a prize or benefit to mail survey respondents can help increase your response rate.

Remember, your goal is to gather reliable, relevant, and accurate information; be sure not to taint your respondents' answers by asking leading questions or offering feedback. Always ask open-ended questions with an open mind. The most valuable answers are usually spontaneous, unprompted, and free-form.

*Observation*

Through observation, marketers try to determine how consumers behave as they buy and use a product, or how they are influenced by marketing strategies. The pitfall of observation is that the presence or bias of the observer can influence the subject's behavior.

### Recipe for the Perfect Focus Group
- Assemble 6 to 10 people who represent your target customer
- Gather in an informal, relaxed setting
- Add one interviewer/moderator with good listening skills
- Ask open-ended questions
- Listen as participants share ideas, respond to one another, and stimulate one another's thinking
- Guide discussion gently for no more than one hour
- Consider videotaping the session for later review

The market research test: Imagine you have answered all of your most pressing marketing questions. Can you set your market strategy with confidence? Do you know exactly what your customers want and will pay for?

Museums, department stores, and even professional sports venues use observation to understand their visitors' movements and needs. Most retail stores use check-out scanners or other simple computer software to keep track of buying behavior. Tracking past customer behavior often helps to predict their future behavior.

**Creating a Survey? Try These Tips**
- Keep questions short, simple, and to the point
- Make it very easy for the respondent to complete
- Use a rating scale of 1 to 5 (1 = strongly disagree; 5 = strongly agree)
- Surveys should take no longer than 5-10 minutes to complete
- Be careful not to bias the answers with your question construction
- Offer respondents some reward for completing the survey (money, discounts, lottery ticket, prize)
- Say thank you!

### Conduct Secondary Research

After conducting a situation analysis, many small businesses learn that the majority of the information they need can be found through secondary research. However, it is not uncommon for entrepreneurs to use a combination of secondary and primary research. Secondary research can lead to the use of primary research to gather limited, specific information.

Typical information sought through secondary research is market size, location, and growth patterns. Businesses also use secondary information to get a better quantitative understanding of their customers: where they live, how numerous they are, their income brackets, educational level, and buying patterns.

Finding secondary research is simply a matter of investing the time to seek it out at public sources and talking to people. Below is a condensed resource list for collecting secondary data. Several books offer valuable listings of secondary data of all kinds. We highly recommend *Find It Fast* by Robert I. Berkman. Also, there is an extensive resource guide in the *NxLeveL™ Business Plan Workbook and Resource Guide*.

## Using the Internet for Market Research

The sources of quality secondary data are almost limitless. You can find the most current sources of information on the Internet. If you do not have a computer and an Internet account, do not despair—many public libraries, chambers of commerce, and community colleges offer free Internet access.

Some entrepreneurs and big businesses are posting market research questionnaires on the Internet. For as little as $500, you can put a questionnaire on the Web, and get answers to your questions in a few days (rather than the four to six weeks traditional questionnaires require). Quick response time is critical to getting to markets more quickly than your competition. Check out the M/S database marketing site at http://www.msdbm.com.

## Major Sources of Secondary Data:

- Public libraries
- University libraries
- Government (federal, state, local) departments and agencies
- U.S. Department of Commerce
- Trade associations
- Industry associations
- Chambers of commerce
- Local newspapers
- Business periodicals: *Business Week*; *Wall Street Journal*; *Journal of Commerce*; *Inc.*
- *American Marketing Association Bibliography Series* (Chicago)
- *Communications Abstracts* (Sage Publications, Inc./Beverly Hills, CA)
- *Journal of Marketing* (Chicago)

## Analyze Data and Prepare Final Summary

The purpose of analysis is to interpret and draw conclusions from the data you've collected. The more completely you wish to understand your market or survey findings, the more rigorous your research design and data analysis must be. The most comprehensive form of data analysis uses statistical models to test the validity of the findings. (Inexpensive statistical computer software packages can perform this type of analysis.)

However, for most small businesses it will suffice to gather the data, and work to draw reasonable conclusions from them. Here are some hints:

- Challenge the validity of your findings
- Check the information for completeness and timeliness
- Recheck to ensure the findings are representative of the larger population
- Assign value and weight to the findings
- Review your findings with a mentor or industry expert

That last recommendation is especially important. It is crucial to seek insight and feedback from some experienced business person throughout the course of your entrepreneurial venture. It's also a good idea to write a brief, informal summary of your findings that contains your conclusions and your action plan. Revisit this summary frequently, and compare it to new conditions in your market.

*Ask questions and seek answers!*

At the end of the market research process, your business should be able to incorporate your findings into a market strategy. Your target market and marketing mix should flow logically out of your market research process.

## Drawing Conclusions: How Big is Your Market?

After gathering your primary and secondary research, you should be able to answer the following questions:

- Who are your target customers?
- Where do they live?
- How much do they earn?
- What is their educational level?
- What do they spend annually/monthly on your product or service?
- During what time of year do they buy?
- What are their saving patterns?
- What are their spending patterns?
- What are their leisure activities?
- What is their family structure?
- What are their numbers: by city, county, and state?
- What is the amount of your product/service they buy annually/each visit?
- What motivates your customers to buy?
- Who are your best prospects?
- Should you emphasize yourself, your quality offerings, your selection, your price, or merely the existence of your business?
- What media do they read, watch, or listen to?

### Old, New, Inexpensive, and Innovative Market Research Methods

- Enclose pre-stamped envelopes with mail surveys
- Tap into the knowledge of the reference librarian at your local library
- If you are already in business, prepare a questionnaire for your existing customers
- Talk with other business people in your area and benefit from their expertise
- Get online and use browsers such as Yahoo! to research your key words
- Create snappy, brief surveys for people who use products or services like yours: look for them in parks, malls, ball games, downtown, at the beach...wherever they may be!
- Be honest and friendly
- Read advertising and marketing industry periodicals; they often contain valuable research findings

## Market Analysis

Competitors, economic trends, and industry standards are the major factors that compose a business's external environment. Although these external conditions are out of your control, understanding them allows you to navigate around obstacles and towards opportunity. How? By tailoring your marketing strategy to the changing demands of your environment.

The goal of market analysis is to help you understand your environment, determine the level of attractiveness of a given market or industry, identify competitors' strengths or weaknesses, and identify your business's strengths and weaknesses.

Looking at your environment is only half the picture; you also need to look at your internal capabilities. These include experience, knowledge, skills, financial resources, and technical excellence. If you analyze your internal and external environment and devise a strategy that maximizes your strengths and minimizes your weaknesses, you will be far ahead of the game.

---

*Turnstile Advertising*

*While waiting to enter an Orlando Magic basketball game, Martin Hering, an advertising professional, saw an amazing opportunity. He noticed that as fans walked through the entrance turnstiles, they always looked down. He realized that he'd discovered a unique place to put advertising messages! On that fateful day in Orlando, the idea for the Turnstile AdSleeve was born.*

*Martin had the benefit of a professional background in advertising and media. When considering new business opportunities, he wisely focused his efforts on his area of expertise: promotions and advertising. Before leaping forward with this novel idea, he would rely on market research to tell him whom he would sell his ideas to, and the size of his potential market of advertisers and sports venues. He would rely on market analysis to tell him who his competitors were, what his core competencies were, and how attractive the professional sports mass advertising industry was for his business.*

*With some advice from an entrepreneur and the help of an engineer, Martin developed the Turnstile AdSleeve, and inaugurated his company, Entry Media, Inc.*

---

## NxLEVEL™ TECH TIP

One of the most promising new market research strategies is the use of customized phone cards. How does it work? Here's a typical scenario: You contact a phone card marketing company and purchase 500 customized phone cards imprinted with your company's logo. You mail them to targeted customers, along with a number they can call to activate the card. When the customer calls, he or she is asked to respond to a survey lasting approximately five minutes. After the survey is complete, the customer has 30 minutes of free long-distance time left on the card. It is reported that the use of phone cards in marketing surveys results in a response rate two or three times higher than that of traditional surveys. Best of all, phone cards are inexpensive and yet are perceived by customers as having a high value. Therefore, receiving a free long-distance phone often leaves the customer with a positive feeling about your company. Phone cards are available in various increments ranging from ten minutes to half an hour, or even longer. A good preliminary Web site at which to investigate phone card marketing is http://www.mhacom.com.

# Competitive Analysis

You may think that competition exists only to make your life difficult, but the truth of the matter is that competition is the reason business opportunities exist! When market needs are not being met, opportunities arise for businesses that create unique ways to satisfy them. Capitalizing on such opportunities is one way to gain a competitive advantage.

To identify these opportunities, businesses usually perform some form of a **competitive analysis**; this means assessing your potential market's overall attractiveness. A competitive analysis has three components: industry analysis, competitor analysis, and SWOT analysis.

## Industry Analysis

Industry analysis identifies how attractive your industry is, and helps you compete more effectively if you decide to enter the market. Using a scale of 1 to 5 (1 being the least and 5 being the highest), rate the degree to which the criteria listed below apply to your industry.

The factors that determine an industry's attractiveness are:

- **Easy entry.** This describes how many barriers there are for new businesses trying to enter the market. High production costs, long set-up times, complex technical knowledge requirements, and logistical challenges are examples of barriers to entry. The greatest barrier is a competitor with a large marketing or cost advantage. A low score here means that your industry is very difficult for new competitors to enter.
- **Level of competition.** This describes the number of competitors in the market and the nature of their competition. When a market is mature and sales are leveling off or decreasing, competition is at its most intense, and the chances of gaining an edge (or even entering the market) are slim. Revenues might be falling, technological breakthroughs are few, and businesses begin to compete on the basis of price alone.
- **Availability of substitutes.** This describes how easily customers can use substitute products from other industries to satisfy their needs. An example would be customers of rental car companies who fly low-cost, commuter airlines rather than driving.
- **Buyer leverage.** This describes the bargaining power that buyers have over businesses in the market. If buyers have many choices and spend comparatively little on products in the industry, their bargaining power is high. They can drive down the price and heavily influence the content of the product.
- **Supplier leverage.** This describes the amount of bargaining power that suppliers have over businesses in the industry. A business that relies on a limited number of large suppliers is vulnerable to price increases and suppliers dictating the terms of the sale of inputs. This can make a market less attractive to businesses by raising their costs and reducing their ability to control their markets.

Insights gained through market analysis help set the business's course

Calculate the total points for your industry, and look below for an explanation of your score.

- **17-25 points.** Your industry is very competitive, so be prepared for an uphill struggle! Unless the potential rewards are great enough to offset the risk and cost of competing in this industry, you may want to consider industries in which there is less competition.
- **10-17 points.** Entering this industry won't be easy, but it may well be worth the trouble. There may be real challenges in several areas, but these are offset by opportunities in other areas. Look before you leap!
- **5-10 points.** Can it be true? Do industries like this exist? Yes, but not for long! If you're lucky and clever enough to have identified an industry that has low competition, is relatively easy to enter, and is in its most immature stage, you should move, and move fast!

## SWOT Analysis: How Does Your Business Rate Within Your Industry?

SWOT means examining your business's **S**trengths, **W**eaknesses, **O**pportunities, and **T**hreats, and comparing them to those of your competitors. This is particularly important for entrepreneurs who are considering entering a market for the first time. Unless you're looking for a long, expensive, frustrating struggle, you'll want to avoid challenging your competitors head-on by competing in areas in which you share core competencies.

*For Martin Hering and his business, Entry Media, Inc., a SWOT analysis would show just where Entry Media could compete most profitably in the crowded and competitive sporting venue promotions industry. The SWOT analysis for Entry Media might look like this:*

### Entry Media, Inc.

*Strengths:*        *Expertise in promotions and advertising.*

*Weaknesses:*      *The sports advertising industry is huge and highly competitive.*

*Opportunities:*     *Currently no advertising placement on entrance turnstiles. A unique place for advertising.*

*Threats:*          *Once the idea catches on, Entry Media will have to move even faster to shore up contracts with advertisers and sports venues.*

*Through SWOT analysis, Martin determined that the market was ripe for his idea and that if he didn't move on it immediately, his window of opportunity would close.*

**Market research** tells you who, where, and how large your potential market is

**Market analysis** tells you how that market operates and if you want to operate a business in that environment

## Competitor Analysis

This is a SWOT analysis of your competitors, both actual and potential. You can gather information about your competitors in many ways. Call them up and ask the questions a potential customer would ask. Try to find out what their strengths are, how long they've been in business, and what new product or services they'll be announcing in the future. You might also talk to other businesses who have dealt with them. Regardless of how you gather your information, get it from a wide array of sources to ensure that it's accurate and up-to-date, and make sure it includes the following information:

On what basis will you compete in your market? The goal of your business is to find and exploit its competitive advantage

- **Product.** What are your competitors' products? How are the products unique? What needs do they meet? What types of packaging do they use?
- **Pricing.** What price structures do your competitors use? How are they positioned?
- **Promotion.** How do your competitors promote their products or services? What is their advertising message?
- **Placement.** Where do your competitors locate their businesses and why? Where do they sell their products or services? How do they distribute their goods?

Answering these questions will form a picture of whom your competitors are targeting and why, and may help you predict their future plans as well as their response to your business's entry into the market. It can also yield valuable information on marketing practices your business can emulate or improve upon.

## Drawing Conclusions: Do You Want To Compete in This Industry?

You've just completed your first competitive analysis. Each of the three elements—industry analysis, competitor analysis, and the SWOT analysis for your own business—has given you new insight into your core competencies. Now, complete the process by drawing some conclusions about how and where to compete in your industry. This is the first step in creating your marketing strategy.

Remember, you are choosing the direction that will guide all of your strategic marketing. Be clear and condense it down to a simple concept that is expressible in ten words. If you can't do this, chances are you need to beef up your knowledge of your market and your customers, and fine-tune the purpose of your business.

*The core concept for Martin Hering's Entry Media, Inc.? "To provide unique, effective sporting venue promotion to clients."*

## Look Before You Leap

It's time to review your findings (preferably with a business mentor), and challenge your assumptions, just as you did with your market research. Ask yourself if have the quantity and quality of information you need to invest your money confidently in your business idea. If you have any doubts, reassess your mission and your findings. You may want to look at your business in a new way, or look for other business opportunities.

## Conclusion

The more competitive your industry, the better you will have to be at finding ways to create value for your customers and exploit the weaknesses of your competitors. Market research and analysis provides the information you need to identify marketing opportunities and problems, understand buyer behavior, and develop marketing strategies. This is an ongoing process, because your competitors, your industry, and your business's strengths are continually changing.

You don't have to rely solely on your intuition or spend thousands of dollars on market research and analysis; there is a great deal of free and valuable market information available to the entrepreneur. Your task is to define what you need to know, and seek answers in an organized and creative manner. With determination and follow-through, your market research and analysis will guide the creation of a successful and original marketing strategy.

Know your strengths and your competitors' weaknesses.

# Chapter 27
# MARKET OBJECTIVES, STRATEGIES, AND TACTICS

*About This Chapter:*
- *How objectives, strategies, and tactics fit together*
- *The marketing process*
- *Successful entrepreneurs use marketing aggressively*
- *Marketing strategy*
- *Choosing tactics*

## Introduction

Imagine a world without marketing. There are no displays of glossy new cars in a showroom. No friends-fly-free airline tickets. No speedy drive-through oil change service. No ten cent per minute telephone calls. No ATM card purchases at the grocery store.

We buy from the businesses that offer products and services like these because they give us what we want in the most convenient and cost-effective way. This chapter explains how to use marketing objectives, strategies, and tactics to create products and services that customers want.

*Customers vote with their dollars*

## How Objectives, Strategies, and Tactics Fit Together

### Strategic Focus on Customers' Needs

Suppose that a business believed its customers needed a better mousetrap, simply because it could build one. It might put huge amounts of time and money into designing a hand-carved mahogany mousetrap complete with digital readout, a detachable tripod, and an AM/FM radio that works even in the shower. It's safe to say that despite all the company's efforts, customers wouldn't buy the mousetrap. Why? Because they'd realize that the old-fashioned mousetrap works just as well (if not better), and costs a lot less! Businesses that set their objectives and strategies without first looking to their customers' needs are doomed to failure.

*Businesses use strategies and tactics to achieve their objectives*

Businesses that focus solely on improving productivity and designing new products around new technology suffer from a **product orientation**; they sell what they produce, rather than catering to their customers' needs.

In contrast, most successful businesses have a **customer orientation**; they design their marketing strategies around the needs of their customers. They carefully research and segment individual customer markets, then they customize their pricing, product, placement, and promotional strategies to fit these segments.

Successful businesses invariably tailor personal selling techniques to the buying styles of customers. This practice is so important that we've dedicated two entire chapters to it: Chapter 4 *A Customer-Driven Philosophy* and Chapter 32 *The Art of Selling*.

## The Marketing Process

Your marketing mix is only as strong as its weakest link

## Successful Entrepreneurs Use Marketing Aggressively

For most entrepreneurs, the goal of marketing strategy is to gain control of a tiny slice of a much larger market. Having fewer resources requires entrepreneurs to choose their battles carefully. As a small business, you have the flexibility and speed to use unconventional tools and strategies. There are no set rules or precedents to follow as you create your strategy. Be creative, innovative, even outrageous!

---◢---

*Tina's Custom Coffee Stand*

*The concept was new in Denver: An espresso coffee stand that offered coffee made from the best and freshest beans, mixed any way you can imagine. Simple espresso? No problem! Double no-foam latte with almond flavor? Sure! In Tina's words, her **core concept** was "To provide high-quality coffee the way people want it."*

*Tina's stand was located on the ground floor of a high-rise office building in downtown Denver. Her target customer profile? The coffee-loving business person who likes to network and schmooze. Her customers would come from her building and others nearby. She envisioned her coffee stand as the perfect place for customers to get the espresso drink they wanted while enjoying time away from the office. Tina's goal was to be the most customer-friendly, classy espresso stand in her area.*

## Marketing Objectives

Before you can set your marketing objectives, you must take the following steps:

### Clarify customer needs

Your market research collected raw information about who your customers are, where they live, what they spend, and why they buy. Now, condense this information into short, clear statements and draw up a **customer profile** that clearly describes, in as much detail as possible, who your customer is.

No business has endless resources to experiment with different concepts and marketing mixes, so make sure that your customer profile perfectly fits your core marketing concept. A **core concept** spells out your business's purpose in 15 words or less, and sets the direction for your marketing efforts.

### Set objectives

Marketing objectives arise from market research and market analysis. Suppose you estimate your market to be worth $200,000 in sales each year; you might decide that a realistic marketing objective would be to control 15% of that market, or have $30,000 in sales in the next 12 months. Or, because of fierce competition, your marketing objective might be to have a certain number of customers in the first six months. Other marketing objectives include:

- Achieving a percentage growth rate in sales, customers, or market share
- Adding more variations of existing products to existing markets
- Entering a new market with an existing product
- Introducing a new product
- Diversifying into different areas of business

### Setting boundaries for your objectives

Setting boundaries around your marketing objectives will sharpen your focus. These boundaries might include specific sales targets in units, dollars, or market percentage. Here are some useful boundaries to consider:

- Create a timetable for your promotional, pricing, product, and distribution strategies, and choose points in time at which you'll measure and reevaluate these strategies.

Marketers continually challenge and revise their goals and strategies

- Establish performance goals and standards for each marketing strategy. How many sales will it generate? How much time or money will it save? How many new customers will it attract? How many new distributors will it produce?
- Create budgets for your promotional, pricing, product, and distribution strategies. Decide how much to spend on each marketing tool over a specific period of time, how to track and tally expenses, and how much money to reallocate if the need arises.
- Evaluate your marketing strategies by asking how successful each element of the marketing mix has been. Is your product satisfying customer needs? Are you effectively using service to enhance your product? Is your pricing method profitable? Is your distribution network cost-effective, and does it perform as you planned it would? Are your promotional messages hitting your intended targets? Are they generating sales while staying within your budget?

———————————◆———————————

*Starbuck's coffee was a couple of blocks away, and always had a line. Tina knew her service had to be faster and more personal than theirs.*

*Tina's customers wanted fast, excellent service, and they wanted their espressos made exactly to their liking. She was the nearest espresso source for the 1,600 people who worked in her building and the three adjacent buildings.*

*She estimated that in these four buildings there was a total of 250 espresso drinkers, each of whom drank at least one coffee drink per day. She had to earn these people's loyalty quickly and completely! Tina's* **marketing objective** *was to control 60 percent of this market within six months, which would give her 150 regular customers.*

———————————◆———————————

## Marketing Strategy

There are many different ways to achieve your marketing objectives; several of the most useful are listed below.

### Segmenting Your Market

Businesses commonly divide their market into **market segments**; these are groups of customers with similar needs and characteristics. Unlike mass marketing, which aims to sell a single product to as broad a group of customers as possible, the purpose of market segmentation is to identify a **target market**, which is the market segment whose needs a business tries to anticipate and satisfy.

You'll recognize your prime target market if it:

- Is large enough to generate profits
- Has unique characteristics and is measurable and definable

**Control is critical to successful marketing**

- Has growth potential
- Is accessible
- Has needs that are not being met

To segment markets, group your potential customers by needs, desired benefits, behavior, and lifestyle characteristics. Using these criteria, try to divide your prospective customers into three or four viable segments. Which of these segments is the most attractive? Which one would you like to focus on first? Second? Third?

*Tina did research by talking with others in the business, reading beverage industry journals, and attending a gourmet food and beverage exposition. She discovered that there were many different types of customers within the espresso drinking population. Based on this information, she segmented her morning customers into three segments with the following names:*

- *"The high-caffeine, high-calorie Herberts" preferred traditional espresso drinks and sweet snacks = 50% of her market*

- *"The high-caffeine, no-calorie Susans" preferred espresso drinks with low- or nonfat milk, and healthy fruit or nonfat snacks = 40% of her market*

- *"The decaf, low/no calorie 'healthy' Heathers" preferred decaf coffee drinks with low- or nonfat milk, healthy fruit or nonfat snacks = 10% of her market*

*These segments and their numbers guided Tina in stocking and promoting her coffee stand. After a month in business, it became clear that her information was on target.*

A **niche market** is a small slice of a larger market. It has distinct characteristics and needs, but is usually too small to support large, established businesses. For this reason, niche markets provide unique opportunities for entrepreneurs; it is much easier to target niches than to enter a mass market.

## Positioning Your Product or Service

**Product positioning** determines which niche your product will fill. The positioning statement communicates the exceptional benefits and features of your product, and tells your target customer exactly why he or she should buy from you rather than from your competitors.

As you create your positioning statement, ask yourself if your offering and its positioning in the market:

- Offers a benefit to your target audience that really matters
- Delivers a real benefit
- Truly separates you from your competitors
- Is unique and difficult to copy

A major difference between business success and failure is market strategy

Segmentation strategy: a football team doesn't try to tackle all players on the opposite team, just the quarterback, running back, or the receiver

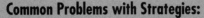

## Common Problems with Strategies:
- Not sticking with the strategy long enough
- Not testing the strategy before implementation
- Not challenging the assumptions and data on which the strategy is based
- Not focusing the strategy on specific goals
- Not adequately controlling the budget for strategy implementation
- Not understanding what customers value

A crystal-clear positioning statement can be the key to all marketing efforts

Clever entrepreneurs don't settle on the first or even the second positioning statement they come up with; they keep searching for the perfect positioning statement until they are completely satisfied. Excellent positioning doesn't come easily. It demands that you look at a lot of information and think clearly. The better you understand your market and your customers, the closer you'll come to the perfect positioning statement.

### Identifying Your Competitive Advantage

Your business's **competitive advantage** comes from offering more value to your customers than your competitors. Value can come from, among other things, a higher quality product, lower prices, better service, or more convenient distribution. Some additional examples of competitive advantage are:

- A new technology
- A specialized customer niche
- Unique distribution channels
- Production cost advantages due to better sourcing, location, or processes
- A stronger base of financial resources through cheaper debt
- A unique brand identity

If you are able to provide more innovative and personalized customer service, you have a competitive advantage over your larger competitors. Therefore, you might position your business accordingly (provided, of course, that you are certain your customers value personal service, and that you do in fact have the ability to deliver it).

In some cases, a business may decide not to enter a given market because it cannot find a position that gives it a competitive advantage.

*Tina had a powerful competitive advantage. She was conveniently located, and offered truly personalized service. Both of her nearest competitors positioned themselves differently; Starbuck's aimed to serve many customers very quickly, while the espresso cafe around the corner was a neighborhood "hang-out" joint. Tina's cart was different; she positioned her business to be the highest quality, most personalized coffee service around. What tactics did she use to achieve this? She knew all her customers by name. She kept a Rolodex file for all of her regular customers. On*

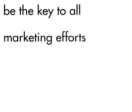

*each card she noted the customer's favorite drink and birthday. She also gave out "frequent sipper" punch cards. Her customers got a point each time they bought an espresso, and at ten points they got a free one. Through her use of the "frequent sipper" program and old-fashioned friendly service, Tina created powerful customer loyalty.*

## Choosing Tactics

Marketing tactics are the specific actions businesses take to produce, price, place, and promote their products or services.

Measuring the results of your marketing tactics improves the effectiveness of your marketing budget by allowing you to separate the winning tools and strategies from the losers.

How can small businesses do this? Easy. Ask your customers where they heard of you. You can ask them in person, in a brief questionnaire, or train salespeople to inquire as they take orders.

Chapters 28 through 31 *Product, Price, Promotion,* and *Placement* discuss each element of the marketing mix in greater detail. These chapters also outline specific marketing tactics for entrepreneurs.

*Just as Tina needed a strategy to guide her selection of product offerings, her pricing, and her placement, she needed a shrewd promotional strategy to help achieve her objective of controlling 60% of her market, and to communicate to her customers her position as the best, most personalized espresso provider around.*

*With the help of a graphic designer, Tina created the "Espresso Update." This short, easy-to-read page contained information on the "bean of the week" and a coupon for a discounted espresso drink. Tina updated it frequently and faxed it to customers late in the afternoon so they could redeem the coupon first thing in the morning. Later, when her goal was to increase her afternoon sales, she began faxing coupons to her customers at two o'clock in the afternoon.*

### The Importance of Consistency

When implementing market strategies and tactics, persistence is of utmost importance. You may be lucky enough to see instant results, but more likely, it will take considerable time and effort.

Maybe those flyers you distributed last week haven't yielded any new customers, or that promotional package you sent to your distributors hasn't increased orders as much as you'd forecasted, but don't get discouraged. Give your marketing tools a chance to work! While some marketing tactics deliver instant gratification in the form of more sales, others might take six months or a year to yield their bounty. Unless you give them the time to work, you'll never know if they *do* work.

## NxLEVEL™ TECH TIP

With the success of Internet auction firms like eBay and Amazon.com, some entrepreneurs are test-marketing their products at auctions in order to see what people are willing to pay, and how buyers react to their products. You can sell the same item over and over again at an auction site, varying the pictures, opening bid, and description; this may tell you which marketing messages get the most response, and which prices are seen as reasonable. This is an inexpensive means of collecting feedback and gauging your customers' willingness to pay, and unlike many other marketing strategies, it can bring in money while you're doing it! The drawback? It can be hard to find any rhyme or reason in buying patterns at Internet auctions, and the information you gain can seem meaningless in the absence of any solid grounds for comparison with your target population. Still, if you find that every time you offer your product at an auction, it sells for at least 10% more than your tentative retail price, it's a good indication that you can afford to raise your price!

## Conclusion

Why do you need marketing? Because without it, you won't know what to sell, where to sell, whom to sell to, or what price to charge. Researching markets, identifying your target customer, and positioning your product or service to maximize your competitive advantage are crucial to marketing success. Having done these things, selling becomes much easier.

By understanding and utilizing marketing objectives, strategies, and tactics, you will create a business that can take on the competition…and win!

# Chapter 28
# PRODUCT

*About This Chapter:*
- *What is a product?  What is a service?*
- *Branding your product or service*
- *Product entry strategies*

## Introduction

Why do we buy products and services?  Because they meet basic survival needs like eating, safety, or shelter.  We also buy products that make our lives easier, make us look or feel better, or project an image we like.  We buy to influence other people, and to feel differently about ourselves.

Entrepreneurs must think creatively and expansively about what their products represent to their customers.  For example, a ski hat might be the warmest on the market, but how does it look and feel?  How durable is it?  What image does its label communicate? Does the manufacturer back up the hat with a return policy? A business that understands the many facets of buying behavior is in the strongest position to succeed.

The purpose of this section is to help you create a product strategy.  It describes how to create a plan for what you will offer, how you will package it, and what services will enhance it.

## What is a Product?  What is a Service?

Technically speaking, a product is a bundle of attributes and benefits designed to satisfy customer needs.  A product can be a service, too.  Services deliver benefits like time savings, convenience, expertise, labor, or comfort.  A product can even be a combination of a tangible item and intangible services.

Products and services often do much more for us than they were designed to do.  Laptop computers make word processing away from the office possible, but they also make us feel up-to-date, "plugged in," and more in control of our work schedules.  The personalized prescription service at your local pharmacy allows you to receive the medicine you need, when you need it; but it also gives you the feeling that you are safe and cared for.

## The Product Basics

The first thing that a business must decide is what products and services to offer. For the entrepreneur, this idea usually comes from a hobby, an area of expertise, or professional experience. The best product ideas are those that meet existing or new customer needs in innovative ways, improve upon an existing product or improve its packaging or promotion.

*Your product line*

A **product line** is a group of products offered by a single company. Kellogg's various breakfast cereals; Boeing's line of jets; and the gravel, seedlings, soil, and shovels at your local garden supply store are all examples of product lines. The auto mechanic who repairs used Nissans and Toyotas is an example of someone who offers a line of services.

All businesses must decide how many products to offer, whether to add new products, and how to position their product lines. These are decisions regarding product strategy; they set the medium- and long-term direction for a business's products.

Another strategic decision is the **depth** of the product line. This describes the number of different sizes, models, or flavors within the product line. A bakery that decides to add new types of doughnuts is extending the depth of its product line.

The **breadth** of the product line describes the diversity of products a business offers. A bakery that decides to branch out and offer frozen pizza crusts and bread sticks is extending the breadth of its product line. Adding new products can be risky, particularly for new businesses. New products require marketing and operational skills beyond the business's core competencies. That's why it is important to revisit your business's strengths and your long-term market objectives before extending a product line.

*Select a product or service you are interested in, or one that is in your area of expertise*

---

*Catharine Paine managed several real estate properties outside Portland, Oregon. She managed them very well; she knew how to deal with clients and was familiar with legal restrictions, tax issues, and environmental and safety codes. In the spring of 1996, she had the opportunity to join a partner in developing a chain of 1950s-style hamburger and malt shops. Her partner also came from the commercial real estate industry, so they figured that between the two of them they could find prime locations, build cost-effective and attractive structures, and manage their properties expertly. They moved quickly, and two months later their first restaurant was open in time for summer.*

*Fifteen months later, they were out of business.*

*What happened? Catharine and her partner knew everything about real estate, but nothing about dealing with vendors, food preparation, selling, staff training, and customer service. They were completely reliant on the manager they'd hired to run the restaurant. They spent all of their time dealing with property management issues and scouting out their new locations.*

*By the time they realized their mistake, it was too late. They were entering the fall season, sales were slowing, and their revenues for their second summer were simply not enough to carry the business through the winter.*

---◆---

The lesson? Know your area of expertise and your capabilities. Perfect what you are doing first, then expand incrementally while building upon your strengths. You can learn many new things, but not all at once. Pace yourself!

### Where do new product ideas come from?

Skillful adaptation means learning from the mistakes and successes of others. For instance, competitors can be a valuable source of inspiration for new products. In many cases, it is the second, third, or even fourth imitator who succeeds with someone else's product idea. The fourth imitator succeeded because he or she was able to learn from the mistakes of others. Investigate products that your competitors have introduced and abandoned. Why did they abandon them? What were the product's strengths and weaknesses? What can you "borrow" from those ideas?

## Recipe for the Perfect Product Mix

Clever businesses constantly look at the tangible and intangible benefits their products deliver. Why? To make sure they're hitting their target audience with the right product. If they aren't, they work quickly to revise their product offerings, using market research to keep track of who and where their customers are, and what their lifestyles are like.

The next section identifies the major elements of the product mix. These variables are just as important for a small business as they are for a large business.

## Packaging

Distinctive packaging helps to communicate your product's image and attract your target customers' attention. Businesses that offer a line of products often design similar packaging (shape, color, size) in order to tie the line together in the minds of customers. Packaging also serves the basic function of protecting products, and providing information to customers about use, ingredients, quantity, and expiration date.

Clever packaging design can also increase sales. Many businesses achieve success by devising new ways to package existing products. By changing the packaging, they reposition the product in the minds of customers, hit new customer segments, and even open new channels of distribution.

Consider these examples:

- Coffee offered in single-serving pouches
- Business computers made user-friendly and repackaged as personal computers
- A container of mixed wildflower seeds sold as "Garden In a Can"
- Shower gel in a tube with a hook on the end

- Soap on a rope
- Toothpaste in a stand-up container
- Dijon mustard in a squeezable container
- Juice in a box
- Sunblock on a string worn around the neck
- Popcorn in a pouch for microwave cooking

## Service Enhancements

Service is one of the least expensive and best ways for small businesses to compete with larger businesses. Why? Because small businesses enjoy much closer customer contact than larger competitors. Customers would rather be treated like a valued friend than like a number, and most are willing to pay a little extra for the pleasure!

Consider the service ideas below and think creatively to come up with some of your own.

### Customer Service Tricks
- Know and greet your customers by name!
- Compile a customer database with (at least) each customer's name, birthdate, special requests, and usual purchases.
- Offer free or low-priced delivery.
- Set up a fax and phone help/information number.
- Create a "frequent customer" program, with rewards for repeat purchases.
- Create a colorful, brief, informative customer newsletter.
- Attach helpful tips and tailored promotional messages to invoices.
- Have convenient, flexible hours that fit your customers' schedules.
- Offer free, convenient parking.
- Give away free samples.
- Send birthday greetings and offer birthday discounts.
- Offer free demonstrations and installations.

## Making Profits with Mini-Marketing

Many businesses are shifting away from mass markets in favor of **mini-markets** that demand customization and direct interaction with customers. Mini-marketers know their customers individually by name, address, telephone number, income, lifestyle, and brand preferences.

Mini-marketing is a product of the new information economy, and it offers great opportunities for entrepreneurs. Thanks to computers, fax machines, and the Internet, businesses can know their customers as never before, and take the guesswork out of creating marketing strategies.

How do entrepreneurs go about using mini-marketing?  By compiling a customer database.  This can be a simple Rolodex of names or a computer database (many inexpensive and easy-to-use database programs are available).  Being aware of who your customers are and what they buy allows you to deliver the type of service they need.

---

*A perfect example of mini-marketing comes from brothers Jason and Matthew Olim, founders of The CD Guys, an Internet-based business that sells compact discs.  They offer the latest CD releases, but they also offer something traditional music retailers don't: expert, detailed information about nearly any recorded music or musician, and truly customized service.  Using their own software, they "follow" customers who browse through the Web site's pages of artists and information.  Simultaneously, they provide promotional and informational messages tailored to fit individual customers.*

*The CD Guys group their customers based on their purchases and interests.  Post-purchase, they follow up with their customers via e-mail to share information about new releases and sales promotions.  Their strategy has paid off!  They registered 70,000 customers in their first five months, and average almost 13,000 visitors to their Web site each day.  The key to their success? Aggressive, highly targeted marketing!*

---

## Branding Your Product or Service

A **brand** is a name or symbol that represents a product.  Evian water, the Saturn car, the Bic pen, and STP motor oil are familiar examples of brands.  A **brand image** is communicated by a product's benefits, its packaging, its advertising, and the services delivered along with it.  In order to differentiate their products from all the similar products on the market, small businesses must create a unique brand image.  An established brand associated with a quality product is a very valuable asset!

**Branding** means telling the "story" of your business and your product in a compelling and colorful way—one that will give people reasons to buy your product instead of someone else's. Although you lack the resources of larger competitors, you can create powerful branding strategies by learning from powerhouses like Proctor and Gamble, Kraft, and Coca-Cola. These corporations have succeeded in part by creating products with distinct "personalities" that often become as important to the customer as the product itself.

For instance, think of all the Coca-Cola commercials you've seen and heard in your life. Think of the catchy advertising jingles, the bold red-and-white cans, the billboards showing ice-cold glasses of bubbly Coke. The "story" of Coca-Cola has been told to us countless times and in countless ways...many times without our knowing it! The result? All of us know what a can of Coke looks and feels like, and many of us will seek it out even when there are many other drinks to choose from.

This is branding at work. In the case of Coke, it has been amazingly successful. In fact, some say that Coca-Cola is the only true global brand—it is instantly recognizable by more people in the world than any other!

### Choosing a Name
The first step in establishing a brand is usually taken—sometimes unwittingly—when the owner chooses a name for his or her company and product. What makes a good name?

- It should suggest product benefits (e.g., Sunkist, Mr. Clean, or Beautyrest mattresses)
- It should fit the brand image: Nissan Pathfinder (adventure), Round Table Pizza (cozy food for friends and families), Ding Dongs (silly, playful food for kids)
- It should be easy to pronounce and recognize
- It should not be previously registered with another company

### Choosing a Brand
How do you decide what your brand should be? As with most marketing decisions, you should begin with your target customers. What makes them buy your type of product? Is it a luxury or a necessity? What motivates your target customers overall? Are they concerned with being trendy? Are they budget-conscious? Are they hurried? What product traits or features do they value? Does your product's price, authentic quality, freshness, durability, flexibility, or ease of use make it special enough to be bought regularly?

Your product's brand is also determined by your company, and people who work there. What kind of business are you running? What "personality" do you want your business to project? What message do you want to communicate? The purpose of asking questions like these is to find those qualities that will instantly mean something to your customers, and make them the core of your brand.

"Coca Cola is the most valuable brand in the world." —Fortune Magazine

Brands give people an emotional reason to buy

Next, write your branding statement. For a small ice-cream maker, this might be: "Sarah's Ice Cream is about being happy, youthful, and spontaneous." Having come up with a branding statement, make sure that this statement guides everything your company does, so that your brand image is clear, consistent, and immediately obvious to your customers. Your company logo, company colors, packaging, labels, business cards, retail space, and even your pricing and promotional messages, should communicate your brand in the same way.

### Brand management

How do you keep your brand image fresh and meaningful to your audience? That's where **brand management** comes in.

Consider Levi's: branding is a huge part of their strategy for success. How else can the company make its blue jeans stand out from the hundreds of other pants available to consumers? When you take a closer look at Levi's branding strategy, it makes a lot of sense. Their primary target market for blue jeans is teenagers, a very fashion-conscious group. This means that their business depends on staying in tune with teenagers, and being responsive to teens' fickle notions about what is "cool." Since this changes from one year (or one day) to the next, Levi's pays close attention to what teens are watching, listening to, doing, reading, and wearing. Then it creates products, commercials, and retail displays that reflect these trends.

> "It is not beneath the dignity of any business person to imitate, adapt, and improve upon the innovations of other companies." —Gordon A. Baty, author and entrepreneur

## Tips for Creating Your Brand

- **Create a plan.** How will the product be conceptualized, packaged, distributed, and promoted?
- **Design your product with care.** Think about your customers' values and preferences, then use shape, color, design, and potential uses to differentiate your product.
- **Name your product with power.** Buzz words are the key to consumer recognition and recall.
- **Package your product creatively.** Use the package to convey your message.
- **Look at the big picture.** Everything that has to do with your business should project a consistent identity.
- **Use merchandising.** Pay attention to product presentation on the shelf.
- **Expand your offerings.** Use product array to create a theme.
- **Consider what you can vary in your marketing or product mix.** Remember that certain elements must stay the same to be true to your brand.
- **Watch your competitors.** What values do their brands offer?

Levi's commitment to this young and fast-moving market segment means that it must be quick to perceive trends, and must respond to them at lightning speed. It must design new styles of jeans and new commercials to sell them, and get its jeans into stores before the next trend comes along. As you can see, Levi's brand guides a great deal of its operating procedures!

### Brand is reputation and relationship

What a brand really boils down to is reputation, which is earned through experience and interaction with customers. However and wherever your company interacts with customers, that is where your brand and your reputation are established. This is why knowing your company's personality and values—and by extension, your brand—is so important: it gives you the script for the role that you must play every time you interact with your customers.

## Product Entry Strategies

You've spent weeks or months developing the vision for your business, and even more time analyzing your market. You've designed your product or service, positioned it, and formulated just the right marketing mix to support it. But how do you introduce it to the market?

Entrepreneurs often have very slim budgets with which to introduce their offerings to the market, so they must use all their wiles, energy, and creativity at this early phase of the business. Every new product, whether it is an unprecedented innovation or a simple revamp of an existing product, requires a careful entry strategy to ensure its success.

The primary purpose of a marketing strategy is to establish a new brand or product with customers, wholesalers, distributors, and retailers. This means building a distribution network to make the product readily available to customers, and then persuading customers to try it for the first time.

*Think of your entry strategy as an introduction to new friends...your customers*

---

**Recipe for successful product introduction:**
- **Overall marketing objective.** Establish distribution, introduce the product, encourage trial.
- **Product strategy.** Differentiation from competitors; highlight unique advantages and benefits.
- **Promotional strategy.** Build brand awareness and differentiate product "personality."
- **Distribution strategy.** Build distribution network to make product easily available.
- **Pricing strategy.** Start at lower prices to encourage trial, then slowly increase prices.

Customers are attracted to new products that have a price, quality, or service advantage over other products. When businesses establish a new product in the market, they must use each element of the marketing mix to communicate the same message and support their efforts. This ensures a consistent, more memorable message for customers.

A wonderful moment occurs when a new product enters its growth period and becomes profitable. This is a time to savor your success...but not for too long! If your product is truly innovative, competitors will take notice and attempt to offer similar products. Even if it is not an innovative product, this is the time to consolidate your gains and reinforce your product's position. Focus your marketing efforts on getting repeat purchases and continuing to attract first-time users. Successful strategies include:

- Thank-you notes to customers
- Following up on customer calls and visits to gauge satisfaction
- Newsletters with company and new product information
- Mailings to past customers, offering discounts tailored to prior purchases
- Frequent buyer programs with discounts

Such strategies remind your customers why they bought from you in the first place, and encourage them to buy from you again. Remember: It is five times cheaper to sell to existing customers than to go out and find new ones!

## Conclusion

Your product strategy begins when you decide what products or services to offer, based on what your market research has shown you about your customers' needs and tastes. Next, find ways to make your packaging, warranties, image, and service enhance your product. Once you identify this mix and the unique "personality" of your product, stick with it. After you test your customer and market with periodical market research, commitment to a sound branding strategy is one of your best tools for success.

It costs more to get new customers than to keep existing customers

# Chapter 29
# PRICE

*About This Chapter:*
- *Price and profit*
- *Determining your costs*
- *Setting your prices*

## Introduction

For businesses of all types, pricing is the ultimate measure of marketing skill. It requires marketers to juggle their costs of doing business, the price sensitivity of their target customers, and the impact of their prices on competitors. A good pricing strategy maximizes profits while providing the greatest possible value to customers.

This section introduces the major calculations involved in pricing your products, and reviews the pricing strategies most applicable to entrepreneurial ventures.

## Price and Profit

This might seem too obvious to point out, but price is the key to your product's profitability. **Profit** is total revenue minus your total costs. **Total revenue** is your price times the number of units you sell. Therefore, price directly affects profits.

In the mid-1970s, price became the most important element of a business's marketing mix. Economic recessions, foreign competition, market fragmentation, new price structures, and government deregulation of large industries (such as airlines and telephone service providers) created more intense price competition than ever before in American business history.

Before you price your product or services, you must thoroughly research the standard pricing practices of your industry. Your market analysis should provide this information. You can also review trade journals and trade association documents, and talk with other firms in your industry.

Price: the key to

profitability

## Determining Your Costs

It doesn't matter how good you think your intuition is. Before you make any decisions about what to charge your customers, you need to know what it costs you to produce and deliver your product or service. This is especially important for sole proprietors who will have additional people working for them at some point.

## Basic Cost Concepts

**Fixed costs** are expenses that a business has regardless of the quantity of units it produces. For example, the cost of installing a commercial oven is the same regardless of the number of loaves of bread baked over the lifetime of the oven.

**Variable costs** are expenses that vary in direct relation to the amount of products produced (for example, the cost of labor and raw materials used to make the product, plus the cost of sales and distribution).

**Total costs** are the total expenses of producing and marketing a product. Total costs are the sum of total fixed costs and total variable costs.

### Typical Variable Costs
- Inputs and supplies
- Overtime wages
- Depreciation on equipment
- Sales commissions

### Typical Fixed Costs
- Salaries and wages
- Vehicle leases and maintenance
- Office equipment
- Marketing expenses
- Rent
- Utilities
- Payroll taxes
- Office supplies
- Machinery and equipment
- Land
- Insurance

**Break-even analysis** pinpoints the level at which total revenue equals total cost. As the volume of units sold increases beyond this **break-even point**, a business begins to earn profits. To identify your break-even point, calculate your costs and your revenue. Below are the basics of price calculations:

*Total revenue = Price x Quantity*

*Total cost = Total fixed costs + Average variable cost per unit x Quantity*

The break-even point occurs when:

*Price x Quantity = Total fixed costs + (Average variable costs x Quantity)*

Looking at the same equation a different way, the quantity needed to break even is:

$$\textit{Break-even quantity} = \frac{\textit{Total fixed costs}}{\textit{(Price - Average variable costs)}}$$

Sam Granville knew a great business opportunity when he saw one. One hot day in July of 1999, he passed a newly constructed house on the eastern shore of Maryland. The house stood out starkly on the large, nearly barren lot. The small maple and pine saplings around the house accentuated how empty the land looked. Sam thought that the property needed a mature shade tree to give it a sense of hominess and history.

His idea: expand his small landscaping business into a tree relocating business. The target customer: Owners of new houses and developers of subdivisions. His product: Beautiful, healthy, mature trees that would add badly needed charm to new construction sites.

Once he completed his preliminary market research, Sam began working on his marketing plan, and calculating the costs and prices for his services. He knew what the market would bear in terms of price, but what would it really cost him to relocate 1/2-ton trees?

Sam began by calculating the cost of moving a single tree. He estimated that on average, it would take him two to four hours to move a single tree. He figured that in his first six months, he would be able to move 30 trees a month. His costs broke down as follows:

| Variable Costs (per tree moved): | | |
|---|---|---|
| Labor (1 helper, 4 hours per tree @ $15.00/hour) | $ | 60.00 |
| 1 tree spade and tractor operator (3 hours @ $30.00/hour) | | 90.00 |
| Diesel fuel for crane & tractor (15 gallons per job @ $1.90/gallon) | | 28.50 |
| Fertilizer & burlap | | 250.00 |
| Tree | | 250.00 |
| Miscellaneous office expenses (phone, fax, supplies) | | 20.00 |
| **Total Variable Costs** | $ | 698.50 |
| **Fixed Costs (per month):** | | |
| Miscellaneous landscaping equipment (shovels, mini-tractor, winches) | $ | 2,000.00 |
| Office equipment (computer, desk, chair, etc.) | | 3,000.00 |
| Rent | | 300.00 |
| Tree spade lease payments | | 250.00 |
| Tractor lease payments | | 200.00 |
| **Total Fixed Costs** | $ | 5,750.00 |
| | | |
| Total cost of relocating 30 trees a month ($5,750.00 + 30 trees x $698.50) = | $ | 26,705.00 |
| Total revenue for relocating 30 trees ($1,500.00 x 30) | $ | 45,000.00 |
| **Net Profit** | $ | 18,295.00 |

*Note that Sam's fixed costs remain the same regardless of how many trees he moves. He has already leased his mechanized tree spade, and bought his computer and his landscaping equipment. However, his total costs rise over time because his variable costs (labor, gas, and trees) go up as he moves more trees.*

*Sam calculated his total revenue for a given price level. If he charged $1,500 per tree, and moved 30 trees a month, his revenue would be $45,000 per month. At 20 trees a month, his monthly revenue would be $30,000. Thus, Sam reaches his break-even point when he relocates between seven and eight trees. After that point, he begins to earn profit.*

*Sam's calculation for break-even quantity is below:*

$$\text{Break-even quantity} = \frac{\text{Total fixed cost}}{(\text{Price} - \text{Average variable cost})}$$

$$\text{Break-even quantity} = \frac{\$5,750.00}{(\$1,500.00 - \$698.50)} = 7.17 \text{ trees per month}$$

---

# Setting Your Prices

Setting your price begins with considering your pricing objectives. Are you primarily interested in your own cost issues, undercutting or matching your competitors' prices, or building customer demand and loyalty? Or are you aiming to achieve a particular return on your investment?

Carefully researching the effect of your prices—and adapting your strategy where necessary—will help you achieve any of the objectives listed above.

Three of the most common pricing strategies are described below. You should be aware of each of these strategies and the impact that prices will have on your customers and competitors. Pricing is not an exact science; often, businesses experiment with several different price levels before settling on a pricing strategy. They also may adjust their prices frequently (though not so often as to frustrate customers). Many entrepreneurs combine several of these approaches to reach the optimal pricing strategy.

### Cost-Based Pricing

Cost-based pricing is the most common, simple, and low-risk pricing method because it is based on a known factor—cost. Cost-based pricing requires that businesses total all of their costs and add a **target return** to determine the sale price. A target return is usually expressed as a percentage of total costs.

**Cost-based pricing** ignores the impact of consumer demand on prices. Thus, you might end up with a price that is out of sync with the market. Cost-based pricing tends to work well in industries in which consumer demand and competition are reasonably predictable.

*Sam Granville Calculates His Price Based On His Target Profit Margin*

*No doubt about it, Sam had a leg up on the competition. He had grown up on a fruit farm, and knew just about everything there was to know about caring for trees. He knew from his market research that he could charge an average of $1,500 per tree. But he wanted to calculate a price based on his costs and his target profit margin of 40%.*

*After calculating his costs, he decided to use cost-plus pricing for his services. This was the simplest method he knew, and he figured if he needed to change his strategy later, he could. Below are his calculations, which he based on moving 30 trees in one month, with a target profit margin of 40%. Sam used the following equation:*

$$\frac{(Units \times Variable\ cost\ per\ unit) + Fixed\ costs}{Units} \times Profit\ \%\ desired = Per\ unit\ price$$

$$\frac{(30\ trees \times \$698.50) + \$5,750.00}{30\ trees} \times 1.40\ Profit\ margin = \$1,246.00\ (price\ per\ tree)$$

## Competition-Based Pricing

Many businesses alter their prices based on competitors' prices. This is particularly common in large, highly competitive industries like airline travel, soda pop, and crude oil. The risk in this type of strategy is that your competitors' cost structure might be significantly different from your own.

**Follow-the-leader pricing** sets prices at the level of an industry's price leader. This pricing structure is common in industries that sell highly standardized products—like farm commodities, industrial raw materials, or computer floppy disks—because these industries tend to be dominated by a few large companies.

**Pegged pricing** establishes a business's prices in line with industry-wide norms; it tends to occur in industries in which there is no clear price leader. Businesses using this method might use the industry norm as a starting point, then offer a slightly higher (**premium**) or lower (**economy**) price to establish a niche within the industry. Having done this, the business works backwards to calculate if it can make an acceptable profit at that price level.

In pricing based on **projected responses by competitors**, businesses consider the response of their competitors prior to taking action. Businesses may set very low prices to discourage new competitors from entering the market, or they may set their prices at mid-range levels in order to discourage competitors from starting a price war.

You may want to develop some "what if" pricing scenarios based on anticipated competitor responses. For example: "If my competitor responds by lowering its prices, I can afford to lower prices by ___ percent."

Experimenting with different price levels is often nearly impossible for new businesses; it can take time and resources that the business just cannot afford. However, you do have a few options. For instance, you might try setting slightly different prices in different geographic areas, or creating intermediate models of your products so as to test the price sensitivity of your customers and competitors. You can also offer short-term discounts to see how the price affects demand for your products.

## Retail Price

Although retailers do not produce the goods they sell, they still have labor costs and overhead; their selling price must cover these costs and offer an acceptable level of profit. Retail price is generally established by multiplying the wholesale price by a given percentage. A retailer using a 25% mark-up would buy Sam's trees at $1,246.00 and sell them at $1,246.00 + $311.50, or $1,557.50. Many retailers double or triple the wholesale price.

## Consignment Selling

Consignment means placing your product in the custody of a retailer who pays you only after the product sells. The producer retains ownership of the products and is responsible for them until their sale. The producer and the retailer negotiate sales commissions and payment terms. The average commission is 25 to 40 percent of the wholesale price.

## Distributor Price

A distributor is an intermediary who buys a large volume of products at wholesale prices and resells them to retailers, who then offer the products to the end user. Because distributors buy in large quantities, they receive a volume discount, and then mark the product up by 25 to 40 percent, depending on the industry.

## Price Adjustments

**List price** is the "official" price that businesses charge, from which they subtract any discounts. The list price is seldom the same as the final selling price; adjustments are usually made to the **trade** or **distribution channel partners**, and to the final customer.

Businesses offer discounts of all types to buyers who meet criteria that reduce selling costs. Strategic discounting can increase sales or "even out" seasonal demand.

**Quantity discounts** are a powerful way for businesses to increase the amount of units they sell. Generally, businesses offer lower prices to customers who buy in bulk.

**Trade discounts** are given to distributors or representatives when they perform some of the marketing functions—such as advertising, promotions, or technical support to customers—ordinarily performed by the manufacturer. Trade discounts are often used as a leveraging tool for new products in distribution channels or retail outlets.

**Seasonal discounts** can encourage customers to make purchases during off-peak selling times, which helps to lower inventory levels when demand is down.

Businesses can offer **cash discounts** to customers who pay for purchases by cash rather than credit. This is often used by manufacturers and their distribution channel partners to encourage speedy payment of bills and to minimize accounts receivable.

## Coordinating Price with Other Elements of Your Marketing Mix

No matter which pricing strategy you use, it must be consistent with the other elements of your marketing mix. Summarized below are issues to consider as you link your price to the other three elements of your marketing mix:

- **Product strategy.** Is your price in line with your customers' perception of quality? If not, then you should consider lowering your prices, improving your quality, or increasing your efforts to educate customers about your product's quality.

- **Distribution strategy.** Is your product's price consistent with the image of your distribution channels? High-priced, premium products should be distributed selectively, while economy products should be distributed intensively to maximize their availability to larger, price-sensitive markets. Even more important, is your price distributor-friendly? Are you using distributor discounts to increase the chances that your distributors will effectively recommend and sell your product?

- **Promotional strategy.** Is your advertising message consistent with your product's price level? If yours is a premium product, is your advertising image one of quality and service? If it is an economy product, is your advertising image one of value? Are your sales promotions undercutting your pricing strategy and profitability? Are coupons or price discounts encouraging only short-term business by fickle customers?

## NxLEVEL™ TECH TIP

One of the benefits of the Internet is that it lets you search for products similar to yours, so that you can check out your competitors' pricing strategies. (You can even pose as a customer, and e-mail pertinent questions to your competitors!) For more general information on pricing strategies, try the following Web sites:

**How to Price Your Products and Services** (gopher:// www.sbaonline.sba.gov/00/business-development/general-information-and-publications/obd5.txt). This page from the Small Business Administration provides good, basic advice regarding pricing strategies.

**Internet Marketing** (http://www.popco.com/hyper/internet-marketing/). Until recently, the Internet Marketing discussion list was an active, free-flowing discussion of marketing on the Internet. It's gone now, but you can read the archives of these discussions at this site. They'll help you learn more about marketing your products or services on the Internet.

**Business Owner's Toolkit** (http://www.toolkit.cch.com/) has a great deal of information on pricing strategies, as well as links to sources of important secondary data, such as their "Power Tools" database.

Use the Internet to compare competitors' pricing

Businesses use market
research to "test the
waters" of customer
needs

### Common Pricing Errors

- Basing price on current, artificially low overhead costs instead of anticipating how overhead might rise over time.
- Assuming that because you are the newest competitor on the block, you must have the lowest prices.
- Trying to compete head-to-head on price with larger competitors. Try instead to offer higher quality, or more attentive service.
- Basing prices on manufacturing costs instead of the value of your product to consumers, which may be quite a bit higher!
- Failing to include in the price an allowance for warranty costs, future service, research and development costs, cost of capital, dealer discounts, and sales commissions.
- Ignoring the way customer demand for the product will change at different price levels. Would sales volume increase if you lowered prices by 10 or 20 percent?
- Failing to use some form of **market skimming**, in which you enter a market with a high price until you have satisfied demand or attracted competitors, then lower the price gradually.

## Conclusion

Pricing requires complete understanding of your customers, costs, and competition; and it can determine the success or failure of your product or service. It's no wonder that businesses spend so much time measuring costs and tracking their customers' reactions to different prices.

For entrepreneurs, the most critical element of pricing is understanding costs. Once you know exactly what your fixed and variable costs are, you can select the pricing method that is best for you. Different industries demand different pricing strategies. Try to understand the most common and effective practices in your industry, then tailor your strategy to fit your business. Pricing your product or service need not be confusing or intimidating—you can learn the basics and build your skills as you go!

# Chapter 30
# PROMOTION

*About This Chapter:*
- *The basics of promotional strategy*
- *Managing your promotions*

## Introduction

If you are starting or growing a business, you must use promotion to catch and hold people's attention. Even the best product or service won't sell if people don't know it exists! This chapter gives you the basic information that you will need to promote your business effectively.

## The Basics of Promotional Strategy

Like every other element of the marketing mix, successful promotion requires a strategy. How do you go about creating a promotional strategy? By selecting the mix of promotional tools you will use to communicate your message. The **promotional mix** comprises advertising, sales promotions, and publicity.

First, set your promotional objectives. If you are introducing an original product, your objectives will be quite different than if you are adding another product to your line, or competing in an established product category. Most entrepreneurial ventures introduce new products, or create a new spin on an existing product.

Your first objective is to make your target customers aware of your product. The goal? To attract a solid base of loyal customers who will spread the word about you to friends and neighbors.

Your promotional message is the beginning of your dialogue with your customer

---

**New Product Promotional Objectives**
- **Raise awareness** by focusing on advertising
- **Create positive attitude** through public relations, networking, advertising
- **Encourage product trial** through sales promotions, coupons, free samples
- **Influence existing buyers to buy and buy again** through powerful personal selling, advertising, consistent follow-up

## Advertising

Advertising is the most well known, expensive, and flashy method of communicating messages about a product, service, or company. Advertising messages may serve to raise awareness, influence customers to buy, or increase a product's visibility. You can use advertising to promote your individual products, your company's image, or both.

### The advertising planning process

Creating an effective advertising message can be expensive and time-consuming. Once you've decided to advertise, you must decide which media to use, what message to convey, which image to project, how often to run your message, and how much to spend. To get the most out of your advertising dollars, you should:

- **Identify your target audience.** Your target audience is defined by your market research and your market analysis. These findings should guide the content, style, and placement of your advertising. Review Chapter 26 *Market Research & Analysis*.

- **Set your objectives.** Typical advertising objectives are to reach a certain percentage of the target market, increase the target customer's awareness of your product/business, or achieve a certain level of sales. Setting clear goals will let you gauge whether you have gotten your money's worth after the fact. Industry sources, newspapers, and radio and television stations can provide good estimates of the monthly sales patterns for your industry. They know what their demographics are, which can help you to set realistic objectives.

- **Set your advertising budget.** Your advertising budget is part of your promotional budget. How much you allocate depends on your objectives and your resources. It also depends on how widely and how frequently you want your message to be heard.

- **Design your advertising strategy.** This is the most creative part of advertising management, and it relates directly to your positioning strategy. How will you encourage your customers to buy? What will your message and your medium be? Will you use humorous short radio spots to highlight how speedy your service is? Or will you use a simple, classy color image to convey premium quality?

---

**Advertisements contain most or all of the following elements:**
- Information about product benefits and characteristics
- Images and/or symbols that make a strong, positive, visual impression
- Emotional or rational appeals to buy or test a product
- Humor
- Spokespersons
- Competitor comparisons

---

### The Promotional Planning Process

Set Promotional Objectives

Assess Outside Factors

Develop a Promotional Strategy

Create Mix of Promotional Tactics

Design Mix of Promotional Tactics

Evaluate Results of Promotional Efforts

## Selecting Your Advertising Media

Media are the outlets that carry advertising messages, such as television, radio, magazines, newspaper, billboards, direct mail, or the Internet. Today, businesses have more choices of media than ever before; all of these options have distinct benefits and drawbacks. For most small businesses, the main criteria for selecting an advertising medium are cost, speed, and effectiveness.

- **Television ads** communicate through sound, color, and motion. Cable TV stations target viewers who have very specific interests, and their advertising rates are comparatively low. Home shopping channels are also a great way to promote and sell products with very little risk or expense.

- **Radio** provides flexible coverage of a wide range of audiences. You can choose the best time, day, and station to reach your target audience, and then hit them with multiple ads. The cost of radio advertising has risen much more slowly than any other major advertising medium, so local radio advertising can be a very cost-effective way to spread a message. Radio stations have staff and equipment to help produce ad spots, but be sure to write your own message; you don't want to sound just like everyone else!

- **Newspapers** are great for running short-term price promotions and coupon offers to very specific audiences. Newspapers reach a relatively upscale audience, and target specific geographic regions. By placing different coupon ads in various local papers, you can measure which is most effective. Newspaper ad salespeople can advise you on the best placement, day, size, and length of run for your ad.

- **Magazines** are a very effective way to reach a narrow target audience. There are magazines for just about every special interest you can imagine, and they are often read more than once by more than one person. Small businesses can often negotiate to use lower cost "remnant" space in magazines when it is available.

- **Direct marketing** is one of the least expensive (per sale generated), most flexible, and fastest growing advertising methods; it includes direct mail, door-to-door sales, telephone marketing, and online marketing. With these direct methods, businesses can target their audience, personalize their marketing, earn higher response rates, generate repeat sales, and compete with larger businesses.

- **Signage:** Billboards, buses, parking meters, gas pumps, and even turnstiles at sporting arenas can display your advertising message. These are among the least expensive media. Messages must be clear, short, and quickly noticeable to be effective. Carefully placing signs where target customers live, shop, and commute is an excellent way to hit a target market.

- **Yellow pages:** People who use the yellow pages are especially hot prospects because they are in a buying mood. Businesses may place listings in different sections. One advantage of this medium is that small businesses can appear to be as big as their larger competitors.

- **Classified ads** are less expensive than traditional ads and can contain more information. Classified ads are often offered at a discount to advertisers who use frequent listings. If you see classified ads in your local paper or favorite magazine for your type of business, you could profit from placing ads there too.

Reach the most people the most times for the least cost

How can you select the right medium for your message and your budget? You should judge all media by the exposure they offer to your target customer. **Reach** describes the percentage of your target market that sees your message. **Frequency** describes the number of times individuals in your target market see your message.

Different advertising media can have different impacts depending on your audience and your advertising content. By using reach and frequency information, you can estimate how much it costs to advertise per customer you contact. This gives you a standard with which to compare your advertising choices.

Once you've selected your advertising tools, you need to decide when to use each one. If yours is a seasonal product, you should coordinate your message with your customers' purchase cycles. Advertising messages can be aired in a few large bursts at scheduled intervals, or spread over a period of time to maintain customer awareness. For businesses that wish to introduce a new product, the frequency with which an advertising message is heard is more important than the reach. It takes several exposures to a message before people even absorb it, much less take action on it! Businesses use a "burst" strategy when they want to create an early and intense impact on customer awareness. Seasonal businesses and businesses offering short-term sales promotions often rely on this strategy.

## NxLEVEL™ TECH TIP

**Most of us have received dozens of promotional ballpoint pens, keychains, coffee mugs, and baseball caps from companies interested in winning or keeping our business.**
If you want get the word about your business out to the public and increase customer goodwill, but aren't too excited by the thought of manufacturing dime-a-dozen promo items like those mentioned above, have a look at the possibilities listed on the **Nerd World Media Internet Subject Index** (http://www.nerdworld.com/nw929.html). The is one of the largest hand-categorized indexes of the Internet, featuring over 300,000 Web sites organized into 10,000 categories. It offers hundreds of links to every conceivable type of promotional product manufacturer. You can find inflatable blimps, golf balls, phone cards, belt buckles, cookies, screwdrivers, umbrellas, pasta, air fresheners, bottled water, holograms, and thousands of other items...all of which can be imprinted with your company name and logo!

*Sales promotions*

Businesses that sell consumer products offer **consumer promotions**, which are short-term (usually) incentives to encourage buying. They print coupons, organize sweepstakes or contests, and offer free samples or rebates to encourage new use of their products or services.

---

*Vance's Vans and Trucks bought and sold used vehicles in Cheyenne, Wyoming. Business was always slow in early summer, and they expected a big influx of used trucks for the fall. Vance needed to come up with a sales promotion that would increase cash flow through the slow season and make room for new inventory in the fall. He decided to invite customers to trade in tractors, trailers, and even snow plows towards the purchase of a truck. His only restriction was that the vehicles had to be less than five years old and in good working condition. Vance had a cousin in the tractor business, so he could resell the equipment more easily than his customers could.*

*Vance's promotion would last three days, on the weekend following the Fourth of July. His target audience? Men between the ages of 21 and 50. His advertising medium? The local country & western radio station. With radio ads running three times a day (at a cost of $300 each), he felt sure that he could get the message out to at least 50% of his target market in the week preceding his sale. He was right! By the end of the sale, he had nearly cleared his lot of trucks, and made a deal to sell to his cousin 20 snow plows, 13 trailers, and a lawn mower.*

---

**Trade promotions** are incentives that businesses offer to retailers and wholesalers for stocking their products. These can include cash allowances for promotional efforts, or discounts for volume or seasonal purchases. Some businesses even hold sales contests or sweepstakes to encourage channel members to make their best effort to sell a product.

## Importance of Different Promotional Elements in Different Industries

|  | Consumer Goods | Services | Industrial Products |
|---|---|---|---|
| Advertising | Med/High | Med | Med |
| Sales Promotions | High | Med | Med |
| Personal Selling | Low | High | High |
| Publicity | Low/Med | Low/Med | Low |

## Direct marketing

Any direct marketing strategy must begin with the right list of recipients. These lists can be bought from brokers or generated in-house. The goal of direct marketing is to make it as easy as possible for customers to buy.

Mail order catalogues are another story altogether. Undertaking a full-scale catalogue is best for businesses that have a large enough base of actual or prospective customers (in the range of 25,000) to pay for quality catalogue design, production, and a large mailing.

Red and black are the
best direct mail colors

**Tips for creating a powerful direct mailing include:**
- Use brightly colored envelopes and high-quality graphics
- Write your recipient's name in LARGE print
- Do several repeat mailings
- Ask for the order in the headline
- Make your offer very hard to refuse
- Compile or purchase your mailing lists carefully
- Keep your writing simple and direct
- In your text, compel your reader to action
- Include an order form
- Make it easy to read, convenient, and full of variety
- Print important information in a second color
- Include an easy-to-use response form
- The best months for direct mail are January, February, and October
- Offer free gifts; emphasize your warranty or "no questions asked" return policy
- Project your response rate and plan for supplies accordingly

Smaller businesses can create a simpler, shorter catalogue, but the commitment is nearly as large. Printing prices go down the more catalogues you print, so this project is not for the unprepared or uncommitted. Here's some more information about catalogues:

- Black and white printing is the least expensive
- 25,000 copies of a two-color catalogue cost approximately $20,000, or 80 cents each including postage.
- First try a smaller test run, then increase volume as you smooth out problems

## Public relations

Public relations refers to the organized efforts that businesses undertake to present themselves in a positive way to customers, government officials, stockholders, lenders, and other businesses.

**Publicity** is unpaid communication about a business or its product or service in the mass media. Because it is unpaid, publicity is the most credible of promotional sources; this makes it an excellent promotional tool for small businesses.

How can you generate publicity? By preparing a **press release** for radio, newspapers, magazines, or local television stations. Join your local trade associations, Chamber of Commerce, and community clubs; and take or make opportunities to speak in public or write articles for newsletters. Other great ways of generating publicity for your business include:

- Co-sponsoring local sporting or charity events
- Participating in local fundraisers by donating prizes or time
- Hiring local students to be interns
- Giving lectures to local trade organizations or chambers of commerce
- Sending your small business story to your local newspaper or trade association

*Publicity can be the most credible promotional message of all*

### Trade shows

One of the best ways to promote your offerings to the customers most likely to need them is at trade shows, exhibits, or industry fairs. The people who attend these events are serious prospects who have come to do some pre-purchase information gathering.

*Everything you do at trade shows should be geared towards generating sales!*

### Trade Show Tips

- Visit shows before you display at one; this way, you can gather information on competitors, selling techniques, new products, and display tricks.
- Research and categorize your prospects before you attend: find out which companies or buyers are your best prospects, drop them a note ahead of time telling them where you'll be (enclose a map or a picture of your booth), and invite them to stop by for a sample or gift.
- Design and print brochures or fliers.
- Create catchy displays that fit your marketing image: use video, film, slides, music, lights.
- Visit trade show display companies ahead of time to get ideas.
- Attract passersby with merchandise, selling abilities, and your charm.
- Set up your own booth, or share a booth with a seller of compatible products.
- Staff your booth with enough friendly, charismatic, knowledgeable people to give quality attention to prospects.
- Throw a party for hot prospects in your hotel suite.
- Create a trade show budget and track all expenses.
- Follow up on all prospects within ten days.

### Word of mouth

Word of mouth is a positive reputation spread from person to person—the happy result of promotional momentum created over time. Products that perfectly satisfy your customers' needs—complemented by creative, excellent service—make a lasting impression that your customers will gladly pass on to others.

Word of mouth advertising can grow out of messages that originated in other media like radio, direct mail, or magazines. Distributing brochures to every customer and creating a catalogue reinforces your relationship with customers and increases the likelihood that they will mention you to others. The best way to get recommendations? Ask for them!

### Networking

Chances are, if you've got the gumption to start your own business, you also have the ability to interact with a wide variety of people. Use it! Continually widen your circle of contacts to include possible investors, customers, consultants, bankers, employees, vendors, distributors, and other entrepreneurs. Take every opportunity to speak publicly; when you do, give out lots of business cards and collect lots of business cards. Always follow up on new contacts with a brief note, then a phone call. You can even create a networking schedule for yourself that includes lunch dates, follow-up notes and calls, lectures, charity events, trade shows, classes, and seminars. Set aside some time to work on these things every week.

### Newsletters

Newsletters enable you to keep up a valuable dialogue with your customers. In order to be effective, newsletters should be published regularly and consistently, contain important information and up-to-the-minute news, be easy and enjoyable to read, communicate your image, and provide solutions for your customers' problems. Even businesses on small budgets can hire a professional designer to help create an inexpensive, attractive newsletter.

### Brochures

Brochures allow you to go into greater detail about your business and its products or services than almost any other promotional medium. People expect detailed information in brochures, so be sure to deliver it to them in a compelling way. You should also:

- Include photos of your products, or of jobs you've completed
- Use color photos or images to increase your customers' retention
- Use the same logo or company headline on the cover as you use elsewhere
- Include your experience, skills, and training
- Include your telephone and fax number, address, business hours, and e-mail address
- Include additional information and price sheets in a pocket on the back page
- Consider shooting a video brochure a two- to five-minute introduction to your business

The purpose of the brochure is to attract and inform

# Managing Your Promotions

Because small businesses have less money to spend on promotions, they must make sure that what they *do* spend is as effective as possible. Here are the necessary steps in managing promotions:

### Set your promotional budget

Creating a promotional budget entails allocating funds to each element of your promotional strategy. You can do this in one of two ways: either decide on your total budget, then divide it among each of your promotional tools; or set the spending levels for each element, then total that to arrive at your promotional budget.

Before you can do this, however, you need to prioritize each of the elements you intend to use. First, create a wish list of what you would like to achieve with each element, then tally up the total cost of this ideal promotional budget. Next, decide which of these promotional elements are most important, and estimate how much money you can afford to allocate to each of them. If the amount seems too low, don't despair! Chances are, you can make your promotional dollars go a lot further than you think.

### Create your promotional calendar

Creating a timeline for the use of your different promotional tools enables you to plan your budget more efficiently, focus your efforts, and prevent "gaps" in your promotional efforts. Usually, a promotional calendar lists when promotions and events will occur, how long each will last and what its purpose is, and the total budget for each event.

### Measure the effectiveness of your methods

Entrepreneurs must make the most of their limited time and money, and the only way to know what worked and what didn't is to measure results. One sure way to get information is to ask customers how they heard of you.

Ask yourself:

- Is the message that my promotional efforts communicate the right one?
- Is this message consistent with my product positioning strategy?
- Have I reached my target audience?
- How has each component of my promotional mix affected sales?
- How do my customers feel about my message?

You can gather information about the effectiveness of your promotional tools by surveying customers, counting coupons, measuring the number of participants in contests or sweepstakes, and computing sales levels during short-term promotions.

Your promotional efforts require careful management to reach the right people with the right message at the right price

A well-defined promotional calendar keeps you on track

### Free/Low-Cost Promotion Methods

**Barter** allows you to trade your products or services for ad space. For instance, even if your local newspaper doesn't want your product, it might need something else for which you can trade. Trade with the person who has what the newspaper needs and you'll get some ad space for less than you'd pay ordinarily. (Keep in mind that radio and television advertising space is always negotiable.) There's even a magazine called *Barter News* that is dedicated to informing people about barter.

Businesses that use **cooperative advertising** receive cash fees from larger companies for mentioning brand names in their promotional efforts (e.g., a painting contractor who puts the name "Dutch Boy" or "Sherwin-Williams" in his or her brochure).

### Promotional Tips for Entrepreneurs:

- Use the front and back of your business cards to promote your business
- Make colorful and/or oddly shaped business cards
- Send humorous promotional postcards
- Offer samples, seminars, demonstrations
- Think community involvement: help organize 10k runs, fundraising activities; network and get your business's logo and name out there
- Sponsor offbeat, memorable events
- Join trade associations, chair committees, speak at community events
- Offer gift certificates
- Use trial sizes to encourage sampling
- Contact past customers and invite them in when you have new products
- Get leads by sponsoring a breakfast with a high-profile local speaker, and inviting local entrepreneurs who aren't direct competitors
- Deliver speedy service, product updates, and promotional info to customers via fax or e-mail
- Use online computer bulletin boards
- Use a toll-free telephone number to increase your response rate
- Look for cut-rate advertising in regional editions of national magazines; also newspapers' "zone" editions offer discount prices and provide excellent exposure
- Home shopping networks can spread your product's virtues far and wide with little direct cost
- Use telephone hold time to air snappy, enjoyable prerecorded marketing messages

You can also save money by designing print ads yourself, and keeping them clear and concise. Perhaps you can't afford a high-impact, full-page ad, but good copy and ad design can pack just as powerful a punch in a half- or quarter-page ad.

**Personal letters** are a great way to introduce yourself to carefully researched prospects. Write a customized letter for each of your prospects, and include specific information about what your product or service can do for them. Be sure to follow up with another letter and a telephone call or visit.

**Fliers** are a very economical way to spread the word about your business to people in your area. Use your unique style or humor to present the facts and inform your customers why they should buy your product. Select a basic idea, combine it with an appropriate photo or graphic image, then explain more fully what you are offering.

### Promotional Tricks Worthy of the Entrepreneur

Now that you understand the basics of promotional strategy, throw out your traditional thinking about how businesses promote themselves. Start looking for **short cuts**. For entrepreneurs, textbook promotional techniques are just the jumping-off point to more unconventional, low-cost techniques. The only things that should constrain your creativity are your budget and time restrictions.

## Conclusion

Look for the most creative, cost- and time-effective ways to promote your products or services. Be sure to choose methods that are consistent with your positioning strategy, and tools that communicate the same message as the rest of your marketing mix. And remember: even the best promotional strategies won't help a business that offers poor quality, bad service, or unwanted products. Start with a great product, a good understanding of your customer, and let your passion for your business fuel an inspired promotional campaign.

# Chapter 31
# PLACEMENT

*About This Chapter:*
- *Placing your product or service: distribution strategy*
- *Selecting your distribution strategy*
- *Placement strategies for entrepreneurs*

## Introduction

This is the final element of the marketing mix: the fourth P, which refers to the placement or **distribution** of the product. Distribution describes all activities involved in moving goods from producer to customer. In the broadest sense, a distribution system includes taking orders, packaging, inventory management, storage, transportation and follow-up service. Good distribution systems are cost-effective, reliable, accurate, safe, and able to satisfy customer needs.

All businesses rely on some form of distribution network to sell and deliver their products or services to their customers. They might take care of distribution themselves, work with **intermediaries,** or use some combination of the two.

This chapter will introduce you to the basics of distribution, and highlight some of the most effective distribution strategies for entrepreneurs.

## Placing Your Product or Service: Distribution Strategy

Distribution strategy means choosing the most cost-effective means of delivering the product to your customer. The strategy must fit the rest of the marketing mix (the product, price, and promotion). Imagine a premium jeweler trying to sell its goods at K-Mart, or a manufacturer of bargain clothing trying to sell its goods through industrial selling agents, or a gasoline company selling door-to-door. Each of these businesses would miss selling opportunities and drive costs beyond the competitive marketplace.

Businesses that use too many intermediaries end up setting their final selling price above what their customers are willing to pay.

Service businesses must also distribute their offerings. Where will your clients come to get their taxes prepared? Will they contract with you directly? Will you set up an office? Will you use fax, e-mail, and the telephone to deliver services?

## NxLEVEL TECH TIP

**In the eyes of many experts, the most important aspect of a successful e-commerce business is maintaining excellent warehousing, distribution, and fulfillment functions. If you're not in the best position to do this, you may wish to consider outsourcing these functions.**

If you need help with inventory, tracking sales and shipments, or hooking your system to a warehouse or fulfillment center, it's best to turn to a systems integrator, a consultant who specializes in building retail or business-to-business Web sites. You can get referrals for systems integrators and warehouse companies from the **Information Technology Industry Association of America** (www.itaa.org), or the **Council of Regional IT Associations**, which is accessible from the same site. You can try IBM's Net.Commerce site (www.software.ibm.com/commerce/net.commerce), or Microsoft's site (www.microsoft.com), or check with your industry's trade association. For more information on the best ways to set up the back end of your Web site, visit **www.clearcommerce.com/eguide**, a comprehensive guide designed to help merchants, financial institutions, commerce service providers, ISPs, and others conduct business electronically.

### Distribution and Small Businesses

Few businesses have the time, money, or expertise to deliver their products directly to their customers. By hiring professional distributors, or outsourcing certain distribution tasks, they can enter new markets more easily. They can even hire other companies to package, store, and deliver their goods, while they focus on customer service, product design, or promotion.

Another major challenge for small businesses is gaining entrance into traditional distribution channels. A good example of this is the prohibitively high **slotting fees** that many grocery chains charge to producers in order to put their products on the shelf. Luckily, there are ways for small businesses to bypass these obstacles and distribute their products more quickly than ever (door-to-door, home shopping networks, classified ads, mail order, the Internet, and fax-on-demand, to name a few).

### Distribution Basics

Businesses in every industry rely on distribution partners, who help them move their products through the **distribution channel**, which is the avenue by which the product travels from manufacturer to final customer. This channel consists of a group of independent businesses, including manufacturers and wholesalers.

**Channel partners** are businesses that act as intermediaries to help buy and sell, assemble, store, display, and promote products. They are called "partners" because they cooperate and coordinate their efforts to maximize their effectiveness. These partners are specialists at getting the right product to the right place, at the right time and for the right price.

In the distribution game, if you miss the mark, you miss your market

## Types of Channel Intermediaries

- **Retailers** buy products from manufacturers, distributors, and wholesalers, then mark up the price to cover their costs and make a profit.
- **Wholesalers** buy and sell bulk merchandise to other wholesalers or retailers. They never sell directly to the public. Their expertise lies in repackaging, storing, and reselling particular categories of goods. An example would be a wholesaler that buys all types of dried fruits and nuts in bulk, repackages them into smaller bags, and sells them to grocery chains.
- **Distributors** buy merchandise from manufacturers and resell it to wholesalers, retailers, or sometimes directly to the final customer. A good example of a distributor is the Northern California coffee company, Peet's Coffees. They buy coffee beans direct from growers and roast the beans themselves. Peet's then sells to wholesalers, who repackage and relabel the coffee to sell to retailers. Peet's also sells directly to customers in their own coffee shops.
- **Agents** charge a commission to facilitate sales between manufacturers and their final customers. Agents do not take title to the products they deal with; they simply represent businesses and their products. **Manufacturers' agents** sell a business's product in a specific geographic region, usually on an exclusive basis. **Sales agents** are different in that they often have more control over setting prices and terms of sale. It is not uncommon for them to take over all or part of the marketing effort for a product, including promotion and distribution strategy.
- **Brokers** specialize in particular product categories and have the least amount of direct involvement with the manufacturer and end users. Brokers unite buyers with sellers, and have only short-term relationships with each. Like agents, they do not take title to the products they broker.

## Basic Channels of Distribution

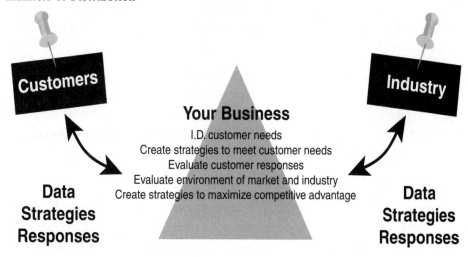

## Selecting Your Distribution Strategy

Like any business strategy, distribution strategies require that you know your objectives, your time and budgetary constraints, and the pros and cons of your alternatives. Distribution objectives include achieving service goals, increasing speed to market, ensuring safety and reliability, or reducing costs. Do your customers value speedy delivery? Does your product require technical support? Do you need to retain complete control over the handling and delivery of your product?

You must identify which distribution option is best for your product, set your strategy, and measure the results. In some cases, traditional distribution channels might not be feasible, and you will have to seek more "entrepreneurial" methods.

*The Macatawa Pickle Company*

*In 1975, Mort Fabrikant started making spicy sweet pickles at his summer cottage in western Michigan. With the help of his daughters, he made them every season and gave them to friends for Christmas and birthdays, and as housewarming gifts. They got rave reviews, and before long, people were calling up to see if they could buy extra pickles! Mort's daughter Katrina said, "Dad, it's time to go into business." All his friends and neighbors agreed! Thus, the idea for the Macatawa Pickle Company was born.*

*Unfortunately, Mort didn't have time to make and sell pickles all day long. How could he sell his pickles without giving up his day job?*

*After a few phone calls and several trips to the library, Mort had the production problem licked. He learned about a small food processing company that would prepare, package, and label his pickles. The real problem was distribution!*

*He called all the major grocery chains in western Michigan and the Chicago area and kept getting the same story: No room for more pickles. Mort would have to come up with another plan if he wanted to share his pickles with the world.*

*One day, while thumbing through a magazine in his doctor's office, he had a flash of inspiration. He would bypass grocery stores altogether and sell pickles through a small classified ad in a magazine. If orders came in, he could package them and send them himself with very little overhead. If they didn't...well, then he'd have to look for another distribution strategy. After several days, he finally settled on this classified ad:*

> *The World's Best Pickle Discovered in Macatawa, Michigan!*
>
> *The secret is out: From the fertile green gardens and sunny lake shore of Macatawa, Michigan comes the ultimate gourmet snack and condiment: The Macatawa Pickle. Pickled and jarred once a year in the sunshine of July, but enjoyed all year long. For your first jar and a recipe book, call 1-800-MACATAW, and ask for Mort.*

Here are some guidelines for deciding if your business needs distributors:

- Customers are scattered geographically and require speedy, small quantity deliveries
- Products require little or no technical selling
- Basic repackaging or customization is required to fit local customer needs
- Distributors are traditionally used in your industry

Your distribution strategy will vary according to whether you produce consumer goods, industrial goods, or services. The next section reviews the basics of distributing in each industry.

## Distributing Consumer Goods

Consumer goods are products that are produced and sold to the final consumer. These products include everything we buy in the supermarket, as well as bicycles, running shoes, and accordions. Here are some of the distribution methods used in consumer product industries.

- **Direct marketing.** Some businesses avoid intermediaries altogether by marketing their products directly to their customers through door-to-door sales, their own retail stores, telephone or catalogue orders, or the Internet. By selling direct, your business controls how your products are sold and serviced. You can remain on top of changes in your market, and respond quickly to customer needs. Direct selling can also be faster and cheaper (in the case of telephone and catalogue sales) than any other distribution method. One of the most important elements of direct selling is keeping a database of past, present, and prospective customers.
- **Manufacturer to retailer.** Most producers of consumer products rely on intermediaries to sell their products. However, large manufacturers that sell to large retailers like K-Mart or Macy's may bypass wholesalers entirely. Businesses choose this strategy because retailers often provide storage and logistical support more cheaply and effectively than wholesalers. On the other side, this gives the retailers more control over the terms of their transaction with the manufacturer.

Other businesses distribute their goods to retailers through wholesalers or other intermediaries. This strategy is used by larger manufacturers that sell to many small retailers. Wholesalers can be particularly helpful to businesses introducing new products. They can use their leverage and expertise in the industry to push the product into retail outlets. Businesses can also use agents and brokers to sell to wholesalers or retailers. These intermediaries operate on commission only, and can be a handy replacement for a small business's in-house sales team. They can present a line of products professionally, coordinate in-store promotions, and share their expert knowledge of markets and customers.

### Distributing Industrial Goods

**Industrial goods** are manufactured products that are sold as inputs to businesses who make them into finished products.

*Careful selection of intermediaries can make your business more profitable*

- **Direct marketing to other businesses.** This type of distribution is much more common in industrial markets than in consumer markets. Most industrial manufacturers have only a few, very large customers to whom they can sell directly. Many industrial products are more expensive and complex than consumer products. They also figure prominently in the production of other products, and must meet certain quality standards and be delivered on time. In short, buyers and sellers in industrial markets are tied together closely in a partnership. In-house sales forces, telemarketing, and catalogues are the major ways that industrial manufacturers market direct to their customers.
- **Manufacturer to intermediary.** For industrial products, wholesalers and agents can provide a more cost-effective way of selling many small products to smaller customers. Intermediaries can also help get a new product established among industrial customers. They can even provide technical and promotional support, depending on the terms of the contract.

### Managing Your Intermediaries

Begin with a clear, simple contract that covers the following:

- Sales staff and quotas
- Pricing policy—flexibility in offering discounts, etc.
- Minimum reorder and inventory quantities
- Geographical territory to be covered
- Handling of house accounts
- Training and technical support for the distributor
- Terms of payment
- Management of service and repairs
- Return policy
- Reports and feedback from distributors on sales and market conditions

### How to Evaluate Your Intermediaries

Once you've decided to use intermediaries, your next task is to evaluate their:

- Selling ability
- Record for paying bills on time
- Promptness and accuracy in handling orders
- Compatibility with your business's operating style

- Willingness and ability to offer marketing feedback
- Dun & Bradstreet credit rating

## The Benefits of Sales Representatives

A professional representative can be the best friend a small business has. They are easy on a business's cash flow since they add no fixed costs to the business. They are usually paid on commission, or when they make a sale; they may even pay for products in advance. They are specialists in the product category and geographic region in which they operate, and are likely to know the industry and prospective customers better than you do. Outside reps may have special technical knowledge of products and be able to offer better technical support or service than you can. They can also help shoulder the responsibility of promotions and advertising.

### The downside of sales representatives

It all sounds too perfect...there must be some disadvantages to using sales reps. And there are! Your product might be just one of many product lines that the rep carries; lacking the right incentives, yours might get lost in the shuffle. Some representatives require a great deal of support to sell effectively. Lastly, sales representatives can be difficult to train, monitor, and motivate. It may take a strenuous effort to get your money's worth.

### Finding and recruiting excellent representatives

The first step in building a first-rate sales team is finding the right people to staff it. Trade journals, directories, and magazines can provide information about who the major representatives are, what lines they carry, and what types of customers they serve. There are also national and local representative and dealer associations, and lists of representatives maintained by local and state chambers of commerce. Lastly, businesses that deal in products similar to yours might be able to recommend a good representative for a given territory.

### When Selecting Reps

- Evaluate selling technique, contact base, and technical know-how
- Make sure the rep's personality is compatible with your business
- Review his or her track record
- Observe a sales call and watch the rep in action
- Clearly define your sales expectations
- Get reliable references
- Hire them for a 3-month trial period, then assess the results

## What You Should Do for Your Reps

- **Contact your representatives at least once a week.** Check on progress, resolve questions, or just chat to keep each other in the loop.
- **Give each representative a good sales manual.** It doesn't need to be anything fancy, but it should contain product specifications, current prices, competitive comparisons, and good product photos. You may also want to include selling angles with arguments and counter-arguments, excellent customer references, reprints of articles and endorsements, and samples.
- **Create an informal representative newsletter.** Use it to announce winners of sales contests, highlight new product developments, answer commonly asked technical questions, and show territory sales volumes. This will keep your reps up-to-date, attentive, and motivated.
- **Give regular and immediate support to representatives.** If they have questions or problems, give them immediate, personal attention. Be prepared to attend initial and major sales calls.
- **Maintain your own record of sales leads.** Do this so you have an ongoing understanding of who your prospects are.
- **Always pay your commissions on time.** Be reliable, accurate, and speedy!
- **Give your sales representatives lots of quality sales leads.** The more prospects they have, the more product they can sell.
- **Follow through with product promises.** If you promise on-time delivery and top quality, deliver it. Give your sales reps the ability to back up their efforts. If they know the product lives up to its promises, they will sell more confidently.

## What Your Reps Should Do for You

- Give weekly updates on prospects and sales efforts
- Prepare regular expense reports and receipts
- Call for product or technical expertise when needed
- Stay current on industry and market trends
- Communicate any customer problems or complaints
- Offer regular feedback on the sales territory
- Be honest and positively represent your business

Take care when selecting sales reps

## Licensing

Licensing is an arrangement whereby a business sells to another business the rights to produce or market its brand name or product. This allows manufacturers to reap the benefits of a product's established reputation and brand without the risk of investing in new products. It effectively transfers the responsibility of marketing and production to the licensee.

*The Joe Boxer Company of San Francisco made its name by selling boxer shorts and pajamas made out of fabric printed with unusual motifs such as chile peppers, glow-in-the-dark lightbulbs, fish, and fruit. They grew and grew, and began selling their shorts in Joe Boxer mini-stores nestled in the men's department of major stores.*

*Then they got the idea of offering sheets and pillowcases. Since they had no experience manufacturing and distributing linens for beds, they contacted one of the biggest names in the bedding game, Martex. After two months of negotiations, they sold the idea and signed a licensing agreement. Martex bought the rights to use the Joe Boxer designs on sheets they manufactured, and used its existing distribution network to place the sheets in department stores across the United States. Joe Boxer knew the secret of good licensing: by focusing on what they did best, they expanded their product line and increased their revenues, without increasing costs or exposure to risk.*

## Placement Strategies for Entrepreneurs

Now for the good news: aside from all the traditional distribution methods, entrepreneurs have another collection of tools available to them. These require a little more energy and creativity to use, but the rewards speak for themselves. Unconventional distribution methods can be very effective and inexpensive. Many small businesses have successfully differentiated themselves by using distribution channels like the following; consider these as a starting point for your own ideas:

- Consignment selling
- Mail order catalogs
- Classified ads
- Fax-an-order
- Telephone/voice mail orders
- Overnight delivery
- Home shopping networks
- The Internet
- Bundle your products with related products, and "piggyback" on their distribution

Remember: Your goal is to break away from precedents in order to devise a cost-effective and unique distribution strategy that complements your product positioning (as well as the other elements of your marketing mix), and delivers value to your target customers.

*H$_2$0 Repairs of Glendale, Arizona*

*Without a reliable source of water, it doesn't take long for crops to wither in the hot Arizona sun. For farmers in Arizona, the only thing as important as an efficient irrigation system is a skilled person to ensure that it runs reliably and smoothly.*

*Jaime Rodriguez is their man. He began H$_2$0 Repairs after working for ten years at a large irrigation management firm in Glendale. He had worked with nearly every type of irrigation system around, and knew all of the major customers in western Arizona. With his lean business (himself and two partners), Jaime was able to offer faster service and lower prices. Furthermore, his was a very specialized business; his only service was repairing the pump that feeds water into the rest of the irrigation equipment.*

*The first-year marketing objectives for H$_2$0 Repairs were to repair or upgrade, on average, ten irrigation systems a month, or have at least 500 billable hours a month. The marketing strategy focused on small- and medium-sized farms. Jaime wanted to position H$_2$0 Repairs as the least expensive, most reliable, local source of irrigation pump expertise.*

*The pared-down marketing plan contained the following marketing mix strategies and tactics:*

| Marketing Mix Element | Strategy | Tactics |
|---|---|---|
| Product | Specialize in offering the most reliable and expert repair of pumps for farm irrigation systems | Set fee estimates; guarantee all work on pumps for 30 days or free repair |
| Price | Offer customers lower prices and more flexible payment options | Charge $25.00/hour plus parts, undercutting largest competitor by 15% |
| Promotion | Raise awareness of H$_2$0 RepairsÕ specialized expertise, lower priced yet speedy and reliable service | List business in the yellow pages in three places: under Farm Equipment, Irrigation Systems, and Repair Services; create an H$_2$0 Repairs brochure to fax to 300 potential customers; include a "bio" page on Jaime Rodriquez and his partners, with details of past projects and testimonials by loyal customers |
| Placement | Deliver services directly and quickly, taking no more than two hours to respond to emergency repairs | Locate office and equipment in southwestern Glendale, Arizona, within 40 miles of the target cutomers; utilize three trucks (privately owned by each member of H$_2$0 Repairs) fully equipped to repair or upgrade five major types of irrigation pumps |

*Jaime created this list of his marketing strategies and tactics within two months of beginning H$_2$0 Repairs. He used it to make sure that the elements of his marketing mix worked in unison to achieve his marketing objectives. Within his first year, he reviewed these strategies and tactics four times. Was his pricing on target? Was his promotional brochure the right medium with the right message? Was his location ideal for his customers?*

*As his base of customers grew, Jaime expanded the plan to include details of projected sales, revenues, and expenses. He knew there might come a time when he would need outside financing for additional equipment. He also knew that before long he would need to expand his team of service experts. For H$_2$0 Repairs, the marketing plan was a launching pad for growth and success.*

## Conclusion

The success of your business depends on reaching the greatest number of your target customers, so a great deal of thought and research should go into selecting the best method of placing your product or service. A distribution strategy that fits your product positioning and the rest of your marketing mix will bring you one step closer to achieving success.

# Chapter 32
# THE ART OF SELLING

*About This Chapter:*
- *The evolution of sales techniques*
- *Professional sales people*
- *Selling and channels of distribution*
- *Optimizing sales opportunities: six steps to sales success*

## Introduction

Regardless of your background, you can learn to be a confident, effective salesperson, and develop a selling style that will distinguish you from your competitors. Your approach should fit your personality, highlight your expertise, and be as comfortable to you as a well-worn glove. This chapter presents some of the best sales techniques for entrepreneurs.

## The Evolution of Sales Techniques

Sales techniques have changed a great deal during the 20th century. Perceptions of salespeople have shifted dramatically; many people used to consider selling a profession for shifty people who used deceit and manipulation to make the sale, even if the customer didn't need the product. A good salesperson was one who could "sell ice cubes to an Eskimo."

Fortunately, things are different now. Today, salespeople listen, understand their customers' needs, and provide solutions. They sell quality products that are guaranteed to perform, and back them up with excellent customer service. They offer a value-added approach, which means providing a service or an association that customers value as much as, or more than, the product itself.

Enlightened salespeople understand that long-term success means keeping customers satisfied after the sale; it costs more to get a new customer, or to win a disgruntled customer back, than it does to sell to an existing customer.

To become successful, you must develop and hone your own selling style

## Professional Sales People

Being a salesperson offers fun, excitement, financial rewards, and fulfilling, long-term relationships. Many people want to be involved in sales, and most people can be taught to sell. Characteristics businesses look for in salespeople are:

- High energy
- Self-motivation

- Ability to understand the big picture

- Persistence and perseverance
- Technical knowledge
- Good communication skills
- Good listening skills
- Ability to use product
- Ability to meet customer needs

## Selling and Channels of Distribution

Your choice of distribution method depends on how your target markets traditionally buy similar products. Do they buy direct or from distributors? Sales agents? Retailers? Do they buy in bulk? Do they require technical support, or after-sales service? Answering these questions will help you pick the right distribution channel for your product.

---

*On Robert Chavez's 55th birthday, he decided to make some changes in his life. For twelve years, Robert had been working in the service department of a large office equipment manufacturer based in Tempe, Arizona. He was responsible for all service follow-up activities in the Phoenix area, so he knew that the biggest customer complaints involved service response time, equipment reliability, and price. Robert and his office manager, Anna Gambera, felt they could meet customers' needs better than their employer could.*

*Their plan: to become independent sales representatives for a competing office equipment business, and sell and manage their own service contracts. At a trade show they attended, Anna and Robert had been impressed by the people they met from a large American copier manufacturer; the product was high-quality, and the company was aggressively expanding into the western states. Anna drew up a proposal to the company, defining the territory and the terms of their customer service contract. Meanwhile, to hone his skills, Robert enrolled in a five-week copier repair course. They decided to call their new business "Copiers West."*

Selling today is 100% customer-driven

---

## Optimizing Sales Opportunities: Six Steps to Sales Success

Whether you handle sales yourself or work through an intermediary, you must understand the principles of good selling.

### Step 1: Prospecting and Prioritizing Accounts

Before proceeding, determine:

- Your target customer profile: size, location, needs, problems, goals
- What unique value your business offers target customers
- How your offerings are better than those of competitors
- What resources you have to encourage consumers to buy your product

Consider all the possibilities; if necessary, seek advice from associates who are familiar with you and your business. Think about sales possibilities locally, in the United States, in the world. Next, step back and sort your list of potential sales prospects into the following categories:

- **Short-term/long-term prospects.** The short-term list includes prospects you can develop immediately. Long-term prospects are larger organizations that require more time to build relationships. (Note: Creating a timeline that outlines each step of the selling process can keep your sales efforts for long-term prospects on track.)
- **Most profitable/least profitable.** Analyze each prospect's profitability. You may find that larger accounts provide less profit per unit of sale, but more profit overall; whereas small accounts provide more unit profit, but require greater effort and time.
- **Prestige accounts.** High-profile accounts provide great exposure for your business; unfortunately, everyone else wants these prestigious accounts too! You may decide to make less profit on some of these accounts, or even make them a loss leader, just to get your name associated with them.

Next, develop your sales targeting strategy. Which accounts should you target first? Which are critical to your long-range goals, and which are the bread-and-butter accounts?

### The value of networking

There's no doubt that networking often has a negative connotation—each of us has been the target of someone's obnoxious networking scheme! However, positive, unobtrusive networking is critical to a business owner's success. The key is to network in a respectful, professional, mutually beneficial, and genuine manner.

Joining organizations or clubs in your field is an excellent way to meet new people and prospects. If you are a sole proprietor, these organizations can introduce you to like-minded people, and give you an opportunity to keep up with new business developments. Chapter 27 *Marketing Objectives, Strategies, and Tactics* discusses networking tips for entrepreneurs in greater detail.

### The value of the computer

Computerizing sales information saves money and streamlines selling activities. Entrepreneurs can develop prospect and account information on computer software, and update sales targets as priorities change. Good account information makes your efforts more professional and organized.

Many inexpensive software packages are available to help small businesses manage business functions such as purchasing, accounting, payroll, and financial planning. They are designed for people who don't have a great deal of computer experience. Training seminars, books, and computer consultants can provide additional help.

---

*By June, Robert and Anna were in business, and the battle for customers was in full swing. Most businesses in the Phoenix area already had copiers and service contracts with larger competitors. Robert and Anna knew that their higher-quality copiers and superior customer service would convince their customers to switch. The problem was getting in the door!*

*They decided to target businesses with less than 100 employees. Then, they began cold calling in person.*

---

### Step 2: Planning and Preparing for Sales Calls

Successful sales calls require thoroughly researched selling plans before you approach your first target customer. Whether for a simple sale (a call on one person who is capable of making the buying decision), or a complex sale where multiple buying influencers take part in the decision, proper sales call planning is the biggest part of the selling process. Face-to-face selling time is very short; planning allows salespeople to maximize their time with buyers by asking the right questions and presenting relevant information. It allows them to sell their products by solving problems.

Prospecting is an everyday job

*Analyzing buyers*

Before you can sell, it is important to understand how different people participate in the buying process. A few examples are listed below:

- **Decision-maker.** This buyer will be able to say "yes" or "no" to your proposal. In a simple sale, the buyer usually makes the decision. In a complex sale, the decision-maker is not readily available or identifiable. The decision-maker is often swayed by several other buying influencers.
- **Gatekeeper.** Gatekeepers don't make the final decision (though they may want you to believe they do). Their purpose is to screen potential suppliers and gather information. This role is often played by purchasing agents and attorneys.
- **Guide.** This buying influencer wants your product or service and will be a strong coach or ally who can provide inside information about the buying process. If there isn't a guide available, develop one!
- **User.** These people use your product or service. They do not make the final purchase decision, but they do have strong influence over purchase decisions.

These influences are interconnected. For example, you may have a great relationship with the decision-maker, but the user will kill the sale if she or he doesn't like the way your product performs. Or, if the gatekeeper denies you access to the decision-maker, you can concentrate your promotional efforts on the user, who has the power to activate the purchasing process.

*Buyer orientation*

People make buying decisions in many different ways. However, there are some general "types" that you can expect to encounter:

- **Security.** This buyer has a desire to keep things stable and does not want any risky propositions. When calling on a security buyer, you should minimize his or her exposure to risk and make him or her feel comfortable.

- **Power.** These buyers want to be recognized for their position and influence, and may abrasively assert their authority and capability. They may not be fun to call on, but they do make decisions and get things done!
- **Relationship.** This buyer likes people, and tends to be very open and friendly. Relationship buyers expect you to socialize a bit prior to getting down to business. This is great if they can make a decision, but not so great if they waste your time!
- **Enlightened.** This type of person makes informed decisions by gathering facts and weighing the alternatives. Being well informed and knowledgeable about your product will serve you well when calling on this buyer.

Salespeople must try to understand the buyers' mindset. What would make your customers' work easier? What would save them time? What makes them buy? Why won't they buy? Selling products from the customers' point of view results in a more successful sales call.

Sell from the customer's point of view

## Step 3: First Contact

The objectives of your first contact with prospective customers are to make a positive first impression, pique their interest, and glean information that will help you make the sale.

To this end, you should prepare open-ended, probing questions; effective questioning leads to quality information. Here are some suggestions:

- **New Information.** Use new information questions to find out about customers' business issues, discrepancies between their current and desired state, and to uncover missing information. "Describe to me, show me, explain to me..."
- **Feelings.** Use these questions to discover desires, values, and intense feelings about issues related to your product or service. "What is your opinion…How do you feel about...?"
- **Confirming.** Use confirming questions to verify whether you've made the proper assumptions, or drawn the correct conclusions.
- **Agreement.** Use this type of question to obtain agreement on an action that will close the sale. "Do you intend, agree, plan...?"

---

*In their initial visit, Robert and Anna focused on gathering the following information about prospective customers:*

- *The type of business*
- *How satisfied they were with the copier and the service arrangement*
- *The name of the purchase decision-maker*

*At the cold call, Copier West demonstrated:*

- *Knowledge of the prospect's copier needs, problems, costs, and issues*
- *Knowledge of their competitors' offerings*

Sales strategies are critical to your success

- *Their expertise, and the quality of their product*
- *Their ability to deliver excellent customer service and maintenance*
- *The savings in cost from switching to Copiers West*

---

### Step 4: Make the Presentation

After listening carefully to your customers' needs and problems, begin by framing a **concept** of your product or service. Why? Because buyers often buy concepts of what the product will do for them, rather than the product itself. A man who buys a new red Ferrari is not buying a car; he's buying power and prestige. If he simply wanted a car for transportation, he would buy a Ford or Honda, like millions of other car buyers!

Think about your last significant purchase. Were you buying the product, or what the product would do for you? Understanding the concept behind your product or service will help you plan your sales strategy and presentation.

You should also give information about your product's **features** and **benefits**. Features describe how the product looks and performs. Benefits describe how the product meets a need or solves a problem. Develop your own feature and benefit statements for your business. Remember to sell benefits, not just features.

Talk about the features;

sell the benefit

What should a professional presentation look and sound like? Here are some basics:

- **Appearance counts.** Wear clothing appropriate to your industry. If you are in the golf business, a polo shirt and casual pants will do nicely. If your clients are bankers, a suit is in order.
- **Attitude counts.** A professional, sincere, honest, and energetic approach is best.
- **Your first comment counts.** Begin with a key question or strong statement—based on your research and/or the first call—that shows your client how your product or service will solve problems or provide tremendous benefits.
- **Presentation of benefits counts.** Show your clients what's in it for them!
- **Creativity counts.** Canned sales pitches don't go far with today's sophisticated clients. Use your creativity to develop a unique presentation.
- **Rehearsal counts.** Don't go in cold; practice ahead of time.

### Step 5: Objections

If life were perfect, every client would immediately purchase everything you pitched. Unfortunately, clients invariably have some objection, or a reason they don't wish to buy. A good salesperson anticipates customer objections and is prepared to respond to them.

Some typical objections are:

- Your price is too high
- I need to talk this one over with my team
- I don't think your program will solve my problem
- I am satisfied with my current supplier and don't want to change

- Your competition has better delivery times
- Your company hasn't been around very long
- I've heard you have financial problems
- I had a bad experience with your company last time

Below is a four-step process to overcome objections.

1. **Listen carefully** to gather information on the problem.
2. **Acknowledge the problem** to show your understanding of the customer's issues.
3. **Explore the problem** by asking questions and clarifying meaning.
4. **Respond to the objection** by recommending a solution.

You may have to repeat this process many times in the course of a sales call. You should also keep in mind that the first few objections may not be the real issue at all. Persistence pays off, but only when matched with civility and an honest desire to solve your clients' problems.

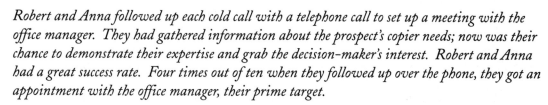

*Robert and Anna followed up each cold call with a telephone call to set up a meeting with the office manager. They had gathered information about the prospect's copier needs; now was their chance to demonstrate their expertise and grab the decision-maker's interest. Robert and Anna had a great success rate. Four times out of ten when they followed up over the phone, they got an appointment with the office manager, their prime target.*

*With their preliminary information in hand, Robert and Anna approached the appointment with the confident attitude that the customer was ready to buy. In every meeting, the rule was to ask questions and listen more than they spoke. They used high-quality pictures of their copiers and a simple chart to present the comparative cost savings of their service contracts over their competitors'. They also made a point of knowing what their prospect's objections might be ahead of time, and preparing solutions for them:*

| Customer objection | Copier West's solution |
|---|---|
| *The hassle of switching equipment* | *Free installation and training, first month free* |
| *Lost time for copier upgrade* | *Same day installation and training* |
| *Need to see copier before committing* | *Nearby showroom with all models and equipment* |
| *Difficulty of getting out of existing service contract* | *Free paperwork prep, explain ease of getting out of no-obligation copier lease agreements* |
| *Fear of using more complicated equipment* | *Demonstrate why Copiers West is easier to use, more ergonomic* |
| *Concern about service delays from smaller provider* | *Money-back guarantee if longer than two-hour repair response time* |

*By presenting their information confidently, and offering benefits that solved their prospect's problems, Robert and Anna earned the respect of office managers. Once they had this, they became the prospect's partners and valued consultants. Then they would listen as the prospect asked questions and raised objections. They always probed for more information when met by an objection. Their goal was to be responsive to the prospect's concerns and needs, and let the prospect gradually arrive at the realization that Copiers West was the obvious choice for cost savings and better service.*

Prepare and be on target

*With their warm personal style and expert approach, Robert and Anna were able to get a foot in the door. They asked the right questions, listened carefully, and presented solutions. Their business grew and grew. They had become truly successful salespeople!*

---

### Step 6: The Close

The biggest reason for lost sales is the failure of salespeople to ask for the order. Why is this? The two major reasons most people won't ask for orders are fear of failure and fear of rejection. Nobody likes to feel like a failure, or to be rejected by other people. However, in all likelihood your client isn't rejecting you personally, nor have you failed personally. There are many reasons why clients don't buy, especially during the first try: they may not have the authority to sign a purchase order, they may have bought a month's allotment the day before, or they may want to get to know you better before doing business with you. There are almost as many reasons as there are customers.

Remember, if you have a quality product or service that is fairly priced, you have no reason to fear the reactions of the buyer!

Here are a few of the many methods used to close a sale:

Welcome objections as you would opportunities

- **Basic close by using an application form.** Begin by asking the customer a question from the application. Write in the answer. Proceed to the next item. As long as the customer does not stop you, you've made a sale.
- **Close by offering alternate choices.** Offer alternatives: "Do you prefer green or blue?" "Would you need two of these, or three?" When a prospect makes a minor decision, the major decision is close.
- **Close by constructing a balance sheet.** For indecisive prospects, remark that a tally of the reasons for and against the concept will make the decision for them. Take a sheet of paper, draw a line down the center and help the prospect to list the reasons for buying your product/service.
- **Close by asking questions.** For a procrastinating prospect who is reluctant to make a commitment but won't tell you why, ask questions: "Is there something you don't understand about my company or our product?" "Is there anything I didn't make clear?" Summarize the presentation one question at a time.
- **Close by citing examples.** People will listen to stories. Describe the experiences of customers you've satisfied in the past.

- **Close by isolating the objection.** Change a prospect's "I'll think it over," to a specific objection. Remark that the prospect obviously wouldn't spend time thinking it over unless he or she was seriously interested. When that is confirmed, say "Just to clarify my thinking, what aspect of this program do you want to think over?" Then probe until the objection is isolated.

- **Close using prospect's objection.** Hear your prospect out, and get a full explanation of the objection. Get the prospect to agree that this objection is the only thing standing in the way of a sale. Then, overcome the objection with facts.

- **Close with a closing question.** If a prospect asks whether it's possible to get what you're selling in such-and-such a way, don't answer with a "yes." Instead, ask the prospect if that's the way he or she wants it. If the prospect answers "yes," the prospect has bought.

*Uncover the underlying problem preventing the sale...and solve it*

## NxLEVEL™ TECH TIP

Your Web site is like a salesperson that represents your business to the entire world, so you want to make sure that it targets the right customers, makes a good first impression, is able to answer any question about your product or services, and does its utmost to complete the sale. Here are some tips that will help make your Web site the perfect salesperson:

- The name and address of your Web site are extremely important, so choose them carefully. Go with a short, striking name that is easy to remember and easy to spell.

- Rapid response is the most important factor in attracting and retaining online business. Reply to your customers' questions and comments within 24 hours, or you're liable to lose them!

- Keep adding to and improving your Web site from the day you launch it. Constantly promote upcoming offers and features so that users will return again and again.

- Keep things simple. Avoid complicated or cluttered sites that serve to "hide" important information. Everything the customer needs to know about your business should be easily accessible. And when you're responding to customers online, learn to express yourself concisely so that you don't waste their time.

- One of the best ways to create an online presence is to e-mail electronic newsletters and magazines—which are eternally in need of new information—and volunteer content on a regular basis.

- The more links you have to other, similar sites, the better. Try to find free links, or "trade-outs," where you offer a link to a site and they provide one in return. Make sure all links appeal to your target audience!

*Persistence, perseverance, and practice!*

### Hi, It's Me Again!

Well, you made eight personal sales calls on the prospect, sent twelve faxes answering technical questions, met seven people on the purchasing team, and spoke with the vice president in charge of the project. You revised your formal offer three times and the last one—finally—was accepted. Congratulations!

Now it's time to get back to your customer and say, "Thank for your business!" Ask whether there are any problems; if there are, give them your immediate attention. A satisfied customer is the best source for new business. In fact, your new customer is a hot prospect right after making a purchase! This is an excellent time to sell something to go along with the previous sale. These so-called **add-ons** could be additional colors, sizes, or complementary products. Remember, it takes a lot less to get a reorder or an add-on than it does to get a new customer!

## Conclusion

Nothing happens in business until somebody sells something. Very few people are born salespeople, but very few people can't learn to be good company representatives. Selling should be fun, challenging, exciting, and financially rewarding. By learning selling skills, doing your homework, and developing your own style through practice, there is no reason why you can't be successful at asking for the order…and getting it!

## Chapter 33
# AN INTRODUCTION TO THE INTERNET

*About This Chapter:*
- *Birth of the Internet*
- *Anatomy of the World Wide Web*
- *Connecting to the Internet*
- *Hurry up and wait*
- *Buying and selling online*
- *Online security*
- *What's next?*
- *Why does it matter?*
- *Where to learn more*

## Introduction

The Internet has become such an integral part of our society that it is hard to believe it has only existed since 1992. Since that time, the Internet has brought enormous changes to almost every area of life, but nowhere has the Internet had a more revolutionary effect than in the world of business. From conceiving and researching new ideas, to manufacturing, to marketing and selling, there is scarcely any aspect of business that remains unaffected by the Internet; and there is scarcely any type of business that cannot benefit from using this powerful tool.

In the next chapter, we'll discuss e-commerce advantages and strategies. For now, let's take a brief look at the history—and probable future—of the Internet.

## The Birth of the Internet

The Internet grew out of an experiment begun in the 1960s by the U.S. Department of Defense (DOD). The DOD wanted to create a computer network that would continue to function in the event of a disaster such as a nuclear war. If one part of the network was damaged or destroyed, information could be rerouted throughout the rest of the system. In this way, data back-up was built into the network. This first network was called ARPANET (Advanced Research Projects Agency). It linked scientific and academic research centers and was the foundation of the Internet.

In 1985, the National Science Foundation (NSF) created NSFNET, a series of networks for research and education communication based on ARPANET protocols. NSFNET was a national backbone service, offering free access to any U.S. research and educational institution. At the same time, regional networks cropped up to link individual institutions with NSFNET.

NSFNET grew rapidly as people discovered its potential for fast information-sharing, and new software tools were invented to make using the network easier. Large businesses like Sprint and MCI began building their own networks, which they linked to NSFNET. As commercial firms and other regional network providers took over the operation of the major Internet arteries, NSF withdrew from the backbone business. In 1991, the NSF eased restrictions on commercial use of the Internet, and the floodgates began to open.

NSF also coordinated a service called InterNIC, which registered all addresses on the Internet so that data could be routed to the right system. This service has now been taken over by AT&T and Network Solutions, Inc., in cooperation with NSF. You can learn all about searching for and registering Internet domain names, or URLs (uniform resource locators) by going to http://www.networksolutions.com.

The World Wide Web (the "Web") is a component of the Internet. It was developed in 1992 by CERN, the European Laboratory for Particle Physics, as a networked information project. This project has become a universe of network-accessible information, both in words and pictures, available on the Internet. Through the use of software, a set of **protocols** and **conventions**, **hypertext**, and **multimedia** techniques, the Web is easy for anyone to roam, browse and contribute to. World Wide Web documents contain content that, when selected, lead to other documents. Put simply, the Web is an Internet-based computer network that allows users on one computer to access information stored on another through the world-wide network.

Sometimes, the terms "Internet" and "Web" are used interchangeably, as in "I'm surfing the Net" and "I'm on the Web."

## The Anatomy of the World Wide Web

The World Wide Web (WWW) is the portion of the Internet that features graphic displays; a Web page is a graphic display stored as a file in computer memory. Web page graphics are based on a comparatively simple programming language called **HTML (hypertext markup language)**, which allows colors, fonts, and pictures to be used where only text messages were possible before. By adding an easy-to-use interface to the Internet, the programming language **HTTP (hypertext transfer protocol)** opened up the Internet to a whole new group of users, and allowed them to jump instantly from one page to another. The result was a truly revolutionary means of presenting information.

The first Web browser was called Mosaic. It was created by the National Center for Supercomputing Applications at the University of Illinois at Urbana/Champaign. This is where a smart young entrepreneur named Marc Andreesen, the co-founder of Netscape Communications, worked as a student; he was a member of the team that created Mosaic. Most people agree that Mosaic made the Internet accessible to the masses.

*The World Wide Web: a user-friendly graphical interface to the Internet.*

*The Internet is a global network of computers that share information, using agreed-upon standards.*

> **Choose your ISP carefully!**
> The most important criterion for selecting an ISP is customer support. How accessible is their technical support team by phone? How quickly do they answer or call back with help? How fast and reliable is the connection to the Internet? How responsive are they to problems with your account or billing questions? Unless you are a technical wizard, you will rely heavily on your ISP for troubleshooting... probably more often than you'd like! Make sure they offer the best possible support.

## Connecting to the Internet

To use the Web you need a computer with a modem, a Web browser, and a connection to the Internet. If you already have a computer at home, the way to start is by choosing one of the many **Internet service providers** (ISPs) in your area. These can be companies like US West, AOL, Sprint, WorldCom/MCI, Earthlink, Sirius, or Concentric. These services include all of the set-up software you need, and provide an easy system with which to log on to and navigate the Web. ISPs generally charge about $20 a month for unlimited Internet access, as well as an e-mail account and free space for hosting a small Web site.

## Hurry Up and Wait

As of this writing, there are millions of Web sites comprising hundreds of millions of Web pages. Unfortunately, many people find that accessing information and images on the Web is annoyingly slow—so much so that some people refer to the Web as the "World Wide Wait." Most people connect to the Web using dial modems over telephone lines. Because the capacity, or **bandwidth**, of telephone lines is relatively low, sending and receiving electronic data can take a long time. If you use a telephone-based modem and your Internet connection speed is of primary concern, check with your local telephone carrier for faster connections. For a fee (and if your line is in a qualified area) you can take advantage of the higher speeds offered by Digital Subscriber Line (DSL) or Integrated Services Digital Network (ISDN) technology. Check with your local telephone carrier or ISP.

Ambitious start-ups and established corporations alike realized early on that with faster connection speeds, the commercial possibilities of the Internet would increase many times over. Faster connection speeds make it possible to view movies, listen to CD-quality audio, and shop from media catalogues online. Simultaneously, much attention has been given to "convergence"—the joining of television-like technology with computer and Internet interactivity. Quickly evolving technologies are making this possible.

Browsers like Netscape Navigator or Microsoft Explorer are computer programs that allow you to view Web pages on your computer screen and move around on the Internet.

New types of connections to the Internet, like fiber-optic, satellite and cable TV lines, have increased bandwidth dramatically, making the Web more powerful. In coming years we'll be able to shop, work, play, research, watch, listen, and communicate over the Internet faster and with fewer hassles than ever before.

## Buying and Selling Online

What's a URL? A Uniform Resource Locator is the equivalent of an address on the Internet. It tells your Web browser where to look for a specific file (or page) on the Internet.

Some of the most successful online ventures have taken existing business models and souped them up with the speed and convenience of the Web. The Internet provides an opportunity for tiny new retailers to launch themselves with minimal cost and minimal time. There's no need to lease retail space when your shop is a colorful and engaging page on the Internet. And there's no need to buy a fancy point-of-sale register or hold tons of inventory in a warehouse when you can collect e-mail orders that you turn right around to your suppliers, who drop-ship products directly from their warehouses.

Many of the earliest and fastest successes in online retailing involved sales of commodity products like books or greeting cards. Commodity products are widely available, vary little in quality of manufacture, and are generally bought by consumers exclusively on the basis of price. Such products are perfect for sale online; when shopping for these types of items, most buyers don't need to hold, taste, touch, or smell them. They just need to be able to read the card or the book and feel as if they're getting the best possible price. Both of these things can be achieved online. *Voila...the perfect model for a business!*

---

*Sparks Fly!*

*Sparks.com is an online "store" where visitors can browse and buy actual greeting cards, which the business then envelopes, stamps, and sends to the chosen recipient.*

*Located in an old warehouse in San Francisco, California, Sparks.com serves customers who visit their Web site. Sparks.com customers communicate via data streams and click on different areas of the Sparks.com site, telling the company what card to send to whom.*

*Sparks.com is a perfect example of the blending of strong branding, good service, and a commodity product offering. In many ways, what Sparks.com is doing is the future of this type of business.*

---

## Online Security

Although online shopping is increasingly popular, many consumers worry about sharing private information like a credit card number online.

In order for online commerce to be truly successful, customers must feel that online merchants are trustworthy and reliable, and that private information such as credit card numbers will not be misused.

For this reason, many companies are racing to create secure Internet payment systems. At the moment, the most widespread payment method is one that involves the creation of a secure socket layer (SSL) and a form where credit card numbers can be gathered and processed by one or more financial institutions in real time.

## What's Next?

What about the fun stuff—television-like programming, 3-D gaming, or high-quality music online? Some of the most exciting improvements to the Web are in the area of multimedia. One company, RealNetworks, has developed the RealPlayer. Providers of entertainment, information, and news can deliver audio and video to everyone with the RealPlayer software installed on their computers. Admittedly, the quality of the video image is much smaller and more jerky than that of your television, but it is the best example of where the Internet is headed. Web sites like abcnews.com and espn.com are currently using this technology to deliver breaking news.

*The Sparks.com brand*

*The Sparks.com store greets visitors with a home page (http://www.sparks.com) that has a very distinct look and feel. Its colors, typefaces, and images work together to communicate the Sparks.com brand: slightly retro, fun, and classy. There is a certain 'punchy' look to the page that correctly anticipates the mood of most customers, who are probably in a rather celebratory mood! Visitors immediately grasp how to get what they want: the navigation bar offers links to "How It Works," "Your Account," and "Help." Along the left-hand side is another navigation bar with which you can access more specific product-related categories: "Father's Day," "Wedding Wishes," and "Graduation." Most important, very prominently displayed on this first page is a link to a page where you can open an account, or sign in if you are an existing member. Like most other online retailers, Sparks.com strives to make buying online quick, reliable, and secure.*

*First-time visitors are guided through a series of screens in which they fill out user profile forms, choosing a user name and a password for their new account. From there, visitors browse and select their cards, and customize the message on the inside. Sparks.com offers several different options for shipping, sending the card either to the customer or to a recipient of choice. They'll even take care of postage and mailing!*

**More great stuff:**
- www.industrystandard.com
- www.wired.com
- www.redherring.com
- www.home.cnet.com
- www.zdnet.com
- www.ask.com

## Why Does It Matter?

The sky is the limit when it comes to where the Internet is headed. It is amazing to consider the number of people and the quality of the minds that are driving these new technologies forward. Because of the demand for higher speed, more valuable services, and richer online experiences, there is an incredible rate of innovation and evolution in these growth industries. This spells tremendous opportunity for entrepreneurs who put themselves in the right place at the right time, and stay one step ahead of the game.

## Where to Learn More

The Online Education site at http://www.web-action.com/remottr.html offers information on just about every conceivable aspect of the Web. Its extensive links will connect you to sites with detailed, user-friendly information on using search engines, designing Web pages, attracting repeat visitors to your site, and countless other topics; as well as numerous tutorials and training sites.

---

*The Impulse Buy Online*

*Sparks.com understands the tendency towards impulse buying and last-minute rushing to send greeting cards, and by catering to this tendency has built a multimillion dollar online business. The Internet is a perfect medium for such a business; it is accessible to people at work and at home, and makes selecting and sending a card quick and easy. For Sparks.com customers, the service they receive is more than worth the price they pay.*

*Sparks.com encourages customers to buy by offering free shipping, thousands of cards to choose from, handwritten or typed personal messages, same day mailing for orders received by 4 P.M. Pacific Standard Time, gift certificates, and "first card free" offers.*

---

## Conclusion

The Internet offers a variety of tools for you to consider as you research, create, build, and sell your business idea. Faster connection speed means that you can access more information more quickly than ever before. It also means that more of your customers are online than ever before. These are the questions you should be asking yourself as you get more familiar with the Internet:

- How can I learn about my customers?
- How can I communicate with them online?
- How can I deliver more value to them?
- How can I earn more revenue, cut costs, and increase profits?

For answers to these and other questions, surf different Internet Web sites to see what established businesses as well as tiny, new start-ups are doing online. Get familiar with this new landscape, and stay familiar, because things are moving ahead quickly...online!

# Chapter 34
# E-COMMERCE

*About This Chapter:*
- *What is e-commerce?*
- *Customer service online*
- *Planning your first Web site*
- *Online marketing strategies*
- *Online advertising*
- *Telling the Web about your site*
- *Search engines*
- *What are Web directories?*

## Introduction

E-commerce has changed the way people do business. The traditional view of technology as a support or operational tool has given way to new business models. Today, technology is a major driver of business strategy and profit. The result is a complete transformation in the economics of transactions. Online business is growing at a rate that surprises even the most optimistic industry experts. According to the *Wall Street Journal*, businesses spent $43.1 billion on Internet-based purchases from other businesses in 1998; this figure is expected to double or triple in coming years.

On the Internet, a tiny start-up company can sell to customers all over the world—most of whom it would be unlikely to reach by any other means—and it can do so without having to invest in multiple store locations and inventories. In general, the cost of doing business on the Internet is comparatively low; for each dollar they spend on fixed assets, successful Internet retailers can usually generate two or three times what a standard retailer generates.

E-commerce benefits customers, too. They can shop at any time of the day or night, without waiting in lines, or driving around in search of a parking place. In fact, studies indicate that a good percentage of Internet shopping takes place after 10 P.M. Web sites also offer more information about products than most stores, and they offer it to thousands of prospective customers at once!

Although the importance of e-commerce is growing, this doesn't mean that offline business models are outdated. You still need to know your customers, manage your finances, and sell your goods aggressively and intelligently. The Internet is not for everyone, and not everyone who is already in it will succeed.

## What is E-Commerce?

E-commerce is the delivery of information, products, services, or payments via telephone lines or computer networks. It's a tool that allows consumers and businesses to cut costs while improving the quality of goods and increasing the speed of transactions. At its most basic, e-commerce means buying and selling products and information in the world's fastest growing market, the Internet.

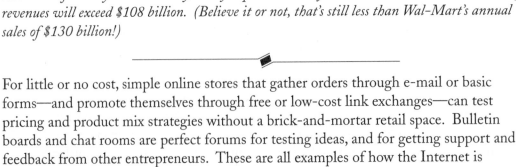

### Examples of Online Services

- **Wells Fargo** (http://www.wellsfargo.com): Banking, bill payment, financial management
- **Preview Travel** (http://www.previewtravel.lycos.com/home): Travel reservations, tickets, and information
- **Internal Revenue Service** (http://www.irs.ustreas.gov): Online tax filing

### Examples of Online Retailing

- **Amazon** (http://www.amazon.com): Books, CDs, videos, auctions
- **Peapod** (http://www.peapod.com): Groceries
- **Key West Seafood Co.** (http://www.keywestseafood.com): Fresh seafood
- **Athleta** (http://www.athleta.com): Women's sports clothes and equipment

*Amazon…Amazing!*

*In July of 1995, Amazon.com launched its online bookstore. Based in Seattle, Washington, the online "store" had no retail space at all—just a Web site that offered big discounts on books, and a well-designed, easy-to-use interface. What Amazon had going for it was a renegade spirit, a keen sense of branding, and very low initial operating expenses. In its first year, Amazon sold just over $500,000 worth of goods, but sales increased dramatically and quickly. At the time of this writing, Amazon reportedly has sales in excess of $360 million!*

*Many people credit Amazon with igniting online consumer sales by helping to teach consumers that it is safe to buy online. Today, analysts predict that by 2003, annual e-commerce industry revenues will exceed $108 billion. (Believe it or not, that's still less than Wal-Mart's annual sales of $130 billion!)*

For little or no cost, simple online stores that gather orders through e-mail or basic forms—and promote themselves through free or low-cost link exchanges—can test pricing and product mix strategies without a brick-and-mortar retail space. Bulletin boards and chat rooms are perfect forums for testing ideas, and for getting support and feedback from other entrepreneurs. These are all examples of how the Internet is simultaneously a powerful business platform, marketing tool, and information resource for entrepreneurs.

# Customer Service Online

It used to be that most entrepreneurs were in competition with no more than a few regional rivals. Online, your competitors may number in the hundreds, and come from all over the world. Competition on the Web is so fierce that many of the most successful Web retailers are intentionally losing money in order to gain market share and develop a loyal customer base. Their goal is to gain a substantial market share over time, and they are willing to lose money in the beginning to do it.

If this strategy doesn't appeal to you, don't worry—there's more to selling on the Internet than offering the lowest price. If pricing was all that mattered, prices would be roughly equivalent across the Internet. However, studies have shown that prices vary greatly for identical items, which suggests that many online shoppers attach a relatively low importance to price versus branding, visibility, and trustworthiness.

Why is this? It may be due to the fact that people are not yet used to buying over the Internet. They may find it intimidating, they could be worried about fraud, and they're afraid of being disappointed. To overcome these misgivings, they want to be assured of fast shipping, excellent communication, and no hassles or confusion. This means that if you can offer the best, most reliable customer service around, you can compete with companies many times larger than your own. Many Internet entrepreneurs say that the secret to successful online selling is to attract customers by any means necessary, then deliver excellent customer service to win their loyalty. Eventually, the cost of attracting new customers will be outweighed by revenues generated by repeat customers.

Make no mistake: Online customers expect the same level of customer service they receive offline—if not more! According to a recent study by BizRate.com, a firm that tracks customer satisfaction with e-commerce transactions, quality of customer service was the top factor in determining whether a customer returned to a particular online merchant. For some companies, the rapid growth of online sales has outpaced investment in structures that support customer service, resulting in declining customer satisfaction. To reverse this trend, many businesses are trying to replicate real-world customer service online.

## Keeping in Touch

One of the biggest complaints customers have with e-commerce is the difficulty of getting in touch with online businesses. They complain that phone numbers can be hard to find on Web sites, and if called, may not be answered. Also, customer e-mails often get no response for days on end, or receive an automated response that does not properly answer the customer's question.

To avoid the frustration this lack of contact causes, and to assure customers that your company is legitimate, it's essential to hire and train customer service representatives to answer your phone. Many prospective customers call simply to ensure that the company actually exists; if you have knowledgeable, friendly people staffing your phone lines, these calls present a perfect opportunity to promote your product or service in a way that directly addresses the individual customer's needs.

*Receiving great customer service is the primary concern of online buyers*

One way to provide low-cost customer support is through **up-leveling**. In this system, customers are initially referred to an automated online information source (e.g., the Frequently Asked Questions (FAQ) pages one sees on so many Web sites). If the customer cannot find the appropriate answer, he or she is invited to send an e-mail message. As a last resort, the customer can be given a phone number to talk to a representative. If you design your FAQ page properly, and your e-mail responses are prompt and helpful, up-leveling can dramatically lower the time you or your staff spend on the phone.

## Planning Your First Web Site

Spending time online is the most important thing you can do while planning your Web site. The only way to know what works and what doesn't is to visit a lot of sites. First-hand knowledge of good online business models comes from searching for businesses online as if you were interested in buying from them. Which online stores are easy to use, and why? Which aren't, and why not? Which Web sites are visually appealing? Which sites load the fastest?

For information on Web design basics, do a search on "Web design," "Web development," or "interface design" and visit the sites that come up. Take detailed notes on what you discover, and soon you'll have strong ideas about what type of functionality and design you want for your own site.

Once you've begun to educate yourself about the Web (a process that can and should continue indefinitely), the next thing to consider is what you can do to meet your customers' needs that can't be done face-to-face. What new products or services can you offer people on the Web? What type of convenience factors are important to your prospective customers?

Building a Web site or a Web-based business begs the same questions as building a business offline. Make sure your Web strategy is as detailed as your offline business strategy. Consider:

- Business objectives
- Attractiveness of market opportunity
- Target market
- Competition
- Customer needs
- Your business's strengths and weaknesses

Think in the broadest terms you can, ignoring the costs and technical hurdles of building your dream site. Make a list of what you would ideally provide to your customers, based on your knowledge of their needs. With this list in hand, and your growing knowledge of the possibilities (from your frequent Web surfing), you now have a starting point for your site.

Visit a lot of Web sites to find out what works and what doesn't

## Requirements for Building a Web Site

The next step in Web development is assessing what you require to build your site. There are many Web development shops and interactive agencies that are experts in this process. These companies range from one- or two-person design shops, to large agencies with teams of designers, programmers, strategists, and client managers. As a small business, your best bet is to search your area for the former. And surprisingly enough, the best place to find a Web design shop is on the Web!

Once you've gathered a list of five or six shops (or more, if you have the time), set up appointments with each of them. Evaluate their capabilities, design sensibilities, and costs. Be sure to look at sites they have already developed and ask for customer references. There is no charge for this first meeting, and you'll be amazed by how much you can learn in the process.

Issues to address include:

- How quickly do you need a functioning Web site?
- Can you do a phased development, launching additional features as you have more time, money, and skills?
- How much money can you budget for creating a Web site?
- What business tasks do you want to accomplish online?
- Who are the customers you want to reach online?
- What information do your customers need?
- Which online business model do you want to consider?
- Will you seek advertisers for your site?
- Do you want to record what users do on your site?
- How often do you want information on your site to change?

The budget question is an important one. Since Web sites can be built by just about anyone, and everyone approaches the task differently, there is a wide range of costs for Web development. You could design and launch your own Web site almost for free. Conversely, a well-designed **promotional Web site** (with no e-commerce functionality) might cost a few thousand dollars, and could take one to two months to design and build.

A **transactional (or e-retailing) Web site** with database technology that allows your customers to browse your products and make credit card purchases could cost you around $75,000, or a whole lot more. Transactional sites can take four months to a year to develop. Sites like this can either be developed by your company (if you want to hire an entire Web team); or can be built, hosted, and maintained by other companies that specialize in doing just that.

**Content sites** that entertain and inform users often take content from print and publish it online. This can require editing, reformatting, and rethinking the entire presentation of that content. These sites have more pages (sometimes thousands of pages) and can take six months or more to develop.

## Online Marketing Strategies

The remarkable success of the Internet means that it's very, very crowded! Somehow, you have to get your Web site noticed so that people can see what you have to offer. This means marketing. The most successful "e-tailers" spend massively on advertising and marketing, both online and offline. Some, like Amazon.com, have virtually become household words. It's not uncommon for Internet businesses to spend more than half of every dollar they earn on attracting new customers! For online businesses, short-term profits must often be sacrificed to the long-term goals of market share, consumer trust, and branding.

A good place to start is with your offline marketing. All of your packaging, letterhead, and other business materials should have your URL prominently printed on them. Word of mouth is a powerful tool, too; tell your customers and friends that your Web site just went up, and explain what service or incentive it offers. Consider handing out little printed announcements of your Web launch.

Figure out what customers want from your business, and find a way to deliver it online

### What Kind of Site Do You Want?

- **Promotional.** Creates awareness, stimulates demand, promotes your brand
- **Transactional.** Allows customers to buy products or services online
- **Content.** Entertains or informs visitors

The best way to attract traffic to a Web site is by offering things on it that people want. Figure out what your customers want from your business, and find a way to deliver it to them online. If they want to learn more about your products or services, create a section on your site where they can get more details with a minimum of difficulty. If they want to be able to schedule appointments with you, put your e-mail address in an obvious position on your first page. Other valuable content and functionality to offer online includes:

- Company contact numbers and address
- Directions to your business
- Frequently Asked Questions page
- Product/services information
- A question or feedback mechanism
- An ordering mechanism

The best Web sites use clean design, with simple graphics that load quickly. Using elaborate frames, multiple browser windows, or streaming media can crash browsers and frustrate your visitors. Frustrated visitors rarely return for a second look!

# Online Advertising

Adweek magazine claims that in 1998, advertisers spent $1.9 billion on online ads, surpassing the total spent on outdoor billboards!  Some companies are willing to pay as much as $200 in marketing costs for each new customer they attract, their logic being that the long-term value of a loyal customer is worth far more than this initial expenditure.  This principle is well worth remembering, provided you understand that you can succeed on the Internet without spending millions.  Although you should definitely think twice before competing directly with huge e-tailers like Amazon.com or CDNow.com, there is still plenty of room on the Web for innovative, creatively marketed products.  A unique e-commerce business targeting a comparatively small niche market can often control that market in an incredibly short time, and with a minimal outlay of advertising dollars.

## How Online Advertising is Different

Almost everyone agrees that online marketing is quite different from its traditional counterpart.  Many experts feel that online advertising should be interactive, and must offer some sort of reward for the consumer's time and attention.  This reward can be as simple as gratified curiosity: one insurance corporation devised an interactive banner advertisement featuring a very short questionnaire, into which interested users entered their age and annual income to receive an estimate of how much money they'd need to retire.  This unusual, compelling ad resulted in a response rate twice the industry average!

Businesses are constantly devising new strategies for online advertising.  While most experts agree that standard advertising techniques can be inappropriate for the Web, there's not much agreement about what works and what doesn't.  Also, credibility problems arise because many advertisers take advantage of the Internet's tendency to blur the boundaries between objective information and promotional hype.  The result?  Some consumers are liable to mistake objective information for hype, or vice versa; while others may be unwilling to trust any information they find on the Web.

Just as for any other form of advertising, the regulations of the Federal Trade Commission's Division of Advertising Practices apply: online ads cannot be deceptive, and any objective claims they make must be substantiated.  More than almost any other type of commerce, e-commerce depends on consumer trust, so be honest, fair, and deliver on your promises!

## Don't Interrupt!

In his book *Permission Marketing*, Yahoo! Inc. Vice President Seth Godin argues persuasively that the online entrepreneur cannot rely on the old tactics of what he calls "interruption marketing"; instead, Godin advocates giving the customer something in return for his or her time.

This notion of "interruption" is one of the major differences between Internet advertising and traditional advertising.  If a consumer wants to avoid advertising interruptions while watching television or listening to the radio, he or she must take an active step like changing the channel, turning the volume down, or leaving the room.  By contrast,

Internet advertisers usually require that the consumer take an active step (i.e., clicking on a banner or icon) to see the advertisement; therefore, online ads must coax consumers to interrupt their Internet experience willingly. In this respect, Web marketing has more in common with direct mailings than it does with electronic media such as radio or TV. This is why the idea of permission marketing is a sound one. In effect, the prospective customer agrees to view an advertising message in return for receiving a product, a discount, or a coupon. You might give away a free duffel bag or mouse pad (imprinted with your logo and URL, of course!) to everyone who registers with your site, or to everyone who buys from it. A less costly strategy would be to appeal so strongly to a customer's curiosity or sense of humor that he or she is drawn to click on your ad. Obviously, there are many possibilities. This is a great time to be creative! As an entrepreneur, you know better than anyone how valuable time is, so ask yourself what would compel you to take time out to look at an ad.

Another new Internet marketing concept is the somewhat unappetizingly named **viral marketing**. This refers to an offer or premium so exciting that consumers pass it along to their friends. The potential for word of mouth advertising on the Web is huge, so if you offer a terrific deal, chances are you'll get noticed fast!

### Direct E-mails

In general, direct e-mailing is not at all popular with online consumers. Many of the junk e-mails (or "spam") people receive offer miracle cures, dubious financial opportunities, or pornography. This inappropriate use has resulted in a certain amount of guilt by association for legitimate marketers. It's also true that a busy person who has to answer 15 or 20 e-mails is likely to respond with hostility to an unsolicited junk e-mail. In fact, due to customer demand, some ISPs allow their subscribers to block unsolicited e-mails!

Does this mean you should never send out mass e-mail messages? Not necessarily. If you serve a small niche market, such as model train enthusiasts or collectors of movie ephemera, an e-mailing list of persons currently involved with model train or film newsgroups, discussion groups, "chat rooms," or list services could be invaluable. (In fact, one of the reasons people join such groups is to increase their exposure to related products and services.)

Your best bet is to identify your target market as narrowly as possible, compile or purchase the appropriate mailing lists, and then send an interesting, brief, unobtrusive e-mail that introduces your business and relates it to the recipient's particular interests. Another possibility is to offer regular updates on your company, or a subscription to an online newsletter—information that is resented as unsolicited junk mail is valued when it comes in response to a request! For this reason, your Web site should have an icon that customers can click on to be added to your mailing list; this enables you to reach thousands of current and prospective customers at a fraction of the cost of traditional direct mailing.

Keep the "spam"

in the can

## The Six Levels of Business Use of the Internet

In the course of delivering Business Internet and Technology training to thousands of small businesses since 1996, members of the Qwest WOW Technology Outreach Program and the Qwest eBITS Business Internet & Technology Solutions group have observed the following levels of business participation in the Internet:

1. Unaware and doesn't care: Management knows little or nothing about the Net, doesn't care to use the Net and believes the business will survive and thrive without making use of the Net. Small businesses of all sorts are beginning to realize that this can be a dangerous and fruitless position.

2. Aware but not online: Business has been exposed to and is aware of the power of the Internet, but is not yet connected. A clever business can be a major player on the Internet at this level.

    - Beg, borrow, or buy Net time from others including family, friends, library, or the local community college. Obtain and use a free email account such as Hotmail, Yahoo Mail, or Qwest.Net Mail.
    - Add your business information to the Web sites of other organizations including the chamber of commerce, convention and visitors bureau, industry sites, and industry publications.
    - Sell products through e-malls, free e-stores such as Bigstep or Freemerchant, auctions sites such as E-Bay, or through an Amazon.com Z-Store.
    - Place your business information with online yellow pages such as Qwest DEX (www.qwestdex.com)
    - Use the Net to research purchasing options and broaden your supplier base to a global market.

3. Online and using major Internet tools and features: At this level, a business does all the above tasks on its own computer and Web connection and broadens its use of the Internet. This might be a good opportunity to network the office, especially if you are bringing in high-speed connectivity such as DSL, Cable, T-1, or ISDN. Networking allows you to share printers and other office equipment and access information on multiple computers.

4. Create a Web site: There is no good reason for a business to not have a Web site. Many companies such as Tripod, Xoom, Freemerchant, Bigstep and others offer free Web space and free Web page building tools. Most Internet service providers offer a limited amount of free Web page space to their customers. Fee-based Web sites cost as little as $10-$15 per month. Once you have your permanent domain name, create linking relationships with organizations identified in level two.

5. Create a commerce-enabled Web site: There are an increasing number of free e-commerce options suitable for a small operation. Tripod, Bigstep, and Freemerchant are only a few of the companies offering free e-commerce options. Fee-based commerce sites such as Yahoo Store and Sitematic offer easy to use online-based Web and catalog building tools. *continued...*

Where will your business fit in?

6. Run an in-house Web server: At level six, you become your own Internet service provider by running your own Web server. This is a major task for most small businesses. You gain flexibility but inherit all the tasks, responsibilities, and costs formerly shouldered by your ISP. Only businesses with fairly deep pockets and strong internal technical talent should consider operating at level six.

Be sure to check out the eBITS Web site: www.ebits.org

## Telling the Web About Your Site

How do you let the population of people surfing around on the Web know about your site? Lots of ways—most of which are free, quick, and easy! The first step is registering with search engines and creating appropriate titles, or "metatags," for your pages. These simple HTML descriptions tell search engines what sort of information is on your site. Search engine "spider" applications pick up your metatags and list your site when key words are entered.

For an excellent and detailed description of how search engines work, go to http://www.go.com (formerly Infoseek) and search for information on the Infoseek search engine tool.

"What's New" Web pages are another fast way to promote your site. These pages list sites that have only recently come online. This used to be the only way to advertise your new Web site, and it is still quite popular. Check out the following locations:

- **Netscape What's New** (http://www.netscape.com/home/whats-new.html). Netscape publishes sites that are unique, or that are a good example of Web page design.
- **Open Market** (http://www.directory.net/). This site provides a daily listing of new commercial sites on the Web. They turn around their new submissions in about a day.
- **Page Classifieds** (http://ep.com/). Under the category "announcements," there is a "Web announcement" listing where you can take out a classified advertisement for free. They can also create a free classified service for your site.

You may wish to announce your Web page address to all major search engines and directories with one submittal. SubmitIt! (http://submitit.com) allows you to choose up to 400 search engines and directories.

# Search Engines

Search engines are the most popular way to find information on the Web. Users type in what they are looking for, and the search engine lists sites that contain matching words or phrases. This doesn't necessarily mean that you will find what you're looking for immediately. The fine art of creating the ideal search engine is still being perfected, as evidenced by the random and sometimes downright strange places you find yourself online!

There is an important element to incorporate on your page before you list your site. Make sure the "title" of your html document is as descriptive as possible about the content of your site. For example, the title for a site promoting a catering business might say, "Sarah Jane's is a full-service gourmet catering service located in downtown Bloomington, Indiana."

- **Alta Vista** (http://www.altavista.digital.com/). With up to 21,000,000 sites indexed, Alta Vista is another "must" for your site. Pay close attention to the instructions: you only need to add your "top" page and Alta Vista will find the rest.
- **WebCrawler** (http://webcrawler.com/). A robot search of the Web.
- **HotBot** (http://hotbot.lycos.com) This search engine is part of the Lycos Network, and includes links to both the HotBot and Lycos directories.

# What are Web Directories?

Web directories are indexes to various places on the Web, listed alphabetically by region, or by subject. The most effective sites are listed by subject or category. Because you want the most people to see your site listing, it is very important to choose the category carefully. Take some time to acquaint yourself with each directory service and how it works before you submit your site. This will help you choose the best category for your site, and could very well mean the difference between 10 and 100 visitors to your site per day!

- **Yahoo** (http://www.yahoo.com/). More people begin their Internet browsing at Yahoo than at any other page, so you will definitely want your site listed here. Yahoo is a little different from search engines in that it is a directory—a listing of sites compiled by people, not software. To be listed on Yahoo, you must submit your site and a description of its contents. Yahoo will place your site in its directory under the proper category, as well as on its "What's New" page.
- **Go.com** (formerly Infoseek). Like Yahoo, Go.com contains listings of sites by category. It's another very important place to have your site listed.
- **Internet Mall** (http://www.mecklerweb.com/imall/). If you sell over the Internet, this service will list your site for free.

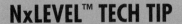

## NxLEVEL™ TECH TIP

### Useful Web Resources

**Net-Happenings** (http://www.mid.net:80/NET/). This is a newsletter sent out to a mailing list, and also archived on the Web. You can announce anything about the net here; all postings are moderated. To subscribe, e-mail to majordomo@is.internic.net, with the phrase "subscribe net-happenings" in the body.

**Net Surfer Digest** (http://www.netsurf.com/nsd/index.html). An overview of new and interesting Web sites.

**Banister's Submit-It** (http://www.submit-it.com). One-stop service submits your site to many places on the Web at once. Excellent time-saver; however, you can't tailor your listing for each site. Great for those who want a lot to happen fast.

**A1 Index of over 650 Free WWW URL Submission & Search Sites** (http://www.vir.com/~wyatt/index.html). Here is a list of Web sites that will take your announcement. There are no descriptions (so you have to search to see what is appropriate). Great for ideas.

Here are a few books that list URLs for interesting and useful Web sites:

**New Riders Official World Wide Web Yellow Pages** (http://www.mcp.com/nrp/wwwyp). This enormous book lists thousands of sites.

**Walking the World Wide Web** (http://www.vmedia.com/shannon/shannon.html). The most recent edition had 200 pages of Web sites. The author (Shannon R. Torlington) provides an extensive writeup for each site listed in the book. Published by Ventana Press.

**Internet Roadside Attractions** (http://www.vmedia.com/ira.html). Also published by Ventana Press, this book specializes in things to do on the Internet.

**Free Stuff from the World Wide Web** (http://www.coriolis.com/coriolis). This book contains many sites that provide free stuff on the Web.

**How to Grow Your Business on the Internet** (http://www.coriolis.com/coriolis). This book has a good chapter on Web resources.

- **Galaxy** (http://galaxy.einet.net/galaxy.html). A must for any Web site. As with Yahoo, choose your category carefully.
- **W3** (http://www.w3.org/hypertext/datasources/bysubject/overview.html). A thorough directory of many Web sites.
- **Starting Point** (http://www.stpt.com/). Another super spot to have your site listed.
- **The Yellow Pages** (http://theyellowpages.com). You can submit your site only by e-mail to admin@theyellowpages.com. Include your category, URL, and a two- to four-sentence description.

- **Lycos** (http://www.lycos.com/). Lycos gets its listings by automatically searching the entire Web. Do nothing and it may find you anyway! But you can ask the Lycos program to search/list your site ASAP. Lycos has 11,000,000 listings, so ASAP may be 3 weeks!

## Conclusion

No matter how big or small your business is, and no matter what products or services it offers, the odds are that you can improve its sales and visibility by going online. Even if you're not yet ready to set up a fancy e-commerce site that accepts credit cards, a well-designed, informative Web page can attract potential customers you'd never reach otherwise, as well as suppliers, distributors, investors, employees...even buyout offers!

Certain experts believe that most businesses will be unable to succeed and grow without expanding into e-commerce. Whether or not this is true, there is no doubt that staying offline in coming years will make it increasingly difficult to compete effectively. Since you're committed to growing your business, why not start right now to get acquainted with one of the most powerful tools at your command?

## Chapter 35
# OVERVIEW OF FINANCIAL STATEMENTS

*About This Chapter:*
- *Basic accounting concepts*
- *Limitations of financial statements*
- *The income statement*
- *The statement of owners equity*
- *The statement cash flows*
- *Financial statement analysis*

## Introduction

Accounting is the process of measuring, recording, and communicating financial information. **Financial statements** are the means of communicating this information. Users generally fall into two categories: **internal users** include owners and managers, who need to get feedback about decisions they have made, evaluate performance, and identify planning opportunities and needs; **external users** include bankers, investors, partners, governmental agencies, and competitors. For them, the information helps in evaluating potential investments, determining credit worthiness, or assessing taxes.

Financial statements tell the story of what happened to the business over the past year. Comparative statements also include information from previous years. Sometimes, financial statements are prepared as a forecasting tool. These are called **pro forma statements** and result from the budgeting process.

## Basic Accounting Concepts

It is easier to understand financial statements if you understand the basic principles of accounting.

### Historical Cost Principle

The **historical cost principle** states that all amounts must be recorded at the exchange price of the transaction at the time it occurred; they are not adjusted for changes in market value. For example, suppose a business bought land in 1978, at a price of $50,000. In 2000, the land is worth $250,000, but only the historical cost of $50,000 appears in the financial statements. Why? Because fair market value estimates are subjective and change frequently.

How much?

Financial statements

reflect historical cost, not

current market value

## Economic Entity Concept

The **economic entity concept** calls for the separation of accounting records and information of a business from those of all other entities, including owners. Let's say a sole proprietor buys a computer for personal use. Even if business funds are used for the purchase, the computer does not belong in the business's financial statements. If the computer had been purchased for business use, the expense would be included on the financial statement.

———————◆———————

*Louisa Egan was a shrewd and knowledgeable business woman who operated a busy travel agency in Peekskill, New York. She specialized in customized adventure travel packages, and knew her clients—and the destinations she recommended to them— personally.*

*By the fall of 1998, she felt she'd reached the point of diminishing returns. She decided to close her office space and manage a small pool of her favorite clients from her home office.*

*Within six months, she was bored. She'd simply had enough of the travel business! She began to toss around other business ideas with her daughter, Anne, who had just graduated from business school. Louisa decided she wanted to start a new business that would create and sell a tangible product, and that she could pass on to Anne when she retired.*

———————◆———————

## Accrual Versus Cash Accounting

A business hires an attorney to do legal work. The attorney completes the legal work in December and the business pays the bill in January. Thus, the attorney has a revenue and the business an expense. Will the revenue and expense be recorded in December or January?

Under the **accrual basis** of accounting, which states that revenues and expenses occur when the action takes place—even if cash changes hands on a different date—the transaction would be recorded in December. Under the **cash basis**, which states that revenues and expenses occur when cash changes hands, the transaction would be recorded in January.

The accounting profession recommends the use of the accrual basis, but most individuals and some small businesses use the cash basis, which is usually easier to understand.

## Full Disclosure Principle

This principle mandates full disclosure of events and circumstances that affect the user of the financial statements. This is done in the statements themselves, or in attached footnotes. As a result of recent lawsuits, the amount of disclosure required has been increasing.

When?

The accrual method says to record revenues and expenses when the transaction takes place

# Limitations of Financial Statements

Although financial statements are the accepted means of communicating financial information about a business, there are limits to their usefulness.

## Historical Cost Principle

Accountants chose this method to make accounting information more reliable, but it also can make the information irrelevant. Who cares how much something cost 50 years ago? Isn't it more important to know how much it's worth today? You won't find that amount in the financial statements.

## Off-Statement Transactions

Despite attempts to make financial statements comprehensive, many transactions are not reflected in financial reporting. This can result from the complexity of the transaction, barter transactions that are not recorded in the books, or the correct application of accounting principles that allow certain transactions to be "off-statement."

## Use of Estimates

Perhaps you think accounting is an exact science? Most of the time it is, but accountants often make estimates of income taxes due, bad debt losses, and many other figures. (Of course, accountants must always strive for fair reporting of financial information.)

## Garbage In, Garbage Out

Financial statements are compiled from the company's daily records. If the recordkeeping is shoddy, the financial statements will be too.

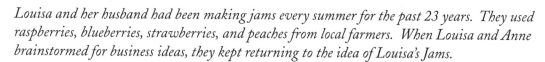

*Louisa and her husband had been making jams every summer for the past 23 years. They used raspberries, blueberries, strawberries, and peaches from local farmers. When Louisa and Anne brainstormed for business ideas, they kept returning to the idea of Louisa's Jams.*

*Anne researched the market for specialty jams and talked to several gourmet food representatives. She made an estimate of overhead expenses, and the amount of jars they'd have to sell to make a profit. The numbers seemed realistic. She and her mother decided to go for it.*

*Anne then negotiated a long-term lease of an old bottling and commercial kitchen facility just outside town. Attached to the back of the building was a warehouse space. The facility needed a lot of work, so Anne negotiated with the owner to get the first six months free in exchange for restoring it.*

*Anne calculated that Louisa's Jams could produce 10,000 jars of jam during its summer months of production. The busiest month would be June, when local farmers harvested blueberries and strawberries.*

*It would be a seasonal business since it would only operate its production facility during the summer. In winter, the business would only need warehouse space to hold inventory and a small office space to manage sales, finance, and marketing operations.*

*Anne figured they could rent out their excess kitchen capacity during the "down" months, which was most of the year. Revenue from these subleases would cover the maintenance and overhead costs for the large facility. In fact, depending on how well she managed the facility, the subleases could end up providing Louisa's Jams with some serious income.*

*She asked around, and came up with three local businesses that were interested. One was a small catering company called Peekskill Caterers.*

## The Income Statement

**Revenue** is the money generated by such earning activities as selling a product, charging rent, or receiving interest on a loan. **Expenses** are the cost of resources used in the process of earning revenue, such as insurance, advertising, wages, and payroll taxes. An **income statement** is a summary of the revenue generated and expenses paid during a given time period. It has a simple formula:

### Revenues - Expenses = Net income

This general formula can be expanded to provide more detail:

| Your Business Income Statement For the Year Ended December 31, 1999 | | |
|---|---|---|
| Sales | | $450,000 ❶ |
| Less: Cost of goods sold | | (200,000) ❷ |
| Gross Profit | | $250,000 ❸ |
| Less: Operating Expenses ❹ | | |
| Wages expense | $80,000 | |
| Payroll tax expense | 20,000 | |
| Insurance expense | 5,000 | |
| Rent expense | 24,000 | |
| Advertising expense | 3,000 | |
| Utilities expense | 1,400 | |
| Depreciation expense | 1,300 ❺ | 134,700 |
| Net Operating Profit or Loss | | $115,300 |
| Other gains and losses: | | |
| Interest revenue | | 700 |
| Interest expense | | (1,200) |
| Net Income Before Taxes | | $114,800 |
| Less: Income Taxes | | 30,000 ❻ |
| Net Income | | $84,800 ❼ |

**ITEM 1—Sales.** Revenue for retail, wholesale, and manufacturing is earned mainly through sales. In the service business, it is called **Fees earned** or **Services revenue.** Notice that there is a separate category, called **Other gains and losses**, which includes earning activities other than your primary operations.

**ITEM 2—Cost of Goods Sold.** The major expense for retailers, wholesalers, and manufacturers is **cost of goods sold**, which is the cost of the products the business sells. This sounds simple enough, but there are many variations to consider. For example, assume that you buy some inventory items for $5.70 each, and later buy some more for $5.90 each. When you make a sale, how will you calculate cost of goods sold? Should it be $5.70 or $5.90? If you can identify the specific products sold, you can answer the question easily. If not, you must use one of three assumptions: 1) the first in are the first out (FIFO); 2) the last in are the first out (LIFO); or 3) an average of the two.

Manufacturers must consider three different costs in their cost of goods sold:

- **Direct materials**—those materials that become an integral part of the product. For a furniture manufacturer, this would include wood and hardware.
- **Direct labor**—the cost of labor spent creating the product. In the case of the furniture manufacturer, it would be the cost of the workers who build the furniture.
- **Overhead**—encompasses all manufacturing costs not already included in direct materials or direct labor.

The income statement is a summary of actions which took place during a given time period

**ITEM 3—Gross Profit.** This is the amount remaining after covering the cost of the products sold. When you subtract all expenses from the gross profit, the result is net income (or loss).

**ITEM 4—Operating Expenses.** All expenses (other than cost of goods sold) incurred in your major line of business (e.g., wages, rent, advertising, payroll taxes, utilities, and depreciation). You can group these expenses into subcategories if you wish. For small businesses, operating expenses normally include all expenses except cost of goods sold, interest, and income tax. These expenses are separated because they are significant for financial analysis.

Revenues - expenses = net income

**ITEM 5—Depreciation Expense.** In common usage, depreciation represents the decrease in value of an asset. Accountants use depreciation to spread the cost of equipment, buildings, and tools over the life of the asset. The cost of these items is an expense of doing business, just like wages or rent, but the equipment has a longer useful life and so should not be shown as a one-time expense. Let's say your business bought a piece of equipment for $25,000 and you expect to use it for 25 years. Is this an expense of doing business? Yes, but we record the expense over the item's 25-year useful life.

There are several methods of calculating depreciation, but most small businesses use one of two methods allowed under federal income tax laws: the **straight-line method**, or the **Modified Accelerated Cost Recovery System** (MACRS). The straight-line method is simple. To calculate it, one simply divides the cost of a piece of equipment by its estimated useful life. In the example above, depreciation expense is $25,000/25 years, or $1,000 per year.

**ITEM 6—Income Taxes.** Income taxes are an expense of doing business, but whether or not you may include this on your income statement depends upon the legal structure of your business. Income taxes are not considered an expense for sole proprietorships or partnerships, because the taxes are levied on the owners rather than on the business. Income taxes *are* levied on corporations, so they appear on the corporation's income statement.

Manufacturers have three parts to cost of goods sold: direct materials, direct labor, and overhead

**ITEM 7—Net Income.** We have worked our way to the **bottom line**. Again, for the income statement, that means:

$$\text{Revenues - Expenses = Net income}$$

Remember: As revenues go up, so does net income. As expenses go up, net income goes down. Therefore, selling as much as you can while keeping expenses as low as possible is fundamental to success.

---

*After the first year of operation, Louisa and Anne realized they'd underestimated the amount of money needed to operate their business. The cost of upgrading their facility and maintaining the old equipment was considerably more than they had expected. Anne sat down and calculated that if the business invested in new bottling equipment, it would save on the cost of continually repairing the old, run-down equipment (that she thought had been such a bargain) and would result in a larger and more reliable production capacity.*

*The cost of the new equipment was over $50,000; it was time for Louisa's Jams to look for external financing. They needed to clean up their financial statements, fine-tune their business plan, and create what Anne called, "A really well-thought-out financing proposal!"*

---

## The Balance Sheet

The balance sheet shows the business's financial situation on a given day *only*. The formula for the balance sheet is:

**Assets = Liabilities + Owner's equity**

**Assets** are economic resources owned by the business, purchased with funds supplied by creditors or owners. **Liabilities** are amounts owed by the business to creditors. **Owner's equity** is amounts owed by the business to the owners.

The balance sheet presents the total of what the business owns, and divides up the assets:

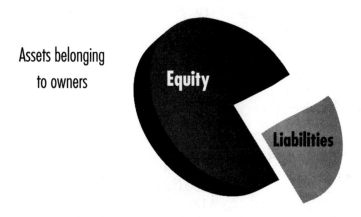

Assets belonging to owners

**Equity**

**Liabilities**

Assets belonging to creditors

The balance sheet presents the total of what the business owns and who has a claim to those resources

Most often, owner's equity is described as the amount left over after liabilities are subtracted from assets. Though accurate, this is perhaps not the most helpful way to think about equity. Recall the discussion of the economic entity concept: If the business is a separate economic entity from the owners, then the owners are just like all other creditors. Funds loaned to the business by creditors must be repaid someday, and creditors generally expect to earn interest on their loans. By the same token, owners hope to get back the amount they put into the business, plus some profit. Thus, equity represents the amount the business owes to the owners for amounts invested, plus profit.

◆

*Louisa was new to the process of gathering the data to update financial statements. When she operated her travel agency, she left all the "number crunching" to her accountant and her business manager. But this time, working with her daughter, she was fascinated. She was curious to find the answers to some nagging questions, like:*

- *Which jams were most profitable? And what type of products would be most profitable to offer in the future?*
- *Were her costs in line with those of her competitors?*
- *How much debt could her business afford to carry?*
- *How attractive was her business to potential investors?*
- *Had the business broken even yet?*
- *Was her daughter doing a good job of managing cash?*
- *What portion of the earnings came from renting out excess kitchen capacity?*

*Updating the business's financial statements gave her the answers to these questions. It was also a powerful reminder of why Louisa's Jams was profitable, and helped prepare the business to seek additional capital.*

◆

Equity represents the amount the business owes to the owners for amounts invested plus profit

**Your Business**
**Balance Sheet**
As of December 31, 1999

**ASSETS:**

Current Assets: ❶

| | | |
|---|---|---|
| Cash | $ 35,000 | |
| Accounts receivable | 70,000 | |
| Inventory | 120,000 | |
| Other | 12,000 | $ 237,000 |

Property, Plant & Equipment: ❷

| | | |
|---|---|---|
| Land | $ 80,000 | |
| Buildings | 250,000 | |
| Equipment | 175,000 | |
| Less: Accumulated Depreciation | (105,000) ❸ | 400,000 |

Intangible Assets: ❹

| | | |
|---|---|---|
| Patents | $10,000 | |
| Goodwill | 60,000 ❺ | 70,000 |
| TOTAL ASSETS | | $ 707,000 |

**LIABILITIES:**

Current Liabilities: ❻

| | | |
|---|---|---|
| Accounts payable | $ 45,000 | |
| Wages payable | 32,000 | |
| Other | 6,000 | $ 83,000 |

Long-term Liabilities: ❼

| | | |
|---|---|---|
| Notes payable | | $ 245,000 |
| TOTAL LIABILITIES | | $ 328,000 |

| | |
|---|---|
| **OWNER'S EQUITY:** | $ 379,000 ❽ |
| *TOTAL LIABILITIES AND EQUITY* | $ 707,000 |

Assets = Liabilities +

Owners' Equity

**ITEM 1—Current Assets.** These are resources the business owns and expects to convert into cash or use up within one year of the balance sheet date. Segregating assets provides information about the short-term ability of the business to make payments and stay in business. In our example, your business owns assets that it expects to convert into $237,000 cash in the next year. That is to say, in addition to the $35,000 of existing cash, accounts receivable will be collected, inventory will be sold, and other assets will be converted into cash for a total of $237,000.

**ITEM 2—Property, Plant, and Equipment.** Includes assets expected to last more than one year. Remember, though, that these assets are listed at historical cost. Thus, in our example, $250,000 is the cost of the buildings when they were acquired, not their market value today.

**ITEM 3—Depreciation.** Depreciation has already been discussed as a means of spreading the cost of long-term assets over time. How much cost has been expensed in the past is the function of the **accumulated depreciation** amount listed on the balance sheet. In the example, accumulated depreciation is recorded as $105,000. Therefore, out of the total cost of buildings and equipment of $425,000, there remains $320,000 of depreciation expense to record in the future. (Note: Land is not depreciated, because the life of the land is infinite.)

**ITEM 4—Intangible Assets.** Intangible assets have no physical presence. You can touch the piece of paper that legally represents a patent, but you cannot touch the patent itself, because it is merely a legal concept. The most common intangible assets are patents, copyrights, franchises, trademarks, organization costs, and goodwill (see item 5).

The brand name and logo for Louisa's Jams falls into this category. How important to Nike is their "swoosh," or Ronald McDonald to the McDonald's Corporation? Very important indeed! And yet these assets might not be large amounts in the financial statements. Intangible assets are recorded at historical cost; the only cost to Nike of the "swoosh" was probably a fee to the graphic design firm that designed it. Furthermore, intangible asset costs are expensed in a manner similar to depreciation, called **amortization**. The amount on the balance sheet is the original cost less accumulated amortization. It may not be a very big number, but may represent something very important to the company.

*Intangible assets are recorded at historical cost*

This creates problems for small businesses trying to obtain financing. What if the most valuable asset the business owns is a patent? The patent appears on the balance sheet as the cost of obtaining it (i.e., total attorney and filing fees, or the purchase price if you bought it from someone else). However, research and development costs are not included. Thus, your most valuable asset appears on your balance sheet at a fraction of its worth to the business!

**ITEM 5—Goodwill.** Goodwill is another intangible asset. Suppose you buy a company with a reputation for great customer service; chances are, you'll pay more because of that reputation. The excess payment represents an estimated dollar value for goodwill.

*Goodwill is the intangible value of a business*

**ITEM 6—Current Liabilities.** Current liabilities are debts to be paid within the next year.

**ITEM 7—Long-term Liabilities.** These are debts due more than one year from the balance sheet date. They often include notes payable to the bank and investors.

**ITEM 8—Owner's Equity.** For a sole proprietorship, the owner's share of the business is listed as one amount, usually called **capital**. A partnership follows the same format, except that one capital amount is listed for each partner.

The owner's equity for a corporation is divided. The amount invested into the corporation by the stockholders is **capital stock**. Profits owed to the owners are **retained earnings**.

*Anne decided to do a cost/volume analysis to answer her mother's questions about how the business was generating its profits, and how close she was to recouping her initial investment.*

*Louisa's fixed and variable costs included the following items:*

<table>
<tr><td align="center">Fixed costs:</td><td align="center">Variable costs:</td></tr>
<tr><td align="center">Lease payments, salaries,</td><td align="center">Hourly wages,</td></tr>
<tr><td align="center">equipment maintenance,</td><td align="center">jars, labels,</td></tr>
<tr><td align="center">equipment depreciation,</td><td align="center">lids,</td></tr>
<tr><td align="center">insurance,</td><td align="center">berries, sugar,</td></tr>
<tr><td align="center">marketing, advertising</td><td align="center">gelatin</td></tr>
</table>

*Anne calculated that for every $4 jar of jam they sold, variable costs were $0.55 and fixed costs were $1.45. This meant that each jar generated $2 of profit. If the business continued at its current sales levels, it would repay its initial investment by the end of the year. Louisa was very happy to hear this.*

*By looking at the balance sheet, Anne calculated that the business's debt/equity ratio was a healthy 25%. This meant that for every dollar asset held by the business, only $0.20 was borrowed! Many businesses would feel that this was too little debt, and that by borrowing more money to grow operations, the business could generate a better return.*

*Anne and Louisa felt that the business could afford to carry more debt, and that the new bottling equipment would make the business stronger and more profitable.*

## Statement of Owner's Equity

The statement of owner's equity can be viewed as a bridge between the income statement and the balance sheet. The income statement details the income-producing activities of the business over a specified time period and delineates net income. Since net income is for the benefit of the owners, the statement of owner's equity adds it to the amount already owed to the owners. The adjusted owner's equity amount is then listed on the balance sheet.

The format differs somewhat depending on ownership structure. For sole proprietorships, the statement will appear as below. Partnerships use the same format, but with a capital account listed separately for each partner.

```
           The Sole Proprietorship
          Statement of Owner's Equity
        For the Year Ended December 31, 1996

    Beginning capital              $70,000
    New investment by owner         10,000
    Net income                      50,000
    Withdrawals                    (40,000)

    Ending capital                 $90,000
```

*A corporation should use the format below:*

```
              The Company, Inc.
          Statement of Retained Earnings
        For the Year Ended December 31, 1996

    Beginning retained earnings   $100,000
    Net income                     250,000
    Less: dividends               (150,000)

    Ending retained earnings      $200,000
```

*As Anne and Louisa updated the business's statement of cash flows for the past year's operations, they found the following:*

- *25% of the business's revenue came from leasing out its excess capacity.*

- *For any given month, the business had an average cash balance of $50,000. This was more than it needed on hand.*

- *The business earned 75% of its operating revenues in September, when its largest customers paid for orders.*

*Anne and Louisa concluded that they should buy the new equipment in October, when the business had its largest cash reserves. They also lowered their target amount of money to borrow, deciding that they could afford to reinvest a larger portion of profits in the business. In essence, they had underestimated the business's ability to pay for its own expansion. They also realized that they were earning a lot of cash from their sublease. If they could more aggressively manage that area of the business, they calculated they could increase overall revenues by 10%. In the future, Louisa's Jams would lease out excess warehouse space and bottling capacity. They also considered offering their tenants a fuller service facility, including commercial food production planning and budgeting assistance.*

# Statement of Cash Flows

When businesses use the accrual method of accounting, they gain very useful information about their past, present, and future financial situations. The accounting profession believes the accrual basis is better than the cash basis. However, it's nice to have a simpler explanation of how the business acquired and spent cash. This is the purpose of the **statement of cash flows**; it presents the amounts, sources, and uses of cash inflows and outflows. No new data is required to create this statement; the information is derived from the other financial statements. This may sound straightforward, but preparing a statement of cash flows is often a very difficult task in which amounts recorded using the accrual method must be converted to what they would have been had the cash method been used. Most small businesses have their accountants prepare this statement!

The statement of cash flows presents the amounts, sources, and uses of cash inflows and outflows

**Your Business**
**Statement of Cash Flows**
**For the Year Ended December 31, 1996**

| | |
|---|---:|
| Cash flows from operations: ❶ | |
| Net income | $90,000 |
| Depreciation expense | 50,000 |
| Increase in accounts receivable | ( 80,000) |
| Increase in inventory | ( 40,000) |
| Decrease in accounts payable | ( 10,000) |
| Cash provided by operations | $ 10,000 |
| | |
| Cash flows from investing activities: ❷ | |
| Purchase of new equipment | $ ( 55,000) |
| Sale of old equipment | 40,000 |
| Cash used for investing activities | $( 15,000) |
| | |
| Cash flows from financing activities: ❸ | |
| Proceeds from new borrowings | $ 135,000 |
| Principal payments on borrowings | ( 85,000) |
| Payment of dividends | ( 30,000) |
| Cash provided by financing activities | $ 20,000 |
| | |
| Net increase in cash | $ 15,000 ❹ |
| Cash balance 12/31/95 | 20,000 |
| Cash balance, 12/31/96 | $ 35,000 |

**ITEM 1—Cash Flows from Operations.** The statement of cash flows is divided into three categories. The first category details cash inflows and outflows from operations. There are two ways to present this information; we have shown the indirect method above. Your accountant may choose to use the direct method, but the result is the same either way: what net income would have been under the cash basis of accounting.

The indirect method can be very helpful in understanding the difference between net income and cash flow. Ever thought, "I have a large net income but no cash! How can that be?" Let's review the example: The business had $90,000 of net income. (This number is taken directly from the bottom of the income statement.) We must adjust this amount so that it accurately reflects the amount of cash held by the business today. First, net income includes depreciation expense, which is a process of cost allocation and has nothing to do with cash. (The cash was spent years ago, when the business bought the equipment.) Since depreciation does not cause additional cash to be spent, we can add it back to net income. Next, we'll look at three crucial operating accounts. Accounts receivable from customers have increased over last year's level, meaning that many of our sales have not yet materialized into cash. Inventory is higher than it was the previous year, so we must have used some of our cash to build up our inventory. Accounts payable have decreased, so we must have used cash to pay off more debts than normal. The statement of cash flows has helped us see that we have lots of net income, but not much cash on hand, thanks to slow collections, increased inventory, and fewer outstanding bills.

**ITEM 2—Cash Flows from Investing.** For small businesses, these inflows and outflows relate primarily to buying and selling property and equipment.

**ITEM 3—Cash Flows from Financing.** The final section lists cash flows from financing activities, including borrowing, paying off debts, issuing stock, and paying dividends.

**ITEM 4—Net Increase in Cash.** The statement concludes with the net change to cash during the year, which should equal the difference between the cash balance at the beginning and end of the period.

## Financial Statement Analysis

It doesn't do any good to get information if you don't use it! In this section, we will discuss the financial statements used to analyze a business. The purpose of this analysis is to:

- **Forecast the future.** Financial statements are historical documents, and historical data can be used to identify trends and forecast the future.
- **Make comparisons.** How well is the business doing? Is $1,000,000 net income high or low? Is $400,000 too much debt? To put your business in the proper perspective, you need to compare your information with that of other businesses, with your industry as a whole, with previous years, and with your expectations.
- **Answer questions.** If the net income is low this year, why is it low? If the answer is, "Because sales have dropped," why have they dropped? Keep asking questions until you get to the heart of the matter.
- **Get feedback about decisions.** Feedback helps you determine the financial outcome of your management decisions.
- **Be knowledgeable.** Keeping on top of your financial situation enables you to be proactive rather than reactive.

- **Present your story.** Discuss your analysis with your banker and CPA. Not only can they offer advice, but they'll be impressed with your efforts.

Financial analysis is very useful, but it does have limitations. First, if you compare your financial results to those of other businesses, remember that using different accounting methods can cause results to vary. Don't waste time comparing apples and oranges! Second, comparing your business to one many times its size might not be relevant. Last, don't fall into the trap of concentrating on effects; keep digging until you find causes.

It isn't easy to get financial information about other small businesses; often, only published industry data are available. Some trade associations publish averages and make them available to members. There are also general sources, which you can find in your public library, or obtain from your banker or CPA. The most well-known publications include:

- *Annual Statement Studies*, published by Robert Morris Associates.
- *Key Business Ratios*, published by Dun & Bradstreet
- *Almanac of Business and Industrial Financial Ratios*, published by Prentice-Hall.

If you decide to compare your business with published industry data, keep in mind that these are averages from which there can be wide deviation.

Now, let's look at four types of analysis: vertical analysis, horizontal analysis, ratio analysis, and cost-volume-profit analysis.

## Vertical Analysis

In this method, each item in the financial statement is expressed as a percentage of a selected base amount. Net sales are used as the base amount on the income statement, and total assets are used on the balance sheet. Consider the example below:

| Your Business Income Statement For the Year 1999 | | |
|---|---|---|
| Net Sales | $250,000 | 100% |
| Cost of Goods Sold | (130,000) | 52% |
| Gross Profit | 120,000 | 48% |
| Operating Expenses | 100,000 | 40% |
| **Net Income** | **$20,000** | **8%** |

| Your Business Balance Sheet 12/31/99 | | |
|---|---|---|
| **Assets** | | |
| Current Assets | $100,000 | 25% |
| Property, Plant & Equipment | 260,000 | 65% |
| Intangible Assets | 40,000 | 10% |
| Total Assets | $400,000 | 100% |
| | | |
| **Liablilities** | | |
| Current Liabilities | $80,000 | 20% |
| Long-term Liabilities | 180,000 | 45% |
| Total Liabilities | $260,000 | 65% |
| | | |
| **Owner's Equity** | $140,000 | 35% |
| Total Liabilities and Equity | $400,000 | 100% |

The percentages show the relative size of each component. You can then view these percentages in relation to previous years. If operating expenses for our sample business are typically 31% of net sales, then you know that some investigation of expenses is warranted. If current assets are usually 35% of total assets, what has changed? Also, vertical analysis is helpful when comparing your business to a business of a different size, or to industry averages. Instead of comparing the numbers, compare the relationship of the numbers. Is your gross profit of 48% average for your industry? How do long-term liabilities comprising 45% of total assets compare to your competitors?

## Horizontal Analysis

Horizontal analysis uses percentages over time rather than down the financial statement. Choose a base year, and express amounts for all other years as percentages of the base amount. Suppose we choose 1997 as the base year. Consider the following sales figures:

| Year | 2000 | 1999 | 1998 | 1997 |
|---|---|---|---|---|
| Sales | $186,000 | $180,000 | $126,000 | $120,000 |
| | 155% | 150% | 105% | 100% |

As you can see, sales tended to increase by five percentage points per year, except in 1999. Investigating the reason for the large jump in 1999 might give you information that will help you plan current marketing strategies, or you could follow the historical trend and budget 2001 sales at 160% of the base, or $192,000.

*Horizontal analysis moves across time rather than down financial statements*

## Ratio Analysis

A ratio is the comparison of one amount to another. Standard ratios can be grouped into three categories:

### Liquidity ratios

Liquidity ratios are a measure of a business's short-term ability to pay current (and unexpected) debts. Bankers analyze these ratios before approving short-term business loans.

**Working capital** $=$ Current assets - current liabilities

**Current ratio** $=$ $\dfrac{\text{Current assets}}{\text{Current liabilities}}$

**Quick ratio** $=$ $\dfrac{\text{Cash + Marketable securities + Receivables}}{\text{Current liabilities}}$

These three ratios reflect activities that are crucial to making a profit in your business.

**Working capital** is the money you need to pay your bills until inventory is sold and receivables are collected. The **current ratio** is another expression of working capital, but because it is expressed as a ratio, it represents the relationship of current assets to current liabilities, rather than an absolute amount. After all, working capital of $40,000 may be plenty for one business, and woefully low for another.

Since needs differ from business to business, there are no established minimums or maximums for the current ratio. However, there may be a rule of thumb for your industry. For each business, there is a level at which the ratio is too low and there is a serious risk that current debts cannot be paid. If current ratio is too high, it may mean that the business is keeping too much excess cash, not collecting receivables, or storing too much inventory.

The **quick ratio** is a refinement of the current ratio. It removes inventory from the calculation because inventory is the least liquid of the current assets.

**Gross profit** $=$ $\dfrac{\text{Net income}}{\text{Net sales}}$

**Inventory turnover** $=$ $\dfrac{\text{Cost of goods sold}}{\text{Average inventory}}$

**Receivables turnover** $=$ $\dfrac{\text{Net credit sales}}{\text{Average net receivables}}$

Earlier, we defined **gross profit** as net sales minus cost of goods sold. Here, we express gross profit as a percentage of net sales. This percentage is very important for making marketing decisions, determining cash needs, and assessing profitability. High-volume discount stores like Wal-Mart keep their gross profit percentages down and try to make up the revenue by increasing their sales volume. This strategy seldom works for small businesses, so it's important to keep an eye on this ratio! If your gross profit percentage declines, it means either that sale prices are dropping, cost of goods is increasing, or the mix of what you are selling has changed.

The **inventory turnover** ratio shows the average number of times inventory turns over (is sold) during the year. Of course, a grocery store should have a much higher ratio than a manufacturer of hand-crafted boats, because people buy groceries more often than they buy boats. Many small businesses get into trouble when their inventory sits and sits; a decreasing inventory turnover ratio will alert you to this problem. If inventory is turning over rapidly, it may mean that customer demand is barely being met, and expanding the business is in order.

Discuss your analysis with your broker and CPA

Your credit policies affect your **receivables turnover** ratio. Granting credit to slow-paying customers makes the ratio decline; this might explain why your business is always short of cash. A high ratio may mean that you are too rigid about credit terms and are losing sales.

### Capital structure ratios

If you consult published industry sources, you will find several ratios that measure capital structure. Here are the most common:

$$\text{Debt to total assets} = \frac{\text{Total debt}}{\text{Total assets}}$$

$$\text{Debt to equity} = \frac{\text{Total debt}}{\text{Total equity}}$$

The ratios measure the percentage of assets funded by borrowing. The remaining amount represents funding by the owners. For example, if your business's **debt to total assets** ratio is 65%, it follows that 35% of the total assets were purchased with your money. These ratios determine the relative riskiness of your capital structure. Carrying large amounts of debt increases the risk of insolvency (inability to meet long-term financial obligations), and necessitates current payments for interest and principal. A **debt to equity ratio** of ten to one indicates greater risk than a ratio of three to one. Not enough debt may indicate a too-conservative business that is missing golden opportunities.

### Profitability ratios

These ratios relate earnings to available resources. You might think of these as answering the question, "How well did I do, given what I had to work with?"

$$\text{Return on sales} = \frac{\text{Net income}}{\text{Net sales}}$$

$$\text{Return on assets} = \frac{\text{Net income}}{\text{Total assets}}$$

$$\text{Earnings per share} = \frac{\text{Net income}}{\text{Average \# of common shares outstanding}}$$

**Earnings per share** applies only to corporations and must be reported on the income statement. This ratio helps an individual shareholder understand what the corporate net income means; it does not mean that a dividend will be paid immediately in this amount. For some businesses, return on equity is a more appropriate ratio.

## Cost-Volume-Profit Analysis

Cost-volume-profit analysis is a very useful tool for entrepreneurs who want to see how expenses change when sales volume changes.

To perform this analysis, divide expenses into variable expenses (which change in total amount given changes in sales volume), and fixed expenses (which stay the same despite changes in sales volume). Here is a picture:

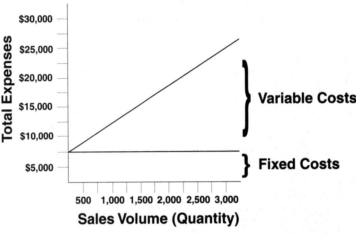

Most small businesses' expenses are fixed, with the exception of cost of goods sold. Suppose a retail shoe store is open 60 hours per week, and its owners have determined that one worker is needed during every operating hour. The cost of paying for 60 hours of work is fixed, no matter which employee receives the pay. The monthly rent is also fixed. Other major expenses, such as utilities and advertising, might change from month to month, but probably don't vary much if the owners are working within a budget. Thus, the only variable expense is the cost of the shoes that are sold.

Now, if we add to our graph a line depicting total sales, we can see the break-even point: that point at which total sales dollars and total expenses are equal.

Most small businesses find their expenses are fixed, with the exception of cost of goods sold

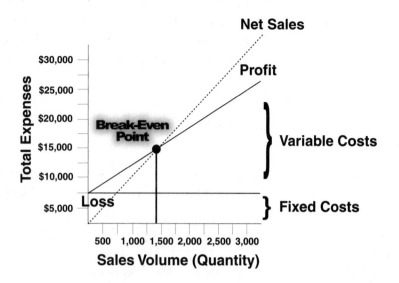

We can calculate the break-even point using the following formula:

**Break-even point**      =      $\dfrac{\text{Total fixed expenses}}{\text{Contribution margin per unit}}$

The contribution margin is the sales price per unit minus the variable expenses per unit.

**Contribution margin**      =      Sales price per unit - Variable expense per unit

It is the portion of the total sales price per unit that goes towards paying off fixed costs. We can adjust the formula to add a desired net income.

**Break-even point**      =      $\dfrac{\text{Total fixed expenses + Desired net income}}{\text{Contribution margin per unit}}$

Assume the following for the shoe store:

| | |
|---|---|
| Average sales price per unit | $ 30 |
| Variable cost per unit | $ 10 |
| Total fixed costs per month | $ 3,000 |
| Contribution Margin | $ 30     ($30-$10) |

The break-even point for the store is 150 units, calculated as follows:

$\dfrac{\text{Total fixed expenses}}{\text{Contribution margin}}$      =      $\dfrac{\$3,000}{\$20}$      =      150 units

If the owners hope to make $2,000 net income per month, they must sell 250 pairs of shoes.

$$\frac{\text{Total fixed expenses + Net income}}{\text{Contribution margin}} \quad = \quad \frac{\$3,000 + \$2,000}{\$20} \quad = \quad 250 \text{ units}$$

Now let's change things around and see what happens. What if total fixed expenses increase by 20%? 280 pairs of shoes must be sold to maintain the desired $2,000 in net income.

$$\frac{\text{Total fixed expenses + Net income}}{\text{Contribution margin}} \quad = \quad \frac{\$3,600 + \$2,000}{\$20} \quad = \quad 280 \text{ units}$$

*Profitability ratios relate earnings to the resources available*

## NxLEVEL™ TECH TIP

**To find answers to your accounting and tax questions, try searching on-line. You can even download the tax forms you need.**

- **Guide to Payroll Taxes** (http://www.payroll-taxes.com/)
- **Rutgers Accounting** (http://www.rutgers.edu/Accounting)
- **Small Business Accounting** (http://sbinformation.about.com/smallbusiness/sbinformation/msub18.htm)
- **Legal information and software** from Quicken (http://www.quicken.com/taxes/)
- **Small Business Tax Guide**, by Intuit (http://www.intuit.com/turbotax/taxcenter/ttbill1.html)
- **Reference Guide to Tax Sites** (http://www.el.com/elinks/taxes/)
- **IRS official site for information and downloading forms** (http://www.irs.ustreas.gov/cover.html)

**Tips on how to create budgets and address other financial issues can be found on the Internet through careful searching.**

- **Cash Planning Tips** (http://sbinformation.miningco.com/smallbusiness/sbinformation/msub18.htm)
- **Business library of on-line articles**, search by topic (http://www.anjoch-investors.com/library.htm)
- **Small Office Tips** (http://www.smalloffice.com)
- **Quicken's Personal Finance Page** (http://quicken.aol.com)

What if the cost of shoes goes up, or we have to lower our sales price, so that the contribution margin decreases $4 per unit? Now we must sell about 313 pairs to meet our goal.

$$\frac{\text{Total fixed expenses + Net income}}{\text{Contribution margin}} \quad = \quad \frac{\$3{,}000 + \$2{,}000}{\$16} \quad = \quad 312.5 \text{ units}$$

However, note that most businesses sell a wide variety of products, so using an average contribution margin per unit won't help you calculate needed volumes by product. Also, identifying which costs are variable and which are fixed is not always easy.

───────────────◆───────────────

*Louisa's Jams presented a financing proposal to four local banks. It stated that the company wanted to borrow $30,000 to pay for new bottling equipment, and that based on its projected sales (growing at 20% a year), it could repay the principal with interest in 20 years.*

*The business was approved for a $30,000 loan one month later. The time Louisa and Anne had put into planning their business and creating and using their financial statements paid off! They had a firm grasp on their business's profitability and cash flows, and were excited to be able to bring Louisa's Jams to an ever-growing audience.*

*They were fast becoming the most famous mother/daughter business team on the East Coast!*

───────────────◆───────────────

## Conclusion

Gathering and analyzing financial information is vital to running a healthy business. Successful entrepreneurs depend upon this information to make decisions. In Chapter 36 *Keeping Books and Records*, the accounting process will be discussed in greater detail, as will organization and business recordkeeping.

# Chapter 36
# KEEPING BOOKS AND RECORDS

*About This Chapter:*
- *It's a dirty job, but...*
- *What makes a good accounting system?*
- *Accrual versus cash accounting*
- *The paperwork*
- *Types of accounting systems*
- *The modules of an accounting system*
- *Tax considerations*
- *What records do you need to keep?*
- *How to choose a bookkeeper*
- *Using an accountant*

## Introduction

Donald Peterson seemed like a nice guy and a good bookkeeper, but he is now serving a 105-month federal prison sentence for embezzling millions of dollars from small businesses. At first, he wrote company checks to himself under a different name. Later, he took on a partner and gave him blank documents to create forgeries. If an employer got wise, Peterson moved to another business and assumed a new identity. He hid his thefts by "cooking the books" and handing his employer false financial statements. Incredibly, he said that few owners asked to see the bank statements, and none looked at the canceled checks. Peterson said that perhaps the theft was a "good learning experience," and helped to make his victims more careful business people.

Unfortunately, embezzlements from small businesses happen every year. In many cases, the theft could have been prevented if the business owner understood and paid attention to his or her accounting system.

This chapter is not intended to make you an accounting expert or solve all your accounting problems. The goal is to help you understand what accounting systems do, how they do it, and your role in managing them.

## It's a Dirty Job, But...

You probably didn't start a small business so you could stay up nights keeping books. Although someone has to do it, it doesn't have to be you; there are many good bookkeepers and accountants out there! But, as Donald Peterson's story shows, it is very important that you understand your accounting system and carefully review its results.

Why do you need accounting? First, there are legal requirements for keeping books and records. The federal government demands that you maintain records to support the amounts entered on your tax return. Second, bankers and lenders require that records be kept. Last, accounting is a means of gathering the information you need to run your business.

A quick word about terminology. You will hear people talk about accounting, recordkeeping, and bookkeeping. All three terms are used in this chapter. What is the difference? In common usage, not much. All three terms refer to keeping track of business transactions. The important thing to note is that all three terms refer to systems involving accounting books and records. The records are source documents that support amounts entered in the books.

Why do we need

accounting?

- Tax information
- Lenders
- Owners

---

*Fitness is big business in Miami. People are willing to pay for the best aerobic classes, latest cardiovascular equipment, and most challenging personal trainers. Sally Garcia was a certified aerobics instructor and personal trainer who worked as an independent contractor at several of the city's best gyms. After getting divorced, she took three months off to travel with friends. During that time, she assessed her professional life and decided she was ready for a bigger challenge.*

*Sally had talked with enough clients to know that most felt the fitness clubs in her area were too loud and impersonal. All 23 of her clients longed for a smaller, more personal club, and told Sally that they would be willing to pay up to 50% more for such a luxury.*

*She decided to make her move.*

---

## What Makes a Good Accounting System?

### Cost vs. Benefits of Information
Can you manage your business using a standard accounting system? Customizing standard systems, or creating new systems to fit your needs, can be time-consuming and expensive. Some questions to consider: How much detail do you really need? Is it worth the cost of getting it? Is it really important?

### Keep It Simple!
Simplicity is the key to a good accounting system; complicated systems often don't get used! Try to eliminate duplication of effort, summarize whenever possible, and set up procedures to eliminate guesswork and uncertainty.

Keep your accounting

system simple!

## Owner Involvement

The best accounting systems are those developed and operated under the watchful eye of the business owner. You needn't do the work yourself, but you must understand the system and be able to interpret the output. Remember, the more involved you are, the better your accounting system will function.

## Internal Controls

A good accounting system includes **internal controls**—policies and procedures that safeguard business assets, promote the objectives of the business, assure reliability of the financial statements, and facilitate compliance with laws and regulations. Internal controls vary by business, but here are some basics:

*Internal controls help you safeguard your assets*

### The control environment

This is a matter of setting an example. If the business owners perform their work carefully and with integrity, employees are more likely to do the same.

### Authorization

Make sure that all business transactions are authorized by the appropriate person. This does not mean the owner should make every decision. Delegation is an effective management tool, but you must clearly state to vendors, banks, and others what authority is being delegated and to which employee.

### Segregation of duties

This is often difficult for small businesses with few employees. However, good control comes from having authorization, recordkeeping, and custody activities performed by different people. (**Custody** refers to receiving or shipping goods or handling cash.)

### Physical controls

This includes such things as padlocked doors, safes, and identification cards for personnel. Blank checks and other documents should be pre-numbered, and locked away when not in use. Cash should be deposited daily.

### Tickler systems

A tickler system helps you keep track of current bills and orders. This can be a red folder for current orders, or a computer program that produces a daily report of due bills.

### Audit trail

A trail of evidence links amounts in the books with source documents. We will discuss examples later in the chapter.

### Monitoring/review

The business owner should consider if the internal controls are effective. Are they really being used? If so, do they accomplish everything they're supposed to? A yearly review by a CPA is also recommended.

*Sally opened her health club, Lunar Gym, in September of 1997. The business was a logical outgrowth of her passion for fitness. She never claimed to be a business woman; she knew nothing about accounting, so she relied on her general manager to take care of all business-related tasks, including keeping the gym's books.*

*Sally priced her gym memberships slightly higher than her competitors. She offered full club memberships, as well as class-only punch cards. When she felt she needed to increase her membership numbers, she would place an ad in the local paper and offer a discounted membership rate. In this way, Sally managed all of the club's marketing efforts.*

*She knew that her management style was "seat of the pants" at best. But the business seemed to be profitable. The rent was getting paid, her clients seemed happy, and she had the best instructors and the fullest aerobics classes in town.*

*Then, one day in 1999, her bank called to say it would not cover any more bounced checks.*

## Accrual Versus Cash Accounting

In the last chapter, we briefly discussed the difference between the cash and accrual methods of accounting. Under the accrual method, revenues and expenses are reported when the activity occurs, regardless of whether any cash has been exchanged. The cash method calls for reporting revenue when cash is received, and expense when cash is paid.

Accountants like the accrual method because it gives more information and is more accurate when matching revenue with the expenses associated with generating that revenue. However, the accrual method is generally more difficult than the cash method. For this reason, most individuals and many small businesses choose the cash method. Even more common is for small businesses to use a "hybrid" method of accounting—one that uses the cash method for some transactions and the accrual method for others, depending on what type of information the owners need. For example, if you were very concerned about how much your business owes to creditors, you could use the cash method except when it comes to accounts payable.

Some businesses fall under federal income tax rules that require use of the accrual method. Bank loan requirements may also call for the accrual method. If you're not sure whether to use the cash or accrual method, seek professional advice.

### Debits and Credits

One accounting equation that always must be kept in balance: Assets = Liabilities + Owner's Equity. You can check this equation after entering new amounts in your books, but there's a quicker method. Suppose you had a clean sheet of paper for every asset, liability, owner's equity, revenue, and expense account. Draw a vertical line down the middle of the paper, dividing it in half. Now you can record increases to that account on one half of the paper and decreases on the other. At the end of the period, you can total both sides and see what change occurred in the account. Doing these increases and decreases in the following manner results in another accuracy check.

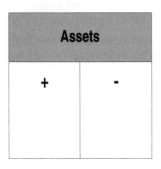

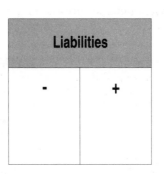

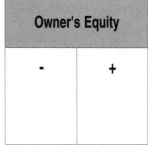

Debits on the left, credits on the right

Notice that the plus and minus are reversed on the two sides of the balance sheet equation. Now, when you record business transactions, your left sides will always equal your right sides. Suppose your business buys a new computer for $2,000 on account. Assets have increased because the business now owns a computer, so $2,000 goes on the left side of the Computer page. Liabilities have increased because the business now owes $2,000, so this amount goes on the right side of the Accounts Payable page. You have recorded $2,000 on a left side and $2,000 on a right side. After every transaction, you can check to see if your "lefts" equal your "rights." If not, you have made an error.

Instead of talking about lefts and rights, accountants gave them special names: debits and credits. Debit means the left side of the accounting sheet, credit means the right side. Debit in and of itself doesn't mean increase or decrease, good or bad, high or low...it just means left!

It is important to note that the debit and credit system does not protect against every type of error. For example, if you record your computer purchase with a debit to Computer for $2,000 and a credit to Accounts Payable for $200, this error will show up as soon as you try to balance the books. However, if you mistakenly record a debit to Computer for $200 and a credit to Accounts Payable for $200, the debits and credits will be equal and the error will not be caught automatically. The same holds true if you forget to record the transaction, or record it twice; the only errors the debit and credit system can spot are those that leave the books out of balance.

Debits and credits can get very confusing! Fortunately, manual and computerized accounting systems are set up so that you can enter amounts into the system and the debits and credits are calculated automatically.

### Calendar vs. Fiscal Year

You must also select an accounting year for the business. It is most common to use a calendar year-end, but other dates may be more appropriate for your business. An accounting year that ends on a date other that December 31 is usually referred to as a **fiscal year**. Some businesses choose a fiscal year because of business seasonality, or to gain income tax advantages. This is a good point to discuss with your accountant.

# The Paperwork

This chapter began by stressing the importance of documenting business transactions. Let's take a look at some of the typical paperwork used. You may not need all of these forms for your business, or you may need additional paperwork; remember, every recordkeeping system is unique.

Here are some of the forms your business may need

| Document | Use | Information Included |
|---|---|---|
| Invoice | The seller's request for payment. This is the "bill" | Seller's name and address<br>Invoice date<br>Buyer's name and address<br>Description/quantity of goods sold<br>Dollar amount per item and in total<br>Credit terms<br>Method of shipment<br>Payment due date |
| Purchase Order | The buyer's request for goods | Buyer's name and address<br>Date<br>Seller's name and address<br>Description/quantity of goods desired<br>Expected price of the goods<br>Special shipping instructions |
| Receiving Report | Indicates that goods have been received | Date<br>Description/quantity of goods received<br>Seller's name and address<br>Condition of goods received<br>Name of person who received the goods |
| Checks | Authorize payment out of a bank account<br><br>Serve as evidence that a bill has been paid | Date<br>Check number<br>Business name and address<br>Payee's name<br>Dollar amount<br>Description of check purpose<br>Authorized signature |
| Cash Register Tape | Give daily sales totals | Date<br>Description of item sold<br>Per unit price of items sold<br>Total sales amount<br>Method and amount of payment<br>Change required |
| Time Cards or Tickets | Help determine wages owed to employees | Employee name<br>Time period<br>Pay rate<br>Hours worked, by day<br>Total hours worked<br>Supervisor approval |
| Payroll Authorizations | Document employee status and pay information | Employee name and address<br>Date of hire<br>Pay rate<br>Job title<br>Authorized work hours<br>Benefits information<br>Method of payment<br>Who hired the employee |

# Types of Accounting Systems

Your accounting system helps you keep track of financial information. You collect the data, record them, classify and summarize them, and report them in the form of financial statements. You need an organized method of doing this to avoid reporting incorrect or misleading information. Accounting systems can be as simple as your checkbook, or complicated enough to baffle a bunch of physicists. Let's take a look at some common systems.

## Journals and Ledgers

The debit and credit scheme tells if you have kept your books balanced after each transaction. If you wish to use this method, you need a place to record debits and credits and summarize them for the year.

Business transactions are very repetitive. Sales are made daily, bills are paid every month, payroll is weekly or bi-weekly. This repetition means that the bookkeeper must enter the same debits and credits over and over. Can you make the process simpler? Yes, by having a special journal for each type of transaction. Here are the most common:

| Journal Name | Purpose |
| --- | --- |
| Sales Journal | To record all sales on account |
| Purchases Journal | To record all purchases of merchandise on account |
| Cash Receipts Journal | To record all cash received |
| Cash Disbursements Journal | To record all cash paid out |

*The debit and credit scheme tells you if your books are balanced*

All systems, manual or computerized, use journals and ledgers. Generally, the journal is used to accumulate transactions. A ledger keeps track of each account. Sales, cash disbursements, and other transactions are recorded daily in the journals. Each month, the journals are totaled and posted in the ledger.

You will also need a General Journal for recording transactions that don't belong in one of the special journals. Below are examples of these special journals; remember, you can customize them to fit your needs.

| *Sales Journal* | | | Page 2 |
| --- | --- | --- | --- |
| Date | Customer | Invoice No. | Amount |
| 1/11/96 | Jayco, Inc. | 96-35 | $ 1,200 |
| 1/12/96 | Davis Glass | 96-36 | 2,800 |

The Sales Journal lists all sales on account. Cash sales are listed in the Cash Receipts Journal. Notice the "trail" that is left by putting the invoice number in the Sales Journal. If you wish to find out more information about that sale, you know which invoice to examine.

The Cash Disbursements Journal is similar to a check register, but more detailed

| Purchases Journal | | | | | Page 5 |
|---|---|---|---|---|---|
| Date | Supplier Name | Invoice No. | Accounts Payable | Purchases | Supplies |
| 1/9/96 | Ajax Corp. | A10345 | 725 | 725 | |
| 1/9/96 | OfficePlace | 237 | 122 | | 122 |

The Purchases Journal records purchases of inventory and supplies on account. Cash purchases are recorded in the Cash Disbursements Journal. Some businesses record inventory purchases in the Inventory account rather than the Purchases account.

| Cash Receipts Journal | | | | | | Page 2 |
|---|---|---|---|---|---|---|
| Date | Cash | Sales | Accounts Receivable | Customer Name | Other | Description |
| 1/4/96 | 1,100 | | 1,100 | Ajax Company | | |
| 1/5/95 | 125 | 125 | | | | |
| 1/6/96 | 55 | | | | 55 | Cash Rebate |

Cash receipts are recorded in the Cash Receipts Journal. You can set up columns to represent the typical sources of cash for your business. Our example includes a column for cash sales, receipts from credit customers, and a catch-all for miscellaneous receipts.

| Cash Disbursements Journal | | | | | | Page 3 |
|---|---|---|---|---|---|---|
| Date | Check No. | Cash | Accounts Payable | Customer Name | Other | Description |
| 1/7/96 | 101 | 437 | 437 | Baker Supply | | |
| 1/8/95 | 102 | 500 | | | 500 | Rent Expense |

The Cash Disbursements Journal is similar to a check register, but provides more detail. Again, you can include a column for any frequently used account.

You will need a General Journal for recording transactions that don't belong in one of the special journals

| General Journal | | | | Page 21 |
|---|---|---|---|---|
| Date | Account Description | Ref. | Debit | Credit |
| 1/11/96 | Equipment | 120 | 3,000 | |
| | Notes Payable | 214 | | 3,000 |

The General Journal is used to record debits and credits for transactions that do not belong in one of the special journals. These transactions are entered in the order in which they occur; many small businesses leave this task to their outside accountants.

The journals tell the bookkeeper what to do to the accounts. Recall that each account is like a piece of paper divided in half vertically. If all these accounts are put together in one book, it is called the General Ledger. The account for Cash might look like this:

| Cash | | | | | | Account No. 101 |
|------|------|-------|---|------|------|--------|
| Date | Ref. | Debit | | Date | Ref. | Credit |
| 1/04/96 | CR2 | 1,100 | | 1/07/96 | CD7 | 437 |

Notice the account number 101, as well as the account title of Cash. As directed by entries in the Cash Receipts and Cash Disbursements Journals above, $1,100 has been added to the debit (left) side and $437 to the credit (right) side of the Cash account. The "CR2" reference in the Cash account shows the source of this debit and refers us to page 2 of the Cash Receipts Journal.

Does it seem like the same number has been written in two places? It has! A trail is being established in case others need to follow in the future. Although the journals and the General Ledger contain the same numbers, they are organized differently, allowing us to find information readily. If you wish to see how a particular transaction was recorded, you should consult the journal and find the transaction by date. To see what happened to a single account during the period, you turn to that account page in the General Ledger.

## Computerized Accounting Systems

Oh, the tedious tasks computers can do for us! We enter a single amount and the computer places it in the proper journal, records a new total in the General Ledger, and gives us up-to-date financial statements. But are computerized systems right for every business?

In their simplest form, computers do the mechanical tasks of adding and subtracting, while the bookkeeper does most of the brainwork. More complex systems are capable of providing management with information much too difficult to accumulate by hand. Most businesses need something in between.

In order to use a computerized accounting system, the business must have access to computer hardware and software. In general, we can think of computerized accounting software as belonging to one of the following groups.

*Many software companies and trade associations offer specialized computer accounting systems*

- **Spreadsheets.** These programs are widely available and relatively inexpensive. Popular packages include Microsoft Excel, Lotus 1-2-3, and Quattro Pro. Spreadsheet programs are like large worksheets with rows and columns that you can set up to look just like the journals and ledger accounts described above. The more complex the business, the more difficult it may be to customize a spreadsheet program. However, many small businesses choose to use spreadsheet programs because their accounting needs are not extensive and the programs are affordable.

- **Point-of-sale terminals.** You know those scanners that most grocery and department stores use at the checkout stand? They are sophisticated computerized accounting systems. Data about merchandise are programmed into the computer, and every transaction automatically updates inventory records. This tells management what is moving fast or slow, and what needs to be ordered. The program also automatically updates the accounting system by recording sales and cash received. These systems are expensive, but they can save money by helping to eliminate errors at the checkout stand.
- **General packages.** Several companies sell computerized accounting packages that can be adapted to most businesses. Prices vary greatly with the sophistication of the system. Leading sellers are Quicken, QuickBooks, and Peachtree. Some packages offer accounts payable, accounts receivable, and payroll modules, while others (like Quicken) are much simpler and include only a basic check register and cash receipts book. However, the simpler packages may not have good audit trails.
- **Industry-specific.** Many companies and trade associations offer computerized accounting systems designed to fit the needs of businesses in a particular industry. These systems often include project or inventory control modules. There are specialized systems for restaurants, retailers, wholesale nurseries, construction companies, and many other businesses.

Whether a computerized accounting system is right for your business is often a matter of cost versus benefit. If the benefit you will receive is greater than the cost of installing and using the system, then it is a good idea. Remember to define "cost" very broadly; take into account dollars, time, and frustration! Implementing a new computer package can try your patience; there are likely to be misunderstandings, incorrect results, and baffling error messages at first. You should continue recording information manually until you overcome the initial problems with your new system.

If you decide to use a computerized accounting system, think about the following before making your selection:

- What are the hardware requirements?
- How easily can the system be modified to suit my needs?
- Does this company have support personnel to help me if I have problems?
- What happens if my needs expand? Can I add additional modules to this system?
- How user-friendly is the system?
- What types of training are available?
- Does the system produce the types of reports and documents I want?
- Who will work with this system in my business? Do I need to hire someone?
- Are other local business owners using this software?

*There was a big problem. Sally realized that her general manager spent most of her time managing the front desk. She was unqualified to be keeping books, and had little interest in the financial operations of the business. Sally found that her manager had been keeping only the most basic of records, and that the club had been bouncing checks regularly for the past six months! She looked back over the last two years of operation and wondered if she was making any money. If so, where was it? Could she afford the upgrades to the club's facilities she'd been planning? Would she be able to get financing, or was her credit ruined?*

*Clearly, she needed to sort things out and take a good hard look at her business's finances.*

### Write-It-Once Accounting Systems

Certain manual accounting systems allow you to write one amount on a special carbonized form and update several books at once. For example, before writing a check to a supplier, you would place forms representing the cash and accounts payable accounts below the check. When you write the check, it automatically transfers the amount as a reduction to those accounts, eliminating errors that occur when amounts must be written in more than one place.

### Check Registers

The simplest form of accounting system, which is often sufficient for the needs of a small business, is a check register. These differ from your personal check register in that many columns are provided to record the source of cash receipts, or the reason a check was written. Monthly totals allow you to prepare a simple income statement, but it can be difficult to prepare a balance sheet from this information. You may need some help from your accountant!

## The Modules of an Accounting System

Whether computerized or not, accounting systems are often divided into several modules. By module, we mean a part of the accounting system that requires special paperwork and accounting tasks. Larger firms might have a whole department for each of these parts. Active smaller businesses may have a different bookkeeper assigned to each module.

### General Ledger

Details from all other account modules are fed into the General Ledger; you might consider it the control module. Every account is given a unique account number, which is listed in a document called the Chart of Accounts. You can assign numbers however you like, but accountants use a standard scheme. It is best to use systematic account numbers like this:

| Type of Account | Begin Account # with: |
|---|---|
| Assets | 1 |
| Liabilities | 2 |
| Owners' Equity | 3 |
| Revenues | 4 |
| Expenses | 5 |

Account numbers can help you create special reports. For example, let's assume Wages Expense has been given the account number 520. By extending the account number to indicate location and department, we can create reports by location or by department. You might record information for Wages Expense in account 520-05-12.

520     Indicates Wages Expense
05     This expense is from the Albany store
12     These wages are for employees in the auto repair department

### Inventory

Inventory accounting can be very difficult and is beyond the scope of this book. The total amount recorded for inventory is the multiplication of two numbers: the quantity of goods times the cost per unit. Ideally, your inventory is turning over quickly, but this does make the accounting process more difficult. There are several methods used to determine the quantity and the cost of goods sold. This is a good subject to discuss with your accountant!

### Accounts Receivable

One accounting tool that gives valuable information about credit customers is the **Accounts Receivable Subsidiary Ledger**. Controlling accounts receivable is crucial to maintaining an adequate cash position. Remember that each account is like a single sheet of paper on which information from the journal is recorded. The Accounts Receivable account includes debits for all sales made on account, and credits for all payments received. However, it is not separated by customer. That information would be very helpful for identifying slow-paying customers and determining if future credit sales should be made. The Accounts Receivable Subsidiary Ledger keeps the credit sales and payment information by customer.

### Accounts Payable

The **Accounts Payable Subsidiary Ledger** helps keep track of amounts owed to vendors. The total of all balances in this ledger should equal the balance in the Accounts Payable controlling account in the General Ledger.

*What Lunar Gym needed was someone whose sole responsibility was to keep the books, manage finances, and safeguard the business's assets. This person would steer Sally's operations by providing professional financial guidance on what she could afford and how she could maximize her financial returns.*

*Previously, Sally had assumed that her financial records, however sparse, were accurate. She thought they might come in handy someday when she sought additional financing to improve her facility. She was in the process of realizing (perhaps too late!) that financial records are essential for day-to-day management.*

*Her first move was to hire Cindy Evangelista, a CPA and freelance financial planner, to help get the books in order. Cindy happened to be a member of the gym, so Sally negotiated a barter exchange for her time: Cindy would receive a lifetime club membership and would be kept on retainer for a monthly fee of $150.*

## Property, Plant, and Equipment

A thorough list of all long-lived assets must be maintained. These records allow calculation of depreciation expense, and help record subsequent disposal of assets. A subsidiary ledger, tied in total to the account balances in the General Ledger, is often kept for these assets. The subsidiary ledger should include date purchased, name of supplier, a description of the item, check number, and amount. Separate ledgers are often kept by type of asset (e.g., equipment, vehicles, building, furniture). An item should be removed from the ledger only if it is physically removed from the business (i.e., junked, sold, traded in, or destroyed).

## Payroll

Payroll accounting is complicated by all the federal, state, and local rules you must follow. Trying to find out what information to keep, and how and when to report it, can be a big headache! You should consider hiring a bookkeeping service for payroll accounting, even if the rest of your accounting modules are handled internally. Many companies offer these services; you can have them perform all the payroll functions (updating employee records, writing payroll checks, preparing payroll tax reports) or you can do some of the work yourself and let them handle the more complicated tasks.

Typically, the components of a payroll system include a **Payroll Register**, which summarizes the payroll for the period, including employee name, hours worked, pay rate, total gross pay, deductions, and net pay; and an **Employee Earnings Record**, which keeps the payroll information listed above for each employee. They also collect sales tax from customers and payroll taxes from employees, both of which must be forwarded to the government.

Accounting for payroll is complicated by all of the federal, state, and local rules

## Tax Considerations

How the business is taxed depends on how it is organized

Businesses pay sales taxes, property taxes, income taxes, payroll taxes, excise taxes, and taxes disguised as licenses and fees. It can be pretty overwhelming to sort through all the tax requirements. It is also far too much information to present in this book, so this is another area where you will need help! However, we can provide some general knowledge about income taxes and payroll taxes.

### Income Taxes

How a business is taxed depends upon its form of ownership. Your business can operate as a sole proprietorship, a partnership, or a corporation. There are also some variations of these forms, such as limited partnerships, S-corporations, and Limited Liability Corporations (LLCs). Here's how federal income taxes apply to these organizations:

- **Sole proprietorship.** Business income or loss is included in the personal income tax return of the sole proprietor; the business does not pay income tax. The sole proprietor includes a Schedule C in his or her personal return, which is due April 15. The sole proprietor may also be required to pay quarterly estimated income taxes and self-employment taxes.
- **Partnership.** Business income or loss is included in the income tax returns of each of the partners; the business does not pay income tax. (This applies both to limited or general partnerships.) The partners list partnership income or loss on Schedule E with their personal returns. The partnership must file Form 1065 by April 15. Partners may need to pay quarterly estimated income taxes and self-employment taxes.
- **S-corporation.** These work very much like a partnership for income tax purposes. Business income or loss "flows through" to the individual tax returns of the corporate owners. Form 1120S must be filed by March 15 and the owner may be required to make advanced payment.
- **Corporation.** The business's income is taxed. The shareholders do not pay income tax on profits earned by the corporation, but when shareholders receive a dividend from the corporation, they pay personal income tax on that amount. The corporation files Form 1120 and pays its income tax by March 15. Corporations may be required to pay quarterly estimated income taxes.
- **Limited Liability Corporation.** LLCs are not taxed directly, so they enjoy the pass-through tax benefits of partnerships and S-corporations.

Fortunately, income taxes are based on the same general accounting concepts used to prepare your financial statements. Unfortunately, some of the specific rules are different, so you cannot simply take your business income statement and forward it to the Internal Revenue Service! The differences between your income statement and your tax return fall into one of three categories:

1. Amounts on your income statement that are not allowed on your tax return.
2. Amounts on your tax return that are not usually included on your income statement.

3. Amounts included on your income statement and your tax return, but in different years.

Our income tax system is very complicated. It is the result of a political process and sometimes changes with the political winds. Very few small businesses prepare their own income tax return. A discussion of the professionals who can help you with this chore appears later in this chapter.

## Payroll Taxes

Payroll taxes are imposed on the employee or the employer.

| Paid by the Employee | Paid by the Employer |
|---|---|
| Federal Income Taxes | State and Federal Unemployment |
| State Income Taxes | Social Security (FICA) |
| Social Security (FICA) | |

Many states impose accident insurance or worker's compensation taxes on the employer. There may also be county or city taxes, as well as taxes supporting public transportation.

Our income tax and social security systems are on a "pay as you go" basis. Companies and individuals do not wait until income tax returns are due to send in the tax owed. Instead, the government collects the money throughout the year. For employees, this is done by employers, who act as collection agents for the government. The employer must withhold the taxes from the employee's paycheck and forward the amount to the government. This duty must be taken very seriously, as the government will prosecute violators. Do not consider money withheld from employees as available to meet other business debts; penalties for failure to make timely tax payments are high.

The employer has several forms to prepare in regard to payroll:

| Form # | Name | Description |
|---|---|---|
| 941 | Employer's Quarterly Federal Tax Return | Reports federal income and social security taxes withheld from employees and social security taxes imposed on the employer. *These forms are due one month after the end of the quarter.* |
| 940 | Employer's Annual Federal Unemployment Tax Return | Used to report federal unemployment tax for the year. |
| 8109 | Federal Tax Deposit Coupons | Used to make deposits of withheld income and both employee and employer shares of social security taxes. Also may include deposits for federal unemployment insurance. |
| W-2 | Wage and Tax Statement | Given to each employee to detail earnings and amounts withheld. *These must be sent to employees no later than January 31st. A copy is also forwarded to the government.* |
| 1099 | Wage Statement | Given to contract employees. |

There also may be forms required by state and local governments.

The timing of deposits for payroll taxes is based on the amount due. Requirements are subject to change, so get the current information from the IRS or your accountant.

———————————◆———————————

*One of the first pieces of equipment Sally had purchased before opening her health club was a computer check-in system called an "Aerobitron." The computer had cost her almost $7,000, and was supposed to record members' visits, membership dues and other receivables, accounts payable, and other vital business information.*

*Unfortunately, Lunar Gym's front desk staff rarely entered information into the system. Most worked at the check-in desk as a result of barter arrangements, and had not been trained on the system. Often, Sally would pass the front desk and realize that the Aerobitron hadn't even been turned on!*

*Sally liked to find clever ways to save money, but it was beginning to look like her shortcuts in personnel and other areas were costing more than they were saving!*

*Had Sally taken the time to be thoroughly trained on the system (or to have her front desk manager receive proper training), the Aerobitron would have been a valuable tool for Lunar Gym. It had many customizable options, and included in her monthly service contract were staff training and customer support. She had failed to use either.*

*Sally worried that the Aerobitron mess wasn't the only mistake she had made. How many others would she discover?*

———————————◆———————————

## NxLEVEL™ TECH TIP

**There's nothing worse than spending hours updating your computer records, only to lose everything to an error or crash.** An exciting new product called **GoBack** monitors every change to your hard disk, logging these changes to a buffer system for storage. This lets you repair any error on your system— including those resulting from virus attacks, software problems, and system crashes—and resurrect deleted files and directories. The length of time GoBack allows you to travel into your computer's past depends on how much of your hard drive you allocate to the program; 10% is usually sufficient to go back one week. For a free demonstration of GoBack, visit **Wild File's Web site** at http://www.go-back.co.uk.

## An Accounting Checklist

As the owner of a small business, you are very busy! You know you need to devote some time to accounting, but what should you do first? The following is from a very helpful checklist published by the Small Business Administration (Management Aids Number 1.107, *Keeping Records in Small Business*).

### Small Business Financial Status Checklist (What an Owner/Manager Should Know)

*Daily*

1. Cash on hand.
2. Bank balance (keep business and personal funds separate).
3. Daily summary of sales and cash receipts.
4. That all errors in recording collections on accounts are corrected.
5. That a record of all monies paid out, by cash or check, is maintained.

*Weekly*

1. Accounts receivable (take action on slow payers).
2. Accounts payable (take advantage of discounts).
3. Payroll.
4. Taxes and reports to state and federal government (e.g., sales, withholding, social security).

*Monthly*

1. That all journal entries are classified according to like elements (these should be generally accepted and standardized for both income and expense) and posted to the General Ledger.
2. That an Income Statement for the month is available within a reasonable time, usually 10 to 15 days following the close of the month. From this, take action to eliminate loss or increase profits (Adjust markup? Reduce overhead expense? Pilferage? Incorrect tax reporting? Incorrect buying procedures? Failure to take advantage of cash discounts?).
3. That a Balance Sheet accompanies the Income Statement.
4. That the bank statements are reconciled.
5. That the Petty Cash account is balanced (the actual cash in the Petty Cash Box plus the total of the paid-out slips that have not been charged to expense total the amount set aside as petty cash).
6. That all Federal Tax Deposits, Withheld Income and FICA Taxes and state taxes are made.
7. That Accounts Receivable are aged.
8. That Inventory Control is worked to remove dead stock and order new stock (What moves slowly? Reduce. What moves fast? Increase.)

Set up a tickler system to ensure your checklist is followed

# What Records Do You Need to Keep?

What records you keep and how long you do so depends on your motives. Generally, we keep records either to meet laws and regulations, or so we have data to review when trying to make business decisions. You will need some past records during your business planning process and when you analyze trends. The records are also very important for documenting the financial history of a business when it is being sold. Income tax regulations require that records be kept during the three-year period that your tax return is subject to IRS audit. Sometimes, your records from seven years past may also be useful for tax purposes.

There isn't a complete, standard list of records and retention times that everyone follows, but here is one idea. Your accountant can help you modify this list to fit your business needs.

| Type of Record | Retention Period |
| --- | --- |
| Bank Statements | 7 years |
| Business Licenses | Until Expired |
| Check Register Tapes | 3 years |
| Check Registers | Keep Permanently |
| Cancelled Checks | 3 years |
| Financial Statements | Keep Permanently |
| General Ledger | Keep Permanently |
| General Journal | Keep Permanently |
| Inventory Records | 7 years |
| Invoices (Accounts Payable, A/P) | 3 years |
| Invoices (Accounts Receivable, A/R) | 3 years |
| Property, Plant & Equipment Records | Keep Permanently |
| Purchase Orders | 3 years |
| Receiving Reports | 3 years |
| Tax Returns | Keep Permanently |
| Time Cards or Tickets | 3 years |
| Travel Expense Records | 7 years |

# How to Choose a Bookkeeper

As a small business owner, you probably don't want to handle all the bookkeeping tasks yourself. You need to find a good bookkeeper, but how? Of course, you should follow the general procedures and consider the issues applicable to hiring any employee, but there are some special considerations when hiring a bookkeeper.

Choosing a bookkeeper:

- Job description

- Experience

- Knowledge

- Check references

1. **Write a job description** stating which modules in your accounting system, and which specific functions in those modules, are the responsibility of the new bookkeeper. Some bookkeeping positions are "full-charge," which means the person works with every accounting module. How many days per week will you need help?

2. **Make sure applicants have the right type of experience** to do the job. You do not need to hire the most experienced applicant, but you should judge if the applicant will be able to handle his or her level of responsibility. Do you have other bookkeepers on staff who will supervise and train the new employee, or will this bookkeeper be in charge? Do you need someone to come in and start from scratch, or are your systems in good working order?

3. **Check accounting knowledge** with tests or interview questions. Your CPA can help you design questions appropriate for the job description.

4. **Consider the requirements** of your current computerized accounting program. Is it important that the new bookkeeper be familiar with that program? Or do you want someone who can help select a computerized accounting program and design your internal controls?

5. **Check references!** Be sure previous employers were happy with the person's performance. You can also talk to them about what tasks the employee did, and compare them to the job description you've written. It can be difficult to discover a dishonest bookkeeper in advance, but you won't know anything if you don't ask questions.

# Using an Accountant

Very few small businesses can get by without some professional accounting help. There are many services to choose from.

## Accounting Services

- **Bookkeeping.** You can hire a bookkeeping service to do any or all of the tasks required in your system, including accounts receivable, accounts payable, and payroll.

- **System design.** You may need help designing an accounting system and internal controls.

- **Income taxes.** You will almost certainly need help planning for and preparing your income tax returns!

Very few small businesses can get by without some professional accounting help

- **Write-up.** You may be able to maintain the books yourself, but you'll probably need help putting together the financial statements and other reports. Some firms will help you design your accounting system based on the software they use. You give the firm your accounting information in the form of input sheets, and their personnel enter it into the computer.
- **Auditing.** As your business grows and prospers, you may need an independent audit. Sometimes an audit is required by loan agreements or when a business is to be sold.
- **Temporary services.** Perhaps all you need is some help getting through the year-end closing of your books, or preparing your annual budget. Maybe you have a busy season when extra help with accounts receivable or inventory would be great. Consider using one of the temporary service agencies in your area.

---

*The next day was not a good one for Sally. She and Cindy met early in the morning to review the business's records. She was relieved that she would soon get to the bottom of her difficulties. She had confidence in Cindy, whom she knew was bright and honest. But Sally was afraid of the other problems waiting for her. How bad was the situation?*

*It was bad. Sally's front desk manager had been throwing away bills, incorrectly recording expenses and revenues, and failing to collect membership dues in a timely manner. They pored through all the files and receipts they could find. Most were crammed into two large folders in the bottom of the front desk. How could Sally have been oblivious to such a disaster happening right under her nose?*

*One of their most disturbing discoveries was that Lunar Gym had more than $10,000 in outstanding accounts payable, and for each day she didn't pay, she was being charged late fees. Her desk manager had prepared an accounts payable ledger, but most of the bills were not recorded in it. Sally dug a little deeper and found a pouch full of checks for membership dues that had never been deposited. No wonder she was bouncing checks!*

*She felt completely responsible for not having taken a larger role in the day-to-day operations of her business. Sally resolved that things would change that very day.*

---

## Who Can Do This Work?

There are several types of accounting professionals. Their services and rates vary according to their qualifications.

**Certified public accountants (CPAs)** are the only accounting professionals who can perform an independent audit. They are skilled, well-trained accountants who offer auditing, income tax planning and preparation, estate planning, financial planning, and write-up services. Although their rates may seem high, they can often save you money by refining your accounting system or helping you reduce income taxes.

Some states have other professional accountants who are not CPAs. These may include **public accountants** and **licensed tax consultants**. These individuals have also passed rigorous examinations and been licensed by the state. They may not perform an independent audit, and while most are glad to help you with tax return preparation, not all offer income tax planning services. As their name implies, licensed tax consultants specialize in income tax return preparation. Public accountants can be very helpful in designing your accounting system, performing weekly or monthly bookkeeping chores, or doing payroll.

There are also many bookkeeping firms with well-trained staff ready to perform bookkeeping functions for you.

---

*The next afternoon, Cindy reported more problems. She had discovered a total of $8,000 in uncashed checks for membership dues. She was worried that the business had underreported its profits and might have a sizable tax bill for the next quarter.*

*However, Sally and Cindy made some quick calculations, and were pleasantly surprised by what they found. If they collected all the gym's outstanding accounts receivable, deposited all of the "lost" membership dues, and negotiated for more time with their largest creditors, the gym could pay its taxes and begin to operate in the black by year's end.*

*They both agreed that the next step was finding a new qualified, motivated, and trustworthy front desk manager to replace the existing manager...and quickly!*

---

### How to Work with Your Accountant

If you remember that most accountants charge by the hour, you will be diligent about giving them organized, complete financial information. Many small-business owners bring their data to the accountant without any preliminary preparation at all, sometimes even in a shoebox. This will cost extra! Perhaps you have decided that your time is valuable enough that you are willing to pay the accountant to organize your records. That's fine, as long as you remember that you still have to involve yourself with the outcome. Monitor the system to see that it's functioning correctly, and review the financial statements carefully.

Your accountant will be better able to help you if he or she has a good understanding of your business. An accountant specializing in clients from your industry will understand the accounting issues businesses like yours face, but will still need to know particulars about your goals and financial situation. You must be very candid with your accountant, so find someone you can trust. Professional accountants keep strict confidence regarding client information.

If you hire an accountant to help design an accounting system, be very clear about the information you need. Some accountants focus on income tax requirements, and will design a system that responds primarily to those laws. Your accounting system should address management information first and tax requirements second.

---

*In their final analysis, Sally and Cindy also realized that Lunar Gym was undercharging for its club memberships. Not only could her market bear a higher price, but she was not currently generating enough revenue to reach her target profit level.*

*They also decided that the club shouldn't expand until it was getting the most out of the space it had. This meant utilizing unused space to generate extra revenue for the club. For instance, using the childcare room for massage therapy during off-peak hours would even out the club's revenue stream throughout the day, and offer clients move services.*

*Within a month, Sally had hired a new manager, who was responsible for maintaining club membership records, paying the bills, depositing membership dues, and working closely with Cindy to input data for the business's general ledger and financial statements. Before starting full-time at Lunar Gym, the manager attended a one-and-a-half-day training seminar on the Aerobitron and a two-week refresher course on bookkeeping. Three weeks later, all of the front desk staff were trained and using the Aerobitron like champs!*

---

## Conclusion

Accounting is complicated, time-consuming and detailed, but extremely important for your business. In addition to providing information needed to run your business, your accounting system is the basis on which you will supply your tax information.

No one expects you to turn you into an accountant overnight, but as a business owner you must be involved in and knowledgeable about your accounting process. Don't let a Donald Peterson take advantage of you!

# Chapter 37
# BUDGETING

*About This Chapter:*
- *What is budgeting?*
- *Why should you have a budgeting system?*
- *Why don't all businesses use a budgeting system?*
- *The budget cycle*
- *How are budgets used?*
- *What makes a good budgeting system?*
- *Types of budgets*
- *Feedback from your budgets*
- *Flexible budgets*
- *Performance measures*

## Introduction

Earlier, we discussed the benefits of business planning. You need a map to judge how far your business has come and how much further it has to go, and a good budget is the best map there is.

Budgets are an integral part of your business plan and financing proposals. A banker is not likely to approve a loan without reviewing and understanding your budgets. Budgets are also useful for communicating plans; they can help keep employees on the same track as the business owner.

## What is Budgeting?

Budgeting is the process of converting into numbers the strategic and operating decisions you make in your business plan. The budgeting process is a component of your planning process and can prove very valuable in itself. Strategies, tactics, and objectives are determined and then future sales, expenses, and cash flows are forecasted.

Budgets are the outcome of the budgeting process. They guide purchasing, scheduling, marketing, personnel, and financing activities. Note that the operative word is "guide," rather than "control." The budgeting process involves educated guesswork, not absolute accuracy. When deviations occur, the results are evaluated, more planning is done, and forecasts are adjusted.

A banker isn't likely to approve a loan without reviewing and understanding your budgets

## Why Should You Have a Budgeting System?

### Get to Know Your Business
While preparing budgets, you must look at every aspect of your business, so you get to know it very well. This familiarity is handy when opportunities arise or changes occur.

### Always Be Prepared
Unexpected situations can cause you to be reactive rather than proactive. You certainly cannot anticipate every challenge your business will face, but the more knowledgeable you are, the easier it is to understand what actions to take.

### Fuel Creative Ideas
By examining your business closely, you can find opportunities to reduce costs, improve products, and increase efficiency. The budgeting process draws attention away from the daily routine of doing the work, and focuses your attention on how the work is done.

### Provide Benchmarks
Without budgets, a business has no means of determining success or failure. Benchmarks aid in charting progress.

### Uncover Potential Bottlenecks
If getting raw materials is a problem in manufacturing your product, the budget process is likely to reveal it, allowing you to plan purchases to avoid such problems.

### Coordinate the Parts of the Business
Budgeting helps ensure that all functions of the business are moving in the same direction. Many small business owners have difficulty expressing their goals to their employees. Thus, employees act according to what they believe the owner wants, but sometimes have the wrong idea. When preparing budgets, objectives are expressed in writing.

### Involve Employees in the Business
People do a better job when they care about their work. Involving employees in the budgeting process links them emotionally to the business.

------◆------

*Peekskill Caterers was owned and operated by Sarah Erhenberg and her business partner, Jason Spears. They leased a commercial space from another local business, Louisa's Jams, which operated in a large kitchen with lots of extra workspace and an attached warehouse. They paid a monthly fee for rent, and for use of the cooking equipment. They also got the benefit of Louisa's daughter Anne's accounting expertise.*

Be prepared: unexpected situations can cause you to be reactive rather than proactive

*The only restriction on Peekskill Caterers was that during the month of June, the peak production month for Louisa's, they had to relinquish use of the facilities. That was fine with Sarah and Jason, both of whom enjoyed taking a full month off each summer.*

*Sarah and Jason were enthusiastic about catering, and were completely dedicated to making Peekskill Caterers the best catering service in the Hudson River Valley area.*

*Their specialty was preparing what they called "Epicurean adventures," meals prepared in a variety of ethnic styles, using the freshest ingredients and most authentic herbs and spices. Their best-selling dishes were Pan-Asian feasts, combining plates of curries, barbecued satays, vegetarian maasalas, and dumplings. They prepared these dishes with a unique flair, incorporating their favorite influences from French and Cajun cuisine.*

---

## Why Don't All Businesses Use a Budgeting System?

If budgeting is such a good idea, why don't all businesses do it? Consider this conversation between a small business owner and her SBDC counselor:

Business Owner: We're just too busy to take time out for budgeting.

SBDC Counselor: Why are you so busy?

Business Owner: I don't know. It just seems like we never have the right materials or the right workers here, so I'm always trying to put things together at the last minute.

SBDC Counselor: Well, maybe you'd have a better idea of what to expect if you prepared budgets. Then you could be sure the right materials and people are here when you need them.

Business Owner: Yeah, maybe. But it's not that simple. Our business is pretty complex.

SBDC Counselor: Sometimes the best way to work with something complex is to break it down into its simplest parts.

Business Owner: But it's too hard to figure out some of the information I'd need.

SBDC Counselor: It's true you can't get it perfect, but you can still come up with valuable forecasts. And it would help you identify things about the business that need your attention.

Business Owner: Well, I know my business inside and out. I don't need a budgeting system to tell me what's going on.

SBDC Counselor: You'd be surprised what turns up when you force yourself to look closely at every aspect of your business.

Business Owner: Even if that's true, I don't want to face those things right now.

*A business without budgets has no way to measure success*

It is difficult to jump into a new process, so owners and managers who have never tried budgeting are likely to shy away from it. If you have ever suffered through an ineffective budget process, you are probably not inclined to go through it again!

## The Budget Cycle

Don't think of budgeting as an activity you do for a few days and then ignore. Recall the planning process:

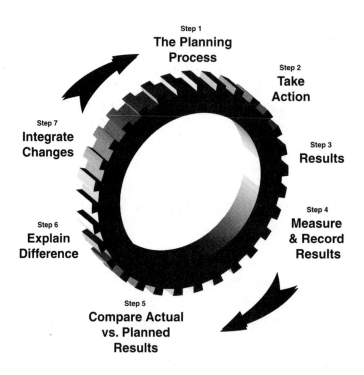

The cycle never stops. First comes planning, then those plans are put into operation. Next comes feedback and evaluation, which lead to changes and more planning, which starts the cycle all over again. Budgeting is part of the planning, analyzing, and evaluation functions within this process.

## How Are Budgets Used?

It is said that financial statement analysis doesn't give answers, it just creates questions. The same is true when evaluating budgeted versus actual costs. If budgeted labor costs were $140,000 and the amount spent was $152,000, a variance of $12,000 results. The obvious question is, "Why did labor costs go over budget?" Perhaps a special order came in and workers were added to get it out on time. Or maybe labor costs were higher than anticipated. Whatever the explanation, this knowledge helps the planning process and keeps the business on track.

Comparing budgeted and actual results can also help you judge employee performance. This is called **responsibility accounting**. Try to associate business activities and costs with the individual controlling those costs. This way, budget reports can be generated by function or by person and used for performance evaluation.

---

*Sarah and Jason had been inundated with catering jobs for the winter holiday season, yet they were not generating enough profit. In fact, when they looked over their income statement and cash flow records with Anne, they found that they had lost $500 the previous month and nearly $900 the month before that. What was going wrong? Anne suggested that they review their pricing and budgeting procedures.*

*When Peekskill Caterers bid for a job, they'd estimate the number of hours of the actual job and the number of hours needed for prep time. Usually, Sarah would just add a few extra hours to the party time to arrive at a total number of billable hours. Then she'd calculate the total cost of the food, and combine the amounts to create a flat fee for the job.*

*Peekskill Caterers bought most of its high-quality ingredients from local farmers or butchers, and was often able to negotiate bulk rates. But if they needed special cuts of meat or seafood, they had to order in advance and pay more. And sometimes, they'd end up rushing to the local gourmet food store to get supplies they'd forgotten or run out of. Sarah rarely incorporated these costs into her estimates.*

*Anne asked the partners how they incorporated overhead into their bids.*

> *"Overhead? Oh, you mean like rent and stuff?"*
> *"Yeah. How do you allocate those costs in your bids?"*
> *"Well, we figure that just comes out of our hourly fee. We don't make any special provisions to cover things like that. It seems too complicated and messy."*

*Anne rubbed her forehead and poured herself another cup of tea. "We're in for a long morning," she thought.*

---

## What Makes a Good Budgeting System?

If you have participated in a poor budgeting system, you probably can tell what made it so bad. But what makes a good budgeting system?

A good budgeting system fuels creative ideas, provides benchmarks, and coordinates the functions of the business. It accomplishes these things with the least amount of turmoil and the greatest degree of communication. Here are some more things to look for in a budgeting system:

### Get Everyone Involved

A participatory process increases acceptance. The person performing a task is in the best position to evaluate that task and help set budgeted amounts. Budgets that come from the top, with little input from employees, are likely to meet resistance. You might hear things such as "He doesn't know what I have to go through here," or "Let's see her come down here and do this."

When using a **participatory budgeting process**, be sure to keep owners and top management involved. No one will take the process seriously if the owners don't seem to care.

### Make Sure Budgets Get Used

It is very frustrating to put lots of time and energy into a budgeting process, only to see the completed budgets sit on a shelf and gather dust. If that happens, it will be very difficult to get participation in the future. Also, since the evaluation portion of the budget cycle is not occurring, valuable information for future planning is lost.

### Evaluate Performance

Variances between budgeted and actual amounts can identify unproductive behavior and help employees make corrections, but be sure to explore variances thoroughly, rather than immediately using them to fix blame. It is very important to do performance evaluation in a positive manner. Punishment might motivate your employees for a little while, but the possibility of a reward is better in the long run.

### Create Desired Behavior

When budgeting, remember that budgets can cause certain behaviors. Let's assume your salespeople will receive a bonus if their sales exceed the budgeted amount. If you set the budget too low, your sales staff will believe that they can easily meet the target and will thus have little incentive to work hard. If the target is too high, they may think it is impossible to meet and give up without trying. Either way, you've caused behavior opposite to that which you desired.

Making realistic **budget assumptions** is very difficult. You may not get it right the first time, but the feedback you get will help you to hit your targets the next time around. That is the benefit of the continuous budget cycle.

### Allow Creativity and Flexibility

Budgets should bend, but not break. If the system is too rigid, the participants won't think creatively. That is what you find when you prepare a budget by simply taking last year's numbers and increasing them by some percentage. Of course, you shouldn't ignore past figures; comparison of budgeted costs and actual costs in previous years is very valuable. However, your budgeting should encourage new ideas and must not be too dependent on past assumptions.

### Document Assumptions

Budgeting involves making assumptions about the future. Write these assumptions down; you will need them when evaluating variances, and to explain your budgets to your banker and other outside parties. You may think you will remember your assumptions, but several busy months later, it just isn't that easy!

The best budgeting system? The one that gets used!

## Use What You Have

Try not to create extra work for yourself. Many computerized accounting systems have the capacity to accept budget amounts and produce reports comparing budgeted to actual figures. Using these systems lets you concentrate on content rather than form.

You should design your budgets to reflect your accounting system, or make changes in your accounting system if it will result in more useful information. Remember to let your planning process—*not* your accounting system—guide what you do.

———————◆———————

*Anne found that Peekskill Caterers had no formal budgeting process at all. They had lots of business, though; with proper budgeting and pricing, they could easily operate in the black.*

*Anne gathered the following information about Peekskill Caterers:*

- *Theirs was a seasonal business. They generated 65% of their total revenue during the peak holiday season between November and December, and during July and August when many people entertained at their summer houses in the Hudson Valley.*
- *When catering for ten or more people, they hired a helper at $12 per hour.*
- *30% of their food supply costs came from last-minute trips to the gourmet food shop.*
- *For the past three seasons, they had underestimated projected sales by at least 40%. This explained their last-minute shopping for supplies, and their feeling of never having enough time to plan for personnel needs or supplies.*
- *Over the same period of time, they had overestimated their projected sales for the slow winter months by at least 30%. They failed to account for the higher cost of produce during these months, or for the higher utility costs for heating their space.*
- *In total, Peekskill Caterers had been underestimating their costs by as much as 15%.*

———————◆———————

## Budgets Should Fit your Business

A budget should fit the needs of your business. Are you short on personnel? Prepare a work schedule with an accompanying budget. Is it difficult to get a particular component of your finished product? Time to do a purchasing budget. Do advertising costs seem to have a life of their own? Budget your advertising costs. Whatever is vital to efficient, effective operation of the business should be included in the budget process.

You can prepare budgets for any timeframe you desire. A budget for the next year, detailed by month, is very common. Some businesses budget for longer time periods; this has the advantage of encouraging thinking beyond the short term.

> Budgets should bend but not break

# Types of Budgets

## Master Budget

The master budget is the compilation of all the budgets prepared by various departments in the business. We often break these down into two groups: operating budgets and financial budgets.

### Operating budget

The operating budget is the part of the master budget that deals directly with operations. This includes sales, production, cost of goods sold, and operating expenses.

### Financial budget

This budget deals with how the business is financed. This includes cash budgets, capital budgets, and projected financial statements.

## Cash Budget

This is the most vital budget for most small businesses. It shows expected cash inflows and outflows, and is often called **cash flow projections**. It enables you to anticipate cash shortages and do something about them before they occur. These budgets are discussed in detail in Chapter 38 *Cash Flow Management*.

## Capital Budget

The capital budget has the longest time horizon. Capital budgets refer to acquisition of land, buildings, and equipment. Estimating future revenues and expenses can help determine whether or not the acquisition is a good idea.

## Flexible Budget

A flexible budget is actually several budgets in one. It includes a range of activity levels. For example, you might prepare the master budget three times, assuming sales of 50,000, 60,000, and 70,000 units.

## Continuous Budget

At the end of each month, a new month is added so that a budget for the next 12 months is created.

# Preparation of an Annual Budget

Walt, owner of Walt's Machine Shop, wishes to develop a cash flow projection for his business. He starts with a first-quarter sales forecast. This is a critical component of the cash flow projection, because all other budgets are driven by forecasted sales.

| Months | Jan | Feb | Mar | Total |
|---|---|---|---|---|
| **Product/Service #1** | | | | |
| Units Sold | 30 | 40 | 50 | 120 |
| Price per Unit | $300 | $300 | $300 | $300 |
| Total Sales | $9,000 | $12,000 | $15,000 | $36,000 |
| **Product/Service #2** | | | | |
| Units Sold | 70 | 70 | 80 | 220 |
| Price per Unit | $500 | $500 | $500 | $500 |
| Total Sales | $35,000 | $35,000 | $40,000 | $110,000 |
| **Product/Service #3** | | | | |
| Units Sold | 2 | 2 | 2 | 6 |
| Price per Unit | $3,000 | $3,000 | $3,000 | $3,000 |
| Total Sales | $6,000 | $6,000 | $6,000 | $18,000 |
| **Total-All Product/ Service Sales** | $50,000 | $53,000 | $61,000 | $164,000 |

The projected number of sales tells how many units must be made or bought, which in turn dictates how many workers will be hired, and what labor costs and other expenses will be paid. And once these things are known, cash inflows and outflows can be forecasted. It all begins with the sales forecast!

A word of caution: Don't inflate sales estimates just to make the business look good. (If the business really isn't profitable, perhaps you should abandon it!) On the other hand, overly conservative sales forecasts may cause you to undercapitalize. Insufficient inventory may be ordered, or not enough people hired.

Basing all other budgets on the sales forecast can lead you back to the beginning. For example, if your sales forecast leads to a negative cash position, you may wish to come back to sales and see if you have been too conservative. Changing the sales units will affect all your other budgets and perhaps lead to a positive cash balance. However, avoid the temptation to determine the cash balance you want and juggle the sales forecasts until you get that amount.

Walt sells on a cash basis, meaning cash or checks only—no credit cards and no accounts receivable. If this were not the case, Walt would have to factor in the discount rate he paid to the bank on his credit card sales, and he could add the actual cash he received each month from collections of his accounts receivable—not the sales amount.

Remember, budgeting is a continuous cycle. When you examined your marketing strategies, you probably made some initial sales projections. Now you can refine them. Later, after you compare actual results to your budgets, you may need to revise the figures for future months.

The sales budget above uses a very simple format; you can add more detail if desired. In your business plan, you already determined a pricing strategy. Now, you need to add quantity. Often, history is used as a base and projections are made from there. Gathering sales history may be a simple matter of reviewing your records, but it can be complicated if you want to look at data by product or product line. Many small businesses do not keep this information. If you think it would be useful, you can change your recordkeeping system to give you this information.

An alternate method is to multiply total sales by your product mix ratio. For example, suppose you estimate that 65% of your sales normally come from your first product line, 20% from a second line, and 15% from a third; these percentages give a rough estimate of sales history by product. You should use percentages of sales dollars to do this. You can also use an industry average; we discussed sources of these averages previously.

When forecasting sales, pay particular attention to past trends in the industry and your business. You may relate a past trend to what was happening in your marketplace and learn something valuable for the future. If you find a trend that you don't expect to be repeated, you should not use it.

Knowing your product's position in its life cycle is very helpful when forecasting sales. Also, if your product is seasonal, that should be reflected in your forecasts.

*Walt's Machine Shop: Cost of Goods Sold Budget*

| Months | Jan | Feb | Mar | Total |
|---|---|---|---|---|
| **Product/Service #1** | | | | |
| Units Sold | 30 | 40 | 50 | 120 |
| Cost per Unit | $45 | $45 | $45 | $45 |
| Total Cost | $1,350 | $1,800 | $2,250 | $5,400 |
| **Product/Service #2** | | | | |
| Units Sold | 70 | 70 | 80 | 220 |
| Cost per Unit | $150 | $150 | $150 | $150 |
| Total Cost | $10,500 | $10,500 | $12,000 | $33,000 |
| **Product/Service #3** | | | | |
| Units Sold | 2 | 2 | 2 | 6 |
| Cost per Unit | $300 | $300 | $300 | $300 |
| Total Cost | $600 | $600 | $600 | $1,800 |
| **All Products/Service Total Cost** | $12,450 | $12,900 | $14,850 | $40,200 |

Recall that cost of goods sold should reflect the cost to the business of the product it is selling. Service businesses do not have this expense. Retailers and wholesalers should check manufacturer and distributor catalogs or recent invoices for cost information, then make a few refinements. The cost per unit used to forecast cost of goods sold should be reduced by expected cash or quantity discounts, and increased by freight charges. In other words, use the net amount you expect to pay.

Manufacturers usually prepare a **production budget**, which shows how they expect to produce the projected sales units. Manufacturers incur three costs for the units they produce: direct materials, direct labor, and overhead. There are many ways to incorporate these costs into the cost of goods sold projection. You may wish to add more detail to your schedule. In the example above, the projections are in the simplest form: Walt's Machine Shop has included only direct materials in its cost of goods sold budget. Labor and overhead costs have been forecast separately and included in the operating expenses budget. This simple presentation doesn't follow the accounting technique known as "full absorption costing," which calls for all three manufacturing costs to be included in the cost per unit. However, Walt's is using these budgets internally, so the simpler version is good enough.

Often, it is helpful to have additional schedules which support the amounts listed in your operating expenses budget

Manufacturers might also consider that they have three types of inventory: raw materials, work-in-process, and finished goods. Walt's has chosen to ignore this because their jobs are relatively short and the amount of work-in-process is never very large. If costs are tied up in work-in-process for a long time, this will affect the cash flow projections, and the cost of goods sold budget should reflect this. Walt assumes all his expenses will be on a cash basis.

The next step for Walt's is to budget operating expenses. Similarly, Walt assumes his expenses will be on a cash basis, and he will not have any accounts payable or other accrual expenses.

*Walt's Machine Shop: Operating Expenses Budget*

| | Jan | Feb | Mar | Total |
|---|---|---|---|---|
| **Labor** | | | | |
| Salaries and Wages | $30,000 | $30,000 | $30,000 | $90,000 |
| Payroll Taxes & Benefits | $8,695 | $8,695 | $8,695 | $26,085 |
| **Total Labor Expense** | **$38,695** | **$38,695** | **$38,695** | **$116,085** |
| **Non-Labor** | | | | |
| Occupancy Expenses | $3,355 | $3,480 | $3,355 | $10,190 |
| Outside Services | $650 | $650 | $650 | $1,950 |
| Insurance | $200 | | | $200 |
| Advertising | $300 | $1,050 | $300 | $1,650 |
| Miscellaneous | $100 | $100 | $100 | $300 |
| **Total Non-Labor** | **$4,605** | **$5,280** | **$4,405** | **$14,290** |

You can have as much detail as you wish in your operating expenses. Walt's has divided their costs into labor and non-labor, but you can use any categories that make sense for your business. It's often helpful to have additional schedules supporting the amounts listed in this budget. For example, Walt's may have a schedule giving the details of occupancy costs.

Be sure to distinguish between fixed and variable expenses when preparing operating expense forecasts. **Fixed costs** remain the same no matter what you forecast for sales, while **variable costs** change with changes in sales volume.

### Cash Flow Projections

When combined, the sales forecast, cost of goods sold budget, and operating expenses budget lead to the cash flow projections.

| Months | Jan | Feb | Mar | Total |
|---|---|---|---|---|
| Total-All Product/Service Sales | $50,000. | $53,000 | $61,000 | $164,000 |
| Total-All Product/Service CGS | 12,450 | 12,900 | 14,850 | 40,200 |
| Total Labor Expense | 38,695 | 38,695 | 38,695 | 116,085 |
| Total Non-Labor Expense | 4,605 | 5,280 | 4,405 | 14,290 |
| **Net Cash Flow** | **-5,750** | **-3,875** | **3,050** | **-6,575** |

This first quarter cash flow projection provides valuable information to Walt. He knows that his cash initial position starting the quarter must be at least $6,575 just to survive his anticipated first quarter cash shortfall.

Walt would complete his annual budget by projecting quarters 2, 3 and 4 in the same manner he did with quarter 1. By combining all four quarters, he would complete his annual budget.

We cannot overemphasize the importance of managing your cash; Chapter 38 *Cash Flow Management* is entirely devoted to this topic.

### Projected Income Statement, Balance Sheet, and Statement of Cash Flows

The projected income statement, balance sheet, and statement of cash flows are prepared as previously described, and are not included as examples here.

Performance reports compare budgeted to actual amounts

---◆---

*A perfect example of Peekskill Catering's difficulties was a Thanksgiving dinner they catered for a party of 12. When Sarah wrote up the invoice for the event, she estimated that her costs broke down as follows:*

- *10 hours of work time @ $20 per hour*
- *$250 in food costs*
- *$350 for wine and champagne*

*When Anne worked with her, reviewing receipts and overhead expenses, they found that her actual costs were:*

- *20 hours of work time (3 hours of research, menu planning, and client management; 10 hours of prep and shopping; 7 hours of cooking and clean-up).*
- *$350 in food costs, including special orders and last-minute runs to the gourmet food store*
- *$350 for wine and champagne*
- *$40 in overhead expenses (including rent, kitchen supplies, utilities, gas, insurance, and taxes), calculated as a percentage of number of hours spent in the kitchen.*

*Sarah had undercharged her client significantly! By totaling her expenses rather than approximating them, Sarah recognized what a difference a budgeting system could make. She also realized that with Anne's help, she and Jason could price their services correctly and generate greater profits.*

---◆---

# Feedback from Your Budgets

Budgets are used to get feedback about business operations. This is done by preparing performance reports that compare actual results to budgeted amounts and show **variances**. Variances can then be investigated and corrective actions taken, if necessary.

For many small businesses, performance reports for the business as a whole are sufficient. However, if your business is organized into functional departments (e.g., sales, production, and shipping) or according to product line, or if you have more than one location, you should prepare reports for each department. The more detail you have, the more feedback you get. The danger is that you can get buried in too much detail.

When complex organizations prepare performance reports, they usually start at the bottom of the business and work up. Each report rolls into another report until you get to the report showing the business as a whole. For example, let's assume that Walt's has organized the sales staff into regional offices. The salespeople in each region report to a regional director, who reports in turn to the marketing manager at the main office. Walt's prepares monthly performance reports by region and in total. The reports for January included the following:

*Sales Performance Report for January*

| Total Sales | Budget | Actual | Variance Over (Under) |
|---|---|---|---|
| Region 1 | $10,000 | $12,000 | $2,000 |
| Region 2 | $25,000 | $24,000 | ($1,000) |
| Region 3 | $15,000 | $16,500 | $1,500 |
| Total Sales | $50,000 | $52,500 | $2,500 |

*Sales Performance Report for January*

| Region 2 | Budget | Actual | Variance Over (Under) |
|---|---|---|---|
| Salesperson 1 | $15,000 | $12,000 | ($3,000) |
| Salesperson 2 | $10,000 | $12,000 | $2,000 |
| Total Sales | $25,000 | $24,000 | ($1,000) |

Notice that the report for Region 2 feeds the report above. The budgeted and actual amounts in the Region 2 report match the figures listed in the report for all sales. Remember, the important thing is to break down the data to get feedback about the business.

Difficulties are often encountered with allocation of costs common to all levels of the business. For example, if Walt's prepares performance reports by functional area (sales department, production, administration, etc.), what should they do with the cost of the copy machine or receptionist, or the other things the departments share? These common costs could be placed in a single performance report, or allocated to various departments. If you don't allocate and the costs are excluded from all performance reports, then no one will be looking at those costs to see if they are in line with the budget.

It is important to investigate the cause of variances before jumping to conclusions. A variance that looks bad at first may actually result from something good, or vice versa. Walt's performance report for January:

| Region 2 | January Budget | January Actual | Variance Over (Under) |
|---|---|---|---|
| **COST OF GOODS SOLD** | | | |
| **Product/Service #1** | | | |
| Units Sold | 30 | 42 | |
| Cost per Unit | $45 | $40 | |
| Total Cost | **$1,350** | **$1,680** | **$330** |
| **Product/Service #2** | | | |
| Units Sold | 70 | 65 | |
| Cost per Unit | $150 | $157 | |
| Total Cost | **$10,500** | **$10,205** | **($295)** |
| **Operating Expenses** | | | |
| Labor | | | |
| **Salaries & Wages** | **$30,000** | **$32,000** | **$2,000** |

It is easy to assume that all expenses over budget are bad, and all savings under budget are good. However, "bad" and "good" are determined by how well you are meeting your business objectives. For example, if you take the above performance report for Walt's at face value, you might think that something is wrong regarding Product 1, in that January expenses were higher than budgeted.

However, notice that this excess occurred because more units were sold than expected. In fact, the company managed to decrease costs per unit. This is good, isn't it? Doesn't every business strive to cut costs? Sure, but how this gets done is important too. Suppose the unit cost decreased because the purchasing manager bought cheaper, lower quality goods. If Walt's has identified its market niche as producing high-quality, long-lasting products, these purchases do not fit Walt's objectives. But if Walt's goal is to become the discount machine shop in the area, they fit very nicely!

Often, variances are interconnected. For example, the report for Walt's shows that salaries and wages in January cost $2,000 more than budgeted. Why did this occur? Perhaps it resulted from the actions taken by the purchasing manager. If inferior materials were used, there may have been difficulties completing the product. Perhaps laborers had to work overtime to fix problems that occurred, and overtime pay was not anticipated in the budget. Or maybe the extra labor cost had nothing to do with the materials used. Walt's sold more units in January than expected. This might have resulted from a special order that could only be produced after hours, and overtime pay was necessary.

Which variances should you explore in more detail? This is a difficult question. It usually isn't possible to evaluate every variance. Some businesses investigate all variances above a certain dollar amount, while others look at the relative size of the variance rather than absolute dollar amount. For example, a variance of more than 5% from budgeted dollars might be investigated, while a variance only 0.5% different might not be. The problem is that some variances are caused by more than one phenomenon, so a small variance might be masking several larger variances that balance each other out. There might be something important to learn from these factors.

We have a tendency to focus our efforts only on expenses with actual amounts higher than budgeted. You also can learn a great deal when costs are under the budgeted amount. You can determine which are beneficial actions and use this information to improve your processes and products.

As you can see, preparing the performance reports is the easy part...figuring out what the reports are telling you is much more difficult!

---

*After a few meetings with Anne, Sarah and Jason adjusted their sales forecasts for the coming season, taking into account sales for the preceding three seasons. They calculated their total overhead expenses and budgeted them for each month of the next year's operations. Overhead increased during peak winter months, when they had higher electric and gas costs.*

*They decided to allocate their overhead expenses to catering jobs based on a five-month year of operations. They had so few jobs during the remaining seven months that the business had to be able to generate its total income during peak months.*

*With better sales projections for the coming season, Peekskill Caterers would be able to order the correct amount of supplies ahead of time. They could buy more supplies at lower bulk rates, and make fewer trips to the pricey gourmet food shop. Since a certain amount of last-minute purchases were inevitable, they added an additional percentage to their total supply costs.*

*Peekskill Caterers also budgeted for hourly kitchen and serving personnel; annual kitchen supply needs like bowls, knives, and aprons; health coverage; gas for their truck; and insurance.*

*The couple finished their meeting with Anne by creating a simple computer spreadsheet template for their budgets. This way they could easily track overhead costs and supply costs, to make sure they were meeting their projected budgets.*

*Sarah and Jason left the meeting feeling more in control of their business than ever before, and confident that they could maintain their budgets and return Peekskill Caterers to profitability.*

## Flexible Budgets

Let's say Walt budgeted sales of 2,800 units in March. If actual March sales units totaled 3,200, how would Walt's performance reports look? Well, certainly actual sales would exceed budgeted sales. Wouldn't this also cause many of his actual expenses to be above budget? You would expect Walt's cost of goods sold to be above the budgeted cost. Perhaps his labor would have a positive variance. Remember our earlier discussions of

### NxLEVEL™ TECH TIP

**One area in which it's often possible to cut your business's costs is shipping.**

Depending on how soon you want a package to be delivered and where it has to go, shipping costs can vary dramatically. By comparing the rates and levels of service offered by different carriers, you can achieve substantial savings every time you ship. This process just got much easier, because it's now possible to get comparisons of shipping rates online by visiting **http://www.intershipper.net**, a free service that locates the best rates among carriers such as USPS, UPS, FedEx, RPS, DHL, and Airborne. The quotes are based on how quickly you want the item to be delivered, and how far away the destination address is. This site also allows you to track packages sent via a variety of carriers at one site, instead of visiting tracking sites for each carrier.

Performance measures focus attention on the actions that drive operations

fixed and variable expenses? Wouldn't you expect positive variances for all variable expenses? The question then becomes: Is actual cost greater than budgeted cost by the amount you would expect?

Flexible budgets can help answer this question, because they reflect actual sales volume. They recast the original budget, using actual sales volume as a base. Next, the flexible budget is compared to actual results so as to eliminate the overall change in sales volume from the variance analysis. It is then apparent what happened to variable expenses given the sales volume achieved. Some of the January performance report for Walt's could be redone like this:

| January Performance Report | | | | |
| --- | --- | --- | --- | --- |
| **Region 2** | **January Budget** | **Flexible Budget** | **January Actual** | **Variance Over (Under)** |
| **COST OF GOODS SOLD** | | | | |
| **Product/Service #1** | | | | |
| Units Sold | 30 | 42 | 42 | |
| Price per Unit | $45 | $45 | $40 | |
| Total Sales | $1,350 | $1,890 | $1,680 | $(210) |
| **OPERATING EXPENSES** | | | | |
| **Labor** | | | | |
| Salaries & Wages | $30,000 | $30,000 | $32,000 | $2,000 |

For Walt's, as for most businesses, cost of goods sold is a variable expense. Therefore, it changes with changes in sales volume. The original budget is redone so that budgeted units sold match actual units sold. Actual sales volume is multiplied by budgeted cost per unit. This focuses on cost of goods rather than volume. The original performance report showed a variance of $330 over budget, which is to be expected because sales volume was higher. The flexible budget shows a variance of $210 under budget. This means that given the sales volume, Walt's had a lower cost of goods sold overall.

Notice that the original budgeted amount and the flexible budget for salaries and wages did not change. Walt's pays its employees a salary plus overtime pay. Unless overtime occurs, this expense is fixed; it does not change with changes in sales volume. Thus, assuming no overtime pay, this expense is budgeted at $30,000, no matter what level of sales is anticipated or achieved.

## Performance Measures

Many companies utilize **performance measures** in addition to their master budgets. These measures focus attention on actions that drive operations. Often, these data are not included in the accounting system, and new procedures need to be established to collect them. Machine downtime, customer orders received by day, number of product defects found, and work-in-process time might be tracked over time so that developing trends can be analyzed.

This helps you to evaluate progress made toward attaining your objectives. Although objectives must be measurable, it doesn't always make sense to measure them in terms of dollars and cents. Instead, objectives can be evaluated using performance measures that are meaningful to the people using them.

## Conclusion

The budget process might seem difficult and time-consuming, but the benefits definitely outweigh the costs. Without this process, you don't have any benchmarks, no way to see if you are doing better or worse than expected. You might wander like Alice through Wonderland, never sure where you are or where you're going. And unfortunately, going down the rabbit hole usually means going out of business!

# Chapter 38
# CASH FLOW MANAGEMENT

*About This Chapter:*
- *Reasons for holding cash*
- *The cash flow cycle*
- *Internal controls for cash*
- *Preparing cash flow projections*
- *Managing excess cash*

## Introduction

Cash is the lifeblood of business, so you must pay careful attention to your cash flow. This is particularly true for small businesses, which tend to be undercapitalized. This means the business operates on a very tight budget, without a great investment of funds—the equivalent of living from paycheck to paycheck. Careful cash management keeps the business from becoming delinquent on its debts and protects its credit rating.

It is equally important to manage your cash position carefully when the business is flush with cash. Idle cash doesn't help profitability, but planning for growth presents cash flow management challenges; you might encounter a cash drain in the beginning as you establish new markets or open new stores. Good times or bad, careful **cash flow management** is an essential part of every business's success.

Cash is the lifeblood of business

## Reasons for Holding Cash

Why do businesses hold cash? In general, there are three reasons:

1. To meet current and upcoming planned expenditures.
2. As a precaution against unexpected expenditures or a drop in revenues.
3. To meet contract or regulatory requirements, such as compensating balances mandated by a loan agreement.

The amount of cash you hold depends on your attitude about risk. How much of a chance are you willing to take that you will not have enough cash to meet your obligations? What size of safety margin makes you comfortable? Remember, there is a trade-off between risk and reward; if you keep an extra $10,000 in your checking account "just in case," you might be missing opportunities to use that cash to earn a greater profit.

Of course, some businesses would love to have an extra $10,000, but their checking account balances never get above $500, and they often make deposits just in time to cover checks. Obviously, these businesses have a greater risk of cash shortages.

*Baked Alaska, Inc., a backpack and purse design company, has a very common problem: it is a small business with big customers who can all but set their own payment terms. Like many small manufacturers, Baked Alaska buys its supplies frequently, and in small quantities. It cannot afford to buy 1,000 yards of canvas, even though doing so would significantly lower its per unit costs. Instead, Baked Alaska buys fabric and trim every few weeks, sews its backpacks, and replenishes its supplies as production warrants. The business survives by making its products in comparatively small batches, so that it doesn't have to carry inventory, and can quickly change its designs to stay on top of trends.*

*While Baked Alaska makes frequent purchases, it doesn't have frequent inflows of revenue. The problem comes from Baked Alaska's largest clients, like Macy's and Clothestime. These businesses often take 90, 120, or even 180 days to pay their accounts. That's a six-month loan that Baked Alaska is making to giant, national retailers!*

*Baked Alaska is in for some serious cash flow problems.*

## The Cash Flow Cycle

The cash flow cycle (also known as the cash-to-cash cycle) represents the length of time that cash is tied up in business operations. If the cycle is shortened, cash will be freed to begin the cycle again or to be invested in other projects. The cycle looks like this:

Manage your cash flow cycle!

**Step 1**
**Purchase Merchandise on Account**

**Step 2**
**Sell Merchandise to Customers on Account**

**Step 3**
**Collect Cash from Customers**

**Step 4**
**Pay Supplier for Merchandise**

Therefore, how long cash is tied up in business operations is a function of 1) how long your inventory sits before being sold; 2) how long it takes your customers to pay; and 3) how long before your suppliers are paid. Managing cash flow means managing these activities. To shorten the cycle, you can speed up sales, speed up collections from credit customers, or slow down payments to suppliers.

## Managing Inventory

**Total inventory cost** is a function of two variables: the quantity of goods in inventory, and cost per unit. You must consider both when managing inventory. You can reduce your investment in inventory by decreasing either the quantity you hold, or its cost. Reducing inventory's per-unit cost calls for careful attention to the purchasing function. A manufacturer must also monitor labor and overhead costs.

Businesses hold inventory to meet actual and potential customer orders, to guard against supplier shortages, to corner the market, or because they have taken advantage of **quantity discounts** offered by suppliers. A bad reason for holding inventory, but a very common one, is that the business has not taken the time to manage it properly.

**Ratio analysis** is a means of evaluating how effectively the cash flow cycle is being managed. Inventory turnover ratio:

How often does your inventory turn over?

**Inventory turnover** $\quad = \quad \dfrac{\text{Cost of Goods Sold}}{\text{Average inventory}}$

This ratio tells the average number of times inventory turns (is sold) during the year. We can convert this into days by dividing the inventory turnover ratio into 365 days:

Average days in inventory $\quad = \quad \dfrac{365 \text{ days}}{\text{Inventory turnover ratio}}$

For example, assume the following for Blodgett Brass Company:

Inventory turnover $\quad = \quad \dfrac{\$\,3,900,000}{\$\,300,000} \quad = \quad 13 \text{ times per year}$

Average days in inventory $\quad = \quad \dfrac{365}{13} \quad = \quad 28 \text{ days}$

On the average, Blodgett's inventory is in stock for 28 days before it sells. Whether this is high or low depends on the environment in which Blodgett operates. They should consider industry averages, their geographical location, their financial history, and any other special circumstances. However, if they wish to decrease the cash-to-cash cycle, Blodgett may try to turn their inventory more often than every 28 days.

How can they do that? The obvious answer is to increase sales. Another way is to reduce inventory by eliminating obsolete and slow-moving products. Careful evaluation of what sells and what doesn't is vital to this process.

Good buying decisions have a substantial impact on inventory levels

Good buying decisions have a substantial impact on inventory levels. For each item in your inventory, you must consider how many to buy and how much to pay. Also, there are several mathematical models you can use to help determine the optimum level of inventory to hold, and how much and when to order. One is the **Economic Order Quantity (EOQ)** model. (You can find out more about EOQ in many business math books.) The EOQ formula calculates the optimum quantity of inventory to order, based on the cost of ordering and storing the goods, anticipated sales, and per unit cost. There are also many computer programs that can help you determine ordering strategies.

Some businesses have turned to **just-in-time delivery (JIT)** systems to reduce inventory levels. These systems attempt to get inventory to your operation just in time to be used or sold. This significantly decreases inventory levels and reduces the cash flow cycle. This may be easier said than done, however; the process requires special cooperation between you and your suppliers, and is very difficult for businesses with wide swings in sales volumes. Many firms have implemented some of the just-in-time concepts and modified the process to suit their needs. You can find many books and articles about JIT systems.

---

*Baked Alaska didn't have a problem with delinquent bills, nor with the choice of accounts to which it sold. Baked Alaska's problem was that it was not being adequately compensated for the time its money was tied up in accounts receivable. Therefore, the solution was to create a better accounts receivable strategy.*

*Baked Alaska's owner, Antonia Bolt, sat down with her accountant and looked closely at her prices, the dollar amount of her largest customers' orders, and the average collection period. They were unhappy when they found that Baked Alaska's average collection period was 103 days, but they were not shocked; payment terms that extended into the next season were not at all uncommon in the industry. Antonia realized that she couldn't change the way the industry operated, but she could change what she charged her customers. This way, she could bank the difference, and create a working capital "cushion" to fund her daily operations.*

---

### Managing Accounts Receivable

Managing accounts receivable means balancing the risks and rewards of your financial and marketing goals. New credit customers may help you meet sales goals, but if they prove to be slow payers, the cash flow cycle may be lengthened and your financial position weakened. However, if you don't offer good credit terms, you may lose sales.

Ratios can help you evaluate the effectiveness of your credit policies.

Receivables turnover ratio:

$$\textbf{Receivables turnover} = \frac{\text{Net credit sales}}{\text{Average net receivables}}$$

This ratio indicates the average number of times receivables turn (are collected) during the year. This can be converted into days by dividing the ratio into 365 days:

$$\textbf{Average collection period} = \frac{365 \text{ days}}{\text{Receivables turnover ratio}}$$

Here's another example for Blodgett Brass Company:

$$\text{Receivables turnover} = \frac{\$ 7{,}200{,}000}{\$ 650{,}000} = \text{about 11 times per year}$$

$$\text{Average collection period} = \frac{365}{11} = \text{approximately 33 days}$$

On the average, Blodgett's customers take 33 days to pay. As with Average Days in Inventory, Blodgett must consider their environment before evaluating whether this ratio is high or low. If they wish to decrease the cash-to-cash cycle, Blodgett should try to reduce the average collection period for their receivables. To do this, Blodgett should review their:

1. Criteria for extending credit
2. Credit terms offered
3. Collection activities

If your business sells to customers on account, you need to monitor who gets credit and how much they get. When considering credit for your customers, use the same methods bankers use when evaluating a loan applicant. Here is a brief summary:

- **Credit history.** Review credit history for new and repeat customers; don't assume that circumstances remain constant for your customers. Pay close attention to customers who ask for increased credit, or request special terms or extended credit. Many agencies can supply credit histories and ratings.
- **Character.** Evaluate your customer's intention to pay by checking the business's reputation and references.
- **Capacity.** Capacity refers to your customers' ability to pay the debt. Look at their past and present financial reports, and observe their current operations.
- **Collateral.** Usually, there is no collateral for an accounts receivable transaction. You may be able to retrieve the merchandise, but that is not always possible.
- **Conditions.** Consider general and local economic trends.
- **Capital.** Customers with a solid financial position are less likely to default.

It isn't likely that your credit evaluation will eliminate all bad debts. It is difficult to judge the likelihood that a customer will be a collection problem, and even good customers can fall on hard times. All you can do is try to reduce the risk by performing credit evaluations diligently.

Your business should have clearly written procedures stating what information is required from credit applicants, and which employees have the authority to grant credit.

The credit terms you offer customers include the credit period and cash discounts. Extending the time before customers must pay lengthens your cash flow cycle, so that your bills may come due before expected receipts from your customers. Remember that

What is your average collection period?

If your business sells to customers on account, you need policies to monitor who gets credit

there is a cost to having funds tied up in receivables; the money can't work for you until you get it! If you shorten the credit period, your customers might either become delinquent on their accounts or buy elsewhere. Determining the optimum credit period may take some experimentation. It's wise to review what your competitors are doing.

**Cash discounts** are given for early payment of invoices. For example, you might offer your customers terms of "**2/10, net 30.**" This means that customers paying within 10 days of the invoice date will receive a 2% discount. Otherwise, the normal payment period is 30 days. Businesses offer cash discounts to attract customers and to reduce the average collection period. The discount given is the price the business pays for these benefits. Two percent may not sound like much, but remember that it is causing customers to pay 20 days sooner than they would without the discount.

The part of credit sales that business owners like least is trying to collect from delinquent customers. There are collection agencies who will do this for you, but they charge a high fee; most businesses resort to this only after other efforts have failed. How much effort you put into collecting receivables is a trade-off between the time and money it costs versus the cash lost if you fail to collect.

---

*Antonia and her accountant discovered that Baked Alaska had a substantial amount of inventory, without even knowing it! Some of its oldest customers were specialty boutiques that only sold merchandise on consignment. They would display backpacks in their stores, and write a check to Baked Alaska for a percentage of the retail price when they sold one.*

*This meant that Baked Alaska's backpacks were sitting in stores without generating any revenue. Antonia's accountant totaled the value of the merchandise in these accounts, and it came to over $1,000. Antonia and her accountant decided that it was crazy to have backpacks sitting on consignment when Baked Alaska was unable to fill all of the straight sale orders coming in, so she decided on the spot to discontinue all consignment sales.*

---

The best strategy is not to let accounts become delinquent in the first place. Careful review before extending credit will help. Also, an effective billing system will ensure that customers receive timely, accurate invoices. If customers believe you will notice if they are delinquent, they are more likely to pay on time. Errors on invoices can cause disputes and delays, so you should make every effort to avoid them.

One effective tool for managing collections is to age your accounts receivable. An **aging report** lists receivables by how long they have been outstanding. Here's an example.

The part of credit sales that business owners like least is trying to collect from delinquent customers

| Bullfrog, Inc. Accounts Receivable Aging Report January 30, 1999 | | | | | |
|---|---|---|---|---|---|
| Customer | Total Due | Under 30 Days | 30-60 Days | 61-90 Days | Over 90 Days |
| Acme, Inc. | $1,400 | $1,200 | $200 | | |
| BitCo | $3,570 | $2,070 | $850 | $650 | |
| Cox Corporation | $2,090 | | | | $2,090 |

Use an aging report to identify slow-paying customers

The aging report allows you to identify slow-paying customers, follow up on collections, and evaluate credit and collection policies.

Many retailers shift the credit risk and collection burdens away from themselves by accepting credit cards. National credit cards, such as VISA and MasterCard, offer revolving credit financing to consumers. The retailer, after making the sale to the consumer, turns in the credit card charge slip and receives 95 to 98 percent of the total credit charge. The institution that issued the credit card bears the risk of nonpayment. To become a credit card merchant, you need to fill out an application and sign an agreement with a bank or other financial institution offering the service. These institutions offer many different services and terms, so check around before signing an agreement. Talk to your banker, other merchants, and your SBDC counselor for some ideas. Or, if you have a newly registered business, look in your mailbox. The financial institutions will find you!

Some businesses speed up collections—and reduce the cash flow cycle—by using a lockbox plan in which customers send their payments to a local post office box that is opened daily by bank personnel. The amounts clear the bank quickly and thus are available to the business sooner. The bank may charge a fee or require a compensating balance for this service. This arrangement is normally used by businesses with a large volume of payments.

You can also shorten the cash-to-cash cycle by assigning or factoring accounts receivable.

**Assigning** receivables means using them as collateral for a short-term loan. (This is also known as pledging your receivables.) The lender reviews the collectibility of your receivables and lends you some percentage of the total. You repay the loan, plus interest, as you receive payments from your customers.

**Factoring** receivables means selling them to a financial institution. The factoring agreement may be on a "with recourse" or "without recourse" basis. If factored with recourse, you still have a collection risk, because the financial institution may seek funds from you should collections be less than anticipated. If factored without recourse, the financial institution cannot seek additional funds from you; as you can imagine, the financial institution will be very careful before entering into this type of transaction, and will charge you more if they determine your receivables are "high risk." Factoring does not result in a loan and no interest is paid. The factor's fee will be the difference between the accounts receivable sold and the cash the factor gives you. One advantage of factoring is that the factor typically assumes all administrative responsibility for collection. Customers send payments directly to the factor. Some businesses see this as a way to reduce overhead costs by eliminating accounting tasks.

Assigning and factoring your receivables are both effective ways of speeding up cash inflows. However, these methods can be very expensive. Interest rates charged on short-term loans for which receivables are assigned will usually be several points above the prime rate. Factoring can be even more expensive: depending on the quality of the receivables, the factorer may offer as little as 80% of the face value. Factoring is not generally recommended for small businesses unless the receivables are of very high quality, with little collection risk, and the business owner needs cash quickly.

---

*Antonia had researched her competitors' payment terms, and her accountant knew what their money could be earning were they to put it back into operations or into other market investments. Within minutes, Antonia and her accountant worked out Baked Alaska's new payment terms. They were as follows:*

- *Prices for all Baked Alaska backpacks would increase by 10%*
- *"5/10" cash discounts would be given for early payment of invoices (that is, a 5% discount for accounts paid within 10 days)*

*Customers paying after 30 days would be charged interest on their orders. Alice decided to factor these terms into the initial order price for her largest customers, who routinely took more than 30 days to pay. This way, the company would earn interest on its outstanding receivables.*

*Antonia decided to see how the new terms worked for six months. At that point, she would evaluate Baked Alaska's receivables and cash flow, and fine-tune the strategy as needed.*

---

## Managing Accounts Payable

The final component of the cash flow cycle is how long it takes to pay your bills. This is the part of the cycle you should try to extend, but only within reason! You do not want to become delinquent on your bills, but you do not need to pay too quickly either.

Using a ratio to monitor this process is more difficult than for inventory or receivables, because your suppliers are likely to offer a wide variety of credit terms. However, you may find it helpful to compute the average time to pay for purchases.

Average time to pay for purchases:

365 days divided by $\dfrac{\text{Total purchases}}{\text{Average accounts payable}}$

Blodgett Brass has the following ratio:

365 days divided by $\qquad \dfrac{5,100,000}{490,000}$ = about 35 days

Do your suppliers offer cash discounts for early payment? Should you pay early enough to take the discount? These points were discussed in relation to accounts receivable; everything said there is now true for you, but from the customer's perspective! You have to balance the advantage of taking the discount versus the disadvantage of giving up the money sooner.

A **tickler system** is very helpful in controlling payments to creditors. Ideally, bills are paid when due (or, if cash discounts are taken, just at the end of the discount period). A tickler system can help you do this. Bills to be paid are sorted by when they are due. This allows you to know what funds will be needed when, and to be sure that those funds are available.

## Internal Controls for Cash

**Internal controls** help safeguard assets and ensure the accuracy of financial information. Internal controls are not meant simply to guard against theft and embezzlement; they also reduce the number of honest errors made, help locate errors before it is too late to fix them, and help employees operate efficiently.

The objectives of internal controls for cash include:

1. To assure that all cash that should have been received was indeed received, deposited, and recorded properly.
2. To assure that all cash disbursements were authorized and properly recorded.
3. To assure that cash balances are secure and adequate.

### Authorization

Every business transaction must be authorized by someone. For cash, this is usually accomplished by having **authorized check signers**. Your bank maintains a **signature card** that must be signed by all persons whom you've authorized to sign checks. Usually, the business owner will be an authorized check signer, but it is important to have additional persons on the signature card. (What if the owner is out of town when the payroll checks must be signed?)

Many businesses require dual signatures on checks above a certain amount. For example, the business may require two signatures on checks greater than $5,000 and on all checks to owners and employees.

Check signers should carefully review what they sign. Many cases of embezzlement occur because the business owner simply signs anything the accountant put in front of him or her, without reviewing the information. Checks to be signed should be presented to the check signer with supporting documents attached. Examine the invoice and compare amounts, payee, and dates before signing the check. If you don't recognize the payee, ask questions or look at your authorized vendor list.

Businesses that issue many checks sometimes use computer-generated signatures or a check-signing machine. In such cases, internal controls must safeguard the use of the computer program or check-signing machine so that no unauthorized persons have access. Having a machine sign the checks for you does not reduce your responsibility to review supporting documents!

### Reconciling Bank Accounts

It is essential that businesses **reconcile** their monthly bank statements with the cash balance on the books. Too often, this internal control is put off until the task becomes so burdensome that it is dismissed forever. If it is not done for several months, mistakes are harder to find and the whole process becomes very frustrating. One small business owner neglected to reconcile his bank statements for more than six years! Challenged by friends to prove he could do it, he finally took a whole week for the task. His account reconciled to within two cents, but that is a lucky exception—his technique is not recommended!

Reconciling items is often simply a matter of timing. Deposits in transit are deposits you made that have not yet been posted by the bank. Outstanding checks are those that have not yet been cashed by the payee. You have already deducted these amounts from your cash balance but they have not been taken out of your account by the bank. Service charges may also be a reconciling item, as the business often does not know the amount of the charge until it receives the bank statement.

Your banker can help you develop a bank reconciliation form. In fact, many banks include a form on the back of the monthly bank statement. A particularly useful method is to reconcile both the bank balance and the balance per books to the correct amount of cash. Here is an example of a bank reconciliation in this format:

| Your Business Bank Reconciliation March 31, 1999 | | | |
|---|---|---|---|
| Balance per bank statement | $3,500 | Balance per books | $2,900 |
| Deposits in transit | 490 | Service charge | (15) |
| Outstanding checks | (1,075) | Error recording check | 30 |
| **Correct cash balance** | **$2,915** | **Correct cash balance** | **$2,915** |

This format is useful because it indicates the correct amount of cash. This is the cash balance that should be included on the balance sheet. In this example, the business must adjust its books for the service charge of $15 and the error of $30.

Bank statements should be mailed directly to the employee responsible for reconciling the bank statements. Other personnel, especially those charged with writing checks or keeping the accounting records, should not have access to the statements.

It is essential that businesses reconcile their monthly bank statements

## Segregation of Duties

Segregating duties is a very important internal control for cash. The goal is to have different people performing authorization, recording, and custodial functions. Do not permit one employee to handle a transaction from beginning to end. In particular, the person who handles the cash should not be in charge of recording the amounts in the books. Here are some ideas for segregating duties in a business with plenty of people to cover all the tasks. Most small businesses don't have the luxury of going to this extreme, but you can use this model to help you segregate the tasks as much as possible.

Segregating duties is critical for controlling cash

*Segregation of duties for cash sales*

| | |
|---|---|
| Handles central cash register | Person 1 |
| Closes register at end of the day and reconciles cash in the drawer to total sales | Person 2 |
| Prepares deposit slip | Person 1 |
| Makes deposit daily and compares deposit slip to cash report prepared by Person 2 | Person 3 |

*Segregation of duties for checks received in the mail*

| | |
|---|---|
| Opens mail and makes a list of checks received | Person 4 |
| Prepares deposit slip | Person 5 |
| Updates accounts receivable records | Person 6 |
| Compares the information from Persons 4, 5, and 6 | Person 7 |

*Segregation of duties for cash disbursements*

| | |
|---|---|
| Prepares checks | Person 8 |
| Signs checks and reviews supporting documents | Person 9 |
| Mails checks | Person 9 or 10 |

*Segregation of duties for bank reconciliation*

| | |
|---|---|
| Prepares bank reconciliation | Person 11 |
| Reviews bank reconciliation | Person 12 |

## Physical Controls

Cash is easy to lose, so steps must be taken to safeguard it. This includes controls for unused checks and cash on hand.

Storing cash in a safe is a good idea, but be sure to control access to the safe combination, and how money is placed into and taken out of the safe. There is safety in numbers, so you should have more than one person present when cash from the safe is handled. An even better physical control for cash is timely deposits; Get the cash off the premises and into the bank. Banks have made it very easy for their customers to deposit cash daily with special merchant windows and night deposit boxes. Bank deposits should be made by the business owner, a trusted employee, or, even better, by two employees together.

It is important to safeguard unused checks. Lock them in a desk or safe and allow access only to authorized check signers or the person who prepares the checks. Checks should be pre-numbered so that you can account for every check in the series. Voided checks should be defaced so they cannot be used again.

## Controls for Cash Registers

Cash registers can be very valuable internal control devices. Remember, you have good internal control when there is a third party involved in the transaction. This is the case when cash registers are used, because the customer can see the prices of items being purchased and review the total sale and change given. This is why many cashiers are instructed to hand the cash register tape to the customer.

Electronic **point-of-sale systems** that use scanners can help eliminate mistakes or theft as long as prices are entered correctly in the system.

When there are cash shortages or overages, be sure to identify who had responsibility for the register at the time. Not only is there concern about theft, but such situations may indicate that additional training is necessary or that your procedures are flawed. When there are too many hands in the till, reconciling shortages or overages becomes very difficult. The best solution is to have one person assigned to one cash register, with no other employee authorized to use that register, but this is seldom possible. Many companies use employee identification numbers that are logged into the register before use, and make a point of providing a new cash drawer at the beginning of each shift. In any case, it should be made very clear to employees who has authority to operate the cash register and who does not.

In addition, some employers use surprise cash counts to test if internal controls over cash registers are appropriate and whether employees are following those controls.

## NxLEVEL™ TECH TIP

**Preparing Your Cash Flow Statement (http://www.onlinewbc.org/Docs/finance/cashflow.html).**
This page is part of the SBA's Online Women's Business Center, which is one of the best resources for entrepreneurs—whether male or female—on the Internet. "Preparing Your Cash Flow Statement" defines cash flow and good cash management, and takes into account your operating cycle. The site also provides a cash flow worksheet, complete with instructions that you can save to your hard drive! There are also several pages on cash flow projections, including instructions and worksheets to help you prepare short-term projections, long-term annual projections, and long-term strategic projections.

**MathWiz** is a versatile, easy-to-use financial calculator with spreadsheet-style input for cash flow analysis, amortization, and loan repayment schedules. MathWiz's financial functions include net present value (NPV), future value (FV), internal rate of return (IRR), payment amount, periods, and payback. The system includes multi-term amortization tables, calendar date calculations, and trigonometry and basic math functions. Other features include roll-back, cut and paste, save, and a "paper tape." You can download a trial version at http://www.informatik.com/math.html.

# Preparing Cash Flow Projections

There are many different types of budgets, including budgets for sales, cost of goods sold, and operating expenses. These budgets serve as the basis for a budgeted income statement, a balance sheet and—most important of all—the cash budget (also known as cash flow projections).

The information comes from the other budgets, but is organized so that cash is highlighted. Preparing a cash budget can help you anticipate cash shortages or plan for using excess cash.

The **cash flow projection** is often confused with the income statement. Remember that your income statement may reflect the accrual basis of accounting, whereas cash flow projections reflect cash coming in and going out.

It is important to realize the difference between the statement of cash flows (an accounting statement) and your cash flow budget. The statement of cash flows and the cash flow projections are presented in different formats; the statement of cash flows generally shows what happened in the past, while the cash flow projection is concerned with the future.

## Timing of Collections and Payments

Below is an example of cash flow budgeting for Walt's Machine Shop. The format used is the same as that in the business plan workbook that accompanies this text. In this example, the worksheet for Walt's Machine Shop breaks sales into two parts: sales made for cash, and sales made on account. This is necessary to reflect the delay between making a sale on account and collecting the cash. To do this, Walt's estimated how customer payments will flow into the business. In addition, Walt's offers credit customers terms of 2/10, net/30. If customers pay invoice amounts within 10 days, they receive a 2% discount off the invoice amount. Otherwise, the entire invoice amount is due within 30 days and no discount is given. Amounts owed after 30 days are past due. In this case, it is necessary to estimate what percentage of customers will pay in time to earn the discount. The discounts allowed are subtracted from the estimated collections on accounts receivable.

Walt's has estimated that 60% of sales are for cash, with the remaining 40% on account. The historical collection pattern for credit sales is as follows:

| | |
|---|---|
| Customers paying within 10 days | 65% |
| Customers paying after 10 days but within 30 days | 25% |
| Customers paying after 30 days but before 60 days | 8% |
| Customers not paying at all | 2% |

Historical patterns are often used to forecast cash collections. Any discounts allowed are subtracted from projected sales dollars, as are any bad debts expected. This determines the amount of expected cash collections.

The cash budget is also known as cash flow projections

| Months | January | February | March | Qtr Subtotal |
|---|---|---|---|---|
| **(A) Beginning Cash Balance** | $25,000 | $12,840 | $2,469 | $25,000 |
| **Cash Receipts** | | | | |
| Cash Sales | $30,000 | $31,800 | $36,600 | $98,400 |
| Collect Accounts Receivable | | | | |
| *Within discount period* | $12,740 | $13,504 | $15,543 | $41,787 |
| *After discount period* | $5,000 | $5,300 | $6,100 | $16,400 |
| *Collected in following month* | $1,550 | $1,600 | $1,696 | $4,846 |
| Sales of Fixed Assets | | | | |
| Miscellaneous Income | | | | |
| **(B) Total Cash Receipts** | $49,290 | $52,204 | $59,939 | $161,433 |
| **Cash Disbursements** | | | | |
| Cash Purchases (Merchandise) | $12,450 | $12,900 | $14,850 | $40,200 |
| Pay Accounts Payable | | | | |
| *Labor Expenses* | $38,695 | $38,695 | $38,695 | $116,085 |
| *Owner Withdrawals* | $1,500 | $1,500 | $1,500 | $4,500 |
| *Non-Labor Expenses* | $4,605 | $5,280 | $4,405 | $14,290 |
| *Purchase of Fixed Assets* | $250,000 | | | $250,000 |
| *Debt Payment - old* | | | | |
| **(C) Total Cash Disbursements** | $307,250 | $58,375 | $59,450 | $425,075 |
| **Net Cash Flow (B - C)** | ($257,960) | ($6,171) | $489 | ($263,642) |
| **Adjustments to Net Cash Flow** | | | | |
| (+) New Debt | $200,000 | | | $200,000 |
| (+) New Owner Investment | $50,000 | | | $50,000 |
| (-) New Debt-Interest Paymts | ($1,500) | ($1,500) | ($1,500) | ($4,500) |
| (-) New Debt-Principal Paymts | ($2,700) | ($2,700) | ($2,700) | ($8,100) |
| (-) New Owner Withdrawals | | | | |
| **(D) Adjusted Net Cash Flow** | ($12,160) | ($10,371) | ($3,711) | ($26,242) |
| **Ending Cash Balance (A + D)** | $12,840 | $2,469 | ($1,242) | ($1,242) |

We must also consider potential discounts in relation to accounts payable. Walt's has a place in the budget for cash purchases and purchases on account. However, in this example, all purchases are made for cash and therefore only one line is needed in the cash flow projection. If it is significant, consider the timing of how you usually pay for your purchases and any discounts you expect to receive.

*The answer was clear: Baked Alaska needed a closer match between the timing of its expenditures and its collections. Altering its pricing and accounts receivable strategy was just half of the equation. How could it improve its management of accounts payable?*

*Antonia realized that she was authorizing the purchase of supplies several times a season. There didn't appear to be any good reason for this. Why should the business buy supplies more than once a season, if the products it produced during that season stayed the same and she knew what its orders were ahead of time?*

*Baked Alaska divided its year into five seasons, each with a different collection of backpacks and purses. This gave the company a competitive advantage over other small designers that offered only three collections a year. Baked Alaska designs were always cutting-edge, and commanded attention from sales representatives and buyers alike.*

*Antonia decided that the company had to start projecting sales levels, and planning well in advance for the supplies it would need. This way, she could make fewer high-volume purchases, and negotiate better prices from suppliers. She also decided to negotiate 30 to 60 day payment terms with all of her suppliers. She figured the increased cost of carrying accounts payable would be more than offset by the money the business saved in bank fees and bad credit.*

*Her accountant agreed. One year later, they reassessed the business's cash flows, and were pleasantly surprised to find that average accounts receivables were down to 72 days, profits were up 8%, and Baked Alaska hadn't bounced a single check in the previous 12 months!*

## Operating Expenses

In general, your cash flow projections include the same operating expenses shown on your operating expenses budget and your budgeted income statement. Depreciation expense is an exception. We include this on the budgeted income statement because we are trying to allocate over time the cost of long-lasting assets. However, depreciation expense has nothing to do with cash, so it doesn't belong in the cash flow projections.

## Owner Withdrawals

An area of cash flow projections often missed by small businesses is owner withdrawals from a sole proprietorship or partnership. If the owner has other sources of support, it may be an acceptable budget assumption that he or she will not withdraw cash from the business. However, if the owner needs cash withdrawals to survive, these should be included in the cash flow projections worksheet. Many small businesses fail in part because the owner underestimated or did not anticipate personal cash requirements. Budgets have a way of coming true, so if you don't budget any compensation for yourself, you might not get any!

Cash flow projections can be very useful when evaluating alternatives for your business

One area of cash flow projections often missed is owner withdrawals

### Borrowings and Cash Balances

The cash flow projections worksheet has a place to record anticipated new borrowings and payments on debt. Notice that in January, Walt's plans to buy some new equipment. The purchase is shown as a cash outflow, and the money borrowed from the bank as an inflow. This format makes it easy to see whether the business will generate enough cash to repay its loans. (Don't forget to budget interest and principal payments.)

Walt's has a negative cash balance projected for the end of March. Armed with this information, he can take steps to prevent the problem. Perhaps he will have to forego his withdrawal, postpone some purchases, or borrow on a line of credit at the bank.

You may need to consider **minimum cash balance requirements**. Some businesses have a policy of not letting their bank accounts dip below a specified dollar amount. You may have balance requirements established in a loan agreement. Look at the ending cash balance for each month of the cash projections and consider whether minimum cash balances will be maintained. If not, look for ways to bring additional cash into your business.

### Assumptions

Remember that these are just estimates. Don't get caught up in tremendous efforts to make your budgets absolutely precise. Simplifying assumptions is acceptable! If your business experiences very few bad debts, you might wish to ignore these in your forecasts. If you do make assumptions about your projections, however, be sure that they are reasonable and document them in writing. This is helpful when explaining your projections to outsiders, like your banker, and allows you to remember why you used a particular number! Later, you should compare your assumptions with what actually happened to see if you must alter your assumptions for future cash budgets.

### Playing the "What If" Game

Cash flow projections are very useful when evaluating alternatives for your business. This is especially true of projections made using a computer spreadsheet program. You might wonder, "What if we were able to increase our sales by 15% next year?" Adjust your sales and expenses accordingly and put the new estimates in your cash flow projections worksheet to see the effect on your cash position.

## Managing Excess Cash

What a wonderful feeling to have excess cash! But what will you do with it? You can't just let it sit around. How should you invest it?

First, surplus cash is cash that is not required to meet current obligations. Many businesses have a targeted or minimum cash balance that they believe they need. Recall that businesses hold cash in order to conduct daily operations and as a precaution against the unknown. If you find your cash balance exceeds this minimum, there are several things you should consider before investing those funds:

- Is this a temporary surplus, or is this amount continually available?
- What financial requirements are coming, and when? Income taxes? Employee bonuses? Balloon payments on debt?
- How much of a risk are you willing to take with this money?
- How much time are you willing to devote to managing this cash?

Answering these questions will help you select the best type of investment. The first two questions address the issue of **liquidity**. Liquidity means the ability to convert an investment back into cash easily. Do you need an investment that allows you to withdraw the funds quickly? Sometimes you can anticipate when you will need the cash; if you know that you will have a big tax bill to pay in March, you can choose an investment that allows withdrawal at any time, or that expires by March.

Every investment has some element of risk, but some have more than others. The amount of risk you wish to take determines what type of investment is right for your excess cash. Risks investors take include:

- **Default risk**— the risk that the issuer will be unable to make interest or principal payments on schedule.
- **Liquidity risk**— the risk that the investment cannot be sold at a reasonable price on short notice.
- **Return risk**—the risk that the market price of the investment will go down.

Of course, there is a drawback to buying investments that have relatively little risk: reward and risk are inversely related, so investments with less risk will yield smaller returns. If you want a greater return, you usually have to accept more risk.

It is important to consider whether your excess cash is there temporarily or permanently. Short-term and long-term investing strategies differ. Long-term investments may include expanding your business or buying another one. Other chapters in this book discuss these options, so short-term investments will be discussed here. In all cases, you should consult your banker and investment counselor for advice.

Here are some of the most common investments on the market:

- **Interest-bearing.** Many banks offer money-market and other business bank accounts, which pay interest at a rate higher than savings accounts. Although these accounts may not yield the highest return on your investment, they are generally safe, liquid, and very easy to arrange.
- **Certificates of deposit.** CDs usually pay a slightly higher interest rate than a bank account, but you give up some liquidity. They are sold with a fixed term, and there is a penalty charge for early withdrawal. This investment may be appropriate when you have surplus cash for a known period of time.

How should excess cash be invested?

- **Government securities.** Generally considered to be secure, Treasury bills sold by the United States Government have maturities of 91 days, 182 days, or one year. However, there is a ready market for T-bills, so they can be sold with as little as one day remaining to maturity. The safety of this investment means the interest rates are relatively low. The federal government also issues Treasury bonds, which have maturities of three to five years. They are considered more risky than T-bills, and may be less appealing for a short-term investment. Lastly, many state and local governments issue bonds, which pay interest that is not subject to federal income tax. Municipal bonds carry lower interest rates because of this tax advantage.

- **Commercial paper.** Commercial paper is unsecured short-term promissory notes issued by corporations. It is the way large companies borrow money from you. This is normally done only by the largest companies, like Ford Motor Credit Corporation. The maturity is usually 60 days or less, but the minimum investment can be very high. It is not easy to sell commercial paper once you have it, so you should plan to hold it until maturity. Interest rates on commercial paper reflect the fact that the investment is unsecured, and the borrower is not the federal government. Accordingly, interest is higher than that for T-bills.

- **Money-market funds.** These funds pool the resources of many investors and purchase short-term securities, such as T-bills, CDs and high-quality commercial paper. A fund allows the investor to diversify holdings without having to buy each investment individually. The fund shares are liquid and easily obtained, often without a commission.

- **Mutual funds.** These operate like the money-market funds described above, except that they invest in stocks, bonds, or some combination thereof. Some are very large and invest only in fairly safe securities. You can also find highly specialized funds that invest exclusively in a certain industry or in growing companies. The relative risks and rewards of these funds vary; you will need to do some research before choosing one. Mutual fund share prices are subject to market swings, so you should be careful to choose one that matches the risk you are willing to take.

## Conclusion

If cash is the lifeblood of business, then consider yourself the doctor. Give your business a check-up by doing cash flow projections, and prescribe ways to make it healthy by managing the cash flow cycle. The importance of these procedures cannot be overemphasized. If you do not pay attention to cash flow, the long-term prognosis for your business is poor!

## Chapter 39
## FINANCING YOUR BUSINESS

*About This Chapter:*
- *Financing needs*
- *Debt or equity?*
- *Choosing debt or equity?*
- *Using a business plan as a financing proposal*
- *Determining how much you need*
- *The C's of credit*
- *Tips for developing a successful banking relationship*

## Introduction

The most common reason given for the high failure rate of small businesses is lack of adequate **capital**. Capital is any asset that a business uses to create value and generate profits, including financial resources, equipment, or even employees. **Working capital** describes a business's most liquid asset, cash. This is the type of capital that growing businesses usually lack. A business can't survive without cash to invest in people, equipment, and supplies; and to pay its expenses. All business owners need to know how to obtain capital; it is rare indeed that a business does not need additional capital to grow!

The first step: understand

capital requirements

## Financing Needs

The first step is to understand why your business needs financing. At what stage of development is your business? Are you planning a new venture, just getting started, expanding a successful venture, or managing a business that has matured? This section describes typical reasons why businesses seek financing.

### Research & Development Money

Small business is the source of many innovative products and services. But to investigate and realize innovations, an entrepreneur needs **seed capital** or **pre-venture financing**. This type of capital can fund market research, technical research, strategic planning, and product development. Early stage funding is usually too risky for lending institutions, so it is generally provided by the owners of the business or investors.

### Start-up and New Growth Financing

Start-up costs include professional fees, inventory, equipment, deposits, marketing materials, and working capital. (The list of costs is different for an existing business.) Growth-related costs might include upgrading equipment to expand capacity, compensation for additional employees, research and development for new products, bulk purchases of supplies or inputs, or additional working capital to support larger orders with longer payment terms.

## Purchase a Business

Some entrepreneurs elect to buy an existing business or a franchise. In addition to start-up costs, other items such as **goodwill** must be financed. Goodwill might include an established brand name, patents, trademarks, copyrights, or a favorable location. It may also include expertise or knowledge possessed by the people within the business. An entrepreneur who buys an existing business usually finances only the portion of the purchase price that is linked to **tangible assets** like equipment, inventory, or buildings. Goodwill is usually financed by the owner under a separate financing contract, or by the purchaser in cash.

## Seasonal Working Capital

Seasonal working capital is used to cover seasonal fluctuations in expenses. Often, the demand for a business's products and services varies from month to month, and season to season. Ski resorts, which rely on the winter months to generate all their revenue for the year, are a good example During the summer, ski resorts must overhaul their equipment and groom ski slopes, which means they have many expenses but little revenue. Such businesses often require seasonal financing to supplement working capital.

## Permanent Working Capital

Permanent working capital is funding that a business requires on a regular basis to cover such expenses as payroll, debt repayment, utilities, marketing campaigns, and rent. It is rare that a business can fund its expansion solely from its own profits; therefore, it must increase its working capital with outside financing of some sort. Loans for seasonal capital are usually paid back within one year. Permanent capital loans are financed as a **term loans,** and repaid over several **terms** or years.

Your business may need both. Take a look at your sales records for the past year or more. Are there seasonal fluctuations in revenue? Do you have different levels of expenses at different times of the year? Differentiating between permanent and seasonal working capital needs will help you to calculate how much money your business needs.

A final note about working capital: One of the most common reasons small businesses fail is an inability to anticipate working capital requirements. Often, small businesses suffer from a disproportionate level of cash versus fixed assets, so they depend on daily receipts to meet operating expenses. If income from sales slows, creditors may force the business into bankruptcy.

Choosing flexible forms of assets, like renting property and equipment instead of buying it, allows a small business to keep more of its capital liquid.

## Equipment Acquisition

A business's existing equipment can serve a limited number of customers, so expansion often means buying new equipment. Commercial banks usually provide this type of loan.

## Real Estate Acquisition

An established restaurant operates in a building it has leased for 15 years. The owner of the building decides to sell, so the restaurant owner buys the building to ensure long-term use of the business site. This is an example of real estate acquisition.

---

*The Fireman, the Idea, and the Collar*

*In 1995, at age 18, Michael Quinn became one of the youngest firemen in San Francisco Fire Department history. An ambitious fellow, he soon signed on for additional training, and earned a seat as the Emergency Medical Technician (EMT) on his engine team. Mike was often first at the scene of an accident, evaluating injuries and administering first aid.*

*Mike routinely stabilized injured people for transport to the nearest hospital. In his first year, he stabilized over 150 people for spinal cord and neck injuries, using a temporary neck brace called a C-collar. Mike felt that these collars were poorly designed. They came in only three sizes, and in the hustle and bustle of the accident scene, he and other EMTs often made mistakes in estimating the size of the injured person's neck. Frequently, they had to fit and refit collars until they found the proper size. And each time they removed and refit a collar, the potential for additional injury increased.*

*Mike knew there had to be a better way!*

---

# Debt or Equity?

Business assets are financed by either debt or equity financing.

## Debt

Debt is a direct obligation to pay an asset (usually money) to a creditor who supplied your business with an asset. The creditor expects to be paid **interest** on the debt. The amount of debt payments depends on the amount borrowed, the length of the loan, and the interest rate.

**Short-term loans** are for less than one year. These are almost always seasonal working capital loans. The most flexible form is called a **line of credit** and allows the entrepreneur to borrow money as needed, up to an approved limit. This is like having a credit card that expires in a year, but with a much lower interest rate! As funds are repaid, the line of credit is replenished and the funds can be borrowed again.

**Intermediate-term loans** are for three to seven years, and are used for permanent expansion of working capital or to acquire equipment. The loans are generally at a fixed interest rate, and may include a penalty for early repayment of the principal.

**Long-term loans** are for ten or more years, and are usually for real estate transactions or equipment purchases. These loans are generally at a **fixed interest rate**, although **variable rate loans** may be available.

Virtually every small business loan through a bank is a **secured loan**. This means that the business, or the business owner, has pledged assets as collateral for the loan in case the business is unable to repay its debt. An unsecured loan simply means that no collateral has been pledged. Very often, people will obtain **unsecured loans** from family or friends. Your business must be a very low-risk one to obtain an unsecured loan from a bank!

---

*The Quinn Collar is Born*

*By September 1997, Mike and a friend, who was an engineering student, made a sample of what they called the Quinn Collar. The changes they made to the basic design of the emergency C-collar were few, but critical. Instead of coming in three different sizes, the Quinn Collar was adjustable.*

*Mike tested the idea on ten other EMTs he knew in various engine companies throughout the city. He spoke with a friend who was a neck and spinal cord specialist, and incorporated his feedback. Once again, a few minor adjustments were made and everyone felt that the collar was a remarkable breakthrough in C-collar design.*

*Mike's engineer friend was able to make test models of the new collar, but needed more time and expert assistance to create a design for mass production. In the next several months, they borrowed $2,000 from family members to pay attorney fees for patent protection.*

*Next, they enlisted the help of Mike's girlfriend, a recent graduate of business school, to help them write a business plan. They had a bankable idea, but they needed help and money. The three of them decided to form a partnership, and began calculating the amount of capital they would need to launch the business.*

---

You can use debt or

equity financing

## Equity

Equity involves no obligation on the part of the business to repay money. However, the individual supplying the money becomes an owner, or an investor in your business.

If your business is a **partnership**, then the person or group who has invested in your business becomes either a **general** or **limited partner**, and has rights as negotiated and outlined in your partnership agreement.

If your business is a corporation, the investor becomes a holder of either **common** or **preferred stock** in the business, and can exercise the powers of a stockholder as defined in your bylaws. Preferred stockholders receive any dividends (a percentage of profits) paid by the business before common stockholders.

## Choosing Debt or Equity

Let's look at the respective advantages and disadvantages of debt and equity financing.

### Ownership

A business owner who uses equity to finance a business is granting the investor a share of future profits, and the ability to exercise some control over business operations. The loss of control is permanent unless you have negotiated a **buy-out clause** that allows you to buy the shares back from the investor at an agreed-upon price. In the best cases, the right investor can provide the business with additional management expertise.

An owner may lose control under debt financing if the loan agreement contains **restrictive covenants** such as limitations on payment of dividends and salaries, a mandatory compensating savings account balance, or a required minimum level of inventory.

How do you decide between debt and equity financing?

## Obligation to Repay

Debt financing places pressure on the business to make scheduled loan payments to repay principal and interest. During start-up and early growth, an expanding company may have difficulty meeting these obligations.

## Tax Considerations

The interest portion of a loan payment is tax-deductible, but the principal portion is not. Dividends paid to any owners, including passive investors, are not tax-deductible.

## Capital Structure

Capital structure is the mix of debt and equity financing a business uses to fund its base of assets. Equity is a permanent source of funds, while debt is always temporary. Acquiring equity financing also increases the asset portion of your business's balance sheet. It need not be paid back, because it is not a debt.

The higher the percentage of debt financing a business uses, the greater the monthly payments it must make to repay that debt. This increases the risk that the business's cash flow will not be adequate to meet debt payments.

Carefully managed debt can carry many benefits, most notably **financial leverage**. Leverage exists as a result of the fact that interest payments, or **interest expense** of debt financing, is a fixed cost agreed upon at the outset of the debt contract, (e.g. a fixed rate term loan, equipment loan, or mortgage) and is held steady over time, while the business's operating income may rise. This means that the business has the borrowed funds at its disposal to invest, producing a greater return than what it must pay on its debt. In this positive scenario, the business benefits.

Unfortunately, if the business operations are not as profitable as forecasted, the business will earn a lower return and have difficulty meeting its fixed debt obligations.

## Industry

Every industry defines a given a **debt to equity ratio (D/E)** as standard or acceptable. Creditors are reluctant to provide debt to businesses with D/E ratios outside this range. Talk to your banker, accountant, or local Small Business Development Center representative to determine the norm for your industry. Both creditors and investors will have their own ideas about how much risk is associated with your business. Risks specific to your business may also include geographic and technological considerations.

---

*How Much $$ to Launch The Quinn Collar?*

*Mike and his partners laid out their business objective: to market a unique, patented C-collar for the temporary stabilization of victims of neck and spinal cord trauma. They would contract the actual manufacture of the collars to a medical supplies manufacturer, and would negotiate to have their C-collar distributed by an existing network of medical supplies distributors. This would result in a "lean and mean" operation that leveraged its most valuable asset: the patent on the Quinn Collar. They hoped that if things went well, a larger medical supplies company would buy the rights to the patent.*

*They began by using common sense, educated guesswork, and industry research to calculate how much financial capital it would take to launch their new venture. They took into account sales projections for their first three years; operating expenses for years one through three; any start-up costs for equipment, research, and development; attorney's fees; and marketing. They also took a look at the average asset to sales ratio of other small medical supply businesses. With this work complete, they settled on the sum of $150,000 for their first two years of operations, assuming they achieved their target sales level of $200,000 in that period of time. They decided to pursue a bank loan for $60,000 of the $150,000 needed. Their calculations for their asset requirements broke down as follows:*

| | |
|---|---|
| *Cash* | *$50,000* |
| *Accounts receivable* | *35,000* |
| *Inventory* | *45,000* |
| *Total current assets* | *130,000* |
| *Total fixed assets (computer, office equipment, etc.)* | *20,000* |
| *Total assets* | *$150,000* |

## Timing

When seeking equity capital, the length of time before a business gets a response or receives capital varies widely. It's almost always a much longer wait when a business is seeking debt.

## Cost of Proposal

Any business that is seeking financing of any kind (including financing from friends and family) must prepare a **financing proposal**. No matter how great your business and how certain the success of your idea, no business speaks for itself. A financing proposal communicates your business's financial position, the quality of its management, and the degree of risk it offers potential lenders and investors.

You should consider obtaining assistance with the preparation of financial statements and projections, preparation and review of legal documents, and research for marketing and technical information. The cost of these services varies a great deal depending upon the amount of assistance you need and the area of the country in which you live. Get help from your lawyer, CPA, SBDC representative, or business consultant.

When obtaining debt capital, you may not require legal services until it is time to sign the loan agreement. Before searching for potential investors, meet with your attorney to verify that you are in compliance with state and federal securities regulations.

### Owner Preferences

A business owner who wants to retain absolute control will have a difficult time working with an investor. On the other hand, an owner who sees advantages to having another voice in management may welcome the right investor.

Raising equity capital requires good sales and communication skills. You are selling your business's promise of profitability, and yourself as a qualified manager of your business.

Before pitching your business, take stock of yourself. How will growth in your business affect your personal goals, your family, your employees, and your current customers? Are you prepared for the responsibilities of a larger business? Remember: Change, both good and bad, is inevitable during periods of high growth.

### Lending Community and Potential Investors

Can your business really service an additional debt? If the lending community is reticent, equity financing may be the best alternative. If equity seems like an attractive option, can you offer an attractive rate of return to an investor? Test the reaction of potential investors.

## Using a Business Plan as a Financing Proposal

A comprehensive business plan is the starting point for preparing a financing proposal.

### Develop Your Business Plan

The preparation of a complete business plan enables you to predict your financing needs instead of approaching your banker each time a need presents itself. It is advantageous to anticipate all financing needs and present them as a package. This is another reason to update your business plan annually.

The essential starting point: The NxLeveL™ Business Plan

### Identify Possible Sources of Financing

Once you have calculated how much financing your business needs, begin shopping for sources. Don't approach these sources until you know the exact needs of your business. How much money do you need? When? How quickly will you be able to repay it? Will you need additional money later? Acceptance guidelines vary from one financial institution to the next, so try to learn about the person or organization you intend to approach. Find out what information they specifically require. Here are some of the things you should know about funding sources before you approach them:

- To whom should you submit your proposal?
- What specific information will they want from you?
- How are decisions about financing made?
- When will the decision be made?
- What types of businesses/industries have they lent to or invested in before?
- If they don't supply the funds, can they help you find other financing?

## Unconventional Financing Techniques

- **Barter financing:** set up a mini-business within a similar, existing business space.
- **Landlord financing:** negotiate to have your landlord pay for some needed upgrades, add that to the rent and amortize it over the life of your business's lease; or negotiate free rent for a piece of the business.
- **Use other people's credit:** if you can't get sufficient credit, have an acquaintance's business buy the inventory or supplies you need, then pay the total back according to the supplier's terms.
- **Contract financing:** if yours is a service business, negotiate to have customers prepay services through one-year, all-inclusive contracts.
- **Concession sales:** if you are a retailer, sublease part of your retail space to vendors whose products complement your own.
- **Staged financing:** look for financing in stages, starting with enough to help you get your business up and running so that you can prove its profitability.
- **Trade credit:** negotiate aggressive payment terms and credit from your suppliers.
- **Leverage future commitments of business:** (as documented in letters from customers) to increase your business's credibility and likelihood of receiving financing from a bank.
- **Buy a business instead of starting one from scratch:** there are many ways to finance the purchase of an existing business. It is not uncommon to be able to negotiate financing from the seller for as much as 80% of the purchase price, or to repay the purchase price incrementally from future cash flows. It is also easier to get bank financing for an existing business than for a start-up.
- **Set up a home office:** save on office space rent and get home business tax deductions.
- **Participate in a small business incubator:** many state and local governments sponsor incubators by providing below-market rent and low-cost support services to small businesses.

Here are some additional questions for bankers:

- What other services can they offer your business?
- Does the bank make SBA-guaranteed loans?
- Does the bank participate in other government loan programs?
- What is the handling charge on credit card receipts?
- Can they supply your business with a line of credit?

## Prepare a Financing Proposal

The financing proposal is a marketing document prepared in order to obtain capital for your business. It should educate the lender about your business, and make the lending decision easier by showing that you understand the factors that determine your business's success, and have carefully reflected on your objectives and your strategies for achieving them. It should also demonstrate proactivity in achieving goals and avoiding pitfalls. The next section of this chapter discusses the specific contents of a financing proposal.

## Customize Each Financing Proposal

What questions should you ask your banker?

Although you are technically the bank's customer, you can increase your chances of obtaining financing if you bear in mind that you are selling the promise of your business to the bank. In other words, approach your financing proposal as you would any marketing effort: first, get to know the customer (keeping in mind the questions listed above), then tailor your proposal so that it speaks directly to the customer's interests, concerns, and needs. You should also personalize your proposal with the name of the person receiving it, the name of the financing source, and specific references to financing programs offered.

## Outline of a Financing Proposal

### Cover letter

This is a one-page letter on business stationery, addressed to the person who will be reviewing your financing proposal. You may wish to thank the person for previous conversations, and confirm any future appointment.

### Summary of financing request

This first page should quickly and clearly summarize the major points of your proposal. Specifically, it should cover the purpose of the financing, the amount and terms requested, the source of funds for repayment, and the collateral offered.

### Use of proceeds

Your financing source will want to know how you'll use the money. This is an opportunity to highlight the amount of capital invested by existing owners, and the use of business funds.

### Collateral offered

If you are seeking a secured debt, list the assets that you will use as collateral and their current market values. (Note: These values must be based on sound reasoning.) Collateral for your loan is negotiable, so don't begin by offering every asset you own! (Skip this page if you are seeking equity financing or an unsecured loan.)

### Investor return

This is your opportunity to present to the investors the financial return they can expect on their investment. You should state if you will have an option to buy out their investment at a future date for a predetermined amount. (Skip this page if you are seeking debt financing.)

November 20, 1999

Ms. Priscilla Frauenzimmer, Loan Officer
Westside Bank
San Francisco, CA

Dear Ms. Frauenzimmer:

As agreed in our recent conversation, I am presenting on behalf of my firm, Quinn Collar, a formal loan proposal for your consideration. As discussed in the body of this document, the loan requested is in the amount of $60,000. The following repayment schedule of this amount is proposed:

(Insert proposed repayment schedule here)

The loan will be used for the following applications:

(Insert intended application[s] here)

In support of this request, the following documents and exhibits are enclosed:

(Insert list of enclosures here)

It is my understanding that a variable interest rate equivalent to X percentage points above the prime rate would apply to the approved loan.

Thank you for your consideration. I eagerly await your reply.

Sincerely,

Michael S. Quinn, Partner
The Quinn Collar
San Francisco, California

Your financing proposal is a sales document!

## Business plan

Your entire business plan is part of your financing proposal. Additionally, financing sources will most likely ask for supplemental information such as:

- Tax returns (last three years)
- Accounts receivable and/or accounts payable agings
- Management information
  - Resumes for all key personnel
  - Personal financial statements for all owners
- Market research studies
- Other information you feel is relevant to the business or loan request

# Determining How Much You Need

Small-business owners are often unsure about how much financing to request. The amount is based on future projections, and we are all rather uneasy about predicting the future! It's fine to ask a loan officer, "What is your reaction to the amount I am seeking?" but not to ask "How much can I borrow?" This section discusses the two most important considerations in determining how much funding to request.

## Type of Financing

The amount you request depends on how your business will use the funds, and the type of collateral you can offer.

Be prepared before seeking financing!

The amount available for financing the purchase of a piece of equipment may be determined by a bank rule limiting such loans to 75% of the purchase price. The financing of real estate and fixed assets is usually limited by a maximum percentage of the transaction.

Determining the amount needed for permanent working capital or seasonal working capital is more difficult, since it depends on the accuracy of your financial forecasts.

## Cash Flow Projection Is Always the Key

The **cash flow forecast** defines the amount of money you need to borrow, particularly for working capital, and demonstrates the monthly payments that the business can afford. The number of years required to repay a loan depends on the length of financing being sought. A one-year cash flow projection may be sufficient for a seasonal working capital loan, but a five-year loan to expand working capital requires a three- to five-year forecast.

# The C's of Credit

How do creditors make lending decisions? Here are six factors that lenders consider when evaluating your financing proposal.

## Credit & Financial History

The financial history presented in your financing proposal should include your personal credit history, as well as a summary of your business's financial performance to date. Your business's financial history should include clear financial data tables and text. Include sales, cash flow, profits, and key financial ratios like the Current Ratio, the Inventory Turnover Ratio, and the Receivables Turnover Ratio. (These and other measures of financial performance are presented in more detail in Chapter 38 *Cash Flow Management*.)

Do you know what a credit check will reveal about you and your business?

Do you know what a credit check will reveal about you and your business? If not, have a credit company perform a check so you'll know what to expect. Banks and other lending institutions routinely check the credit history of potential borrowers. As a small business owner, you should expect to have the credit check cover you and your business. You can order a copy of your personal credit history by contacting organizations like TCI Credit Bureau or EQUIFAX. Either will send you a copy of your credit report for a small fee.

## Character

The soundness of a small business loan is often more dependent on the trustworthiness of the owner than the track record of the business. Your reputation in your area is important, so you should provide excellent local business references.

## Capacity

Bankers expect a business to be able to make loan payments from its profits. **Capacity** refers to the ability of the business to repay the loan with cash generated from operations. Your financial projections address this concern, but bankers are also influenced by the past financial history of your business. If your business has been no more than marginally profitable in the past, but your projections are optimistic, you may have difficulties convincing a professional lender that your business will be profitable in the future. Good past performance is the major criterion by which a lender will judge your financing proposal.

## Collateral

If your business can't make its loan payments because of poor sales or low profits, the bank will satisfy the debt by taking title to the collateral—the assets you pledged to the lending institution as security for the loan. Collateral is necessary to obtain a loan, but collateral without capacity or secure value usually results in a negative answer to a financing proposal.

## Conditions

How will future economic trends affect your business? You assessed this and other risks in your business plan. Now, you should share these assessments with your banker.

## Capital

Are you committed to your business? The banker wants to see a commitment, both in terms of time and money. You are asking the banker to supply debt financing for your business. The banker is watching your **debt to equity ratio**. How will you or your business provide the equity portion of the project you are seeking to finance?

---

*Quinn Collar Financing Strategy*

*After several months of research and business planning meetings, Mike and his partners settled on the following:*

- *They projected $60,000 in sales the first year, $140,000 in year two.*
- *They estimated their net profits would be 15% of sales, or $9,000 in year one and $21,000 in year two.*
- *They negotiated with a manufacturing contractor to extend credit on production, resulting in estimated accounts payable of approximately 10% of sales.*

- *Each of the three partners would invest $15,000 of his or her own money in the business, in exchange for 5,000 shares of common stock.*

- *They would approach their local bank for a short-term line of credit of $30,000.*

- *They would apply for a mid-term loan from the bank for $60,000.*

- *In exchange for the loan, Quinn Collar would agree to the bank's two loan requirements: 1) The business's Current Ratio (current assets divided by current liabilities) must not fall below 1.80; 2) No more than 60% of the business's financing would come from debt (stated another way, the business's total debt versus total assets should not be greater than 60%). If Quinn Collar failed to meet these requirements, they would have to repay the loan immediately.*

### The Quinn Collar Projected Balance Sheet (at end of year one)

**Assets**

| | | |
|---|---|---|
| Cash | $50,000 | |
| Accounts Receivable | 35,000 | |
| Inventory | 45,000 | |
| Total Current Assets | 130,000 | |
| Fixed Assets | 20,000 | |
| Total Assets | 150,000 | |

**Debt and Equity**

| | | |
|---|---|---|
| Accounts Payable | 6,000 | (10% of $60,000 sales) |
| Credit Line | 30,000 | |
| Total Current Liabilities | 36,000 | |
| Long Term Debt | 60,000 | |
| Total Debt | 96,000 | |

**Equity**

| | | |
|---|---|---|
| Common Stock | 45,000 | ($15,000 x 3 partners) |
| Retained Earnings | 9,000 | (15% of sales) |
| Total Debt and Equity | $150,000 | |

# Tips for Developing a Successful Banking Relationship

## Deal with Banks Located Close to Your Business

You will be more inclined to visit your banker, and vice versa, if he or she is local. Choose a more distant banker only if local bankers do not understand your business needs. Local banks generally have a commitment to supporting local businesses, and are therefore more receptive to local loan requests.

## Make an Appointment with the Right Person

Whether your goal is to obtain preliminary information or to present your financing proposal, identify the right person to talk with at the bank, then make an appointment.

## Select a Banker Whom You Feel is Comfortable with You

You should feel like your banker will listen to your concerns. By the same token, you want a banker who tells you his or her concerns. It's very frustrating have a financing proposal turned down, but receive no explanation!

## Select a Banker Who is Interested in Your Type of Business

Find a banker who either has existing clients in your industry, or expresses interest in learning more about your industry. A knowledgeable banker can offer you advice, and advocate approval of your financing proposal.

## Ask the Banker for Advice About Your Situation, Not Money

During any meeting with your banker, ask for advice. Bankers meet with many business owners, and see how various owners deal with problems. Your banker is also knowledgeable about local attorneys, accountants, and business consultants.

## Present a Complete Financing Proposal

Want to make a good impression on your banker? Make sure your financing proposal is complete the first time! The majority of entrepreneurs approach bankers with incomplete or poorly executed proposals, so this is your chance to shine.

## Tell the Truth

The financing proposal is a marketing document; it presents your business situation in a positive light based on fact. If you try to hide facts about your business, you are probably going to be unsuccessful. Disclose problems at the beginning and work to overcome them. Otherwise, the banker may think you are incompetent or dishonest. Either way, you won't obtain the loan!

## Uses and Benefits of Loan

The banker is looking at the capacity of your business to repay the loan. Show the banker how you will use the proceeds of the loan to improve this capacity.

### Be Flexible

If your banker suggests that you modify your proposal, listen carefully. The suggestion might not work for your needs, but the banker would not make a suggestion if it wasn't important to the process.

### Be Patient

Entrepreneurs think bankers take too long to make decisions, and bankers think business owners are always in a hurry. Before submitting your proposal, find out how long the process will take, and then provide the information needed by your banker. Finally, realize that the process may take longer than anticipated. The lesson is to start the process well in advance of when you need the financing.

### Do All of Your Banking at the Same Bank

Some entrepreneurs are always shopping banks in hopes of saving service fees or getting a better interest rate. It always pays to shop around but having done so, choose one bank to supply all your services.

At the end of the day, the decision to lend you money depends on the financier's confidence in your management ability

## NxLEVEL™ TECH TIP

**Finding capital for your business can be simplified by looking online.**

- **The Foundation Center Online** is the premier clearinghouse for information on raising money from foundations (http://www.fdncenter.org/index.html)

- **"A Hitchhiker's Guide to Capital Resources"** (http://www.inc.com/incmagazine/archives/02980741.html)

- **Banking through Nations Bank** small business home page (http://www.nationsbank.com/smallbiz/)

- **Bank One Small Business Solutions** (http://www1.bankone.com/busbank/)

- **Key Small Business Solutions** (http://www.fedmoney.com/)

- **Federal Money Retriever** (http://www.fedmoney.com/)

- **Virtual Finance Library** Ohio State, (http://www.cob.ohio-state.edu/dept/din/overview.htm)

- **FinWeb**, financial economics site (http://www.finweb.com/)

- **Venture Capital**, subscribe to their listing (http://www.adventurecapital.com)

- **US Small Business Administration** (http://www.sbaonline.sba.gov/intro.html)

- **National Business Incubation Association** (http://www.nbia.org/nurture.htm)

## Recommend Business Associates to Your Banker

Once you have developed a good relationship with your banker, demonstrate support by referring other business owners to him or her. Bankers need to make good loans, so they appreciate referrals to good business owners.

## Conclusion

Begin immediately to implement the concepts covered in this chapter. Develop a good relationship with your banker, start "working" your personal and professional networks, and make sure you have an excellent business plan.

Approach your next search for financing by taking the following steps:

- Determine why you need financing
- Select debt or equity. If debt, determine what type
- Develop a well-researched, straightforward financing proposal
- Present a customized version to each potential source of financing
- Be persistent!
- Be professional
- Demonstrate confidence and integrity
- Know your financing target
- Maintain close relationships with financing sources

Determine the amount you need before approaching possible financing sources

# Chapter 40
# MONEY SOURCES

*About This Chapter:*
* *Conventional sources of funding*
* *Other sources of money*
* *Other innovative sources of financing*

## Introduction

Entrepreneurs often think only of banks when they look for financing, but there are plenty of other options. This chapter provides information about the alternative money sources available to small, growing businesses.

## Conventional Sources of Funding

### Personal Funds

National studies show that four out of every five new businesses are launched with the personal funds of the owner. Personal funds include:

* **Savings.** This includes money in a savings account, a money-market account, a certificate of deposit, or even a shoebox under the bed.
* **Investments.** Besides stocks and bonds, this includes stamps, coins, jewelry, and precious metals.
* **Life insurance.** Many life insurance policies allow you to borrow against the cash surrender value of the policy.
* **Second mortgage.** You may be able to borrow a percentage of the equity you have in your home; this includes refinancing your house or taking a second mortgage loan.
* **Personal loans.** You may be able to obtain a personal "signature loan" at your bank or credit union.
* **Spouse income.** Determine how much is available on a monthly basis to help finance your business needs. You can invest this monthly amount in your business, or use it as the basis for obtaining a loan.
* **Family and friends.** While not really a source of personal funds, your family and friends may provide capital because of your personal relationship with them.
* **Credit cards.** Credit cards should be considered only as a last resort.

Four out of five new businesses are started with the owner's personal funds

---

*The School Teacher Turned Coppersmith*

*Ryan Mikus was a high-school teacher in Kalamazoo, Michigan for 29 years. When he wasn't correcting tests or coaching soccer, he was indulging in his passion for coppersmithing. He had a studio in the old barn at the back of his property, where he made lamps and candlesticks. He particularly admired the styles of the copper masters active in the Arts and Crafts movement, which was popular during the late 19th and early 20th centuries. When he retired in 1997, he decided to try to turn his hobby into a business. His mission: to create an array of elegant, original hand-crafted copper lamps, vases, and candlesticks.*

*After several months of perfecting his designs and production techniques, Ryan was ready. He decided to sell his lamps under his own name, inscribing each one with the words: "Hand-crafted in the studio of Ryan Mikus, Kalamazoo, Michigan."*

*He took his three best lamps to well-known home design stores in Kalamazoo, Holland, and Detroit. He was surprised and inspired by the overwhelmingly positive feedback. "How much for ten like this?" one store buyer asked. "How many can I have by Christmas?" another inquired. Ryan knew it was time to begin building his business.*

*First, he would need financing to buy materials, upgrade equipment, and buy a computer.*

---

## Financial Institutions

This section examines financial institutions that provide the **debt capital** or **debt financing** needed by small businesses.

**Debt financing** means that an individual incurs an obligation to pay back money that has been lent to his or her business. Sources of debt financing often require some form of asset as **collateral** to ensure that the debt will be repaid.

### Banks

Different banks serve different markets. Small community banks focus on serving local businesses; a large commercial bank with hundreds of branches operates quite differently.

Savings banks tend to specialize in home mortgages and automobile loans. This doesn't mean you can't approach them for a business loan, but it is not their major business line.

Commercial banks are interested in business loans. Their loan officers are accustomed to processing business loan applications, and are familiar with other financing options if you don't qualify for a loan from their bank.

It is important to understand that banks usually don't make loans to businesses in the start-up phase; they prefer to make a government guaranteed loan. (Government-guaranteed loan programs are discussed later in this chapter.)

Commercial banks are interested in business loans

### Credit unions

Credit unions are started and managed by employees of a company, members of a labor union, or other groups. If you or a family member belongs to a credit union, you may be able to borrow some of your needed capital from it.

### Consumer finance companies

Consumer finance companies make small personal loans that are 100% secured by collateral. They charge higher interest rates and processing fees than banks and credit unions, but are more flexible about approving financing requests.

### Commercial finance companies

Commercial finance companies focus on business loans and operate similarly to consumer finance companies. They also make SBA-guaranteed loans. Examples of these institutions are AT&T Capital, GE Capital Credit, and The Money Store.

### Leasing companies

Leasing companies rent fixed assets to businesses and individuals. A lease is merely a long-term agreement to rent. There are three kinds of leases:

- **Financing leases** are the most common. The lessee maintains the equipment and may have the right to buy the equipment at the end of the lease.
- **Operating leases** are also called maintenance leases. The lessor is responsible for the maintenance of the equipment.
- **Sale and leaseback** is similar to a financing lease. The owner of a fixed asset sells it to another party, who then leases it back to the original owner.

---

*Ryan Mikus needed a computer powerful enough to track production and inventory, maintain his sales files, surf the Net for supplier and design ideas, and manage his financial records. He had been selling a few lamps a month, but did not yet have enough revenue to buy a computer and printer. After talking with several computer resellers, he discovered two options for financing computer equipment.*

*If he took a loan out and bought the equipment, he would have a new **asset** (the computer) as well as a new **liability** (the loan to pay for the computer) on his **balance sheet**. He'd have to maintain the computer, and **depreciate** its value on his balance sheet over time.*

*If he signed a lease for the computer equipment, he would not own the equipment. Thus, it would not appear as an asset on his balance sheet, and neither would the corresponding liability of the loan. Instead, he would pay a monthly lease payment, which would be recorded on his books as an **expense**.*

*Ryan was new to the business of financing and leasing, so he enlisted the help of his accountant (his brother-in-law, Bob). After reviewing Ryan's credit worthiness, cash flow projections, and equipment needs, Bob recommended that Ryan go with the lease. His had several reasons for this recommendation:*

- *Ryan could immediately record the cost of the computer equipment as an expense, thus lowering his business's net taxable income*
- *His lease payments would conveniently include all down payments, taxes, installation, insurance, and maintenance*
- *The computer supplier would provide all service and technical assistance, allowing Ryan to focus on creating his lamps*
- *The lease would allow Ryan to update his computer when better technology came on the market, or to replace his equipment if it no longer fit his needs*

*After Ryan and Bob researched different kinds of leases, they negotiated a **closed-end operating lease** with a company in Kalamazoo. This was a two-year lease with a monthly payment of $350.00; it included all maintenance, equipment substitutions, and a cancellation clause. At the end of the lease period, Ryan would not own the computer, and would be free to upgrade to newer equipment or—cash flow permitting—to buy different equipment elsewhere.*

---

Here are some of the advantages and disadvantages of leasing:

### Advantages of a lease
- A lease seldom requires a down payment.
- Your business will not have a liability on its balance sheet.
- You may be able to make payments over a longer term than with a loan.
- You can upgrade high-tech equipment by ending one lease and starting a new one with new equipment.

### Disadvantages of a lease
- A lease almost always costs more than a loan.
- You probably won't own the asset at the end of the lease.
- The business does not have an asset on its balance sheet.

There are three kinds of leases: financing, operating, and sales/leaseback

## Checklist for Leasing Agreements

- **Cost of the lease.** How much is each payment? When are payments due? What is the real amount of rental fees or interest? Is there a grace period before you are assessed charges? What is the total amount you will pay over the lifetime of the lease?
- **Extra costs.** Must you pay security deposits? Installation charges? License fees? Taxes? Penalties for early cancellation of the lease?
- **Lease flexibility.** What are the provisions for skipped or late payments?
- **Service.** What maintenance and service will be provided, and by whom? Is there a guarantee for the equipment? Must you pay for servicing? Will you receive a refund for downtime if the equipment fails?
- **Insurance.** What level of insurance coverage is included in the lease? Will you be assessed an insurance fee, or be billed separately by the insurance provider?
- **Equipment upgrades.** What are the provisions for upgrading or replacing equipment during the term of the lease? How much will it cost you?
- **Residual value.** What will the equipment be worth at the end of the lease period? (This directly affects your lease payments.)

*Small Business Administration*

The U.S. Small Business Administration (SBA), which was created in 1953 to assist small businesses, offers both direct and guaranteed loans.

The term **direct loan** simply means that the SBA makes the loan directly to the small business. A **guaranteed loan** is where a financial institution makes the loan to the small business and a portion is guaranteed by the SBA. The following information is taken from SBA materials; it briefly discusses the average number of employees or annual sales volume you must have to be considered a small business by the SBA.

- **Manufacturing.** Maximum number of employees may range from 500 to 1,500, depending on the type of product manufactured.
- **Wholesaling.** Maximum number of employees may not exceed 100.
- **Service.** Annual receipts may not exceed $5 to $14.5 million, depending on the industry.
- **Retailing.** Annual receipts may not exceed $5 to $13.5 million, depending on the industry.
- **Construction.** General construction annual receipts may not exceed $7 to $17 million, depending on the industry.
- **Special trade contractors.** Annual receipts may not exceed $7 million.

- **Agriculture.** Annual receipts may not exceed $0.5 to $3.5 million, depending on the industry.
- **CDC loans.** An optional size standard applies: net worth of $6 million or less and average annual net earnings of less than $2 million.
- **LowDoc.** Under $5 million in sales and less than 100 employees.

### Certified Development Companies

A Certified Development Company (CDC) is a nonprofit organization sponsored by state or local governments, or by private interests. The purpose of a CDC is to contribute to economic development by making government loans. The exact nature of these loans varies. Contact your local Small Business Development Center (SBDC) or Chamber of Commerce to find the CDC that serves your area.

### Community Development Loan Funds (CDLFs) and Community Development Financial Institutions (CDFIs)

The most famous of the financial institutions involved in this type of lending is South Shore Bank in Chicago. To find out who makes community development loans in your area, call the Community Capital Association at (215) 923-4754.

### Rural Economic & Community Development

The Rural Economic & Community Development (RECD) is a federal agency that offers loan programs for small businesses in rural areas.

## Federal Loan Programs

### SBA 7(a) Loan Guaranty Program

This is the largest of the SBA loan programs; it paid over $10 billion in loans in federal fiscal year 1995. The 7(a) loan program was designed to help small businesses obtain long-term financing for needs such as working capital, machinery, equipment, fixtures, leasehold improvements, building acquisition, and construction. The loan is made by a private lender to a small business, and the SBA guarantees a percentage of the loan. On January 1, 1995, the maximum amount guaranteed by the SBA was reduced to $500,000.

Special variations of the SBA 7(a) program include:

**LowDoc.** A variation of the 7(a) program for loans of $100,000 or less. This program finances new or existing businesses, and places less emphasis on collateral. It features a rapid approval process (usually two or three days). The following is taken from a current SBA brochure.

The LowDoc Program is for loans of $100,000 or less

- LowDoc is for small business loans of $100,000 or less
- The applicant completes the front of a one-page SBA application; the lender completes the back
- Lenders require additional information from the applicant
- For loans over $50,000, the applicant includes a copy of U.S. Income Tax Schedule C, or the front page of the corporate or partnership returns for the past three years
- Personal financial statements are required for all guarantors

**GreenLine.** This loan program provides a term commitment of up to five years for a revolving "line of credit" loan to finance the cash cycle of your business. The SBA will guarantee a maximum of 75% of your bank loan with a dollar limit of $750,000. Your business must meet the same eligibility criteria required for a 7(a) loan, and is subject to a first lien on the assets being financed (e.g., inventory, receivables, contracts) as collateral. Personal guarantees are required. Secondary liens on machinery and equipment, real estate, and personal assets may also be required.

**Women's Prequalification.** This program provides greater access to capital for women-owned small businesses. The maximum loan request is $250,000.

**CAPlines.** This program helps small businesses meet their short-term and cyclical working capital needs. The SBA guarantees 75% of the line of credit (up to a maximum of $750,000) with a maximum maturity of five years.

### Guaranteed loans

Both of the loan programs described in this section are available through commercial banks. The small business must be "export-ready."

**Export Working Capital Program.** The SBA will guarantee up to 90% of a loan with a maximum of $750,000. Loans are for twelve months, with two annual renewal options. The loan may be used as described below:

- Pre-shipment working capital (to finance the labor and materials for manufacturing or purchasing goods for export)
- Post-shipment exposure coverage (to finance foreign accounts receivable generated from export sales)
- Combination of pre- and post-shipment financing

**International Trade Loan.** This is a long-term loan program for small businesses engaged or preparing to engage in international trade. The SBA can guarantee a maximum of $1 million for facilities and equipment, and $250,000 in working capital.

Export programs for

small business

### Direct loans

The maximum amount of these loans is $150,000, and they are available only to applicants unable to secure a bank loan or a 7(a) loan. Direct loans are intended for businesses in high unemployment or low-income neighborhoods, Vietnam-era or disabled veterans, handicapped persons, and low-income individuals. Direct loan funds are very limited, and applicants are generally placed on a waiting list.

### SBA 7(m) MicroLoan Program

These direct loans are made through intermediary lenders (generally nonprofit organizations with experience in lending and technical assistance, such as a CDC). This short-term loan has a maximum of $25,000 and is usually given to small businesses owned by women, low-income individuals, or minorities. Some intermediary lenders may require borrowers to undergo training or business counseling. Loan proceeds may be used to buy furniture and fixtures, machinery and equipment, inventory, supplies, and working capital.

## SBA 8(a) Participant Loan Program

Eligible small businesses must be 8(a)-certified firms. These loans are either direct, or made through lending institutions with the SBA guaranteeing the loan. Loan proceeds may be used for fixed assets or working capital.

## CDC Programs

Certified Development Companies (CDC) are sponsored by state or local organizations

**502 Loan Program.** This loan program provides long-term, fixed-asset financing to small businesses in rural areas. Contact your local CDC to determine if your business is eligible. Eligibility criteria include the type of business and the population of the community in which your business operates. The loan is processed by a CDC.

**504 Loan Program.** This loan program supplies long-term (10 to 20 years), fixed-asset financing through a CDC. Typically, 504 loans are provided as follows:

- 50% by an unguaranteed bank loan
- 40% by an SBA-guaranteed loan
- 10% by the small business borrower

Contact your local CDC to obtain more information.

## RECD Programs

**RECD Intermediary Relending Program.** The Intermediary Relending Program (IRP) makes loans to small businesses and other legal entities in cities that have a population of less than 25,000. The loans are made by intermediaries such as CDCs, or other nonprofit organizations. The loan can finance up to 75% of a project, with a maximum of $150,000. Loan recipients must document their inability to finance the project through commercial credit or other government programs. This program often appears locally under the name Rural Development Fund.

**Business & Industry Program.** The Business & Industry (B&I) Loan Guarantee Program encourages commercial financing of rural businesses. The business owner applies through a commercial financial institution, and together they submit an application to RECD. Most types of businesses in cities with a population of less than 50,000 are eligible. There is no official minimum loan, but loans typically begin at the SBA 7(a) maximum and can be as high as $10 million.

## Other Government Loan Programs

### State, county, and city

The loan programs offered by state and local governments vary greatly from state to state. Many counties and cities have established **small loan funds**; check for such programs in your area. Local governments may operate the program themselves, or through another agency, such as a CDC, that has experience managing loan programs.

### Revolving loan fund

Local and regional revolving loan funds were originally capitalized with grants from the Economic Development Administration, the HUD Community Development Block Grant Program, and other sources. These loans take a subordinated security position to a loan from a private lender. Loans are limited to eligible borrowers in particular counties or cities. Standards and rules vary from region to region.

With equity capital, you sell a portion of your business

## Other Sources of Money

The previous section discussed sources of debt capital that are frequently used by small businesses. This section covers some less common sources of debt capital, as well as sources of equity capital.

### Equity

*Preliminaries*

If you decide to seek **equity capital**, remember that you are selling a portion of the ownership of your business. If your business is presently a sole proprietorship, it will have to become either a partnership or corporation. This is a complex issue, for which you should seek legal counsel.

If your business is a partnership, the provider of equity capital will become a partner. How much of your business the investor will own is a matter of negotiation. You should have a written partnership agreement that thoroughly details the rights and obligations of each partner. Most partnerships are general partnerships. Limited partnerships have specific accountability and tax considerations; if you intend to form a limited partnership, you must consult an attorney who is experienced in these issues.

If your business is a corporation, the source of equity capital becomes a stockholder in the corporation. A corporation may issue preferred stock in addition to common stock. Preferred stockholders do not vote at stockholder meetings. It is also possible to issue more than one class of common stock—some of which do not have voting rights—or to sell the investor warrants or rights for shares of stock in your business.

Limited liability companies (LLCs) are an increasingly popular form of business ownership. If you are interested in obtaining equity capital in conjunction with an LLC, consult a knowledgeable attorney.

Be aware that obtaining equity capital is a more time-consuming process than obtaining debt capital. Sources of equity capital demand more information and take longer to review it, and you'll need help from attorneys and accountants to complete the process.

### Venture capitalists

Venture capitalists make high-risk investments in young, unproven companies with the potential for very high rates of return.

---

*Seed Ventures Capital Club was started by four successful, retired entrepreneurs who had money to invest and wanted to help other businesses get started in their community. They are especially interested in ventures that banks consider too risky.*

*They prefer to invest in several moderate-sized projects, rather than a few big projects. Their preferred parameters for investment are:*

- *$20,000 to $100,000 per project*
- *Businesses willing to accept and act on their managerial and strategic advice*
- *Service or manufacturing businesses with a strong management team*
- *Businesses that produce high-quality, "old world" services or products*
- *Businesses that draw on the skills of local talent*

*Each member contributes equally to the venture capital fund, which is then invested in start-up businesses they all agree have the most potential. In exchange for investing, they often help steer a company by sitting on a board of directors.*

*Seed Ventures looks for projects that complement their existing portfolio of investments. They enjoy facilitating networking among their businesses, and creating a coalition in which the sum is greater than the parts. When Ryan Mikus's business plan and funding proposal came before Seed Ventures at one of their meetings, they were intrigued, and decided to take a closer look.*

---

## Investment clubs

In some communities, local business people pool their money to make investments in new and established businesses. This allows smaller investors to participate, and larger investors to spread their risk.

Finding investment or venture capital clubs is simply a matter of keeping your eyes open and asking everyone you know if he or she knows whom to contact. Local chambers of commerce are a good source of information. There is no official listing of these groups, which vary in size, investment strategies, and targeted industries. Some are easy to locate, while others maintain a low profile.

———————◆———————

*Ryan Mikus stumbled onto Seed Ventures after researching investment clubs on the Internet and speaking with his Chamber of Commerce. He prepared an executive summary of his business plan, and a cover letter in which he clearly outlined how much funding his business needed. After working closely with his brother-in-law Bob, and an advisor at the SBDC in Kalamazoo, he calculated that he would need $30,000 for the first year of operations. If sales followed as he planned, he would need only $10,000 in year two.*

*Ryan's business plan summary was one of nearly 30 that Seed Ventures received that month. They liked his lucid, straightforward writing style, and they liked his business idea. They decided to meet with him.*

———————◆———————

## Investment bankers

Investment bankers are in the business of providing equity capital (not loans) to new and young businesses. They do this by selling shares of stock in the business to their customers. They rarely deal in amounts less than $1 million, and are interested only in businesses that offer attractive rates of return. They seek out the same types of businesses as venture capitalists, but are not as willing to take risks.

## Private investors, wealthy individuals

Every area has some local entrepreneurs who have been very successful. These people, sometimes referred to as "angels," are a good source of both debt and equity capital for local small businesses. Your attorney, accountant, or banker may be able to put you in touch with such individuals.

## Professionally managed pools

Large institutions often pool their money into a partnership that invests in small businesses.

> Investment bankers are in the business of providing capital to start up and young businesses

## Strategic partnerships

Large corporations often invest in small businesses that will help the corporation enter new markets and provide a return on investment. It is important to understand that the motive is more than profit; they are looking for small businesses that fit into a strategic mission or long-range plan. For this reason, these relationships are commonly referred to as strategic partnerships. There are three common forms for such investments:

- **Stock purchase.** The large corporation buys some of your stock and becomes a stockholder in your company.
- **Joint venture.** The corporation and your business form a partnership, and the corporation provides capital.
- **Licensing agreement.** You retain total control of your business, but sell the corporation specified rights to use/sell your business's products or services.

## Employee stock ownership plans

Employee stock ownership plans (ESOPs) are similar to other methods of selling equity in your business. The difference is that you are selling shares of stock to your employees rather than to outside investors. This provides your business with equity capital to use for expansion, and gives your employees a vested interest in the success of your business. This is not feasible for a start-up company unless it's well financed from the outset.

## Small Business Investment Company (SBIC)

The SBIC Program is the only venture capital program sponsored by the federal government. The SBA licenses private venture capital firms, and these SBICs have a portion of their financing guaranteed by the SBA. They provide equity capital and long-term debt to small businesses that have significant growth potential.

## Specialized Small Business Investment Company (SSBIC)

SSBICs operate much like SBICs, but have additional financial leverage, which is provided by the SBA in return for agreeing to invest in, or loan to, small businesses with socially or economically disadvantaged owners.

IPOs: hot new stock issues

## Initial public offerings

The term **initial public offerings (IPOs)** refers to the first time a corporation offers its shares of stock for sale on a publicly traded stock exchange.

The Securities Act of 1933 began the federal government's regulation of publicly traded securities. The act fulfills two objectives:

1) To provide prospective investors with full and fair disclosure of the character of new securities.
2) To prevent fraud and misrepresentation in the sale of securities.

The Securities and Exchange Commission (SEC) is the agency that enforces federal statutes relating to securities. Any agreement that obligates your business to pay another party a portion of your profits or to make interest payments is a **security**. Thus, the federal government closely regulates the issuance of publicly traded stocks. However, several cost-effective options are available to the entrepreneur seeking equity capital. Consult a securities lawyer before issuing any shares of stock.

### Small Corporate Offering Registration (SCOR)

Forty-two states allow SCOR offerings, which enable small businesses to originate and sell stocks to investors with a minimum of cost and regulation. Most small businesses can raise up to $1 million per year, provided they have equity equal to at least 10% of the amount of capital being raised. Form U-7 is the registration form for corporations that are registering under state securities laws, and are exempt from SEC registration under Rule 504 of Regulation D. The average cost to prepare a SCOR offering is under $25,000.

### Intrastate offering

An intrastate offering is a security offered and sold only to residents of one state. Such an offering is exempt from SEC regulation, but is still subject to the securities laws of the state in which the security is being offered. Such state laws are often called **blue sky securities laws**. In order to qualify for the intrastate offering exemption, your business must be incorporated in the state in which it is making the offering, carry out a significant amount of its business in that state, and make offers and sales only to residents of that state.

There is no fixed limit on the size of the offering, nor on the number of investors who may purchase your stock.

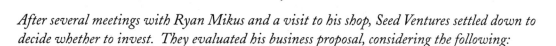

*After several meetings with Ryan Mikus and a visit to his shop, Seed Ventures settled down to decide whether to invest. They evaluated his business proposal, considering the following:*

- *Is there a potential for consistent growth and profits?*
- *Does the business offer a target return on investment?*
- *How strong is the management? Can it be improved?*
- *What are their gut feelings about the business concept and the principal owner?*

*Gut feeling was the most important criterion to Seed Ventures, and they had a good feeling about Ryan Mikus! In addition, they were very impressed with his business plan. They felt his lamps were of the highest quality, his cost and revenue projections on target, and his market potential solid. Their only concern was that Ryan was a sole proprietor. Seed Ventures knew that partnerships had a higher rate of success, and were generally more stable. They decided that they would invest in Ryan's business, but would require that he find a partner who had stronger management skills than he did. They would help Ryan to identify and recruit this partner.*

*Pending this, they would invest $30,000 in Ryan's business in the first year, and $10,000 in the second year. They would then re-evaluate his operations and profitability and make a judgment about whether to invest additional funds.*

*In exchange, Ryan agreed to meet with members of Seed Ventures as frequently as needed to make sure his business was on target. Seed Ventures usually met with their businesses once or twice a month at first, and asked for status reports each month thereafter. They reserved the right to suggest changes to management and strategy. In most cases, this advice was much appreciated and put to good use.*

---

## Other Innovative Sources of Financing

### Suppliers

A supplier can be a source of capital in two ways. First, a major supplier may be interested in providing you with equity or debt capital. A strong motivation for the supplier is often a desire to work with a proven wholesaler or retailer in your geographic area.

Suppliers: sources of capital or favorable terms

Second, you may be able to negotiate favorable terms for your business if the supplier is motivated by having your business in the area. These terms can include discounts, extended payment periods, increased cooperative advertising, or any other concession that helps your business conserve its capital. Your success will put money in the pocket of your supplier.

### Loan Guarantors

Small business owners often find that they cannot support the collateral and capacity requirements of their loan application. As a result, they are turned down for loans, or are offered a smaller loan. You can overcome this problem by finding a third party with assets that can be used as collateral to guarantee your loan payments. This means that the third party assumes the risk of making the loan payments if you default. The cost of such a guarantee varies greatly.

### Loan Brokers

Loan brokers find financing for business owners and other individuals. They often charge a flat fee up front, which you must pay whether you obtain financing or not. Some brokers charge a smaller up-front fee, and then take a percentage of the loan upon approval. You should select a loan broker very carefully. It's a good idea to ask prospective loan brokers for references from businesses they've helped finance.

### Franchising

It is possible to purchase some franchises with little money down and obtain the start-up financing directly from the franchisor. When a direct loan is not possible, the franchisor might guarantee your loan with a lender familiar with the franchisor.

## Owner Contract, When Buying a Business

When selling a business, most entrepreneurs want the buyer to obtain financing so that they can be "cashed out." This is often not possible and the seller must carry a contract for a portion of the selling price. The term, interest rate, and collateral are all negotiable.

### Venture Capital Tips

- Answers to investment requests usually come within 21 days. If you don't get an answer within this time, save your energy—focus on other investors and funding sources.

- Make your calculations simple, clear, and to the point. Investment analysts continually hear pitches for funding, and they respond better to easy equations and simple math.

- Demonstrate that you are at risk. Investors are more likely to consider funding your business if they know that you have a high incentive to succeed.

- Don't pay yourself too much money. Make sure your uses of funding are clearly described, and that the important money goes towards essential expenses. No golf club dues, expensive lunches, or exorbitant salaries!

- Have a plan for getting to market. Venture capitalists want to see concrete, aggressive plans for generating sales and earning profits. They want to know your exact timetable for entering the market, and how long it will take to become profitable.

- Toot your own horn! Highlight any awards or media coverage you've gotten, and point to larger, established organizations with whom you have done business or partnered.

---

*With Seed Venture's help, Ryan met Betsy Dykstra, a 31-year-old business development manager for a major lamp company in Holland, Michigan. She was in operations for two years and had managed sales for the last three. She also had an MBA from Michigan State. Ryan's business was exactly the kind she had been wanting to work with, and she and Ryan hit it off well. They made good partners.*

*The partnership between Ryan and Seed Ventures also worked well. In the first six months, he met with members of Seed Ventures more than ten times, getting guidance on establishing wider distribution, investing in additional equipment, and evaluating a possible move to a better-equipped workspace. By the end of his first year of operations, the business was breaking even and Ryan's lamps were being sold in fine furniture stores and gallery stores throughout*

*Michigan, Illinois, Indiana, New York, California, and Colorado. By doing his homework and writing a good business plan before searching for funding, Ryan gained a new partner who filled in his weak spots, investor "angels" who funded his venture, and a promising business.*

---

### Grants

There are a few grant programs for small business owners. This section describes two programs of the federal government that are operated through the SBA.

#### *Small Business Innovation Research (SBIR) Program*

The SBIR Program began in 1982. It is designed to stimulate technological innovation, and gives small businesses the opportunity make proposals to meet the research and development needs of the federal government. Eleven federal agencies participate in the program, and the SBA publishes solicitation announcements on a quarterly basis. There are three phases to the program.

- Under Phase I, a small business can receive up to $100,000 to develop a prototype or otherwise prove its concept.
- Under Phase II, a small business that successfully completed Phase I can receive as much as $500,000 to develop the prototype for production.
- There is no government funding for Phase III, where the product is actually placed into production.

#### *Small Business Technology Transfer (STTR) Program*

This program started in 1992, and is similar to the SBIR program. The small business submitting an application must collaborate with a nonprofit research institution.

## Conclusion

There are many ways to finance a new business. However, you must first know exactly how much money your business needs, and what its projected revenues and expenses are. With a well-researched business plan and a carefully written funding proposal, you can find just the right source of funds. Remember: Perseverance, excitement, and confidence in your idea will inspire prospective lenders and investors to become as enthusiastic about the promise of your business as you are!

# PART X
# DEAL-MAKING

## Chapter 41
## NEGOTIATING AND MAKING THE DEAL

*About This Chapter:*
- *What is negotiation?*
- *Power in negotiations*
- *Anatomy of negotiation*
- *Common negotiating strategies*
- *Making the deal*
- *Your negotiating partners*

## Introduction

Your success as an entrepreneur depends largely on your ability to make deals, close and manage sales, and—most important of all—get paid. Honing your negotiating skills is the first step in this process. This chapter introduces several theories of negotiating, and describes the basic concepts that govern negotiations. The approaches presented here are used throughout the business world.

Before we go any further, it's important to understand that negotiation doesn't have to be intimidating. It is fundamentally about identifying interests, being personable, and talking with people! The more relaxed and confident you are, the easier it is for others to deal with you, and the more likely you are to achieve your goals. Most people assume that the strongest negotiator always has the most power. If you believe this, consider the following:

Understand the process and negotiate your way to business success

- There would be no negotiation unless both sides anticipated a benefit.
- The goal of negotiation is to create a new situation that is better than the old one.
- Agreements made under pressure last only while one party feels weaker than the other; when the weaker party gets the opportunity to back out, the agreement falls apart.

A strategy that is useful in most situations is the joint problem-solving approach, commonly referred to as win-win. This approach creates an open, honest dialogue between the negotiating parties. It forces negotiators to attack the problems, rather than each other. Don't forget: Negotiation needn't be combative to produce results!

## What is Negotiation?

You may not consider yourself a skilled negotiator, but whether you realize it or not, you negotiate every day. Many business activities—including personnel management, signing leases and contracts, buying supplies, and acquiring capital—require negotiation. Even when you debate which restaurant to go to with friends, or bring your car to the repair shop, you are negotiating in some way. Everyone negotiates, but as you've no doubt discovered, some people are much better at it than others!

If you're like most people, you try to avoid the conflicts that can arise from the negotiation process. Certainly, negotiating is sometimes a nerve-wracking process in which resolution comes at the expense of one of the parties. The highly competitive nature of business demands that companies negotiate in order to survive, so it's not surprising that negotiations can become quite difficult when the stakes are high and the outcome uncertain. Negotiations can also be complicated by conflicting personalities, delicate egos, cultural differences, time crunches, and worst of all, a sole emphasis on personal gain.

But it can be different. Negotiation can produce solutions that neither side could have achieved independently. It can create enduring agreements, enhanced partnerships, and higher benefits for all. In fact, negotiation can be open, straightforward, and even fun!

How does this happen? Good negotiators understand themselves and what they want out of the process, but they also try to find where their own interests and those of their counterparts overlap. They take into account the other side's interests and perspectives, and use their negotiation skills to resolve conflict and create common solutions. In the process, they develop an objective perspective that helps them to overcome hurdles.

Like any other skill, negotiation can be learned and practiced. Clear goals, confidence, and knowledge all affect your ability to negotiate deals; understanding what good negotiators do and why they do it will help you achieve great results.

## Power in Negotiations

You have just read a description of the traits of the most effective negotiators. However, many negotiators never use any of these approaches and are still able to make incredible gains. No doubt you've witnessed this, or perhaps even done it yourself. By virtue of having the upper hand, one can dominate the negotiation process, put forth inflexible demands, and achieve one's goals. This demonstrates that the role of power, the context of the process, and the relationship of the participants all determine the outcome, regardless of the approach one follows. Still, we can understand and work with these constants without resorting to threats, bluffs, or power plays—none of which will produce the best and most enduring settlement.

### The Power of Relationships

Many negotiations have as much to do with the relationships of the parties involved as they do with the issues being negotiated. This may seem like an obvious point, but it is one that is very often ignored. The fact is, when we speak about the relationship between two sides, we are not simply speaking about a buyer and a seller, or a landlord and a tenant. We are speaking about each side's power to protect its interests and achieve its goals. Power in a negotiation isn't simply defined by authority or strength; it can also exist as a result of:

*The goal of negotiating is building strong and lasting agreements*

- Expertise, or access to information
- The amount of "currency" a person possesses (i.e., things valued by the other side)
- The level of interest in a continued relationship
- Past achievements or track record
- The ability to satisfy goals elsewhere or by other means
- Courage and confidence

Most important, power can be created in the course of the deal-making process as the result of one participant being a better negotiator than the other. Here are a few basic principles of power:

- Power is always relative and limited, never absolute
- Power can be real or perceived
- Power can be exercised without action
- Power is often only as strong as it is believed to be
- Using power always involves risks
- Power dynamics change over time

Think about your own past negotiation experiences. Consider the actual and perceived balance of power between you and your counterpart. What was the outcome? What conclusions can you draw? Did actual power or perceived power play a larger role in the outcome? Chances are, perceived power played a larger role. In most negotiations, your power is dependent upon your ability to identify or create it, and use it.

## The Power of Context

Let's say the largest landlord in town negotiates a lease with a tenant. The tenant is new to town, unfamiliar with the market, and has few choices of apartments to rent. The landlord, a long-time resident, owns many apartments, and has many people interested in renting from her. Who do you think has more power to determine the outcome of the negotiation? As this scenario demonstrates, the relative power between the negotiating parties has a great impact on the process. Other factors—including the timeframe for decision-making, the economic or social outcomes, the participants' public image, and the past and present relationship between the participants—all affect negotiations. Perhaps the most important factor is whether or not the negotiating parties have any interest in a long-term relationship.

## The Power of Perception

As the following story illustrates, people can enter negotiations with wildly divergent ideas of the issues involved.

———————————◆———————————

*A tenant who works outside her home and has no pets believes that the sole criterion for her prospective landlord's rental decisions is a tenant's ability to pay the highest rent possible. In fact, the landlord is more interested in the security of the building. For this reason, the landlord would rather rent to someone who is in the building more often and has a dog. Therefore, the tenant's perceptions have limited her understanding of the context of the negotiation and weakened her position.*

As this example demonstrates, negotiations are conducted on the basis of perceptions. This is why communication between the parties is so essential and so difficult. People instinctively give weight to their assumptions without being aware of it. Two sides may enter a negotiation with completely different perceptions about their relationship and the elements of the deal. Negotiators who understand this use open communication to separate fact from fiction and to identify common ground.

### The best negotiations occur when:
- Both parties wish to have a long-term relationship
- Both parties perceive that they rely on one another for mutual gain
- Both parties have strong leaders who can accept or enforce an agreement
- A third party is able to offer objective insight and guidance
- Both parties are truly motivated to find a solution
- Both parties understand the underlying issues
- There is a large area of perceived common ground
- There is trust between the parties
- The negotiators listen to one another

### The Power of Hope

What each side hopes to achieve by negotiating, and how confident each side is of reaching a favorable settlement, has tremendous impact on the negotiation. It is generally accepted that:

- People with high hopes achieve better outcomes
- Skilled negotiators with high hopes earn better outcomes regardless of the amount of power they possess
- People with high hopes can direct negotiations better than people with lower hopes
- High initial proposals improve the quality of the final settlement
- People with the lowest hopes tend to make the most unnecessary concessions
- People with high hopes make several small concessions to reach agreement

Higher aspirations focus attention on what could be, rather than on what is or what has been. This opens the door for creative thinking.

*The higher your aim, the better your outcome!*

# The Anatomy of Negotiation

What is the "anatomy" of negotiation? It is the series of events and processes that occur in every negotiation. As anyone who has tried to negotiate the sale price of a new car knows, negotiation is a process that requires time and patience. No matter who you are or what approach you take, the process generally contains the same phases. These include setting an agenda, voicing demands and offers, working to minimize differences, and closing the deal. Ideally, each of these stages builds upon the gains made in the previous stages, allowing the two sides to move closer to an equitable agreement.

As you read the following list of negotiation phases, think back on your past negotiating experiences and ask yourself: What occurred at each stage? How did you behave? Were you aware of the process in which you participated?

## Stages of Negotiation
1. Parties independently decide to negotiate.
2. Parties mutually present reason for negotiation.
3. Parties explain wants and needs.
4. Parties present demands or proposals for agreement.
5. Parties review and test proposals.
6. Parties narrow the field.
7. Parties bargain for final settlement.
8. Parties arrive at an agreement (verbal or written).

## Hard and Soft Negotiators

Different people take different approaches to negotiating. Some naturally seem to favor a "hard" approach, while others prefer "soft" negotiations. What does it mean to be a hard or soft negotiator? Hard negotiators are competitive, unyielding, and focused exclusively on their own interests. Soft negotiators are submissive and focused on the interests of their counterpart.

Most people perceive the process of negotiation as a contest of wills that the hardest negotiator always wins. It is largely because of this that many people dislike negotiating, and rightly so. Why would you want to go head-to-head with a hard negotiator if your own style is soft?

However, there is a middle path by which a cooperative or flexible negotiator can succeed. This more balanced negotiator is capable of furthering his or her own interests while creating a beneficial solution for both parties.

Short-term gain equals

short-term agreement

The best negotiator is neither hard nor soft

## NxLEVEL™ TECH TIP

**The new technology laws that have made "digital signatures" possible has resulted in a trend towards online contracts. Although this may be a valuable capability in some situations, we suggest that the following guidelines be adhered to when using the Internet as a medium for conducting negotiations, or entering into contracts.**

When you enter into purchase and sale agreements online, make sure that you receive an acceptance of your offer from the seller or its electronic agent via e-mail.

When you accept an online offer that has been conveyed to you by a specific method, use that same method to communicate your acceptance of the offer, unless the other party specifically instructs you to communicate acceptance by some other method.

Clearly stipulate that a contract will become binding only when all terms have been reduced to "writing" and "signed" by both parties. Make it clear whether "writing" is to mean an electronic document authenticated with a digital signature; or a document that is printed on paper and signed in ink. Also, clearly stipulate that the contract will only come into existence when the last party to sign it communicates the fact that he or she has signed the contract.

---

*Some people believe that life is first and foremost a ruthless struggle that none but the strong and selfish can—or should—survive. In reality, history has shown that it is more often cooperation that ensures survival, both of individuals and of societies. No discussion of cooperation would be complete without presenting the well-known example of the Prisoner's Dilemma, which demonstrates the common anti-Darwinian situation wherein the unanimous pursuit of selfish interests among individuals results in the worst possible outcome for all.*

*Two prisoners are arrested together and placed in separate cells. They are questioned separately by the authorities; each prisoner can either claim innocence or accuse the other prisoner and be released. If both claim innocence, both will be released. If each "defects" and accuses the other, both will be punished. However, each prisoner must act without knowing which course of action the other will choose.*

*For the unfortunate souls trapped in this grim situation, there exists a middle course where one prisoner defects and is released, and the other claims innocence and is punished. This is known as a "zero-sum" outcome, in which one prisoner's gain is matched by the other's loss. Clearly, then, if both prisoners pursue their own interests in hopes of a zero-sum outcome, they will fare worse than if they'd cooperated by both claiming innocence!*

---

The table below highlights common traits of hard and soft negotiators. It also demonstrates how stereotypical behavior limits success. Can you find any points of intersection between a hard and a soft negotiator? How can an agreement be achieved?

| Negotiating Styles and Behaviors | | | |
|---|---|---|---|
| **Events in Negotiation** | **Competitive** | **Cooperative** | **Submissive** |
| Setting the Agenda | • Tries to negotiate on home turf<br><br>• Focuses debate on own issues<br><br>• Ignores other party's demands | • Tries to negotiate on neutral turf<br><br>• Focuses other party's issues as well as own<br><br>• Listens to others party's demands | • Negotiates on other sides's turf<br><br>• Focuses on other party's issues<br><br>• Concedes to other part's demands |
| Voicing of Demands and Offers | • Requires other party to make first offers<br><br>• Returns with very high demands, low offers<br><br>• Exaggerates own position, ignores other side's | • Interchanges offers and demands with other party<br><br>• Returns with moderate demands and offers<br><br>• Shares reasons for interest in specific items, seeks same from other party | • Presents recent offers or demands on other party's terms<br><br>• Returns with low demands and high offers<br><br>• Concedes to other party's priorities |
| Final Bargaining | • Concedes only on items of low value or interest<br><br>• Pushes for large concessions from other party | • Pursues equal concessions from both sides<br><br>• Pursues mutually beneficial settlement | • Concedes to other party's demands<br><br>• Makes large concessions |

Aim for flexibility and confidence!

This exercise is a self-diagnostic test designed to help you understand your behavior patterns during negotiation. With this knowledge, you can practice and improve your skills. Above all, aim for flexibility and confidence!

## Common Negotiating Strategies

The following section explains some of the more commonly employed negotiating strategies and the assumptions that support them. As you will note, these approaches are separated not so much by the degree to which they are hard or soft, but by the way in which they define the nature of the relationship between the negotiating parties.

### Roll Over, Rover

People who use this strategy pursue a positive relationship at any cost. They tend to focus on minimizing differences and points of conflict, and to value long-term relationships at the expense of immediate, concrete gains.

### Winner Takes All

In this case, the negotiator seeks a win-lose (or "zero-sum") outcome at the expense of the business relationship. Negotiators who use this approach are aggressively competitive, and might utilize threats or bluffs to the point of misrepresenting their goals. There is often little trust between the negotiating parties, and minimal interest in maintaining the relationship. Parties engaging in such negotiations exclusively pursue their own interests, attempting to gain as much information as possible about the other side, while giving away as little as possible about themselves. Unfortunately, this is the strategy that most people envision when they think of negotiations. However, most business negotiations are aimed at building relationships. For this reason, agreements that produce large, short-term gains for one party fall apart if they fail to satisfy both parties' needs.

*The zero-sum game limits negotiations and outcomes*

### Make Like an Ostrich

Some people plunge into negotiations with teeth bared and claws sharpened; others simply plunge their heads into the sand. When the issues are too messy and they perceive the benefits to be negligible, they act like an ostrich and ignore the process completely. In such situations, neither immediate gains nor the relationship between the parties is of particular importance.

### Three-Legged Race

This approach is neither hard nor soft. Instead, it combines the best of both approaches by being hard on the problem and soft on the participants. Like kids in a three-legged race, joint problem-solvers work together to reach the goal that they both desire. They make every attempt to approach problems side-by-side, and work towards a positive outcome for all. Hence, this strategy emphasizes both the relationship and the concrete outcomes of the negotiation process.

Participants who use this approach are open with each other, and are thus able to cooperate. As the name implies, the parties are dependent upon each other and are eager to achieve a positive, win-win outcome.

# Making the Deal

It is a long journey from your initial negotiations to the final signature that closes the deal. To be a successful negotiator, you must understand that with each step you take, you are moving either one step closer to an agreement, or one step farther away. Closing the deal requires successful completion of each stage of negotiation. Remember: Making the deal is a process, not an event!

## Interests vs. Positions

The first step in negotiation is to identify where your interests lie. It is amazing how often people fail to accomplish this simple task! When you have clear goals, you project a confident, professional image that gives your counterpart a reason to take you seriously.

Note that your interests can be very different from your position. Your position is what you say you want (more money, a faster turnaround time, a larger order size). Your interests are the things that motivate you to take your position (your needs, concerns, hopes). It's important that you understand the difference; negotiators who don't may spend a great deal of time quibbling over positions, only to end up with an agreement that barely satisfies their interests.

To prepare for negotiations, list your interests in order of their importance. These interests are the currency in which you will be dealing, so determine how much each is worth in relation to the others. Next, consider all the options that would satisfy your interests. How many ways can your interests be met? What are you willing to do to get what you want?

## What About the Other Side's Interests?

You must also identify the interests of your counterpart. How does he perceive the issues? What are her personal and business priorities? The more you discover, the more you'll be able to influence your counterpart.

You should also explore those terms of the deal that would satisfy your counterpart's interests, and the point at which he or she no longer has an incentive to negotiate. It is in your best interest to discover as many options as possible. You can enhance your bargaining position if you are able to conceive of options that your counterpart hasn't considered.

Try to present possible approaches to reaching an agreement. Asking "Why not..." and "What if..." questions can reveal your counterpart's underlying concerns. For example, you might ask a supplier, "Why not deliver our orders by the 15th of each month?" If the supplier responds by saying, "Because we're at capacity for truck delivery mid-month, and it'd cost too much to increase capacity just for you," then you have identified that one of the supplier's major concerns is cost. This gives you a concrete issue to address.

Be hard on the problem and soft on the participants

## The Obstacle Course

You're sitting face-to-face with an investor, banker, or supplier, and somehow things just aren't working. Perhaps you are unable to communicate with one another, or maybe you feel intimidated by the other party. Either way, there seem to be insuperable barriers to an agreement. What should you do?

First of all, don't give up! Now is when the real work begins. This is the heart of the negotiation process: getting through the obstacle course to achieve your objectives. The following strategies can help.

### Name the Enemy

If the other person resorts to a manipulative tactic, your best weapon is to recognize it and name it! Confronting these tactics will destroy any power they have over you.

Here are several common manipulative negotiating tactics. Can you think of others?

- **Stonewalling.** The negotiator refuses to budge from his or her position, rejects your proposals, and is indifferent to your efforts to communicate.
- **Bullying.** The negotiator attempts to intimidate or threaten you into giving in. This person may wage an assault on your credibility, your proposal, or your authority.
- **Deception.** The negotiator tries to trick you into giving in, taking advantage of your good faith by providing misleading or false figures.

How can you recognize these tactics? First, make sure your counterpart's data and positions are congruent. Read the person's body language, facial expressions, tone of voice, and actions. To the careful observer, these offer a great deal of information about a person. Naming disagreeable tactics as soon as you see them can improve your sense of control and confidence.

### Use Your Power

No matter how weak you consider your negotiating position to be, you are likely to have more power than you think. Even if you lack any formal authority or economic power, there are many power points you *always* have, including:

- The power to negotiate fairly and intelligently
- The power to build or reject a relationship
- The power to choose whether to sign the deal
- The power to point out the consequences of a failed agreement
- The power to deflect attacks by refusing to retaliate
- The power of your coalition with others who share your interests
- The power to demonstrate a way out of the conflict

### Open Your Ears!

If you really listen to what the other person is saying, you might find that an obvious solution has been right in front of you all along. Don't be tempted to use the time when your counterpart is speaking to formulate a clever response, or to plan your next entrepreneurial venture. Being a careful listener is the best advantage you can have.

To be a better listener, frequently summarize what the other person is saying, and ask for more information. Be patient. Realize that the payoff for listening is the ability to understand where interests intersect; this is how enduring agreements are made.

### Get in the Other Person's Shoes

Rather than getting frustrated with and retaliating against your counterpart's tactics, try stepping into his or her shoes for a moment. Try to understand and appreciate his or her point of view. (Be aware that doing this does *not* require you to make any concessions.) Not only is this approach beneficial to you, but it can also disarm your counterpart. Chances are, the last thing he or she expects you to do is shift perspective and momentarily join the "enemy."

When you consider another person's opinion, you have an opportunity to identify issues on which you agree. You may find that you have the same time pressures, cost considerations, or even the same personal dislike for negotiating! Whatever it is, recognize it and use it to form a bond.

### Lighten Up and Laugh!

Why get stressed and worn out by negotiating? After all, there is a beneficial side to it, or you wouldn't be doing it. The way you approach negotiations can have a big effect on the results, so why not have a positive, easy-going outlook?

Humor can disarm even the most adversarial opponent. Take the opportunity to lighten up the discussion when possible. This can build trust and create a more hospitable environment.

### Fall Back and Regroup

When negotiations get tense, people often retreat to their positions instead of focusing on their interests. They simply react, without thinking or listening to the other side. Many negotiations fall apart at this stage.

You have the power to break this deadlock and get back on track. How? By stepping back from the table, putting aside your assumptions and emotions, and looking at the negotiation as an outside observer would. Having cleared your head and gained insight, you'll be ready to engage more effectively than ever.

Remember that you have as much right to set the pace of negotiations as your counterpart does. Exercise this right whenever you feel the need to. Collect yourself, reflect on the issues, and decompress. This will give your counterpart a chance to do the same.

One way to buy yourself some time is to say nothing. Silence is one of the most powerful tools a negotiator can use; it gives the other person nothing to argue with, and may throw off his or her momentum. This consolidates your power, and forces the other side to adapt to your pace.

Another valuable way to slow down the process is to review the progress you have already made. Try summarizing the proposals that were put forth up to that point. Taking notes is helpful as well; it gives you a reason to pause periodically throughout the negotiation, while showing that you take the process seriously.

### Get Off the Hot Seat

No matter what the other person says, never make an important decision on the spot. Good negotiators always fall back, regroup, and go to a safe location to make their decisions. In this context, "safe" describes a place where you have no pressure to agree to a given settlement. If pressured, try responding, "Let's close this deal after my lawyer/ partner has had a chance to look over it." Or "You've obviously put a lot of time into this, and I'd like to do the same before I answer." One of our favorites is, "I always get a good night's sleep before I sign a contract."

Even if you only have a few minutes to make a decision, you should still allow yourself some space and time to review your options. Never let yourself be pressured into a decision by a deadline imposed by the other side. If you feel this happening, test the deadline—you'll soon find out how serious it is. Remember: A decision made under pressure may be one you regret later.

*Beware of imposed deadlines*

## Walking Away from the Table

By using the strategies above, you demonstrate your commitment to the deal-making process. However, there may come a point at which your best alternative to reaching an agreement is to stand up and calmly walk away from the negotiations. Knowing your "walk-away" threshold in advance strengthens your position, and gives you a solid footing from which to judge the other side's proposals.

Different people reach this point under different circumstances, and at different points in the process. How do you decide when you will walk away? One thing you can do is consider the costs—in terms of time, money, relationships, productivity, personal integrity, and emotions—of walking away versus continuing to negotiate. As a general rule, it's time to think seriously about walking away from negotiations when:

- Your counterpart's ethics clash with your own
- You are being forced to accept a deadline you cannot meet
- Your counterpart is greedy and will make no compromises whatsoever
- You believe that your counterpart is unwilling or unable to follow through on his or her part of the deal
- You can achieve greater results elsewhere
- You distrust or dislike your counterpart to the point that you cannot justify a continued relationship with him or her
- Economic conditions lower the value of the deal to your business

# Your Negotiating Partners

In the course of running your business, you are very likely to enter into negotiations with each of the following types of people. The basic information presented here will help you to be confident, professional, and well prepared.

## Lawyers

When hiring lawyers, the issues usually involve price. Most lawyers price their services in one of two ways:

- **On contingency.** The lawyer's payment is based on a percentage of the damages you win in a lawsuit.
- **Straight fee.** The lawyer's payment is based on hourly work.

Fees are always negotiable, so collect fee information from several lawyers prior to negotiating. Generally speaking, it helps to like and trust the lawyer you hire to represent your interests. Lawyers can be valuable advisors when you are negotiating with other parties; just remember that your lawyer is there to give you legal advice, not to handle the negotiations for you!

## Bankers

There are many types of banks; some serve consumers and some serve businesses. Your goal is to find a bank that understands your needs and has your interests at heart. Bear in mind that unlike many negotiating partners, banks are limited by a number of business factors:

- They must require signatures of the principals on unsecured loans
- They must perform balance sheet tests of business customers
- They avoid long-term debt
- They must charge higher rates for riskier loans
- They require collateral—such as real estate or other assets—to secure loans

## Venture Capitalists and Investors

Without a doubt, investors have a leg up on the average small business owner for one simple reason: they negotiate deals more often than most other people. Work with your lawyer when negotiating with prospective investors!

Some issues you will encounter when negotiating with investors:

- **Share of equity.** This refers to the percentage of ownership the investor will have in your business.
- **Mix of straight versus convertible debt.** Convertible debt can be exchanged for equity (stock) in the company. Straight debt is simply money the business owes to a lender, and grants no rights of ownership to the business.
- **Consulting agreement.** This obligates the business to "buy" a given amount of consulting time from the investor.

Other issues include rights of first refusal on any sale of management stock, right to veto any new financing, and preemptive stock purchase rights. Be sure to document any agreements on paper, and have your lawyer review them before you sign anything.

## Suppliers

Most negotiations with suppliers relate to a specific transaction, and involve price, quality, delivery time, and units. Since you will probably rely heavily on your suppliers, it is wise to choose a supplier who shares your values and standards, and with whom who will enjoy working. For more information on managing relationships with suppliers, see Chapter 45 *Purchasing, Warehousing, and Inventory Management.*

## Customers and Buyers

Customers are the final consumers of your product or service, while buyers purchase goods to alter and/or resell. Negotiations with customers are different from other negotiations in that they should be guided primarily by your interest in cultivating a long-term relationship. If you are in a service business, you will probably be negotiating contracts that include price, delivery time, and project terms. Negotiations with buyers are identical to those with suppliers; major issues include payment terms, late payment options, specification changes, and contract changes.

## Employees and Contractors

In negotiations with employees, the major issues are compensation, benefits, and duties. A major consideration is the goodwill you hope to engender between you and your employee. For this reason, it's best to know as much as possible about the person's interests, goals, and ambitions before entering into negotiations with him or her. For more information on this subject, see Chapter 24 *Managing Human Resources.*

Your relationship with contractors will probably be more limited, and negotiations will focus on cost, parameters, and deadlines. As with other negotiating counterparts, you should have as much information as possible about your prospective contractors before negotiations begin.

## Landlords

At some point, most entrepreneurs will have to negotiate a lease with a landlord. Usually, landlords want to earn as much money per square foot as possible. Rent generally covers a fixed period of time, and often includes several add-ons (e.g., ground fees, maintenance, year-end charges, and cleaning deposits). All of these fees are negotiable.

## Conclusion

Negotiating and deal-making are processes that require the participants to reach an agreement that maximizes the benefits for both sides. The win-win approach to negotiating yields more for everyone: it creates trust and respect between you and your counterpart, increases mutual gains, and enhances your prospects for profitable business deals in the future.

When both sides are willing to address issues directly and honestly—instead of wasting time on posturing and self-aggrandizing bluster—they usually find that a mutually satisfying agreement is easy to reach. Agreements reached in this way tend to last longer, and are more beneficial to both parties. For every deal you hope to close, joint problem-solving is the best path to follow!

# Chapter 42
# MANAGING THE DEAL

*About This Chapter:*
- *What is contract management?*
- *Nurture your partnerships*
- *How to exceed expectations*
- *Staying in touch*
- *Got a problem? Fix it!*
- *At the end, start over again!*
- *Review, review, review!*

## Introduction

Congratulations! You've just negotiated the best possible terms and signed a groundbreaking deal. Now you have a contract to manage. Whether you've agreed to provide a product or service, or to receive a product or service from someone else, your job is the same. You must ensure quality performance that meets or exceeds the terms of the contract, and maintain open communications between you and your partner.

A signed contract is a priceless asset for your business, particularly if it's with a major customer. It is surprising how many business people, exhilarated with the thrill of the hunt, neglect deals they've closed! Your contracts represent a promise of future deals, but only if you manage them professionally. This chapter shows you how to do so.

## What is Contract Management?

**Contract management** means implementing practices that keep your contractual relationship running smoothly, such as scheduling meetings with your partner, setting performance checkpoints, creating a stable operating environment, and establishing a method of achieving goals despite the uncertainties of your market. Delivering exceptional performance under contract requires continuous, consistent management. Ideally, you and your partner will get to know and trust one another during this process.

## Nurture Your Partnerships

Nurturing a contractual partnership means understanding each other's performance standards, time constraints, business priorities, and management culture. How does your "partner" business make and implement decisions? What are its competitive strengths? What does it value in its business dealings? Understand these things, and you will be able to meet requirements before they are requested of you.

Careful contract management ensures championship performance

The first step is to review the terms of the contract with your partner. You should agree on how and when each side is to perform its part of the deal, and how each will verify and measure progress. Here are some additional suggestions:

- **Review** the timetable for successful completion of the contract
- **Break** the contract into smaller pieces based on the timetable and performance goals (e.g., units to be delivered, deadlines to meet)
- **Determine** how and when to communicate
- **Define** the responsibilities of each participant
- **Identify** contingency plans for managing breaches of contract, and late or substandard performance
- **Define** the margin of error allowed for performance targets
- **Establish** meeting times and dates to review the status of the contract

## Create a Contract Specialist

It's an excellent idea to make someone within your business responsible for keeping track of the issues related to this contract. On a day-to-day basis, this person will ensure your business's compliance with the terms of the deal, and become the communication link between your business and your partner. This needn't be the employee's only job, and you needn't create a new department or a fancy title; you simply need to formalize responsibility and accountability for managing contracts.

*Designate a Countess of Contracts, Viscount of Value, or Sultan of Surpassed Expectations*

Who you designate depends on the nature of the contract. Does managing the contract require specific technical knowledge or good people skills? Does it require daily contact, or only weekly or monthly contact? Who in your business has the skills, attention to detail, and time to do the job well?

Creating a contract specialist calls for the same logical steps you used to create your management structures: identify your needs and goals, allocate responsibility and authority, set standards for performance, and create yardsticks to measure performance. Sound familiar? We hope so!

## Making Sure You Receive Exceptional Service

Let's talk for a moment about how to get the most out of the contracts you sign with outside providers such as bookkeeping services, manufacturers, maintenance, technical support, sales management companies, or market research firms. Things to keep track of include:

*Make sure you get what you pay for*

- The timeliness with which they deliver
- The means by which you communicate your needs and expectations
- How invoices are received and organized
- Opportunities for their product or service to enhance your product or service
- How their product or service is inspected to meet quality standards
- How problems with quality or performance will be overcome
- How, when, and by whom final payment is authorized
- Ideas for negotiation of future contracts

# How to Exceed Expectations

Next, let's focus on managing your performance as the provider. Given the choice between simply meeting the terms of your contract or exceeding them, always do more rather than less! We've already discussed the importance of maximizing the value you offer your customers. In this case, your customer is the person or business with whom you've signed a deal. These relationships are crucial to your business's performance, so you should value and nurture them as you do your customer relationships.

Depending upon your type of business, exceeding expectations can mean different things. If you write software, exceeding the contract might entail taking extra time to tailor a software program to a particular customer's needs. If you are a producer of specialty sauces and your customer is a small chain of cafés, exceeding expectations might mean researching wines that complement the food on your customer's menu. Finally, if you are a tax preparation consultant, exceeding expectations might mean paying a house call to help your customer organize his or her documents.

Play by the rules of the game

Here are several of the most basic ways to exceed expectations:

- **Be speedy and professional.** All companies should deliver rapid, professional service when and where their customers need it. The better you know your customer, the better you'll be able to anticipate needs and meet them in advance of being asked. Exceeding expected delivery time is one of the most powerful statements you can make, but you should never sacrifice quality and professionalism for speed!
- **Follow up on service.** Check with your partner (either in person or over the phone) to make sure that any questions or issues were resolved. Once again, a great deal of your business's success rides on your ability to look back on your performance with a critical eye and accurately rate how effective it was. Was it timely, appropriate, and professional?
- **Minimize the unnecessary details.** Make sure your invoices aren't cluttered with petty extra charges for small spare parts or minor service details. Are there potential irritations on your invoices? If you think so, your customer probably does too!
- **Share your expertise.** Just as you want your suppliers to enhance your business's competitiveness, you should work to make your customers more competitive. Share your knowledge with them, and look for ways to increase its value to them.
- **Always be accessible.** You can do this by being physically located near their office, or by making yourself easily accessible via phone, fax, or pager.
- **Get involved.** Your personal commitment to your partner is a strong indicator of professionalism, reliability, and the importance you place on the relationship.

Rules can mean the difference between having a venture or an adventure on your hands

## Staying in Touch

Communication is so important to nurturing your business relationships that it bears special discussion here. When we say communication, we're not talking about the occasional phone call from you to your partner; we're talking about an ongoing dialogue in which you and your partner coordinate performance, review targets, and work to improve your relationship. Personal relationships evolve with personal contact, so every opportunity you have to speak with your partner is an opportunity to improve cooperation and performance.

You have many means of communicating with business partners, including:

- Personal visits
- Toll-free phone line
- Fax machine
- Semi-social meetings
- Cellular phone
- Newsletter
- E-mail
- Beeper
- Regularly scheduled meetings

Consider creating a Web site that offers standard product or service assistance, or carrying a beeper so that you or your contract manager can be reached anywhere. Or how about creating an update notice that you fax to your client every week?

As valuable as these suggestions are, scheduled communication should never replace impromptu, face-to-face communication. By communicating with your partners more effectively than any of their other partners, you will distinguish your business as special, and gain yet another competitive advantage.

## NxLEVEL™ TECH TIP

As we mentioned above, staying in touch is essential to business relationships. If your business obliges you to travel often, and you can't delegate the responsibility for contract management, you might want to consider signing up for AT&T TeleTravel Service, which is designed for entrepreneurs with heavy travel schedules.

By calling an 800 number and entering a code, you can turn an ordinary phone booth into a sophisticated telecommunications center with access to voice mail, a message service (for both domestic and international calls), FlightCall for airline flight status information, three-way conference calling, language interpretation for more than 140 languages, sequential calling, and speed calling. The service costs $25 per year plus a per-minute charge. Contact AT&T for more information.

## Got a Problem?  Fix It!

It is human nature to avoid ugly or embarrassing situations.  No one enjoys feeling uncomfortable or making mistakes.  However, when you ignore problems, they tend to grow.  At some point in your business dealings, you will make mistakes—all businesses do!  But don't worry: you can improve and grow by learning from these mistakes.

Consider this scenario: you ship an order to a customer five days late, and when it arrives your customer calls to tell you that you sent too few of a certain item.  What do you do?  Identify the problem and take responsibility for it.  As the president of your business, any problem, large or small, is ultimately your responsibility.

Problems don't fix themselves

Here are the fundamentals of crisis management and problem resolution:

- Identify the problem
- Recognize your partner's frustration or annoyance
- Understand what caused the problem
- Take full responsibility
- Fix it—fast!
- Meet with your partner in person and explain how you will prevent the problem in the future

Partners who feel that you've treated them with respect and given them the attention they deserve are some of the best allies your business can have.  Likewise, people who feel that you have dealt with their problems professionally may become some of your most loyal customers.  Speedy and sincere resolution of problems helps your business to learn, grow, and develop long-term relationships.

## At the End, Start Over Again!

One of the most important components of contract management is a built-in potential for change and improvement.  Look ahead and ask yourself:

- How can you better serve your partners' needs or enhance value?
- How can they better serve your needs?
- Which needs have not been met?
- How can you improve communications?
- How can you collaborate to streamline performance?
- Where does synergy exist between your businesses?
- How can you sell them another deal?

Learn from this contract to improve the next

Always look at current work as laying the foundation for a future contract.  Leverage your existing relationships, and look for ways to form others.  Develop a track record and loyal business partners, and you will have a solid foundation upon which to grow.

## Review, Review, Review!

The importance of reviewing your business's performance cannot be overemphasized. You can only improve in the future by understanding and critiquing your past performance. This applies to all aspects of your business. Reviewing your performance in a contract entails:

Sometimes looking back is the best way to move forward

- Reviewing actual versus anticipated results
- Identifying strong and weak points
- Identifying opportunities for change and improvement
- Establishing a timetable for the next contract period.
- Soliciting and listening to feedback from your contract team
- Creating a "mini" business plan for the contract for the next year, comprising goals, tasks to be delegated, cost, and timetable.

## Conclusion

Ensuring your business's consistent, high-quality performance of contractual obligations requires allocating specific responsibilities within your business, and encouraging open communication between yourself and your business partners. By properly valuing and managing contractual relationships, you can gain a competitive advantage in even the most competitive markets.

# PART XI
# MANAGING GROWTH

## Chapter 43
## MANAGING GROWTH

*About This Chapter:*
- *Why grow?*
- *Understanding your personal goals*
- *Updating your business plan*
- *What is managed growth?*
- *Tools for growth: management reporting and controls*
- *Strategies for growth*
- *Financial considerations*
- *Utilizing capital for growth*

## Introduction

Some businesses grow without any deliberate effort on the part of their managers, simply by taking orders, delivering products, and collecting payment from an expanding base of customers. Other businesses grow because their management made a strategic decision to do so. This may involve finding additional financing to expand product offerings, increasing production capability, extending geographic reach, or tapping into new markets.

The biggest challenge confronting you as an entrepreneur is to grow your business intelligently and deliberately. Too often, entrepreneurs leave their future to fate, surfing market trends and congratulating themselves for being in the right place at the right time. They let the market determine how fast their businesses grow. Unfortunately, they have it all backwards!

This chapter will help you master the forces that affect your ability to manage growth. First we'll explain why you might want to grow, then discuss the tools and strategies you'll need.

## Why Grow?

You've figured out the best way to operate, you've mastered pricing, and feel you are serving your customer better than anyone else. Why would you change anything, let alone face higher risk and increased debt by trying to grow?

There are many reasons why businesses choose to pursue growth:

- To dominate the competition
- To increase profits
- To take on new challenges

- To hit the break-even point sooner
- To achieve economies of scale
- To get volume discounts on inputs and materials
- To enhance the company's status and prestige
- To acquire a broader, more diverse customer base
- To reach more attractive customer segments
- To improve customer service by being more accessible, having more resources, and offering lower prices

The benefits of growth aren't limited to your market presence or bottom line. Well-managed growth can mean exhilarating and fulfilling times for your entire business team.

---

*Let's Learn Edutainment*

*When the call came, Joe McGuire wasn't prepared for it.*

*It was a job offer from June Video, a fast-growing video production company based in Los Angeles. They were expanding operations, and wanted to grow their office in Joe's hometown of Atlanta, Georgia.*

*June Video knew everything about recording and editing video and sound pieces for other businesses; now they were developing their own video and CD-ROM titles, which they would market under their own name. They were impressed by Joe's extensive editorial and project management experience, and wanted him to head their new children's video department. This meant managing new projects, and helping with June's transition into producing original material. They offered him a generous salary, and invited him to hire his own team.*

*It was the best job offer Joe had ever received, but the timing couldn't have been worse. Six months earlier, he had left his full-time job as an editor at a children's book publishing house in order to dedicate himself to his own small production company, Let's Learn Edutainment. In that time, Let's Learn had already completed and sold two educational videos, and had many other projects planned.*

*Joe loved working for himself. He wanted to stay in his business and make it grow, but he was worried that he lacked the time, money, and personnel to do so. "Maybe this is a sign," he thought. "Maybe I should just hang it up and take this terrific job!"*

*What he really needed to do was reassess his business before making any decisions.*

---

## Yes, But Should I Grow?

So you know all about the benefits of growth...for some businesses. But does that mean you should grow, too? Will your business honestly perform better or achieve more by being larger than it is now? What will be the cost of growth?

There are two schools of thought on this subject. One says, "The bigger, the better!" You must dominate your market and spread your company's business over the widest base of customers possible. This philosophy has fueled globalization and acquisitions within many of the largest businesses in America.

The other school of thought says, "Small is beautiful." Being small and specialized lets businesses target niche markets and tailor their products to customers better than their larger competitors. This approach seems to be validated by the development of the fastest-growing segment of the American economy: small business.

Think carefully before you leap into the task of growing your business. Growth simply for the sake of growth will waste precious resources and energy. As your business evolves, your goal should be to grow only as much as will allow you to increase profits.

Likewise, your strategic choices should be calculated to increase competitiveness and customer loyalty. To achieve this, you need not necessarily be larger than you are now. Remember, companies in all segments of the economy are trying to mimic small businesses by downsizing, reorganizing, re-engineering, and teaming their employees. If you can better serve your market by being small, then by all means stay small!

Grow only if it delivers additional and proportionate competitive advantages and opportunity for profitability

## Understanding Your Personal Goals

Clearly, the profitability and financial health of your business are determining factors in how, when, why, and if it grows; but your motivation, inspiration, and commitment are also important. What's the point of running a growing business if you don't enjoy it?

As you plan for growth, reflect upon your personal goals. Ask yourself:

- What motivated me to start my own business?
- What do I want to accomplish through this business?
- Will growing this business help me achieve my vision?
- What things do I like most about my business?
- What things do I dislike most about my business?
- What things do I value most about being in business?

Try to identify areas where your interests, skills, and vision have changed, and consider the impact of growth on your personal goals.

Grow to increase profits

## Updating Your Business Plan

Let's say that after careful review and consideration, you decide that now is the time to grow. The next step is to review and revise your business plan. Even the most carefully researched, ingeniously written business plan becomes obsolete when conditions change. Your customer's profile or market segment can shift, economic conditions can change, your competitors can introduce groundbreaking products, or a new technology can emerge.

This is why you must periodically update your business plan. And you must certainly update it before you set out to court additional financing. Ask yourself the following questions; your answers will guide the evolution of your new and improved business plan:

- Are my original goals for the business still reasonable?
- What threats and opportunities does my business face?
- What are my business's strengths and weaknesses?
- Are my assumptions still valid?
- Can I measure my progress according to my original standards?
- Am I meeting quality and service goals?
- Does my business plan accurately reflect my business today?
- What resources does my business require to achieve its goals?
- Are my customers' needs being expertly and uniquely served?
- Can my business operate more efficiently that it does currently?

Remember, all or part of your business plan will be used by investors, customers, bankers, suppliers, partners, consultants, and employees to gauge its profit potential. Think of the growth phase you are entering as an entirely new business. Look at your new challenges and opportunities, and set new goals for yourself. By updating your business plan, you are creating the document that will guide this exciting phase of your business. Also, this may very well be the tool that attracts the additional financing you need for growth!

Ask yourself these questions:

- Is my business moving in the right direction? Have I hit my targets?
- Does my product or service truly reflect my business's strengths?
- Who are my customers? Why do they buy my product or service?
- Who are my competitors? What do I offer that they do not or cannot?
- Am I serving the customers I targeted in my business plan?
- Has the competitive landscape of my market changed?
- Have my customers' needs changed? Has my ability to meet their needs changed?
- Has cost structure and pricing in my industry changed?
- Are there any new technologies that affect my ability to compete?

## What is Managed Growth?

Successful entrepreneurs distinguish themselves not only by a keen understanding of their markets, but also by their ability to plan their growth. How do they do this? They identify trends likely to affect the business environment. They plan for their financial needs, and begin laying the groundwork for additional financing long before they need it. They create management controls to sustain performance, and utilize budgets to safeguard cash.

True, many businesses succeed simply by going with the tide. However, such success is rarely sustainable, and is usually based on circumstantial factors. Failing to manage growth can affect every area of your business's performance. Major pitfalls include:

- Experiencing only limited, short-term growth
- Inability to maintain consistent performance standards
- Unprofessional behavior
- Low employee moral, and high employee turnover
- Loss of profitability
- Loss of customer loyalty
- Diminished quality of products
- Slowdown in business learning and competitiveness
- Inability of overworked leadership to provide direction
- Cash crunch and bankruptcy
- Inefficient use of resources
- Stress and burnout
- Loss of focus on core objectives
- Poor communication among employees

It's sad but true: many businesses get a bad name by being unprofessional, overworked, unfocused, and unable to provide quality customer service consistently. Why? Because they fail to plan for the future. Don't become so intoxicated by big orders and exploding demand that you fail to equip your business for long-term survival!

## No Pain, No Gain

Many people don't like change, and it's quite true that change can often be downright frightening. On the other hand, the most exciting and positive events seem to happen in times of crisis: people develop new skills, challenge themselves, and discover their potential. Growth without uncertainty and crisis is simply not possible. This doesn't mean that your business can't grow unless it's subjected to some disastrous near-meltdown. By "crisis," we simply mean a point at which you must let go of old ideas in order to adapt to new circumstances. It's always difficult to do this, but the rewards speak for themselves.

*Sustained growth means being equipped for long-term survival*

---

*Joe telephoned June Video and arranged to speak with them the following Monday. He said he needed the weekend to evaluate their offer.*

*He had to think fast, but carefully. First, he took a hard look at his business. He knew what his current revenues and expenses were, and he had projections for upcoming projects. But he didn't have a clear picture of his business model. Who was his ideal customer? What sort of project was most suited to his strengths and interests? Which production duties had to be done by Let's Learn, and which could he contract out to other businesses? Should he grow his business?*

*Joe had never taken the time to update the business plan that he'd created over two years ago, when he was working full-time for the children's book publisher and Let's Learn had only done a few small projects. He decided that before he made a move, he would rewrite his business plan.*

———————————◆———————————

Watch for warning signs of too much growth

### Warning: Slow Down!

Believe it or not, there is such a thing as too much growth. Too often, businesses go from booming sales to bankruptcy because they fail to notice the warning signs of out-of-control growth. Here are some problems that signal trouble for growing companies:

- Cash flow problems and difficulty paying bills
- High employee turnover
- Overlooking the details of running the business
- Customer complaints
- Failure to focus on the business's core competencies
- Diminished quality of products and services

Are you overlooking any of these warning signs in your business? Since managed growth is the easiest to sustain, why not create safeguards to keep your business on track? Why not limit your business to a set level of customers, a specific geographic region, or a particular order size?

These limits need not be permanent; they merely restrict growth to a manageable level for a given period of time, to keep the business operating within its maximum performance range.

## Tools for Growth: Management Reporting and Controls

Before we discuss how to put your investment capital to work in a given growth strategy, let's review the tools your business will use to manage its growth.

### Cash Management

Aside from enabling you to pay your bills, cash on hand indicates the health of your business. Good cash management strategies show potential investors that you know how to run a profitable business, and will be able to service your debt. This is why you should cultivate relationships with prospective sources of financing while your business is doing well.

Your ability to manage cash skillfully determines your business's ability to grow. On the other hand, poorly managed cash can drain your business's vitality in the blink of an eye. Here are several of the biggest drains on cash that a business can have:

- Interest payments on debt
- Cash tied up in excess inventory
- Uncollected accounts receivable

Projecting, monitoring, and conserving cash is not one of the more exciting parts of managing a business, but it can be the most important! If you're not good at tracking spending and calculating your cash balances, enlist the help of someone who is. Here are some basic cash management tips:

- Work out a format with your accountant that fits your business's needs
- Schedule your accounts receivable by major accounts
- Pinpoint collection problems one by one
- Schedule major cash payments by supplier
- Plan for cash flows at least six months in advance
- Review and update your cash flow plan weekly
- Deal with cash shortages before they occur
- Use your banker as a partner

*Your ability to manage cash determines your business's ability to grow*

---

*Joe spent the entire weekend researching and rethinking his business plan. When he had reviewed the marketing aspects of his business, he committed them to paper. He wrote, revised, took a break, and checked his work several times. Finally, he condensed it into a mission statement:*

*"Let's Learn Edutainment is committed to designing the highest-quality, most creative multimedia learning tools. Let's Learn products surpass national and state educational standards and incorporate cutting-edge technology. Let's Learn creates value by conceiving original ideas for presenting educational material, and expertly managing teams of in-house and contracted professionals to bring these ideas to fruition."*

*In thinking through this mission statement, Joe had identified Let's Learn's greatest strengths: conceptualization of new projects, and assembling teams of people to perform the production work. He decided to focus on pitching concepts and projects to large, national content providers. Since most content creators were expanding into multimedia formats, he would create multimedia content. His projects could be made for any medium, including print, video, audio, CD-ROM, and the Web.*

*Joe estimated that in order to meet his professional targets and personal income goals, Let's Learn would have to produce, on average, eight major projects a year. That would require that he move out of his home office into a larger office space, hire two additional project managers, and invest in new computer equipment.*

*The project seemed to get bigger and bigger the more Joe looked at it! If he was serious about these goals, he would need a clear, aggressive growth strategy. It would be a lot of work, but Joe was eager to face new challenges. He felt confident that his business could continue to be profitable and grow.*

*By Sunday morning, he had made the decision to turn down June Video's job offer. The decision about how to grow Let's Learn would be a lot more difficult.*

---

## Good Management Skills

When we talk about the management of a growing business, we're talking first and foremost about its leader...you. The success or failure of your business hinges on your ability to:

- Delegate
- Think strategically
- Manage resources
- Manage people
- Manage time
- Closely manage complex issues

Your task is to ensure the internal health of your organization during these turbulent, exciting times. This means creating a system of checks and balances that will allow your business to perform consistently, professionally, and profitably.

## Good Team Building

The key to being a good leader is creating a good team. This means gathering committed and inspired people who can work together toward common goals. As discussed in Chapter 23 *Team Building and Leadership*, these people need not all be full-time employees, but they do need to be aligned on goals and in close communication with one another. Your role as the leader of your business is to delegate the responsibility and authority necessary to perform key tasks. If you hope to grow your business, you cannot do it alone. So start building a high-performance team now!

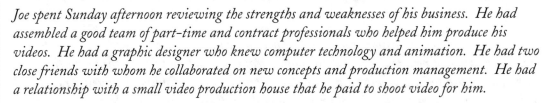

*Joe spent Sunday afternoon reviewing the strengths and weaknesses of his business. He had assembled a good team of part-time and contract professionals who helped him produce his videos. He had a graphic designer who knew computer technology and animation. He had two close friends with whom he collaborated on new concepts and production management. He had a relationship with a small video production house that he paid to shoot video for him.*

*But Joe felt like he never had enough time to manage projects efficiently. He was often too busy to record his project hours and materials expenses; several times he'd even failed to bill his clients for work he completed!*

*He realized that what Let's Learn needed most was:*

- *A business manager to organize project billings and expenses, payroll, overhead expenses, and equipment repairs.*
- *A team of three full-time project managers*
- *An ongoing, reliable alliance with a video and audio production house, to achieve economies of scale, consistent quality, and reliable project completion dates*
- *Office space*
- *Better time management*
- *Project prioritizing and resource scheduling*
- *Equipment upgrades*

*He calculated that these things would cost Let's Learn over $300,000 for the first year. He knew he couldn't afford to borrow that much money. How else could he finance his growth?*

---

### Good Time Management

Understanding time management will improve productivity and performance, lower your stress level, and enhance relationships with employees, suppliers, and customers. Your family might even appreciate the benefits of a calmer, more organized you!

Here are some basics of time management. First:

- Identify how you spend your time
- Identify wasted time
- Identify your "high-performance clock"—those times of day when you are most productive. Use this time for your most demanding tasks, and reschedule all others
- List your personal priorities

Then:

- Work with a team
- Rank tasks by importance
- Delegate authority and responsibility when necessary
- If possible, complete your tasks in a single session

## NxLEVEL™ TECH TIP

Here are a couple of Web sites that may help you to manage your growing business.

- **Outsourcing Interactive** (http://www.outsourcing.com/) offers information on strategic leveraging of outsourcing resources and capabilities. This site features outsourcing products, advisory services, training programs, and issue sessions; a discussion area; outsourcing information tools; an online archive of outsourcing articles, briefing papers, and statistics; and a summary of the Outsourcing Institute's Survey of Outsourcing Users.

- **Business Know-How** (http://www.businessknowhow.com/bkhtips.htm) is an interactive newsletter for home office and small business owners who are looking for inspiration or practical suggestions on starting or managing a successful business. It is also a place for home office and small business owners to share the insights and expertise they've acquired with others. (And if you're wondering whether you're really getting the most out of your time, this site even has a link to a form that will automatically calculate the value of your time in dollars and cents!)

- Set aside an appropriate amount of time to finish your tasks
- Get regular exercise to keep your mind and body tuned

## Strategies For Growth

Your business is profitable, you're up-to-date on the dynamics of your market, and you know the direction in which you want to go. You are inspired and your team is excited! Now you want to take your business to the next level, either by increasing your customer base, tapping into a new market, or offering additional products or services. You need a strategy to accomplish this. If your business is like most, it will need additional financing at this stage. Here are the factors that differentiate growth strategies:

- Level of risk
- Speed at which they allow growth
- Cost of growth
- Implications for the future of your business
- Degree of management control they allow you to retain in your business

---

*It was Sunday night. The next morning, Joe had to give June Video his answer.*

*Suddenly, he realized that the perfect solution was right in front of him. Why not take advantage of their interest in him by proposing a partnership between June Video and Let's Learn Edutainment?*

*Both companies would benefit from the partnership. Let's Learn could move into June Video's office space, share their receptionist, and contract them to do all video and audio recordings. Let's Learn would save money by not paying rent and would have, in effect, its own in-house production studio.*

*In exchange, June Video would get an in-house content creation department. Joe would bring along his team, and give June Video first rights on jointly marketing Let's Learn's titles. June Video would also expand its revenues through the additional production work, and they'd learn the content creation and project management business from the inside out.*

*It seemed like a perfect strategy. Joe calculated that if June Video liked the idea, he would need only $150,000 for the first year of growth. After that, he calculated that the business would be self-sustaining, and able to pay additional managerial salaries out of earnings.*

*When Joe made the pitch to June Video on Monday morning, they liked the idea enough to request a face-to-face meeting. They liked the idea of sharing office space, and having Joe and his entire creative team onsite, and they really liked the fact that he would bring four projects already in the works. In this first meeting, both businesses agreed that the idea looked promising for both companies' growth plans.*

---

# Financial Considerations

If you are going to grow, you will probably need more money than your business can generate. Managing a growing business requires cultivating external financial resources *before* you need them.

What does this sort of planning entail? Making intelligent decisions about your business's financial needs, and getting access to external **seed capital** when you need it.

External financing for your growing business can come from:

- Individual investors (the public)
- Private investors (wealthy individuals)
- Professional investment funds (venture capitalists)
- Foundations (grants for special causes)
- Corporations (joint ventures and equity investments)
- Commercial banks
- Investment banks

Additional internal financing for your business can come from:

- Reinvestment of profits from sales
- Sale of assets
- Credit from suppliers (extended payment terms)
- Customers (payments in advance)
- Employees (stock purchase plans, wage/salary concessions)

Use your knowledge about your business to select the methods of financing that is right for you. You may choose a source of financing based on the length of time the funds are available, the costs involved in acquiring them, or the amount of control over your company you are able to retain.

Securing capital will require selling investors on your track record, business plan, employees, personal vision, professionalism, and prospects for growth. Here is a checklist for use in the capital acquisition process:

- Update your business plan
- Document your business's track record
- Identify new opportunities, problems, and challenges
- Show your business plan to prospective investors and ask for feedback
- Identify how much money you need, over what period of time
- Review your financial and marketing ideas
- Update your targeted sources of financing often
- Be straightforward, direct, and honest
- Be confident and optimistic, but realistic
- Show conviction and passion

Begin now to cultivate external financial resources

You may ask, "How am I supposed to be confident and direct when this entire business is so new and uncertain?" Consider this: There are far fewer successful entrepreneurs out there than there are sources of financing, and there are more eager investors than there are profitable ventures in which to invest. For this reason, if you've demonstrated your ability to manage a profitable and growing business, you have every reason to be confident.

———————◆———————

*After his first meeting with June Video, Joe was overjoyed. There seemed to be a good fit between the companies, and he looked forward to their next meeting, in which they would hash out the details of the plan.*

*But Joe realized that the partnership didn't solve his growth management issues. Would sharing a receptionist, hiring additional project managers, and using larger production facilities help him use his time better? He had a feeling that his problems ran deeper. He always felt pressed for time, and worried that he was not using what time he had wisely. If he had this much trouble managing his own time, how could he manage a larger team for his growing business?*

*Joe decided he needed help in managing his time and delegating responsibility, so he attended a seminar on time management, which was sponsored by his local Chamber of Commerce. There, he learned that he needed to break down how he actually spent his time.*

*Joe created a job description for himself and each member of his team. This was a simple list of duties and responsibilities that each person needed to perform. It prioritized tasks and outlined how projects would be scheduled and monitored.*

*Joe's job description reminded him that his greatest value to Let's Learn was in high-level strategic planning and project promotion. Therefore, he would focus his efforts on coming up with new project ideas, pitching projects to buyers and distributors, creating alliances, and prioritizing and scheduling production. All other tasks (including billing, expenses, payroll, training, and day-to-day contact with contractors) he would delegate to other employees.*

*He decided that since the early morning hours were his most productive, he would use that time to focus on his most demanding tasks, like writing scripts and storyboards, creating new ideas, and budgeting projects. In the afternoon, he would do all other tasks.*

*Now that Joe was plotting a course for Let's Learn's growth, he wanted to set a good example for his team, and make his business as professional, reliable, and fun as possible.*

———————◆———————

## Utilizing Capital for Growth

Once you've decided to pursue additional financing for your business, you need to decide how to put the new funding to work for you. Consider the following costs and benefits of some additional growth strategies:

## Acquisition

Strategies for growth through acquisition of an additional business depend on:

- Tax considerations
- The business goals of the participants
- The industry/type of companies involved
- The regulatory environment
- The amount of assets involved

The starting point for growth by acquisition is an evaluation of your potential acquisitions:

- Cash flow
- Assets
- Sales, cash, profitability, and break-even projections
- Market position
- Management team
- Organizational culture
- Unique advantages of merging (synergy with your business)
- Legal considerations
- Management of the new business entity

<aside>Banks judge your business on the basis of its profits, not its sales</aside>

## Joint Venture/Partnership

Growing by entering into a partnership is an increasingly common strategy of big and small businesses alike. This entails choosing a partner with complementary skills, technologies, customers, or products, to achieve things neither business could do alone. Joint ventures are very popular ways to:

- Minimize risk
- Achieve economies of scale
- Create synergies
- Gain technical know-how
- Expand geographic reach
- Acquire patented products, technology, or processes
- Expand the customer base
- Lower costs by pooling expenses
- Increase product offerings

Just because you manage a small business doesn't mean that a joint venture or partnership can't offer you the same benefits it offers bigger companies. All of the benefits listed above apply to your business just as much as they apply to the Microsofts and GEs of the world. They help you serve your customers, be profitable, and increase your competitiveness in the market. Alliances and partnerships can be as complex or simple as you choose to make them, but the principle always remains the same: You need to identify what each side contributes to and takes away from the deal.

Other methods of achieving growth include going international, franchising, and enlarging your product line or geographic area

---◆---

*June Video had what they wanted. Rather than hiring an additional employee, they had created an entirely new in-house team of producers. Within three weeks, Joe had hired his two friends and his graphic/computer artist as part of his full-time team. Within three months, the joint June Video/Let's Learn production team had finished its first video project, called "Freddy Frog in the Amazon." They were in the process of adapting it to CD-ROM. Members of both teams worked well together, and continually learned from one another.*

*Joe McGuire could hardly believe his luck. Nine months before, owning a full-time business had been just a dream. Now he'd negotiated a partnership with a national production house, applied for and received his second round of financing, and was managing his own team. Joe was delegating responsibility, managing his time, and cranking out projects like a true pro. What's more, he was lined up to achieve his personal income goals for the year. Let's Learn sure had come a long way! Joe was proud of his efforts, and prepared himself for the exciting year of growth and challenges that lay ahead.*

---◆---

## Conclusion

The biggest challenge growing businesses face is maintaining professional, consistent performance. All too often, they fail to serve customers, move away from their core competencies, and experience cash management problems. In the worst cases, they lose control of their profitability, resulting in a crisis where their very survival is on the line.

Your business plan and your personal objectives are perhaps the most important things to consider as your business grows. Businesses that fail to prepare a cohesive plan can fall into the trap of reacting rather than acting. By reaffirming your vision for your business, can you tap into the essential motivation and inspiration that fuels long-term growth.

# Chapter 44
# DEALING WITH LARGE ORGANIZATIONS

*About This Chapter:*
- *Doing business with the government*
- *Government small business programs*
- *How to work with prime contractors*
- *Dealing with big business*

## Introduction

Imagine if your little company received a bid invitation from the U.S. Forestry Service, who needed 25,000 Ranger's hats delivered over the next six months. It would double your business! You'd feel excited and a little frightened, and you'd probably ask yourself: What do I need to do to win the bid? Aren't there a lot of rules when you deal with the government? Can I produce that many hats in six months? Will they pay me on time?

Dealing with large businesses and the government can be both enticing and daunting. It entails some risk, and requires you to make changes in the way you normally do business. You may have to put more resources on the front end in your marketing efforts, prequalification procedures, and budgeting. Your administrative costs may be higher due to the increased recordkeeping and procedural requirements of the larger organization. Also, some big businesses and the government are slow to pay invoices, which may put a strain on cash flow. However, with careful planning you can learn to meet the requirements of doing business with larger organizations.

## Doing Business with the Government

- The U.S. Government is the largest purchaser of products and services in the world. Of the $250 billion the government spends annually on procurement, nearly 20% goes to small businesses.
- There are 1,200 U.S. Government buying offices around the country. There is probably one fairly close to you.
- The U.S. Government buys almost everything, so it's likely that it will buy what you make.
- Government agencies are able to make small purchases (less than $2500) using the Government Purchase Card, which means improved cash flow to those companies that accept credit cards.
- Doing business with the U.S. Government may help you diversify your markets.
- There are government-sponsored programs such as the Procurement Technical Assistance Centers (PTACs) to help small businesses do business with larger businesses.

## Government Small Business Programs

During and after World War II, it became evident that the government needed suppliers of all types of goods and services in the event of emergency. As a result, the Small Business Act of 1958 was enacted to require that more contracts are awarded to small business owners. The government recognizes three types of small businesses:

Small is beautiful

- **Small Business.** The Small Business Administration has given each industry a NAICS (North American Industry Classification System) Code, which is categorized by the number of employees, or a maximum amount of annual revenues.
- **Small Disadvantaged Business.** This classification requires first that you meet the SIC code standards above. At least 51% of your business must be owned and managed by socially and economically disadvantaged people. This group includes Black, Hispanic, Asian, and Native American minorities.
- **Women-Owned Small Business.** To qualify, your business must meet NAICS code standards and be 51% owned, managed, and controlled by women.
- **HUBZone Business.** This program provides contracting preferences to small businesses located in and hiring employees from historically underutilized business zones.

The U.S. Government has allocated a percentage of procurement dollars to be spent with small businesses. Some bids are offered *only* to small businesses. There is also the Small Business Administration's 8(a) Program, to which only small, disadvantaged business firms may apply.

———————◆———————

*Jane Hayward and Karen Summers, both former office managers, started their company after they coordinated several office moves for their respective employers. Their company, Interlink, Etc., manufactures lightweight office furniture on wheels. Hayward and Summers decided to bid for a government contract to supply office furniture after finding out about the government's program for woman-owned businesses. Their successful bid to provide office furniture for the regional Social Security Administration offices in Texas and Oklahoma netted them over $100,000 in sales in their first year of business!*

———————◆———————

### Government Market Study

Now that you know how profitable government business can be, how do you go about attacking this market?

First, determine which government offices are located near your business. (Be careful not to stretch your boundaries so far that you risk failing to perform; this will endanger future government business opportunities.) As you look at your geographic opportunities, consider the following guidelines:

- **Size.** Consider your size and the geographic area you can handle. If you are a very small business, you may want to select a small area at first. If you are already a larger business, you may want to go for an entire state.
- **Location.** Where are you located in relation to government facilities? Large, populated areas have more government opportunities than smaller, rural areas.
- **Experience.** How much experience do you have, and how good are you at what you do? If you are new and still learning, you may want to stay close to your core competencies. If you have been in business a long time and enjoy a good market share, you may want to expand your customer base.
- **Type of business.** If you can manage your business from a distance, your selling area can be much larger.

### Where are Government Buying Offices?

After assessing how large a geographic range you can handle, identify the **government buying offices** within your targeted geographic area. There are ten regions grouped by the Small Business Administration. Identify your region, then go to your local Small Business Administration Office and ask for a listing of the buying offices in your region.

### Government and Personal Selling Techniques

Now is the time to meet with the appropriate people in the buying offices and start the sales process you learned in Chapter 32 *The Art of Selling*.

- Contact the office of Small Disadvantaged Business Utilization (OSDBU) of the agency you wish to do business with. The staff can provide you with a directory of agency buying locations and advise you on the types of goods and services that the agency regularly purchases. Many agencies promote outreach programs and offer "how to" publications that provide assistance in understanding their procurement programs.
- Register in PRO-Net, and SBA database of small business contractors and their areas of business. Agency contracting officers and prime contractors search the database to find small business sources and subcontractors. Firms can easily register from the SBA website.
- Agency purchasing office maintain source lists for the goods and services that they buy. Firms can be included on the agency's Solicitation Mailing List Application simply by completing a Standard Form 129 with the agency.
- Wherever possible, arrange marketing visits to agency project and program personnel.
- Provide catalogues and brochures to key personnel within the agencies.
- Participate in agency market research by attending pre-solicitation conferences.
- Many federal agencies hold small business fairs that emphasize how to do business with the government and provide information regarding their program activities. Some have the added feature of making on-the-spot purchases from small business attendees.

*Look at geography first*

*Sell, sell, sell*

- Contact your closest PTAC (Procurement Technical Assistance Center) and talk with a Marketing Assistance Specialist about your company and the type of product or service you provide.
- Follow-up—This is as important as the meeting itself. You need to work with your SBS to ensure you have been added to the automated bidders list. Keep following up to determine if there are additional business opportunities.
- Contact the requisitioner—It is the buyer's responsibility to ensure the products and services meet the requisitioner's needs. If you have a new product, you may need to meet with the requisitioner. This can be arranged through your SBS.

## Submitting an Offer

After you have completed the steps above, it will take the buying office a couple of weeks to get your company loaded into its automated bidders list. Once in the database, you must wait until a requisition comes in for the items or services you sell. (The automatic bidder list rotates offers among the bidders, so that the same bidders are not always selected.)

There are three types of solicitation:

1. Small purchase procedures, which are for procurements of $25,000 or less. The procedure is called a **Request for Quotation**. Your response is called a quote.
2. Sealed bidding procedures, which call for an **Invitation for Bids**. Your response is to offer a bid. The government uses sealed bids in the following situations:
   - There is sufficient time for the sealed bid process.
   - No additional information or discussion needs to take place.
   - More than one sealed bid will be received.
   - The bid is based on price, or price-related criteria. A firm price contract will be awarded if your sealed bid is accepted.
3. Negotiated procurement procedures, which are used when procurement is expected to be over $25,000. You will receive a **Request for Proposal** and will be expected to submit both a **technical proposal** and a **price proposal**.

## How to Prepare an Offer

Although you may have prepared hundreds of commercial offers during your career, doing business with the government can be both different and difficult. Here are some things to keep in mind:

- **Always respond.** Respond even if you do not offer a bid. This is very important, because "no response" names are deleted from the bidders list.
- **Be on time.** The government does not accept late submittals.
- **Complete all paperwork.** If you are unable to answer a question, contact the appropriate official for assistance.
- **Be careful.** Don't overlook any items that might affect your price.

If you follow these simple guidelines and are patient, thorough, and professional, you are in a good position to be considered for the contract award.

## How to Win a Government Contract

Here are some keys to winning government contracts:

- **Be responsible.** Have your financial affairs in order, be prepared to submit references for similar work, meet delivery schedules, and have the technical skills and equipment necessary to do the work.
- **Have the best proposal.** While the best price will always be the major factor in determining if a company is awarded a federal government contract, there are several other factors that will influence a contracting official's decision. Past performance is becoming a significant factor considered when awarding contracts. Even though a company may not have federal contracting experience, references from previous non-federal buyers may influence a federal purchasing official who is attempting to secure the best product or service for the government. Best value is another factor federal contracting officials use when awarding a contract. For instance, does a company offer faster delivery, a better warranty or possibly more service for the same dollar.

*When Ken Dyer decided to expand his computer reselling business from commercial clients to the government, he knew that he would have to change his approach to selling. After consulting with a friend who had experience as a state agency buyer, Ken contacted his local government buying office and scheduled a 15-minute presentation in which he emphasized the cost advantage of dealing with a local reseller. He made sure that he followed up with the buyer, and submitted a sealed bid well in advance of the due date. After waiting three months, Ken was elated to find out that he had won the bid to provide computers to the state's Division of Motor Vehicles while the division phased out its outdated equipment.*

## Types of Contracts

Here are the major types of governmental contracts:

### Firm fixed-price contract

The contractor agrees to supply a particular product or service at a fixed price that won't change during performance. This is probably the most commonly used government contract.

### Fixed-price contract with economic price adjustment

Allows the price to be revised in case of a specific economic contingency. There is usually a limit to upward adjustment, but none to downward adjustment.

### Cost-plus-fixed-fee contract

All of the contractor's costs are paid by the government, plus a fixed fee. The amount of the fee is negotiated prior to award, and doesn't change during the contract regardless of any changes in the cost of performance. This arrangement gives the contractor very little incentive to control costs, since the fee remains the same whether actual performance costs are high or low. It can only be renegotiated if there is a change in the scope of the work.

### Cost-plus-award-fee contract

Provides for reimbursement of all allowable costs incurred during performance, and for both a base fee (profit) and an award fee (more profit).

### Time and materials/labor-hour contract

Used by the government to buy labor at a fixed price (including all overhead, general and administrative expenses, and profit), and materials at cost.

### Indefinite-delivery contract

These are generally used to procure common supplies, commodities, or repair services. There are three classifications:

1. **Definite quantity contracts** provide for delivery of a known quantity of a supply or service over a known period of time.
2. **Requirements contracts** provide for the filling of all requirements for a specific supply or service during a specified contract period. The quantity to be bought during the contract period is unknown at the time of award. This type of contract guarantees the contractor that all requirements for the supply or service contracted will be purchased from his or her business, and specifies a maximum amount to be procured. Deliveries are scheduled on the basis of orders placed with the contractor.
3. **Indefinite quantity contracts** provide for a contractor to furnish an indefinite or unknown quantity of a supply or service during a fixed period of time. They specify a minimum quantity the government will purchase, and a maximum quantity the contractor must deliver during the contract performance.

There is an infinite variety of contracts, most of which are based on the types above. It is paramount that you understand the terms and conditions of each bid request prior to submitting your bid. Why? Because you will be bound to the terms and conditions stated in your submittal. Failure to understand the type of contract can cost you dearly!

## Post-Award Activities

Congratulations—you won the bid! Now what? Here are a few pointers:

- Complete all paperwork exactly as requested
- Immediately report any problems that occur, always citing "cause and cure" (what happened and why, how and when you will fix it)
- Deliver exactly what was purchased, exactly when promised

- Keep the lines of communication open
- Thank them for their business!

### The Mentor Program

The Department of Defense's "Mentor-Protege Pilot Program," established by Section 831 of Public Law 101-510, has a threefold purpose. First, it gives major contractors an incentive to help small, disadvantaged businesses perform contracts. Second, it establishes business relationships between major contractors and small, disadvantaged businesses. Third, it increases the participation of small, disadvantaged businesses. The major advantages are:

- Aid from the mentor in management or technical matters
- Loans
- Cash purchases
- Advance payment

In other words, you have access to the resources of a larger firm. If this type of arrangement appeals to you, pursue it.

## How to Work with Prime Contractors

Prime contractors are those "Big Business" companies—like IBM, Bechtel, and Lockheed—that are always being awarded huge contracts. Why does this affect you? Because when these giants are awarded major contracts, they are required by law to subcontract a portion of the work to small and disadvantaged businesses!

All the marketing and sales techniques mentioned previously come into play here. Since prime contractors operate under the government's "Rule Book for Procurement," many of the same principles apply:

- **Do your paperwork**. Paperwork is very important to government contractors, a fact borne out by the mass quantities of paperwork government contracts require: certified payrolls, written change proposals, materials submittals, quality control plans, and much, much more. Most contractors dislike paperwork for two reasons: first, many don't know how to do it; second, it costs them money. If you work with contractors, be prepared to do your share correctly.
- **Talk to them just as you would any other client**. The subcontracts manager needs to know what is going on in order to keep supervisors and the government advised.
- **Do the work on time and on schedule**. This is the best way to ensure repeat business.

Here are some of the most important differences between the government procurement and prime contractor procurement systems:

Service is the name of the game

## NxLEVEL™ TECH TIP

For entrepreneurs seeking information on government contracts, FedBizOpps (www.fedbizopps.gov) has been designated as the single source for federal government procurement opportunities that exceed $25,000. By signing up to automatically receive procurement information, by solicitation number, selected organizations and product service classification, you can react more quickly to procurement opportunities because you are better informed. The FedBizOpps web site provides assistance by e-mail and a toll-free helpline. The site also links to several other highly useful sites dealing with government procurement.

Big business—big sales?

- **Bid openings**. Contractors are generally not required to hold public bid openings or disclose bid opening results. Some do have public openings, and some don't.
- **Solicitation publication**. Contractors are not required to publish solicitations in the government's website, www.FedBizOpps.gov.
- **Determinations of non-responsibility**. Prime contractors are not required to refer determinations of non-responsibility to the Small Business Administration for review.
- **8(a) and other government programs**. Prime contractors don't use the Small Business Administration's 8(a), SDB or HUBZone Programs Program to make awards to small, disadvantaged businesses.
- **Full and open competition**. The Competition in Contracting Act, which states that the government must allow all responsible sources that request a solicitation package to submit a bid, doesn't apply to prime contractors. They must achieve effective price competition, so they need only enough bids to ensure a fair, reasonable price.

## Dealing with Big Business

Like government agencies, large private companies have standards for procedures, policies, and professionalism. It helps to remember the following:

- No matter what business you are in, your business is service. Determine what your big business partners want and deliver it.
- As a smaller company, your core competencies include speed, focus, and teamwork. Use them to your advantage when dealing with big business.
- As a niche or specialized company, do what you do best. Be honest about your capabilities and stick to your specialty.

Note: Competition is very, very keen when you attempt to sell your product or service to companies in the Fortune 1000. Unless you have a one-of-a-kind product, or a unique service, the Fortune 1000 may not be where you want to market your goods.

## Know Thyself

If you have thoroughly and honestly assessed your human, financial, and physical (plant and equipment) strengths, and think you are ready to tackle the bigger clients, go to it! Remember to assess not just your current situation, but your ability to expand while keeping the quality high and the price competitive. If you can do all this without disrupting relationships with current clients, you might be ready to move into the big time!

## Doing Business with Big Business

Dealing with big companies can greatly benefit your company in many ways. Here are a few examples:

- By selling directly to big business, you indirectly enter new markets. This may help diversify your markets.
- Your company can learn from its association with large professional companies.
- A long-term contract with a large company can stabilize your cash flow.

## Marketing and Selling

All the approaches to marketing and personal selling mentioned elsewhere in this book apply to big business. The key is to commit to a marketing plan, and be patient and persistent.

Let's take a moment to review the key elements of marketing strategy, and focus in particular on specific strategies for targeting larger companies. Once again, the first step is understanding your customer. Start by answering these questions:

- What is the nature of my customer's business?
- What is the single most important competitive factor for them?
- What is their core competency?
- Who are their competitors, and where is their industry headed?
- What do they look for in partners?
- What is their "culture"?
- What is their buying process? Who are the decision-makers, users, gatekeepers, and influencers? (For detailed discussion of this, see Chapter 32 *The Art of Selling*.)

Look at the business from every possible angle. Imagine that their issues are your issues (since they will be if you win their business). With these insights in mind, tailor the four P's of your marketing mix (Product, Price, Placement, and Promotion) to the large corporation's needs.

*Ramona Davies is one of only a few "trend gurus" who regularly provide their clients in the consumer products industry with up-to-date market information and reliable predictions of what the next trend will be. Ramona started her career at an international consulting firm, doing marketing studies focused on the food products industry. By gaining expertise in the coffee segment, and building a rapport with several major clients, she was able to start a marketing forecasting firm that focuses on the coffee industry. Because she proved her worth to her clients while she was still working for the consulting firm, the large businesses felt comfortable continuing their relationships with her when she started her own business. By leveraging her market intelligence, Ramona is able to do business with major corporations in several countries.*

## Partnering with Big Businesses

Increased risks, global competition, new technology, and the demand for faster cycle times have created a climate in which businesses are partnering more than ever. However, joint ventures and partnerships have been used for a long time by entrepreneurs eager to expand their businesses or enter new markets. Other reasons small businesses partner include:

- Gaining access to new technology or expertise
- Broadening their geographic scope
- Achieving economies of scale
- Building synergy with complementary skills, products, or processes
- Increasing sales
- Side-stepping or complying with trade regulations
- Pooling costs and performing innovative joint research
- Learning new things from larger partners

A **joint venture** is a business entity composed of two or more active business partners. These are also called **strategic alliances** or **partnering agreements**, and can involve a wide variety of business, nonprofit, or governmental organizations.

When considering a partnering agreement with a larger business, the first stop should be your attorney's office. The key to a successful agreement is understanding what each side wants, needs, and brings to the partnership. Know what your choices are, and tally the costs and benefits of each (financial as well as strategic, including competitive risks and benefits) before you enter any agreement. Also crucial for a successful partnership is a good fit between each party's personality and business culture.

If you have a product or service big business wants, it may come to you. Big business wants quality, professionalism and reliable relationships with their partners. Offering these things is the way to compete successfully for contracts with big businesses.

## Conclusion

If you decide it is time to go after government and big business contracts, prepare to do things differently. These large organizations have their own way of doing things, so there will be more paperwork and bigger challenges. The key to a successful business relationship is to lead with those characteristics that give you a competitive advantage: clear focus, speed, teamwork, and individualized customer service.

# Chapter 45
# PURCHASING, WAREHOUSING, AND INVENTORY MANAGEMENT

*About This Chapter:*
- *The purchasing process*
- *What is a contract?*
- *Quality control*
- *Planning your warehouse*
- *Inventory management*
- *Cost control and performance audits*
- *The power of information technology*

## Introduction

**Purchasing** is a systematic process by means of which businesses buy the raw materials and components that they use to manufacture their products and run their offices. The goal of a good purchasing strategy is to get the right quantity of a high-quality product, at the right time, and with the right level of service. This process is crucial to your success, because careless purchasing can result in problems—such as late delivery or shoddy materials—that affect your company image, production turnaround, and customer satisfaction.

With the advent of information technology, it is easier than ever to track costs, lower the price of your product, and increase your competitiveness. The result? Businesses of all sizes have realized that the total cost of materials goes far beyond the initial price tag, and purchasing has become a much higher priority. Closely allied to purchasing are the concepts of **expediting** and **quality control**, which assure that products and processes run smoothly and efficiently, and result in a high-quality end product.

In this chapter, we'll also discuss the issues involved in creating organized, efficient **inventory management** and **warehousing** systems.

## The Purchasing Process

What can you do to make sure that you get the best deal? It takes more than a call to the company with the biggest ad in the yellow pages! You should develop a plan that takes into account each step in the purchasing cycle, including:

- Finding qualified suppliers
- Evaluating cost and quality
- Deciding what to produce yourself and what to contract out
- Ensuring prompt and proper delivery (expediting)
- Setting and measuring quality standards

- Controlling transport costs
- Understanding the Uniform Commercial Code

## The Operations Manual

In a large corporation, every department has its own standards and procedures, which are set down in a large manual that explains how to do things "by the book." (Perhaps the very reason that you have chosen to blaze a new trail is your dislike of this red tape. Does this mean that you can eliminate these procedures? Of course not! To run at maximum efficiency, your business requires a certain amount of paperwork and systems.)

Creating a purchasing manual allows you to track the activities that occur in and out of your business. Your manual should include information about:

- Generating materials requests
- Preparing a pre-qualified bidders list
- Evaluating bids
- Expediting/quality control activities
- Evaluating transportation alternatives
- Information technology

- Identifying prospective suppliers
- Soliciting bids
- Assigning purchase orders
- Controlling inventory
- Paying invoices
- Audit procedures

This process is represented in the following table:

### Simplified Purchasing Cycle

| Step | Initiator | Document | Receiver |
|------|-----------|----------|----------|
| 1. | Anyone in company who has authority to request materials | Materials Request | Warehousing Department |
| 2. | Warehousing Department | Purchasing Request | Purchasing Department |
| 3. | Purchasing Department | Bid Request | Suppliers |
| 4. | Suppliers | Bids | Purchasing Department |
| 5. | Purchasing Department | Purchase Order | Supplier |
| 6. | Expediting Department | Expediting Report | Purchasing Department |
| 7. | Quality Control Department | Quality Control Report | Purchasing Department |
| 8. | Supplier | Packing | Warehousing Department |
| 9. | Transport Company (Supplier) | Bill of Lading | Warehousing Department |
| 10. | Supplier | Invoice | Finance/Accounting Department |
| 11. | Finance/Accounting Department | Payment | Supplier |

This chart is far from complete, but it can serve as a guide to get you started. The purpose of creating your own purchasing manual is to tailor your operations to your needs.

## Evaluating Potential Suppliers As Partners

As Vince Lombardi once said, "Winning isn't everything—it's the only thing." Change that to, "Price isn't everything—it's the only thing," and you have the philosophy of many people in business. But price *isn't* everything, so it's wise to consider these additional factors when evaluating potential suppliers:

Can you communicate with your suppliers?

- Quality
- Service
- Technical/financial strength
- Reputation
- Quantity
- Cultural fit
- Location
- Communications

You need to know that your suppliers can meet or exceed your expectations once they have your purchase order. Visit their facilities and meet the people with whom you will be dealing. Find out how they do things, and evaluate their technical and financial capabilities against those of rival companies.

Another good reason to visit your suppliers is to see if they have a good cultural fit with your business. Do they believe in on-time delivery? Do they run a smooth operation? Is their plant clean, well ordered, and efficient? Most important of all, can you communicate with the owner and his or her management team? You should get answers to these questions before buying from a vendor.

## As Long As It's Quality

A vice president of a small manufacturing company discusses the issue of quality: "We don't compete with off-the-shelf goods that come a dime a dozen. We market our company on our ability to understand our customers' needs and build them a system that is second to none in quality. If that means buying another company's materials and incorporating them into our design, then that's what we do. Our aim is to provide the highest quality product, and we do this by utilizing good purchasing and quality control practices. It must be working, because over eighty percent of our customers come back!"

This company produces value-added components and relies on its vendors to provide the commodity-type (low-margin) items that make its system complete. Because the company has a relatively small plant, its core competencies lie in producing the more complex items; therefore, it subcontracts the less profitable components. The lesson? Specialize in what you do best, and invite other companies to do the rest, and you will get the most out of your company's resources.

### Prioritize!

Purchasing needs fall into four basic groups:

- Raw materials (items used in manufacturing)
- Disposables (daily usage or indirect materials)
- Fixed assets (equipment, trucks, desks, etc.)
- Out-of-ordering (specialty items)

You should set up a purchasing system that prioritizes these categories as they relate to your business. As your business grows, this system will become more and more important.

## What is a Contract?

A contract is an agreement that outlines the promises made by your company and those with whom you do business. To make a contract legally binding, there must be:

- An offer
- An acceptance
- An exchange of value
- Execution by an individual with legal authority

Meeting these requirements reduces the headaches involved in purchasing. By putting everything down in writing, you and your vendors are literally on the same page.

There are many different kinds of contracts. For our purposes, we can classify them as follows:

- Prime contracts
- Employee contracts
- Subcontracts
- Purchase contracts
- Management contracts
- Leases
- Purchase orders

Purchase contracts, purchase orders, and subcontracts are of primary importance to your purchasing activities, and thus are defined here:

- **Purchase orders.** This is a buyer's acceptance of a seller's offer to perform work for a stated price. When the buyer agrees to the terms, the purchase order becomes a valid contract. If the buyer changes any of the terms, the purchase order becomes the buyer's counteroffer to the seller's proposal, and becomes binding only if the seller accepts the counteroffer. Here is an example of a purchase order:

| Purchase Order | | No. | |
|---|---|---|---|
| | | Date | |
| | | Page | |
| | | Requisition No. | |

| Acting as Agent for (Insert name of client) (Address) To: | Ship To: |
|---|---|

| Item No. | Quantity | Description | Code or Equip. No. | Unit Price | Cost |
|---|---|---|---|---|---|
| | | | | | |
| | | | | | |
| | | | | | |
| | | | | | |

| Confirming Order Placed With: | Total Value | $ |
|---|---|---|

| Cost Code | Inspection Required o YES    o NO | Payment Terms | |
|---|---|---|---|
| Invoice Instructions Send    # | Copies of Your Invoice with Original Bill of Lading | Shipper | Origin |
| To: | | Ship Via | Weight |
| | | Shipping Terms | |
| | | Promised Shipment | |
| | | By | Phone |
| | | Title | |

- **Purchase contracts.** This is an agreement between a buyer and a seller to provide goods or services for a price. A purchase contract differs from a purchase order in that it originates from the seller. It is used for purchases that are complex and of high value.
- **Subcontracts.** A subcontract is a legal agreement in which you, acting as the prime contractor, enter into a contract with a subcontractor who will help you perform part of a project. The subcontractor's legal obligations are only to you—the prime contractor—and not to your customer. There are two types of subcontracts: those for materials and those for services. In some cases—such as engineering and production of components—a subcontract may involve both. A typical services subcontract is displayed on the following page.

| SUBCONTRACTOR | SUBCONTRACT |
|---|---|
| ADDRESS | |
| | REGISTER NO. |
| CONTACT | EFFECTIVE DATE |
| TELEPHONE | SUBCONTRACT NO. |
| LOCATION OF WORK | ISSUING OFFICE |

THIS SUBCONTRACT is entered into as of the ___ day of ___ ,20 ___ , between ___ (Contractor) and the above named Subcontracor. All work specified below, which is a portion of the work and services to be performed by the Contractor for ___ (Owner), shall be performed by the Subcontractor in accordance with all the provisions of the Subcontract, consisting of the following documents:

1. WORK TO BE PERFORMED:  Except as specified elsewhere in this Subcontract, Subcontractor shall furnish all plant, labor, materials, supplies, equipment, transportation, supervision, technical, professional and other services, and shall perform all operations necessary and required satisfactorily:

2. COMPENSATION:   As full consideration for the satisfactory performance by Subcontractor of this Subcontract, Contracter shall pay to Subcontractor compensation in accordance with the prices set forth in and with the payment provision of this Subcontract.

| CONTRACTOR: | SUBCONTRACTOR: (Insert Name) |
|---|---|
| Authorized Signature | Authorized Signature |
| Print Name | Print Name |
| Print Title | Print Title |

## Rules of Conduct: The Commercial Code

The Uniform Commercial Code (UCC) is the current U.S. law of commerce.  It is a codification of common law, which coalesced over hundreds of years from customs used by merchants and traders to settle their disputes.  You should become familiar with it, as the UCC covers every purchase that you make.

A contract can be oral, written, or implied through the actions of two parties.  Be aware that when you send a purchase order to your vendor and your vendor complies with it, you have entered into a legal agreement.

Two terms that appear again and again in the UCC are "reasonable" and "in good faith." These concepts should guide you when you consider your legal obligations under a contract. If you have a problem with your order, you should make every effort to resolve it in good faith. Everyone makes mistakes, and sometimes it's better to take a small loss than to lose a valuable business partner over a petty dispute.

## Materials and Services

There is probably no such thing as a company that produces every raw material and component on its own, or provides all of its own services. However, many companies are original equipment manufacturers (OEMs), which buy materials and integrate them into a product that others use in their completed products. Note that some of these products are also finished goods (e.g., tires, which are used by car manufacturers as well as sold to the general public). One of your challenges is to determine which components would cost less if you bought them from a vendor instead of making them yourself. This process gives you yet another way of controlling costs.

You should also consider which services to contract out. Service contracts can include anything from engineering to janitorial services. You should accept bids for these services just as you would for raw materials or components. It's also important to keep tabs on service work, and conduct periodic checks on the quality and delivery of your service contractors.

## International Purchasing

If you are considering buying materials produced outside the United States, be careful! Ideally, you should visit foreign vendors just as you would domestic suppliers. You should definitely check references from their clients, both in their home country and the United States; the key issues here are quality and efficient delivery. Careful investigation will help you to judge foreign vendors on terms similar to those you use to evaluate domestic vendors.

Be sure to seek the advice of bankers (trade letters of credit), custom brokers (for bills of lading, government regulations), and others in this field.

## Expediting

Expediting means moving an order along quickly and efficiently. It is not enough to buy something and hope that it will show up! The goal of an expediting department is to ensure that suppliers follow through on their commitments regarding scheduled shipping dates. To achieve this, your expediting department should:

- Follow the instructions outlined in your purchasing manual
- Periodically report the status of materials that are due to be shipped
- Alert management to any mistakes or delays that could affect the order
- Visit supplier factories as needed to verify status of materials
- Identify and resolve problems that might delay final shipment
- Coordinate deliveries with other vendors involved in a given project
- Submit a final report on the vendor's performance

UCC is the U.S. law of commerce

From the moment your purchasing department receives a request for materials, the expediting function should kick into gear. This means involvement with the purchasing department on tendering bids, awarding purchase orders, and checking on the order well before its delivery date.

If you need an order to arrive more quickly than originally planned, regular dialogue with your suppliers can make it easier for them to make an early delivery. If you call your vendors only when an order arrives late, they will not be as aware of your evolving needs.

At first, the purchasing and expediting group may comprise only one employee. However, as your business grows, it pays to divide this activity into two separate functional areas.

## Quality Control

In the context of purchasing, quality control refers to checking the quality of an order prior to delivery. It is particularly necessary when your products are specially ordered or highly engineered (such as fixed assets or out-of-order, custom-made goods). Quality control should start before a purchase order is issued, and continue with periodic checks to ensure that the materials in question meet specifications.

Your quality control department should:

- Follow the instructions outlined in your purchasing manual
- Visit supplier factories as required to verify materials specifications
- Identify and resolve specifications problems that affect product quality
- Alert management to any mistakes in design or production
- Submit a final report on the vendor's performance

As noted above, quality control procedures include visits to your vendor to check on specifications. For example, if your vendor is producing valves that will be used under hydrostatic pressure by your customer, you should make sure that the valves' dimensions, thickness, and strength meet your contractual specifications. If the valves were not sufficiently thick to withstand the pressure, the entire system your client ordered would be subject to failure! These activities should be conducted on a periodic basis well before the delivery date. This way, while your vendor is in the process of producing and filling your order, you can catch mistakes before they become more costly for you or your supplier to fix.

## Planning Your Warehouse

What would your dream warehouse look like? Would it span three football fields, have an automatic retrieval system, and be so squeaky clean that you could not find a speck of dust in the place? Where would you put it? Perhaps right next to your largest customer, so that you could deliver your product by sending it down a chute? This is a fantasy for some, but there really are facilities like this in the United States!

In determining your warehousing strategy, should you merely consider your material and delivery needs and weigh these against your available storage space? Of course you should take this into account, but you might also consider options located across your distribution network (i.e., your vendors, wholesalers, distributors, retailers, and customers). Any or all of these entities may have warehousing capability, and because of their size or geographic location, they may be able to lease space cheaper than you can. When evaluating prospective suppliers, wholesalers, and distributors, why not pay heed to their warehousing capabilities in order to determine if they can help lower your costs?

*Gayle Goodman owns a small manufacturing company in the Midwest. She recently performed a survey of prospective distributors. Some of the companies she evaluated were strictly distributors, some were also manufacturers, and some were brokers. Among the many criteria she considered was warehousing capability. Gayle was interested in increasing sales volume, but she was already operating at full capacity and had to use her warehouse for materials rather than for finished goods. Furthermore, she had determined that storage was not one of her business's core competencies. Therefore, she wanted to find distributors who would hold her product. Gayle visited the companies she'd surveyed, and selected four with whom she formed partnerships. All four had adequate warehouse space and computerized inventory systems.*

There are two approaches that you can use when determining your warehousing needs: internal or public warehousing. Internal warehousing allows you much greater control over your inventory, but requires you to incur greater fixed costs. Public (or rented) warehousing offers less control, but involves significant cost benefits in that there is no capital investment required in land or the warehouse itself. If you are in an area with very efficient and dependable transportation, public warehousing is a viable option.

Warehousing can be divided into two types: manufacturing and storage. The former is a place to keep raw materials and work-in-process; the latter is used to store finished goods until they are ready to be shipped. You can expand your manufacturing warehouse capabilities by linking with vendors who will hold components for you until you need them. Your storage warehouse capabilities can be increased by transferring finished goods to wholesalers, distributors, and customers. Either way, your goal is to develop partnerships that lower your carrying costs, allowing you to focus on your core competencies.

### Documents
Documentation is a very important part of the warehousing and inventory control process. Requisition and purchase order forms for materials and services are provided in Exhibits 1 and 2.

*Exhibit 1: Purchase Order*

| Requisition, Purchase Order and Blanket Order Release | | Requisition No. | | |
|---|---|---|---|---|
| | | Date | | |
| Dept. | Requested By | To Be Used For | | Required By |
| Acct. No. | Cost Center No. | | Approp. No. | Deliver Att. of |
| Special Instructions | | | | Approved By |
| Quantity | Part No. | Description | | Unit Price |
| | | | | |
| Vendor Name and Address | | Taxable o | Exempt o | Our Purchase Order Number |
| | | Confirming to | Date | |
| | | Terms and Conditions | | |
| | | FOB | | |
| | | Payment Disc | | |
| | | Other | | |
| For Our Use Only Vendor Performance on this Order | | Buyer Authorization | | |
| Quality | Prices & Terms | (Must be signed to be valid) | | |
| o Good | o As on Order | | | |
| o Rejected | o Different | | | |
| Delivery o As Requested o Late o Unauth. Split | Actual Lead Time in Weeks | | | |

*Exhibit 2: Requisition Order*

| Service Industry Requisition and Purchase Order | | | No. | |
|---|---|---|---|---|

| Date | ○ Stock | ○ Nonstock- Forms Control | ○ Nonstock- Purchasing |
|---|---|---|---|

| Responsibility Center No. | Requested by | Approved by (over $1,000) |
|---|---|---|
| | Approved by | Approved by (over $5,000) |

| Charge to: | Deliver to: |
|---|---|

| Quantity Requested | Quantity Issued | Unit of Issue | Stock or Form Number | Description (in detail) | Unit Price | Total Price |
|---|---|---|---|---|---|---|
| | | | | | | |

| Date | Filled By | Remarks |
|---|---|---|

| Vendor Name and Address | TAXABLE ○ | EXEMPT ○ | OUR PURCHASE ORDER NUMBER |
|---|---|---|---|
| | Vendor No. | | |
| | Confirming to | | Date |
| | Terms and FOB | | Payment Disc. |
| | Conditions Other | | |
| | Buyer Authorization: | | |
| | (Must be signed to be valid) | | |

Vendor Please Note: Unless you provide us written expressed exception to the contents of this order, we assume you agree and will pay your invoice accordingly.

## Big or Small, Here or There

A warehouse can range in size from a small back room to a huge distribution complex. When choosing a location for your own warehouse, or recruiting businesses with warehousing capabilities of their own, try to strike a balance between the size and the location of the warehouse. Do you want one large warehouse in each market that you serve, or do you want many small facilities? Remember: You want to sell your product on price and delivery terms that are equal throughout your market; whatever warehouse size and location you choose, your goal is to provide the best delivery and service to your customer.

Your warehouse location may depend on what you produce

Where should you locate your warehouse(s)? This depends on the following factors:

- The size of your products
- How much you sell in a given period of time
- The location of your office
- The location of major suppliers
- The location of your customers
- The transportation available to you
- The business cycle for your products
- Personal preference

If your product is very complex or large, it's best to locate your warehousing facility close to your materials sources. In this case, relatively few items leave your facility, so the benefits of being close to multiple sources outweigh the cost of faster transport. You might think about having an efficient and dependable means of transportation at your disposal, so that you do not compromise delivery to your customers.

If you sell large quantities of your product or it is relatively small, it would be wise to locate the warehouse nearer your market. In this scenario, your turnover is higher, so the benefits of faster delivery outweigh the cost of bringing raw materials to your plant. If you determine that your customers' needs outweigh your need to have materials close to you, a warehouse close to your end-users would make sense.

## The Perfect Warehouse

The condition of your plant is a reflection of how you do business. Your warehouse plan should make space for everything that goes on inside your building. This includes space for materials storage as well as material handling equipment.

Your location, design, and orientation can all aid you in maintaining a well-ordered warehouse. Does your warehouse need rail car access? How large will receiving and storage areas be? Will it have one story or two? By anticipating your physical warehousing requirements in advance, you can avoid problems that might prevent you from keeping your warehouse in order.

You should keep a path clear to all of your materials and finished goods, so that you can access them at a moment's notice. In addition, schedule regular maintenance for your material handling equipment so that you will have fewer breakdowns.

To run a warehouse smoothly, your employees need to know how to use the inventory control system. If your employees are well trained, they will be the strongest link in your system!

It's also a good idea to look into various security systems; keyless entry systems, video monitors, and related items can help prevent theft. Likewise, your information system can keep track of inventory, and identify discrepancies and theft.

## Product Life

The internal environment is one more factor that you must consider when you plan your warehouse. Products differ in their resistance to the elements. For example, if you manufacture aerosol-based goods or food products, you must be conscious of temperature. You must certainly take humidity into account if you locate your warehouse on the Gulf Coast. And what about the cold in Montana or Minnesota? Or the rain in Oregon or Washington? If you do not take these factors into account, you could end up with damaged or spoiled goods!

———————◆———————

*Warehousing in Phoenix*

*Let's suppose you intend to open a warehouse in Phoenix, Arizona. The hot, dry desert climate is ideal for storing some types of goods, and disastrous for others. Obviously, if your product requires temperature control, you will have to make sure that your warehouse has an air-conditioning system. Another consideration is something that is found in every desert climate: dust. If your products must be stored in a high-purity environment, you might be forced to rent a relatively modern (i.e., more expensive) building, because older buildings in the Phoenix area are usually not built to withstand the elements. In fact, many structures in Phoenix still use a "swamp cooler" to beat the heat of summer. The lack of weatherproofing also results in cracks along doors and window frames, so when the hot desert winds come rolling across the state, you can be sure that dust will penetrate the building! As you can see, maintaining the proper temperature and air purity is not always easy when operating a warehouse among the cactus. What problems will you face in your location?*

———————◆———————

## Breakage

You cannot entirely avoid breakage, but you can plan for these incidents and resolve them efficiently. What should you do when you experience inventory damage? Consider the following points:

- **Recovery systems.** Try to refabricate damaged items. If the damage is minimal, can you repackage or resurface your product? If a finished product is damaged beyond repair, can you recycle some of the parts and run them back through your production line? If possible, incorporate into your system a way to reprocess damaged goods, or at least obtain salvage value.

- **Inspection.** "Who's to blame?" is the first question asked when someone discovers damaged goods. Blame aside, you should have your staff check for breakage when deliveries arrive, when goods move into and out of your warehouse, and throughout the production cycle. Teach employees that inspection and damage avoidance are an important part of the job.

- **Reconciliation with suppliers or transporters.** What can you do when goods are damaged in transit from your supplier? Proper documentation is essential to obtaining credit or remuneration for the damages. Emphasize this point with your receiving department as a part of quality control.

## Inventory Management

When setting up an inventory control system, you should first consider what inventory you will need—and what problems might occur—during the various phases of your production process. You might plan your inventory strategy like this:

- Anticipate inventory needs based on market expectations
- Determine the company's goals, and develop an inventory policy consistent with those goals
- Train employees to follow guidelines
- Set up an information system that links all of your departments
- Compare inventory levels with actual materials usage

### How Much Inventory Do You Need?

When considering your inventory needs, how can you be sure that you do not stock too much or too little of a particular material? The methods used to solve this problem range from the traditional **economic order quantity (EOQ)** to the most recent theory on inventory management, **just-in-time delivery (JIT)**. The trade-offs in cost, time, and customer service are key factors in your decision to maintain certain inventory levels. To begin with, consider the following criteria:

- Inventory investment
- Material needs
- The effect of inventory practices on profits
- Your competitor's cycle times
- Inventory control through an integrated information system
- Customer service
- Carrying costs

Here is a sample of an inventory control sheet:

| | | | | | | | | | | |
|---|---|---|---|---|---|---|---|---|---|---|
| | | | | | | | | | | |

**Inventory Control Sheet**

| Inventory Date | | | | | | Page No. | | | | |
| Area/Storage Location | | | | | | Type Inventory | | | | |
| Commodity Description | | | | | | Commodity Code No. | | | | |

| Part Number | Part Descrip. | Unit of Measure | Physical Count Quantity | Book Balance Quantity | Reason for Difference Code | Inventory ABC Class | Annual Usage | Usual Reorder Quantity | Usual Safety Stock | Unit Cost |
|---|---|---|---|---|---|---|---|---|---|---|
| | | | | | | | | | | |
| | | | | | | | | | | |
| | | | | | | | | | | |
| | | | | | | | | | | |
| | | | | | | | | | | |
| | | | | | | | | | | |
| | | | | | | | | | | |

*Rosann Brummell runs a company that produces golf clubs. She estimates that it costs her $50.00 to place an order. Her expected demand for the year is 2,000 units, and she has determined that her cost per unit will be $10.00. She has calculated that her carrying cost is equal to 20 percent of the unit cost. By plugging each of these values into the formula, she finds her EOQ:*

*Rosann's economic order quantity is 316 units, which means that she should order 316 units at a time. To calculate your range of possible economic order volumes, set up a matrix with a range of **expected annual demand** on the x-axis, and a range of **unit costs** on the y-axis. By manipulating carrying cost and ordering cost variables, you arrive at a dynamic picture of your economic order possibilities. You can then choose which order quantity best fits the expected demand and costs for each material you need.*

EOQ = economic order

quantity

The EOQ method uses inventory averaging to give you an initial inventory level. This should satisfy your inventory needs in the majority of production situations. However, it does not provide latitude during periods in which you have exceptionally high or low

The old and the new:
EOQ and JIT

Just-in-Time: just more savings!

demand. To prevent back orders and stockouts, consider carrying a safety stock; this is a buffer of raw materials that you continually carry in case the demand for your product spikes upward unexpectedly. To determine your safety stock for a given product, estimate your best-case sales scenario and hold extra inventory to use in that situation.

The EOQ method also gives you a way to place an order between your estimated upper and lower inventory requirements for a given time period. Once you have decided on these levels, you can set reorder points that tell you when to place your next order for each material, thereby avoiding over- or under-ordering.

## Just-in-Time Delivery

Another inventory management philosophy—one that has revolutionized inventory practices in the past decade—is just-in-time delivery. As mentioned earlier in this chapter, a JIT delivery system is one in which raw materials are delivered as needed. This results in little or no inventory being held, as the goods are immediately incorporated into the production process. If you operate in an area that is rich in suppliers and efficient transportation, this might be the best way for you to manage your inventory.

Large American corporations such as Motorola now have comprehensive JIT programs that extend upward to their vendors. They have formulated a term called "preferred vendor status," which means that their vendors subscribe to rigorous quality, production, and delivery standards. They are expected to deliver goods with zero defects, in the right quantities, and at the right time. Some companies that use a JIT system receive shipments on a daily or even hourly basis!

You might say, "That sounds great for major companies, but I could never keep up with the demands JIT would make on my business." It is true that JIT delivery requires you to be on the ball and keep your mistakes to a minimum. However, with proper materials planning—and electronic links to your customers and suppliers—it can be done. At a minimum, you might strive to emulate this system by reducing the time that your materials sit in your warehouse, thereby minimizing carrying costs.

The JIT delivery system requires the use of smaller warehouses, with more frequent deliveries and smaller order sizes. And efficient transportation becomes even more important under the JIT system. Also, your inventory management system is critical in giving you up-to-the-minute information on customer orders.

*Control costs by keeping inventory levels to a minimum*

If you make it your goal to subscribe to the JIT philosophy, your vendors will continually be holding inventory for you. These materials and components are, in essence, your work-in-process, and are stored by your vendors until you give them the go-ahead to deliver it.

---

*A Multi-Million Dollar Mistake*

*Chemical facilities are among the most complex production systems in the world. Depending on their size and purpose, they can take years to build and can require dozens of subcontractors. One such facility located on the Gulf Coast was forced to shut down in the late 1990s because of faulty valves. Upon inspection, it was found that the failed parts came from a third party—a foreign supplier—who had not been approved by the master contractor. The subcontractor who purchased these valves cost everyone from the contractor to the client millions of dollars in lost performance incentives, refitting expenses, and lost product revenue. By cutting corners with an unfamiliar product, the subcontractor gained in the short run, but lost big in the long term; this mistake cost the firm its reputation and any hope for future business. The foreign vendor who supplied the faulty parts lost a foothold in the American market. The chemical company not only*

*Find a suitable environment for your product*

*lost revenue, but also lost customers due to late delivery. All of these problems could have been avoided if purchasing, expediting, and quality control procedures had been put in place and followed.*

---

# Cost Control and Performance Audits

Cost and performance auditing is the process of evaluating and improving your company's efficiency. There are two kinds of audits: internal (by your accountant), and external (through a public accounting firm). The advantage of an internal audit is that it costs less to perform. An external audit is relatively expensive, but often identifies problems that your own staff might not.

Reduce costs and pass the savings on to your customers

A comprehensive audit involves looking into every aspect of your organization for possible areas of cost cutting and control. Through this process, you can find out whether materials orders are being matched with requests, or if one of your employees might be stealing from you.

Have you ever heard of an audit that didn't find anything wrong? Of course not! That's why this can be an intimidating process. But that shouldn't stop you from taking advantage of this valuable tool. Audits that are performed correctly can reveal everything from small errors, to gross inefficiency, to fraud.

## Quantifying and Controlling Costs

Your plant is up and running, and your product is selling like hotcakes—you can relax, right? Actually, this is the perfect time to root out problems in your system! This is particularly true with inventory management. You can improve your bottom line by examining where waste occurs. In some cases, you might be running at maximum efficiency with your own resources, but your competitors might be out cutting deals with suppliers and customers to hold manufacturing and finished goods inventory for them. This is no time to miss the boat! You might consider examining your total distribution system—from your vendors to your plant to your customer—for ways to minimize the amount of inventory that you hold. By doing this, you can concentrate your efforts on producing the best product possible, and let the transportation experts alleviate your warehousing load by providing a smooth path from your vendors to your customers.

Here are some questions to ask yourself: What is the optimum size of your warehouse? Do you need one at all, or can you get by with a simple receiving area? Can your suppliers provide you with varying order quantities on an as-needed basis? Your total costs go down as warehouse size decreases. In fact, if you convert some of that warehouse space into additional production capacity, you might increase your turnover and your profits. And by ordering on an as-needed (JIT) basis, you will reduce your carrying costs—another plus. Critical to this process is an efficient and dependable transport company that is willing to carry smaller loads more frequently. On the customer delivery side, the same holds true: you must be able to ship your product out the door soon after it is packaged and ready to go.

By helping you focus on what you do best, inventory management lets you reduce costs and pass the savings on to your customers, so nobody will be happier than your customers if you make this work!

## The Power of Information Technology

Set as one of your goals the immediate establishment of a complete information system that ties together all of the ideas discussed in this chapter. Information technology has evolved to the point where you can buy very powerful hardware and off-the-shelf software at an affordable price. The object is to integrate your purchasing manual with your information technology system. This information system generates valuable data, facilitating better management practices.

Information systems also sustain lines of communication between different departments in your company. As such, they provide a paper trail of your activities. Growth necessitates periodically evaluating your purchasing, expediting, and quality control activities to improve efficiency and control costs.

## Conclusion

As we have shown in this chapter, purchasing, warehousing, expediting, and quality control and inventory management are critical to the success of your business. Your company may not have as much in-house warehousing capability as its larger competitors, but by developing business partnerships with your vendors and customers, you can seize the opportunity to use their warehousing space, thus lowering costs. This means ordering in smaller lots on a more frequent basis and shipping your finished goods inventory soon after it comes off the line. This philosophy is called just-in-time delivery: we call it just plain common sense! So modernize your purchasing procedures, shrink your inventory, increase your turnover, and minimize your warehousing costs. Your competition will wonder how you do it!

## Chapter 46
# CONGRATULATIONS AND BON VOYAGE!

*About This Chapter:*
- *The nature of profit*
- *The journey ahead*

As an entrepreneur, you are one of the folk heroes of business. You create jobs, launch innovative products, and spark economic growth in your community. You turn risks into opportunities, fueling a more productive economy.

Having completed this course, you deserve a hearty pat on the back for a job well done. You have examined your business concept, confronted challenges, and planned for future growth. You have developed your skills and knowledge, and joined thousands of other entrepreneurs whose dynamic leadership leads to national economic growth and community vitality.

## The Nature of Profit

Entrepreneurs are free from the traditional limits of standard pay for standard work; they invent their work, their product, and the way they do business. But all the same, entrepreneurs are bound by the laws of profitability, which state that a business must generate more money than it spends.

Cash left after all expenses have been paid is profit, which can be allocated to the owner(s), or reinvested to help grow the business.

Your business earnings must compensate you for the risks you have taken, and for the time, energy, and personal savings you invested in the business. But such compensation is not the only reward of being an entrepreneur. Independence, creative freedom, and the fun of growing a business offset the long hours, risks, and uncertainties that entrepreneurs face.

### Customer Orientation

Any profit generated by your business is the result of satisfying your customers' needs. How much will people pay for a product or service that meets their needs? That depends on the reliability, innovation, and amount of convenience your product or service delivers.

To satisfy your customers, you need to understand them thoroughly. In short, your business must fit your customer like a glove. We think this customer orientation is essential to success.

"There is only one success—to be able to spend your life in your own way."
—Christopher Morley

## Learning and Entrepreneurship Go Hand in Hand

Success doesn't come simply from knowing what your personal strengths are. It also comes from understanding and overcoming your weaknesses. Entrepreneurship is a continuous cycle of questioning, analyzing, and learning. Did you achieve your objectives last time around? What could you have done better? Who might have been able to help you? What will you do next time to improve?

You needn't become an expert in every area of business management, but you do need to understand enough about each element of your business that you can ask the right questions to ensure that business tasks are being done well.

You should never ignore areas of your business that intimidate or confuse you. Each aspect of business can be easily managed when it is broken down into smaller parts. Taking the time to ask questions and seek help makes every problem soluble. Once you have done this, you can make choices about allocating responsibility, resources, and if need be, engaging the services of experts. You should not declare any area of your business "off limits" to careful scrutiny.

In the course of growing your business, you will continually upgrade your knowledge and improve your skills. Can you imagine anything better than overcoming challenges, learning new things, and increasing the profitability of your business?

Continuous learning is critical to entrepreneurial success

## Find a Partner, Create a Team

Committing yourself to acquiring new skills doesn't mean that you have to do everything yourself. Collaboration is an essential ingredient of creativity and efficiency. When you feel overwhelmed by the challenges you face, the insight and support of others will fuel you to continue onward and upward. Surrounding yourself with people who have complementary skills and different points of view will save time, increase the credibility of your business, and improve the decisions you make. In short, by creating a pool of talent your business can draw on (through formal partnerships, team building, or informal mentoring arrangements), you increase the likelihood that your business will continue to succeed.

## The Impact of Technology

Data management and communication tools are becoming more user-friendly and affordable. Many software applications for communications, word processing, database management, graphics, presentation, and networking are pre-packaged to help you solve your business problems. Training in these systems is readily available in most communities. If you have not yet availed yourself of these powerful business tools, now is the time to start!

## Ethical Issues

Business ethics are principles of right and wrong that go beyond questions of mere legality. Fair-minded entrepreneurs are respectful of their obligations to customers, employees, suppliers, investors, and their community. This sense of integrity and honesty must inform the day-to-day operation of your business. The reasons are simple: Ethical business decisions engender the loyalty and respect of your customers, employees, and suppliers; they protect you from potentially disastrous legal problems; and they give you an enormous competitive advantage!

## Community Involvement

No business operates in a vacuum. You are part of the community in which you work; your current and future customers, suppliers, employers, and investors are also part of your community. When you give something back to your community, you gain the economic and personal benefits such actions produce, and your community reaps the benefits that only entrepreneurs can bring to the table.

## The Beauty of the Business Plan

At the risk of repeating ourselves, researching and writing a thorough business plan is the most valuable thing an entrepreneur can do.

A business plan should be compelling, easy to read, and informative for anyone interested in financing, supplying, or working with or for your business. The ideal business plan is both an inspirational narrative and a blueprint.

For growing businesses, the business plan is particularly important. You are working to serve a larger pool of customers, maintain your quality, and juggle resources and time; a business plan controls and guides these efforts. It is a benchmark against which you can gauge your progress and your effectiveness.

*Writing a business plan is the most important thing an entrepreneur can do*

## Many Paths to Follow

We hope that in the process of preparing your business plan, you've gleaned some answers to your most pressing questions. Has your business achieved its original objectives? Has your mission changed? Have the needs of your customers changed? Are there weaknesses in your business's management?

As you can see, there are many paths you might take from here. We hope that participating in NxLeveL has given you a better understanding of the basics of marketing, financing, producing, and planning for growth.

## Welcome to the NxLeveL™ Training Network

The NxLeveL™ Program for Entrepreneurs is a broad, national network of kindred spirits and fellow innovators. To date, thousands of people have emerged from the NxLeveL Programs. These entrepreneurs have completed business plans and are ready to take the next step in growing their businesses.

The most valuable asset NxLeveL™ gives its participants is access to other people who have participated in and taught programs; their combined business and life experiences constitute a golden resource. By sharing ideas and supporting one another, entrepreneurs learn from each others' mistakes and explore new ways to achieve their goals. They also enjoy the comfort of knowing that others have experienced similar challenges, risks, and rewards.

You can participate in this network by visiting the Web site maintained by the NxLeveL™ Training Network, and by building on the relationships you formed with your fellow class participants. Furthermore, local trade associations, chambers of commerce, and Small Business Development Centers sponsor many events for small businesses. Attend them, contribute to them, and benefit from them!

We are proud to welcome you into the NxLeveL™ network of entrepreneurs, and look forward to your contribution to our success stories and innovative entrepreneurial solutions!

## The Journey Ahead

You are embarking on a journey into the world of entrepreneurship, where opportunities and rewards are as numerous as the risks and challenges you'll encounter. On this journey, initiative, creativity, and ingenuity triumph. Being a successful entrepreneur begins with finding your unique strengths and interests. Once you've done this, you must use them to your best advantage, by building your business around them. When you love what you do, you work harder, with more creativity and efficiency; this gives you a powerful competitive advantage.

Having taken the time and expended the energy to study the basics of entrepreneurship, you now have more tools with which to build your business and ensure the chances of its success and profitability.

The entrepreneurial vision is a powerful force; it can transform the quality of your life, the goals you achieve, and the legacy you leave your family and community. When you combine this vision with your expanding knowledge of business, your entrepreneurial journey becomes fun, fulfilling, and profitable.

# PART XIII
## APPENDIX

# GLOSSARY OF TERMS

*The business world is filled with specialized terms. Understanding the business vocabulary will enables you to understand entrepreneurial concepts, and to feel less threatened by the language in business discussions.*

*This section makes it easy to look up common business terms and defines acronyms frequently used in business.*

**accounts payable.** Money owed for inventory, supplies, and other expenses.

**accounts receivable.** Money owed to a business by customers.

**accrual basis.** A method of accounting in which revenues are recorded when earned and expenses are recorded when incurred, no matter when cash changes hands.

**active investment.** An investment in which one is actively involved in earning money, such as owning and operating a business.

**aging report.** A list of accounts receivable according to the length of time the unpaid balance has been owed. Aging allows businesses to identify slow-paying customers, manage collections, and evaluate credit policies.

**amortization.** The process of liquidating a cost over a long period of time (e.g., a home mortgage) by periodically making a payment that reduces the principal amount.

**arbitration.** A system administered by the court system to resolve disputes; it is increasingly used instead of litigation.

**articles of incorporation.** A document filed with a state's Department of Commerce stating why a corporation is being formed and what type of business it conducts; and serving to register the corporate name.

**asset valuation.** A method of business valuation that calculates the total assets of the business (building, property, machinery, etc.) to arrive at a value for the business.

**assets.** Any items of value owned by a business; items on the balance sheet that reflect value owned including cash, accounts receivable, notes receivable, property, and property rights.

**assumed business name.** The name under which a business operates. Most states provide for registration of assumed business names, which protects the name from misuse by others. Also known as a "fictitious" or "trade" name.

**balance sheet.** An itemized report listing assets, liabilities, and owner's equity at a given point in time.

**bid pricing.** Pricing used by organizational buyers in which requests for proposals invite interested sellers to bid on a set of specifications.

**bill of lading.** A shipping contract that outlines the terms of a shipping agreement and the means by which goods will be shipped.

**blue sky law.** A law regulating the sale of securities, real estate, etc., especially designed to prevent the promotion of fraudulent stocks.

**boilerplate.** The detailed standard wording of a contract. Also known as "fine print" or "standard clauses."

**brand.** A name or symbol that represents a product.

**brand image.** The customer's impression of a brand.

**break-even analysis.** Identifies the point at which total revenue equals total costs and profits are zero.

**break-even point.** The sales level at which neither a profit is earned nor a loss incurred. The basic break-even formula is: S (break-even level of sales) = FC (fixed costs) + VC (variable costs). Analyzing the break-even point helps to predict the effects of changing costs or sales levels on income.

**breakdown forecasting.** Looking at one's largest population of customers, then breaking that group down by qualifying criteria such as age, income, and preferences to define the level of sales expected from target customers.

**brokers.** Professional intermediaries who bring buyers and sellers together. Brokers do not have formal or lasting relationships with either party, and are often used by businesses that need not maintain a full-time sales force.

**buildup forecasting.** An estimate of the size of each market segment; the estimates are added to arrive at a sales forecast.

**business trust.** An unincorporated association organized to conduct business for profit. It is operated by a board of trustees for the benefit of certificate holders.

**buy/sell agreement.** A contract that sets forth the terms and conditions by which associates in a business can buy out other associates.

**bylaws.** An agreement among shareholders of a corporation for the structure of the business. Bylaws typically set forth provisions for the annual meeting, size and manner of election of the board of directors, number and duties of the officers, voting requirements for merger, and similar matters.

**capital stock.** The total stock authorized or issued by a corporation.

**capital.** Cash and/or material assets (e.g., tools, property, and equipment) owned by or used in a business.

**carrying costs.** The cost of tying up money by holding inventory, plus additional costs like taxes and insurance on inventory.

**cash and carry wholesalers.** Wholesalers that sell from warehouse facilities. Buyers pay cash and transport their own merchandise.

**cash basis.** A method of recording income and expenses in which each item is entered when received or paid.

**cash discount.** A discount given to buyers who pay bills within a specified time.

**cash flow.** The movement of cash into and out of a business.

**cash flow projection.** A financial planning document used to predict cash flow.

**cash receipts.** Cash generated from sales, accounts receivable, and loans.

**certified public accountant (CPA).** An accountant certified by a state examining board as having fulfilled the requirements of state law to be a public accountant.

**CFR.** See **Code of Federal Regulations**.

**channel partners.** Businesses that act as intermediaries to help other businesses buy, sell, assemble, store, and display products.

**channel(s) of distribution.** See **distribution channel**.

**chart of accounts.** A document listing the ID numbers of each account.

**civil law.** The body of laws regulating ordinary private matters, as distinct from laws regulating criminal, political, or military matters.

**closely held business.** A business owned by a small number of persons (usually under 25) whose interests in the business (shares, stock, partnership certificate, LLC memberships) are not publicly traded.

**Code of Federal Regulations (CFR).** The general and permanent rules of the federal government as published in the Federal Register.

**COGS.** See **cost of goods sold.**

**collateral.** Assets pledged to a lender to secure or support a loan.

**common law.** Law created through judicial application of precedent.

**competitive analysis.** Measurement of a competitor's strengths and weaknesses.

**compound interest.** Interest earned on the principal and on previously accumulated interest.

**consumer database.** Demographic or financial information about individual consumers gathered from applications for credit, drivers' licenses, or telephone service records.

**consumer promotions.** Short-term sales promotions to consumers.

**continuous budget.** A budgeting technique in which twelve months are always shown, with a new month added constantly.

**cooperative advertising.** Advertising in which manufacturers and retailers pool their resources to promote both the product and the store. The manufacturer offers retailers an allowance to advertise the manufacturer's product, allowing retailers to include the name of their store.

**copyright.** The exclusive right to reproduce, sell, publish, or distribute literary or artistic work (i.e., works of authors, composers, and other artists).

**corporation.** A group of persons authorized by the state to function as a separate legal entity with privileges and liabilities distinct from those of its individual members.

**cost advantage.** A type of competitive advantage in which a business reduces costs below those of competitors, and is thus able to lower prices or channel savings into other areas.

**cost of goods sold (COGS).** Costs associated with the sale of a product or service, which may include materials, freight, direct labor, and overhead.

**cost-plus pricing.** A basic pricing method in which a business determines its costs, then adds a percentage to achieve a desired profit margin.

**cost-type contract.** A contract providing for payment to a contractor of allowable and reasonable cost plus a profit.

**CPA.** See **certified public accountant**.

**CPS.** See **current population survey**.

**criminal law.** Concerns the rights of society versus the actions of individuals.

**culture.** The beliefs, norms, values, and customs that define a business.

**current assets.** Cash or other items convertible to cash within one year, or items that will be used up by the business within one year (i.e., cash, inventory, short-term notes receivable, and accounts receivable).

**current liabilities.** Monetary obligations due to be paid within one year (e.g., accounts payable, wages payable, taxes payable, current portion of long-term debt, interest, and dividends payable).

**current population survey (CPS).** Monthly survey conducted by the Bureau of the Census. It provides estimates of the number of persons working, the number unemployed, and related employment data.

**current ratio.** Current assets divided by current liabilities, indicative of whether or not a business has sufficient current assets to meet its current debts. The higher the ratio, the more likely it is that a business will be able to meet its current obligations.

**customer orientation.** A primary focus on the needs of customers.

**dealer.** A distribution channel intermediary who is granted the exclusive right to sell a company's products in a franchise agreement.

**debt capital.** Business financing that normally requires periodic interest payments and repayment of the principal within a specified time.

**debt to equity ratio.** The relationship of creditors' money to owners' money in a business, indicating the extent to which a business is dependent upon borrowed funds.

**demographic data.** Statistical information on population characteristics, including age, income, occupation, marital status, education, and location.

**depreciation.** The portion of the cost of tangible operating assets (such as buildings or equipment) recorded as expense for the accounting period; results from spreading out the cost of long-lived assets over several years.

**direct labor.** For a manufacturer, labor costs that can be directly traced to the products.

**direct loans.** Loans made by the Small Business Administration directly to a small business.

**direct mail.** Presenting a product or service to the customer via mail without the use of middlemen.

**direct marketing.** Presenting promotional information to potential consumers via door-to-door selling, telemarketing, direct mail, catalogue, or the Internet; any presentation of a product or service directly to the consumer without the use of a middleman.

**direct materials.** For a manufacturer, those materials that become an integral part of a finished product.

**direct response.** Marketing that asks for an order and aims for instant and measurable results, allowing the consumer to consummate the sale without outside interaction.

**direct writer.** A type of insurance agent who represents only one insurance company.

**discretionary income.** Amount of spendable or savable income available after providing for basic necessities such as shelter, food, clothes.

**distribution channel.** A group of independent businesses composed of manufacturers, wholesalers, and retailers; it delivers what the customer wants, when and where they want it.

**dividend.** A share of profits paid to stockholders of a corporation.

**double taxation.** Taxation of corporate net income and stockholder dividends.

**dropshippers.** Wholesalers who take title to the merchandise but do not take physical possession. They obtain orders from wholesalers and retailers, and forward these orders to the manufacturer who sends the goods directly to the wholesaler or retailer.

**durable goods.** Products used over time (computers, CDs, dishwashers).

**duties.** Import taxes based on a given country's preset tariff rate.

**e-commerce.** The buying or selling of products, information, or services over the Internet.

**economies of scale.** A mass production concept: the more goods are produced with the same machinery and overhead, the lower the per unit cost of the goods.

**EIN.** See **Employer Identification Number.**

**Employer Identification Number (EIN).** An identifying number of a business entity, obtained from the IRS by filing application form SS-4.

**equity capital.** An investment received in exchange for partial business ownership. The investor's financial return comes from dividend payments, and from growth in the net worth of a business.

**equity.** The amount of the owner's investment in the business; what remains after total liabilities are subtracted from total assets; also called "net worth."

**estoppel.** A rule of law requiring that a party who leads another party into believing that a contract exists between them must perform as per the terms of that contract.

**expediting.** Moving orders quickly and efficiently by ensuring the supplier's commitment to a scheduled shipping date.

**expenses.** The outflow of assets by an entity in order to operate; expenses are subtracted from revenues to determine net income.

**factoring.** A method of financing in which a business sells its accounts receivable at a discount for cash.

**feasibility study.** Determines if a business opportunity is worth pursuing.

**Federal Insurance Contributions Act (FICA).** Legislation under which taxes are levied for the support of Social Security.

**FICA.** See **Federal Insurance Contributions Act.**

**financial intermediary.** A financial institution that acts as the intermediary between borrowers and lenders. Banks, savings and loan associations, finance companies, and venture capital companies are major financial intermediaries in the United States.

**financial statements.** Accounting reports that generally include a Balance Sheet, an Income Statement (also called a profit & loss statement), a Statement of Owners' Equity, and a Statement of Cash Flows.

**financing lease.** A lease that usually does not provide for maintenance service, is noncancelable, and lasts the expected economic life of the asset.

**fixed (interest) rate.** An interest rate that does not change during the life of the loan.

**fixed costs.** Costs that do not vary significantly with the volume of output or sales (i.e., utilities, rent, depreciation, interest, administrative salaries). Also, costs that are constant regardless of quantity of products or services sold.

**fixed-price contract.** A contract that provides for a specified price (or, in some cases, an adjustable price) for supplies or services, usually within a stipulated contract period. Such a contract places maximum risk and responsibility upon the contractor.

**flexible budget.** A budget that includes a range of activity levels, used to compare with a budget that reflects actual sales volume.

**focus group.** A group of 6-12 people interviewed by a professional who asks open-ended questions for the purpose of gathering data about their preferences, opinions, beliefs, and experiences. Also, a group of potential consumers who participate in a structured discussion of a product or service.

**freight forwarder.** A person or firm that arranges to pick up or deliver goods per instructions from a shipper or consignee.

**full-time workers.** Generally, workers who work more than 35 hours per week.

**general ledgers.** A business record that includes details of all accounts.

**general partnership.** Two or more persons who jointly own a business. General partners participate fully in management of the business, and their liability is personal and unlimited.

**goodwill.** Intangible assets of a business, generally referring to the difference between the business's market value and the market value of its net tangible (appraisable) assets.

**gross profit.** Net sales (gross sales less returned merchandise, discounts, or other allowances) minus cost of goods sold; also referred to as "gross margin."

**groupthink.** A tendency towards reactionary, consensus thinking that limits the ability of a group to investigate or appreciate issues and alternatives.

**guaranteed loan.** A loan made by a financial institution to a small business with a partial guarantee given by the Small Business Association.

**historical cost principle.** An accounting principle stating that all costs must be recorded at the exchange price of the transaction at the time it occurred.

**income statement.** A financial report showing revenues earned, expenses incurred in earning the revenues, and the resulting net income or net loss; also referred to as a profit and loss statement.

**independent agent.** An insurance agent who offers policies from a variety of companies.

**independent contractor.** A self-employed individual who has his or her own business; has many occasions to do freelance work for others; and is responsible for his or her own acts, contracts, and tax withholdings.

**indirect forecasting.** Gathering of data relating to a target market, in the absence of specific information about that market.

**industry profile.** Pertinent information about a specific industry, such as its size, trends, growth potential, and history.

**informal capital.** Financing from an informal, unorganized source. Includes informal debt capital such as trade credit, or loans from friends and relatives; and informal equity capital from informal investors.

**infrastructure.** In business management terminology, the managerial support structure that surrounds the direct management team (e.g., advisors, consultants, lawyers, accountants, bankers, and insurance agents).

**infringement.** A breach of a law, right, or obligation.

**initial public offering (IPO).** The first offering of stock in a company to public investors.

**institutional advertising.** Advertising that is "non-promotional," meaning that it stresses features and benefits related to the identity of a business, rather than promoting specific merchandise or services.

**intangible assets.** Those assets that literally cannot be touched; these include a business's goodwill, customer lists, and patents.

**intellectual property.** Ownership or exclusive rights to processes or other products of intelligent thought, such as trade secrets, copyrights, patents, or trademarks.

**intensive distribution.** Distributing a product through many retail outlets. Usually used for low-cost "convenience" products.

**intermediaries.** Businesses or individuals who help a product move through the distribution channel from the manufacturer to the customer.

**internal controls.** The policies and procedures a business establishes to assure reliability of its accounting records, to safeguard its assets, and to promote its objectives.

**Internet.** A global network of linked computers that share information using agreed-upon communication standards.

**Internet service provider (ISP).** Commercial companies that provide access to the World Wide Web, often for a monthly fee.

**inventory.** The raw materials, work-in-process, and finished goods (including merchandise purchased for resale) intended for internal consumption or sale; an asset listed on a business's balance sheet.

**investment bankers.** Bankers who arrange long-term financial transactions for their clients, often guaranteeing the sale of securities within a certain amount of time and at a specific price.

**IPO.** See **initial public offering.**

**ISP.** See **Internet service provider.**

**JIT.** See **just-in-time delivery.**

**joint liability.** Where one joint debtor has the right to insist that a co-debtor be joined in the liability. The liability is required to be apportioned among the debtors.

**joint venture.** A business entity comprising two or more active business partners. Also known as "strategic alliances" or "partnering agreements."

**just-in-time delivery (JIT).** The practice of producing the exact amount of products needed by customers and delivering them at the exact time they are needed. Businesses that buy from JIT suppliers minimize inventory holding costs and decrease their turnaround time.

**K-1.** A tax form given to LLC members, showing their share of profit or loss.

**key-person insurance.** Life insurance taken out by a business on an essential or very important employee, with the company as beneficiary.

**leasehold improvement.** Any improvement made to leased property. Such improvements become the property of the lessor at the end of the lease, and are categorized as an intangible asset to the lessee.

**letter of credit.** A bank document guaranteeing the availability of funds (or guaranteeing a loan up to a specified amount) that can be drawn on by a business's creditor (or supplier) under specific terms and conditions.

**liabilities.** A business's short- and long-term debts.

**liability insurance.** Insurance covering losses arising from injury or damage to another person or property.

**licensing agreement.** A legal contract in which a licenser grants the use of specific property rights to a licensee in return for royalty payments.

**limited liability company (LLC).** A business entity that is a hybrid between a partnership and a corporation. They are highly flexible, provide limited liability to their members, and are not subject to double taxation.

**limited partnership.** A partnership that allows for general and limited partners; limited partners are usually liable for debts only to the extent of their investment, and have limited or no control over management.

**line extensions.** Additions to a business's offerings that deepen the existing product line (i.e., offer more varieties of the same products or services) rather than broadening it (offering more varieties of different products or services).

**line of credit.** Short-term financing (usually from a bank) that is available for a business to borrow against as needed, and that must be repaid within a specific time.

**liquidated damages.** Consequences of breaching the terms of a contract, as set out in that contract.

**liquidity.** The readiness and ease with which assets can be converted to cash without a loss; generally describes the degree of solvency of a business.

**list price.** The price that appears on a product line sheet or a catalog, or is quoted by a salesperson. This is a business's official price before any discounts. This is also known as the final selling price.

**LLC.** See **limited liability company**.

**long-term debt.** Loans scheduled to be paid back over a period longer than one year.

**long-term liabilities.** Debt that will not mature within the next year.

**loss leader.** Merchandise or services sold at a loss to increase customers, sales of related items, or customer awareness.

**MACRS.** See **modified accelerated cost recovery system**.

**manufacturers' agents.** Agents that sell a company's product in a particular geographic area, usually on an exclusive basis. They do not take title to the goods they sell and earn their money through commissions. These agents also carry the product lines of other manufacturers and sell only to wholesalers, retailers, and industrial buyers.

**market.** A population segment comprising actual or potential buyers of a particular product or service.

**market analysis.** Gathering of data that tell how attractive a given market is for your business.

**market research.** The process of gathering information to make strategic business decisions.

**market segment.** A unique, homogenous sub-market of a larger market.

**market share.** The percentage of a market's total sales (in units or dollars) that a business receives.

**market skimming.** Entering a market with a high price until one satisfies demand or attracts competitors, then gradually lowering the price.

**marketing.** All activities meant to influence the sale of goods and services to consumers.

**marketing mix.** The four variables that a business can use to achieve a competitive advantage and sell to a **target customer**. These are product, price, placement, and promotion.

**marketing plan.** A document describing how a business will market its products or services; contains information on target markets, product positioning, competitive advantage, and the marketing mix.

**mark-up.** The percentage by which a product's price is increased to achieve a desired profit margin. This is used with cost-plus pricing, and is expressed as a percentage of the price of the product.

**mass merchandisers.** Stores that sell at lower prices than department stores and specialty boutiques, and offer a broad assortment of products.

**MBDC.** See **Minority Business Development Centers**.

**mediation.** A nonbinding means of settling a contractual dispute through negotiation.

**merchandising.** The planning and promotion of sales by presenting a product to the right market at the right time.

**merchantability.** An implied warranty stating that goods are fit for normal use and are of the same quality as similar items produced by others.

**merger.** A combination of two or more businesses into one.

**mini-marketing.** The practice of marketing strategies on individual customers.

**Minority Business Development Centers (MBDC).** Established to increase the number of minority-owned businesses, help existing firms expand, and minimize business failures.

**minority-owned business.** For the purposes of the Bureau of the Census's 1987 Characteristics of Business Owners (CBO) survey, businesses owned by Blacks, Hispanics, Asians, American Indians, Alaska natives, and other minority groups.

**mission statement.** A written statement broadly describing what a business hopes to achieve.

**modified accelerated cost recovery system (MACRS).** The system of calculating depreciation used for income tax reporting.

**net income/loss.** The result after subtracting all expenses and taxes from total revenue.

**net present value.** A calculation of what future dollars are worth today.

**net profit.** Sales minus variable costs and fixed costs. Net profit is used as a starting point to measure return on investment for specific products or businesses.

**net worth.** The total assets of a business minus its total liabilities.

**networking.** Making contact with a variety of people in related fields to foster communication with additional contacts, or to provide information that goes beyond the reason for the initial contact.

**niche market.** A special segment of a market, often defined in terms of particular buyer characteristics, which a given business is particularly well suited to target.

**noncompetition agreement.** A contract that restricts an employee or owner from competing against a former business or employer. These contracts are permitted if they are limited in time and geographical area.

**nondisclosure agreement.** A contract whereby a person or company agrees not to disclose trade secrets.

**objectives.** The goals a business wishes to achieve.

**Occupational Safety and Health Administration (OSHA).** A federal agency under the Department of Labor that issues standards and rules for safe working conditions, tools, equipment, facilities, and processes; and conducts compliance inspections.

**Office of Small and Disadvantaged Business Utilization (OSDBU).** Located within nearly every federal department to assist minority-owned businesses with selling to the government.

**operating agreement.** An agreement among the members of a limited liability company, or parties to a partnership, that serves much the same function as a corporation's bylaws.

**operating lease.** A lease that usually provides for maintenance service, is cancelable, and lasts less than the expected economic life of the asset.

**operational planning.** A planning process focused on short-term actions (usually one year).

**organizational chart.** A chart diagramming the managerial structure of a business, designating specific areas of responsibility.

**OSHA.** See **Occupational Safety and Health Administration.**

**OSDBU.** See **Office of Small and Disadvantaged Business Utilization.**

**outsourcing.** The buying of parts of a product to be assembled elsewhere, or the hiring of independent contractors to assist with business operations.

**overhead.** The regular ongoing operating expenses of a business, including rent, utilities, upkeep, taxes, administrative salaries; costs not directly associated with the product/service.

**owner's equity.** The amount owed by a business to its owner.

**part-time workers.** Employees working fewer than 35 hours per week.

**passive investment.** An investment in which one is not actively involved in generating money, such as a savings account or the stock market.

**patent.** Governmental granting of exclusive rights for a specified period of time to the inventor of an invention or process.

**performance bond.** An indemnity agreement to protect against loss due to breach of contract; also called a "contract bond."

**performance reports.** Reports to management that compare actual results to budgeted amounts and indicate variances.

**permission marketing.** An online marketing concept stating that the marketer must work to gain the Internet user's "permission" to present an advertising message.

**personal financial statements.** Financial documents of an individual, often requested by financial institutions from the borrower or guarantor of a loan; generally includes a balance sheet and tax returns from the prior three years.

**personal guaranty.** A contract where the individual acts as a surety or guarantees the obligations of another. Most often used by lenders dealing with a closely held corporation, where principal shareholders must sign personally.

**personal selling.** An element of the promotional and sales mix that involves one-on-one communication between a sales representative and a customer.

**point-of-purchase displays.** Promotional displays in stores (e.g., window displays, display racks, and banners).

**pollution prevention (P2).** A program businesses can implement to reduce or eliminate generation of hazardous and nonhazardous wastes.

**preferred stock.** A special class of stock, often non-voting, which is given priority over common stock as to dividends.

**price promotions.** Short-term discounts offered by manufacturers or retailers to encourage customers to try a product.

**primary data.** Original data collected by a business to answer specific questions about a market. Primary data collection methods include focus group interviews, surveys, and questionnaires.

**prime contract.** A contract awarded directly by the federal government.

**principal.** The dollar amount originally borrowed or financed, on which interest is paid; also referred to as the "face amount" of a loan.

**private offering.** Solicitation of sale of a security to a few persons, at a low enough dollar amount that federal or state registration is not required.

**pro forma.** An estimate of future results from a present set of assumptions.

**product extensions.** New variations of existing products. Extensions can be revised or repositioned products.

**product life cycle.** The phases a product or service goes through as a result of changes in consumer demand and competition. Phases include introduction, growth, maturity, and decline. These affect the marketing strategy a business uses.

**product line.** The collection of products or services that a business offers.

**product orientation.** A focus on product or production methods instead of customer needs. This can lead to producing products that customers do not want.

**product positioning.** The way a product is priced, promoted, and placed in the market. Businesses use positioning strategies to maximize their competitive advantage and differentiate their offerings from those of competitors. Products are frequently "repositioned" to highlight a new feature, or to target a new market niche.

**product.** All of the tangible and intangible features and benefits offered by a business. This can be a physical product or a service.

**profit.** The financial gain resulting from revenues after all expenses have been paid.

**profit margin.** The amount of each sales dollar that represents net income, usually stated as a percentage; net income divided by sales.

**promotional allowance.** Price discounts offered by a manufacturer to retailers in exchange for advertising the manufacturer's products. See **cooperative advertising**.

**promotional mix.** The strategies and tactics a company uses to communicate the benefits of its products or services to target customers. These include advertising, personal selling, public relations, networking, sales promotions, and direct mail.

**promotional Web site.** A Web site that creates awareness and stimulates demand, but does not have online sales capabilities.

**proprietorship.** The most common legal form of business ownership (about 85% of all small businesses are proprietorships). The owner's liability is unlimited in this form of ownership.

**psychographic data.** Data dealing with the activities, interests, and opinions of a target population; in marketing, such data are valuable in understanding target consumers' buying decisions.

**public offering.** A general solicitation for participation in an investment opportunity. Interstate public offerings are supervised by the Securities and Exchange Commission.

**publicly held corporation.** A corporation whose stock is traded publicly, and is therefore registered with the Securities and Exchange Commission.

**qualitative data.** Marketing data that cannot be quantified or counted, such as political beliefs, preferences, and experiences.

**quantitative data.** Marketing data that can be measured and subjected to statistical analysis (e.g., monthly earnings, number of children, amount of rent paid).

**quick ratio.** "Quick assets" (cash and other assets immediately convertible to cash) divided by current liabilities. Lenders use this ratio to measure the ability of a business to meet current debt obligations.

**responsibility accounting.** A method of accounting that associates business activities and costs with the individual responsible for those costs.

**retained earnings.** A corporation's accumulated, undistributed earnings.

**revenue.** The money generated by such earning activities as selling a product, charging rent, or receiving interest on a loan.

**rule of entry.** A formal policy by which a family member must have gained a certain amount of work experience with other companies before he or she may join the family business.

**sale and leaseback.** An arrangement in which a business sells an asset while simultaneously leasing the asset back from the purchaser.

**sales agents.** Extensions of manufacturer's sales force. These intermediaries have more authority to set prices and terms of sale than manufacturer's agents, and may even take over a manufacturer's entire marketing effort. Sales agents specialize in specific types of products and operate primarily in industrial goods markets.

**sales forecast.** Predicts how much of a product or service will be sold over a period of time.

**SBA.** See **Small Business Administration**.

**SBDC.** See **Small Business Development Centers**.

**SBIC.** See **Small Business Investment Company**.

**SBIR.** See **Small Business Innovation Research Program**.

**SCOR.** See **Small Corporate Offering Registration**.

**SCORE.** See **Service Corps of Retired Executives**.

**secondary data.** Market information that has been gathered and published in readily available form.

**secured loan.** A loan for which the borrower has pledged assets as collateral to the lender.

**seed capital.** Funding required in the early or growth stages of a business to finance market research, strategic planning, technical research, and product development.

**selective distribution.** The practice of distributing goods or services through a limited number of intermediaries and outlets. This enables manufacturers to have greater control over the way their products are sold.

**Service Corps of Retired Executives (SCORE).** An SBA volunteer management assistance program, providing counseling, workshops, and seminars for small businesses.

**short-term debt.** Loans that are due within one year.

**short-term interest rates.** Interest rates for short-term borrowing, usually for a term of one year or less.

**SIC Code.** See **Standard Industrial Classification Code**.

**simple interest.** Interest paid on the principal of a loan only, rather than on the principal plus accrued interest.

**situation analysis.** A preliminary look at the market data available, which tells one whether additional information is needed.

**slotting fee.** A fee required by a retailer for stocking an item.

**Small Business Administration (SBA).** A federal agency established to provide prospective and existing small businesses with advocacy, financial assistance, management counseling, and training.

**Small Business Development Centers (SBDC).** Established by Congress in 1980 to join federal, state, and local governments; the educational community; and the private sector in making management assistance and counseling available to existing and prospective small business owners.

**Small Business Innovation Development Act of 1982.** Federal statute requiring federal agencies with large extramural R&D budgets to allocate a certain percentage of these funds to small R&D firms.

**Small Business Innovation Research Program (SBIR).** A grant program for small businesses that are working to meet the research and development needs of the federal government.

**Small Business Investment Company (SBIC).** A federal venture capital program that uses private venture capital firms and SBA-guaranteed financing.

**Small Corporate Offering Registration (SCOR).** A program in which security offerings that are exempt from registration with the Securities Exchange Commission can meet state registration requirements with a minimum of cost and regulation.

**sole proprietorship.** An unincorporated one-owner business, farm, or professional practice.

**squeeze-out.** Techniques employed by one or more owners of a business to remove another owner.

**Standard Industrial Classification Code (SIC Code).** A numerical code that identifies a business based on its type of business or trade activity.

**stewardship principle.** The principle that members of a family must meet higher standards of conduct and performance in a family business than non-family employees.

**strategies.** Plans devised in order to achieve objectives.

**stream of earnings.** A method of business valuation that derives a company's value from its profit, earnings, or cash flow (or their multiples or present values).

**subcontract.** A contract between a prime contractor and a subcontractor, or between subcontractors, to furnish supplies or services for performance of a prime contract or a subcontract.

**succession.** The passing of legal authority over a business to new leadership (which usually—but not necessarily—consists of family members in the next generation), along with the transfer of ownership interest (equity) in the business.

**succession plan.** A plan, preferably formal, whereby the controlling owners arrange to pass on authority and assets in the family business to the next generation, or to non-family buyers of the business.

**surety bond.** Bonds providing security from claims filed against a business.

**SWOT analysis.** Analysis of a business's strengths, weaknesses, opportunities, and threats.

**tactics.** Specific actions that support strategies.

**tangible assets.** Those assets that can literally be touched (e.g., equipment, buildings, inventory).

**target market.** A group of potential customers consisting of the most likely prospective buyers of a specific business's goods or services.

**target return.** An established level of financial return on an investment, usually expressed as a percentage of total costs. This guides price setting.

**tariffs.** Taxes on imported or exported goods.

**term loan.** A loan having a due date for repayment of longer than one year; most commonly used for equipment, real estate, or other fixed asset purchases.

**terms.** Conditions or provisions specified for repaying loans or paying invoices; terms usually include the time limit, amount to be paid, and any discount.

**test marketing.** A way to experiment with a new product or marketing strategy before attempting to act on a larger scale. Test marketing is used for short periods of time.

**tort.** A wrongful act causing injury to a person, for which a civil action may be brought to recover damages.

**total revenue.** The total amount of money generated through sales.

**trade discounts.** Discounts offered to wholesalers or retailers who perform certain marketing functions on behalf of the manufacturer.

**trade promotions.** Incentives that businesses offer to retailers and wholesalers for stocking their product.

**trademark.** A symbol, letter, device, or word that identifies a product; it is officially registered, and grants exclusive legal use to its owner or manufacturer.

**transactional Web site.** A Web site that allows customers to browse products and make credit card purchases online.

**turnover.** The rate of speed at which items are sold.

**unsecured loan.** An uncollateralized loan backed only by the borrower's signature.

**up-leveling.** A system of answering customer inquiries through informative automated responses and e-mails, the goal being to cut down time spent answering phone inquiries.

**variable (interest) rate.** An interest rate that changes during the term of the loan.

**variable costs.** Costs that change significantly in direct proportion to the volume of output or sales.

**venture capital.** Money used to finance new or unusual undertakings.

**vertical integration.** The strategy of controlling many or all of the sourcing, manufacturing, and distribution tasks required by a business.

**viral marketing.** A form of online marketing in which an offer or incentive is so attractive that Internet users spread it to one another through word of mouth.

**warranty.** A promise or representation made about goods that becomes part of the deal, and creates an expectation that the goods will conform to that promise.

**Web.** See **World Wide Web**.

**work done for hire.** A doctrine stating that ideas created while employed or commissioned are owned by the employer or commissioner.

**working capital.** Resources available to cover short-term expenses, as determined by subtracting current liabilities from current assets.

**World Wide Web.** A user-friendly portion of the Internet that allows the use of "pages" featuring graphic displays, fonts, colors, animation, audio, and the like; and permits users to jump instantly from one page to another.

**zoning.** The division of an area into zones that restrict the number and types of buildings and their uses.

# Index

## U

## V

## W

## Y

## Z